Sing and Sing On

Chicago Studies in Ethnomusicology

A series edited by Philip V. Bohlman and Timothy Rommen

Sing and Sing On

SENTINEL MUSICIANS AND THE MAKING OF THE ETHIOPIAN AMERICAN DIASPORA

Kay Kaufman Shelemay

The University of Chicago Press   CHICAGO AND LONDON

The University of Chicago Press, Chicago 60637
The University of Chicago Press, Ltd., London
© 2022 by The University of Chicago
Published 2022
Printed in the United States of America

31 30 29 28 27 26 25 24 23 22   1 2 3 4 5

ISBN-13: 978-0-226-81016-4 (cloth)
ISBN-13: 978-0-226-81002-7 (paper)
ISBN-13: 978-0-226-81033-1 (e-book)
DOI: https://doi.org/10.7208/chicago/9780226810331.001.0001

Library of Congress Cataloging-in-Publication Data

Names: Shelemay, Kay Kaufman, author.
Title: Sing and sing on : sentinel musicians and the making of
    the Ethiopian American diaspora / Kay Kaufman Shelemay.
Other titles: Sentinel musicians and the making of the Ethiopian
    American diaspora | Chicago studies in ethnomusicology.
Description: Chicago ; London : The University of Chicago
    Press, 2022. | Series: Chicago studies in ethnomusicology |
    Includes bibliographical references and index.
Identifiers: LCCN 2021035771 | ISBN 9780226810164 (cloth) |
    ISBN 9780226810027 (paperback) | ISBN 9780226810331
    (ebook)
Subjects: LCSH: Ethiopian Americans—Music. | Ethiopians—
    United States—Music. | Musicians—Ethiopia. |
    Musicians—United States. | Music—Social aspects—
    United States.
    | Music—Social aspects—Ethiopia. | Music—Political
    aspects—Ethiopia. | Music—Political aspects—United
    States.
Classification: LCC ML3560.E83 S53 2022 | DDC 780.89/928073—
    dc23
LC record available at https://lccn.loc.gov/2021035771

♾ This paper meets the requirements of ANSI/NISO Z39.48-1992
(Permanence of Paper).

To musicians of the Ethiopian American diaspora,
past, present, and future

Sing on,
Child of innocence, sing.
Sing,
The life-giving mother silenced,
Sing. Sing on,
Daughter of peace, sing.
Sing, the father
For a forbidden truth condemned,
Sing. Sing on, and forward,
Child of sacrifice, sing.
Sing,
Abortive cry against darkness,
Sing. Sing.

SOURCE: Tsegaye Gabre-Medhin, *Oda Oak Oracle: A Legend of Black Peoples, Told of Gods and God, of Hope and Love, and of Fears and Sacrifices* (London: Oxford University Press, 1965), 68.

Contents

List of Plates * xi
List of Figures * xiii
List of Tables * xv
Editorial Policies * xvii
Preface: FUNDAMENTALS. Toward a Concept
of the Sentinel Musician * xxi

Section I. Frameworks

1. THRESHOLDS. Ethnography, History, Biography * 3
2. MOBILITIES. People and Music in Motion * 29
3. SENSES. Ethiopian Sensory Thought and Practice * 49

Section II. Processes

4. CONFLICTS. Revolutionary Musical Lives * 77
5. MOVEMENTS. Pathways to Asylum * 99
6. COMMUNITIES. Places and Politics in Diaspora * 121

Section III. Transformations

7. SOUNDS. Performing Identity, Mobility,
and the Ethiopian Sound * 149
8. SIGNS. The Genealogy of Orchestra Ethiopia
at Home and Abroad * 171

9. CREATIVITIES. Musical Invention and
Diasporic Challenges * 204
10. HORIZONS. Rediscovering Heritage and
Returning to Homeland * 229

*Afterword: Sentinel Musicians
in Global Perspective * 257
Acknowledgments * 267
Appendix: An Overview of Ethiopian Diaspora
Communities across the United States * 277
Glossary * 289
Notes * 297
Discography * 379
Interviews and Communications * 385
Field Notes * 389
Bibliography * 391
Index * 417*

Plates

Plate 1.1   Map of the Horn of Africa * 6

Plate 1.2   Political map of Ethiopia (2020) * 9

Plate 1.3   Library of Congress interviewees * 16

Plate 1.4   Library of Congress interviewees * 17

Plate 1.5   Bezawork's CD *Lemenor* * 21

Plate 2.1   The Either/Orchestra with Teshome Mitiku * 30

Plate 2.2   Church of Saint George, Lalibela, Ethiopia * 38

Plate 2.3   "Saint George and Scenes of His Martyrdom,"
            by Nicolò Brancaleon * 40

Plate 2.4   *Arba Lijoch* * 45

Plate 3.1   Christmas ritual, Lalibela, Ethiopia * 50

Plate 3.2   Saint Yared * 54

Plate 3.3   Procession with sacred altar tablets, DSK Mariam Church,
            Washington, DC * 62

Plate 3.4   Moges Seyoum * 64

Plate 3.5   *Azmari* in procession * 68

Plate 3.6   Ashenafi Mitiku * 72

Plate 4.1   Imperial Bodyguard Orchestra * 81

Plate 4.2   Ali Birra * 84

Plate 4.3   Telela Kebede and family * 90

Plate 4.4   Gish Abbay *Kinet* * 94

Plate 5.1   Amha Eshete * 102

Plate 5.2   Elizabeth and Martha Namarra * 106

Plate 5.3   Getatchew Gebregiorgis * 113

Plate 5.4   Selam Seyoum Woldemariam * 115

Plate 6.1   U Street, Washington, DC * 126

Plate 6.2   Ethiopian immigrants and establishments,
            Washington, DC * 127

Plate 6.3   Addis Ababa Restaurant * 131

Plate 6.4   Dukem Ethiopian Restaurant billboard, Addis Ababa * 133
Plate 6.5   *Masqal* celebration, New Riverside Park * 134
Plate 6.6   ESFNA 2008 sociocommerscape * 135
Plate 6.7   Dukem Ethiopian Restaurant * 137
Plate 7.1   Mulatu Astatke * 151
Plate 7.2   *Dawal* at Lalibela, Ethiopia * 156
Plate 8.1   Halim El-Dabh * 177
Plate 8.2   John Coe * 179
Plate 8.3   Tesfaye Lemma * 182
Plate 8.4   *Reunion*: Melaku Gelaw, Charles Sutton,
            Getamesay Abebe * 185
Plate 8.5   Orchestra Ethiopia * 190
Plate 8.6   Dukem Ensemble * 197
Plate 9.1   Mount Dashen * 205
Plate 9.2   Yehunie Belay and Hillary Rodham Clinton * 215
Plate 9.3   Meklit Hadero * 217
Plate 9.4   Abebaye Lema and choir * 222
Plate 9.5   *Merigeta* Tsehai Birhanu * 226
Plate 10.1 Musicians in Washington, DC * 238
Plate 10.2 Henock Temesgen * 240
Plate 10.3 Wayna Wondwossen * 248
Plate 10.4 Munit Mesfin * 249
Plate A.1   Betelehem "Betty" Melaku * 278

Figures

Figure 1.1 Narratives of musical historical time * 25
Figure 8.1 An overview of the multiple lives of Orchestra Ethiopia * 174

Tables

Table 3.1   The seven senses according to the Ethiopian highland oral tradition * 55

Table 3.2   The seven senses as listed in an Ethiopian dictionary * 55

Table 3.3   Sequence for performing the *Mahlet* * 57

Table 5.1   Musicians' migration to the United States, interim stops, and status * 117

Table 6.1   Ethnic place-making in the heterolocal urban setting * 128

Table 6.2   Venues for ESFNA 1997–2020 * 136

Table 7.1   The *yäfidel qərs'* (conventional signs) * 159

Editorial Policies

In order to make this book as accessible as possible to nonspecialists in Ethiopian studies, I have made a number of editorial decisions on the transliteration of terms, names, lyrics, and quotations.

Words from Amharic and Ge'ez

Words from Amharic and Ge'ez are transliterated using a simplified version of the system found in Wolf Leslau's *Concise Amharic Dictionary*.[1] There are seven vowel sounds in Amharic, of which five for the most part correspond to English vowel pronunciations: *a* (as in "ah"), *i* (like "ee" in "feet"), *e* (like "a" in "state"), *o* (as in "nor"), and *u* (like "oo" in "boot"). The vowel *ä* is pronounced like the sound one makes while hesitating in speaking and which is represented in writing by "uh." The vowel *ə*, represented by the schwa, has a pronunciation approximately like the *e* in *roses*.

The glottal stop, represented by ', corresponds to the pronunciation of the initial sound of the English "uh-uh." It can occur between vowels in some words such as *Ge'ez*. The slight rounding of consonants is represented by a *w* following a consonant.

Most of the Amharic consonants are the same as, or close to, English sounds. In an effort to limit diacritical markings, I will differentiate only consonants that are "glottalized" or "ejective," that is, pronounced with the stream of air coming from the lungs shut off by closure of the glottis. These include *t'*, *ch'*, and *p'*. The consonant *q* is always glottalized, and I represent the glottalized *s* as *s'*. A consonant corresponding to the sound "ni" in "onion" is marked as *ñ*. Since many words are spelled with different characters representing the same sound (notably *s* and *h*), I do not distinguish between the different consonants that are pronounced the same. All consonants can be lengthened (geminated), and I have endeavored to follow the geminations indicated in Thomas Leiper Kane's *Amharic-English Dictionary*.[2]

Amharic and Geʻez words and terms are presented italicized in the main text. The glossary presents all terms in correct transliteration, followed by a popular spelling in parenthesis if one is commonly used, as in *Gəʻəz* (*Geʻez*). The main text follows this pattern at the first use of a term, with the popular spelling used thereafter. The reader should be aware that many different spellings are used for the same Ethiopian term, and an effort has been made here to choose the most common among them to facilitate web searches. Other Ethiopian languages such as Afaan Oromo are transcribed according to the source at hand.

Ethiopian nouns may or may not have a plural marker, and it is common to use a singular form when the plural is intended. Plural form is not consistently used in Amharic and can be confusing. In this book, I use the singular form only (e.g., *azmari* as both singular and plural). I do not indicate plurals by attaching an English *-s* to an Ethiopian word.

Names

Names of people, places, and ethnic groups are spelled according to the most common English-language usage. If a person has chosen a particular spelling for his or her own name, as indicated on websites or on recordings, I use it. (One exception is the idiosyncratic French spellings used in titles of *éthiopiques* recordings, which will be reproduced in references in the discography, but not in the text.) Personal names that do not have a popular or preferred spelling have been transliterated using the system employed for terms.

Ethiopians are customarily referred to by their first names, a tradition I observe in discussions within the text after a first reference to the individual's full name. I have also cited and alphabetized Ethiopian authors' entries in the bibliography by their first names. Changing the order creates confusion, since the second name is not a family name but the first name of the father, and a third name may be added, which is the first name of the paternal grandfather.

Calendar and Dates

The Ethiopians use a calendar that is approximately seven and a half years behind the Western calendar. Thus, the millennium, celebrated in the year 2000 of the Ethiopian Calendar (EC), occurred in September 2007.

Unless specifically marked EC, all dates are given according to the Gregorian calendar.

Quotations from Interviews, Song Lyrics, and the Literature

The primary data on which this study is based include quotations from interviews as well as song lyrics, proverbs, and poetry. Interviews with Ethiopian American diaspora residents were conducted mainly in English and transcribed in full; a few interviews were conducted in Amharic, some with the assistance of translators. I have edited quotations lightly to reduce redundancies and grammatical infelicities and used ellipses to indicate when a word or clause is deleted. I have not otherwise altered commentary by research associates.

Song lyrics are provided in both Amharic and English translations when appropriate, with the source of the text and translation credited. When sources cited provide song texts in Afaan Oromo and other regional languages, I quote them as given.

In the case of quotations from various scholarly and secondary sources, any terms included there will be spelled as they were in the original source even if it deviates from standard spellings.

Fundamentals

TOWARD A CONCEPT OF
THE SENTINEL MUSICIAN

Wanna

GENERAL MEANING: Chief, principal, important, primary

MUSICAL MEANING: Fundamental tone; tonic

This book explores the lives of musicians from Ethiopia and adjacent regions of the Horn of Africa, beginning in the years preceding the 1974 Ethiopian revolution and extending through well over four unsettled decades that followed as a global Ethiopian diaspora emerged. The experiences of musicians in the throes of exile and resettlement chronicle music making in deeply unsettled times. But this story also offers lessons that extend beyond the boundaries of the experiences recounted here and that transcend the history of the region from which these individuals come, as well as the locales in which they have resettled.[1] These musical lives under duress provide grist for a reappraisal of the roles of musicians in the rapidly changing societies of which they are a part. They testify to the power of musicians' agency through and beyond music making to reshape the world around them.

As a cover term for the complex range of musicians' actions and activism that I detail in this book, I introduce the concept of the "sentinel musician." I coined the phrase after repeatedly witnessing the powerful roles that musicians of the Horn of Africa have played at home and in diaspora, environments in which they have both guarded and guided the communities of which they are a part. However, my use of the word *sentinel* is also inspired by precedents within the Ethiopian tradition itself.

Shortly after being named Ethiopian regent in 1917, Ras Tafari Makonnen founded the Imperial Bodyguard. After his coronation as Emperor Haile Selassie I in 1930, he renamed the unit of his personal guards *yänəgus təbbäqa*, (the king's guard) or *yäkəbr zäb* (honor guard).[2] The highly trained militia with infantry battalions and an artillery brigade under the direct control of the emperor was early on regarded as "the most capable unit in the Emperor's armed forces."[3] In 1930 as well, the emperor established the Imperial Bodyguard Orchestra as his resident musical ensemble. The Imperial Bodyguard Orchestra, and later a Jazz Band, were lauded by many, and over the decades they launched the careers of a number of Ethiopia's most revered musicians. But although the Imperial Bodyguard was founded to guard and protect the emperor, and although in the late 1950s it established a security system and thwarted two coup attempts, its leaders also proved to be critics of imperial power, most notably as the leading protagonists of an unsuccessful 1960 coup attempt mounted while the emperor was on a visit to Brazil. As we will see in chapter 4, musicians of the Imperial Bodyguard Orchestra also were implicated in the 1960 coup attempt.[4] The power of sentinel musicians can therefore move in various directions, sometimes protecting and lauding the powerful but, at other moments, offering critique and even active political resistance.

A sentinel musician galvanizes processes that produce large, if sometimes ephemeral, social events and groupings; here we can invoke the concept of assemblages to refer to emergent social wholes in which the parts retain their autonomy.[5] Musical and nonmusical activities of a sentinel musician often interact, but each sentinel musician retains his or her own agency and, in the face of new contingencies and opportunities, constantly adjusts to new settings and rapidly changing conditions. Forced migration renders musical agency an exceedingly dense subject, with shifting spheres of influences and challenges. Over time, a sentinel musician can generate a range of social processes, whether by producing musical sound, performing a ritual, establishing new musical groups and institutions, or serving as a link in multiple and interacting networks.

Musicians are well known to have been important conduits for information in many societies, such as the *jeli* of Mali, who transmit knowledge available nowhere else.[6] The same is true in Ethiopia, where the *azmari*, itinerant musicians who accompanied themselves on bowed lutes or plucked lyres, have for centuries transmitted historical information, offered social commentary, and spread news of recent events. Musical sound played a role in a variety of unexpected settings: feudal lords in the Ethiopian past are said to have used "musical signatures" to verify their identities as the senders of written documents. Messengers were evidently taught a secret musical code to sing when delivering a written message in order to confirm its source.[7]

In Ethiopia and many places across the African continent, musicians also played musical instruments as official sources of communication as well as surrogates for speech.[8] Even instruments that did not perform as formal speech surrogates were associated with communicating text. The name of the Ethiopian flat kettledrum, the *nägarit* (*negarit*), for instance, is derived from the verb *näggärä*, "to speak, inform, or announce."[9] The *negarit* was in the past sounded to assemble a community to hear official proclamations, with two drums suspended on the right and left of a mule's back, respectively, and struck by men with mallets walking along each side. The drum could announce the entry of a dignitary; it was also sounded to summon troops into battle. When this practice ceased in the mid-twentieth century, the name of the "talking" drum was given to the official Ethiopian government publication for federal laws, known as the *Nägarit Gazeta* (*Negarit Gazeta*: lit., the drum gazette).[10]

In numerous Ethiopian contexts and throughout the Horn of Africa, singers and instrumentalists have long been acknowledged as pivotal figures: they guided the transmission and performance of cultural traditions in domains ranging from worship to entertainment while offering inspiration and comfort during times of hardship. Sometimes musicians achieved this impact by singing wordless tunes and sounding instrumental melodies; at other moments they performed lyrics with double meanings, a verbal practice known in Ethiopia as "wax and gold."[11] The wax is the literal, outer meaning of sounded or written words, while the gold is the hidden, inner meaning. This system of double meanings in Ethiopian speech, literature, and song makes it possible for a musician to take an ambiguous position on the subject or political event at hand. I have taken inspiration from this system of double meanings to contextualize better the single-word chapter titles of this book; I have inserted a simulated "wax and gold" heading at the beginning of each chapter containing an Amharic word that has been used with both a general and musical meaning. Such practices are the heritage and responsibility of musicians, part of both their performances and their multiple roles in society.

But at no time is the role of the musician more heightened than in times of conflict, when music and its performance anchor deep and often irreconcilable meanings within everyday life. We can take as an example an Ethiopian bass guitarist who, during the revolutionary years of the 1980s, performed in a northern Tigray People's Liberation Front (TPLF) cultural troupe. She recalls her work as serving as a musical voice of the political organization that ultimately overthrew the Ethiopian military regime in 1991:

> I write songs and I act in dramas. I write and read poems and I compose music — very easy cultural songs . . . I am now armed with a bass guitar and am serving the revolution as much as the comrades on the war front with their bullets. I know that art is war by itself.[12]

Other musicians who play traditional instruments, such as the six-stringed lyre, the *krar*, consider their instruments to be weapons of resistance and dissent as well: "In my generation, people used the *krar* to fight. They sang songs about how to save the country."[13]

The word *sentinel*, derived initially from efforts to guard against aggression or theft, had its origin in sixteenth-century European military settings, referring to someone or something that stands watch or keeps guard. Yet both the word *sentinel* and the rapidly proliferating concepts associated with it over the centuries capture musicians' initiatives in surprisingly fruitful ways. The etymology of the word *sentinel* remains uncertain, but apparently originally stems (due to its connection to perceiving or watching) from the Italian verb *sentire*, "to hear," itself likely derived from the Latin *sentire*, "to feel or to perceive by the senses."[14] If the ability both to hear and to perceive keenly is vital to the success of all sentinels, few have more sensitive perceptual skills than do musicians. Indeed, in recent scientific studies, musical training has been credited with enhancing human cognitive development, including the ability of musical activities to sharpen neural networks associated with focused attention.[15]

Within Ethiopia and adjacent regions, one finds a deep-seated association between those who serve as guards and those who pass long hours in music making. These individuals range from the shepherds who watch over crops and livestock in the countryside to the guard who protects an urban compound around the clock while performing on the flute and other instruments. In general, the historical role of musicians in perceiving events and recording their observations through song and narration remains heightened today across the Horn of Africa, where oral transmission serves as an important channel for communication in the present and for conveying memories from the past. An Ethiopian musician's capacity for nuanced observation is surely shared by many across different geographical and historical boundaries, a topic that will shadow the following pages and be further discussed in the afterword.

The close connection between sentinel capacities and the role of the senses is further highlighted in the Ethiopian language, Amharic: the word *həwas* (*hiwas*) refers to a physical sense or sensation, while *səmmet*, translated as "sensibility or emotion," is derived from the verb *sämma*, "to hear, to listen, or to perceive."[16] The sensory aspects of a sentinel musician's role emerges both in discussions with Ethiopian musicians and in the literature, where there are deep historical and cultural connections evoked among concepts of the senses (*hiwas*), emotions (*səmmet*), and listening (*sämma*).[17]

The word *sentinel* can also encompass musicians' emerging roles over time in different settings, expanding from its connection with standing watch. Early on in Europe there were poetic references to the roles played by what were termed "sentinel stars," which poets lauded as keeping watch and guiding travelers along their way. Thomas Campbell's "The Soldier's Dream," proclaims:

> Our bugles sang truce—for the night-cloud had lowered,
> And the sentinel stars set their watch in the sky;[18]

We will see that some musicians played important sentinel roles in guiding other musicians through the course of their migrations abroad, effectively serving as "sentinel stars" in a variety of circumstances.

Over time, *sentinel* has accrued numerous additional meanings, including in medical domains, where a sentinel node has long been considered a primary marker of the spread of cancer.[19] Musicians and their music making parallel many of the old and new meanings of the word *sentinel*, as musicians serve as guards, guides, and nodes in emerging networks, all the while "sounding" dimensions of change in the communities of which they are a part.

So, I will use the neologism "sentinel musician" throughout the following pages to designate a musician who has served his or her society with vigilance, drawing on heightened sensory powers of perception and an ability to shape sound. A sentinel musician watches and listens with care, and at pivotal moments may offer warnings or commentaries through his or her performance. Some sentinel musicians have quite literally led the way as they migrated to new locales, establishing transnational networks, founding new institutions, and undertaking numerous initiatives in community building. Not all the actions of sentinel musicians are overtly musical; many are political, institutional, and social. At the same time, the most powerful sentinel musicians retain an ability to pivot among multiple domains and to re-invent themselves as situations demand. All of these activities require a full measure of agency, including the ability to be creative under adverse circumstances, and a willingness to extend oneself on behalf of the welfare of others. Musicians often take the initiative to offer emotional support to the displaced, much of their impact arising from the deep-seated power of their music to shape emotional comfort and healing.

The powerful role of music and musicians within society has been a subject addressed by many in the past, including the celebration of music as an "annunciatory vocation" by French social theorist Jacques Attali.[20]

Attali argued that we should view the musician as "a creator" who "changes the world's reality," and went on to suggest that "music is prophecy," with the musician acting simultaneously as "reproducer and prophet."[21] While I will not argue here that musicians are prophets, such suggestions have in fact been made regarding Ethiopian musicians. Ethiopian oral traditions emphasize that in the past at moments of crisis, officials at all levels used to ask "*Erranna men ala?*" (What do the shepherds say?):

> If there are things that have gone wrong in the community, if there are prophecies of what is to come, critical and prophetic views are said to be expressed in the songs of young shepherds. Oral tradition has it that [Emperor] Menelik [1844–1913] benefited a lot from the views, criticisms, and warnings of these shepherds. Thus, it could be said that there was a tradition of governance in Ethiopia which always gave room and paid attention to these voices.[22]

An introduction to an album of Ali Birra, an Oromo musician revered for the last half century, in fact lauds his ability as "an artist with an international vocation . . . who is also a prophet, witness of his century and of African heritage."[23]

Throughout the following pages, we will encounter several types of agency exercised by musicians. These include musical agency applied directly through musical creativity and performance; action or task agency that effects outcomes in musical domains by producing concerts, aiding musicians, and initiating ensembles; and finally, social agency, actions that shape domains outside the world of music itself.[24]

The Ethiopian concept of agency, *ammakayənnät*, translates as "the state or condition of being one who straightens, corrects, or equalizes."[25] However, this term is also used to convey the idea of agency as an ongoing process, as indicated by the statement translated from Amharic that "sand is made from rocks by the agency of water."[26] The Ethiopian term *ammakayənnät* also implies an effort by an agent such as a musician to mediate a social process in motion. In this way, the Ethiopian concept resembles that about which recent sociological inquiry has argued that "the key to grasping the dynamic possibilities of human agency is to view it as composed of variable and changing orientations within the flow of time."[27] Taking the dynamic nature of time into account, this book embraces a broad definition of agency as "the socioculturally mediated capacity to act."[28]

The protracted making of the Ethiopian diaspora requires tracing the role of musicians over the course of decades and in multiple locales. At all times, the agency of these mobile musicians has been exercised against formidable odds, whether emotional, political, or economic. Most of the individuals discussed and quoted in these pages struggled in their daily lives while they continued to devote untold hours to organizing and performing music. That much of their musical activity is generated through individual initiative does not lessen its social impact. Indeed, these musicians demonstrate powerfully that "to understand music as performance means to see it as an irreducibly social phenomenon, even when only a single individual is involved."[29]

At times musicians spearhead initiatives outside the musical domain altogether, founding institutions and organizing events that serve their communities. Most of the musicians discussed in the following chapters are engaged both within and beyond the boundaries of music making as community organizers and cultural agents. They employ performance to bring people together and in order to establish and sustain community values and moral standards.[30] These musicians work closely with others who endorse the power of the performing arts—including those engaged with theater, sports, and food. Yet they also recognize that "the first aim of the refugee is to survive, and having done that, that initial goal is quickly replaced by the general ambitions of life."[31]

Enacting and enabling musical performance can, in different situations, redress grievances, evoke long-forgotten memories, and help recreate the world anew. Musicians, especially those displaced by circumstance, combine their musical prowess and sensory acuity to exercise leadership and moral authority through sound. This book tells some of their stories in the following chapters.

Chapter Contents

The book is divided into three sections, each containing several chapters. The first section, titled "Frameworks," includes three chapters detailing the theoretical, methodological, and historical background for the rest of the book. Chapter 1, "Thresholds," provides an overview of political issues that sparked the great Ethiopian forced migration of the 1970s, as well as the multilocale and long-term research that tracked this process over the course of decades. Chapter 1 introduces theoretical frames that underpin the entire study, setting forth multitemporal and biographical studies as powerful sources of original data and new interpretations.

The two subsequent chapters of section I discuss the conceptual fields and histories necessary to understand sentinel musicians' lives. Chapter 2, "Mobilities," summarizes the factors that have set Ethiopian musical lives into motion within five main historical contexts: (1) imagined mobility, catalyzed by and sustained through myth, legend, and literature; (2) physical travel, whether involving departure for distant places or encounters with mobile individuals from elsewhere; (3) forced migration, processes provoked by sudden traumatic events such as natural or political disasters; (4) voluntary migration, mobility born of individual choice; and (5) virtual mobility, movement through channels of communication and auditory media. While these mobilities have histories emerging in different periods, one can also find evidence of their interactivity until the present day.

Chapter 3 of section I, "Senses," brings the history of sentinel musicians and their performances into dialogue with sensory studies. Exploring the impact of Ethiopia's sensual environment on musical perceptions and performance, the chapter presents a little-known framework of seven senses in the region and surveys the continued influence of Ethiopian Orthodox Christian belief and materiality on the sensory associations of many present-day musicians and dancers.

Section II, "Processes," includes three chapters that detail the ways in which musicians' lives were set into motion and experienced before and during the tumult of the revolution, continued through the protracted migration process, and amplified while founding new communities abroad. "Conflicts," chapter 4, explores musicians' experiences as agents of political action and dissent in the years leading up to the revolution; details musical lives under frightening political conditions, including arrest, imprisonment, and threats of death; and documents moments of opportunity within a climate of fear.

Chapter 5 of section II, "Movements," moves forward in time to narrate how musicians circumvented Ethiopian repression and made their ways abroad. The chapter details the experience of the first Ethiopian musicians to arrive in Washington, DC; charts varied pathways to asylum; and traces opportunities for defection, including those during a high-profile 1988 concert tour intended to offer Ethiopia's thanks to the international community for support to the homeland during the severe famines of the early 1980s.

The processes through which new Ethiopian communities arose in a cross section of American urban areas and the role of music and musicians within them is the subject of chapter 6, "Communities." This chapter discusses the active engagement of musicians in founding new religious institutions, in establishing networks and venues for musical performance, and in integrating music into community life. An appendix to the book presents additional historical and ethnographic details about Ethiopian diaspora communities located across the United States.

The third section of the book, "Transformations," contains four chapters that chart the ongoing life of Ethiopian music and musicians in the North American diaspora. Chapter 7, "Sounds," explores ways in which mobility manifests itself in diasporic musicking. The chapter also discusses vocal and instrumental musics as interactive styles; the manner in which the emotions are embedded and conveyed through diasporic musical performance; and sonic markers of ethnicity.

The genesis and transformations of a musical ensemble across boundaries of homeland and diaspora is reconstructed in chapter 8, "Signs." Inspired by methods gleaned from prosopography and actor-network theory, this chapter brings together individual testimonies to produce a "historical ecology" of Orchestra Ethiopia, a traditional folklore ensemble that has existed in multiple permutations both in Ethiopia and in diaspora.[32] The chapter reveals a textured history of unexpected collaborations across musical, ethnic, and national boundaries.

Chapter 9, "Creativities," chronicles new and lively initiatives among diaspora musicians in domains ranging from sacred music to popular styles as well as challenges to these creative efforts. From efforts to Americanize Ethiopian Orthodox chant to Afro-futurist musical explorations, this chapter maps hidden connections between seemingly separate musical scenes and the manner in which sentinel musicians work through musical creativity to reshape their social environments.

The transnational flow of funds and the growing number of returnees from diaspora to Ethiopia are the subjects of chapter 10, "Horizons." This chapter provides a close reading of the sentinel roles of musicians who have returned home following decades of residence abroad in North America. The chapter explores the impact on younger musicians of visits to the homeland they either left as children or knew only through their imaginations. The reverberations of Ethiopian music and musicians outside Ethiopia with growing new audiences claim attention here, as does the central role of the *éthiopiques* CD series in this process.

In sum, the book moves from the intellectual framework of section I, to tracking the rapid processes of change before, during, and after the Ethiopian revolution in section II, to exploring the many transformations experienced in the lives and music of musicians in section III. Along the way, the reader may want to consult the glossary for elucidation of Ethiopian terms. The discography lists recordings commercially released on CDs and LPs and provides links to the many recordings online of music and musicians discussed throughout these pages.

The afterword, following up on the central topic of this preface, summarizes the impact of sentinel musicians as they move outside their own communities to assume roles as cultural icons and sonic guides for new listening publics. A concluding discussion of the roles of musicians from other times and locales explores ways in which they, too, have served as sentinels.

SECTION I
Frameworks

Thresholds

ETHNOGRAPHY, HISTORY, BIOGRAPHY

Wazema
GENERAL MEANING: Prelude, beginning, initial part
MUSICAL MEANING: Musical liturgy for the eve of a holiday

Hundreds of musicians left the Horn of Africa as part of a forced migration that began in the mid-1970s and continues to reverberate more than forty-five years later.[1] Of the millions of refugees who departed from Ethiopia, Eritrea, and Somalia for destinations worldwide during this period, musicians constituted only a small and, on the surface, seemingly inconsequential number. However, the neglect of the role of music in forced migration in general, as well as the lack of attention to the contributions of individual musicians caught up within these upheavals, conceals important insights available nowhere else. Under conditions in which societies experience conflict and through the adverse circumstances in which people are forced to move and reestablish themselves elsewhere, many musicians assume social responsibility and emerge as agents of both deeply desired continuities and innovative changes. As explained in the preface, I term these individuals "sentinel musicians."

The neglect of the plight of refugees by music scholars, as well as by humanists in general,[2] has not just limited our knowledge of the expressive culture of forced migration; it has resulted in a very inadequate understanding of the trying conditions migrating musicians encounter and the many contributions they make in confronting them. Music, always ephemeral and challenging to study, becomes even more elusive when the musicians who conceive and perform it are set into motion under threatening circumstances. If mass displacement can be said to "render refugees indistinguishable" one from the other, even more rarely have their voices been heard.[3] The following pages seek to bring these lives into focus and their sounds into earshot by bringing to the fore tales, testimonies, and music of individual musicians and their communities. While not all musicians can be said to function as sentinels, so many offer this leadership that it commands our attention.

The sheer number of people forced to migrate also makes it all the more difficult to apprehend on an individual level the traumas that refugees experience. Within these circumstances, music provides a channel through which both individual and collective memories are transmitted and remembered. Periods of exile experienced by individuals are rarely perceived by outside observers as anything more than fleeting moments within the larger flow of collective time. As a result, each disrupted existence, devastating for the person involved, tends to be dwarfed from the perspective of what historians have termed the *longue durée*, the temporal patterns that shape historical trends over the course of generations and even epochs. The experience of migration within individual musical lives deserves much greater attention than it has received to date. Musicians' mobility leads me to follow an approach set forth by historian Stephen Greenblatt, who has suggested that

> mobility must be taken in a highly literal sense. . . . Only when conditions directly related to literal movement are firmly grasped will it be possible fully to understand the metaphorical movements: between center and periphery; faith and skepticism; order and chaos; exteriority and interiority. Almost every one of these metaphorical movements will be understood, on analysis, to involve some kinds of physical movements as well.[4]

A migrant's life constitutes an extended transition—days, months, and even years—during which everyday existence is disrupted and in flux. The migratory experience begins well before the moment of departure and extends long after arrival in a new place; it carries with it challenges that test individual fortitude and transform worldviews.[5] Displacement reshapes most aspects of a refugee's life and, in many cases, continues to exert its power on subsequent generations. One finds evidence of forced migration's impact echoed in the musical expression of many diaspora communities over the course of generations, whether reenacted through the resonance of African American spirituals or performed through the haunting sounds of the Armenian *duduk*.[6]

Migration, quite simply, reshapes both sound worlds and senses of self. An Ethiopian Oromo verse describes this transformative experience in straightforward fashion, observing that "our girls who travel, they sing the songs of others" (i.e., the Adare and the Amhara songs).[7] The introduction of new music surely brings with it new concepts and values, enabling times of displacement to shift social boundaries and alter the status quo. But forced migration also demands ingenuity, necessitating that musicians both protect the transmission of valued traditions and innovate to accommodate new circumstances.

From Homeland to Diaspora: Processes of Mapping and Naming

Where does a migrant come from? This seemingly straightforward question is in fact quite complex to answer, particularly among those who have experienced forced migration. How many refugees from Saigon, who fled South Vietnam in the early 1970s, today refer to their former home as "Ho Chi Minh City," as it was renamed in 1976 after its fall to what was formerly known as North Vietnam? The name by which one identifies one's home underscores the manner in which the present may either acknowledge or obscure one's past. One Oromo woman forced to leave Ethiopia recalled,

> Isn't it amazing that I feel that this [the United States] is my country? The country where I was born is like in the back of my head. If there had been peace in my country, I could have been someone else. . . . It crosses my mind sometimes and it makes me sad.[8]

Many conflicts have shifted national borders and prevented access to former homes, as is the case in the Palestinian-Israeli conflict, where disputed territory is known as the West Bank or Judea and Samaria, depending on one's national identity or political affiliations. The Horn of Africa offers a series of conflicts perpetuated in nomenclature that reflects the shifting nature of ties to historical homelands. (See plate 1.1.)

The recent mass population outflow from the region dates from the mid-1970s as a direct outcome of the Ethiopian revolution. From the mid-1970s onward, waves of refugees crossed Ethiopian and Eritrean borders into the Sudan and Kenya, from which many eventually made their way to destinations across the world. Some joined the few Ethiopians already living abroad, mainly Ethiopian students from affluent families who had been sent for education as early as the middle of the twentieth century and who had settled in small numbers in the United States, England, Italy, and the Netherlands.[9] Thousands of Beta Israel (Ethiopian Jews) fled the region beginning in the later 1970s, many trekking overland to seek asylum in Sudanese refugee camps, from where they were later airlifted to Israel in 1981.[10] Departures of Ethio-Somalis across the border to Somalia accelerated during and after the 1977 Ethiopian-Somali war, with

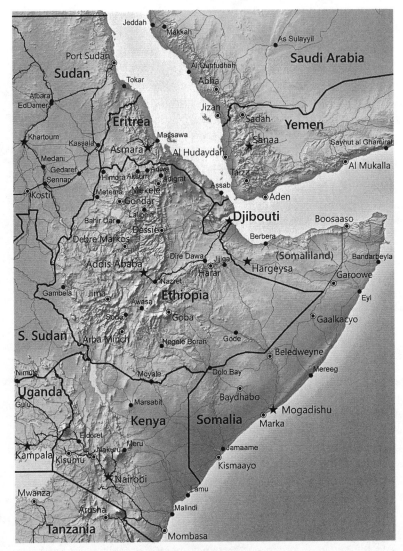

PLATE 1.1 Djibouti, Eritrea, Ethiopia, and Somalia share the peninsula that
extends off northeast Africa south of the Arabian land mass.
Courtesy of Scott Walker, Harvard Map Collection.

many later migrating to US cities such as San Diego and Minneapolis–St.
Paul.[11]

The end of the Ethiopian revolution brought yet another spike in migration. After the fall of the revolutionary government in 1991, a large wave
of Ethiopians left for destinations abroad, some of whom settled in the
United States and others in Australia.[12] The Eritrean civil war ended in

1991 with the official independence of Eritrea from Ethiopia in 1993, leaving Ethiopia landlocked and with a gaping wound in the Ethiopian polity as well as ongoing armed conflict.

Although many of these migrants came to the United States, firm and accurate numbers are very difficult to come by. Figures vary greatly among authoritative sources. While the Migration Policy Institute estimated as of July 2014 that approximately 251,000 Ethiopian immigrants and their children were living in the United States, this number vastly underestimates the total numbers of Ethiopians and is generally considered to undercount even those living at that time in Washington, DC, alone.[13] Moreover, whatever census figures exist do not embed information about refugees' places of origin in the Horn of Africa or their nationalities beyond the general rubric "Ethiopian."

To acknowledge nationalities in conflict as well as numerous dates and places of departure, this book speaks often of the Horn of Africa instead of referring solely to Ethiopia. This is despite Ethiopia's domination of the region both geographically and politically and its position at the ethnographic center of my own multisited research. Like most discussions of forced migration, this one confronts the challenge of portraying complex relationships, past and present, that link perceived peripheries with centers, all of which have been in flux and subsume a wide range of ethnic communities with distinctive identities, different belief systems, and disputed histories.[14] Writing about a contested region, or even just a part of it, presents great complexities if one wishes to be inclusive without eliciting anger all around.

Ethiopia itself has long been home to numerous ethnic communities, although the intense diversity was overshadowed by the political and cultural dominance of the highland Amhara and the Ethiopian Orthodox Tewahedo Church, both greatly diminished in power since the overthrow of Emperor Haile Selassie I by a Marxist regime in 1974. This history has led to substantial Amhara migration and, as a result, to Amhara majority status in many Ethiopian diaspora communities in the United States.[15]

While the 1974 revolution dislodged longtime Christian Amhara political, religious, cultural, and economic hegemony, it did not resolve longstanding ethnic conflicts. A new political system, "ethnic federalism," organized in postrevolutionary Ethiopia in 1994, defined political sovereignty primarily by ethnicity vested in the "nations, nationalities and peoples" of the country.[16] The Ethiopian Constitution from that date states,

> A "nation, nationality or people" . . . is a group of people who have or share a large measure of a common culture or similar customs, mutual intelli-

gibility of language, belief in a common or related identities, a common psychological make-up, and who inhabit an identifiable, predominantly contiguous territory.[17]

There are in the twenty-first century approximately eighty ethnocultural groups in Ethiopia, divided among ten ethnically defined regions.[18] (See plate 1.2.) Among the ethnicities officially named as a "people," "nation," or "nationality," the Oromo, the Amhara, the Tigrinya speakers, and the Somalis are numerically the largest groups.[19] One thus finds that ethnicity was reified in late twentieth-century Ethiopian cartography and consciousness, mixed with "the public celebration of ethnic diversity."[20] While those living in the homeland had by the 1990s become familiar with "culturalism pluralism . . . as the Ethiopian condition,"[21] there was considerable diasporic ambivalence about the politicization of ethnic boundaries in the homeland. Diasporic Ethiopians also had to struggle to calibrate their own senses of Ethiopian identity—national, ethnic, and religious— within very different contexts abroad. Thus there are a wide array of concerns about personal identity and ethnicity across the diaspora, especially given that changing Ethiopian governmental policies during and after the revolution had invested ethnicity with new political valence.

Sensitivities in the Ethiopian American diaspora are also shaped by the impact of racial divides and a heightened racial discourse in the United States. Race (*zär*) and racial (*yäzär*) identity are also implicated in concepts of ethnicity in Ethiopia but have not been historically foregrounded to anything approaching the awareness of race in the United States. Ethiopians living in the American diaspora in the twenty-first century sometimes use the term *race* rather than *ethnicity* or *ethnic community* in discussing ethnicity.[22]

Very few musicians interviewed related stories of discrimination in Ethiopia associated with colorism. However, one older immigrant of partial Agau descent from the central highlands recalled an experience early in his career when he was refused a musical position because of his dark complexion:

> I wanted to be hired as a musician, so I went to Hager Fikir (Patriotic Association). They said, "You're too black to be on stage . . . your complexion is too dark, you won't be suitable for this stage." And they sent me home. . . . If you want to know the truth, I was quite a good-looking fellow.[23]

In the past, the term *Habesha* was used by Ethiopian Christian highlanders and Eritreans as a self-designation for Ethiopian.[24] But with the indepen-

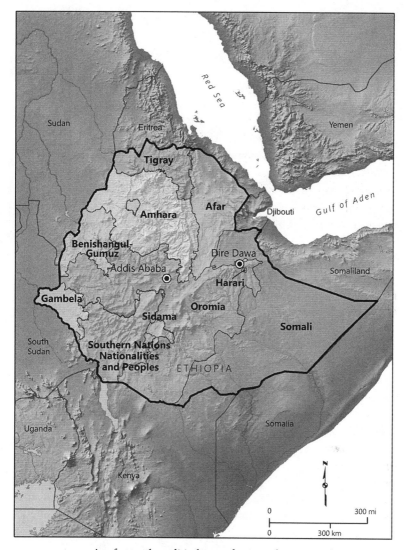

PLATE 1.2 As of 2020, the political map of postrevolutionary Ethiopia is based on a system of ethnic federalism with ten autonomous ethnic regions and two chartered cities. Courtesy of Scott Walker, Harvard Map Collection.

dence of Eritrea and ethnic federalism's naming of each region according to the majority ethnic community within it, growing ambivalence about the term *Habesha* emerged. Discussion can ensue when this word is used. The accomplished *krar* player from Bahir Dar (Amhara region), Minale Dagnew Bezu, replied to my query about his ethnic background as follows:

MDB: I mean, before we didn't really tell our ethnic backgrounds, we usually say we are Ethiopians. When somebody asks me what my background is, I always say I'm Ethiopian first and, second, I'm Amhara.

KKS: Should I say *Habesha* or just Ethiopian?

MDB: I prefer Ethiopian (chuckles).[25]

One singer of dual Eritrean and Harari descent notes that

> North Africans and Arabs refer to people from the northern part of Ethiopia and Eritrea, who have the same or very similar roots, as Habesha, the Latin form of the word being Abyssinian, as I understand it. At any rate, my being of dual nationalities, Eritrean and Ethiopian, and having band members hailing from both nations, I decided to call my group Abyssinia Roots. I feel the name best reflects our commonalities in language, culture, and tradition.[26]

Prior to and during the revolution, when Ethiopia was divided into fourteen provinces, many would self-identify by giving their natal geographical locale: a Gondari was from Gondar in what was Begemder Province, or a Gojjami was from what was Gojjam Province in the central highlands. Certainly there was always implicit recognition of ethnic descent and status, most notably whether one was part of the then powerful Christian Amhara community. Linguistic and ethnic identities were on some occasions marked by the use of different place names, notably by individuals of Oromo heritage who called Addis Ababa by its traditional Afaan Oromo name, Finfinnee.

At the same time, these different linguistic communities historically overlapped, and many individuals married across ethnic boundaries. Most, especially from urban areas, spoke Amharic in addition to the language of their natal ethnic community, and those who had attended urban high schools and universities also often spoke English. In general, musicians raised in Ethiopia displaced to the diaspora were sometimes uncomfortable discussing ethnicity, perhaps given the emphasis on ethnic identity they had experienced during and after the revolution. But all, both at home and abroad, have certainly given the issue of ethnicity considerable thought.

In interviews, some musicians made it clear that definitions of ethnicity are situational and that musical contexts neutralize ethnic particularity for them as cosmopolitan performers. This seems to especially be the case for Eritrean musicians born when that country was part of Ethiopia and who lived in Ethiopia for years. Guitarist Selam Seyoum Woldemariam recalled that

> music was different for me. I am a global citizen and to me, music has no boundaries. I was an example to everybody, you know? I believe that music is above these things and it would unite all of us. I have both respect, good respect, from both Ethiopians and Eritreans. . . . Yes, there are some problems everywhere. Sometimes I control those things and I don't lose my identity, you know?[27]

Another individual of Eritrean descent who acts as a manager for other musicians insists that

> I don't make that distinction. I mean, you know, we're all the same people, we have the same culture, we look the same, nobody can distinguish who's who. And I grew up and I was born in Ethiopia, so I'm an Ethiopian. It really doesn't make sense to me, the differences.[28]

Some musicians from other ethnic backgrounds raised in Amhara-dominated settings move readily across ethnic boundaries, such as Oromo singer Abdi (Tesfaye) Nuressa, who took care to point out the presence of multiple Oromo communities within what is too often treated as a unitary ethnic category:

> I really don't have a problem with mixing here and there. But there are others who do have problems mixing. . . . But I want to make a point here that we, the Oromo, have a variety of cultures in the music.[29]

During the second half of the twentieth century, the spread of sound recordings and various broadcast media as well as the founding of state "cultural ensembles" brought the existence of multiple ethnic music and dance styles from across Ethiopia front and center into national consciousness. The display of ethnic musics and dance at national events as well as at urban hotels and restaurants to attract tourists increased the emphasis on traditional (*bahelawi*) music.

While this book and the larger project on which it draws had its genesis in Ethiopian studies, my own work over the years has purposefully expanded from its early focus on the Ethiopian highlands to incorporate a wider range of people and music representative of modern Ethiopia and the region as a whole.[30] This has been an important correction of focus as multiple populations have moved back and forth across the borders (past and present) of the modern state of Ethiopia and included people from regions who have, during the years of this study, achieved independence (Eritrea) or who aspire to various degrees of self-determination (Oromo). Dislocations for reasons of conflict or natural disaster have also increased border crossing in a region that has long been in a state of perpetual motion.

Many of the individuals who participated in this study have deep sensitivities as well as differing opinions about how they wish to be identified in terms of national identity and ethnicity. I will use the designation "Ethiopian" when referring to the Ethiopian state and its citizens of many ethnic backgrounds, unless I am discussing an individual with a different citizenship or who self-identifies in another way; when appropriate in these instances, I will refer to Amhara, Oromo, Eritrean, Somali, and other ethnic or national identities. But a central challenge of writing about this region and, in particular, its diaspora communities, is the volatility of issues surrounding ethnicity.

Conflicts in the homeland have reverberated internationally, where extensive communication networks amplify their impact and then resound back to the Horn of Africa. Many of these debates at home and abroad are given voice through musical performances and can arouse strong responses, such as the protests worldwide mounted against concerts by the well-known Ethiopian singer Teddy Afro (Tewodros Kassahun). Teddy Afro's song "Tikur Sew" (lit., Black man), a track from his album of the same title, celebrated the victories of late nineteenth-century emperor Menelik II, who vanquished the Italians at the Battle of Adwa in 1896 and who has long been celebrated for unifying Ethiopia into a modern state.[31] While a hero to many (highland) Ethiopians, Menelik II is perceived by Oromo as the late nineteenth-century conqueror of their southern homelands. Efforts by Teddy Afro to reinvigorate Ethiopian unity with a tribute to Menelik II's victory at Adwa were therefore met with both homeland and diasporic anger:

> The Ethiopian citizens belonging to the largest ethnic group in the country, the Oromo, have started a movement with a slogan "Oromo First." . . . They have also called a boycott against the Heineken beer company, "Boycott Bedele Beer," rejecting a sponsorship accord between the beer company and a renowned artist Teddy Afro to hold a concert entitled "a journey of love and unity" aiming at promoting unity among Ethiopians. They claimed that the artist used to sing songs glorifying Emperor Menilik II, a king the boycott movement believes to be a colonizer of the land of the Oromos. In the end, the concert was canceled.[32]

Competing ethnic and national identities from the Horn of Africa surface in unexpected diaspora settings, as an encounter I had at an Ethiopian restaurant in Washington, DC, graphically demonstrated. During the 2008 Ethiopian soccer tournament, an event celebrated each summer in a different Ethiopian American urban diaspora locale (discussed in more detail in chapter 6), daylong athletic competitions are followed by celebratory concerts that extend throughout the night in Ethiopian restaurants and clubs. Late one such evening in July 2008, I sat on a barstool alongside an Ethiopian colleague at a local DC restaurant listening to musicians performing Ethiopian popular music.

A man sitting nearby suddenly leaned over and, without introduction, gestured to me. Rolling up the sleeve of his shirt, he pointed to a tattoo on his forearm just above the wrist and asked me whether I knew what it was. Uncertain, I shook my head. "It's a map of Eritrea," he said, thereby identifying himself in no uncertain terms as an Eritrean within a very nationalistic, largely Amhara, Ethiopian diasporic musical setting.[33]

Yet if many of the individuals cited in this study discussed their ethnic backgrounds with pride, an equal number pushed back against ethnic separatism and described themselves as multiethnic. One church musician, who discussed his descent from an Oromo father and a mother who was of mixed Amhara, Gurage, and Tigrayan ancestry, qualified his discussion by saying, "But you know, Ethiopia is a mixed community, mixed race. So, you can call me a real Ethiopian, if you like, where all the races are mixed in my blood."[34]

The recent, disputed history of the Horn of Africa therefore provides a complex backdrop for understanding both deep-seated tensions and the interrelated lives of musicians of various ethnic and national backgrounds from the region as they moved abroad. Periods of conflict and resolution have ebbed and flowed. In 2017 and 2018, protests in Ethiopia against the government over arrests of opposition figures resulted in casualties and multiple impositions of a state of emergency. In February 2018, in a process eerily reminiscent of the "creeping coup" that marked the onset of the 1974 revolution with strikes and protests, the Ethiopian prime minister resigned and, soon after, a new prime minister, Abiy Ahmed, was appointed.[35] These fast-changing realities have reshaped my engagement with this project for more than forty-five years; necessitated new considerations of how to approach history through an ethnographic lens; and brought front and center the importance of individual biography and experience to this study. In the following pages, I detail my methods and theories, setting the stage for the chapters that follow.

An Accidental Longitudinal Study: The Research Process

My own scholarly engagement as an ethnographer of Ethiopian music and culture intersected with the beginnings of the Ethiopian revolution in February 1974, which interrupted what I had planned as a full year of musical ethnography in villages of northwestern Ethiopia. I had arrived in Addis Ababa in August 1973 and soon after began fieldwork in the northern highlands conducting my doctoral dissertation research on the liturgical music of the Beta Israel or Falasha, better known today as the Ethiopian Jews in Israel.[36] With the advent of the revolution during winter 1974, the instability and violence across the country prevented me from returning to my field sites in the north, but I remained in Addis Ababa through the end of 1975, an observer of a country in crisis.[37] I was aware of the impact of the revolution on everyone around me as well as the virtual cessation of public musical life; I also witnessed a growing number of surreptitious departures.

When I returned to the United States in 1976, first to the University of Michigan to complete my dissertation and then on to a teaching position at Columbia University in New York City in September 1977, I encountered members of the first wave of Ethiopians forced to migrate to the United States as well as students and diplomats unable to return home to the Horn of Africa when the revolution began. A close friend from Addis Ababa, a distinguished Eritrean monk and priest who had barely escaped Ethiopia during the tumult, arrived in New York City that same month. Ironically, we lived within blocks of each other on the Upper West Side of Manhattan, much closer than our homes had been in Addis Ababa. And, as I noticed with surprise, all around us were growing numbers of newly arrived Ethiopian and Eritrean immigrants.

If a conventional foreign fieldwork model had impelled me to carry out research in highland Ethiopia four years earlier to study Ethiopian musical life, by 1977 the Ethiopian music and musicians settling in around me in North America turned that model on its head. I soon began to visit Ethiopian and Eritrean Orthodox churches in New York, especially the small Ethiopian congregation graciously hosted by the stately Riverside Church just a few blocks down Riverside Drive from my Columbia University apartment. As early as the 1980s, I was able to teach a course that included taking my students to attend an Ethiopian Christmas ritual in the city and to carry out interviews with local Ethiopian church officials and musicians. The proliferation of Ethiopian and Eritrean restaurants in New York and across North America provided public venues in which Ethiopians came together and where Americans could get a taste of Ethiopian food and culture, occasionally with a live musical performance by immigrant musicians. Restaurants, shops, and other community institutions proliferated in other cities, most particularly in Washington, DC, where some of the earliest Ethiopian refugees had settled in the mid-1970s.

Ethiopian and Eritrean communities also popped up in cities across North America, with various ethnic groups from the Horn of Africa following friends and relatives in a pattern of chain migration to various locales. If Washington, DC, came to host the largest number of Ethiopians and Eritreans abroad, large populations also settled in Los Angeles and Atlanta, along with substantial cohorts of Oromo refugees moving to Minneapolis and Toronto. In 1991 a vanguard of Somali refugees arrived in the United States, with a majority finding a home in Minneapolis. By the turn of the millennium, Ethiopians and Eritreans constituted the second-largest new African community in the United States, second only to Nigerians.

I tracked the growth of the Ethiopian diaspora informally at first, then more methodically, beginning what would prove to be a long-term engagement. I carried out participant observation over the years in New York City (1977–90), Boston (1994–present), and Washington, DC (1999–2014).

In the early 2000s, I was able to resume regular trips to Ethiopia while simultaneously expanding my ethnographic observation to a cross section of Ethiopian communities across North America. This enabled me to better appraise homeland-diaspora interactions and, by the mid-2000s, to follow up with musicians who had begun to return to Ethiopia from diaspora. I undertook a series of intensive research trips to major urban areas where Ethiopians had settled across North America and, moving beyond the northeastern United States (Boston, New York, and Washington, DC), made short field trips to Seattle, Los Angeles, Atlanta, Houston, Dallas, Minneapolis, and Toronto. Hundreds of immigrant musicians from the Horn of Africa were actively performing and recording music across the United States and Canada, but the sheer numbers I encountered raised questions about how to approach their presence in the North American diaspora.[38]

During the summers of 2007 and 2008, my appointment to the Chair in Modern Culture at the John W. Kluge Center at the Library of Congress provided an extraordinary opportunity to systematically interview a number of Ethiopian, Oromo, and Eritrean musicians from the DC area. These interviews are part of a collection detailing musicians' migration processes, their music, and its place in their lives that I deposited in the Archives of the American Folklife Center at the Library of Congress.[39] (See plates 1.3–1.4.)

For this project, I purposefully sought to interview individuals across the boundaries of musical genres, generations, genders, and ethnic and

PLATES 1.3 AND 1.4 These photographs include participants interviewed by the author at the Library of Congress during 2007–8 who are discussed or cited in the book. Included in alphabetical order, from left to right and from top to bottom in each plate. Plate 1.3, row 1: Abdi (Tesfaye) Nuressa; Abonesh (Abiti) Adinew; Abraham Habte Selassie; Alemtsehay Wedajo. Row 2: Ashenafi Mitiku; Behailu Kassahun; Beniam Bedru Hussein; Betelehem (Betty) Melaku. Row 3: Bezawork Asfaw; Getahun Atlaw Garede; Getatchew Gebregiorgis; Hana Shenkute. Row 4: Hermela Mulatu; J. C. Jefferson Jr.; Martha Ketsela; Melaku Gelaw.

Plate 1.4, row 1: Mesfin Zeberga Tereda; Minale Dagnew Bezu; Moges Habte; Moges Seyoum. Row 2: Mohaammad Ibraahim Xawil; Sayem Osman; Selam Seyoum Woldemariam; Setegn Atanaw. Row 3: Tekle Tewolde; Telela Kebede; Tsegaye B. Selassie; Tsehay Amare. Row 4: Wayna Wondwossen; Woretaw Wubet; Yehunie Belay; Zakki Jawad.

religious backgrounds.[40] The secular musicians I interviewed were divided between *bahəlawi* (*bahelawi*: cultural, traditional) musicians and *zämänawi* (*zemenawi*: modern, popular) musicians; in many instances, the genre borders are blurred with a single musician performing both cultural and modern music, the latter sometimes termed *bahəl zämänawi* (*bahel zemenawi*) when performance includes traditional melodies accompanied by primarily Western instruments. General references to musicians here, therefore, incorporate those across the full spectrum of musical repertories, including traditional singers and instrumentalists, musicians who transmit popular repertories, and church musicians. However, it is important to recognize that church "chanters do not consider themselves to be musicians in the vernacular sense; that is, they do not perform 'musiqa.'"[41] The highly trained Ethiopian church musicians interviewed were veterans of years of training in Ethiopian churches and monasteries before migrating.

Some interviews included in my Library of Congress collection were recorded in other diaspora communities, including Boston, where historian Steven Kaplan and I completed ten lengthy interviews with the renowned Ethio-jazz musician Mulatu Astatke during our joint year as fellows at Harvard University's Radcliffe Institute for Advanced Study in 2007–8.

Interviewees included individuals closely involved with musical performance although not performing musicians themselves; several made crucial contributions to Ethiopian musical life at home and abroad. Indeed, they surely should be considered to be sentinel musicians, supporting the lives of other musicians and mounting musical performances. These included, among others, the poet and actress Alemtsehay Wedajo, who has written song lyrics for more than forty Ethiopian singers at home and abroad and who has long been an organizer of community events and children's musical activities, and Amha Eshete, a pioneer in Ethiopian sound recordings, ensemble management, and institution building in Ethiopia and in the United States. I also interviewed several non-Ethiopian musicians who were closely involved with the performance and life of Ethiopian music for decades, contributions that provided invaluable historical details otherwise inaccessible.[42]

During the 2007–8 interviews, musicians I queried estimated that there were around one hundred fifty Ethiopian immigrant musicians active in the Washington, DC, metropolitan area.[43] Through personal networks and by circulating letters on various Ethiopian internet sites notifying musicians about the project, I contacted and invited as many musicians as possible to the Library of Congress for interviews. In some cases, musicians holding multiple jobs were unable to spare time for interviews; a few others were unable to participate for personal reasons.[44] The vast majority of the musicians I contacted by telephone or email responded and made efforts to schedule interviews. Biographies of many of these musicians are cited here by permission. Additional interviews dating before 2007 and after 2008 are also cited in the list of interviews and communications.

My active research for this book, both in Ethiopia and in its North American diaspora, formally concluded in 2014, although a 2015–16 sabbatical year at Stanford University provided a welcome opportunity to gather a good measure of information on the Oakland and San Jose diaspora communities and to interview a few notable musicians from the San Francisco Bay Area. I visited Ethiopia a number of times since 2006 and met with several musicians whom I had earlier interviewed and who had returned from diaspora. I have continued to attend additional performances, on virtual media since the inception of the COVID-19 pandemic in spring 2020, and to follow up with various research associates until the present, including sharing materials with my research associates and carrying out a fair measure of dialogic editing. In sum, the materials that stand behind this book encompass more than forty-five years of ethnographic observation and research. They document the manner in which a revolution set in motion a great migration from the Horn of Africa, the revolution's impact on migrating musicians and their lives, and the outcomes of this movement abroad in the United States.

Theoretical Frameworks: When Ethnography Meets History
THE CASE FOR MULTITEMPORAL STUDIES

While historical methods have long been part of the ethnomusicological toolkit,[45] there have been surprisingly few discussions of historical theory and method in ethnomusicology.[46] Ethnomusicologists perhaps assumed that historical approaches are self-evident and do not require the same sort of careful interrogation they habitually have given to other methods and their theoretical frameworks. If ethnomusicologists are to achieve a more textured approach to history, they must give such matters more attention. At the same time, the grounded and often heterogeneous nature of ethnographic data provides challenges to the construction of even conventional linear historical narratives.

When studying forced migration and eliciting the testimonies of refugees, one encounters not just a heterogeneous mix of sites and dates of departure and arrival, but varying degrees of recall of moments along the way that were sources of great emotional duress. These instances require sensitivity when working with refugees, despite therapists' suggestions that patients' "trauma stories" may become a "centerpiece of the healing process."[47] While some musicians freely discussed their refugee experiences and welcomed these exchanges, other interlocutors declined to discuss the migration process and a few showed signs of emotional distress. In these instances, I tried to let the musician lead the conversation in other directions without pressure.

Musicians revealed many fraught moments through testimony and through song. A good example of the manner in which song provides primary testimony is the plaintive ballad "Lemenor" (To exist), performed by Bezawork Asfaw, a revered singer who gained asylum in the United States in 1990.[48] (See plate 1.5.) The song's lyrics recall the traumas of adjustment to life in exile, while the melody reinforces longing for the past by using the traditional *təzəta* (*tizita*) pentatonic mode, an Ethiopian musical marker of nostalgia:

Lämänor əyätäf chərächərkuñ bämədrə	To exist, I'm trying to survive in this world,
Həyəwäten bädästa lämaläfa bəməkrə	Trying to live in happiness.
Səntun səntun səntun ayyähu	How much, how much, how much have I seen?
Sənt asayäñə yäədme mist'ər	How much in all my life time is secret?
Yəhun kämalät bäsətäkər ayəwät'añä kəfam alnagär (x2)	I don't utter bad words except to say let it be (x2)
. . .	
Yähəywätən t'ämäzmaza guzo	But my journey was blocked by difficulties.
Lämäwät'at ləbem täsfan yəzo	And I'm still alive, working hard.
Däkämäñ takätäñ alalkum	I did not say that I am tired,
Lämänor täsəfam alwarät'kum	I have not lost hope to exist.[49]

Musical ethnographers seeking to forge new approaches to history can learn a great deal from the discussions among different schools of historical investigation during the last half century even if one chooses not to adopt a single approach in full. One finds a continual interplay in historical discourse between macro- and microhistorical approaches. Fernand Braudel, a leader of the French *Annales* school of historical scholarship, proposed in the 1950s that historians should speak to "an ever more precise idea of the multiplicity of temporalities and of the exceptional importance of the long term."[50] Braudel's work, especially his notion of "the *longue durée*," sought to expand the temporal backdrop against which both larger-scale events and individual lives are perceived to take place.[51]

Braudel in fact proposed that three levels of historical inquiry be pursued simultaneously: First is long-term "history whose passage is almost

PLATE 1.5 Bezawork Asfaw's title song of her CD *Lemenor* (2002) describes the challenges of surviving in diaspora. Courtesy of Bezawork Asfaw.

imperceptible, that of man in his relationship to the environment, a history in which all change is slow, a history of constant repetition, ever-recurring cycles"; next is the medium term of "slow but perceptible rhythm"; and third, the "traditional history — history, one might say, not on the scale of man, but of individual men, . . . that is, the history of events: surface disturbances."[52]

Studies of the *longue durée* are not common in ethnomusicology because music scholars are not often able to reconstruct the history of oral traditions to the time depth of more than a century.[53] Reconstructions of Ethiopian ritual musics in the oral tradition and their histories going back to the fifteenth century offer rare models of an ethnomusicological exploration of greater time depth.[54] Studies of great time depth are generally attainable only in cultural domains with written historical sources as well as indigenous systems of musical notation.

For the ethnomusicologist, the reconstruction of long-term history is a daunting task because of the constraints of qualitative ethnomusicological methods and data. In terms of its temporal limits, participant observation with living musicians is likely to permit reconstructions and insights that can date back for several generations, only rarely more.[55] Ethnographic data, especially of oral traditions, do not lend themselves easily to digital methods of analysis that are making important contributions to the revival of *longue durée* studies in the twenty-first century.[56]

Most musical ethnographers and anthropologists of music have focused on lives of individuals and the major musical events in which they are engaged, exploring processes of individual musical creativity as well as the interaction of social events associated with performance. For the ethnomusicologist, it is undoubtedly profitable to continue to do shorter-term research of a year or longer—producing what may in retrospect prove to be "episodic histories."[57] At the same time, it is possible to construct medium-term histories when sources and circumstances permit, with a goal of crafting studies that span several or more decades. A medium-term study of this time depth can provide sufficient analytical distance to offer new insights through the interactions of multiple subjects and perspectives. It is also a time period within the range of a single researcher working over the course of a career.[58]

It is a medium-term approach I adopt and advocate in this book, based on a methodology I term "multitemporal." By a multitemporal study, I refer to a research process that draws on repeated ethnographic encounters over a period of decades with the musicians and musical communities studied, revisiting them in different places and under changing circumstances.[59] Each return to the field gives rise to new, deepening insights into particular subjects and events and provides additional narratives and perspectives that can reveal unexpected patterns. The opportunity for ethnomusicologists to establish ongoing relationships with communities and individuals within them opens possibilities for multitemporal studies, including reexposures to materials that may be familiar, but that can suddenly provide evidence of changes over the course of time, as well as new interpretations. Multitemporal research methods enable the ethnomusicologist to understand complex and entangled narratives that help illuminate the "close relationship between subjectivity and temporality" and to approach time as "an *interlocking* of presents, pasts, and futures that retain their depths of other presents, pasts, and futures, each age bearing, altering, and maintaining the previous ones."[60]

As an important component of multitemporal research, musical ethnographers can draw on some of the methods and findings of the field of microhistory, which emerged in part as a response to perceived shortcomings of *longue durée* studies. *Longue durée* studies tend to mask the role of the individual and to omit considerations of human agency. In contrast, microhistories reduce the scale of observation to reveal the complications of individual relationships within particular social settings. Of potential interest to music scholars is the fact that

> microhistorians tend to focus on *outliers* rather than looking for the *average* individual as found by the application of quantitative research methods. Instead, they scrutinize those individuals who did not follow the paths of their average fellow countryman, thus making them their focal point. . . . Microhistorians use these cases to reflect on the workings of the society at large. Nearly all cases which microhistorians deal with have one thing in common; . . . each has much wider application, going well beyond the specific case under examination by the microhistorian.[61]

Microhistory's focus on outliers can resonate with studies of those consummate outliers in almost every society: musicians. The opportunity to study a community of musicians over the course of time and through spatial changes can yield broad insights into musicians' sensibilities, as well as their contributions to their societies. These studies can shed light on musical life in other locales.

If ethnomusicologists have not generally pursued ethnographic research that takes place over long periods, neither have formal longitudinal methods attracted them, likely because longitudinal studies require advance planning that does not harmonize easily with the unpredictable rhythms of individual participant observation. Classical longitudinal studies undertake repeated investigations of the same phenomena or individuals, purposefully revisiting an earlier study or updating data at more or less regular intervals.[62]

Although few long-term studies in music have been defined as such from the outset, a number of music scholars have carried out multitemporal research, returning for follow-up visits with communities and individuals they first encountered in the field. The longitudinal potential of an ethnomusicological study in most cases emerges slowly over time and teaches the researcher what questions to ask. As one astute Eritrean immigrant to the United States with whom I discussed ethnographic method remarked, "If you don't ask, the story stops. You have to ask the right questions."[63]

Anthony Seeger has written about the advantages of long-term research he carried out with the Kisêdjê people of Brazil, with whom he spent more than two years in the 1970s and 1980s, followed by seven short return visits in and after 1994. Listing both the advantages (and disadvantages) of long-term research, Seeger writes that our visits are like a still photograph of a full length film. In spite of our best efforts, we can capture only a fairly brief moment. . . . It is possible to see changes in the community in terms of leadership, languages, music, and almost anything else during 30 years, which can lead to substantially different insights than those made on the basis of a short visit.[64]

The process of multitemporal research may be said to produce a series of "microhistorical" studies that in their interrelationships enable the musical humanist to make significant contributions to historical discourse. This book thus constructs a detailed historical picture of forced migration based on the accounts of life experiences of musicians caught up within that process at different moments in time, establishing multiple internal time lines between testimonies or "narratives." Many of these accounts emerged slowly over decades, but not in chronological order. Multitemporal research demands a lot of sorting and cross-referencing; connections often emerge only when additional information becomes available. In sum, the methodological process is similar to piecing together a very large jigsaw puzzle, one for which the pieces come into view only over time. Even then one never achieves a complete image, because the puzzle's many pieces continue to change shape.

In the following pages, I will set forth testimonies that relate to multiple levels of experience; all are taken from accounts by individual musicians. In the deepest sense, these commentaries, both longer tales and shorter quotations, convey experiences of great importance to individuals throughout the decades of this study.

Musicians' narratives often move from a first level of concern with an individual's life, usually that of the speaker, to connect with a second level of moments in the broader course of community existence, linking individuals and their agency to institutional and collective processes. A third, intersecting or relational level can be reconstructed from observation of musical performances; this performative continuum of musical time shapes both individual and collective musical experience while existing in close dialogue with both.[65] All three narrative levels interact and, in their interaction, produce a composite record of musical historical time and its work in domains of subjectivity. (See figure 1.1.)

Biography as Kaleidoscope

If biographical data and oral traditions recounting life experiences reveal insights about the broader historical continua of which they are a part, musicians' verbal testimonies provide rich details about premigratory ex-

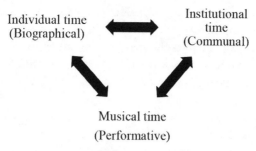

FIGURE 1.1 Narratives of musical historical time.

periences in their homelands, convey otherwise hidden knowledge of the conditions of transit, and broaden understanding of their lives at points of arrival. Through the testimony of many musicians, as well as through their performances, we can compile a multifaceted record of the lived experience of forced migration and its outcomes. These testimonies and performances offer a kaleidoscopic view of multiple lives, their interactions, and their impact on a broader landscape.

In negotiating this move from individual to collective perspectives, I have been stimulated by the field of prosopography, which has advanced methodologies to write "collective biography" based on data drawn from individuals in a population group that the researcher has determined has something in common, such as profession, social origins, or geographic origins.[66] Musicologists and ethnomusicologists have not often drawn on the methods of prosopography, likely because of their tendency to focus on the individual musician, whether a composer or performer. One of the few musical studies utilizing a prosopographical method discusses French composers between 1871 and 1905, investigating processes of identity formation through linking aesthetic choices to aspects of composers' social background, their position in the field, and political perspectives.[67]

Yet if prosopographers have succeeded in compiling copious historical data, they have too often left the reader to do much of the work of making connections. In seeking to avoid this pitfall, I highlight and address the broader themes extracted from the experience of many musicians through the central topics explored in each chapter. The narratives of many musicians stress their experiences in situations of conflict, their roles as sentinel musicians during processes of migration, and their surprising contributions on behalf of the collective good. In virtually every case, musical testimony and events allow us to recapture fleeting moments during which individual musical lives intersected and new relational modalities emerged.

Of particular importance is charting the impact of a number of musicians on their communities and the broader social worlds of which they were a part. Prosopographers have gathered information about a number of individuals to see what it reveals not just about the connections between them but also "how they operated within and upon the social, economic and other institutions of their time."[68] In order to understand better the agency that musicians wield in shaping their own societies, I follow the model of more recent prosopographers influenced by Pierre Bourdieu's concept of cultural fields and who have sought to position a confluence of human actions within "concrete social situations governed by a set of objective social relations."[69] By inflecting this approach with Bruno Latour's more fluid and flexible concept of the social as a process rather than perceiving it as bound to fixed institutions or spaces, I trace the fluidity that characterizes musical lives and performances in diaspora.[70]

When the great variations and nuances in individual biographies are combined, one can extract invaluable overviews of shared experiences. In the following pages, I focus most heavily on biographical data gathered over the decades from fifty-four immigrant musicians, over half of whom received asylum in the United States. Most remain today in the United States, while some have returned to Ethiopia within the last ten to fifteen years. I include six musicians who maintained primary residences in Ethiopia throughout this period while spending long periods in North America for music making, education, or family visits.

These fifty-four musicians practice a wide variety of musical styles. About half of them are in the secular domain as performers of cultural (traditional) musics and a quarter or so in modern (popular) musics. The rest transmit sacred musics of the Ethiopian Orthodox Church and other Christian denominations.[71] Of the musicians interviewed, twenty-nine are singers, twenty-two are instrumentalists, and three are dancers. All the church musicians as well as the traditional musicians from the secular domain combine song, instrumental practice, and dance in their training and performances. Musicians in modern or popular repertories, however, tend to be either singers or instrumentalists.

In terms of age cohorts, the two oldest musicians I interviewed were born in the 1930s and the majority were born in the decades between 1940 and 1980; there are five younger musicians with birthdates after 1980. Age does not appear to correlate in any way with either style predilections or to the degree of musical innovation or conservatism. Traditional musicians are found in all age brackets and some of the most innovative popular musicians are among the oldest; several of the youngest are more conservative in style and repertory.

Musicians' testimonies revealed the strong residue of ethnic conflicts and national sensitivities that arose in the years before and during the 1974 revolution and from the policy of ethnic federalism established after the revolution, during the 1990s. Almost half of the musicians I interviewed in diaspora are of Christian Amhara descent; the rest represent a diverse range of ethnicities and religions today present in the Horn of Africa, some with ambivalent relations to the Ethiopian state, including many of the Oromo and Eritrean musicians. Eleven musicians do not affiliate with a single ethnic group but rather prefer to describe their backgrounds as multiethnic, with ancestry from a variety of communities.

The musicians' narratives provide insights into their individual lives, transmitting evidence of many experiences that are shared. For instance, biographical reminiscences confirmed that most confronted strong parental disapproval of their musical interests early on and encountered active family resistance to their entry into musical careers. Musicians occupy an ambivalent position in Ethiopian society and the Horn of Africa at large, where they are considered to be indispensable yet equally often are reviled. As a result, most had to exercise a full measure of initiative to become a musician; one can only wonder whether the need to express themselves in the face of opposition early on shaped their ability to push back as sentinel musicians during moments of pressure later in their lives. Each, in a different way, demonstrated unusual pursuit of independence within hierarchical and patriarchal contexts. Pursuing a musical career carried substantial risks in Ethiopia and adjacent regions well before the dangers of the revolutionary period. As we will see in the following chapters, Ethiopian secular musicians had long been known for their ability to inspire patriotism; for centuries, traditional minstrels (*azmari*) had performed songs with double meanings (wax and gold) that offered political commentary and thinly masked social criticism. Throughout the documented history of Ethiopia, musicians were noted for their ability to incite resistance, becoming targets of official retribution when they opposed those in power. Church musicians, some of whom were powerful healers, were also both admired and feared for their supernatural powers.

During the Ethiopian revolution, musicians once again became targets of suspicion and discrimination. They faced alternatives whether to cooperate with the military regime or to flee in the face of daily constraints such as curfews and orders against public gatherings that curtailed live performances. As the carriers of news and commentary, musicians were among the first to be adversely affected by the revolution's increasing constraints and violent trajectory.[72]

Musicians in revolutionary and postrevolutionary Ethiopia became musical sentinels both through their music making and through a range of initiatives designed to aid others and enhance their communities' lives. The following chapters recount their efforts before, during, and after the 1974 revolution, providing insights into the changing societies of which they were a part.

Mobilities

PEOPLE AND MUSIC IN MOTION

Səlt

GENERAL MEANING: Line, pathway
MUSICAL MEANING: Mode, melody

The sounds of "The Either/Orchestra," a ten-piece jazz ensemble, spilled out of the storefront in Inman Square Cambridge, Massachusetts, that housed a modest performance space known as the Lily Pad. On that summer evening in July 2010, a medley of Ethiopian big-band pieces dating from the late 1960s filled the air with the renowned Ethiopian-born singer Teshome Mitiku as soloist. Billed as a "secret concert" and a "test run" for the musicians' planned appearance at the Chicago Jazz Festival six weeks later, the band played arrangements of pentatonic melodies in pungent Ethiopian tunings marked by syncopated rhythms, underpinning Teshome's fluid and ornamented vocal line. Several of the songs had been composed by the singer himself in the late 1960s, including "Yezemed ye-bada" (lit., family or others),[1] which voiced sentiments that would prove prophetic, anticipating the displacement of the singer and other Ethiopians in the years to come: "Even if nobody, family or others, comes to my aid, I will make it, even if I go crazy trying."[2]

Both the band and the singer were mobile musicians who had lived and made music in completely separate worlds. Teshome, known abroad mainly to aficionados of Ethiopian music, had been the star singer of the Soul Ekos Band (lit., soul echoes) founded around 1969 in the Ethiopian capital, Addis Ababa. The Either/Orchestra was established in 1985 by a Boston-area saxophonist and composer, Russ Gershon. These unlikely collaborators from different places, times, and musical styles found each other as a result of a convergence of late twentieth-century global politics, a surge of forced migration from the Horn of Africa that included an unusual

PLATE 2.1 Singer Teshome Mitiku (top right head shot) performs
Ethio-Jazz in 2010 with Russ Gershon's (front center) Either/Orchestra.
Either/Orchestra photograph courtesy of Russ Gershon; photograph
of Teshome Mitiku courtesy of Bryan Thompson, Graffiti Photo.

number of musicians, and the circulation by the mid-1990s of Ethiopian
music worldwide through recordings across various media. (See plate 2.1.)

Teshome's early career set this process into motion. Soul Ekos was the
first independent popular band in Ethiopia, organized and managed in
1969–70 by a young musical entrepreneur and record-store owner named
Amha Eshete. Amha recorded the brilliant but short-lived band for his
Amha Record label, which itself survived for barely seven years (1969–
75) and was a musical casualty of the Ethiopian revolution.[3] But in February 1997,

> Amha Record masters were retrieved from remote storage in Greece by
> Francis Falceto, and many of these original recordings became the basis of
> releases within Falceto's French CD series *éthiopiques*, circulated beginning
> in 1997 to an international audience.[4]

Russ Gershon encountered these recordings, which included four songs
performed by Teshome, catalyzing Gershon's deep engagement with Ethiopian big-band music of the 1960s and 1970s.

The pathway to this collaboration was a circuitous one. In 1970 musicians of the Soul Ekos Band ran into political trouble from their association with emerging student protests against the Ethiopian imperial government. After singing an overtly political song with the opening words
"Fano Tesemara ende Ho Chi Minh ende Che Guevara" (Fighter, de-
ploy, like Ho Chi Minh and like Che Guevara), and experiencing several

brief imprisonments, Teshome fled Ethiopia in January 1970 for Sweden. There he pursued his musical career and fathered a daughter who grew up to be the celebrated Swedish pop star Emilia.[5] After decades in Sweden, Teshome migrated again and settled in Washington, DC, in the early 1990s.[6]

If Teshome was one of the first musicians to flee Ethiopia even before the revolution began in 1974, his arrival in Washington, DC, brought him to a new home amid the largest Ethiopian and Eritrean community outside the Horn of Africa. Meanwhile, the Either/Orchestra had been collaborating since the end of the 1990s with Ethiopian musicians in the North American diaspora. A little more than a decade later, the concert at the Lily Pad celebrated the joining of musicians and the repertory that linked their musical lives, only one of many tales of global musical interaction. Yet, while mobility provides an immediate framework for understanding the story of a particular revolution and its international reverberations, an overview of mobility in the more distant past contributes important insights into the full range of encounters that have left their marks on Ethiopian music and its performance over the course of time.

If it can be said that musicians venture "from home on the thread of a tune," music also clears a pathway for these journeys.[7] Indeed, in the Ethiopian language, Amharic, the word *sɔlt* carries the double meaning of "pathway" and "melody."[8] When a musician performs a melody, they both sustain their musical tradition and clear a pathway for sentinel activity. Beyond the ability to evoke shared memories across widely divergent homeland experiences, migratory paths, and diaspora locales, musicians have the capacity both to unite and to divide, to give voice to competing identities, and to sound divergent political positions. A melody can also bring together those who have followed very different pathways as they move from one part of the world to another.

The Horn of Africa

Northeast Africa, with a peninsula that juts into the Arabian Sea resembling the protrusion on the forehead of an African rhinoceros, came to be known during the twentieth century as the Horn of Africa.[9] (See plates 1.1 and 1.2.) With a landscape cross-cut by the dramatic chasms of the Rift Valley, ranging from rugged highlands to inhospitable desert lowlands, Ethiopia presents one of the most forbidding topographies on earth and is not conducive to travel. But the region owes its place in the global imagination as a metaphor for isolation and stasis less to geographical or historical realities than to a memorable phrase once written by eighteenth-century English historian Edward Gibbon: "the Aethiopians slept near a thousand years, forgetful of the world by whom they were forgotten."[10] His words sparked a great misunderstanding of the historical mobility and global impact of peoples from the Horn of Africa when they were disseminated by later scholars whose work reached a general readership, such as Edward Ullendorff's writing on Ethiopia's isolation in his widely read general introduction to the country and its people.[11]

This chapter considers the relationship between spatial mobility and social mobility in historical perspective, drawing on Thomas Faist's criticism that the conventional concept of mobility implicitly suggests a division between high-mobility modern contexts and low-mobility traditional societies.[12] Case studies from the Horn of Africa demonstrate that, although external views of mobility may impose a modern-traditional divide, movement is, in fact, a long-standing process within the area, not restricted to physical movements across national boundaries. In contrast, it is clear that there is a marked distinction between degrees of virtual mobility in traditional and modern societies in this and other areas, with the former constrained by inadequate infrastructures supporting virtual resources.

The Horn of Africa exploded into international consciousness in the 1970s for two reasons.[13] Donald Johanson's 1974 discovery of a skeleton that came to be known in Ethiopia as *Denkenesh*—"Lucy" to the wider world—established the Afar region of Ethiopia's Rift Valley as an important cradle of human history.[14] A few years before this stunning archaeological discovery was made, a series of devastating droughts overwhelmed the region, providing a flashpoint that eventually led to the 1974 Ethiopian revolution and the overthrow of the emperor and to a widespread perception of the entire Horn of Africa as a site of famine and death. Thus, Ethiopia in particular and the Horn of Africa in general became in the global imaginary both a site for the birth of humankind and an equally powerful symbol of the constant threat of mortality. Both perspectives have been reinforced and circulated through musical associations: Johanson named his spectacular archaeological find Lucy after the Beatles' 1967 classic song "Lucy in the Sky with Diamonds," and the songs "Do They Know It's Christmas" (1984) and "We Are the World" (1985) eventually awoke the international public to ongoing famines in the region and generated donations to help affected populations.[15]

Although the Horn of Africa has had a rapidly changing political map, it remained on the margins of the colonial scramble for Africa in part as a result of Ethiopia's successful defense of its independence. Often overlooked was the Italian colonial presence in Eritrea and Somalia from the late nineteenth century, as was Italy's brief occupation of Ethiopia itself between 1936 and 1941. Both the British and the French also had colonial footholds along the coast. In 1960 British and Italian colonial Somalia became independent and joined together to form the United Republic of Somalia.[16] The French Territory of the Afars and the Issas in 1977 became the small country of Djibouti.[17] But it was during February 1974 that uprisings began that led to the overthrow of longtime emperor Haile Selassie I half a year later by a repressive military regime, constituting the biggest political upheaval in the region since the Italian invasion of 1936.

The borders of historical Abyssinia, as Ethiopia was long known, were redrawn through centuries of religious and military expansion south and west that, by the end of the nineteenth century, gave rise to the modern Ethiopian state. The loss of Ethiopia's Red Sea ports followed decades of civil war that culminated in Eritrea's independence in 1993. Border conflicts between Ethiopia, Eritrea, and Somalia have continued to flare in the region well into the twenty-first century.

The 1974 revolution opened a new chapter, as many people of the Horn of Africa were forced to disperse from their homelands and to rebuild their lives abroad. They settled on all continents except Antarctica, with the largest numbers streaming to North America, the primary diaspora research site for this study. Many were refugees who received asylum and others of their number remain undocumented. Today, immigrants from the Horn of Africa are settled across the United States, in locales ranging from Maine to California and from Minnesota to Texas, as well as in Canada.

Exile and Refugeeism in Ethiopian History and Imagination

In 1951 the United Nations Refugee Convention established a single definition of a refugee as someone who is unable or unwilling to return to their country of origin owing to a well-founded fear of being persecuted for reasons of race, religion, nationality, membership in a particular social group, or political opinion.[18] Following this important 1951 convention, human displacement has continued unabated and has commanded international attention. According to the United Nations, by 2015 there were more than sixteen million refugees worldwide.[19] The flood of late twentieth- and twenty-first-century departures from the Horn of Africa resulted in the establishment of Ethiopian, Eritrean, and Somali communities in Africa, the Middle East, Australia, Europe, and — in their greatest numbers — North America. By 2012 US Census data estimated that the late twentieth-century continental African immigrant population in the United States numbered 1.6 million, with immigrants from four African countries (Nigeria, Ethiopia, Ghana, and Egypt) accounting for 41 percent of the total.[20] If mobility has increased dramatically, one of the primary causes in the twentieth and twenty-first centuries has been the surge of refugees as a result of natural disasters, famine, and war.

The concept of refugee has since the mid-twentieth century been an essential part of the international human-rights lexicon, but the term assumes clear meaning for most individuals only when they are thrust into unanticipated motion. The poet Alemtsehay Wedajo, an Ethiopian who received asylum in the United States in 1991, compares the shock of exile to the trauma of birth:

> When you come out of your mother's womb, suffering difficulty,
> When you come to the world you do not know.
> The kind of cry that you cried then when you were born,
> You cry again when you are exiled from (your) country.[21]

But definitions of the term *refugee*, although now officially recognized worldwide, are not necessarily understood in the same way within the history of a given place. Ethiopia provides such an example.

The Amharic word *səddättäñña*, derived from the Amharic root *säddädä*, meaning "to send off, to banish, or to exile," describes someone who is a refugee, displaced person, or an exile.[22] The experience of exile within the homeland is part of the Ethiopian past, dating at least as far back as the late thirteenth century. At that time, potential male competitors for the Ethiopian throne, including sons and other male relatives of sitting monarchs, were exiled from court and sent to secluded, flat-topped mountains in the northern Ethiopian highlands.[23] These isolated sites were subsequently associated with *səddät*, "exile or banishment."[24]

Over the centuries, some Ethiopians were also forced to leave their natal villages because of infectious disease or disability, notably individuals who suffered from leprosy (Hansen's disease):

> Where a family's resources are insufficient to maintain non-productive adults, the sick man must leave his hamlet to become a mendicant, begging from almsgivers at the gates of large and famous churches.[25]

Being sent into exile within Ethiopia thus carried strong and negative associations.[26] Exile outside the country, however, was not a common part of Ethiopian experience before the twentieth century, although there were instances of both voluntary and forced movement abroad to be discussed later in this chapter. A notable exception was the extended period of exile abroad that Emperor Haile Selassie I, along with many other Ethiopians, experienced when they were forced to seek asylum during the 1936–

1941 Italian occupation of their country.[27] The exile of the emperor was viewed as a national disaster and humiliation. So deep was the wound from the Italian occupation and subsequent exile that not all celebrated the return of the emperor from asylum in Great Britain, as one Ethiopian proverb makes clear in no uncertain terms: "A priest who has broken his vow cannot do his priestly duties, so a king who retreated [in the face of the enemy] cannot be a king."[28] The 1974 overthrow of Haile Selassie I's regime and subsequent forced migration of so many Ethiopians marked what has been termed as

> a critical threshold in the history of migration from the Horn of Africa. Most Ethiopians were unfamiliar with the very concept of a "refugee" and repelled by the idea of moving abroad permanently.[29]

A recent survey of Ethiopian song lyrics from the last century indicates that references to displacement or exile were rare in songs composed before the 1974 revolution.[30] Ethiopians never anticipated that they could be forced into exile abroad. Indeed, foreign influences had long been regarded with suspicion, and concerns about exposure to distant cultures were expressed openly in songs about Ethiopian students sent to study in Europe and the United States after World War II:

> My kin, living abroad, beyond the sea, hurry, come
> Your mother and country are longing for you. . . .
> It is no use to brag and tell people that you were abroad
> Unless you achieved something that makes you proud
> We want you to learn skills but nothing else
> We beseech you not to bring us deviant behavior.[31]

If the story of the late twentieth-century Ethiopian abhorrence of exile is not a unique one in human history, it is vital to locate this recent era of forced migration in the context of the experience of mobility in the Ethiopian past.

Modalities of Mobility

Ethiopia provides rich materials for a discussion of mobility with its intermittent population movements. An overview of Ethiopian mobility, coupled with an appreciation of individual pathways that were actually traveled, can provide broader insights into patterns that emerge over time across historical periods and in different locales. Here I give particular attention to John Urry's "mobilities paradigm" and the five interdependent mobilities he calls corporeal, material, imaginative, virtual, and communicative.[32] I have recast his framework to take into account the factors that generate mobility and reflect more precisely the rough chronology of this phenomenon as encountered in the long history of Ethiopia. One finds a close and inseparable relationship between corporeal and material mobility in the African past, rendering problematic Urry's separation of human mobility from modern networks of transport and communications. Needless to say, an ethnomusicological study of music also presupposes communicative mobility as a factor that overlaps with all other mobile categories at various points in time.

First, what I term "imagined mobility" is set into motion and sustained through myth, legend, or literature. Second is mobility embedded in actual physical travel, which subsumes both corporeal and material mobility, whether through human departures for a distant place or through encounters with mobile individuals or objects that come from elsewhere into the home environment; as detailed in the previous sections, more instances of actual physical travel in early centuries came into the region than departed for foreign locales. Travel is also usually conceived to be a temporary process, with the assumption that the traveler is a sojourner who will return home at some moment in the future.

For our purposes here, a third form of mobility, commonly called forced migration, occurs when travel is set into motion by a traumatic event ranging from an encounter with a slave trader to the occurrence of a natural or political disaster. Forced migration usually begins suddenly and necessitates an abrupt departure from the place of residence. Forced migration inevitably embeds a high degree of stress and uncertainty; generally, both the ultimate destination and the possibility of return to the point of departure are unknown.

Various factors can lead to the fourth category of mobility, voluntary migration. Although commonly regarded as a process of mobility born of individual choice and agency, rarely is a so-called voluntary process without precipitating social or economic factors, nor is it without a substantial degree of stress. Although positive conditions at destination may provide incentives for travel just as negative factors at home may spur departure, rarely are voluntary migrations fully a matter of personal choice or individual agency. In large-scale movements of population such as those that gave rise to the Ethiopian diaspora, one can find a mixture of forced and voluntary migrations, often at the same time for different individuals, and sometimes at different moments within the experience of a single person.

A final, fifth category is virtual or mediated mobility, a topic that is the subject of a growing literature.[33] Musicians and their musics prove to be deeply embedded in many virtual channels, and their contents shed new light on the migratory processes that set them into motion.

The history of the Horn of Africa provides rich examples of each of these types of movement. A possible sixth category, recently entering the literature as "return mobility," will be explored in chapter 10.[34]

Whatever modality of mobility is under consideration, it is sure that each occurrence sheds light on power relations of different times and places; the Ethiopian case study is no exception. In short, "mobility and control over mobility both reflect and reinforce power. Mobility is a resource to which not everyone has an equal relationship."[35]

Imagined Mobility

Distant links to the Jewish Middle East are set forth in the early Ethiopian literary work and national epic the *Kəbrä Nägäst* (Glory of the Kings). This heavily elaborated Ethiopian rendering of the biblical tale of Solomon and the queen of Sheba recounts the travels of Makeda, the queen of Ethiopia, to Jerusalem; her subsequent union with King Solomon; the birth of their son, Menelik; and Menelik's later journey as an adult to his father's court, during which he steals the Ark of the Covenant and brings it back with him to Ethiopia.[36] In this origin myth, we find a link between Ethiopia and the world beyond its borders, one that is reaffirmed through repeated travels over time and the importation of objects and people from abroad.

Imagined mobility seems to exist most comfortably when ascribed to the distant past or from a time remembered that is somehow lost in the present.[37] The mobile Ethiopian imagination, in large part a result of its Judeo-Christian background and orientation, is particularly attracted to Jerusalem as an imagined destination of travel. Jerusalem is the focus of many geographical imaginaries in Ethiopian history, inspiring dreams of mobility in several epochs and among various peoples. For instance, in the twelfth and thirteenth centuries, Ethiopians are said to have constructed the rock-hewn churches of Lalibela at the northern town founded by an emperor of that period.[38] (See plate 2.2.) According to the legend of Lalibela's founding,

God revealed his plan to the king in a dream, and commanded him to build a replica of Jerusalem in the place where he was born. Toponomy-

PLATE 2.2 The Church of Saint George is the most famous of the churches hewn from solid rock at Lalibela in northern Ethiopia. Collection of author.

cally this is reflected in the presence of a watercourse called the Jordan (Yordanos)—complete with a monolithic cross and pillar commemorating the baptismal place of Christ himself—and a mount of Olives (Däbrä Zäyt) and Golgotha (Golgata). Lalibela is thus one of the many "Small Jerusalems" in the tradition of Christianity. The Ethiopian tradition connects the erection of the New Jerusalem with the fall of Jerusalem in 1187.[39]

Imagined mobility can later be realized in physical travel. For example, over time the mythical tie to Jerusalem became an aspiration for both Christian Ethiopians and the Beta Israel (Ethiopian Jews) to make pilgrimages to the city.[40] Ethiopian Christians from the early Christian period were committed to visiting the city of Jerusalem; it was traditional for a pilgrim who visited there to have a cross tattooed on her forehead or hand. In the 1860s, a religious dispute between the Beta Israel and European missionaries seeking to convert them to Protestantism resulted in an attempt by a large number of Beta Israel to walk to Jerusalem because they thought that the coming of the Messiah was near. The effort ended after three years near the northeastern Ethiopian town of Aksum, and the pilgrims returned home.[41]

Physical Travel

Ethiopia's mobile contacts with the Christian world abroad are recorded in historical documents and artifacts. From soon after the entry of Orthodox Christianity into the country in the early fourth century, Ethiopia's church was in close touch with the Coptic Church of Egypt and much of the rest of Eastern Christendom.[42] Ethiopian Orthodox Christian clerics visited Jerusalem on pilgrimages as early as the 380s CE, established their own communities and chapels in the Holy Land by the 1400s, and sent Ethiopian representatives to the Council of Florence in Italy (1437–43).[43]

Muslims making the pilgrimage (hajj) to Mecca from various parts of Africa also passed through northeastern Africa in order to reach the port of Massawa, today in Eritrea, from where they crossed the Red Sea to the Arabian peninsula. Some of these pilgrims remained permanently in Eritrea or Ethiopia, becoming part of the local population.[44] In 1529 the imam of a sultanate in the southeastern region adjacent to the city of Harar invaded the Ethiopian highlands. Although the conquest eventually failed, for reasons discussed in more detail later, many were killed or displaced, and the ethnic composition of the region substantially altered.[45]

Ethiopian relationships with Italy and other European nations are linked by travel that stretches back to the Middle Ages. What distinguishes these encounters is that they are reciprocal and set the stage for later contact between Ethiopia and Italy that extended into the colonial period and beyond. The Ethiopian-Italian relationship, for example, began when sea routes spanned not just the Mediterranean, but from the eleventh century forward, the Red Sea and Ethiopian ports as well. Overland caravans linked Ethiopia across the Sudan plain to Alexandria, Egypt, a gateway to Western Europe.[46] From as early as the twelfth century, Europeans were intrigued by rumors of a powerful East African Christian kingdom ruled by "Prester John" and aspired to establish relations with it as a hedge against Muslim power in the region.[47]

If the Ethiopian Orthodox Church was the primary agent for voluntary Ethiopian travel abroad, foreigners also visited Ethiopia early on, including Jesuits who began entering the country in the sixteenth century.[48] There is evidence of substantial exchange between Ethiopia and Italy in the arts, in worship, and in academic pursuits. The Italian artist Nicolò Brancaleon (c. 1460–1526) sojourned for decades in Ethiopia and is known to have introduced new pictorial elements into Ethiopian Church paintings.[49] (See plate 2.3.) The nineteenth century saw yet more contact between Ethiopia and the outside world, notably the arrival of European

PLATE 2.3 The triptych "Saint George and Scenes of His Martyrdom,"
painted by the Venetian artist Nicolò Brancaleon during the three decades he
was employed in the Ethiopian court, is signed beneath the central figure of
Saint George as "I, Marqoryos the Frank [Afrengi] painted this painting." The
signature clearly identifies Brancaleon, who was called "Marqoryos" in Ethiopia,
with the appellation "the Frank" identifying him as a foreigner. Brancaleon's
work demonstrates artistic cross-fertilization, combining Italian Quattrocento
elements with aspects of contemporary Ethiopian style (Marilyn Heldman,
"Catalogue," *African Zion: The Sacred Art of Ethiopia* [New Haven, CT: Yale
University Press, in association with InterCultura, Fort Worth, Walters Art
Gallery, Baltimore, and the Institute of Ethiopian Studies, Addis Ababa, 1993],
188–89). Photo by Paul Henze from the collection of Stanislaus Chojnacki
(Mäzgäbä Seelat: SC-004-015-010), with the permission of Michael Gervers.

Protestant missionaries, who served as mediators between Ethiopia and
Europe. These individuals also expanded the interest of Ethiopian rulers
in the European "arts and sciences," laying the groundwork for the first
Ethiopians to study abroad.[50]

Italians entered coastal Eritrea in the 1890s, a period during which the
rest of Ethiopia escaped colonial domination by virtue of its stunning victory over the Italian army in March 1896 at the Battle of Adwa. Except for
the brief and violent Italian occupation during the six years before and at

the beginning of World War II, the Ethiopian state was officially independent throughout its history.[51]

However, the Italian presence introduced a new form of travel for men
from the Horn of Africa, as military mercenaries. In 1911 the Italians fought
the Ottomans and began an occupation of territory in North Africa that
would later become Libya. At first, they hired mercenaries from their col-
onies in Eritrea and Somalia, but eventually they recruited Ethiopians as
well for service in North Africa. The large number of Ethiopian mercenaries who participated in the Italian campaign in Libya, numbering twelve
thousand from one region of northern Ethiopia alone in the year 1934,
were known as *tərənbuli*, a name derived from the Libyan capital, Tripoli.
A song dating from this period, "Shäggaw Tərənbuli" (The handsome Ethiopian from Tripoli), makes it clear that Ethiopians were attracted to service
both by the historical prestige of the military in Abyssinian society and by
the money they made for fighting abroad. The song likely originated with
an *azmari* (minstrel) but was picked up and popularized by well-known
singers throughout and after the Libyan period.[52]

A second opportunity for Ethiopian men to travel abroad in a military
context occurred during the Korean War, when Ethiopians joined a battalion of the United Nations Forces known as the *Qañäw Shaläqa* (the
Kagnew Battalion), after which the US military base Kagnew Station in
Eritrea was named in 1952.[53] The Ethiopian experience in East Asia is recalled with nostalgia in the song "Japanwan Wodədjə" (I fell in love with a
Japanese [woman]), performed by the legendary Ethiopian singer Tilahun
Gessesse, who had a romantic relationship while on leave in Japan during
his own service in Korea:

> While I was in the Far East, I fell in love with a Japanese [woman]
> I remember burning in her love
> She resembles a flower hanging from the vine
> Her beauty is stunning when one looks.
> There is no one that matches her beauty
> She is the fountain of humbleness and beauty is her culture.[54]

Through song, travel for military expeditions abroad, including tales of
tərənbuli and of beautiful and poised Japanese women, were embedded
into the Ethiopian consciousness.

A second and unexpected chapter of Ethiopian travel and contact with
individuals from abroad was catalyzed by the global imaginary during the
first half of the twentieth century, when Ethiopia's Ras Tafari garnered in-

ternational attention as a powerful symbol of African independence. In the 1920s, Marcus Garvey launched the "Back to Africa" movement, seeking to reclaim Black pride through a return to Africa. In 1927 Garvey was deported from the United States to his homeland, Jamaica. There he and others predicted that the crowning of a Black king in Africa would presage deliverance for all Black people. This prediction was based on passages in Genesis 49:9 and elsewhere in the Bible that compared biblical Israel's (Judah's) power to that of a lion, with later references to Christ as "the lion of Judah." In this context, the coronation of Ethiopian Regent Ras Tafari in 1930 as Haile Selassie I, the Lion of Judah, was greeted by many as a fulfillment of the prophecy.[55]

In the West Indies, one outcome of these events was the formation of communities—some called Ethiopians, others termed Rastafarians—that supported the new Ethiopian emperor. Ras Tafari's accession to the Ethiopian throne as Haile Selassie I was thought to herald the downfall of "Babylon" (white colonial powers) and the subsequent deliverance of Black peoples. Ras Tafari thus provided a central symbol for what became known as the Rastafarian religious and political movement and its associated musical style, reggae. Not only did the Ethiopian Orthodox Church send members of its clergy to open an archdiocese of the Caribbean and Latin America in Trinidad in 1952 (the first time Ethiopian clerics entered this region), but a Rastafarian settlement was approved in Ethiopia by Emperor Haile Selassie I in 1950. These immigrants to Ethiopia lived on land granted them in the town of Shashamane, about 250 kilometers south of Addis Ababa. A 2003 census taken by the Ethiopian Immigration Office estimated that Rastafarians of fourteen nationalities lived in Shashamane. Once a larger population, their numbers declined dramatically when all rural land was nationalized by the revolutionary government in 1975, although hundreds of Rastafarians today remain permanently settled in Ethiopia.[56]

Forced Migration

Forced migration from the Horn of Africa began early on, well before the mass migration sparked by the 1974 revolution. Disturbing historical records reveal early forced removal of people from the region to foreign locales through the Indian Ocean slave trade. Although the slave trade is usually thought of as characterizing West African and trans-Atlantic history, ample evidence shows that peoples from early Abyssinia and adjacent regions were taken as slaves during periods of regional conflict as well as during slave-raiding expeditions from dates early in the Common

Era. Primarily Muslim traders exported slaves from Abyssinian Red Sea ports to Arabia as well as to points as far east as India. Indeed, the son of an Abyssinian slave woman in Mecca is documented as having been one of the first converts to Islam. Named Bilāl b. Rahāb al-Habašī, this man is said to have become the first official *muezzin* to chant the call to prayer from the mosque when it was instituted in the year 623; he is also reputed to have accompanied the Prophet Muhammad on all his expeditions.[57]

The slave trade from the Horn of Africa persisted until the nineteenth century, when it reached its peak. It is estimated that, during the nineteenth century, nearly five hundred thousand slaves were taken from Abyssinia by sea and via overland routes to a wide variety of destinations across the Persian Gulf and the Levant. Unlike the Atlantic slave trade, which had ships solely given over to human cargo, slaves were moved along with other "goods" on boats that crossed the Red Sea and Indian Ocean. Female slaves are said to have outnumbered males, with Ethiopian women desired as concubines in Arabia, Istanbul, and Egypt.[58]

During the first half of the sixteenth century, as already noted, Ethiopia was invaded by Muslim forces from the south led by Aḥmad b. Ibrāhīm al-Ġāzi.[59] This leader of Somali origin captured most of historical Abyssinia, burned and destroyed churches and monasteries, plundered precious materials, and massacred priests and monks; his forces also sold slaves to the East.[60] The invaders were defeated in 1543 with the aid of Portuguese soldiers, who arrived at Ethiopia's request. The protracted struggle devastated the country and interrupted performance and transmission of the Ethiopian Christian liturgy. So serious was the threat to the continued performance of church ritual orders that surviving musicians soon developed and codified a notational system for the liturgy.[61]

Multiple waves of forced migration set off by the 1974 revolution will be the subject of chapter 4.

Voluntary Migration

From the Italian defeat in 1941 through 1959, approximately 553 Ethiopian men and women were sent abroad to study. By the early 1960s, about one thousand students went abroad each year and, by the early 1970s, two thousand left Ethiopia annually to study abroad. In 1970 Ethiopian students were scattered across forty countries and continents, with the largest contingent being the more than seven hundred who were in the United States.[62] Most of these young people were from elite, urban Ethiopian families, and when the revolution began, many were unable to return home or chose not to.[63] They became among the first members of the Ethiopian diaspora, anchoring what are today dozens of vibrant Ethiopian American communities.

Voluntary contact with foreigners at home in Ethiopia had also increased dramatically in the decades prior to the revolution, with a marked impact on musical domains. Here we encounter the manner in which the course of musical life in twentieth-century Ethiopia provides a template of culture change in the country, with the increasing influence of foreign teachers. Emperor Menelik II (1889–1913) made the first moves to establish a modern educational system. Near his final years on the throne in 1908, he founded the Menelik II Lyceum in Addis Ababa, staffed mainly with Egyptian teachers.[64] Clear evidence shows Emperor Menelik's interest in importing new communication technologies: a photograph from Menelik's late years shows the emperor listening intently to an early telephone transmission around 1909, the year he created the Ministry of Posts, Telegraphs, and Telephones.[65]

Brass instruments had been used in the Ethiopian court since 1896, when Czar Nicholas II of Russia sent a full complement of band instruments to celebrate Ethiopia's victory over the Italians at the Battle of Adwa. Several months after the instruments arrived in the country, Ethiopian musicians tutored by a Polish conductor brought from abroad performed "La Marseillaise" before the emperor. According to a contemporary account,

> This brass band took turns with azmaris (traditional minstrels) and Abyssinian horns (meleket and embilta), which are the true trumpets of Aïda, while, in the great courtyard where audiences are held, the timpanists [referring to men playing flat negarit drums], mounted on their mules, drummed those strange rhythms that strike the foreigner so vividly.[66]

These instruments were played intermittently in various eclectic combinations over the subsequent decades at events for the Ethiopian aristocracy, including at court diplomatic proceedings and feasts.

The presence of brass instruments in the court and the expertise of European musicians was of great interest to Menelik's successor, Ras Tafari. On April 16, 1924, Regent Ras Tafari left Ethiopia for a diplomatic and educational journey that included stays in Jerusalem and Egypt, as well as visits to capitals across Europe. A transformative musical moment took place when, during his time in Jerusalem, the regent encountered a large brass band. The performers were forty orphaned youths who had survived the Armenian genocide. (See plate 2.4.) Ras Tafari immediately hired the entire ensemble, which arrived in Addis Ababa on September 6, 1924, with a full complement of instruments. Known as the *Arba Lijoch* (forty chil-

PLATE 2.4 An ensemble of forty Armenian orphans (*Arba Lijoch*)
brought to Ethiopia in 1924 from Jerusalem by then Regent
Ras Tafari. Courtesy AGBU Nubar Library, Paris.

dren), the band required a year of intense rehearsal because many of the
young men were in fact novices on their instruments. The group became
S. M. Negus Tafari's Royal Marching Band (1924–30), the predecessor of
the Imperial Bodyguard Orchestra discussed in the preface.[67]

The Armenian band members were surely not "children," but rather
young male adults ranging in age from eighteen to twenty-five. Their 1924
arrival, accompanied by their director, Kevork Nalbandian, had a major
impact on Ethiopian music from that date forward:

> The *Arba Lijoch* formed the royal imperial brass band of Ethiopia and each
> of the children were allocated a monthly stipend, provided with hous-
> ing and trained by their musical director, Kevork Nalbandian. Nalbandian
> was an Armenian orphan himself, originally from Aintab (modern-day
> Gaziantep) in the southeastern region of the Ottoman Turkish Empire. It
> was Nalbandian who led the *Arba Lijoch* with his musical compositions
> and [Haile] Selassie was so impressed with the band's compilations, he

asked Nalbandian to compose the music for Ethiopia's national anthem. In 1926, Nalbandian composed the Ethiopian Imperial National Anthem . . . and it was performed by the 40 orphans for the first time in public during Haile Selassie's official crowning as Emperor on November 2, 1930 in Addis Ababa.[68]

The band contributed to the already growing interest in foreign musical styles from its performances at most court events and before Ethiopia's army and imperial bodyguard bands. The impact of foreign musicians such as Kevork Nalbandian was cumulative and reshaped several streams of tradition that came after them. Likely these musicians should be included among the numbers of sentinel musicians who helped clear a pathway for new styles of Ethiopian musical performance, including (beyond brass bands) the introduction of jazz, "orchestral" folklore ensembles, and the accompaniment of traditional songs by Western instruments. In chapter 8 we will again encounter the impact of visiting foreign musicians on Ethiopian musical ensembles. Thus, the late nineteenth-century entry of band instruments set into motion a major shift in performance practice within traditional cultural music that had consisted until that time of individual instrumentalists who performed solo or accompanied singers or dancers. Here we witness the stirring of a powerful strain of musical modernism emerging from the cumulative impact of relationships of Ethiopia with the music and musicians of Europe and other cultures of the north and west.[69] It has been suggested that

> the process implanted the hegemony of the notion of "modernity" and its identification with "Westernization" and these, in turn, have brought in their train successive narratives, of economic development, and of environmental fragility and ruin. And these narratives have embedded themselves profoundly in the consciousness of Ethiopians.[70]

Politics are thus deeply embedded in the impact of mobility. That the young members of the Armenian band were of foreign extraction did not preclude them from participating in Ethiopian politics, resulting in an early-twentieth-century instance of musical resistance:

> A story passed down [by one of the last surviving band members] tells us that it was customary for the *Arba Lijoch* to play the national anthem for visiting diplomats. One year, [Haile] Selassie's interior [minister] had summoned the orphans to learn the anthem of Turkey in preparation of the visit of Turkish delegates. All 40 orphans, in protest, refused to learn

the anthem, saying "We will not learn the anthem of a country that killed our parents." After much pleading from the Ethiopian interior [minister], the *Arba Lijoch* eventually learned the anthem. But when the time came to perform it to the visiting delegates, the orphans performed an ethnic Armenian song instead.[71]

Haile Selassie I's cosmopolitan interests would come to be a distinguishing mark of his reign, sending Ethiopians abroad and establishing a reputation for welcoming visitors, with the result that "his economic adviser was an American, his military experts came from Sweden and Belgium, and his bandmaster was a Swiss."[72] The emperor actively expanded the nascent Ethiopian educational system: he founded new schools, hired foreign faculty, and sponsored young Ethiopians for foreign academic training. By the start of the Italian occupation in 1935, more than two hundred Ethiopians had received their college education abroad.

Virtual Mobility

Perhaps no type of mobility is more widespread in the twenty-first century than the virtual, assuming a role as the primary means of communicating a musician's movements and providing access to performances and new recordings across great distances. As is the case of so many communities in diaspora, Ethiopians have in general engaged heavily with information and communication technologies in order to share aspects of their rapidly changing lives and identities, to help forge new communities, and to promote cultural innovation.[73] Virtual networks are resources of paramount importance for diasporic Ethiopians, in ironic contrast with compatriots in their homeland, which ranks low internationally in digital resources and which has on occasion censored homeland websites and restricted communications with sites abroad as well.[74]

For Ethiopian musicians abroad, the internet provides a mechanism through which they can maintain contact with each other and coordinate large events such as concerts and festivals. Websites also become virtual travel sites, providing an overview of musicians' itineraries, concerts, and clips of their newest songs. Such sites offer a type of double mobility, enabling visitors to track a musician's route in real time and to arrange encounters when they visit an area.

Members of the Ethiopian diaspora have used cyberspace to build new networks that replace the ones they have lost through forced migration.[75] Many of these networks are based on shared ethnicity, discussed earlier as an ongoing site of contention among many Ethiopians and their neighbors from the Horn of Africa at home and abroad. A good number of cyberspace affiliations also convene those with shared political affiliations, and many others draw on specific professional associations or interest groups. Especially prominent online is ethnic activity in music and the arts. Even when individual musicians do not have a heavy personal presence in cyberspace, the many institutions and activities to which they are committed are relatively well represented and connect them. In this way, music travels across time and space and is more mobile, in fact, than its performers.

If notions of Ethiopian stasis remain widespread, it is hoped that this brief historical overview has provided evidence for multiple types of Ethiopian mobility across the region and beyond from early dates. The outcome, especially within the last century, has been a proliferation of modernist cultural elements, the history of which is deeply connected to that of contact with individuals and traditions from outside Ethiopia. We will see in the following pages the extent to which musical modernity has its own history in Ethiopia, one of active appropriation.[76] The shock of the revolution and the manner in which so many were forced to depart to an unknown life abroad demonstrate the fragility of memories of large-scale movement from the past as well as from more recent periods.

Senses

ETHIOPIAN SENSORY THOUGHT
AND PRACTICE

Həwas
GENERAL MEANING: Sense
MUSICAL MEANING: Hearing

During their stay in Ethiopia in the second half of the sixteenth century, two Portuguese Jesuits left an account describing an intensely multisensory Ethiopian Christian liturgical performance in a torch-lit church, detailing as well its heightened emotional impact on both participants and listeners:

> They perform nothing from writing, but everything from memory. When they say Matins, apart from the usual torches before the altar, in which grease burns instead of oil, there is no other light in the church, nor in the choir. They chant the psalm-verses, not alternately, but each one all together. . . . No one recites seated; the older men are allowed to lean on wooden props when they are tired. The whole service is in the . . . Ethiopic language. Whatever they say, they accompany with suitable movements of face and body. Thus they speak weeping the words of tears; laughing those of laughter; leaping those of leaping; loudly those of clamour; softly those of silence; in short, whatever they utter, they show with such bodily gesture as to be understood no less through the speaker's signs than through his voice. . . . In these celebrations they carry four or five silver crosses like sceptres in their right hands, and as many thuribles in their left; and many rattles join with the sung psalms and hymns. For the rest, they carry out the divine offices with so much piety and inward feeling that those who are present can hardly restrain their tears.[1]

This description could just as well be of a twenty-first-century Ethiopian Christian ritual, which does not differ greatly from its sixteenth-

PLATE 3.1 The celebration of *Lidet*, Ethiopian Christmas,
at the rock churches of Lalibela, c. 1973. Collection of author.

century predecessor, except perhaps for the absence of torches in all but
the most isolated rural churches without electricity. All ceremonies are
still mounted in the dark hours of the early morning in an incense-filled
church, performed by men leaning on prayer staffs, chanting in Geʻez,
and accompanied by sistra, drums, dancing, and clapping.[2] (See plate 3.1.)
Taking the multisensory Ethiopian Christian liturgy as a point of departure and return throughout, this chapter argues that Ethiopian musicians
draw on multiple heightened senses to communicate with and to engage
their listeners. Through their performances, whether sacred or secular,
across domains of music and dance, and through musical practices that
touch on broader worlds of aesthetics and healing, musicians' practices
and testimonies map the sensory worlds of which they are a part. Both
in twenty-first-century Ethiopia and across its global diaspora, many aspects of this complex sensory world remain intact and continue to inflect
aspects of everyday life.

The argument that liturgy and its musical content are multisensory is
certainly not a new one. Well before the recent sensory turn in the humanities and musical scholarship, scholars of religion recognized the importance of religious ritual as a consummate sensory experience. Decades ago,
historian of religion William Graham asked "if we have not seriously short-
changed both ourselves and our field of study by ignoring or minimizing
the 'sensual' aspects of religious life — the sensory and sensible stimuli and

responses that figure so fundamentally in religious practice of all kinds."[3] Many others have noted the multisensory nature of ritual, sparking lively discourses in fields such as medieval art history, and scholars have moved toward an "anthropology of liturgy" and acknowledge that liturgy often constitutes a "synthesis of the arts *par excellence*."[4]

However, this chapter extends beyond simply acknowledging the sensory to argue not only that musicians transmit a rich domain of sensory information through liturgy but also that these same sensory powers are critical to the efficacy of the sentinel musician. Like many other religious traditions worldwide, the Ethiopian Christian liturgy has had a primary sensory impact in the sonic domain that extends well beyond boundaries of the sacred sphere, influencing many other areas of life. It is unfortunate that studies of ritual too often tend to focus on sensory transmission of theological messages and view sensory content, including musical performance, as contained within liturgical boundaries.[5] In contrast, I will emphasize the impact of liturgically shaped sensoria on other domains of daily life, demonstrating the ways in which the senses move through ritual and its practitioners to multiple other domains, in the process transforming many aspects of life and experience.[6]

Nowhere in Ethiopian culture is the interaction of the senses quite so compelling or so deep a part of Ethiopian consciousness as in the performance of the Ethiopian Christian liturgy, the indigenous musical tradition of the Church that dates from the fourth century. The word for sense, *həwas* (*hiwas*), is linked to all the organs of the body, including the voice box (*yädəms' həwas*: vocal chords, but lit., the voice sense).[7] Given their responsibility to transmit a liturgy that is entirely an oral tradition, Ethiopian Christian musicians must be highly trained. In the past, most spent many years in rural monasteries and specialized church schools to hone their musical skills.[8] The sensory virtuosity of Ethiopian Christian chant provides the historical backdrop necessary to understand the emergence of sentinel musicians in Ethiopian society at home and in diaspora, who, through heightened skills of perception, became keen observers of and communicators about the world around them. This heightened sensory mix has traveled with the venerable Ethiopian Christian musical tradition across the region as well as with mass forced migration abroad.

The Contribution and Impact of Saint Yared

Ethiopian church musicians attribute their multisensory tradition to the legacy of Saint Yared, the mythologized founder of the church's liturgical music. Many accounts of Saint Yared's life and contributions have been passed down both orally and in writing by subsequent generations of musicians of the Ethiopian Orthodox Church, who generally date the saint's life to the sixth century and credit him with composing the entire corpus of Ethiopian Orthodox chants through divine inspiration. Saint Yared is also said to have organized the chants into three modes; to have innovated *qəne* (*qene*), a genre of improvised poetry; and to have invented a system of musical notation.[9] Some credit Saint Yared with originating all Ethiopian music, not just ritual music: "Before Yared, there was no music in Ethiopia. He began it all, after him everything was expanded."[10]

Several tales are commonly transmitted about Yared and are included in the accounts of his life in the Ethiopian *Sənkəssar* (Synaxarium), read annually on commemorative days in the church.[11] One of these stories describes Yared as a very poor student who failed to learn sacred texts and melodies, which resulted in punishments by his uncle and mentor, Gedewon. Discouraged, Yared fled the church school to an outlying area, where, tired from his travels under the hot sun, he sat down to rest under a tree. There,

> he observed how a caterpillar would repeatedly try to climb the tree but would fall before it reached halfway. After several attempts, however, the insect finally succeeded in climbing all the way to the top of the tree where the fruits lay. Yared was highly encouraged by what he saw and felt that he had just learned the greatest lesson of his life. He realized that patience and perseverance were the key to education as well as overall personal success. He immediately returned to the school and apologized to his uncle. . . . Thereupon, Yared's learning faculties underwent a sudden metamorphosis. He changed from a half-wit into the most brilliant mind the city had ever seen. He is said to have memorized the entire scriptures and mastered literally every subject offered on the school curriculum in a single day. After his miraculous graduation, he became a deacon and served at the Cathedral of Holy Zion.[12]

Individuals often cite the story of Yared's encounter with the caterpillar as an inspiration for meeting whatever challenges confront them. Another less widely circulated tale recounts that Yared assigned four of his pupils to teach and spread his system of church music when he retreated to monastic isolation late in his life, modeling a process of institutionalization, development, and propagation of his system of sacred music for his musical heirs. The practice has given rise to "a genealogy of masters from Yared in the 6th century down to Aleqa Mersha in the 20th."[13]

These stories of Saint Yared's persistence and planning in the face of adversity have lent relevance to his story over the generations. His efforts to sustain the Ethiopian Christian tradition inspired the faithful at moments when their tradition was threatened, as during the sixteenth-century Islamic invasion, as well as during the twentieth-century revolution and subsequent forced migration.

The figure of Saint Yared still looms large in twenty-first-century Ethiopian Christian thought and imagination. Many churches in diaspora display paintings of Saint Yared and observe a special "Saint Yared's Day" each year.[14]

The eighteenth-century full-page miniature of Saint Yared in plate 3.2 illustrates two episodes from the saint's life, both of which shed light on sensory aspects of his persona and performance. The upper image emphasizes the primacy of sound and the sense of hearing. Yared's right hand is raised in a gesture of speech while his left hand touches his ear in a manner that signifies listening or hearing as he converses with three birds sent to him from the Garden of Eden. The importance of auditory skills is reinforced by tales about Saint Yared, which link sacred sounds to the cycles of the natural world:

> The legend goes on to say that Yared was led to the Garden of Eden by three angels in the guise of three white birds, and there mastered the songs of the birds, and the sounds of the animals and beasts. Yared, the polyglot of nature's varied sounds, incorporated into his hymns reflections and observations of nature and its kaleidoscopic phenomena, all to the glory of the Creator. Thus, his compositions reflect the periodicity of the seasons, and of the agricultural cycle.[15]

Yared is revered as an authority whose chant and voice were innately powerful. Aesthetic values associated with Yared's performance of liturgical music have over time spread into the secular domain, where "the remark [is] often made of a good singer: his voice makes one cry."[16]

The lower painting in plate 3.2 reveals a largely hidden aspect of music's sensory powers—its ability to ameliorate pain. Saint Yared is seen here performing a chant with sistrum and prayer staff in front of sixth-century emperor Gebra Masqal. So transported are both Yared and the emperor by the sound of the chant that neither is aware that the king's spear has accidentally pierced the singer's foot, opening a bleeding wound. The ability of sacred sound and the musician's voice to transform consciousness and to ameliorate pain resonates across a number of Ethiopian cultural domains.

PLATE 3.2 This miniature of Saint Yared in an eighteenth-century illuminated manuscript presents two important episodes from the saint's life. The upper register portrays the encounter with three birds sent from the Garden of Eden, and the lower, his performance with sistrum and prayer staff before Emperor Gebra Masqal. Ethiopian vellum, tempera, and leather binding 32 × 22 × 6 cm (12 5/8 × 8 11/16 × 2 3/8 in.). Gift of Frank Jewett Mather Jr. (y1951-28). Image courtesy of Princeton University Art Museum.

But here we must pause and address an important issue: while the senses are physiologically universal, they are conceived and defined differently within various cultural arenas. What in fact constitutes Ethiopian conceptions of the senses? The notion of five senses so pervasive in the West proves to be insufficient to discuss Ethiopian sensory notions.

TABLE 3.1 **The seven senses according to the Ethiopian highland oral tradition**

AMHARIC	SENSES	LITERAL MEANING
ayn	seeing	eye
jor	hearing	ear
afencha	smelling	nose
af	tasting	mouth
ej	feeling	hand
eger	walking	leg, foot
abalä zär	sex sense	sex sense (lit., male genital organs, polite term)

SOURCE: Simon D. Messing, "The Highland-Plateau Amhara of Ethiopia" (PhD diss., University of Pennsylvania, 1957), 573.

TABLE 3.2 **The seven senses as listed in an Ethiopian dictionary**

HIWAS	SENSES
r'iy	seeing
semi	hearing
atsenwo	smelling
ti'im	tasting
gesis	feeling

*"And when, to these five, leg and sex organ are added they become seven" (Kidanä Wäld Kəfle, *Mäsahafä Säwasəw Wägəs Wämäzgäbä Qalat Haddis* [A book of grammar and verb, and a new dictionary] [Addis Ababa, 1948 EC], 438, col. 25). I am grateful to Dr. Getatchew Haile, who alerted me to this reference.

The Senses in Ethiopian Thought and Practice

Although there are few written sources that discuss Ethiopian concepts of the senses, an anthropologist working in highland Ethiopia in the 1950s documented a list of seven senses he gathered after extensive ethnographic work with Ethiopian Christian highland populations.[17] Each sense is said to be centered in a corresponding organ, as illustrated in table 3.1.[18] We can also turn to an obscure Ethiopian Ge'ez dictionary for confirmation of this sevenfold typology. (See table 3.2.)[19]

Ethiopian concepts therefore extend the standard (Western) five senses to include the lower extremities and sex organs. Inclusion of the leg and foot is not surprising, for one stands for hours during performance of the Ethiopian liturgy, and leg and foot motions are an integral part of liturgical dance in church rituals. The lower limbs are also engaged in the many processions and pilgrimages that are part of Ethiopian Christian rituals.[20] 'Əgər (leg) can be translated as "motion," linking the senses to processes of pilgrimage in the Ethiopian church and, perhaps ironically, to the process of migration itself.[21] The seventh sense, listed as "sex organs," is entered by Kane under the term *häfrätä səga* (lit., shameful flesh),[22] which he translates as "genitalia."[23]

Sex organs, however, stand in a very ambivalent relationship to liturgical performance. Priests are prohibited from having sexual intercourse the night before they are to lead the liturgy. In the past, women and men entered traditionally round Ethiopian churches separately, women through their own door on the south side and segregated in that area during the ritual. In basilica-style churches more common in modern Ethiopian urban areas and in the diaspora today, men and women usually sit on separate sides, with women on the left.[24] In general, a strong value on gender separation within the church extends to Ethiopian society at large.

Taste provides another example of a sense in an ambivalent relationship with church rituals. The main musical corpus of the Ethiopian church includes chant, instrumental practice, and dance and is performed in the early morning hours on holidays by musicians who are required to fast. After this concludes around 6 or 7 a.m., the more austere Mass follows, chanted by the priests and deacons alone. The Mass contains readings from scriptures and, often, portions read in heightened speech, but it does not utilize choirs, instrumental accompaniment, or dance. The sacrament of Communion, and after the conclusion of the ritual, a sacred meal for clergy and congregation are the most prominent moments when ingestion and a sense of taste are brought into play. Thus, taste is a sense purposefully excluded from the ritual until the moment of the Eucharist, just as women and all connections with sexuality were in traditional practice isolated from the liturgy and its performance altogether.[25]

It must be said that constraints on erotic and taste senses do not render either of these senses entirely absent, even on occasions when Ethiopian beliefs dictate that sensory deprivation should be heightened. For instance, during the Lenten season, all are supposed to undertake daily partial fasts.[26] The liturgy itself also forfeits some of its usual sensory load during Lent, as musicians are required to sing plainchant without instrumental accompaniment or dance during the season. One frequently performed Lenten hymn makes clear "the deeper significance of fasting beyond mere abstinence from nourishment":

> Let the eyes fast;
> Let the tongue fast;
> And let the ears fast from hearing evil.[27]

TABLE 3.3 **Sequence for performing the** *Mahlet*

Qum zema	plainchant
Zəmmamä	to lean on a staff; to move the staff left and right
Märägd	to slap or hit
S'əfat	slapping; unison chant with *kebero* (drum) playing slapping style, accompanied by sistrum
Shəbshäba	to keep time to the music; double time, with clapping

SOURCE: Berhanu Mekonnen, interview by author, June 2, 1975, Addis Ababa; Abraham Habte Selassie, *Saint Yared and Ethiopian Ecclesiastical Music* (Washington, DC: Debre Selam Kidist Mariam Church, 1999), 30–33.

The sense of taste is never far from the fasting mind since it is denied until the Eucharist is celebrated near the conclusion of the Mass. Ethiopian Christianity is well known for its large number of fasts, about two hundred fifty a year, one hundred eighty of which are obligatory, with the rest observed only by the clergy. During these many hours, the congregation is effectively "filled" with overwhelming sensory input from the performance.[28]

Performing the Senses: A Ritual Hierarchy

Church practices implicitly prescribe the order in which the senses unfold during ritual performance. Within the *Mahlet* (a ritual in which chants are performed with instruments and dance), each liturgical portion is repeated,[29] with each repetition increasing its sensory load. A single portion is sung in one of the three modes and is repeated no less than five times; during repetitions 2–5, the text is abbreviated, often represented by a single word or short phrase. This set order of musical repetitions foregrounds the sense of hearing and leads the listener through an auditory pathway marked by increasingly complex textures and intense sounds. (See table 3.3.)

The musicians begin performing a portion as unaccompanied plainchant (*qum zema*), sung solo and often repeated antiphonally either by two soloists or two choirs of singers "on two sides." Plainchant is performed without instrumental accompaniment or body movements. Next, added to the chant rendition are rhythmic motions of the prayer staff and body, known as *zəmmamä*, with the prayer staff pounded on the floor to mark important beats of prescribed patterns.[30] The *märägd* follows, with several internal subdivisions of the chant, each accompanied by sistrum, drum, and dance, at increasing rates of speed. Then one has *s'əfat* (slapping), with a slapping style on the drum to accompany the chant with dance and sistrum. Finally, a section known as *shəbshäba*, with singing, clapping, dancing, and drumming, builds to a climax at which point the sound abruptly ends.

Sound exerts its primacy in other ways as well. Walking toward an Ethiopian church in which the *Mahlet* is underway, one can hear the music long before one arrives.[31] Amplification in Ethiopian churches today at home and abroad, especially in urban areas, contributes to this sonic impact both from a distance and inside, as does the participation of many musicians singing in unison. As the ritual proceeds, women interject high, joyous ululation, blending with the striking of the prayer staffs on the floor, the tinkling of the sistra and thuribles, and the booming of the drums.

It is not surprising that narratives of the Ethiopian liturgy's genesis emphasize the primacy of the ear. Saint Yared, according to learned church musicians, is said to have acquired the liturgy aurally:

> The story is related that one day Yared was carried into Heaven by angels and there he learned his music from the Seraphim—the twenty-four heavenly Priests whose function it was to sing constantly before the throne of God. When he returned to earth, he went directly to the Cathedral of Holy Zion, stood upright in front of the Holy of Holies and began to sing with a loud voice: "Ah! The melody I heard in heaven from the holy angels as they sang 'Holy, Holy, Holy God, the Holiness of Your glory has filled the heavens and the earth.'"[32]

Text does not dominate the liturgy because it is nearly entirely sung.[33] Words and music are coterminous and fused. Although there are liturgical manuscripts with musical notation in the Ethiopian church tradition, they are used only for study and not during performance of the *Mahlet*, which depends entirely on the oral tradition.

The notational system that entered into Ethiopian Christian practice in the mid-sixteenth century was instituted, as noted earlier, to support the chant tradition after the extensive destruction of churches and wholesale slaughter of clergy during the Islamic invasion a few years before; however, many clerics still transmit an oral tradition that Saint Yared himself invented the notational system. In addition, the church notation unites text and tune in a manner that can be interpreted only by individuals who have learned the oral tradition. Each notational sign represents a short melody named by letters from the text with which it is most regularly associated.

The Ethiopian *Mahlet* can surely be characterized as a consummately sonic affair. Yet, once one enters into the church, smell and sight add rich dimensions to what has been heard. The strong odor of incense permeates the space. Most churches provide other sources of rich visual stimulation, including religious paintings, carpets, embroidered vestments, processional crosses, and large ritual umbrellas.[34]

Congregants are required to take off their shoes as they enter the church, moving the sense of touch into consideration. Some bring along a piece of cloth (or in diaspora, warm socks!) to provide a barrier against cold floors. Men and, in recent years, some young women, lean on wooden prayer staffs during long hours of prayer. During some rituals, such as on Epiphany, priests and deacons bless members of the congregation by splashing them with holy water.[35]

The sixth sense—of the feet and legs—assumes importance during the danced repetitions of hymns and during processions. Several different movement styles are extant in Ethiopian Christian liturgy linked to practices in various locales. One is said to connect the motions of the body and prayer staff to the motion of the reeds that grow along the shores of Lake Tana in the country's northwest.[36] The final and seventh sense—sex organs and, implicitly, abstinence from sexual activity—opens up a range of constraints related to patriarchy and the historically limited role of women in the church. Below we will explore the agency of musicians in transmitting the senses across religious, ethnic, gendered, and geographical boundaries.

Transmitting the Senses

The Ethiopian Christian liturgical cycle was a crucial unifying factor in Ethiopian highland society for over a millennium and a half and still plays an important role in many Ethiopian diaspora communities as well as in the postrevolutionary homeland. The Ethiopian church has long reinforced the passage of the seasons as part of its calendrical cycle; it has emphasized traditional values historically associated with the nation; and it has sustained longtime hierarchical patterns of interpersonal and gender relationships.[37]

Here ethnographic observation, individual testimony, historical sources, and iconography allow us to unravel what might otherwise be overlooked connections between the sensory world of the church and many secular domains. The Ethiopian Orthodox Church held a commanding position in Ethiopian society throughout its history, with the emperor at its head. Although the region was long home to many Muslims, especially in Eritrea and regions southwest of the Ethiopian highlands, as well as a number of communities that maintained their own indigenous religious traditions, Christian Amhara hegemony over the centuries across the highland region in particular was powerful. The Church's impact increased in the late nineteenth century when Emperor Menelik forcibly unified what was to become the modern empire, bringing many Oromo and other southern communities under imperial sway. Few, whatever their ethnic or religious background, escaped the impact of Amharization, as the imposition of Christian Amhara values and culture came to be known in the twentieth century. The imposition of Amharic as the national Ethiopian language and the active repression of other languages, especially Afaan Oromo spoken by the region's largest ethnic group, the Oromo, was an additional unifying factor. Twentieth-century communication media and greater mobility between the cities and countryside rendered the impact of Ethiopian Christian sensibilities wider still, other religious orders not excepted. One telling example of this impact is the Oromo ceremony, *Masqala*, where a traditional Oromo seasonal observance eventually blended with the Ethiopian Christian *Mäsqäl* (*Masqal*) observance, the Festival of the True Cross.[38]

In Ethiopia, sensory and aesthetic values are transmitted as lived experience, rarely explicated within systematic texts as is so common in the West. Musical performances, stories of the lives of saints, and proverbs have additionally provided the most important channels for communicating Ethiopian Christian sensory concepts and precepts. It has been said that Ethiopia lives by the proverb, and proverbs are often quoted in conversations in the course of daily life. One colorful example is a proverb that reinforces the religious injunction common to Ethiopian Christians and Muslims against eating pork and links the prohibition at once to realms of hearing and taste: "Pork taints not only him who eats it but also him who hears about it."[39]

Tracking the senses across boundaries requires attention to how these elements come to shape many aspects of habitus, a concept well known from the work of sociologist Pierre Bourdieu.[40]

Bourdieu formally defines habitus as the system of "durable, transposable dispositions . . . as principles which generate and organize practices and representations that can be objectively adapted to their outcomes without presupposing a conscious aiming at ends or an express mastery of the operations necessary in order to attain them." . . . The habitus is sometimes described as a "feel for the game," a "practical sense" (*sens pratique*) that inclines agents to act and react in specific situations in a manner that is not always calculated and that is not simply a question of conscious obedience to rules. Rather, it is a set of dispositions which generates practices and perceptions. The habitus is the result of a long process of inculcation, beginning in early childhood, which becomes a "second sense" or a second nature. According to Bourdieu's definition, the dispositions represented by the habitus are "durable" in that they last throughout an agent's lifetime. They are "transposable" in that they may generate practices in multiple and diverse fields of activity, and they are "structured structures" in that they inevitably incorporate the objective social conditions of their inculcation.[41]

Over time, the interplay of the senses sustained in Ethiopian Christian liturgy can be said to have become part of a "durable disposition" embedded across the broader region's habitus. One can identify a number of powerful agents of this transmission process, among them the position of the Ethiopian emperor at the head of the Church. One notable example of the monarch's ability to shape habitus by decree was the "Christianisation of time," a process through which the fifteenth-century emperor Zär'a Ya'əqob (1434–78) "Christianized" the calendar in an effort that both organized time and dictated the rhythm of believers' lives.[42] The church clergy, especially the nonordained musicians, also played an important role in naturalizing the senses across a sacred-profane divide.

The upper part of the body was perceived as holy, and the lower part, which serves sex and defecation, was considered to be profane. An Ethiopian proverb expresses in metaphorical terms this divided nature of the body by referring to the Ethiopian Christian practice of keeping the *tabot*, an altar tablet, inside the sacred Holy of Holies in every church. (See plate 3.3.) The proverb states, "Above the hips—the *tabot*, below the hips, idols."[43]

Multiple aspects of the ritual process reshaped the senses of everyday life outside the church. Holy water from the church was widely used for healing in many contexts, even by members of other religious groups. If incense played a prominent role in heightening the senses within liturgical performance, it came to be used over time by Ethiopian women to deodorize their bodies during the dry season when little water was available; noble or wealthy women are reported to have used imported church incense (*at'an*, incense) for this purpose.[44]

Musicians played an especially critical role in transmitting sensory norms across multiple cultural domains and, as a result, shaped habitus. Here we will look at three categories of musicians—church musicians, minstrels, and dancers—for insight into their roles in shaping of the senses across a broader population.

PLATE 3.3 Procession with sacred altar tablets at the DSK Mariam Church, Washington, DC, celebrating *Masqal*, the holiday of the True Cross. Collection of author.

Church Musicians outside the Church

Church musicians, the *däbtära* (*debtera*), in Ethiopia were particularly important in conveying the notion of a sacred-secular divide while at the same time instrumental in crossing it. Some church musicians were active as healers, a connection that linked their expressive roles in liturgy to the concerns of daily life.

One church musician, who will remain anonymous, described how he brought the power of liturgical song to contexts outside church, where his singing elicited deep emotion and effected healing:

The only place that people come to cry and then get healing is church. A good number of people kept telling me when I become a participant in the liturgy, they hear that and then healing came through that song. I won't say it is my singing, it is the power of the Holy Spirit, that we call the Word of God, goes into the ear of those individuals and then heals. It is the Word that heals. I have strong belief in that. I do go around people's homes and to the hospital and after I do some prayers, I do some singing for them. I see immediately tears in their eyes. And then the next morning when I call, the first thing they say is, "That song healed my soul."[45]

Because many ailments are regarded as "closely interwoven in the body and spirit of the patient[,] . . . [*debtera's*] activity in the official religion is believed to extend over the ills of the body and over the world of the spirits."[46] These church musicians use herbal remedies, therapeutic performances and incantations, prophylactic amulets, and divinatory texts to mediate pain and cure disease. Despite its widespread practice and perceived efficacy, healing by church musicians has never been sanctioned by the Church, which prohibits exorcising spirits.[47]

Ethiopian church musicians today both at home and in diaspora speak passionately about the encompassing role of Christian ritual in the lives of Ethiopians, linking the importance of sacred song to other realms of experience. Materials such as those of Ethiopian music and ritual suggest that we need to dig deep into aspects of musical performance and to confront differences that exist in conceptualizing the play of the senses across cultural and religious boundaries within a society. Musicians surely can provide entry into understanding these complicated dynamics in most extant traditions. The liturgy attributed to Saint Yared has over the centuries both anchored spiritual life in the Ethiopian church and shaped the sensory world beyond its walls. The tales of Saint Yared also forecast many of the themes articulated in the testimony of Ethiopian musicians in the present.

To become a church musician involves a commitment to decades of study and honing performance skills. A musician must be so deeply engaged when performing chant that he can sustain it for rituals many hours in length while conveying its power to the congregation. Over the centuries, generations of church musicians had to marshal a full array of their senses in liturgical performance, moving beyond singing and listening to incorporating heightened perceptions of touch and movement in instrumental practice and dance. The leader of the musicians, the *märigeta* (*merigeta*), has long commanded special respect for his superior knowledge and leadership. His very title derives from the verb *märra*, which extends beyond leading the singing of chant to carrying responsibility "to lead, to guide, and to point out the way."[48] Here the Ethiopian Christian world of the senses also shapes the role of sentinel musician. If the responsibilities of leading church musicians were always demanding in their homeland, the challenges awaiting in diaspora have proven to be even greater. One can witness the dimensions of this work under pressure in the life story of one master church musician, Moges Seyoum. (See plate 3.4.)

Today a US citizen living in Alexandria, Virginia, *liqä* (*liqa*) *mezemran* (leader of the musicians) Moges Seyoum is an accomplished Ethiopian church musician who for more than the last quarter century has led the performance of the musical liturgy at the Debre Selam Kidist (DSK)

PLATE 3.4 A formal portrait of *liqa mezemran* Moges Seyoum.
Courtesy of Marilyn E. Heldman.

Mariam Ethiopian Orthodox Tewahedo (EOT) Church in Washington,
DC. Under Moges's musical guidance, DSK Mariam Church has become
one of the largest Ethiopian Orthodox churches internationally with argu-
ably the most complete and sophisticated performances of the Ethiopian
Orthodox Christian liturgical cycle in the American diaspora.

Born in 1949 in the Manz region northeast of Addis Ababa (today the
eastern area of the Amhara Region), *liqa mezemran* Moges was steeped in
the Ethiopian musical liturgy from childhood:

My father was a *zema memher* [chant teacher] and a scholar of *zema*
[chant]. I finished the *qal təməhərt* [oral singing school] when I was young,

nine years old. I studied with my father . . . and then came to Addis Ababa to continue my education, *aqqwaqwam* [sacred instrumental practice and dance], *qene* [improvised liturgical poetry], and different things. I became a master for *aqqwaqwam*. Yes, my profession is *aqqwaqwam*. And by this profession I got an award . . . from our majesty, Haile Selassie. I have two brothers, one is a *merigeta* still, and the other finished theological school and is a businessman.[49]

Moges began his liturgical career as a deacon, next became a liturgical musician (*debtera*), and finally became a leader of the musicians (*merigeta*). In 1966, at an unusually young age, he received the title *qangyeta* (the leader of the right-hand side), that is, the musician who leads the right-hand side of the two choirs that alternate as they sing plainchant (*qum zema*). In 1970 Moges began additional studies of theology and law in Greece. One of many Ethiopian students abroad stranded at the start of the revolution, he remained in Greece until he received asylum in the United States in August 1982. He went first to Dallas, Texas, where he joined the friend who had sponsored his immigration, and together they founded an Ethiopian Orthodox church in Garland, Texas. In 1989 he accepted an invitation to help found and lead the liturgy at the new Ethiopian church, DSK Mariam, in Washington, DC. Moges's title then became *liqa mezemran*, an honorary designation indicating that he is most accomplished both as a liturgist and as a musician. *Liqa mezemran* Moges describes this title as meaning "the singers' boss" or "the singers' leader."[50]

Liqa mezemran Moges is an extraordinary musician who has taken his responsibilities as a musical leader to heart and has initiated efforts to sustain Ethiopian Christian liturgical performance outside his homeland. In an effort to ensure that important Ethiopian portions are performed on holidays despite the absence of chant schools in diaspora, *liqa mezemran* Moges recorded and published in 2006 a compendium of annual holiday chants.[51] He also transmitted Saint Yared's legacy by writing a booklet on the saint's teachings and music[52] and devoted years to preparing a volume explicating the Ethiopian notational system.[53] On September 17, 2008, *liqa mezemran* Moges received a US National Endowment for the Arts National Heritage Fellowship for his leadership in performing and preserving the Ethiopian liturgy and its music in the United States.

In diaspora, Moges has taken many initiatives to ensure transmission and performance of the Ethiopian Christian liturgy. He holds a class every Saturday morning as a volunteer to train men from his church to sing important portions of the service for upcoming holidays. In this way he seeks to encourage Ethiopian Orthodox Americans to perform their liturgical heritage, ever sensitive to the reality that most do not know the Ge'ez language nor have the time as immigrants to spend hours in church to acquire the liturgy as they would have done in the Ethiopian past. *Liqa mezemran* Moges further leads the way in efforts to transmit the Ethiopian Orthodox tradition outside the walls of the church in its new American home by arranging public presentations of the liturgy, such as arranging chants and rehearsing a choir that performed at the Sixty-Ninth National Folk Festival in Richmond, Virginia, in October 2007.

> In the American society, we have a plan, you know, to show everywhere. Not in our church only. We have to explain for people and for example, universities. . . . There is the game of promotion.[54]

The Ethiopian Orthodox Church has been aptly characterized as "an institution that has found itself on the fault line between tradition and modernity."[55] *Liqa mezemran* Moges's sensitivity to a changing religious environment derives in large part from his reverence for Saint Yared and his commitment to sustain that heritage in diaspora:

> I would like people to know that our faith is very important and that Yared was very holy. This guy, Yared, was very intellectual. He brought *zema* (chant) from the angels, that's what our tradition says. He was a superman! Nobody today gets to hear angels like that![56]

Ethiopian church musicians such as *liqa mezemran* Moges are not alone in their fealty to Saint Yared. Many Christian musicians performing in the secular sphere are outspoken about the impact of Saint Yared on their own musical practices. They believe there to be historical connections between the heavily pentatonic sound of both sacred and secular modal systems within Ethiopian music:

> By the way, those four *qəñət* (*qenyet*) of the secular music came out of the three modes of Yared. . . . We always claim that the Ethiopian church is a pioneer to the Ethiopian civilization: socially and spiritually. St. Yared is the father of today's Ethiopian music.[57]

Even Ethiopian musicians who grew up exclusively in diaspora and largely outside the Orthodox Church have been influenced by the Ethiopian Christian sound, as one young Ethiopian singer raised in the United States recounted:

I have this one producer who says, "You love that pentatonic, don't you?" And I'm like, really? And I don't even realize how much hearing those sounds has influenced me, but yeah, it's probably more subconscious than conscious.[58]

In addition to their sacred and secular music's shared melodic content, many also link the vocal style in Ethiopian popular song to the singer's traditional background within the Ethiopian Orthodox Church. While praising the extraordinary voice of internationally known Ethiopian singer Aster Aweke, one instrumentalist noted that

> she has retained a lot of traditional elements. Her singing, if you take it out of the background music, it's really more traditional. . . . She always retained that style of church singing. She went to the Orthodox church and so it is there in her singing. . . . And she is lamenting, the typical Ethiopian traditional sort.[59]

Many popular Ethiopian singers attribute their own style to their experience singing in church choirs.[60]

The Sensory World of Secular Minstrels

Like the *merigeta*, who convey the sensory power of sacred music across homeland and diaspora, minstrels (*azmari*, from *zämmärä*, to sing), who sing and play the *mäsänqo* (*masenqo*), a one-stringed bowed lute, and the *krar*, a six-stringed lyre, also extend their intensely multisensory performance practice across many ethnic and religious boundaries in Ethiopian society.[61] (See plate 3.5.)

The historical moment at which *azmari* emerged is not clear; both male and female musicians are mentioned as part of royal encampments, the latter associated with prostitution, in Father Francisco Alvarez's 1520 narrative of his visit to Ethiopia.[62] Alvarez mentioned musicians performing on the *masenqo* for the emperor, although there is some confusion in his description between the one-stringed bowed lute known by this name and the "harp of David," the large ten-stringed lyre, the *bägäna* (*bagana*).[63] Other clear descriptions of the *azmari* are found in the works of travelers such as James Bruce (1730–94), who visited Ethiopia in the later eighteenth century.[64]

Descriptions of *azmari* performances showed the musicians to be among the most accomplished practitioners of the system of double tex-

PLATE 3.5 *Azmari* play *masenqo* in a procession c. 1936.
Courtesy of Itsushi Kawase Private Collection.

tual meanings known as wax and gold.[65] *Azmari* occupied an ambiguous
position in Ethiopian society, admired for their keen powers of observation, commentary, and linguistic skill, but also reviled for their dependence on patronage and mendicancy as well as their deep-seated association with healing in several contexts. These minstrels were extraordinarily
versatile, performing for rich and poor, and were prominently heard at
both sacred and secular events. The ambiguity of their social position was
mirrored by their nasal, ornamented vocal style that blended subtly with
the melodic line of the *masenqo*.

One can gain an overview of the traditional *azmari* repertory that cut
across multiple social and sensory domains through the songs of *azmari*
Tessema Eshete (1876–1964), who traveled to Berlin between 1908 and
1910, where he recorded more than thirty selections.[66] This century-old
collection spans many of the broad range of topics an *azmari* would commonly address. Virtually all the songs include prominent references to
Christian beliefs and figures or contain quotes or paraphrases from the
scriptures; a good number praise specific Christian saints or the Virgin
Mary.[67] Many of the songs praise prominent individuals of the late nineteenth and early twentieth centuries, including Emperor Menelik and his
empress.[68] Other well-known figures, ranging from nobles to a leader of
the merchants, are also eulogized and celebrated, often with an overtly

political tone. Finally, one finds several love songs included, a genre often sung by *azmari*.

Several of the minstrel's songs offer a reflexive perspective on the *azmari*'s career. One discusses the *azmari*'s low social status, noting that "my genealogy is not that esteemed or lofty."[69] Another song touches on issues of mobility, revealing stress on the *azmari* from traveling outside his natal area, asking "How can I take pride in a country that is not mine?"[70] The song "Medina" recounts the secular singer's unsuccessful attempts to qualify as a church musician ("cantor" in the song):[71]

> I studied the Psalms:
> Verse, phrase, word, and syllable.
> They said I should study the Hymns,
> But I couldn't manage to be a *qene* composer
> And write verses worthy of a cantor.[72]

With their knowledge of a wide range of political situations, entry into local intrigue, and communication about current events, minstrels were at risk during times of conflict. When Italy occupied Ethiopia in the late 1930s, many minstrels and church musicians (sorcerers) were considered to be such direct threats to the occupation that they were executed, along with other musicians and healers banned by Italian viceroy Rodolfo Graziani:[73]

> Convinced of the necessity of completely eradicating this evil growth, I have given an order that all itinerant singers, clairvoyants, and sorcerers in the city and its surroundings must be arrested and turned over to the army. Already today we have arrested and eliminated seventy. . . . By special order it has been forbidden for the future—on pain of death—to practice these professions.[74]

Like the church musicians, the *azmari* is engaged both in church-related rituals and in healing ceremonies. Although they do not participate in the liturgy, *azmari* regularly lead processions outside the church on holidays, their *masenqo* heralding the approach of priests and deacons behind them, carrying church regalia, including the *tabot*, followed by members of the congregation. One young *azmari* descended from a lineage of minstrels in the Gondar area of northeastern Ethiopia recalled his father's many performances outside a church in his home village:

> There's a big tree surrounded by rocks and the people gather and the priest preaches. Right then, my father used to play the *masenqo*.[75]

The *zar* cult, a possession cult widespread across the Horn of Africa from Somalia to the Sudan, provides yet another rich setting for the *azmari's* sensory-laden role in interreligious influence and exchange. Held at night to exorcise spirits, the *zar* ceremony features an *azmari* singing and playing the *masenqo* to "warm the ceremonial space" and to accompany drumming, clapping, and ululation.[76] After chewing *khat* (*Catha edulis*), smoking cigarettes, smelling incense, and drinking *araqi* liquor, the *zar* practitioner (*balä zar*) achieves an altered state by performing the *gurri* dance to the accompaniment of the *masenqo* and drum.[77] In short, the *zar* ceremony is also a multisensory event that brings together aspects of indigenous spirit beliefs with Ethiopian Christian influences, such as the use of incense and songs addressing God and the Virgin Mary.[78]

Thus, the *masenqo* tradition and the *azmari* who perform on the instrument present lively examples of intense sensory engagements that cross divides of religion, ethnicity, gender, and class. They trace the genesis of their profession to an ancestor named Saint Ezra, who is said to have played his *masenqo* to relieve the Virgin Mary's pain when dying. "Ezra is the origin of people who play the *masenqo*, my ancestors."[79] Here we find also the underlying connection of the *azmari* with healing and mediation of pain:

> There is the expression "Ezra's *masenqo*." When St. Mary was dying . . .
> this person Ezra was playing *masenqo* and David was playing *bagana* (ten-
> stringed lyre). And then St. Mary was suffering from the pain of death,
> but as she was listening to the beautiful melody, the pain was gone and
> she was passing. You know, she was dying without any pain. They sing it
> [this story] sometimes. They sing it right before they start a performance,
> anytime, anywhere. Even at the wedding party, even at those nightclubs,
> they just don't care about the audience, they just look up to the sky and
> they will just sing. [The song] is full of *qene*, it's full of metaphors. Partic-
> ularly religious.[80]

Azmari have made important contributions to Ethiopian society at home and abroad. But beyond their impact as a group, their performances draw on a sensory base in part derived from and shared with church musicians, one that has had a decisive effect on their society at moments of transition. This realm of the senses also shapes dance.

Ethiopian Dance as Sensory Practice

The inclusion of the legs and feet within the Ethiopian senses bring bodily motion and dance into consideration. Here again, one finds strong, if little explored, connections between dance derived from Saint Yared in the Ethiopian Orthodox Church and the dances of secular life. Dancer Getatchew Gebregiorgis, for years the lead dancer at the City Hall Theatre in Addis Ababa, recalls that he was inspired from early childhood both by Ethiopian Christian liturgical music, as well as by stories of Saint Yared's creativity in conceiving it:

> So, we have priests, they teach everyone in the neighborhood, a bunch of kids together, how to learn Ethiopian letters, and then our books. I did that. I was singing spiritual singing by hearing the priest every time we were in class. You know, he's singing. I listened and I loved it. . . . And then finally I found that Yared was the greatest man, he made melodies, and everything very interesting, so beautiful and amazing. It just stained my soul and spread. And then I found that this is me, this is what I like. This is music, you know? And then I keep going with that, first grade, second grade. I start participating by writing poems, singing . . . and dancing. All the time, yeah.[81]

Ethiopian dancer Ashenafi Mitiku, born in Ethiopia in 1966, performed from his childhood with revolutionary secular music ensembles but also participated in liturgical dance in church. (See plate 3.6.) Raised in a devout Ethiopian Orthodox family, he studied in rural church schools but disappointed his father, who wanted him to become a priest, by becoming a dancer. After moving to a school in Addis Ababa at age twelve, he became a professional dancer with the City Hall Theatre group.[82] Ashenafi gained asylum in the United States in 1993. With a systematic knowledge of dances from a variety of ethnic communities and regions gained from research and videotapes gathered by the City Hall Theatre, Ashenafi has used this knowledge creatively in a variety of folkloric contexts in the United States. At the same time, he attends regular Sunday morning and holiday rituals at DSK Mariam Church in Washington, DC.

Ashenafi is keenly aware of the different use of the senses cross-culturally and notes that

> in Ethiopia, we have a different dance because our dance is neck and shoulder, because religion is very important. People, they don't want to see any sexual movement. . . . If you go to West Africa, they do a lot of movement like the West. Most of the time we do neck, shoulder, and jumping. Our dances actually connect with nature. Əskəsta (shoulder dance) connects with the Blue Nile Falls . . . where the water comes like shaking. . . . And we do one dance called yädoro mədwət (the chicken dance). You put your chin up and down.[83]

PLATE 3.6 Dancer Ashenafi Mitiku (foreground center) performs with colleagues at Dukem Ethiopian Restaurant, Washington, DC. Collection of author.

Secular dances employ special physical and sonic techniques such as shaking all over the body and the sound of heavy inhaling and exhaling. A guttural sound is also employed, known as *gurri*, the same term as that for the trance dance performed during the *zar* cult ritual, during which hand clapping heightens the beat until the spirit connects to the medium. Here we once again find a connection across boundaries of secular and ritual domains.[84]

Conclusion

If there is little literature to inform us about the role of the senses in the Ethiopian past and present, it is clear that liturgical performances and related testimonies provide substantial insights. Musical performances and other forms of oral and aural perception provide important pathways for linking religious concepts and the sensory realm, moving both beyond the walls of the church. No doubt the Ethiopian sensory arena has been shaped by flows from multiple directions, but since the central power of the church in daily homeland religious and political life began to diminish only in the 1970s, the movement from Orthodox Christian practice outward is often dominant. In part through performance, sensory realms associated with music have moved from the liturgy into other domains of Ethiopian cultural life. As an anthropologist who has comparatively documented Amazonian cosmologies and perceptions of the senses summarizes aptly: "Sensory models are conceptual models, and sensory values are cultural values. The way a society senses is the way it understands."[85]

Certainly, a major sensory transition is now underway in diasporic Ethiopian life, as many of the second and third generations of Ethiopian Christians living in diaspora do not speak Ethiopian vernaculars and do not know Ge'ez, nor do they attend the Orthodox Church regularly or at all. The power of evangelical Christianity is particularly strong among Ethiopian youth, who constitute the majority in new Ethiopian evangelical congregations. At a service in an Ethiopian evangelical church I attended in Boston, most wore Western dress, whereas many women wear traditional dress in the Ethiopian Orthodox churches. The music for the evangelical liturgy was provided by a solo guitar, and hymns in Amharic were accompanied by a synthesizer.[86] Although in the early twenty-first century a well-trained generation of priests from Ethiopia still leads the traditional Ge'ez liturgy worldwide, and as is often the case in traditions under stress, tends to emphasize tradition, changes are on the horizon and will no doubt wield an impact in the sensory and aesthetic domains. The numbers of *merigeta* are stretched thin in diaspora and many churches have to hire musicians from Europe or even the Ethiopian homeland to officiate for major holidays.

Yet despite changes underway, Ethiopian musicians today both at home and abroad still speak passionately about the encompassing role of Christian ritual in the lives of Ethiopians, linking the importance of sensual aspects carried through sacred song and dance to other realms of experience:

> When they teach us, they do tell us to be careful in how to sing . . . because we're thinking of the suffering and salvation history of Christ. So when we sing, it is not just for pleasure that we're having. . . . It is fascinating, very unique, and very special. To get the depths and the core of it, you need to be part of it. I don't know if language is adequate enough to explain it. It is embedded in the entire life of individuals in Ethiopia.[87]

Part of the power of musicians who assume roles as sentinels, such as Moges Seyoum, under strikingly new conditions in the twenty-first century, derives from the subtle yet pervasive influence of the historical myth and music of Saint Yared. Although many musicians may no longer serve as guards of Yared's liturgical orders, they continue to act as sentinels of sensory memories that remain in their thrall.

SECTION II
Processes

Conflicts

REVOLUTIONARY MUSICAL LIVES

Chɘqchäqa
GENERAL MEANING: Argument or dispute
MUSICAL MEANING: A rhythm that pits twos against threes

The impact of revolution on musical lives—and that of musical lives on contested political processes—can be fully understood only in relation to each other. Yet in the midst of the turmoil, with ongoing violence, it is difficult for a researcher to gather testimony, not to mention that it is often hazardous for participants to offer it. Although some recent studies explore the relationship between music and conflict, few details have emerged from the experiences of musicians in such situations.[1] This study, extended over the course of decades, provides an opportunity to understand the broader course of revolutionary events and their devastating effect on individuals involved. Although there has been a strong tendency, especially in the popular press, to present the Ethiopian revolutionary period as a musical wasteland, a closer look both confirms the violence done to individual lives and contributes new evidence of unexpected musical activity. One also finds a deep-seated engagement of musicians with political discourse and action over time.[2] This chapter sets forth stories of sentinel musicians past and present, providing details of the conflicts in which they played pivotal roles. Sentinel musicians did not first emerge at the time of the revolution but were a source of musical agency in Ethiopia long before that conflict began.

Political action in the homeland through music in support of competing factions provides a prelude to the revolution and continued dialogues with Ethiopians in exile. Not only does one find multiple phases of conflict over the years between and within the homeland and diaspora, but these events may be perceived differently by those of various ethnic and religious backgrounds who have experienced conflict, exile, and estrangement. This situation has led to the production of multiple narratives in different places and among different constituencies.[3] In the case of Ethiopia, however, it is clear that a deep history of political involvement by musicians continued and accelerated during the revolutionary period and continued abroad as diaspora communities were established and matured.

The Musician's Political Heritage

Although the Ethiopian revolution was a period of challenging political engagement for musicians, it is, on closer examination, a clear continuation of the sentinel roles that musicians had long played in Ethiopian life. This activity began long before the advent of the revolution, through both official musical organizations and individual initiatives; in many cases, one often gave rise to the other. For instance, proximity to power was always a deep yet ambiguous aspect of the life of the *azmari*, as we have already seen in chapter 3. The minstrel's low social status was symbolized by his entry into the court through a door (*yäsarqosh bär*; lit., stealth gate) shared with other employees, rather than through the main gate reserved for the elite and guests.[4] However, the *azmari* was also known as *liqä mäkwas*, a title shared with a pair of notables, who dressed like the monarch and stood on his left and right during ceremonial occasions.[5]

One can cite many episodes from both the distant and more recent past during which music, musicians, and musical instruments were intertwined with royal authority and power. During court processions, as noted in the preface, Ethiopian emperors and other aristocrats were traditionally preceded by numerous musicians, including drummers playing kettledrums (*negarit*).[6]

One would also need to take account of the regular performance of Ethiopian chant, a core part of the Ethiopian Orthodox Christian liturgy, within a church formally headed by the emperor, as a musical complex giving voice to power. So important was the connection of imperial power to liturgical music and scriptures that in the past Ethiopian emperors were portrayed in icons as King David with his lyre.[7]

Musicians other than *azmari* also were active in the imperial court, especially under the twentieth-century rule of Emperor Haile Selassie I. We have seen in the preface that the emperor established the Imperial Bodyguard Orchestra as his resident musical ensemble, an outgrowth of the group of Armenian youths he brought to Ethiopia from Jerusalem in 1924. There seems to be little doubt that Haile Selassie I considered music and the arts in general as an indispensable part of official life and that he marked major political occasions through music. In 1927, as regent, he commissioned an Ethiopian national anthem that remained a national symbol from the time of his coronation in 1930 until the beginning of the revolution.[8] Music had therefore long been a proud symbol of Ethiopian imperial power. The Tafari Makonnen School, founded by the regent in 1925, had musical ensembles and its own school song in Amharic composed by the school's English teacher, H. E. Blata Ephrem; the song premiered in the presence of the regent on June 16, 1925.[9]

Musicians were particularly valued as symbols of patriotism, none more so than those of the Ethiopian Patriotic Association, Hager Fikir (*Yähagär Fəqər Mahbär*; lit., Love of Country Association). A professional theater company founded in July 1935, just before the Italian invasion in early October that year, the Patriotic Association brought together writers, musicians, and speakers at rallies and theatrical events to warn the population of the threat from the Italians and to raise patriotic spirit to resist. A notable aspect of the Patriotic Association from its inception was its professional *azmari* company. Although the Patriotic Association was suspended when the Italians entered the Ethiopian capital, some of its members continued the struggle surreptitiously on their own.[10] After the liberation in 1941, the Patriotic Association was reestablished and housed, rather ironically, in a building that had been used for an Italian officers' club.[11] A powerful member of the Ethiopian government as minister of finance (1941–57) and a fervent nationalist, Makonnen Habte-Wold is said to have been a driving force in founding the Patriotic Association and to have encouraged the revival of the Hager Fikir and related musical events after the Italian invasion. Members of the association performed songs in celebrations he arranged for the emperor and in broadcasts on Ethiopian radio.[12] Makonnen continued to promote the musical and theatrical presentations of the Patriotic Association until he was murdered along with other high government officials during the attempted coup against the emperor in December 1960.[13]

The British suffragette Sylvia Pankhurst, who spent years in Ethiopia, wrote a volume on highland Ethiopian cultural life that included English translations of a number of patriotic *azmari* song lyrics circulated before and during the Italian occupation. Some songs called openly for resistance ("Rally, rally, come together; Ethiopians unite; isn't it unity which wins the day?"), but others masked the message with double meanings in the wax and gold tradition.[14] In the following song that Pankhurst included from the era of the Italian occupation, the text appears to portray officials ordering their followers to build typical rural houses, constructed around a central pole. However, the deeper meaning of this text, the gold, is that the house represents the nation and the pillar without which it cannot be built was the emperor, who was then in exile.

Ras Abeba Aragai ordered his patriots to make the house;
Dedjazmatch Tashome did likewise;
Falleke Lidj Ayhu did likewise;
And also the proud Garasu did likewise . . .
But the pillar had disappeared;
Therefore the house could not be built.[15]

Musicians who had been pressed into imperial service could also become sources of resistance. As we have seen in chapter 3, an *azmari* in particular was always capable of offering a critique of his patrons. That several languages of the region, including Amharic, Ge'ez, Tigrinya, and Somali, could disguise pointed commentary in texts replete with double meanings rendered musicians of all repertoires, of most ethnicities, and across genres, vulnerable to official censure and arrest when their true messages were discovered.[16] Itinerant *azmari* in particular harvested a wealth of information about those for whom they performed and embedded in their songs allusions to the rulers' strengths and weaknesses.[17] An *azmari* was always capable of revealing excruciating detail about political and economic issues that were otherwise taboo, as French scholar Marcel Griaule's description of an *azmari* performance he witnessed in the early 1930s graphically reveals:

> For a long time they [the *azmari*] continued a caricature of the Prince; the soldiers and servants were delighted and alarmed. He took up everything: the management of the domanial property, the tax on coffee, the master's fear of seeing himself dispossessed by the eldest son, the haste he had used in proclaiming as heir his last-born, Yohannes, a turbulent child whose brain was nothing remarkable. He exposed in detail the politics of the campaign for prestige conducted in this . . . country.[18]

In the patriotic era that followed the return of the emperor and the end of World War II, songs in praise of Haile Selassie I's innovations proliferated. The refrains of two such songs were written down by a surviving relative of the late emperor. One song that became popular in the early 1950s had the refrain "Rejoice, my soul, rejoice! Your pride has been restored by Haile Selassie!" And in 1954, when Haile Selassie set off on a lengthy trip to the United States and Europe, a praise song addressing the emperor by his horse's name, Abba Tekel,[19] became a hit in Addis Ababa: "Tekel, hurry back, Tekel hurry back, the people of Ethiopia long to see you."[20]

By midcentury, too, when traditional musicians had resumed their long-standing political roles, international popular music and the Ethiopian

PLATE 4.1 The Imperial Bodyguard Orchestra in Addis Ababa, c. 1951, conducted by Austrian musician and chief music instructor Franz Zelwecker. Courtesy of Francis Falceto and Collection of Tsige Felleqe.

equivalent (*zemenawi*) began to circulate widely in the country. At this time, the emperor set in motion a campaign to modernize the country, spearheading widespread construction of new roads, schools, and hospitals in consultation with international experts.[21] Just as music had from the beginning of his rule been integral to his attempts to inspire support for his innovations, once again song became a channel through which support for those in power was galvanized.

Important musical organizations such as the Imperial Bodyguard Orchestra and the Ethiopian Patriotic Association not only marshaled backing for the emperor but also provided institutional contexts in which promising musicians received excellent training and built their own reputations. (See plate 4.1.) These and other performing groups initiated with imperial support, such as the Haile Selassie I National Theatre and Orchestra Ethiopia (to be discussed at length in chapter 8), at once launched careers of musicians and became training grounds for music used for political purposes.[22]

But, by the late 1950s, the regime was increasingly viewed by many younger Ethiopians as insular, traditional, and manipulative, driven primarily by personal loyalty to the crown. Formal protest of any sort against the emperor was exceedingly dangerous, but songs and their texts provided the possibility of at least disguising strong criticism. In 1960, as noted in the preface, leaders of the Imperial Bodyguard led a coup attempt against the emperor.

Imperial Bodyguard musicians were involved in this political activity. Tilahun Gessesse (1940–2009), a renowned singer of Oromo descent who attained legendary status in his country during his lifetime, joined the Imperial Bodyguard Orchestra as a singer in 1958.[23] In 1960 Tilahun recorded a hit song with the orchestra, "Alchalkum" (I can't take it anymore), that on the surface expressed a lover's complaint, performed in a duet with the well-known female singer Bezunesh Bekele (1935–90). However, "Alchalkum" concealed a protest against the emperor's regime and, after the 1960 coup attempt, Tilahun was arrested and jailed. This strophic pentatonic song, accompanied by a unison orchestral line punctuated with drumming, is emphatically opened by Tilahun, followed by Bezunesh and a male chorus. Both the song's multilayered text, and the arrangement in which individual voices are then supported by a chorus, suggest shared concern about the political situation of the time.[24]

By the 1960s, then, music was heavily involved in two contradictory directions, on the one hand advancing the public face of imperial politics and, on the other, directly conveying anti-imperial activity. Musical initiatives against the imperial state also emerged from quarters not allied with the emperor, particularly among Oromo musicians for whom music provided a potent channel for Oromo nationalism. At the same time, several prominent Oromo musicians, including Tilahun Gessesse and Ali Birra, were able to ride the changing political tides while building major careers in the heart of the imperial musical world. They also became icons in the Oromo world at home and abroad, sentinel musicians who expressed Oromo pride and agency through their music. No better example exists than Ali Birra, whose career began to take shape in the 1960s, a decade before the revolution's start.

A Voice from Ethiopia's South: Ali Birra

A major new Oromo musical initiative began when the merger of several Oromo self-help organizations in 1963 formed the Macha-Tulama Self-Help Association in Addis Ababa.[25] This organization, and the founding that same year of two new musical groups in the southeastern town of Dire Dawa, Urjii Bakkalchaa (Morning Star, later known as Afran Qallo), and Biftu Ganama, are considered to mark "the decade of Oromo national awakening that was followed by the emergence of the Oromo national struggle."[26] From its inception, the Macha-Tulama Self-Help Association attracted Oromo from all regions and religious backgrounds.[27] Although its main objective was to establish schools, health clinics, and roads, along with mosques and churches, meetings, conducted in the Afaan Oromo language, also addressed political issues such as Ethiopian colonial policy.[28] The Oromo musical groups quickly attracted an audience across the Oromo communities and they traveled to various cities to perform at Macha-Tulama meetings.

In 1963 a young Oromo musician who was to become the voice of Oromo resistance, Ali Mohammed Musa, began performing with a youth ensemble from Dire Dawa associated with Urjii Bakkalchaa.[29] At an annual performance celebrating the end of Ramadan, he was invited on stage with the main band to sing. Ali performed the song "Birraa dhaa Barihe" (Spring season), by the renowned Oromo poet Abubakar Musa, which celebrates the end of the rainy season and the beginning of the Oromo spring. The reference to spring carried significant cultural symbolism as a period of new beginnings and a time of hope. The song marks both the singer's adoption of the name "Birra" (spring)[30] and a defining moment in the "spring" of Oromo nationalist aspirations. The song's text with images of long-deferred dreams of spring love effectively masked Oromo political aspirations:

> Spring has arrived!
> Scented flowers in bloom
> What bliss, what a blessing
> Let us fly away.
> Be done with longing
> Go somewhere we live happily together,
> Head over heels in love we are,
> Constantly think and dream of each other.
> Let us fly away and touch down side by side
> There to settle down and live our dreams.[31]

After that first performance, Urjii Bakkalchaa promoted the teenage Ali to singer and tambourine player and from then on he performed with the main band.[32] After being arrested and imprisoned for insulting the emperor of Ethiopia during a band performance that entailed crossing the border to nearby Djibouti,[33] Ali was imprisoned for six months in southeastern Ethiopia and was warned not to sing Oromo songs; after his release, he was detained several more times. As a result of his stressful

PLATE 4.2 Photograph of Ali Birra. Courtesy of Ali Birra and Lily Marcos-Birra.

imprisonment and the trauma of witnessing the hanging of his cell mate, Ali left Dire Dawa for Addis Ababa. There he began to write more overtly political songs, especially "Maal Ja'an" (What did they say?), a call to take up arms and fight government oppression.[34]

However, thanks to a chance encounter with an army officer in Addis Ababa, Ali was invited to join the Imperial Bodyguard Orchestra, with which he made his debut in 1966. Here we witness Ali's remarkable ability to negotiate successfully the ambiguities of living as an outspoken Oromo at the heart of Amhara society. Later, Ali described his position for three years with the imperial ensemble as that of a "*qotugna* singer" (the language of the field hands), a pejorative expression used at the time to refer to the officially banned Oromo language, Afaan Oromo.[35] In his performances with the Imperial Bodyguard Orchestra, Ali insisted on singing songs only in Afaan Oromo: "I was a hot-blooded teenager at the time, and I was rebellious. Even if they killed me, I didn't care at the time. And then I was just doing it in Oromo, and they liked my work. And they took me."[36]

Ali Birra became a sentinel musician whose songs sparked resistance, following a long-standing pattern among musicians in Oromo society dating from at least the late nineteenth century, when the Ethiopian emperor conquered Oromo lands.[37] (See plate 4.2.) Ali left the Imperial Bodyguard Orchestra in 1969 and struck out on his own, making his way through the thicket of imperial censorship until the beginning of the revolution. At that point, the military government changed tactics and appropriated Ali's popularity, suggesting that the revolution had emancipated the Oromo from Amhara oppression. Here we find an example of how a changing political climate could shift official views of a musician and his music, redefining his performances from the realm of resistance to that of governmental support. After a decade in Addis Ababa singing with major bands and appearing regularly in concert at the Harambee Hotel in 1982, Ali married a Swedish diplomat and in 1984 took advantage of his new diplomatic passport to depart Ethiopia.[38]

Transitions: Emerging Pressures and Opportunities

Despite their close association with those in power and use of traditional musical styles to support their positions, official musical ensembles could also at times give rise to innovations. The Imperial Bodyguard Band included a jazz ensemble, one of the first in Ethiopia, and some of its participating musicians subsequently became members of the early popular nightclub band, the Ras Band, taking its name from the Ras Hotel, where they played regularly. In the 1960s, other popular bands began to proliferate, each associated with a different Addis Ababa hotel:

> So, they started playing in those clubs and later on you know, some groups would come out from there and form another group, [one] at the Giyon Hotel. There were a lot of hotels then. And it started to spread slowly. The early days of the revolution saw continued pressure on traditional musicians and the continued growth of popular music, which assumed some of the responsibilities for commentary that had previously emerged from the *azmari*.[39]

As we have already seen, many popular singers encountered political troubles even before the revolution's inception. One, of course, was Teshome Mitiku, discussed at the beginning of chapter 2, who was forced to leave Ethiopia in January 1970 after performing an overtly political song before a large audience at the Haile Selassie I University in Addis Ababa. Harassed by government officials and then taken into custody for several days, Teshome was one of the first musicians to depart from Ethiopia in advance of the revolution, an experience that foreshadowed the difficult political times to come. He recalled that

> the last few years of the 1960s was a very critical time in Ethiopia. Even though the music scene was upbeat, there was also an undercurrent of social discontent. We were not political at all, but we were very popular at the time and people used to come from all corners to watch us. I believe the security people had an eye on us.[40]

The early days of the Ethiopian revolution unfolded slowly, having in-cubated during several years of devastating drought and famine in the country's north. With nerves on edge by late 1973, a massive rise in gaso-line prices in early January 1974 sparked waves of civil unrest: troops mu-tinied, teachers demonstrated, and taxi drivers, along with many others, took to the streets in protest over rising taxes and inadequate wages. The army in the then Ethiopian province of Eritrea, which had sought indepen-dence from the Ethiopian state since it was formally incorporated into the country in 1960, revolted in late February 1974. By March 1974 labor strikes began, along with demonstrations by students and revolts that stretched across the country. Muslims demonstrated for religious equality and for the right to be referred to as "Ethiopian Muslims," not as "Muslims living in Ethiopia."[41]

Thus began, in the spring of 1974, what came to be known as the "creep-ing coup," a period when the military slowly assumed what would become overwhelming power. The process accelerated on April 26, when the army arrested high civilian and military officials, and gained added traction on June 28, when it formed a body known as the Coordinating Committee of the Armed Forces, Police, and Territorial Army.[42] A group of radical offi-cers, led by Major Mengistu Haile Mariam, formed the Provisional Mil-itary Administrative Council, which came to be known as the Derg (lit., committee or council).[43] The climax came on September 12, 1974, when the Derg suspended the Ethiopian Constitution, dissolved Parliament, and deposed Emperor Haile Selassie I.

An Overview of the Revolutionary Years

The course of what had been a relatively peaceful and optimistic revolu-tion turned suddenly violent, however, with the execution of sixty de-tained leaders of the former government on November 24, 1974. In March 1975 the Derg nationalized rural land, which was owned predominantly by the emperor, the aristocracy, and the Ethiopian Orthodox Church.[44] As part of the Derg's campaign for rural land reform, known colloquially as *zämäch'a* (*zemecha*), some sixty thousand students and teachers were sent to hundreds of rural locales to enforce the revolutionary program and establish peasant associations.[45] Many songs were composed during the campaign, and a special *zemecha* choir was organized with two hun-dred members conducted by Nerses Nalbandian, who for decades had been an active member of the Armenian community in Ethiopia and a leader in Ethiopian musical life. The text of a popular *zemecha* song declared:

I am going to the campaign, to the countryside,
To eradicate ignorance from Ethiopia's land.[46]

Soon to follow were the bloodiest years of the revolution, known as the "Red Terror," in 1977–78, when several factions mounted resistance to the Derg and violence racked the streets of Addis Ababa. Thus began a revolution that would continue during the reign of Mengistu Haile Mariam until his overthrow by forces from northern Tigray Province in 1991.[47] The conflict raised a number of difficult challenges for musicians in ways that would forever change their lives. Once the Derg's power was firmly established, many musicians were forcibly swept up into a range of new musical institutions designed to control the population and to endorse government policies. And, as the revolution wore on, an increasing number of musicians sought to escape their country, seeking new opportunities and stability abroad. Each phase of the revolution played out differently in individual lives.[48]

Revolutionary Repression

During the early days of the Ethiopian revolution, most musicians found themselves under great pressure, both psychological and logistical. With the entry of the Marxist military regime, church musicians experienced, along with the rest of the Church hierarchy, a great loss of prestige with the downfall of the emperor, who had headed the Church, as well as severe economic strains stemming from the nationalization of Church resources and land. Church rituals that had traditionally been celebrated throughout the night, with the heart of the chant performance occurring during the very early morning hours, became, under curfews, nearly impossible for clergy to mount and for their congregations to attend.[49]

The government-imposed curfews shifted erratically, at their most extreme extending from 6 p.m. to 6 a.m.; additional mandates forbade groups of more than three or four people to convene in public. The curfews, first imposed in late fall 1973, also closed down private nightclubs and other independent venues for secular musical performance.[50] This brought out into the open what had once been a more subtle process of political engagement and commentary in musical domains that had begun in the prior decade while the emperor was still in power.

Musicians experienced a host of challenges during the revolution. These included confronting censorship and imprisonment, intimidation and violence, forced musical activity on behalf of the government, and forced migration.

One can understand the dimensions of revolutionary trauma only through a close look at individual experiences, turning first to those of Telela Kebede.

Telela Kebede

Born in 1938 in Kenya to Ethiopian parents who met there while in exile during the Italian occupation of their country, Telela Kebede could not have anticipated that she would have to leave her country late in life. Of Amhara descent and Ethiopian Orthodox faith, Telela received an elite education unusual for a woman of her generation at the French Lazarist Mission School in Sidamo.[51] There she sang in the mission choir and began performing publicly in the region. Despite her father's strenuous objections, Telela became an *azmari* (minstrel), performing in local drinking houses.[52]

Telela's reputation as a singer spread quickly, and, when the Haile Selassie I National Theatre was constructed in 1955 and dedicated to mark the silver jubilee of the emperor's coronation, Telela joined as both an actress and a singer.[53] An early exponent of the blurred musical boundaries between genres that would become increasingly common later in the century, Telela crossed over between the institution's *bahelawi* (cultural) and *zemenawi* (modern) ensembles, performing in both styles.[54] Musicians began to amplify traditional instruments, playing electric *masenqo* and *krar* in both cultural and popular music.[55] Telela's versatility was unusual in the 1950s and, with considerable justification, she considers herself as the "first modern singer" of her nation.[56]

In 1974 Telela recorded the song "Lomi Tera Tera" (lit., Lemon quarters) by well-known composer and lyricist Getachew Debalke. The text mourned the death of a mother who had given birth to fourteen children, a wax and gold allusion to "Mother Ethiopia" and the fourteen provinces the country had at the time.[57] However, the song's refrain, "lomi tera tera," which refers to a section of a traditional market where only one product, in this case lemons, is sold, masked a hidden meaning. When sung, the phrase sounds like the Amharic idiom "lomi bäyyätära," meaning "each according to his fate,"[58] implying an uncertain future for the "fourteen children" and the end of national unity:

> *Lomi tera tera* (lemon quarters / each according to his fate)
> *Lomi tera tera* (lemon quarters / each according to his fate)
> I entrust my mother to you
> Fourteen,

She bore from one father
and she raised all
at once, nurse and mother
Yet she cries because not one cares for her now.[59]

Although Telela recalls that the song was intended to criticize the emperor's policies and to express concern about the long-feared secession of Eritrea, both she and lyricist Getachew Debalke were taken into custody by the military forces who were in the process of overthrowing the monarchy.[60] Although Telela was released from the notorious Sendafa prison, north of Addis Ababa, after three months' confinement, Getachew remained in detention for eight years.

For two years after her release in 1974, Telela confronted major personal and economic challenges, scratching together a living by performing privately as an *azmari* in her own home.[61] This resulted in a second brief imprisonment for Telela on the grounds that "bourgeois people came there."[62] Telela eventually returned to a position at the National Theatre, where she performed until the end of the revolution.[63] But as was the case with so many of the other musicians during the revolution, Telela's life continued to be unsettled. After a period of renewed political activism on behalf of human rights in Ethiopia and government-imposed house arrest, Telela left Ethiopia for the United States for nine months in 1992 just after the end of the revolution; homesick, she then returned to Addis Ababa. But once again Telela found herself under surveillance whenever she left the house. Telela's daughter Mimi recalled, "there was a shadow everywhere she went, whether to a funeral, a wedding, or even to church. To continue like that was not good for her."[64] With family urging her to leave Ethiopia, Telela returned to the United States in 2003, where she has since lived with one of her daughters in a DC suburb. (See plate 4.3.)

Telela considers herself a sojourner abroad and hopes to return to Ethiopia in the future. She remains sensitive to music's role in political discourse and the manner in which her own performances in the past put her at risk. At the same time, she views her political activism, both through speech and through song, as an integral part of her sentinel role and responsibility as a musician:

I don't know about politics. But I love my country. I have a friend who, whenever he starts talking, it might be on one subject, but it will end up as politics. Sometimes, I talk what I feel. But whenever I do politics and music, I can express myself, whether in music or theater. People may interpret

PLATE 4.3 Singer Telela Kebede with her daughter Mimi Wondimiye
and granddaughter. Collection of author.

it in whichever way they wish. . . . The interpretation sometimes becomes
whatever they want it to say. So, my performance is a sort of acting. Even
if a person doesn't want to hear it, he can understand.[65]

Revolutionary Musical Life

As the creeping coup increased in momentum, conditions for musicians
deteriorated. Public musical venues such as the Venus Nightclub, which
from 1968 through December 1973 was a popular center of Addis Ababa
nightlife, were forced to close because of the imposition of curfews. Although the Venus Nightclub reopened intermittently until 1978, when its
owners finally managed to leave the country, supplies of food and drinks,
as well as musicians, were often hard to come by.[66]

The revolution brought about enormous social changes that had far-
reaching implications for musical life. By early 1975, many of the high
school and college students, including musicians, who had been sent to
the countryside through *zemecha* to set up peasant associations and raise
political consciousness on behalf of the new socialist regime, had become
alienated; some were driven away or killed when local peasants resisted
new policies and land reform.[67]

Life in urban areas was also increasingly unstable. Musicians recall the difficulties encountered by famous members of disbanded ensembles such as the Imperial Bodyguard Orchestra and the Police Band, some of whom "were begging on the street, they had nothing to live on."[68] Dawit Yifru, a keyboardist and music arranger who was a founding member of the Roha Band that succeeded the Walias Band as featured performers at the Addis Ababa Hilton in 1981, recalled that musicians were forced to perform alongside the atrocities of people being murdered on the streets during the Red Terror in 1977–78.[69]

Later moments during the 1980s were also distressing for Roha Band members:

> Sometimes the revolutionary guards would show up at the Hilton and interrupt with a salute and campaign saying, "Comrades, down with the reactionary!" . . . and Dawit says that the guards tell them to continue their program and leave. The frequency of the atrocities, according to Dawit, forced them to normalize situations.

"Now going back to that period, [it] does not sound real. It looks like a film or a dream," Dawit says.[70] Yet some musicians were able to work through the difficult times. One, who was a student when the revolution began and was imprisoned for protesting the regime, recalls that

> by early 1975, foreign musicians in Addis Ababa were told to leave the country. The Ibex band, then at the Ras Hotel, was on the verge of disbanding when the two foreign musicians they employed were denied work permits. Their lead guitar player was Zimbabwean, Wilson Endru, and the singer was Kenyan. Endru discovered me while I was performing at the Venus Club and told Ibex members that he found them a young guitarist. They contacted me and I joined them. Mahmoud (Ahmed) was the singer. . . . Consequences for not going to *zemecha* were extremely harsh. One could not be employed or go to school. For me, joining Ibex was a blessing in disguise.[71]

Musical life was largely confined to entertaining patrons who remained at local hotels during the all-night curfews. Patrons would arrive before curfew began and either stay in the hotel club or bar all night or rent a room. Moges Habte, a virtuoso saxophone player who was a founding member of the Walias Band that performed at the Addis Ababa Hilton from 1974 to 1981, recalls the ways in which musical changes mandated by Derg policy were avoided by ensembles performing at the hotels:

After the Derg came, things changed. Everything should be a revolutionary music. The Walias [Band] stayed that long because we were playing in
the Hilton. That was an international hotel and we had to play only international music. That's why we stayed there.[72]

The bulk of songs sanctioned by the government during the revolution
were those supporting the political changes.[73] Because political content
was conveyed by song texts, singers, not instrumentalists, were of greater
importance to the performance and, as a result, much more at risk.[74]

Moges recalls that the Walias Band would start playing at 7 p.m. and
end around 1 a.m. People who were not staying overnight at the hotel had
to depart for home before midnight. The musicians had a curfew pass, although driving during curfew was quite risky even with a pass; usually they
spent the night in a room they were given at the hotel.[75]

The musicians who played at hotels tried to make the best of their situation. While performing at the Hilton every night, the Walias Band decided to record themselves live. They bought a tape recorder and brought
it to the Hilton, eventually producing numerous cassettes. They also had
their keyboard player (Hailu Mergia) harmonize the Ethiopian melodies
he played and issued a cassette with solo keyboard renditions that became
very popular.[76]

Revolutionary Addis Ababa saw the opening of bars at which *azmari*
performed, called *zəgubəñ* (lit., close after me), to which people arrived
before curfew and remained until the curfew lifted at dawn.[77] In sum, even
during the revolution there were musical opportunities for musicians of
the top rank:

> Another beautiful period, beautiful music, even within the revolution. . . .
> I am not suggesting that the time was good for this kind of activity. . . . The
> curfew was there, so we adapted to the curfew and people used to come in
> at nine or ten p.m. They wouldn't be out till morning, till dawn. So, people
> got used to this kind of thing. They came and stayed with us. . . . You know,
> before the revolution, people had the choice of going everywhere. They
> would come to this club and then they would go somewhere else, but that
> was not possible.[78]

Forced Musical Measures

After the proclamation that nationalized urban land and buildings in July
1975, the Derg implemented a number of additional urban social and administrative changes, establishing neighborhood administrative units in

Ethiopian cities and towns across the country, termed *qäbäle* (*kebele*; lit., locality, area).[79] Each *kebele* was located within a designated neighborhood and oversaw collection of rents for newly nationalized properties.[80] The local residents who manned these units were heavily armed and over time became increasingly engaged in identifying and detaining individuals suspected of antigovernment activity. The *kebele* were largely responsible for the intense bloodshed during the early stages of the Red Terror, declared by Mengistu Haile Mariam when he became the head of state in February 1977.[81] This edict gave the *kebele* power to exert their control over the local population in an effort to wipe out the EPRP, the Ethiopian People's Revolutionary Party, which had resisted the top-down power of the Derg. *Kebele* competed with each other to score the highest number of executions of counterrevolutionaries, with the numbers of those murdered estimated in the tens of thousands in 1977 and 1978.[82]

During 1977, the year the EPRP was broken, anarchy reigned in Addis Ababa, in other major urban centers, and even in the countryside. Unspeakable horrors were perpetrated on a largely defenseless civilian population for the sake of dogmatic purity, the broad masses, democracy, national integrity, and civilian rule. The government, however, had the urban masses, history, and guns on its side and finally wore down the EPRP, in the process killing, or forcing into exile, thousands of Ethiopia's best-educated and idealistic young people. The Red Terror was so traumatic that subsequently there was virtually no civilian opposition to the Derg.[83]

In addition to its armed control of neighborhood life, each *kebele* was also required to support musical activity, which led to the founding of the *kinät* (*kinet*), a musical troupe established for political purposes. (See plate 4.4.) *Kinet* was derived from a Ge'ez word for art or creativity, and everyone was supposed to participate.[84] There were more than six hundred *kebele* nationally, with outstanding musicians from their respective musical ensembles joined together into provincial troupes.[85] There is no doubt that the *kinet* was the major new musical institution born of revolutionary fervor and that it had a lasting impact on the lives of those who performed as part of them.

The *kinet* emerged as an outgrowth of the founding of COPWE (Commission for Organizing the Party of the Working People of Ethiopia), a committee first established in December 1979.[86] Reports issued during the revolution noted that the *kinet*

> elaborates upon human life and describes various phenomena in a stunning manner; as a result it reflects upon ordinary issues by nourishing them through creativity; thus, it has a vital role in educating and stimulating the

PLATE 4.4 Dancers and *masenqo* players of the Gish Abbay *Kinet*
perform in 1986–87 under a large portrait of the Ethiopian Derg
chairman Mengistu Haile Mariam. Courtesy of Yehunie Belay.

community. The artist who is a creator and performer reveals social reality and exposes hidden issues as well as emphasizing obvious ones. Thus,
art becomes an instrument of class struggle. And its ideological role cannot be overlooked.[87]

More than a thousand revolutionary songs were composed and broadcast on Ethiopian radio in the wake of the revolution.[88] Indeed, music on
other topics, including love songs, were discouraged and even banned.
Many musicians worked actively for the revolution, with hopes, especially
in the early years, that their music would help effect change.[89] Some worked
under pseudonyms, such as lyricist Getachew Debalke, who wrote revolutionary poems after his release from jail, when the censors refused to publish
his work in view of his controversial song "Lomi Tera Tera."[90] In the words
of a speech by the revolutionary leader Colonel Mengistu Haile Mariam,

> With the condition that provides an opportunity for a new cultural devel-
> opment, the production of artistic works that the people once saw only
> from a distance, particularly music, is being announced, starting from the
> *kebele* up to the national level.[91]

Although the Derg sponsored both cultural and Western-style bands
as part of the *kinet*, there were special opportunities for traditional musi-

cians, whose status was raised by government sponsorship. After the Derg assumed power in 1974, the military government used traditional musical performance to extend and solidify its control:

> The military junta (Derg), as part of its socialist principles and Cultural Revolution, encouraged the revival of Ethiopian traditional music including war songs, *fukera-shilella*, which were traditionally used to motivate the warrior ethos.[92]

Many traditional musicians prominent today in diaspora, including a number interviewed for this study, were veterans of the *kinet* system. Leading popular musicians include Abegasu Kibrework Shiota (keyboard) and Henock Temesgen (bass), who played in the Kebele 19 *Kinet*.[93] Ashenafi Mitiku was a dancer in the revolutionary *kebele* Siddist Kilo beginning in the sixth grade, moving several years later to dance with the troupe at the City Hall Theatre.[94] At age thirteen, Bezawork Asfaw joined the *kinet* of her *kebele*, which, without a name, was simply known as *asra sost kebele* (lit., Kebele 13).[95]

Each province also had its own *kinet* that performed at a very high level and drew outstanding musicians from its entire area. *Krar* player Minale Bezu began his nine-year career with the Gojjam region *kinet* named Gish Abbay (lit., the Source of the Blue Nile); after starting as a singer in 1983, he shifted to *krar* and a *käbäro* (*kebero*) drum when his voice changed.[96] A second well-known member of the Gish Abbay *Kinet*, Yehunie Belay, joined that ensemble at age nine in 1977.[97] Virtuoso *masenqo* player Setegn Atanaw performed with Blue Nile *Kinet* in Bahir Dar for seven years and then joined the National Theatre.[98] Tsehay Amare, born in 1974, sang with the Lalibela Cultural Troupe from Wollo.[99]

Beyond providing employment for musicians during the eighteen years of the revolution, with particular support for traditional styles, it has been suggested that the *kinet* played a "pivotal role" in the development of neo-traditional musical performance practices (*bahel zemenawi*).[100] Most of the musicians just mentioned who trained in the various *kinet* emigrated to the United States, where their performance careers have included *bahelawi*, *zemenawi*, and *bahel zemenawi* styles.

The Derg formed other less prominent musical groups, such as one named the Yätäbabbärut (lit., the Cooperative, from *täbabbärä*, to cooperate).[101] As a member of this group, *azmari* Woretaw Wubet built his reputation by performing a Derg-approved song, "My Mother Is Ethiopia," demonstrating his loyalty and devotion to Ethiopia. Woretaw recalls that if you wanted to succeed, if you wanted to do anything in music, you would play what they told you in the way of propaganda military songs. I was able to do this and my songs became very popular.[102]

Woretaw left Yätäbabbärut in 1980 to join the Patriotic Association performing group and remained in Ethiopia until he received a contract to perform in Canada at the end of the revolution in 1991; he received asylum in the United States in 1993. In sum, music making in support of revolutionary goals was quite prominent during the revolutionary period, especially with the founding of the *kinet*. The number of musicians proliferated across musical styles, some eventually making their way into popular circles:

> It was everywhere, you know? Everybody became a singer because they wanted to be like us. And those started to join us, a lot of new singers came from the *kaffetenya* and the *kebele*.[103]

The Revolution's Toll: Bezawork Asfaw's Close Call

The violence of revolutionary Ethiopia took a great toll. Yet, in some cases, music saved the lives of musicians during this period, providing them with employment otherwise unavailable through the various *kinet*. Bezawork Asfaw (b. 1964) was the daughter of an Ethiopian Orthodox Christian priest who was also a bodyguard for the emperor.[104] She grew up singing from childhood at Addis Ababa's Kidist Mariam Church in the Sunday school choir, which shaped her musical development; as it did for many other singers, experience in church choirs was an important factor in her pathway into musical performance. As the daughter of a priest, Bezawork attended choir rehearsals every day at 5 p.m. and sang with the choir on Sundays and holidays in the church.[105] However, the revolutionary environment and the organization of the *kebele* determined her musical future:

> I never had a plan to be a singer, but after the Derg, we had to be in the *kebele*. If you didn't go to the *kebele*, or you didn't have a job, you could not go to school. I was thirteen years old then. We had to go to the *kebele* and we had to do something for the *kebele*. I didn't have any idea about the political, just God gave me a voice.[106]

The *kebele* required everyone to participate regularly, usually once a week, at gatherings called *nikat* (from the verb *näqqa*, to awaken or to be on one's guard), a mass indoctrination session for revolutionary ideology.[107] Bezawork remembers the *nikat* vividly, holding discussions of politics through the period of Red Terror violence and the wars with both Somalia and Eritrea. Instead of going to *zemecha*, Bezawork performed songs for the *kebele*:

> Each of the *kebele* had to have a concert, and then we worked with the National Theatre also, as backup singers. . . . . Our director just took the musicians and went everywhere in the capital. We did work, made money, and then brought the money home to survive. We worked with the orchestra of the Kebur Zebenya [Bodyguard]; we would just sing to give them a break. There would be food, T-shirts, things like that to make money for the government. The times were not good. Although my father did not want me to be a singer, he wanted to see me live. There was no choice because everybody was in jail.[108]

The *kebele* worked closely with the revolutionary government to conduct house-to-house searches, to arrest people whom they suspected to be counterrevolutionaries, and to confiscate arms. Bezawork spent three months in the *kebele* jail during the Red Terror, arrested by *kebele* officials who had gone to her home seeking her brother. When they could not find him, they came to the church and arrested her instead. Arresting one sibling in the place of another was a common practice during the height of the revolution and especially between 1977 and 1979 when "even children, 10–12 years old, also became targets."[109] In the crush of arrests and violence, no record was made of Bezawork's detainment, and she was left to languish in jail. She recalls this traumatic experience:

> It was terrible. Every morning they took people out and killed them. Every time we woke up, we were just crying and praying every time. It was bad, the time we had.[110]

After three months, the small *kebele* jail was impossibly overcrowded, and the guards took people out to interview them. Bezawork was then freed and returned home. Not long afterward, a representative of the National Theatre came and asked musicians to participate in auditions. Bezawork auditioned successfully and became part of the National Theatre while in ninth grade.

Younger than most of her peers, Bezawork continued to perform at the National Theatre throughout most of the revolution. At first, she sang and danced with the cultural ensemble. Four years later, she also began singing with the *zemenawi* band. She moved on to work with the *gwäshämärawi* (lit., percussion band) and even sang for a time with a string quartet. The revolutionary years were frightening ones for Bezawork, who recalls that

> we could not go anywhere. Working night times was so bad. People were dying everywhere, and my family was concerned about me. It was a very scary time.[111]

In 1987 Bezawork was chosen for a large ensemble that would perform for a special international tour, *Həzb lä Həzb* (*People to People*), sponsored by the Ethiopian government. However, her affiliation with the ensemble was discontinued for unstated reasons, and she did not travel with the group abroad.[112] In 1990 Bezawork received a contract to perform in Canada and, with great difficulty, managed to depart Ethiopia, later receiving asylum in the United States.[113]

Conclusion

The revolutionary years beginning in 1974 disrupted most aspects of the Ethiopian musical world of the post–World War II era. These years were difficult ones for musicians, whose lives and careers were unalterably changed. Yet, as noted at the beginning of this chapter, despite popular belief, musical activity did not cease by any means and some surprising new directions emerged.

The big-band era long supported by the emperor through major musical institutions in the 1950s and 1960s ended, as did the proliferation of private music clubs across the capital.[114] But, by the mid-1970s, the best musicians from the major ensembles began to establish smaller, independent instrumental groups with solo singers performing primarily for clients in major hotels in urban areas. With the revolutionary era, too, came a renewed emphasis on traditional music and musical instruments, in part because of the ubiquitous *kinet*, which funneled a large number of young people into musical careers.

During these years as well, the ever-inventive *azmari* experienced a resurgence. After the revolution, when the curfews were lifted, new traditional clubs known as *azmari bet* (minstrel houses) were founded in the Addis Ababa neighborhood adjacent to the Addis Ababa Hilton Hotel.[115] The changing shape of Ethiopian musical life during the revolutionary years shaped that which came after it, both at home and in the emerging diaspora.

Movements

PATHWAYS TO ASYLUM

Wäzäwwäzä
GENERAL MEANING: To shake, to agitate, to move to and fro
MUSICAL MEANING: To dance

Accompanied by the synthesizer and the six-stringed lyre, the 1998 song "Harar Dire Dawa" moves at a fast pace that lends emphasis to its lyrics recounting common routes taken by refugees fleeing revolutionary Ethiopia.

> Fleeing to Harar, Dire Dawa, Djibouti!
> Fleeing to Haraghe, Djibouti, Somalia!
> Fleeing to Sidamo, Moyale, Kenya!
> Fleeing to Illubabor, Gondar, Sudan![1]

With exit visas from Ethiopia largely prohibited by the military regime and the resulting inability of most to leave officially either by air from Addis Ababa or by the single railroad line extending from Addis Ababa to Dire Dawa and then on to Djibouti, escape often necessitated traveling dangerous routes overland through various border areas to Djibouti, Somalia, Kenya, and the Sudan. The song's performer, Abonesh "Abiti" Adinew, recalled that

> I sing of the memory one has of first crossing the border. We already passed so many hardships and then we come to this place. That's what it says and they're calling out every small town in the neighboring country.[2]

The impact of forced migration cannot be underestimated, forging a new relationship to history and what has been termed a shared politics of emotion and subjectivity typical of many diaspora situations and the reappropriation in exile of cultural homelands: "It was only after becoming refugees," writes Mekuria Bulcha, "that many Oromos started to feel, 'see,' talk, and write about and sing the natural beauty of their country."[3]

In this chapter we will trace the divergent pathways musicians took as they left Ethiopia during the revolution and in its wake after 1991. Large-scale migrations are often described in ways that suggest they occur in undifferentiated temporal zones and across similar spatial terrain. The lack of detail in most migration accounts has been criticized by Adelaida Reyes in her monograph on the Vietnamese forced migration, in which she reveals migration to be

> extremely complicated, involving huge numbers of people and many different paths to resettlement, and . . . critical differences between forced and voluntary migrants become crystallized in the interim period between departure and resettlement.[4]

In the case of Ethiopia, like that of Vietnam, refugees have different dates of departure, migratory paths that often require multiple stops of different durations along the way, and different points of arrival; in sum, what appears to be a mass movement of people incorporates many modalities of migration experience.[5] The heterogeneous nature of Ethiopian society, and the conflicts arising among peoples of different ethnic, regional, and religious backgrounds, have also inflected both the ebb and flow of migration at different dates and different routes taken. Although a study of Ethiopian refugees in Washington, DC, during the mid-1980s found that 59 percent went into exile after their imprisonment or loss of family or friends through revolutionary violence, there were also instances of voluntary migration after the revolution ended.[6] In this chapter, I track departures from revolutionary and postrevolutionary Ethiopia both forced and voluntary and shed new light on the different pathways refugees followed.

We can look first at different moments of departure. Many former government officials and others who were at extreme risk because of their past connections to circles of power escaped the country as soon as possible, where they joined the small number of Ethiopians already abroad by the 1970s at universities or in diplomatic missions. In addition, many Ethiopian Christians, especially Christian Amhara from the highland region, were impelled to leave early on as the actions of the Marxist regime dismantled the Ethiopian Orthodox Church's political and economic power. Indeed, a large number of individuals departing Ethiopia during the 1970s and 1980s were Christian Amhara fleeing revolutionary violence after the overthrow of the emperor.

During the period of the creeping coup, the Derg had not yet instituted the draconian measures that would soon foreclose most possibilities of legal emigration. But there was a steady reduction of permits to leave the country, particularly for individuals wishing to leave for Western Europe and the United States, with whom diplomatic relations had been strained in the global power shifts between the United States and the Soviet Union in the Horn of Africa. The Derg also denied access to overseas education, leaving only government officials and their relatives with permission to travel.[7] Thus, when an individual was fortunate enough to obtain an exit visa, he or she often made the choice while abroad not to return. But one individual who departed Ethiopia early in the revolutionary years stands out both for his groundbreaking contributions to musical life in Ethiopia, and, as we will see in the following passage and in chapter 6, his sentinel role in building a new Ethiopian musical community in the United States. This is Amha Eshete, born in 1945, who must be recognized as the first major figure in the wave of Ethiopian musical migrations to the United States that began in the mid-1970s.

Amha Eshete

Amha Eshete began his career in Addis Ababa not as a practicing musician, but as a music aficionado and entrepreneur. He recalls that his first purchase on being hired for his first job was a stereo.[8] His first musical initiative, in 1969, was to found and manage the brilliant but short-lived Soul Ekos Band, which featured prominent singers Teshome Mitiku, Alemayehu Eshete, and Seyfu Yohannes. A year later, Amha opened the Harambee Music Shop, the first record store owned by a native Ethiopian in the capital. (See plate 5.1.) The Italian owner of the other major record store in the city could not keep up with demand for a wider array of music, giving Amha an opening to stock recordings from New York, India, Kenya, and West Africa.[9] On the first day of business, Amha sold half of his store's merchandise. He remembers that "people were thirsty for the hottest acts—James Brown, Jim Reeves, Otis Redding, Wilson Pickett and others."[10]

When Amha realized that there were no Ethiopian records available, he decided to found the first indigenous Ethiopian recording label. There was a very modest history of sound recordings with Ethiopian musicians abroad and in Ethiopia itself, and Ethiopian Patriotic Association held a

PLATE 5.1 Record producer Amha Eshete's sentinel actions have spanned well over half a century. Courtesy of Amha Eshete and photographer Michel Temteme.

monopoly on publishing recordings.[11] Taking this situation into account, Amha decided "after many sleepless nights [he] was determined to take a risk of probable imprisonment and decided to ignore the decree to start producing modern Ethiopian music."[12]

> I had a gut feeling that it was the thing to do. . . . Philips couldn't have done what I did, because they were a big, official company, and a foreign one at that. But I was a young, independent, unknown and gutsy Ethiopian just starting out in the business. I could do things that they would never dare. I thought, nobody's going to kill me for this. At most I might land in jail for a while. I talked my plans over with lots of people at the Haile Sellassie I Theatre and of course at Aghèr Feqer Mahbèr [Hager Fikir, Ethiopian Patriotic Association]. They all warned me that I was headed for serious trouble. There has always been censorship in Ethiopia, even under the Emperor. To publish a newspaper or a book (or a record), you needed a censorship visa from the Ministry of Information. But as they had apparently forgotten all about the imperial decree regulating record production, they had no problem with me issuing my records, just like any book in Amharic or in English. In fact, I was already importing foreign records. I had my first records, two 45s by Alèmayèhu, stamped in India—it was nearby, and cheap. When the records arrived, Aghèr Feqer threatened me, brandishing

the Emperor's order, but without much conviction. They knew that they had produced almost nothing in the past years, and it all just died down.[13]

Amha launched his Amha Records label in 1969. Although the national press in Ethiopia reported on the record publication controversy, officials did not impede Amha's operation. After its launch and during the next decade, Amha produced just under ninety-three 45s, eleven LP albums, and the very first cassette in Ethiopia.[14] He recorded the originals in Addis Ababa and then had LPs produced in Lebanon, Egypt, and Greece.[15] Amha describes the music scene in Addis Ababa during the late 1960s and early 1970s as

> buzzing with the mixture of international sounds, Ethio-jazz, and traditional music. . . . modern Ethiopian music was emerging at an incredible pace even though there was an extensive government control and censorship every step of the way. . . . It was the first time that new and modern night clubs were being opened, record players were being installed in cars, and enjoying music was the spirit of the time.[16]

Amha was at the center of the lively musical world in Addis Ababa, working without role models, learning through trial and error, and often making decisions based on gut feeling.[17] As he recalls,

> I had no experience, for example, on how to negotiate with the artists. . . . I did what I thought was right and fair to me and all the others involved at the time. . . . It was a lifetime experience and believe me it worked because I was able to produce one hundred and three 45s and a dozen LPs in a few years.[18]

Many of Amha's recordings would find renewed life beginning in the 1990s through their remastering and distribution for the *éthiopiques* series, a subject discussed in chapter 10.[19] By the mid-1970s, Amha was deeply engaged in producing records, and in September 1975, he managed to obtain an exit visa in the early days of the revolution to travel to Greece to purchase more professional sound-recording equipment to ship home to Ethiopia. But when Amha arrived in Greece, he learned that the Eritrean singer Tekle Tesfa-Ezghi, featured on his most recent album, had been accused of pro-Eritrean propaganda and thrown into jail; this despite Amha having received clearances to release the album. When Amha's father was also imprisoned soon thereafter, Amha realized that he could not safely return home. He flew then to Washington, DC, and became one of the first refugees seeking asylum from the Ethiopian revolution. Amha also became a major force in establishing a new musical community in the United States, details of which are recounted in chapter 6. One might wish to declare Amha "sentinel musician zero" of the Ethiopian American diaspora.

By 1975 individuals began fleeing the country to prevent their high-school-age children from being conscripted into *zemecha* and sent to rural areas to set up peasant associations and carry out other government projects. Fear of violence in the cities also spurred many to depart, especially during the horror of the Red Terror.

Eritreans began fleeing the violence of the ongoing civil war for Eritrea's independence, which flared anew in early 1974. Many Ethiopian Somalis also fled the region to escape the border war in 1977–78 between Ethiopia and Somalia.[20]

Pathways to Asylum

The choice of a route to leave the country depended on multiple factors, including the level of violence in different sectors at the time of departure and access to a route of egress. For most Ethiopians seeking asylum, there were two main routes to escape during the years of the revolution: traveling west to reach refugee camps in the Sudan or heading south to cross the border into Kenya.[21]

Perhaps the most widely publicized mass movement of Ethiopians out of the country during the early years of the revolution was that of the Ethiopian Jews (Beta Israel), beginning around 1980 from the north of the country to Sudanese refugee camps. By late 1983, the Sudanese camps were filled with refugees of many Ethiopian backgrounds in addition to thousands of Ethiopian Jews from the Gondar area. The conditions in the refugee camps were increasingly desperate and it is estimated that between two and four thousand Ethiopian Jews died in the camps or on their way to the Sudan.[22]

One's proximity to either the northwestern or southern border was the primary determinant of the exit route chosen. During the revolution, an underground structure of multiple organizations such as the EPRP (Ethiopian People's Revolutionary Party) and EDU (Ethiopian Democratic Union) would, whenever possible, try to aid those making their way west to the Sudan.

The United States was the preferred destination for the largest number of emigrants from the Horn of Africa.[23] A majority of these individuals escaped Ethiopia during the revolutionary years through the Sudan, the primary overland route for Ethiopians from the northwest of the country and for Eritrean refugees. The movement of refugees to the Sudan was a dangerous ordeal, requiring a hazardous overland trek through Ethiopia and across the Sudanese desert, followed by interrogation and sometimes imprisonment by Sudanese officials. Frequently the situation became dire, such as when refugees lacked identification cards and were urgently in need of food and medical attention. The Sudan itself was overwhelmed by the tidal wave of refugees and was poorly equipped to handle a problem of such enormous dimensions.[24] Female Ethiopian refugees reported especially frightening difficulties, experiencing instances of sexual harassment and a high risk of rape that compelled them to "employ" a guard, known in Sudanese Arabic as an *etma asher* (lit., after twelve; a husband only after working hours).[25] Destitute women alone with children, an all-too-frequent occurrence, encountered terrible obstacles in satisfying their most basic needs for shelter and food for their families.[26] Some refugees I interviewed were so traumatized by their escapes that they were unwilling or unable to share any details, either finding it too upsetting to discuss or needing to protect the identities of those who had helped them to survive the journey.

By 1991 two-thirds of the 1,066,300 Ethiopian refugees moving through neighboring countries of Africa had left through the Sudan and a third through Somalia; only very small numbers, mainly Oromo from adjacent regions in the southeast and south of the country, escaped to Djibouti or Kenya during the revolutionary years.[27] Sudan also proved to be the location from which the greatest numbers of applicants successfully obtained resettlement in the United States; before 1984, 60 percent of refugees in Sudan who applied for asylum were successful in entering the United States.[28]

Elizabeth Namarra

An overland march to Kenya was the route taken by an Oromo gospel singer and composer Elizabeth Namarra, who grew up in an evangelical Christian home in the Boji area of Wollega in western Ethiopia.[29] Elizabeth's father, an Orthodox Christian who joined an evangelical church as a teenager, often traveled around Oromia seeking converts, taking Elizabeth along with him. Because of her activity as a Sunday school teacher and choir leader for the indigenous Pentecostal Church Mulu Wongel (Full Gospel Believers' Church), which had been deemed illegal by the Ethiopian government in 1967, Elizabeth was targeted by the Ethiopian government during the revolution.[30] She was arrested several times while at church and imprisoned. In late 1983, Elizabeth escaped and fled to Kenya,

PLATE 5.2 Elizabeth Namarra (on right) followed her sister Martha (on left)
to Kenya and then to Minneapolis. Collection of author.

where she joined her sister Martha, who had preceded her; after nearly two
and a half years in Nairobi, she again joined her sister, this time in Minneapolis in 1986. (See plate 5.2.) The trauma of the revolutionary years is still
very much with Elizabeth decades later, especially a sense of displacement:

> Where do I belong? There is a feeling of homelessness, like you don't be-
> long anywhere. . . . They started persecuting me at eleven years of age and
> I had to run away. All Oromo things were on hold for nineteen years.[31]

A number of Oromo who took refuge in Kenya made their way to
Australia; by 1984 an Oromo refugee community was established in Melbourne.[32] The Oromo migratory path through Kenya was quite strenuous
and protracted, often requiring years of waiting between the application
to migrate and the receipt of an Australian entry visa.[33] One Oromo im-

migrant recalled the difficulty of the migratory process, as well as the absence of choice about the destination for resettlement:

> There were Ethiopian agents in Djibouti and many refugees were treated badly by the police there. We remained for three months. . . . But it was too dangerous for us to stay so we decided to go to Kenya. I speak good Somali language so we moved by foot to Hargeysa. . . . We walked through the desert to Mogadishu . . . and across to Hagadera in Kenya. There are no buses in Somalia . . . it was a long and dangerous journey . . . anyone can rob you. There was rebel fighting . . . we saw a lot of people die and wouldn't have survived without the help of Somali people who gave us food and water. . . . In December 1996 we got refugee status and remained in Nairobi for two years waiting for the UNHCR to send us somewhere. In January 1999 they told us we were going to Melbourne where the Oromo community would help us settle. We knew nothing about Australia, only kangaroos. . . . I still haven't seen one.[34]

Other Destinations

Ethiopian communities arose in other locations internationally, established where the possibility of asylum was approved by a host country. Among them was Jerusalem, where the centuries-old Ethiopian church and monastery provided a magnet for an expatriate community that had increased during the Italian occupation of Ethiopia from 1936 to 1941. Great Britain, which had offered refuge to Emperor Haile Selassie I during that same period, hosted a small Ethiopian community that continued to grow during the revolution.[35]

Many places across Europe had welcomed Ethiopian students during the later years of Haile Selassie I's reign and enabled them to remain when the revolution began in 1974. Ethiopian communities had been established early on in many European urban areas, each of which presented challenges for migrants from the differences in ideology and socioeconomic conditions.[36] To date, there have been only a few studies of the Ethiopian diaspora communities in Europe, one of which is Abbink's work in the Netherlands, considered to be among the most desirable European destinations, where training was available for agricultural experts, civil servants, and engineers. By 2006 official figures from the Netherlands counted 10,300 Ethiopian migrants among a total population of 230,000 African migrants in Holland.[37]

Most European sites of resettlement grew out of historical ties between Ethiopia and the European country in question, such as the presence of many Eritreans in Italy, drawing on cultural and linguistic affinity stemming from the longtime Italian colonial presence in Eritrea from 1890 through 1941.[38] A number of Ethiopians and Eritreans who migrated to Italy also moved on to other locales for permanent settlement, as was the case of guitarist Selam Seyoum Woldemariam, discussed later in this chapter, saxophonist Moges Habte, and vocalist Martha Ketsela, all of whom left on a pathway that took them through temporary residency in Italy to eventual settlement in the United States.

Music and Defection: The People to People Tour

Departures continued to mount throughout the 1980s as individuals lost hope for the homeland political situation to change. When, after a great effort, a musician was successful in arranging an exit visa to perform abroad, it opened the possibility for seeking asylum. But an unusual opportunity arose for a number of Ethiopian musicians to travel in 1987 as a result of a concert tour sponsored by the Derg titled *Hǝzb lä Hǝzb* (*Hizb le Hizb, People to People*).[39] *People to People* was Ethiopia's response and national "thank you" to the world for aid given them during a devastating drought and famine that began in 1984. A major event in that effort was *Live Aid*, a sixteen-hour-plus superconcert organized by Bob Geldof and Midge Ure at Wembley Stadium in London and John F. Kennedy Stadium in Philadelphia on July 13, 1985, to raise money for Ethiopian famine relief.[40]

Although the *People to People* tour was conceived by the Ethiopian government as a way to acknowledge aid sent from abroad during the drought, no less important from the perspective of the Derg was the opportunity to expose outsiders to Ethiopian culture in a positive context. The initiative was a substantial one that took more than a year and a half in rehearsals to prepare and required considerable financial resources.[41]

The *People to People* musical show was a set of music and dance numbers about one and one-half hours long, loosely connected by a narrative of travel across the country that sets up encounters with various ethnic communities and their musical traditions. Ethio-jazz musician Mulatu Astatke was contracted to audition the musicians, select the repertory, and organize the performance with assistance from Tesfaye Lemma, the former director of Orchestra Ethiopia.[42] The traditional ensemble alone included approximately thirty-five performers, with six male and female singers, a choir, sixteen dancers, and a number of instrumentalists, including two playing *krar*, three on *masenqo*, two drummers, and a *washint* (flute) player.[43] Additional musicians and stage crews brought the troupe to more than fifty in total.[44] The well-known *azmari* Shambel Belayneh was included, along with several other cultural musicians. A handful of famous Ethiopian singers also were invited to join the tour, including Bezunesh Bekele, Neway Debebe, Tilahun Gessesse, Maritu Legesse, and Mahmoud Ahmed, although at least one other (Bezawork Asfaw) participated in *People to People* rehearsals but was excluded from the tour.[45]

In preparation for the tour, Mulatu traveled to various regions of Ethiopia, deciding which ethnic music should represent the country and which musicians to invite. In the end, Mulatu selected Amhara, Gojjam, Harar, Oromo, Tigray, Wollo, and Wollayta music for inclusion. All these ethnic and regional styles were accompanied by a single ensemble that privileged instruments of the central highlands, some with altered construction such as extra strings and amplification for dance numbers. The instruments differentiated regional styles by emphasizing characteristic rhythms associated with each. Costumes emphasized different and colorful styles of ethnic dress associated with each community. However, the single backdrop featured cultural sites of the highland plateau region, including the ancient stelae at Aksum and one of the rock churches from Lalibela, backed by flat-topped mountains (*amba*) typical of the northern highland plateau landscape.

The troupe performed in major halls in the Soviet Union, England, France, Germany, Hungary, Bulgaria, Sweden, Finland, Denmark, Italy, the Netherlands, Greece, the United States, Mexico, and Cuba. Mulatu anticipated that there might be issues of defection and brought along extra musicians to protect against potential attrition from that cause.

> I had a big responsibility as the musical director of this group. People told me, "Look, Mulatu, people might probably defect. How are you going to handle this?" So what I did was, I always had with me two people, like two great *krar* players, four to five *masenqo* players. I had reserves. Because, you know, if something happens, I didn't want to have a problem.[46]

After arriving in Washington, DC, several musicians let Mulatu know that they planned to defect:

> They came to my room and said, "Look Mulatu, we want to talk to you because there are some guys who want to give us dollars, green cards, and if you want to defect with us you can see we are going to leave." "Wow," I said, "I have a big responsibility and it is not only for me. I cannot go.

Since I represent my country, my people, oh, it's so hard for me. I cannot do this, no."[47]

The police soon arrived, having been advised that people who wanted to defect were being held against their will. The police met with Mulatu, who called the Ethiopian ambassador to consult; after discussion, the ambassador decided that if musicians wanted to defect, they could do so. That afternoon, the troupe performed in Baltimore, and afterward three musicians disappeared. Mulatu spent the next two weeks reorchestrating musical parts to make up for the lost drummer and *krar* player; he also trained another musician on the drum.[48]

Meanwhile, the director of the Ethiopian Folk Dance and Music Ensemble on the tour, Tesfaye Lemma, had a diabetic emergency and was hospitalized in Baltimore on the day of that concert. Local Ethiopians there intervened and assured the Ethiopian ambassador that Tesfaye would rejoin the tour when he recovered. After four days, Tesfaye returned to the tour hotel in Washington, DC, where Ethiopian Embassy staff began closely monitoring his activities, even escorting him to meals. When Tesfaye objected to the surveillance, the embassy sent three security guards to the hotel. At this point, Tesfaye, too, decided to defect and escaped that same evening while the guards were asleep, taking refuge in the home of an Ethiopian friend in the area. After the two-week period during which the emergency rehearsals adjusted the show to make up for the defections, Mengistu Haile Mariam ordered the troupe to cancel performances in Los Angeles and other US cities and to depart for Mexico and Cuba.[49]

The process of defection and the strain of establishing a new life in the United States presented enormous challenges for those who made that decision. Although most requests for asylum were granted, and there was, by the late 1980s, a large Ethiopian American community in the northeastern United States on which refugees could lean, the advantages of newfound artistic freedom were counterbalanced by difficulties. Mulatu felt that the price of defection, losing one's home and life path, was too great:

It's so hard. But the thing is, they defect and then the defection does not really continue to something. It's just nonsense to me. You see that people just live somewhere else. I don't think this is correct. You've got to have some kind of rhythm, you know. So this is what I believe in. Out of those who defected, one probably will be something. Somebody or something. You know, contributing to America or contributing to Ethiopia. But you never know, so this is how it is.[50]

Getatchew Gebregiorgis

Although many refugees were reluctant to provide details of the traumatic experience of escape, defection, and asylum, dancer Getatchew Gebregiorgis spoke openly about his own experience and gave permission to have it published.[51] Born in 1962 in Dessie, a town in the Amhara Region of the highland plateau, Getatchew was from an Oromo family of Orthodox Christian faith. Getatchew grew up in Addis Ababa, where he studied Ethiopian Church music as a child. He found that

> Yared, the greatest man, he made melodies, very interesting, such beautiful and amazing things. It just stained my soul and spread. And then I found that this is me, this is what I like. This is my interest. This is music, you know?[52]

During the Red Terror, Getatchew was accused of being involved in the resistance, was arrested and tortured, and spent two years in jail.[53] He survived and, once freed, learned about an audition at the National Theatre for a dancer and singer; he auditioned and got the job. Getatchew worked through the revolutionary years as lead dancer at the National Theatre and was as a result a clear choice to serve in that capacity for the *People to People* troupe. He was the first in the group to decide to defect.

> I thought they were going to take me back. If I defect where I was suspected of being involved in the resistance and I get caught, I know I'm going to be killed or [hanged] or something. So I took no risks. We were "travel prisoners," we didn't have even our passports, we didn't know where we were or where we were performing. We just suddenly, like a soldier, had to get up, get in a bus, get on a plane. Only when we got there did we find out the country: "oh, this is Germany, oh, ok."
>
> So, finally, when I got here [to the United States], I was looking for an opportunity when I could defect. We had five security people following us, looking at what we were doing, what we said, and whom we called. So I said, "I'm gonna be killed when I get there. So, God, help me get out. You are the one who brought me here, you gave me this life again." I wanted to rise, to show the world who I am. And to show for my people, for freedom.
>
> I remember it was March, a snowy night. I performed at the Kennedy Center then the same night ran from my hotel, with nothing. 3 a.m. in the morning, running, I didn't know where I was going. Looking for freedom. I didn't know anybody. From the hotel I was running the whole night. Around 4:30 or, quarter to 5, I came out by the Washington Monument.

I see the American flag, and the light, and I thought I was dreaming. And I said, "I'm free." I stood and looked at it. I'm laughing, crying, running around. I didn't think about the cold. And I realized about fifteen, twenty minute later, I came to myself, I said, "what am I doing here?" Maybe this place is a sensitive area, a protected area, and I am in jeopardy. I walked away. Now I've got to march somewhere and find somebody to talk to. I kept walking, I didn't know what street it was, but I followed the lights. I got to a street and walked down Pennsylvania Avenue.

And then I saw a place with flags, and I thought it was the United Nations. I said to the guards, "I'm an Ethiopian artist, I've defected, I came out from the group, so can I get political asylum?" "Oh, no, no, this is the wrong place," he responded, "you have to go to immigration."

I'm thinking, where is that place? How do I get there? Finally, something clicks in my mind. I have a friend I knew a long time ago and she has a phone number. And in the middle of the night, I called her. She picked up the phone, I told her who I was. She knew that I was in the hotel with the group and had seen my performance. And I said, "I defect." "Where you are?" And I said, "I'm in the street, on Pennsylvania Avenue, at 19th Street." "Well, I'll come and pick you up." She took me, she saved my life. She's an artist, an Ethiopian.

We met this lawyer who stood up for me and made a free petition to the government of United States of America for immigration. I pledged who I am, what I did, how I came, the story I told you. They gave me political asylum immediately.[54]

Getatchew received asylum in 1988 and began the long process of adjusting to a new life in the United States. In addition to performing at DC nightclubs, restaurants, and Ethiopian community events, he collaborated with other new arrivals to establish a musicians' association in 1989. (See plate 5.3.) When I interviewed him in July 2008, he had recently been elected president of the association. He described his work as a sentinel musician in detail:

We struggle really hard. Without financial support, we cannot reach our goals. We support the community and we did shows to demonstrate our sympathy for the bombing of Badme;[55] we send money to support our families and for the Red Cross. . . . We want to be recognized, to be in the world market as Ethiopians. We want people to know the music where this started, where Yared started. We have to establish this bridge; if we cannot do it, our children will do it. Music is our light.[56]

PLATE 5.3 Dancer Getatchew Gebregiorgis hosts a booth at the 2007 EFSNA tournament on behalf of the Association of Ethiopian Musicians in North America. Collection of author.

Emigration after 1991

The Tigrayan-led government that overthrew the Derg maintained its power over Ethiopia well over two decades after the revolution's official end. One new factor after 1991, however, was that the most stringent travel restrictions were lifted, which made possible travel and voluntary migration motivated by pull factors such as family reunions, educational opportunities, and employment abroad.

Although many Oromo migrated during the revolution, in 1991 many more were soon forced to seek asylum abroad to flee nonstop violence and human-rights abuses by the Ethiopian government against them. The tension between the Oromo and the Ethiopian polity has deep historical roots, and neither the Ethiopian revolution nor the protracted postrevolutionary period effectively addressed the issues at stake in the Ethiopian government's mistreatment of the Oromo, nor of growing Oromo resentment.[57] After a brief period of shared power in 1991–92, the Ethiopian government banned the most active Oromo political organization, the Oromo Liberation Front (OLF), in 2006 as a terrorist organization.[58] As a result, "alleged ties to the OLF may serve as justification for arrest, detention, firing, expulsion, or confiscation of property."[59] Since 2015, Oromo protests against the Ethiopian government have been mounted against the government's proposed expansion of the municipal boundary of the capital, Addis Ababa, into Oromo lands. In 2017 the Human Rights Watch World Report documented widespread crackdowns on Oromo freedoms of expression and association, including the killing of more than five hundred people at large Oromo protests between November 2015 and July 2016.[60] In August 2012 the prime minister of Ethiopia, Meles Zenawi, died at the age of fifty-seven, twenty-one years after overthrowing the military regime, having led the postrevolutionary government since 1991.[61] Hailemariam Desalegn, the minister of foreign affairs and deputy prime minister, of southern Wolayta ethnic descent, succeeded Meles but encountered increasing resistance after several years in power. In 2018 Hailemariam resigned his post in the face of mass protests and was replaced by the first Oromo prime minister of Ethiopia, Abiy Ahmed. After taking office, Prime Minister Abiy released political prisoners, relaxed the state of emergency, negotiated an end to hostilities with Eritrea, and loosened restrictions on the news media.[62]

Eritreans also were forced to leave Ethiopia at several points both during and after the revolution, as well as subsequently from Eritrea itself after independence. The experience of Selam Seyoum Woldemariam provides an example.

Selam Seyoum Woldemariam

A notable instance of forced migration years after the revolution ended was the case of Eritrean guitarist Selam Seyoum Woldemariam. (See plate 5.4.) Born (1954) and raised in Addis Ababa, Selam lived in the city with an Ethiopian wife and family. He forged a career as a successful musician with the Ibex band, which played regularly at the Ras Hotel during the early years of the revolution. After several years, most of the Ibex group departed for the Sudan.

> They were asking us, let's go to the Sudan. . . . They asked us, but me and my bass player, Giovanni Rico, didn't want to go because we were in school then. And we had families. I was married, and Giovanni was married, and we could not do that move. So, we said, "you can go, we will not be going." So that was the birth of the Roha Band. We stayed there, in the Ras Hotel.[63]

The Roha Band moved to the Hilton to perform in 1981 when Walias, the resident band at the time, left for a tour to the United States, where several members defected. The Roha Band quickly filled the vacuum, performing the entire week at the Hilton for a varied clientele.

Yet even with Roha Band's success during the revolution, there were dif-

PLATE 5.4 Guitarist Selam Seyoum Woldemariam (Selamino) performing in the United States in 2010. Courtesy of Selam Seyoum Woldemariam.

ficult moments. Soldiers and security officers would often threaten Selam and extort money. Although the Roha Band managed to tour occasionally during the revolutionary years, they had "a very tough time" getting permission to leave the country and had financial challenges, mitigated by the fact that "it was not only the music that was our source of income; two of us also had music shops."[64]

In May 1998 a full-blown war between Ethiopia and Eritrea broke out as a result of a long simmering border dispute over Badme, a small border town claimed by both countries. In June Selam was arrested without warning and, along with other Eritreans, was deported overnight to Eritrea from Ethiopia. The deportation was unprecedented and shocking: "There was no pattern in what they did."[65]

Selam stayed with his mother in Asmara for a year and was not allowed to rejoin his family in Addis Ababa during his wife's serious illness.[66] He eventually made his way to Italy, where he applied for asylum in the United States, finally arriving in 2000 to join a relative in California. But he decided that he preferred to live in Washington, DC, where he had visited in 1991 on a Roha Band tour and moved there to start a real estate business. His family soon joined him.[67]

An Overview of Migration Patterns

Thirty-one of the musicians I interviewed received asylum in the United States during or after the Ethiopian revolution. Some of their experiences have already been recounted, such as those of Bezawork Asfaw, Amha Eshete, Getatchew Gebregiorgis, Telela Kebede, Elizabeth Namarra, Tesfaye Lemma, Moges Seyoum, and Selam Seyoum Woldemariam; others will appear in the chapters to come. Those who received asylum in the United States often arrived after an interim stop for a period of time in places such as Italy, Greece, Canada, the Sudan, or Kenya. The dates of individual departures and subsequent requests for asylum extend from the earliest in 1975 throughout the revolution, as well as from the postrevolutionary period well into the twenty-first century. (See table 5.1.)

Several younger musicians received asylum when they were brought by their parents to the United States as children. Singer Wayna Wondwossen arrived as a toddler with her mother in 1977; singer-songwriter Meklit Hadero came as a young child with her family in 1982; Debo Band leader Danny Mekonnen arrived in 1981 as an infant with his parents from refugee camps in the Sudan, where he was born; concert producer Tekle Tewolde received asylum with his parents in 1984.[68]

Others received asylum in the United States as young adults through family members already living in the United States. In 1997 singer Abdi Nuressa joined his mother after a decade-long wait for reunion; also in 1997 instrument maker and performer Melaku Gelaw and his daughter, singer and multi-instrumentalist Betelehem Melaku along with their entire family received asylum to join their wife/mother already in Washington, DC.[69] Singer Teshome Mitiku arrived in the early 1990s after his long residency in Sweden, joining his brother, saxophonist Teddy Mitiku.[70]

As we have seen, exiting Ethiopia with a contract to perform was a strategy used by many musicians to seek residency abroad. A good number defected during tours or contractual periods abroad. Beyond those who sought asylum during the *People to People* tour, Moges Habte came to the United States on a band tour in 1981 arranged by Amha Eshete and

TABLE 5.1 **Musicians' migration to the United States, interim stops, and status**

NAME OF MUSICIAN	ARRIVAL YEAR	STATUS	INTERIM STOP(S)
Seleshe Damessae	Early 1970s	Education	
Amha Eshete	1975	Asylum	Greece
Wayna Wondwossen	1977	Asylum	
Henock Temesgen	1980	Education	
Martha Ketsela	1981	Asylum	Italy
Danny Mekonnen	1981	Asylum	Sudan
Moges Habte	1981	Asylum	
Moges Seyoum	1982	Asylum	Greece
Meklit Hadero	1982	Asylum	Europe
Father Tsehai Birhanu	1982	Education	Leningrad
Tsegaye B. Selassie	1982	Education	
Elizabeth Namarra	1983	Asylum	Kenya
Tekle Tewolde	1984	Asylum	
Zakki Jawad	1985	Education	India
Abegasu Kibrework Shiota	1986	Asylum	
"Tommy T" Gobena	1987	Education	
Tesfaye Lemma and Getatchew Gebregiorgis	1988	Asylum	*People to People* tour
Sayem Osman	1989	Education	
Bezawork Asfaw	1990	Asylum	Canada
Mohaammad Ibraahim Xawil	1990	Asylum	Indonesia
Teshome Mitiku	Early 1990s	Asylum	Sweden
Alemtsehay Wedajo	1991	Asylum	
Abraham Habte Selassie	1991	Church sponsorship	Ireland
Woretaw Wubet	1993	Asylum	
Setegn Atanaw	1993	Asylum	
Minale Dagnew Bezu	1993	Asylum	
Yehunie Belay	1993	Asylum	
Ashenafi Mitiku	1993	Asylum	Great Britain
Hana Shenkute	1994	Asylum	
Abebaye Lema	1996	Diversity visa	
Abdi Nuressa	1997	Asylum	
Melaku Gelaw and Betelehem Melaku	1997	Asylum	
Abonesh Adinew	1998	Asylum	
Getahun Atlaw Garede	1998	Church sponsorship	Ireland
Selam Seyoum Woldemariam	2000	Asylum	Eritrea and Italy
Beniam Bedru Hussein	2000	Church sponsorship	
Behailu Kassahun	2002	Asylum	
Mesfin Zeberga Tereda	2002	Diversity visa	
Telela Kebede	2003	Asylum	
Munit Mesfin	2003	Education	India and Namibia
Hermela Mulatu	2005	Education	

NB: This table is a summary of information on migration dates and pathways of forty-three musicians who provided testimony for this project. If no interim stop is listed, the individual came to the United States directly from Ethiopia or did not provide this information.

sought asylum; Abegasu Kibrework Shiota arrived in 1986 on tour and began musical studies at the Berklee College of Music in Boston; in 1993 Minale Dagnew Bezu defected during a cultural tour, as did Yehunie Belay, who soon married an Ethiopian American; and Abonesh Adinew arrived on a concert tour in 1998 and sought asylum.[71]

Although the possibility of leaving Ethiopia for education abroad was dramatically restricted during the revolution, one can find exceptions among the musicians interviewed. A few left Ethiopia for studies in the years just before the revolution, including Seleshe Damessae, a talented *krar* player, who entered the United States in the early 1970s and studied at the University of Vermont.[72] A number of others arrived in the United States for educational purposes, including bassist Henock Temesgen in 1980 and *merigeta* Tsehai Birhanu, who in 1982 came for postgraduate studies at Princeton University direct from prior studies in Leningrad (now Saint Petersburg, Russia).[73] Others arrived to enroll at US secondary schools and colleges, including singer Tsegaye B. Selassie (1982), bassist "Tommy T" Gobena (1987), and music blogger Sayem Osman (1989).[74] Keyboardist and composer Beniam Bedru Hussein came to the United States with the sponsorship of the Mennonite Church, with which he and his family were affiliated in Ethiopia (2000); Munit Mesfin arrived for secondary school in Massachusetts in 2003 after living abroad in both India and Namibia with her mother; and 2005 saw Hermela Mulatu, daughter of Mulatu Astatke, enter the United States for educational purposes.[75]

After the revolution ended, a few accomplished church musicians from the Ethiopian Orthodox Church were sent to clerical positions in Jerusalem and later moved on to Ireland. Both Abraham Habte Selassie (1991) and Getahun Atlaw Garede (1998) pursued studies in Ireland and subsequently entered the United States with church sponsorship.[76]

Some special circumstances helped several musicians survive the revolution at home and then migrate abroad. Traditional dancer Ashenafi Mitiku (b. 1966) grew up in a devout Orthodox Christian family in a rural area of northern Gojjam province. When he was twelve, he went to live with his sister in Addis Ababa and attended school there, where he also danced and drummed in his local *kebele*'s *kinet*. After several years, Ashenafi became a professional dancer with the City Hall Theatre in Addis Ababa, a full-time job where he learned traditional dances from various ethnic communities across Ethiopia and traveled the country to perform them. With the help of an American woman named LaDena Schnapper, who had worked with the Peace Corps in Ethiopia, Ashenafi emigrated to the United States in October 1993. Ashenafi had danced regularly at the Karamara Hotel in Addis Ababa, where he met Schnapper, who helped him process paperwork to leave the country for Great Britain. After a year in England, Ashenafi was able to migrate to the United States, where he became a citizen in 2006. Ashenafi lived in Schnapper's home in Washington, DC, for five years until her retirement and refers to her as "my American mom."[77]

As one reviews the migratory paths of the musicians summarized in table 5.1, one is struck by the variety of pathways and the multiple points where musicians stopped along their way, such as Mohaammad Ibraahim Xawil, who immigrated to Seattle in 1990 from Indonesia.[78] Zakki Jawad, whose experiences will be discussed in chapter 10, came to the United States for education after spending two years studying in India.[79] Only two musicians interviewed won the lottery for US diversity visas, Abebaye Lema (1996) and Mesfin Zeberga Tereda (2002).[80] Thus seventeen years of revolutionary upheaval, along with ongoing repression for a quarter of a century under the postrevolutionary rulers, sparked a large and diverse wave of musical migration.

One study of the Ethiopian revolution has identified three main "vintages and waves" between 1974 and 1991. The first wave was migration before the revolution, a largely voluntary flow involving elites seeking education abroad, which drew to a close with the overthrow of Haile Selassie. The second exit interval shifted dramatically to forced departures, commencing in 1974 and including Ethiopians fleeing the elimination of armed opposition and the consolidation of Mengistu Haile Mariam's power in 1979; the second exit interval also included the outflow in response to the Eritrean conflict, the border war with Somalia, and the Red Terror. The final period extended from 1980 until 1991, marked by the largest exodus between 1984 and 1986.[81] But as table 5.1 makes clear, migration continued apace after the end of the revolution, with nearly half of the musicians in this small sample seeking residency in the United States after 1991.

In seeking to understand why so many refugees from the Horn of Africa sought to come to the United States, a major study shows that more than half (58%) gave US opportunities and conditions as an explanation, another 21 percent cited the presence of family members or relatives in the country, and 11 percent attributed their migration directly to difficult living conditions in the country of application. The rest (10%) stated that they had no other viable alternatives.[82]

According to Koehn's study, two-thirds of the Eritrean émigrés did not arrive directly from Ethiopia and 56 percent of Ethiopians secured their entry visa from a neighboring country in the Horn of Africa; the rest entered the United States via Western Europe.[83] For the majority, there is little doubt that the growing Ethiopian community in the United States was a major attraction and that many chose to migrate to the United States because family, relatives, or friends were already there.[84] Ethiopian refugees settled in a number of North American communities, and the role of musicians in ensuring the growth of them is the subject of chapter 6.

Communities

PLACES AND POLITICS
IN DIASPORA

Debo

GENERAL MEANING: Communal labor
MUSICAL MEANING: Ethiopian American musical ensemble

As we have seen in chapter 5, the first wave of refugees from the Horn of Africa arrived in the United States in the mid-1970s; more sought asylum during the devastating Red Terror of 1977–78 and the wars with Somalia and Eritrea that broke out around the same time. The upsurge of forced migration beginning in the 1970s from the Horn of Africa and from Southeast Asia sparked the passage of the 1980 US Refugee Act as an amendment to the Immigration and Nationality Act.[1]

Processes of forced migration have a number of outcomes, paramount among them the founding of new communities far from the historical homeland, commonly termed diaspora communities. The phenomenon of diaspora is the subject of a substantial literature that has expanded its theoretical orientation and focus as well as its coverage of communities that anchor immigrant lives in new locales.[2] The great migration from the Horn of Africa to North America provides rich case studies of diaspora, incorporating a number of immigrants with different political, religious, and cultural orientations.[3] But if diaspora studies today document subjects ranging from generational differences to return to the homeland, there is no question that "music is central to the diasporic experience, linking homeland and here-land with an intricate network of sound."[4] This chapter provides an overview of the founding of Ethiopian American diaspora communities, with attention to the sentinel roles of musicians and the range of activities and institutions they initiated in this process.

Some Ethiopians arrived in the United States in the decades before the start of the revolution; they were primarily young adults from elite families who came to study at US universities. Those already in the United States during the mid-1970s found their lives suddenly disrupted. One was Elias Negash, who arrived in New York from Ethiopia in 1971. He first moved to Boston, where he attended junior college and planned to study jazz at the Berklee College of Music. But in 1974, with family financial support for his studies interrupted by the revolution's onset,[5] Elias had to relocate to California to live with his brother, then a University of California–Berkeley student. "The plan was really to go for four years and go back home," Elias said, "but I ended up staying forty years."[6] A performer of Ethiopian jazz and world music with the Bay Area Retroz band, Elias worked as a composer and pianist, honing his musical chops by studying music theory at Bay Area colleges and, in the mid-1970s, when the area's first Ethiopian restaurant, the Blue Nile, opened on Telegraph Avenue, by playing the piano regularly there. In the decades to follow, Elias's music circulated in the United States and Ethiopia on solo CDs, and he operated his own recording studio.[7]

The future of Ethiopian refugees was shaped by the traumatic events surrounding their arrival in the United States and the efforts of organizations coordinating their resettlement. Government entities, including the US Office of Refugee Resettlement and private groups such as Catholic Charities USA, initially sponsored the refugees from the Horn of Africa, making decisions about where they would settle. Circumstances required some immigrants to remain in the place of first asylum for only a short time and then move on. The family of musician Danny Mekonnen, for instance, arrived from refugee camps in the Sudan and settled in Fargo, North Dakota; they subsequently moved to Paris, Texas.[8] Of twenty-seven thousand Ethiopians officially documented as having entered the United States between 1984 and 1986, for example, 25 percent went to California and another 25 percent were divided among Maryland, Washington state, New York, Georgia, Washington, DC, and Illinois. The remaining 50 percent were dispersed across other parts of the United States, seeding Ethiopian communities in many US cities.[9] Because the majority of the early refugees were single men without family ties in the United States, Catholic Charities created clusters of refugees to avoid a situation in which a non-English speaking Ethiopian would find himself in an area where he could not communicate with anyone.

We [Catholic Charities] try not to place refugees in a vacuum. We either build the community around them or initiate a plan to resettle x number of refugees of a particular ethnic background in a given group.[10]

These policies ensured that at least some refugees were placed with those of the same ethnic and linguistic background, giving rise to local communities of descent. But in one notable case, the efforts of a single musician had a striking impact on the future of the new Ethiopian diaspora in the United States, notably that in Washington, DC. As discussed in chapter 5, two years after Amha Eshete's 1975 arrival in Washington, DC, he opened the Blue Nile, the first full-service Ethiopian restaurant in the US capital.[11] Even those who were still living in Ethiopia at that time were aware of the musical ferment abroad set into motion by Amha:

> There was a restaurant on Georgia Avenue and Amha Eshete was the one who brought them to entertain here in the United States. . . . Singers and musicians came to America.[12]

By 1982 Amha had also opened the Ibex Club, an establishment encompassing three floors of entertainment:

> The first floor was live jazz, the second floor was modern band with comedians during the band's recess. The third and top floor was huge and we used to have disc jockeys. It was on Georgia Avenue and its capacity was in excess of eight hundred. Eventually, I had the first floor for an Ethiopian live band. Top class Ethiopian artists like Ephrem Tamiru, Bezawork Asfaw, Shambel Belayneh, Ketema Mekonnen, Aster Aweke, and others including band members like Abegasu Shiota, Henock Temesgen, Hailu Mergia, Moges Habte and a few others have performed. . . . One unique circumstance was that my club was the first [and] largest with three floors in the Washington area. It also lasted for over fifteen years unlike many other clubs whose life span is a maximum of two to three years.[13]

Amha remained in Washington, DC, until 1993, when disability from a chronic illness forced him to return to Ethiopia.[14] He died in Addis Ababa in April 2021. He had hoped to travel back and forth between Washington, DC, and Addis Ababa, but his limited mobility rendered the plan impossible. He decided that "going back and forth will make me lazy, neither here nor there."[15] He marveled at the number of Ethiopian musicians who had settled in Washington, DC: "There are more there [in Washington, DC] than here [Addis Ababa] now."[16]

Amha had an early and dramatic impact on many aspects of musical life both at home in Ethiopia and in its North American diaspora. Beyond his extraordinary contributions as a record producer in Ethiopia, whose oeuvre would decades later reach a global listening public through reissues on the *éthiopiques* label, he made an institutional impact through founding one of the first Ethiopian restaurants abroad as well as the first Ethiopian nightclub in the United States. Amha was a vital link in the course of events that resulted in the spread of Ethiopian restaurants worldwide, a process that has made Ethiopian cuisine and music a global phenomenon. His Ibex nightclub had a continued presence in the DC area until it closed in February 1997.

As a result of Amha's work in institutionalizing Ethiopian music performance in Washington, DC, at both his restaurant and his nightclub, he became a sentinel for musicians from his homeland seeking a lifeline abroad and helped jump-start the process of chain migration by Ethiopian musicians to the DC metropolitan area. Amha was the first to arrange for Ethiopian musicians to tour in the United States in 1982–83, devoting a great deal of time and effort to bring the Walias Band over, some members of which sought asylum and remained in the United States afterward.[17] That first tour spanned the nation, visiting Los Angeles, Houston, New York, Boston, and, of course, Washington, DC. Soon after, Ethiopian singers began to arrive on their own, hiring keyboardists who had immigrated to the United States to accompany them. Over the years, individual musicians who came as part of concert tours or arrived independently chose to remain in Washington, DC, did so in large part because of the institutional base Amha had built.

Heterolocal Residential Patterns and the Importance of Ethnic Places

Several characteristics are common to the structure of most Ethiopian immigrant communities. First, most of them share heterolocal patterns of residency with immigrants spread across various neighborhoods.[18] Thus, Ethiopian immigrants lived in different neighborhoods rather than in Ethiopian-only areas. Second, one finds that similar institutions and social organizations anchor most Ethiopian diaspora communities, providing a template through which one can gain a comparative perspective. And third, musicians have played important roles in shaping not just musical events, but institutional and cultural life across these communities. They founded institutions that support other musicians and arts activities and sustain venues such as churches that serve many in a locality. Because of its dominant position as the center of Ethiopian American diaspora life, it is worthwhile to explore the Ethiopian community of Washington, DC, and the metropolitan area of which it is a part for insights.

Washington, DC

The large number of Ethiopians in Washington, DC, has made a particularly indelible impression on new arrivals from the Horn of Africa: "You feel like you're in your own country when you come here," recalls Tefera Zewdie, owner of Dukem Ethiopian Restaurant, who left Ethiopia as a teenager in the 1980s.[19] No other community has the same density of immigrants from the Horn of Africa as does Washington, DC, with an estimated two hundred fifty thousand Ethiopian residents.[20]

Although a few Ethiopian refugees arrived in Washington, DC, as early as 1975, including the notable Amha Eshete discussed earlier, Ethiopian institutional development in the area began to intensify around 1980. The Ethiopian Community Center on Georgia Avenue NW was founded that year, with the Ethiopian Community Development Council established in 1983 as an organization to help resettle refugees in the metropolitan area.[21] Ethiopian musicians arriving in Washington, DC, in the early 1980s noticed the upsurge of Ethiopian-related activity and recall that it directly influenced their decision to settle in the area:

> My ticket was Addis Ababa, Milano, Boston, that's it. . . . Then, when I came to Washington, DC, there were a lot of Ethiopians, Ethiopian restaurants, everything. I changed my mind because I had a lot of friends here, maybe the music business might be here. When the band came here, weddings, show business, restaurants, everything boomed.[22]

In the 1980s, most Ethiopian commercial establishments in Washington, DC, were in the Adams Morgan area centered around Columbia Road and 18th Street. By the 1990s, as rental prices for shops skyrocketed in Adams Morgan, Ethiopian commerce shifted to the U Street corridor converging on 9th Street close to Howard University. In the mid-2000s, the Ethiopian community launched an initiative to officially name 9th Street "Little Ethiopia," a move successfully resisted by African Americans who had long considered that area, the site of the Lincoln Theatre and known as "the Black Broadway" where Duke Ellington performed, to be the heart of Washington's historical African American community.[23] (See plate 6.1.)

By the 2000s, with the explosion of real estate prices in Washington, DC, many Ethiopians moved to suburbs in Maryland and Virginia and new Ethiopian commercial areas began to open. (See plate 6.2.) Eastern Avenue in Silver Spring, Maryland, became a new center, with Ethiopian shops and restaurants, and a second commercial area emerged in down-

PLATE 6.1 On U Street NW in Washington, DC, a mural of
Duke Ellington overlooked Almaz, an Ethiopian restaurant that
closed during the pandemic in 2020. Collection of author.

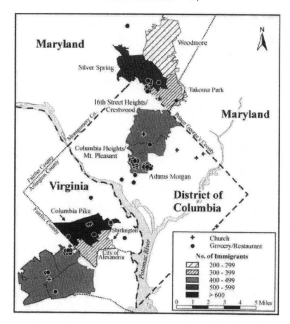

PLATE 6.2 Ethiopian immigrants and establishments in the Washington metropolitan area. From Elizabeth Chacko, "Ethiopian Ethos and the Making of Ethnic Places in the Washington Metropolitan Area," *Journal of Cultural Geography* 20, no. 2 (2003): 23.

town Alexandria, Virginia, and extended into other Virginia suburbs. It has been suggested that Little Ethiopia in Washington, DC, has been displaced by two new Little Ethiopias, one in Silver Spring and nearby Takoma Park, Maryland, the other in Alexandria extending west into Fairfax County, Virginia.[24] Houses of worship were among the institutions founded by Ethiopian immigrants: The Debre Selam Kidist Mariam EOT Church was one of the first, established in 1987 in Washington, DC, and given cathedral status as *Re'ese Adbarat* (Head of Churches) in 2001.[25]

The shaded areas on the map in plate 6.2 identify residential concentrations of Ethiopians in the DC metropolitan area, who constituted less than 20 percent of new African arrivals even in those neighborhoods where they had the greatest concentrations.[26] The various residential areas highlighted in plate 6.2 and the relative numbers of Ethiopians in each, indicate that the largest number of Ethiopians dwelled in Virginia, followed by Maryland, with Washington, DC, in a close third place. These data, gathered by cultural geographer Elizabeth Chacko in the early 2000s, correlate with the demographic information provided by musicians I interviewed who were living in the metropolitan area in 2007–8.

TABLE 6.1 **Ethnic place-making in the heterolocal urban setting**

Ethnic institutions	churches, civic and political organizations, etc.
Ethnic sociocommerscapes	ethnic businesses that provide goods and meeting places
Ethnic arenas	spaces used repeatedly by a community but lacking permanent ethnic markers
Intangible ethnic places	internet sites, radio and television stations, musical recordings, etc.

SOURCE: Elizabeth Chacko, "Ethiopian Ethos and the Making of Ethnic Places in the Washington Metropolitan Area," *Journal of Cultural Geography* 20, no. 2 (2003): 29–30.

The DC metropolitan area exemplifies a residential pattern that can be observed in most other Ethiopian diaspora communities across the United States: as has been noted, residential areas do not coincide with the location of important Ethiopian commercial and cultural institutions. The black dots on the map mark the locations of Ethiopian grocery stores and restaurants and the crosses mark locations of Ethiopian churches. These physical sites serve, to borrow terminology from cultural geography, as "ethnic place makers," which hold both real and symbolic meaning in the construction of Ethiopian diaspora communities.[27] These important sites, separate from the immigrants' homes and workplaces, are where members of the community gather. Sociologist Ray Oldenburg has referred to such places as the "great good places" or as "third places."[28] Oldenburg suggests that the most important function of these places is to unite a neighborhood, but in the case of the Ethiopian diaspora discussed here, third places are most often outside neighborhoods of residence and therefore exercise a very special role in bringing together a dispersed community.

Ethnic Place-Making in the Ethiopian American Diaspora

Chacko argues that urban ethnic identities are not displayed in the residential centers but rather are vested in specific "*places* where community is forged and embodied."[29] She also suggests that Ethiopian diaspora place-making serves as a model for understanding the creation and maintenance of an ethnic community by other new immigrant groups.[30]

Chacko provides a useful taxonomy of the places that generate a sense of community in urban settings characterized by residential scattering, dividing them into four categories she terms ethnic institutions, ethnic sociocommerscapes, ethnic arenas, and intangible ethnic places. (See table 6.1.)

ETHNIC INSTITUTIONS

Ethnic institutions are dominated in the Ethiopian diaspora first and fore-most by churches, an indication of the strong stream of Ethiopian Ortho-dox Christian descent that unites a good number of Ethiopian immigrants. The revolution affected Christian Amhara Ethiopians immediately and, as a result of the many pressures on the homeland Orthodox Church, the ma-jority of the American diaspora Ethiopian refugees during the first years of the revolution were of Orthodox Christian faith. As we have seen, the Ethiopian Orthodox Church has a liturgy that is almost entirely musical, with highly trained musicians singing, playing drums and sistra, and danc-ing. A musician must be one of the founders of a local church because, without a musician, the liturgy cannot be performed. A notable example we already encountered in chapter 3 is the career of *liqa mezemran* Moges Seyoum, who was trained as both a priest and a musician and who co-founded an Ethiopian Orthodox Church in Dallas, Texas, on his arrival as a refugee in 1982. In 1987 *liqa mezemran* Moges traveled regularly to Wash-ington, DC, to help establish DSK Mariam EOT Church in Washington, DC, which has matured into one of the largest Ethiopian churches in the global Ethiopian diaspora.[31]

Only at large churches in major urban areas such as Mariam EOT Church in Washington, DC, does one find a cohort of musicians per-forming the liturgy. But one finds many churches scattered across all Ethi-opian diaspora locales, the smaller ones often staffed by a clergyman who both chants the liturgy and administers sacraments, sometimes assisted by young deacons from the congregation. Although in early years of the diaspora many Ethiopian churches met in buildings lent by other denom-inations, such as Riverside Church in New York City, a number have gone on to purchase existing buildings, including Debre Selam St. Michael EOT Church in Boston and St. Mary's EOT Church in Los Angeles. A few have designed and built their own new structures, including St. Gabriel EOT Church in Seattle. Complicating factors related to church governance and membership have arisen, including conflicted relationships between dias-pora churches and the church hierarchy in Addis Ababa; an alternative pa-triarch was recognized in the United States.[32] In addition, many churches experienced internal tensions and divided into new, competing congre-gations. For this reason, it is not unusual to find several Ethiopian and Eritrean Orthodox Churches in most Ethiopian diaspora communities, as well as increasing numbers of Protestant and evangelical institutions.

Other ethnic religious institutions in the Ethiopian American diaspora include mosques. Muslim Ethiopians who migrated initially tended to affiliate with existing area mosques wherever they settled. Several communities with a critical mass of Ethiopian Muslims of Oromo descent, including Atlanta, Oakland, and Toronto, have established their own mosques.

As we have already seen, ethnic organizations also include community centers that offer social services and support for their communities in transition. Most communities have social-service institutions of various sizes, often named after the Ethiopian ethnic community that they serve.

ETHNIC SOCIOCOMMERSCAPES

Sociocommerscapes include stores, record shops, and most notably in the case of Ethiopian and Eritrean diaspora, restaurants. Some sociocommerscapes are unmarked as ethnic places, such as a Starbucks in downtown Minneapolis that was so packed with Ethiopian, Oromo, and Somali men when I visited one Saturday afternoon in March 2011 that I couldn't squeeze inside.[33]

Ethiopian markets are scattered across many diaspora locales, such as the small Maru Grocery on Bissonnet Street in Houston, Texas, the only Ethiopian shop in a diverse and multiethnic shopping center. Ethiopian sociocommerscapes, including the markets that sell traditional foodstuffs such as spices and Ethiopia's indigenous *teff* grain (*Eragrostis tef*), are also the main venues through which flyers that advertise concerts and other cultural events are circulated.[34] Most of these markets stock sound recordings and DVDs and, on occasion, traditional clothing and a few Ethiopian musical instruments. Only a few Ethiopian shops, such as the California Studio in Minneapolis, marketed only audiovisual materials.[35]

It has been said that cooking and cuisine represent "aesthetic knowledge of identity" and that "the Ethiopian restaurant is the most visible projection of Ethiopia's diasporic community in the West (whether in Amsterdam, London, or Rome or on 18th Street in Washington, DC)."[36] In the diaspora, Ethiopian restaurants provide a sociocommerscape where Ethiopians from different neighborhoods gather and where people from the broader American community also come into contact with Ethiopian culinary and cultural worlds.

Ethiopian restaurants are generally among the first public venues to emerge in virtually any and every American city with an Ethiopian resident able to cook and administer it. These places, well marked and known within their respective urban areas, serve as magnets at which Ethiopians (and many others) converge.

The names of Ethiopian restaurants provide insights into diaspora and homeland politics, ethnicity, and religious orientations. Many take names

PLATE 6.3 Addis Ababa Restaurant in Silver Spring, Maryland (named after the Ethiopian capital city), was one of dozens of Ethiopian restaurants scattered across the DC metropolitan area. Collection of author.

that recall places in the owner's native region of Ethiopia or Eritrea, such as Langano (a lake in Oromia south of the Ethiopian capital), Ras Dashen (the highest mountain in northern Ethiopia's Semien Mountains), Dukem (a small town south of Addis Ababa), or Lalibela (site of the famous rock churches in northern Ethiopia). Certain city names (Asmara, Dire Dawa) signal owners and clientele of Eritrean or Oromo ethnicity, respectively. (See plate 6.3.) Many restaurants use Ethiopian words evoking moods, important dates, and objects: Desta (joy or happiness), Meskerem (September, start of the new year), and Kokeb (star). A few take the name of their owners, such as Zenebech or Rahel. Others are named after Ethiopian Christian holidays and important rituals, or objects associated with food and its presentation, including Fasika (Easter), Demera (ritual bonfire for *Masqal*), Bunna (coffee), and Mesob (large table-height basket that holds a communal food tray). An informal commentary about Ethiopian restaurants in a cross section of American locales provides a colorful overview:

> I fell in love with my first [Ethiopian restaurant] in Boulder, Colorado, in 1990, but sadly, the Colorado foothills offered only one option, as did

Jacksonville. Conversely, Princeton had none, making Manhattan feel like a windfall with eight. Los Angeles, to its credit, had 10 and a Little Ethiopia district lined with banners and bunting. For those few years in the City of Angels, I felt as if we had hit the East African jackpot.

That was before Dallas. . . . By the time we had been here for a year, I'd mapped out 11 Ethiopian restaurants, one Eritrean restaurant, and at least two Ethiopian grocers. . . . The region surrounding [Interstate] 635 and Greenville, the area that DFW International identifies as Little Ethiopia, isn't going to win any awards for quaintness . . . our Little Ethiopia has no banners, no foot traffic, or signposts, and no defined borders, just a very loose concentration of restaurants and retail that, though not showy, provides an introduction to a North Texas immigration story that, for the last 35 years, has gone largely untold.[37]

Ethiopian communities are most publicly represented by their restaurants, and few other Ethiopian third places across the diaspora are also so closely tied to musical life. Many restaurants are venues for live Ethiopian musical performance if any Ethiopian musician is available in the area to perform; otherwise, restaurants play recordings imported from Ethiopia, or increasingly, Ethiopian music recorded in the United States. The DC metropolitan area has countless Ethiopian restaurants and is particularly rich in live musical entertainment on weekend and holiday evenings. Some North American Ethiopian restaurants, such as Dukem on U Street in Washington, DC, are so famous internationally for both Ethiopian food and musical performances that they advertise on billboards in downtown Addis Ababa. (See plate 6.4.)

A number of clubs feature Ethiopian musicians who compete for the same audiences. One summer night in 2008, I went to Arlington, Virginia, to hear a joint performance by two DC singers appearing together at a venue that usually features salsa music. Not until around 11 p.m., when neither the accompanying instrumentalists nor more than a few members of the audience had arrived, did the singers find out that the instrumentalists whom they had hired to accompany them had gone instead to perform at an Ethiopian restaurant just down the road.[38] The performance was canceled.

ETHNIC ARENAS

Places termed "ethnic arenas" are those taken over occasionally to celebrate ethnic events on special occasions but that lack permanent markers of that ethnic presence. Once again, events held by Ethiopian diaspora

PLATE 6.4 Billboard on Bole Road in Addis Ababa advertising Dukem Ethiopian Restaurant in Washington, DC, and Baltimore, Maryland. Collection of author.

communities in such arenas are heavily associated with musical performance.

On holidays traditionally celebrated with outdoor processions, such as *Masqal*, the Festival of the True Cross observed annually in late September, many Ethiopian churches hold ceremonies in local parks they have reserved for the occasion. New Riverside Park, bordering on Memorial Drive in Cambridge, Massachusetts, adjacent to the Charles River, has regularly hosted a *Masqal* ceremony mounted jointly by several Ethiopian Orthodox churches from various neighborhoods of Boston and its suburbs. The event requires considerable diasporic creativity because the bonfire traditionally lit for homeland *Masqal* observances is prohibited by American fire laws. However, the enterprising congregations have fashioned a bonfire-shaped conical structure covered with gold-flecked cloth that reflects the rays of the setting sun, around which the congregation processes, carrying sparklers and candles, singing hymns.[39] (See plate 6.5.)

Other ethnic arenas exist, most prominently the stadiums that host the annual Ethiopian soccer tournaments. In the mid-1970s, small groups of Ethiopians began to gather informally on the weekends in various diaspora locales to play soccer. "We knew each other, somehow we found each other," musician Elias Negash said of the first soccer sessions in the

PLATE 6.5 New Riverside Park in Cambridge, Massachusetts, is an ethnic arena regularly transformed for community *Masqal* observance. Collection of author.

Oakland Ethiopian community when he arrived there in 1975.[40] "Since it was a small community, this was our chance to get together and speak our national language."[41]

Local soccer teams were quickly established by most Ethiopian diaspora communities and, in 1984, the Ethiopian Sports Federation in North America (ESFNA) was established. By 2015 there were thirty-one formally constituted Ethiopian soccer clubs from cities across the United States and Canada. For a week each year overlapping the July 4th weekend until its forced cancellation in 2020 because of the COVID-19 pandemic, the Ethiopian community came together in a different metropolitan area chosen to host the annual event.[42]

Games were played at a stadium rented for the occasion, with musicians contracted both from diaspora locales and from Ethiopia to perform at opening and closing tournament ceremonies, as well as at nightly events held at nearby concert venues and restaurants. Each soccer tournament constructed its own temporary sociocommercial center adjacent to the stadium, erecting rows of tents and booths for vendors selling mementos, recordings, and food, with ample space given over to exhibits for philanthropic and public help organizations.[43] (See plate 6.6.)

A list of the urban areas that have hosted this annual summer event both provides an overview of the major Ethiopian diaspora communities and demonstrates the manner in which sports and music combine

PLATE 6.6 The ESFNA 2008 sociocommerscape constructed alongside
RFK Stadium in Washington, DC. Collection of author.

to bring these new communities together. (See table 6.2.) Major musical
events both open and close the games: An opening "Ethiopia Day" concert typically leads off the tournament, and a festive concert with major
performers is scheduled for the final evening.[44]

The ongoing life of soccer tournaments also provides a map of ethnic divisions among immigrants from the Horn of Africa. In 1986, twelve
years after ESFNA was founded, Eritreans initiated the Eritrean Sports
Federation in North America (ERSFNA) with a mission "to promote and
facilitate the development of amateur sports and cultural events within
the Eritrean and Eritrean-American communities in North America."[45]
A decade later, in 1996, the Oromo Sports Federation in North America
(OSFNA) sponsored its first formal soccer tournament in Toronto, bringing together six participating clubs from several Canadian cities as well as
from Minnesota and Seattle.[46]

All the soccer tournaments, whatever their ethnic or political affiliation,
are major, if temporary, sites for musical performances. Some Ethiopian
restaurants near the games, such as Dukem in Washington, DC, remain
open twenty-four hours a day for round-the-clock socializing and performances during the weeklong tournaments in their area.[47] (See plate 6.7.)

Beyond ESFNA's focus on soccer and music, the organization also has
a social mission as a nonprofit organization dedicated to promoting Ethiopian culture and heritage and to building a positive environment within

TABLE 6.2 **Venues for ESFNA, 1997–2020**

2020	Minneapolis, MN (canceled because of the COVID-19 pandemic)
2019	Atlanta, GA
2018	Dallas, TX
2017	Seattle, WA
2016	Toronto, Canada
2015	College Park, MD
2014	San Jose, CA
2013	College Park, MD
2012	Dallas, TX
2011	Atlanta, GA
2010	San Jose, CA
2009	Chicago, IL
2008	Washington, DC
2007	Dallas, TX
2006	Los Angeles, CA
2005	Atlanta, GA
2004	Seattle, WA
2003	Houston, TX
2002	Hyattsville, MD
2001	San Francisco, CA
2000	Toronto, Canada
1999	Dallas, TX
1998	Atlanta, GA
1997	Atlanta, GA

Ethiopian American communities in North America. The organization aspires to bring Ethiopians together to network, to support the growing Ethiopian business community, and to empower the young by providing scholarships and mentoring programs. The soccer tournaments, as well as other sports activities and cultural events, are vehicles for an increasingly ambitious social mission.[48] In 2018 ESFNA donated funds for relief efforts in Ethiopia to mitigate the impact of yet another drought; for this purpose, ESFNA partnered with Catholic Relief Services and local nongovernmental organizations in Ethiopia. ESFNA also collected and donated funds for flood victims in the Omo River Region of southern Ethiopia and for HIV/AIDS relief across the country.

The soccer tournaments, like almost all immigrant community ventures and organizations, reveal the complexity of diaspora politics, as well as the deep value placed on collective activities that enhance social bonding. The Ethiopian, Eritrean, and Oromo soccer games continued until the advent of the COVID-19 pandemic in 2020 as well-attended annual events, with

PLATE 6.7 A banner announcing 24/7 musical entertainment at Dukem Ethiopian Restaurant, Washington, DC, during ESFNA 2008. Courtesy of Itsushi Kawase.

Eritrean and Oromo games both scheduled for dates that do not conflict with ESFNA. But in 2011–12, homeland political conflicts divided ESFNA and led to a split that resulted in a competing tournament. The annual ESFNA soccer tournament took place in Dallas, Texas, from July 1 to 7, 2012, and a rival tournament was mounted by the newly organized All Ethiopian Sports Association One (AESAONE) during that same week in Washington, DC.[49] The soccer tournaments bring the *sämənna wärq* (wax and gold) metaphor to life—what appears on the surface to be merely a sports event on closer scrutiny reveals multiple layers of athletic, musical, and political competition.

INTANGIBLE ETHNIC PLACES

Much of diaspora cultural life is transacted in virtual spaces, most prominently through the internet, but also though engagement with media such as sound recordings. The internet is central to Ethiopian life in diaspora, both forging a sense of community and promoting cultural innovation. "Information and communication technologies (ICTs) have made transnational, extraterritorial Ethiopian culture a reality, rendering commonplace diaspora contact with the homeland that was previously impossible."[50] By the end of the twentieth century, virtual networks had transformed the experience of diaspora Ethiopians:

> Since 2000, I have watched my Ethiopian American children and their friends maintain almost daily contact with Ethiopia. At (Ethiopian owned) 7–11 [7-Eleven] stores, they buy telephone cards to call friends and families in Ethiopia about day-to-day problems. They keep up with Ethiopian news, politics, and music through a plethora of Web sites. . . . Diaspora Ethiopians send remittances in amounts greater than Ethiopia earns from its coffee exports. . . . The advance of information technology is in large measure responsible for those transnational connections.[51]

A watershed technological event that occurred in 2000 sparked an explosion in virtual communications by Ethiopians, notably digitization of the Ethiopic script and the acceptance of the Ethiopic character set for inclusion in Unicode 3.0 Standard (Unicode Consortium).[52] This invention made it possible for Ethiopians and Eritreans, who read and write in Amharic and Tigrinya, to communicate online.[53]

Ethiopians have been extraordinarily active in posting Ethiopian diaspora recordings and music videos on YouTube, which has become a treasure house for both homeland and Ethiopian diaspora music culture. Many websites stream music and provide discussions of a wide array of Ethiopian musical styles. An informal survey of the online presence of twenty-five diaspora musicians provided insight into three levels of virtual presence. First, nine musicians who perform entirely within the Ethiopian community, but of economic necessity pursue their careers part-time, have no media outlets of their own. In some cases, this is due to less-than-fluent English skills and performances only in Amharic or other vernacular languages of the Horn of Africa. These musicians work largely through personal and community networks and do not have websites, Facebook pages, or Twitter and Instagram accounts. A second group of six perform for Ethiopian audiences internationally and have a presence on websites or Facebook but lack Twitter or Instagram accounts. One of these six has a website only in Amharic and another, only a Twitter account. Third, ten full-time professional musicians or ensembles are active on Facebook and have websites, as well as Twitter or Instagram accounts. Two of this group have their own channels on YouTube. The size and professional preparation of these websites are notable.[54]

A vital source for Ethiopian diaspora communications by the beginning of the twenty-first century was the *Ethiopian Yellow Pages*. Discussed at more length in chapter 9, this publication has morphed from a printed volume for the DC community to an online publication, which, in the words of its founder Yeshimebet "Tutu" Belay, is "more than a book."[55] The volume includes a section devoted to musicians, a contribution of the *Ethiopian Yellow Pages* vice president Yehunie Belay, who is a well-known traditional musician.

Ethiopians and Eritreans living abroad depend heavily on the internet, which increasingly serves as the primary conduit for communications in diaspora.[56] A study of the Eritrean website www.dehai.org, founded during the first years of Eritrean independence (1992–2000), discussed the ways in which the "new forms of technological and geographical mobility are giving rise to new publics and new public spheres that transform the meanings of community, citizenship, and nation."[57] On August 1, 2020, a new channel titled Trace Muzika was launched via the online streaming service habeshaview-app, performing "non-stop music" from Ethiopia and its diaspora. The channel ranks the top 10 Ethiopian songs and includes music from "diverse regions in Ethiopia."[58]

Yet the internet is still not as readily accessible in Ethiopia itself, a result both of an insufficient technological infrastructure and of restrictive government policies. This has particularly been the case since 2005, when many websites and blogs were blocked by the Ethiopian government, restrictions that were relaxed only in spring 2018.[59]

Rounding out the virtual sphere, there are Ethiopian radio and television stations across the diaspora, most started by individual entrepreneurs. We can take as an example Radio DJ Endale Getahun, who in 2016 began the first Ethiopian FM radio station in Aurora, Colorado (KETO 93.9 FM).[60] Endale works "through music." He says, even though "I am not a composer or creator . . . I play and distribute both recordings and live shows."[61]

Music is therefore ubiquitous across these intangible ethnic places as Ethiopians attempt to overcome distances from the homeland and to forge new, virtual social networks among far-flung diaspora locales.[62] Many musicians advertise and distribute their own CDs and DVDs internationally, circulating clips or MP3s on the web.

By the mid-1980s, Ethiopians settled in many cities across the United States and Canada. Although many aspects of diaspora community life that have been noted are shared, a complex interaction of ethnic, cultural, and political factors combine to shape these North American Ethiopian diaspora communities in slightly different ways. Here we will briefly survey some of the major issues that render each community distinctive; the economic and occupational patterns that shape these centers; and complex issues related to religion and gender.

The Politics of Diaspora Life

A range of political issues are never very far from the surface in most Ethiopian diaspora communities. The Ethiopian government's implementation of the policy of ethnic federalism in 1993, which redrew provincial maps and renamed regions according to their majority ethnic population, has resulted in continuing ethnic conflict both in the homeland and in diaspora.

From the earliest years of the diaspora, there were deep ethnic divisions between Ethiopians and Eritreans, an outgrowth of the bitter civil war that contributed to the fall of the emperor and resulted in Eritrean independence in the early 1990s. But, since 2000, Ethiopian-Eritrean tensions have slowly receded, with a rapprochement officially taking place when Prime Minister Abiy Ahmed negotiated a peace treaty between the two nations on July 9, 2018, accelerating a healing process already underway both at home and abroad.[63] This reconciliation was, not surprisingly, celebrated through musical performances in Addis Ababa on July 15, 2018, with the "Declaration of Peace" concert at Addis Ababa's Millennium Hall. There, singer Teddy Afro (Tewodros Kassahun) appeared alongside eight other famous musicians, who performed under giant portraits of the presidents of Ethiopia and Eritrea.[64]

But if Ethiopian-Eritrean tensions have slowly receded in the diaspora, other new tensions have emerged, especially over the growth of Oromo political power in the homeland and efforts toward Oromo autonomy. At the end of the revolution in 1991, forces from northern Tigray province assumed power, with the TPLF (Tigray People's Liberation Front) and EPRDF (Ethiopian People's Revolutionary Democratic Front) established as the ruling parties. After a yearlong attempt at political cooperation between the TPLF-EPRDF and the OLF (Oromo Liberation Front), the new government was threatened by the OLF's growing nationalism. EPRDF forces attacked Oromo peoples in two southern regions of the country, killing and displacing many. As a result, the OLF left the government, further violence ensued, and many more Oromo migrated abroad.[65] A number of displaced Oromo sought asylum in existing Oromo communities such as Minneapolis, Atlanta, and Seattle, where, on arrival, they were described by the receiving communities as "traumatized."[66]

Since the revolution as well, ethnic tensions have increased between

Ethiopians and Somalis from both the Ethiopian Ogaden region and adjacent Somalia itself, who departed the Horn of Africa in response to several waves of conflict. In part because of these tensions, refugees of Somali
descent have tended to remain within their own social networks.

Diaspora communities have also increasingly taken political action and
mounted protests over international events negatively affecting Ethiopia
or its diaspora. For example, a sudden deportation of Ethiopian migrants
from Saudi Arabia in 2013 caused an outcry among diaspora Ethiopians
worldwide, who drew attention to "serious deportation abuses." Initiatives
included a letter to the US State Department delivered to the Dallas federal courthouse by local Ethiopian community leader Mac Mekonnen.
"Our immigrants in Saudi Arabia are being robbed and abused," Mac told
the local press.[67]

Economic and Occupational Patterns

There are shared occupational patterns across diaspora communities. First-
generation diaspora Ethiopians have tended to cluster professionally in
transportation and service industries, taking advantage of ethnic networks
to obtain positions driving taxis, staffing parking garages, and working at
airports.[68] According to members of the community, working as a taxi
driver enabled immigrants to act as their own bosses and was more lucra-
tive than other available employment. Beyond setting one's own schedule,
drivers placed a high premium on being able to park anywhere and felt
that they could balance driving with other commitments such as child-
care or attending classes.[69]

Ethiopians continue to be well represented in the hospitality industry,
many working in restaurants, hotels, and shops. Although an Ethiopian
professional network is growing in business, law, and academia, especially
among Ethiopian Americans of the second generation, many older immigrants remain limited by lack of fluency in English and seek positions in
sectors such as elder care that can accommodate their linguistic and professional skills.

Issues of Gender

Changing gender relations is a cultural arena characterized by both divisions and concern across the Ethiopian diaspora. Many issues confront
women from the Horn of Africa in diaspora communities, including continuing trauma from their journeys to the United States. Marriages made
along the migration route often cannot withstand the pressures of reset-

tlement; in many cases, tension has arisen when wives are younger and more adaptable than their husbands, who are accustomed to homeland patriarchal domination. Resettlement in the North American diaspora presents challenges such as spousal abuse, which prove to be of heightened concern when instances of domestic violence lead to deportation of the abuser.[70] Although a woman in diaspora has the power to call the police, once authorities are involved, a family may be divided and lose a major breadwinner as well. Unlike in Ethiopia, in the diaspora there are no *shämagəle* (elders) who traditionally mediate family disputes. One therefore finds an immigrant community that both suffers from traumas and anger brought with them from Ethiopia and faces substantial challenges in adjusting to gender equality in diaspora life.

Newly founded social organizations try to address such problems. Groups such as the Adbar Women's Alliance (AWA), founded in 1994 in Cambridge, Massachusetts, emerged from discussions among women attending the annual soccer tournaments in the early 1990s.[71] Local resources can also shape the institutions in a single diaspora community. For instance, a decision was made to establish the AWA in Cambridge, Massachusetts, rather than in Washington, DC, because of the numerous universities and higher educational level in the area that founders thought would encourage acceptance of the organization. Despite this carefully chosen locale, traditional community attitudes and issues of domestic violence have often continued. At the same time, women of the Ethiopian diaspora have made important contributions to the institutional and economic lives of their new communities, initiatives that will be discussed in more detail in chapters 9 and 10.

A number of concerns cross ethnic, gender, and religious affiliations among all the immigrants from the Horn of Africa wherever they have settled. Prominent among them is the question of where they will be buried at the end of their lives. This has been an especially pressing matter for aging first-generation immigrants who retain strong emotional ties to their homelands. As a result, many communities in diaspora maintain an old Ethiopian Christian tradition of founding social welfare organizations known as *mahbär* (*mahber*), as well as more recent neighborhood self-help organizations, *əddər* (*edir*) without religious ties.[72] In both cases, members make regular payments into a monthly fund and on the occasion of a death, the costs for repatriation and burial in Ethiopia are covered at least in part for a member.[73]

However, forty years or more of residence in diaspora have resulted in deeper attachments among some first-generation immigrants to the United States, now the homeland of their US children. As a result, there is an emerging trend for first-generation immigrants, especially Eritreans, to be buried in diaspora.[74]

A Comparative Perspective

Despite the prevalence of heterolocal residences in many metropolitan areas, third spaces such as Little Ethiopia in Los Angeles or the emerging Little Ethiopias in Washington, DC, Silver Spring, and Alexandria, provide a density of Ethiopian cultural life that is as exciting for longtime residents as for new arrivals. Singer Teshome Mitiku recalled that

> I came to visit my brother Teddy [in Washington, DC] sometime in the early 90s. When I came here I was shocked. I never thought that such a large number of Ethiopians had migrated to this part of the world. I mean everywhere I went there were Ethiopians. I said to myself, "What am I doing in Sweden? This is where I need to be." Then I went back to Sweden. . . . I gave my apartment to a friend and I was gone. As soon as I arrived here, I got involved in a lot of Ethiopian activities, including music, fundraising for different causes. I became socially involved with the community. That kept me going.[75]

Yet, although there is Ethiopian musical activity across a full range of ethnic places in most Ethiopian diaspora locales, especially on days of religious, historical, and political significance, there are real logistical and economic challenges to uniting these widely scattered communities.

Most Ethiopian diaspora communities have both significant similarities and some striking differences. Some communities may have slightly more residential clustering that results from their cities' smaller geographical spread than do those of the DC metropolitan area, Los Angeles, or the San Francisco Bay Area, allowing ethnic places and sociocommerscapes to generate an abiding sense of community in these locales as well. (See appendix for an overview of selected Ethiopian diaspora communities across the United States.) The earlier immigrants, primarily Ethiopian Christians and Eritreans from the highland region, are better institutionalized and are more comfortable with displaying their ethnic identities. In contrast, refugees of Oromo or Somali descent tend to be more recent arrivals and less numerous except in Minneapolis and a few other diaspora locales. They are less inclined to publicly display their identity, both out of ambivalence about their Ethiopian pasts, and, for many, out of concerns related to emphasizing their Muslim identities in the post-9/11 United States.

In part as a result of the dispersed nature of their residences across large metropolitan areas, Ethiopians in Washington, DC, Los Angeles, and the San Francisco Bay Area tend to have more contact with others across ethnic and racial boundaries than do Ethiopians, Eritreans, and Oromo living in smaller communities in midwestern, southern, and southeastern locales. Similarly, Ethiopians in New York City, for the most part, lack well-defined ethnic places in which they can express their identities. But changing economic and social conditions also reshape relationships within a community and transform local ethnic and class divisions over time, as do both homeland and US domestic politics.

Musicians are present and actively performing in many of the communities surveyed in the appendix, many standing out for the important work they have done on behalf of the traditions they transmit and the communities they represent. But the waves of homeland and diaspora political currents circulating through individual communications and virtual channels are ever volatile, galvanizing political positions that can quickly give rise to disturbing outcomes. Such events have on occasion directly threatened the careers of even the most beloved musicians.

Political controversies can emerge unexpectedly from seemingly innocuous events, with devastating consequences for some individuals. One such diaspora controversy involved a well-known Ethiopian immigrant singer of Gurage descent in Washington DC, Abonesh "Abiti" Adinew. In a diaspora poised to respond to highly charged political issues, a musician became the epicenter of a heated conflict.

Abonesh "Abiti" Adinew

Born in 1970 in a Gurage region about one hundred kilometers southwest of Addis Ababa and a specialist in *bahelawi* (cultural) music, Abonesh has been widely admired for her ability to sing in a variety of Ethiopian languages in addition to her native Guraginya language and to perform in many regional styles. As Abonesh noted,

> I can't talk Somali, but I can sing it. Ethiopia has different ethnicities and they have different cultures, they have different foods, and I like to explain to the people that culture. When you sing Orominya, the dance, the clothes, and everything, the music is different and beautiful. . . . Because if you explain about culture, about life, even about politics, you can explain through music.[76]

During the revolution, just after her ninth-grade year in school, Abonesh was recruited to become a member of the *Kebur Zebenya*, the

Imperial Bodyguard Orchestra in Addis Ababa. She performed with the ensemble until, in 1991, the new government suddenly dissolved the orchestra, arrested some members, and vandalized the ensemble's headquarters, during which many of its recordings were also destroyed. Abonesh then joined the Ras Theatre for two years, moving next to the National Theatre and singing at an Addis Ababa nightclub.

With employment becoming increasingly uncertain, Abonesh followed many other musicians and decided to leave the country. In 1998, while in Washington, DC, on a musical tour arranged by the Ethiopian government, Abonesh sought and received asylum, eventually becoming a US citizen. Well known for her rendition of the song discussed at the beginning of chapter 5, "Harar Dire Dawa," which describes the experience of refugees and the various overland routes they followed to leave Ethiopia, Abonesh quickly established a lively career traveling to perform in various communities. Abonesh and her husband opened a restaurant on 9th Street near Howard University, called after her nickname, Abiti, where she performed regularly for a growing clientele.

Seven years after arriving in the United States, Abonesh returned for the first time to Ethiopia. It was a tense period after disputed 2005 elections, a difficult political moment for Ethiopia and its diaspora.[77] Ethiopians were excited that Abonesh had returned for a visit, and she received a great deal of media attention. During one radio appearance, Abonesh was asked what she thought about the changes in the country since her departure, and she responded positively, commenting that the changes in Addis Ababa looked very good to her. Word of this interview spread rapidly via the internet, and many in diaspora were infuriated by what they perceived as praise by Abonesh for the Ethiopian government.[78]

Upon her return to the United States, Abonesh received death threats and had to hire guards when she performed. She and her husband struggled to keep their restaurant open but were eventually forced to close it as a result of boycotts by patrons angered by the radio interview. Abonesh could no longer perform safely in the Washington, DC, area and, for a time, traveled to sing in Las Vegas, Seattle, and Atlanta and abroad in Sweden, England, and Germany. The pressures of diaspora rage on the singer and her family were extreme.

Despite the disruptions in her life, Abonesh continued to devote herself to important causes, organizing music for a World Refugee Day in Washington, DC, and participating in a fundraising video released by Washington, DC's Kedus Gabriel EOT Church.[79] She made recordings on behalf of AIDS relief and to support a fistula clinic in Ethiopia.[80] "It's like anything she can do to help in her power, she does it," commented her husband.[81]

By 2008, however, Abonesh decided to stop singing Ethiopian traditional music and began to focus exclusively on performing Ethiopian gospel music. A Facebook post by Abonesh stated that "In my future life, I will sing only for MY GOD! I wished for a long time to be a gospel singer. GOD allows this now."[82]

If Abonesh's radio interview and diaspora response had a devastating impact on this singer's life and musical career, other controversies, large and small, have intermittently engaged the growing number of Ethiopian diaspora communities in North America. But, throughout this process of migration and diaspora growth, Ethiopian musicians have continued to make music, their performances suspended between sound worlds of the past and diasporic innovations. The following chapter moves toward a definition of the Ethiopian sound and traces its collective and individual pathways over more than forty years of transformational mobility.

SECTION III

Transformations

Sounds

PERFORMING IDENTITY, MOBILITY, AND THE ETHIOPIAN SOUND

Dəms'

GENERAL MEANING: Sound, voice
MUSICAL MEANING: Instrumental sound or singing voice

Musical sound permeates human experience, standing in an interactive relationship to time, place, people, and technologies. Musical sentinels may choose to safeguard sounds from past experiences, allowing listeners to draw on a full range of bodily memories aroused by sonic-somatic encounters. At many moments and in various contexts, musicians may also take the initiative to guide familiar musical sounds in new directions, combining traces of the past with influences from the present as well as materials from their own imaginations. Each musician, at different moments, and in different places, constructs his or her own musical map, guiding the listener through a range of new experiences of hearing, feeling, and thinking.

My approach to sound builds in part on Ethiopian concepts of the body and senses introduced in chapter 3. As we have seen, there is an old Ethiopian concept of seven senses, one of which is əgər (leg), which can also be translated as "motion,"[1] leading me to include mobility in my considerations of sound. Here, too, I consider "how the full spectrum of sensory experience contributes to our interpretation of sound and music."[2] Perceptions of music among its listeners provide pathways to understanding music's impact, leading one to move beyond music's sonic structure into sensory domains beyond the ear and into what sound tells the listener about the world from which it emerged.

In this chapter, I explore aspects of Ethiopian music making across the prerevolutionary, revolutionary, and diasporic periods, unpacking what these sounds reveal about the cumulative experience of individuals within an unsettled musical world in motion. The broad cover term for sound, dəms' in Amharic, extends across a full spectrum of phenomena that produce sound from the vocal cords (*yädəms' awətarec*) to the amplifier (*dəms' magwaya*). *Dəms'* is used, with some modification, for a broad range of typologies for human speaking and singing as well as for an animal's cry (*dida dəms'*). Musical sound is often performed by a *dəmsawi* (vocalist).[3] Below we will discuss the music of a cross section of musicians who have performed the sounds of the Ethiopian past and present both at home and abroad, exploring music making and its sonic outcomes in relation to mobility; in its relationship to instrumental and vocal resources; in its involvement with the senses and emotion; and as it reveals ethnic identity. These musical initiatives have forged new sonic pathways for the Ethiopian diaspora.

The Sounds of Cultural Mobility

Mobility is both a historical reality and a complex sensory experience, embodied within unconscious awareness termed "proprioception," the perception of the position of one's body. Perhaps no music of the revolutionary and diasporic periods can provide deeper insights into where and how sound maps Ethiopian cultural mobility than that of Mulatu Astatke, the founder of the style known as "Ethio-jazz." (See plate 7.1.) Mulatu, who is quoted in chapter 5 as one of the arrangers of the *People to People* tour, was one of the first Ethiopian musicians to live and study abroad for an extended period, beginning in 1956 as a student at Lindisfarne College in North Wales, followed by musical studies in London. In 1958 he moved to Boston, where he was the first African musician to enroll at the Schillinger House, later to become the Berklee College of Music. By 1960 Mulatu had relocated to New York City, where he participated in the city's lively jazz scene. Although he has maintained his home base in Addis Ababa from the late 1960s, even throughout the revolution and his adult career, he has been constantly in motion across the world, spending long periods in the United States, where his daughter Hermela Mulatu resides.[4]

In the decade before the 1974 revolution, Mulatu crafted a new jazz style joining foreign influences he encountered during his sojourns abroad with sounds both indigenous and foreign from his Ethiopian past. His indigenous sonic heritage included Ethiopian Orthodox Christian liturgical music, as well as secular Ethiopian instrumental and vocal styles, melodies, and rhythms; foreign influences encountered in Ethiopia were a range of Western classical and popular styles. Mulatu's music provides more than a hybrid style, however; it can also be heard as an aural map of his musical encounters both in Ethiopia and various sites abroad. As we will see in

PLATE 7.1 Mulatu Astatke, Addis Ababa, 2018. Collection of author.

chapters 9 and 10, musicians continue to consider Mulatu a sentinel musician and regard his music as a guide and model for their own creativity half a century after his compositions first circulated.

Mulatu's Ethio-jazz has been heard by many as "traveling music," a designation given to his music used for the soundtrack of Jim Jarmusch's 2005 film, *Broken Flowers*.[5] The film tells the story of a middle-aged bachelor (played by Bill Murray) discarded by his most recent girlfriend, who receives an anonymous letter telling him that he has a nineteen-year-old son who may be looking for him. With the encouragement of his next-door neighbor, an Ethiopian immigrant and amateur sleuth acted by Jeffrey Wright, the man embarks on a trip to visit four former girlfriends from about twenty years before, trying to ascertain whether one of them might have had his child without telling him. Jarmusch has acknowledged that he conceived the film's Ethiopian character in order to feature Mulatu's music in the soundtrack.[6] In a pivotal scene in a local coffee shop, the Ethiopian neighbor provides an itinerary for the man's trip, along with maps and a CD of Mulatu's music that he characterizes as "traveling music." The subsequent scenes of travel in the film are accompanied by selections of Mulatu's Ethio-jazz.

The seeds for Ethio-jazz grew in the first instance out of Mulatu's early exposure to a variety of traditional and popular musical styles at home in Ethiopia as a child and teenager. The roots of Ethiopian big-band music were planted early on, in the late nineteenth century,[7] but Mulatu's first exposure was to the early popular band founded in Addis Ababa during the 1940s and the early 1950s at the National Theatre. Some of these groups of that period, such as the "jazz section" of the Imperial Bodyguard Orchestra, played repertories "mixing mambo, boogie-woogie and airy arrangements of Ethiopian tunes";[8] Mulatu recalls hearing these bands at parties and concerts in the capital as early as 1950, well before his departure for England and the United States.[9] But Mulatu's new style also reflected his subsequent exposures to diverse styles of music making in London, Boston, and New York City during the late 1950s and 1960s.

> Ethio-jazz: I just created it myself. It's my own term. I said, "I have to somehow develop this music." Now, if I start fiddling with the modes, the *tizita*, *bati, anchihoye, ambasel*, that's totally how we change Ethiopian music to different worlds. So, what we were really lacking was the harmony. And most of the Ethiopian musical instruments are melody instruments. There are no harmony instruments. So I figured, "How do I make these beautiful tones, our modes, make it sound so nice?" . . . So, I used to spend hours and hours, how to do my progressions, which can fit beautifully to our modes.[10]

"Yäkärmo Säw" (Yekermo Sew), Mulatu's most widely circulated composition in part because of its prominent use in Jarmusch's film, displays important aspects of Mulatu's new compositional style and moreover maps important aspects of his transnational itinerary until his return to Addis Ababa in the late 1960s.

After a brief time in North Wales, Mulatu enrolled in London's Trinity School of Music and explored the panoply of international musical styles surrounding him. While in London, Mulatu heard a great deal of live music and interacted for the first time with Caribbean and West African musicians who were performing publicly for British audiences. He recalled that

Nigerians, Ghanaians were all performing their music nicely. . . . You know, I said, "What are we doing?" I was one of those Ethiopians who have the chance to go travel all over and they find other African countries really respecting their culture, respecting their clothes and playing their music, and so forth. . . . I have to do something of Ethiopian music.[11]

New musical experiences giving rise to Ethio-jazz emerged as Mulatu studied the vibraphone and jazz theory in Boston and then, after his move to New York City, frequented clubs such as the Village Gate and completed a course of study at Harnett National Studios. Particularly drawn to Latin musicians, Mulatu began to experiment with musical fusion, composing bilingual songs that included texts in Amharic and Spanish.[12] As a result, recalls Mulatu,

> I came up with Ethio-jazz at that period. A different direction. Hugh Masekela was doing South African–type music like the blues and Zulu; Fela was doing highlife type. So, they have different concepts of developing African music. . . . But the idea, the concept, came while we were studying, while we were playing with big bands, when we studied the harmony class at Berklee and everything.[13]

Mulatu's "Yekermo Sew" is one of his four compositions in the soundtrack of *Broken Flowers*.[14] "Yekermo Sew" takes its name from a play by the revered Ethiopian poet and playwright Tsegaye Gabre-Medhin (1936–2006), at whose invitation Mulatu's piece was originally composed.[15] Colloquially translated as "A man of experience and wisdom," the title derives from a traditional phrase in Amharic, with Orthodox Christian associations: *Yäkärmo säw yǝblan*, a new year's blessing, translates "May He (God) make us people of the next year!"[16] Mulatu says that he hoped to sustain and convey memories of older Ethiopian traditions through this composition:

> I was really trying to depict the older people, this is what I was trying to get into, because this has this beautiful Ethiopian feeling to this music. This reflects . . . the older people, the last warriors, the fighters, and the earlier people, and how they would sit and listen to the *azmaris* [minstrels] for hours and hours.[17]

Mulatu remembers little of the plot of Tsegaye Gabre-Medhin's play *Yekermo Sew* for which he composed this music, but he recalls that he was inspired by its title.[18] He drew on the Ethiopian secular mode *tizita*

[C–D–E–G–A], a pentatonic scale that is closely associated by later twentieth-century listeners with memory, as well as with feelings of nostalgia and loss. For "Yekermo Sew," Mulatu used *tizita* in what modern Ethiopian musicians term its minor form [C–D–E-flat–G–A-flat].[19] "Yekermo Sew" is set in the modern secular modal system of Ethiopian highland music and reflects theorizations channeled through the framework of Western tempered tunings and music theory in Ethiopian musical institutions established in Addis Ababa by the middle of the twentieth century. Mulatu, however, believes that the piece also conveys feelings associated with the modes of the Ethiopian church, not just the secular music performed by professional minstrels after church ceremonies.[20]

The use of melodic content drawn from traditional Ethiopian musical practice is only part of the musical vocabulary in "Yekermo Sew"; one must also factor in the long-standing jazz practice of musical quotation, as well as the impact of modal jazz in the American scene within which Mulatu lived and worked in New York City. Perhaps most immediately discernible is an external melodic inspiration for the "Yekermo Sew" melody— a composition by Horace Silver.

A pianist of Cape Verdean descent, Silver settled in New York City in 1950 and performed with Miles Davis in the mid-1950s in recording sessions for Prestige Records.[21] Mulatu reports that he did not know Silver personally, nor does he remember seeing him perform live. However, he did hear Silver's music in recordings and perhaps in performances by others and recalls that he felt a connection with Silver's use of "five-tone scales" and the pentatonicism invoked by many other musicians composing in the modal jazz scene during that period.[22] Silver's use of innovative time signatures and Latin-inspired rhythms also appealed to Mulatu, who had learned to play the conga drum and, as noted before, had a predilection for working with Latin musicians and others of African and Caribbean descent. The pervasive use in Ethiopian popular music of what is termed the *chəqchäqa* (*chik chika*) rhythm, with patterns of twos juxtaposed against threes, also rendered Mulatu unusually receptive to a variety of syncopated rhythms from other traditions. No doubt the commemorative aspect of Silver's piece with its dedication to his father was in Mulatu's memory as he sought to write his own nostalgic composition in *tizita* mode for Tsegaye Gabre-Medhin's play.

"Song for My Father" was recorded in 1964 after Silver returned from a collaboration with Sergio Mendes in Brazil.[23] Mulatu therefore either learned Silver's composition from a now-forgotten musical performance he attended in New York City or became familiar with the song through the recordings he heard in various media.[24] In addition to subtly transforming the melody of Silver's composition in its phrasing and rhythm, Mulatu also adapted its ostinato figure, expanding it to a vamp with octave doubling in the bass, thereby reducing its link to Western functional harmony.

In terms of its form, the original version of "Yekermo Sew" leads off with the head based on Silver's melody, followed by a bridge, after which the head is repeated. Solos follow with the return of the head and bridge. A final return of the head ends the piece abruptly. The original recording of "Yekermo Sew" further captures in its instrumentation the technologies of the late 1960s that were new at the time, the period during which the song was conceived and initially recorded. In the first keyboard solo heard in the 1969 recording, Mulatu plays a Fender Rhodes, an electronic piano that was introduced and became popular in that era; its bell-like timbre no doubt attracted vibraphonist Mulatu.[25] The second solo is played on an electric guitar with a "fuzz" pedal, also an innovation of the 1960s, an effects pedal that modifies and distorts the sound.[26] Thus, both the melodic borrowing and the instruments used provide a strong link to Western jazz and popular music of the 1960s.

Although he played the trumpet while in Wales, Mulatu subsequently performed throughout his career as an accomplished vibraphone player, the instrument he had learned at Schillinger House in Boston.[27] Over time as well, most of Mulatu's jazz was instrumental, a strategic choice when he lived at home in Ethiopia during the revolution and when composing vocal music with double meanings in their texts could have invited revolutionary scrutiny and possible retribution. Yet, if one wishes to acknowledge that the vibraphone over time had become Mulatu's musical voice, it is also important to recognize the symbiotic relationship between voice and instruments within Mulatu's music. If Tsegaye Gabre-Medhin's song text provides insight into the world of Ethiopian elders and long-standing Ethiopian Orthodox Christian ethos that Mulatu otherwise sought to convey instrumentally, the composition also provides evidence for the synergy between Ethiopian instrumental and vocal styles.

Vocality, Instrumentality, and the Elusive Ethiopian Sound

The dominance of the voice and the vocality of instrumental styles is a deep-seated Ethiopian musical trait. In interviews, Mulatu attests that he hears the large church drum, *kebero*, as a melodic instrument and compares it to the liturgical chant it accompanies: "It's part of the chanting, it's a melody by itself."[28] In another of his Ethio-jazz compositions, "Dawal," Mulatu uses the instrumental jazz ensemble to evoke the chanting and reciting in the church, as well as multiple other sensory aspects of the ritual:

PLATE 7.2 A *dawal*, such as this one at the rock churches of Lalibela,
is sounded to call the faithful to prayer. Collection of author.

The beginning is free because all of these noises they make are trying to
recall the churches, the deacon, the *merigetas*, and the *dabtaras* . . . even
the incense. It is all the effects. Then the melody comes. It is the melody
that is sung by deacons, and I've heard it that way.[29]

A *däwäl* (*dawal*) is a large rectangular idiophone made of stone, traditionally hung outside Ethiopian churches in the countryside and struck
with a stone to produce a resonant sound that called people to prayer.
(See plate 7.2.)

Mulatu also hears brass instruments as interchangeable with stringed
instruments: "I often imagine the bridge of 'Yekermo Sew' as played by
guitars although it is actually played by horns!"[30] It is therefore not surprising that the prominent use of two tenor saxophones in 1960s and early
1970s Ethiopian jazz and pop are heard by both Ethiopians and outsiders to
sound "more like Ethiopian vocals or Ethiopian traditional instruments."[31]

Just as the concept of voice (*dəms'*) itself serves as a broad cover term
for musical sound, Ethiopian vocal and instrumental quality share timbral
characteristics as well as an affinity for ornamentation, especially when
they perform the same melodic line in an intensely heterophonic texture.
Here, despite cultural and religious diversity, one must interrogate the in-

fluences of Ethiopian Christian musical style on a wide swath of secu-
lar music of the region. Many secular musicians credit their creativity to
Saint Yared, as noted in chapter 3, and one frequently encounters secular
Ethiopian vocal and instrumental styles attributed to the influence of the
Church. This influence extends to the present in diasporic contexts, partic-
ularly among those of Ethiopian Christian descent. One young Ethiopian
American who participates actively in both Ethiopian church music and
popular music commented that he perceives the vocal style and ornamenta-
tion of superstar The Weeknd, Ethiopian Canadian singer Abel Makkonen
Tesfaye, as having been shaped by his background in the Ethiopian Orthodox Church tradition: "Weeknd is an embodiment of the Ethiopian sound.
He is taking nostalgia in his voice and applying it to what he wants."[32]

Attributing aspects of a distinctive, pan-Ethiopian quality at least in
part to the impact of Ethiopian Orthodox Church vocal style may be considered provocative by those of other religious faiths in Ethiopia and the
wider region due to longtime resentment that emerged as a powerful political force in the years before and during the revolution as a result of the
many centuries of Christian Amhara hegemony. All Ethiopian ethnic communities, particularly in the postrevolutionary climate of ethnic nationalism, take pride in the distinctiveness of their musical traditions and, as
will be discussed, recognize distinctive rhythmic and dance movements
as markers of their ethnic identity. This stream of ethnic aesthetics has persisted despite efforts during the revolution to establish a national style, a
movement different in content but not so different in intent from Haile
Selassie I's historical efforts at cultural unity through a process known as
Amharization. It is also the case that some singers of different ethnic backgrounds who grew up in regions outside the highland plateau, such as the
great Oromo vocalist Ali Birra, have vocal styles that are less nasal and
that use fewer ornaments than most highland singers, likely reflecting in
Ali's case the singing styles of southeastern Ethiopia and adjacent regions.

But it is also apparent that much of Ethiopian secular and popular music, especially vocal style, retain a sonic imprint often attributed by insid-
ers to the pervasive influence of Ethiopian Orthodox liturgical chant, not
surprising with the widespread participation of young Ethiopian Orthodox women in church choirs from the 1970s forward. In addition, the engagement of young musicians in revolutionary ensembles between 1975
and 1991 further reinforced a shared sound. It is notable that two of the
most popular male Ethiopian singers from the second half of the twentieth century came from ethnic and religious backgrounds outside the
Christian Amhara community—Tilahun Gessesse and Mahmoud Ahmed.
Both participated prominently in leading national ensembles such as the

Imperial Bodyguard Orchestra and are recognized for representing a national vocal style.[33]

A number of vocal styles were used historically in the Ethiopian Christian liturgical performance, but only three survive in performance today, each associated with a monastery in a different region of the northern highland plateau from which that style originated. By the period of the 1974 revolution, the Bethlehem style, named after the Bethlehem monastery near the central highland town of Debre Tabor where the style is said to have begun and continues to be taught, dominated performance practice in urban church schools and public liturgy.

Yet two more regional styles, Qoma and Achabir, that were founded and sustained at two other highland monasteries, also survive today.[34] These three extant schools of vocal style are distinguished from one another by a subtle range of sonic characteristics, including melismas of different lengths, and in the case of the Qoma style, a noticeably softer, near-falsetto tone quality. The three styles also are distinguished by phrases of different lengths, with Bethlehem's short (*ac'c'ir*) style punctuated by more frequent breaths. In contrast, church musicians of the long (*räjjim*) style associated with Qoma and Achabir perform more sustained phrases, and Qoma is considered to have "repetitions without end."[35]

Indigenous guidelines for Ethiopian Christian vocal style and production are articulated in detail as part of another domain of Ethiopian liturgical practice: the Ethiopian Christian notational system, *mələkkət* (*melekket*). The notation system includes more than 650 signs based on the Ethiopic syllabary, each representing a short phrase of melody drawn from a particular liturgical portion, but there are ten additional signs, known as the *yäfidel qərs'* (conventional signs), which guide aspects of vocal placement and production, articulation, phrasing, and melisma. (See table 7.1.)

Though most secular musicians are not familiar with the conventional signs, they do use similar techniques and, in several cases, similar terminology about vocal style and production. One singer discussed and demonstrated her production of a traditional Ethiopian female vocal style from both the throat or neck (*dəfat*) and the chest (*därät*), commenting that it can also be even deeper, "in the stomach."[36]

Reference to the stomach additionally connects these sonic domains with bodily senses, which were discussed in chapter 3 as having penetrated across different ethnic and religious divisions and will be elaborated further later on. These practices also appear to have been transferred by Ethiopian composers and performers to Ethio-jazz and to the other westernized musical genres and repertories that they perform.

Here we can take as an example the music of a renowned Ethiopian sax-

TABLE 7.1 The *yäfidel qərs'* (conventional signs)

TERM	LITERAL MEANING	MUSICAL MEANING	SIGN
därät	chest	sing in front, straight and loud voice, in the throat	⌣
yəzat	catch or hold	to stop or hold your voice in the middle	.
rəkrək	[etymology unknown]	a vocal slide or tremolo	...
dəfat	to turn downwards when the chant dips	bend the neck, mask the voice	⌢
qurt	cut, be abrupt	press your voice short and downwards, and stop the sound	⊣
ch'ərät	accent	drag or pull the sound and put your neck upward like a bull in harness	)
hədät	go without stopping	deliver it like water that flows	⌣—
qənät	be straight	hold your neck up upright at end of song	)
änbər	to rest, to place	end of a musical phrase	⊂
dərs	[etymology unknown]	soften the voice and let it die away	⋂

SOURCE: Kay Kaufman Shelemay and Peter Jeffery, eds., *Ethiopian Christian Liturgical Chant: An Anthology* (Madison, WI: A-R, 1993), 1:105.

ophonist of Mulatu Astatke's generation, Getatchew Mekuria (1935–2016), whom Western critics have described as playing with an impassioned vocal quality on the saxophone that produced "an ardent, full-throated style . . . blowing in declamatory gusts with a fervent, quavering vibrato."[37] One of Getatchew's most famous performances was a saxophone solo of the Ethiopian *shəllälä* (*shillela*), a traditional song in heightened speech performed by Ethiopian warriors on their way into battle.[38] The vocal *shillela* begins in a high tessitura, descending through a heavily ornamented line as a call to battle. Born in the central highland countryside in 1935, Getatchew learned to play the clarinet when he was thirteen, soon moving on to the saxophone. He recalled that in 1958, when he was performing at the National Theatre as an actor and musician, he

> interpreted the role of a supposed warrior to kill a quantity of Italian soldiers, singing and ranting the war chants. Suddenly, I had the idea to transpose them to the saxophone, or rather to sing them on my instrument for I say the words that I blow at the same moment.[39]

The manner in which Getatchew performed the saxophone has been heard as a "quest for an impassioned, expressly vocal quality,"[40] influencing many other musicians playing other instruments.

The music of both Mulatu and Getatchew were sufficiently ear-catching to have attracted global audiences during the late 1990s and 2000s. If both Mulatu and Getatchew's exposure to a variety of musics reshaped their own musical initiatives, their own hybrid styles surely enhanced their appeal to a diverse listening public and their sentinel impact on other musicians.[41]

The distinctive sound and impact of Ethiopian vocal music will return in discussions of the international spread of Ethiopian music in chapter 10. But here we need to take into account the impact of the international reception of Ethiopian vocal style that can be traced to the circulation of *Ere Mela Mela*, the first Ethiopian album (originally recorded in Addis Ababa in 1975) released internationally in 1986 by an independent Belgian label, Crammed Discs; this milestone sheds additional light on the convergence of vocal and instrumental styles in Ethiopian music.[42] When the album was released as a CD by *éthiopiques*,[43] the shake or tremolo in Mahmoud Ahmed's voice became a subject of comment by listeners. The tremolo described by the church notation's conventional sign *rəkrək* resembles the vibrato later cited as a characteristic of Getatchew's saxophone style:

> It's the quaver that makes the Ethiopian singer Mahmoud Ahmed's voice so arresting. He seizes on a note, brief or sustained, and makes its pitch tremble as if its urgency could barely be contained. . . . That quaver is coupled with emphatic rhythm and grainy determination in a voice that Ethiopians in and out of the country have prized since the 1970s . . . Each quaver rooted the music in Ethiopian tradition while insisting on the universality of passion.[44]

The ostinato played by the instruments in the title song of the album, "Ere Mela Mela," moves along in intervals of close seconds, mirroring the quaver of the vocal melody. Arranged from the traditional repertory, "Ere Mela Mela" was likely inspired by its performance by singer Asnaqetch Werqu (Asnaketch Werku) (1935–2011), a revered female *krar* virtuoso with whom the song was closely associated.[45] The text of the song varies among performances; individual singers personalize their lyrics, a standard occurrence in Ethiopian performance practice. Mahmoud's performance of "Ere Mela Mela" speaks of the somatic impact of unrequited love:

> I'm looking for a solution
> I'm not going to get involved in another love affair
> What room is left for another?
> I can go to all the doctors, it's no use

You are my sickness, because you are not with me.
When I'm too hungry I snack on anything
But to be satisfied, I need to feed upon your love.[46]

"Ere Mela Mela" was acknowledged by foreign listeners for its original sound and was described as "one of those rare albums that unveil a remarkably vital pop-music style from a little-known corner of the world."[47] The song's minor sound in fact resembles the tuning systems known in twentieth-century Ethiopian secular music as *tizita* minor; it also juxtaposes duple and triple rhythms, the ubiquitous Ethiopian *chik chika* beat. The enthusiastic response to "Ere Mela Mela" launched the commercial marketing of Ethiopian music abroad and laid the foundation for its circulation in diaspora.

In all three instances discussed here, as well as in other recordings by Mulatu, Getatchew, and Mahmoud, there are a rich interplay of instrumental and vocal styles and a felicitous blend of local and foreign influences.

Sound, the Senses, and Emotion

We can now turn to the final song on track 15 of the *Ere Mela Mela* CD (reissued in *éthiopiques 7*), which is also featured on other *éthiopiques* volumes in recordings of Mulatu Astatke (*éthiopiques 4*) and Getatchew Mekuria (*éthiopiques 14*), the ballad "Tizita."

This ballad guides us to yet another important component of Ethiopian musical sound: its deep relationship to the senses and to the emotions. One of a genre known as *əngwərgwərro*[48] from the verb *gwərgwərrə*, "to reflect, brood on one's misfortunes; to sing or hum in a low tone of one's sorrows,"[49] *tizita* translates as memory, nostalgia, or "reminiscence." This song of longing was widely performed before and during the period of the revolution and has been actively sustained across the diaspora until the present.[50]

Perhaps the most famous rendition of the song "Tizita" in the last several decades is by Bezawork Asfaw, whose terrifying imprisonment as a teenager during the Ethiopian revolution was recounted in chapter 4. Bezawork's commentary about her own first public performance of "Tizita," as well as the content of the song text, leads us directly into the sensory and emotional impact of a song's distinctive sound.

The turning point in Bezawork's career occurred several years after she joined the National Theatre in 1978, after her release by the *kebele*. Although a very junior member of a troupe of prominent musicians,

Bezawork was asked to sing the song "Tizita" at a special Thursday night concert program:[51]

> I didn't believe I was singing with these people. . . . Everybody was a popular singer. . . . I was just singing "Tizita." And then after I sang, everybody was happy, and everybody was so crazy for "Tizita." It was a big thing for me, and I was shaking. Then, after the second week, . . . everybody was coming, the journalists were coming. . . . I found the spotlight as the queen of "Tizita."[52]

Bezawork has remained the "Queen of Tizita" since her migration to the United States in 1990.[53] Her renditions of the song, usually performed to the accompaniment of a modern band, are both reflective and reflexive in their textual content. Her lyrics on a 2010 recording, composed by the poet Nigussie Te'amwork, deal "with an overall comparison of life in the past versus the present, emphasizing changes observed in human relations and characters. . . . The lyricist portrays *təzəta* as everyone's faithful friend, a way of looking back to yesteryears in which more wisdom and maturity had prevailed."[54] According to Bezawork, the contents of the lyrics are related to her personal life and to the perspective of her decades-long experience in exile. In Bezawork's "Tizita," the past is said to color and shape the present:

Tənantənəm yayä sələnägä yawəqal	One who is aware of the past, can deal with the future
Tarik yastäwalä kät'äbib yələqal	One who is aware of history is more talented than a sage
Zämän yämayshəräwə tarik new təzəta	*Təzəta* is a timeless history
Dägun fit däqəno hulun yämiräta	Putting the good parts ahead; overcoming every barrier
Təzəta tamañ new wärätən əyawəqəm	*Təzəta* is faithful and not temporary
ənd säw lägänzəb botawun ayläqəm	It does not lose its dignity like humans for money
Gänzäb särgäñña näw säw siyaqärəb säbsəbo	Money is ephemeral; one can buy friends with money
Yəhənät gən siyarəq yəmäsəlal täsəbo	But poverty segregates one like an epidemic disease
Kägize gar əbro säw bəzu bimäññəm	Even if man desires a lot in the course of time
Dhənan t'əllo maläf bələh əyasä	To put away the good doesn't make one clever
Yätənantu nägär yədhawə hon zare	That of yesterday is taking place today
ədme lätəzəta nuron ayyähu nore	Thanks to *təzəta* I am still alive to witness this.[55]

Bezawork's "Tizita" lyrics and melody changed, expanded, and contracted in different performances. One performance by Bezawork was not recorded but was described as an improvised, deeply painful, and extended "Tizita." It took place at Amha Eshete's nightclub in Washington, DC, and Amha himself described it as a

> memorable and heartrending version. Visibly smarting from her recent romantic breakup, Bezawork improvised for 45 minutes on the torments of lost love, never repeating a single verse, as if pain heightened her inspiration. The audience was transfixed, somewhere between enchantment and fear, and wondered if all this wasn't going to end in suicide.[56]

There are many versions of "Tizita"; each singer (or their lyricist) crafts a nostalgic text for his or her own version of the song.[57] The poet and lyricist Alemtsehay Wedajo explained that "'Tizita' is one of the very famous melodies of Ethiopia and I wrote six different 'Tizitas' for singers."[58]

The mutability of the "Tizita" text is widely recognized by singers and is alluded to within Michael Belayneh's rendition of the ballad:

Qəne näw təzəta zema näw təzəta	Təzəta is poetry; təzəta is melody
T'əbäb näw təzəta həyəwät näwtəzəta	Təzəta is wisdom; təzəta is life
Zaräwə yäminorut yänofäqu läta	Something to live on during times of nostalgia
Həyəwätəna täsfa məññot əneəwənäta	Life and hope, dreams and reality
Sərana əgat'ami nuronna ət'a fänəta	Routine and occasional, living and destiny
Mänfäsəna səga yätäwogu läta	At times of war between the body and soul
əlfo yämiyaget'əbät t'əbäb näw təzəta	Təzəta is a wisdom that enables you to
	transform the past into beauty.[59]

So well-known is the *tizita* concept that it has been enshrined both in music and in visual arts.[60] One poem articulates the many ways in which pain of nostalgia is linked to bodily processes and emotions, causing pain that eats one's body "like a termite."[61] However, most renditions of "Tizita" discuss the pain of love lost and unrequited desire for a lover, as heard in the text of a classic version of the song recorded by singer Aster Aweke on her first international album, *Aster*. In this case, the cry for love "becomes music to the ear":

> You are my memory, I have no other memory.
> Promising to come, yet breaking this promise yourself.
> Please let him come by horse, softly,
> A man of his kind never uses a mule.

My cry for your love has become music to your ear,
Music to your ear.

Please remember I am haunted by love and affection.
Look at me, I've grown thin because of your love.
I only wish I could be free of your love.
I imagined baking bread in an oven of moonlight.
How could people start gossiping about things I haven't done?
I see him every day in my daily dream.
My obsession with him has become my only food.
I am restless and sleepless in the middle of the night,
I am sleepless.

I wonder where my love is?
I wonder where my love is?
I wonder.[62]

It is clear that both the text and melody of "Tizita" contribute to the song's sensory and emotional response. While Chapter 3 explored the historical role of the senses in Ethiopia and traced deep sensory connections of Ethiopian music making across different eras and repertories, the song "Tizita" reaffirms the manner in which melody, whether or not it is coupled with meaningful texts, continues to catalyze emotional responses.[63] The *tizita* melody and the secular mode or tuning system of the same name with which nostalgia and memory are associated extend to other songs and instrumental pieces in that same tuning. Beyond the mode *tizita*'s uncertain history, it is clear that "Tizita" songs of the revolutionary era and diasporic period arouse memories of the past that manifest themselves in bodily sensations.[64]

Indigenous musical terminology can help clarify the manner in which Ethiopian musical performance is linked to auditory and somatic arousal. In Amharic, *sämma*, "to hear or to listen,"[65] shares a root with *səmmet*, which conveys a range of meanings, including feeling, emotion, sense, sensation, or sentiment.[66] *Səmmet* can also be part of a compound term such as *bəherawi səmmet* (national feeling), an adjective describing someone or something sentimental (*səmmetawi*), or a verb meaning to excite or stir the emotions (*səmmet qäsäqäsä*).[67]

We have already seen in chapter 3 that a typology of bodily organs correlate to the senses (*həwas*, pl. *həwasat*).[68] In one of the only studies of emotion in Ethiopian music, ethnomusicologist Stéphanie Weisser investigated the physical and verbal response of listeners to music of the *bagana*, a ten-stringed lyre used to accompany paraliturgical songs in the Ethiopian Orthodox Christian tradition.[69] Notable for its deep, buzzing quality (produced by leather strips placed between the instrument's bridge and each of the ten strings, creating sympathetic vibrations similar to other chordophones cross-culturally), the *bagana* conveys both through its sound and its material presence a rich history in which the instrument has been said to have power to ameliorate pain (see chapter 3) and to protect the listener against evil spirits. The corporeality of the instrument's sound box is made clear by the oral tradition that the instrument "gives birth" to sounds and is said to symbolize the Virgin Mary.[70]

Weisser summarizes types of self-reports by listeners defining their "inner reactions to music," an expression used as a place holder for affects, emotion, mood, feeling, and arousal.[71] The instrumental introduction to a *bagana* song provides several layers of initial information for the listener, including "the musical 'signature' of the musician and/or the melody to be performed," while serving to prepare the musician physically and emotionally and also draw the attention of listeners.[72] A series of short instrumental ostinatos accompany the poetic text and vocal melody.[73]

In response to questions such as "What do you feel when you play/hear the *bagana*?" posed by Weisser's team during research sessions with *bagana* players and listeners, a range of responses indicated that the sound provoked physical reactions, shaped auditory and tactile perceptions, and triggered a number of associations and memories.[74] Both players and listeners indicated that the *bagana* could make them cry,[75] echoing a centuries-old description of the impact of Ethiopian Orthodox Church music performance cited at the beginning of chapter 3.[76] Others reported feeling vibrations all over their body, of feeling deeply immersed in the sound, and experiencing a "low and mellow sound that penetrates deep into the heart." The *bagana* generated feelings of devotion and religiosity, and one response stated that listening to the instrument was similar to prayer. Some noted that the sound generated memories from the past, such as of "an old man who played in the church when they were a child" or of a deceased father.[77] Although Weisser's study could not argue for a causal link between the formal characteristics of the *bagana*'s sound and emotional reactions to it without further testing, the study's conclusions suggest that structural features of the *bagana* repertoire probably combine with its cognitively constructed identity in order to produce specific reactions.[78]

The *bagana* study provides intriguing insights into the rich range of emotional responses to music among Ethiopian listeners, especially those with a background in or experience influenced by the highland Ethiopian Christian musical tradition. As noted in chapter 3, the correlation of each of the seven senses in the Ethiopian highland oral tradition with an organ or other body part make it vital to consider that Ethiopian associations with body organs extend as well to psychological states and emotions. Most notable are the roles of the belly (*hod*) and of the heart (*leb*). The stomach is considered to be the seat of emotions. Magnanimous emotions are referred to as *hod chäräqa*, literally "the belly is lit up like the moon." Fear, in contrast, is known as *hod babba*, literally "the stomach trembles," conveying that the body shakes. Forgetfulness, *hod gäbba*, can be translated as "the belly swelled," that is, it lost the thought.[79] In contrast, the heart is considered to be the location of the presence or absence of wisdom. A series of expressions indicate that a person (1) has good judgment (*leb ber*, lit., "one who has a silver heart"), (2) is inventive (*leb wäläd*, lit., "child of the heart"), (3) is considered to be inactive or to lack wisdom (*leb mut*, lit., "one whose heart is dead"), and (4) is thought to be an imbecile (*leb defen*, lit., "one whose heart is stopped up").[80]

Vocal style is also thought to be produced deep within the body. Aster Aweke remarked that Tilahun Gessesse sang "from his abdomen down there. And he's got this control. . . . It's so amazing, it's just a gift."[81] The Ethiopian Canadian pop star The Weeknd (Abel Makkonen Tesfaye) has similarly defined Ethiopian aspects of his own vocal style:

> That's how I was raised. My mother, my grandmother, my uncles would play Ethiopian artists like Aster Aweke and Mulatu Astatke all the time in the house. They would drink coffee, eat popcorn, and listen to the music. It's such beautiful music, but I didn't realize how beautiful it was until I left that head space. That's why I feel my singing is not conventional. I mean, if you look at technique, I'm not a technical singer; I know I get bashed by R&B heads 24/7. I'm not here to do Luther Vandross runs. I can't do what Jennifer Hudson does. But the feeling in my music and my voice is very Ethiopian and very African and much more powerful than anything, technically. . . . I let my voice do all the talking. I'll probably do an album one day where it's not lyrics at all, just melodies. . . . That's the Ethiopian side of me. . . . Ethiopian poetry is a different language. I can speak and understand [Amharic], but I can't understand their poetry. When my mother would translate—it's the most beautiful thing ever. I've never been back home to Ethiopia, but when I do go I'm going to make it very special.[82]

Performing Ethnicity

Identity is a multivalent concept in most settings, with musical characteristics generally regarded as able to convey ethnic identity, representing "aspects of social behaviour that relate to the historical origins and cultural repertoire or style of a group."[83] In chapter 1 we explored sensitivities about ethnicity in both Ethiopia and its diaspora; historically, ethnicity was associated primarily with membership in a community that shared language usage, common religious and ritual complexes, and strong historical associations with specific geographical regions. The primary musical markers of an Ethiopian community's identity are first and foremost song texts in an indigenous language.[84] However, there is a strong correlation of specific rhythms and dances with ethnic identity, a subject on which there has been a dearth of research. A notable exception was a two-month expedition during the summer of 1965 by György Martin's team from the Hungarian Academy of Sciences that filmed and recorded dances in eight Ethiopian provinces.[85] The project included "dances of the Amhara, Tigrean, Agaw, Adare, Esa-Somalian,[86] Kullo,[87] and Kaficho peoples, as well as those of six different [Oromo] tribes."[88] Members of several Addis Ababa folklore ensembles established in the 1950s and 1960s also undertook educational initiatives to record and perform dances of various communities, as members of the Haile Selassie I National Theatre, the City Hall Theatre, and the Ras Theatre:

When I was in Ethiopia, the people from the [City Hall] Theatre worked, too, in the countryside. . . . They brought cameras, video, and we watched it. Each dance has a meaning.[89]

Both private and public performances of ethnic music and dance are intended to evoke pride in and nostalgia for these identities. Listening reinforces ethnic identity, as one member of the Oromo American diaspora noted in describing his own daily routine listening to the music of Ali Birra:

Every day, I start my day with his music. I love music, I never studied music, but I hear each of the instruments separately in me. Usually the way I listen, I listen to the drum, the lead, the bass, everything separate in my mind. His music is so deep to me and I don't want to start my day without using his music. In my car now, my daughters, they listen. I put Oromo music on and they listen, they sing with me. His messages are so deep and the music is so deep.[90]

However, one can occasionally encounter ambivalence during public presentations of ethnic musics, as was the case at a major concert celebrating the Ethiopian Millennium attended by thousands in Washington, DC, in September 2007.[91] The event featured a lengthy sequence of music and dance styles drawn from a cross section of Ethiopian ethnicities, leading the concert moderator at one point to sigh and remark: "This will go on until we get through all the ethnic groups."[92] Public performances tend to offer a formal, stereotyped medley of traditional songs alternating with ethnic dance interludes. During the songs, the dancers change into cultural or regional costumes appropriate for the subsequent set.[93]

Sometimes songs performed by well-known singers can convey ethnic pride and affiliation even without distinctive musical characteristics; the use of an indigenous language is sufficient to convey identity. Perhaps no better example exists than Ali Birra's widely circulated song "Oromiyaa," which is considered by many to be the Oromo national anthem.[94] In diaspora locales with large Oromo communities from Melbourne to Minnesota, "Oromiyaa" is broadcast at the start of weekly Oromo radio programs.[95] Ali Birra composed this up-tempo march in a major key while he lived in Sweden.[96] The Afaan Oromo refrain translates:

Oromiyaa, Oromiyaa	*Oromiyaa, Oromiyaa*
Biyya abbaa kooti	My fatherland
Gammachuun koo hir'u	My happiness is never complete
Amman sii arguuti	Until I see you again
Oromiyaa, Oromiyaa	*Oromiyaa, Oromiyaa*
Oromiyaa, Oromiyaa	*Oromiyaa, Oromiyaa.*[97]

Rhythm, Dance, and Ethiopian Identity

Some rhythms are associated with particular ethnic communities. For instance, Tigrayan music is associated by many with a distinctive 5/4 meter, with accents occurring on the second beat. Tempo can also provide a clue to the identity of the music. Instrumental music from Gondar, a former provincial capital in the northwest, often uses a quadruple meter that tends to be performed at a faster pace than that of the region to its south, Wollo, where slower four-beat units are more common.[98]

Much of Ethiopian traditional music is associated with dance, providing aural and kinesthetic ethnic markers for the listener and viewer. Dance styles vary across ethnic communities, with circle dances more common among Oromo dancers, and the Amhara shoulder dance *əskista* (*eskista*) is found across the highlands and beyond. Ethiopian warriors traditionally wore lion manes on their heads and shoulders; folkloric dances of the twentieth century have adapted this practice as a "lion dance," often associated with Oromo dance traditions.[99]

Distinctive movements are incorporated into the dances of Gurage communities, an agrarian people from a zone of the Southern Nations, Nationalities, and Peoples' Region of Ethiopia, which subsumes a number of communities who speak dialects of a language known as Guraginya.[100] The most common Gurage dance encountered in modern folkloric performances is based on a strong duple beat reinforced by a repetitive up-and-down motion of the dancer's arms with hands clasped in front of the dancer. This arm motion is said to mimic cutting the stem of the staple food and commercial crop in the Gurage region, the *Ensete ventricosum*, or false banana plant.[101] There is also a second association with this motion connected to the large number of Gurage who migrated to urban areas, where they became well known for their entrepreneurship.[102] Young Gurage boys were particularly active in setting up shoeshine stands on the streets of Addis Ababa, where their motions shining shoes can be seen to mimic the arm motions of this dance.[103] When Gurage men dance, they pair these stereotypical hand motions with energetic leg movements that are described as looking "like big scissors."[104]

Perhaps no rhythm is more characteristic of highland Ethiopia or more closely associated Ethiopian music and dance across traditional and popular domains than *chik chika*:

> This is actually a 6/8 rhythm and what makes it different are the accents and where they are played. And I don't think *chik chika* was the name given to it by the traditional instrumentalists. I think it was the name given by the modern players. It probably came from the sound he gets from the high hat, the "chik chika."[105]

Chik chika can best be defined as two beats against three—a type of musical argument in which the first beat of each pattern of two and three beats coincides, but the second beat of the two-beat pattern falls between the second and third beat of the three-beat pattern, setting up an off-beat accent. *Chik chika* can be varied to suit the context and desire of the musician:

> A traditional player might play 1–2–3 / 4–5–6 etc., with fast accompaniment of twos. That would be a traditional percussionist playing on the drum [set]. But it could be a lot of things, there are a lot of variations. The feel is the same feel, but with different accents, and with different ways and from different tribes, it's different rhythms. Based on the same six beats, but with different tempos.[106]

Chik chika is heard regularly in Ethiopian popular music across ethnic groups to the extent that it can be said to be a common rhythmic signature of Ethiopian music as distinct from other global popular styles.

Medleys of ethnic musics and dances were performed by the second half of the twentieth century by several folklore ensembles, including Orchestra Ethiopia, an ensemble founded during the 1960s in Addis Ababa. The genesis of this orchestra and its extraordinary life across imperial, revolutionary, and diasporic periods are detailed through the testimony of a wide range of its leaders and participants in chapter 8.

Signs

THE GENEALOGY OF ORCHESTRA
ETHIOPIA AT HOME AND ABROAD

Mələkkət

GENERAL MEANING: Sign, signal, symbol, message, cue
MUSICAL MEANING: Notational signs in Ethiopian chant

This chapter takes a close look at an Ethiopian traditional (*bahelawi*) music ensemble, Orchestra Ethiopia, over the course of decades from its genesis in Ethiopia to its continued life in the North American diaspora. This multitemporal reconstruction is achieved through the lens of multiple biographies that together narrate both processes of continuity and surprising transformations during decades of intense challenge. They reveal (1) the capacity of an ensemble to link musical lives that may otherwise give no evidence of such connections; (2) the manner in which an ensemble is, over time, an entity that continually shifts in its constitution and meaning; and (3) an ensemble's capacity to transcend its own agendas and those of the individuals who have shaped it, revealing unexpected historical and cultural insights.[1]

Throughout Orchestra Ethiopia's history reconstructed here, one encounters repeated signs of the ensemble's struggle for political and economic viability, insurmountable barriers that eventually spelled the group's demise. At the same time, its history reveals processes of intense creativity that include the development of an original system of music writing for the orchestra. Based on "signs" (*melekket*) of the historical Ethiopian Christian notational system combined with diagrammatic, pictographic, and numerical characters from other sources, this hybrid notation is one of a number of Orchestra Ethiopia initiatives that draw on both indigenous and foreign elements.[2] Orchestra Ethiopia can be seen as exemplifying a distinctive Ethiopian modernism that accelerated by the end of the nineteenth century, with a relationship to outside innovations and technologies that would be incorporated into Ethiopian traditions, including religion.[3]

The distinctive form of Ethiopian modernism has been explored within a theory of creativity, known as "creative incorporation," proposed by sociologist Donald Levine, who suggested that Ethiopians have responded historically to foreign influences through a process that absorbs and transforms the new ideas as part of a "tenaciously conserved native tradition."[4] We will explore processes of creative incorporation here as well as in chapter 9 as a stimulating reference point for approaches to new directions in the Ethiopian diaspora.

This chapter begins well after the start of the temporal continuum it reconstructs, narrating first my initial encounter in 1974 with Orchestra Ethiopia and its director Tesfaye Lemma, who began his work with Orchestra Ethiopia in 1966, three years after its founding, and sustained the ensemble through much of the rest of his life (d. 2013). Tesfaye was the crucial link in the orchestra's move from homeland to diaspora.[5]

Expanding on Tesfaye's perspectives at different points in time, as well as through interviews with others, has itself been a multitemporal process. Three narrative strands intertwine, each of which informs the others. First are the stories of a number of Ethiopian musicians engaged with Orchestra Ethiopia and its successor ensembles and with each other over decades. The second are the roles of several foreign musicians whose lives and careers intersected with Orchestra Ethiopia, shaping both their own experiences and the course of Orchestra Ethiopia's history; through this strand of narratives we can understand some of the ways in which Western influences transmitted through individual initiatives became an ongoing part of the Orchestra Ethiopia experience. Third, a series of musical events provides insights into both continuities and shifts in the orchestra's mission and musical style over time. In their interactions, these three sets of narratives intertwine and refract a lively stream of revolutionary, post-revolutionary, and diaspora music history. In sum, this chapter provides a historical ecology[6] of the life of Orchestra Ethiopia, as well as implications for understanding other traditional folklore ensembles in Ethiopia and its diaspora, all part of rapidly changing political, social, and economic scenes.

Beginning in medias res

When the Ethiopian revolution began early in 1974, increasing violence across the country brought my fieldwork in northwestern villages to an abrupt end. Restricted to Addis Ababa, I began to investigate the musical world around me in the capital and soon encountered Orchestra Ethiopia, a musical ensemble that performed in local hotels and appeared on Ethiopian television. The orchestra consisted of musicians playing traditional instruments from different regions and ethnic groups across Ethiopia and incorporated singers and dancers.

I contacted the ensemble and attended occasional orchestra rehearsals held at the Creative Arts Centre of what was then called Haile Selassie I University, and I began taking weekly lessons on the six-stringed Ethiopian lyre, the *krar*. The orchestra director, Tesfaye Lemma, who had returned two years earlier from residencies with the Alvin Ailey American Dance Theater in New York City and composition studies at Indiana University, was a gracious interlocutor. On July 7, 1974, I attended the orchestra's presentation of a new system of musical notation that Tesfaye had innovated in collaboration with orchestra colleagues.

Shortly thereafter, my work with Orchestra Ethiopia lapsed. The revolution was well underway and access to the orchestra was increasingly hazardous after the closing of the university. In 1975 Orchestra Ethiopia disbanded, one more musical victim of the revolution. I had not planned to pursue additional research or to write about the orchestra, although I did find an opportunity to discuss their remarkable notational system in an article.[7]

But as the years passed, I found myself encountering traces of Orchestra Ethiopia time and again. The orchestra came up in testimonies from countless musicians, some of whom had played with the group, and I slowly became aware of the impact of Orchestra Ethiopia and its musicians on subsequent musical events and on other ensembles. This, of course, is a central lesson of ethnography—what seems to be marginal at the outset can in the fullness of time provide entry into other rich topics and new insights. Subsequent ethnography began to provide a more nuanced view of the orchestra's history and shed unexpected light on the interaction among foreign and Ethiopian musicians in its genesis and subsequent life; it also revealed the strong stream of modernism that had reshaped the transmission of traditional Ethiopian musical styles. Furthermore, the "afterlife" of Orchestra Ethiopia, both in Ethiopia and later in the North American diaspora, proved to have important repercussions in multiple domains.

A chronology of the orchestra emerged as a result of testimony from more than a dozen individuals at different times and places. Only in their totality did these narratives reveal the overview sketched in figure 8.1.

Tesfaye Lemma

Born in 1946 in Addis Ababa, where his father served as a chamberlain for the empress in the Imperial Palace, Tesfaye was first educated at the Tafari Mekonnen School and then transferred to a Canadian Jesuit School. Over

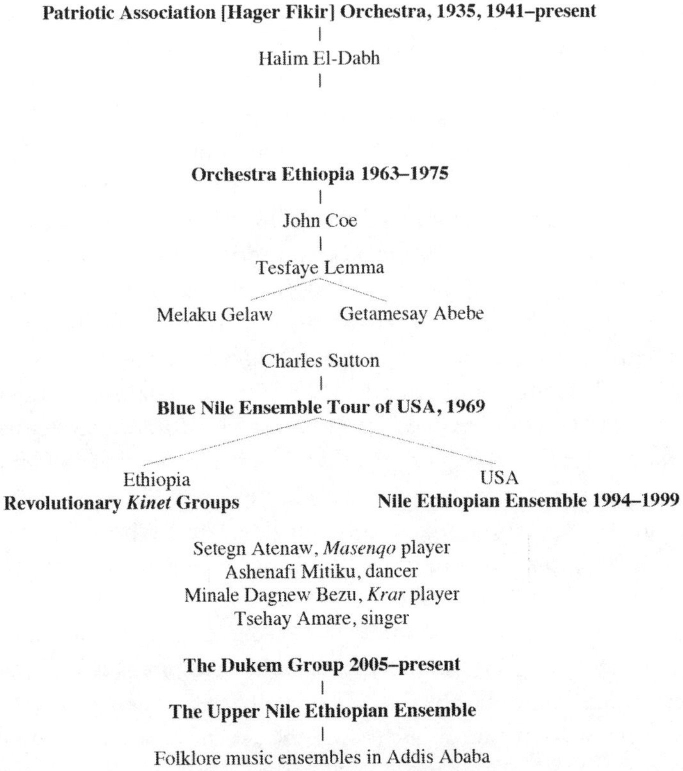

Patriotic Association [Hager Fikir] Orchestra, 1935, 1941–present
|
Halim El-Dabh
|

Orchestra Ethiopia 1963–1975
|
John Coe
|
Tesfaye Lemma

Melaku Gelaw   Getamesay Abebe

Charles Sutton
|
Blue Nile Ensemble Tour of USA, 1969

Ethiopia   USA
Revolutionary *Kinet* Groups   **Nile Ethiopian Ensemble 1994–1999**

Setegn Atenaw, *Masenqo* player
Ashenafi Mitiku, dancer
Minale Dagnew Bezu, *Krar* player
Tsehay Amare, singer

The Dukem Group 2005–present
|
The Upper Nile Ethiopian Ensemble
|
Folklore music ensembles in Addis Ababa

FIGURE 8.1 An overview of the multiple lives of Orchestra Ethiopia.

the strenuous objections of his father, who punished Tesfaye throughout his childhood for his involvement with music, Tesfaye acquired musical experience primarily by attending performances. "There were no musicians in my family. It was ignored . . . and nobody wants to see their child as a musician," Tesfaye recalled.[8]

At an early age, Tesfaye was impressed by hearing the Imperial Bodyguard Marching Band and the performance of its star vocalists such as the renowned Tilahun Gessesse. He recalled that "at that time they played while marching in full regalia through the streets. . . . I would run along beside them all the way."[9] Tesfaye reminisced: "From my childhood I loved music. I used to go to weddings and Epiphany, and one of the Ethiopian music festivals at Jan Meda Square. And I also studied church music."[10] Early on, Tesfaye joined his school band and learned to play the trumpet.[11] Also as a child, he began writing lyrics for songs, and by the time he graduated from high school, he was composing music to go with the lyrics. Most composers in Ethiopia sang as they invented melodies without notation, but Tesfaye would compose by whistling, first imagining the lyrics and then the melody.[12]

Tesfaye recalled being deeply influenced by Emperor Haile Selassie I's commitment to introducing Western culture to Ethiopia:

> We have to learn from the Westerners, otherwise we can't defeat them. We have to bring Western ideas to our country. Haile Selassie was the first king to open officially Ethiopia for Western civilization, and [to] countries like Germany, Russia, America, England, and France. He was the first African king to defeat the Italians. He signed some Greeks and Armenians to come through Djibouti to Ethiopia and opened some shops, restaurants, and these kinds of thing. He organized the Imperial Bodyguard, the first modern army institution. . . . Like Europeans, we organized ourselves through schools, through military police, and through modern institutions. Before him there were no highways, there were no schools, there were no health institutions. Haile Selassie is the founder of Ethiopian civilization.[13]

The notion of an indigenous orchestral ensemble had its roots decades earlier when then regent Ras Tafari first encountered symphony orchestras and other Western ensembles during trips to Europe in the 1920s. Ras Tafari requested that a similar instrumental ensemble be founded in Ethiopia but that it would use indigenous instruments. One of the government's most progressive ministers, Makonnen Habte-Wold, was well versed in European culture and arts.[14] In July 1935, on the cusp of the Italian invasion, Makonnen Habte-Wold founded the Ethiopian Patriotic Association, Hager Fikir, serving as its first president. It was initially a group of *azmari* who gave open-air performances of music as part of short, improvised plays to inspire patriotism. But with the fall of Addis Ababa in May 1936, the association was disbanded, reinstated only after the liberation in 1941.[15] To implement the new musical ensemble, Makonnen called on a former student of the Menelik School trained in European musical instruments, Beshah Tekle-Maryam, to gather traditional musicians.[16] Musicians playing a full array of indigenous instruments constituted an ensemble that staged its first show in February 1942.[17]

An apt example of cultural domestication, the group was intended to be "like the Europeans," but to "make propaganda for the emperor." The initiative is said to have had as its rallying cries "Let's follow our leader. Let's go to school. Let's work together. Let's make unity."[18] According to Tesfaye, the Hager Fikir ensemble drew most of its *masenqo* players from the central highland province of Wollo. "To remember each song," he was told, "since most of them came from Wollo, they gave [it] the name of Wollo song: Wollo Bati, Wollo Tizita, Wollo Anchihoye, and Wollo Ambasel."[19]

Hager Fikir evidently provided a model for the indigenous instrumental ensemble that was later established at the Haile Selassie I National Theatre.[20] Thus, when Orchestra Ethiopia began in 1963, it was not a completely new concept in Ethiopian traditional musical performance, although the orchestra was soon to innovate in many ways.

Orchestra Ethiopia has been said "to have been born of a marriage brokered by enlightened monarch Haile Selassie I between his empire's ancient ways and the institutions of the modern world."[21] Orchestra Ethiopia sought to represent a multiethnic nation through music. The orchestra played traditional music from Ethiopia's many regions in unison, some as lively instrumental arrangements, others with vocal parts, most numbers accompanied by percussion. Musicians wore traditional dress, and dancers changed multiple times into the regional dress of the ethnic community whose music they would next perform.

When he left home during high school in response to his father's view of music as a "trifling and sinful pastime," Tesfaye heard from a friend that the then Haile Selassie I University had established a Creative Arts Centre on campus.[22] The center was headed in 1964 by Philip Caplan, an American speech and drama professor who spent 1963–65 in Addis Ababa as a Fulbright lecturer at the university,[23] and Gebre Kristos Desta, a painter and poet trained at the Academy of Arts in Cologne, Germany, who later started the first National Gallery of Ethiopia.[24] From the start, then, artistic activity at the Creative Arts Centre involved collaboration with foreigners, confirming Tesfaye's recollection that "the university started this Orchestra Ethiopia with the help of Americans."[25]

That the Creative Arts Centre turned to foreign musicians for leadership surely reflects precedents set earlier by the emperor. From the beginning, foreigners worked with Ethiopian musicians to realize the emperor's artistic vision. Although there was resistance from cultural traditionalists and individuals who were concerned about Western cultural domination, the trend of hiring foreign artistic collaborators continued, starting with Egyptian composer Halim El-Dabh.

Halim El-Dabh

Halim El-Dabh was born to a Coptic family in 1921 in Cairo, where he received his first training in Western music, winning first prize at a piano

PLATE 8.1 Halim El-Dabh, Cambridge, Massachusetts, 2007. Collection of author.

competition at the Cairo Opera House.[26] (See plate 8.1.) In 1950 El-Dabh moved to the United States, where he spent much of the next twelve years engaged with various fellowships and educational ventures, building his reputation as an innovative composer and performer before departing for Ethiopia in 1962 with the support of a Rockefeller Foundation fellowship. In Addis Ababa, he first worked on a research project comparing Coptic and Ethiopian Christian Church musics and taught at Haile Selassie I University. El-Dabh recalled that he "taught students to appreciate their own values and culture" and that his goal was to bring together Ethiopian soloists to play in an ensemble to convey "the energy of the Nile Valley." In 1963 El-Dabh received a contract from the university to start Orchestra Ethiopia.[27]

Thirty or forty individuals responded to El-Dabh's public call for musicians and, with financial support from the German Embassy, the group rehearsed and performed its first radio broadcast in 1964 on Radio Voice of the Gospel under the name "Orchestra Ethiopia."[28] Shortly thereafter, El-Dabh convinced the university president to put the musicians on the university payroll. El-Dabh had the orchestra play only traditional Ethiopian melodies in unison to convey a sense of national unity despite the cultural diversity of the ensemble.[29] El-Dabh reminisced about the process of founding the orchestra, which he said, "started in a very spontaneous way."

I became introduced to the *tej bets* [drinking houses] of the area. If an *azmari* was walking down the street and playing his *massenqo*, I would follow him. Wherever I found a group of musicians I would join them. I created a kind of disturbance in the process.... Gradually, the idea spread that I wanted to create an orchestra. As a result, about forty musicians came and camped around my house. Of course, I felt responsible, so I went to the President of the University Kassa Woldemariam and asked if he could put them on the payroll because they were a very great tradition in Ethiopia. He kind of laughed at me.[30]

Undaunted, El-Dabh approached a local radio station, Radio Voice of the Gospel, and arranged for his musicians to record there. The manager of the station contracted to make a small payment to them each time the recordings were broadcast. The German Cultural Institute (Goethe-Institut Addis Abeba) also offered support by hiring the orchestra to give paid performances.

"When I started taking them to Voice of the Gospel to record, they became an entity, relating to each other as a group," said Halim.[31] Now seeing them begin to attract favorable attention and sensing potential in Halim's imaginative venture, President Kassa relented and agreed to put the musicians on the University payroll. Orchestra Ethiopia was born.[32]

El-Dabh chose thirty-three musicians accustomed to playing as soloists and used techniques such as getting one musician to mimic the sounds of another, to train them to play in unison as an ensemble. If the orchestra was shaped by El-Dabh's imagination, he also refused to teach the musicians Western music and consistently stressed the importance of appreciating their own musical values and cultures. El-Dabh's strong commitment to indigenous music both in the classroom and in his work with the orchestra resulted in a large number of traditional musicians being brought to campus.[33]

El-Dabh left Ethiopia in 1964 and returned to the United States, where he became a citizen. He went on to have a long and successful career as a professor at Kent State University, as well as a composer of considerable reputation. El-Dabh did not meet Tesfaye during his stay in Ethiopia. However, El-Dabh did encounter the person who was to succeed him as director of the orchestra and endorsed his hiring. After El-Dabh's departure, Creative Arts Centre director Philip Caplan recruited a Peace Corps volunteer named John Coe to direct Orchestra Ethiopia.

PLATE 8.2 John Coe, Cambridge, Massachusetts, 2007. Collection of author.

John Coe

John Coe, a pianist and former music major from Dartmouth College who was in the first Peace Corps contingent of three hundred volunteers to arrive in Ethiopia in 1962, recalled that "someone said we were the biggest invasion of Westerners in Ethiopia since the Italians."[34] From 1962 to 1964, Coe worked as a Peace Corps volunteer in Jimma, a southwestern Ethiopian city long an important center in the western Oromo region, where he taught English and French and directed plays. (See plate 8.2.) But Coe quickly attracted attention with an appeal directly to Sargent Shriver, the director of the Peace Corps, during the director's official visit to Ethiopia: Coe asked Shriver to buy him a piano to use for musical events. Shriver agreed to his request and Coe managed to purchase an old upright piano in the capital that he transported to Jimma in the back of a horse-drawn cart. Coe soon attracted a lively following locally as Jimma students participated in the theatrical productions he organized. One of the young students who performed and also collaborated on writing lyrics with Coe was none other than Haile Gerima, who would leave Ethiopia with foreign sponsorship to attend the Goodman School of Drama in Chicago and become a distinguished filmmaker in the United States.[35]

Born in 1939, Coe came to the attention of Philip Caplan when he presented a musical at the Creative Arts Centre during Halim El-Dabh's tenure there. Coe had collaborated in Jimma with another Peace Corps volunteer to mount a production in Amharic for which he composed the music based on George Bernard Shaw's 1912 play *Androcles and the Lion*; it subsequently had a successful run in Addis Ababa.

Coe next persuaded the Peace Corps to let him move to the capital to serve as assistant director of the Creative Arts Centre. He inherited a large cohort of orchestra musicians from El-Dabh and tried unsuccessfully to found a glee club. Coe's first composition for Orchestra Ethiopia in 1964 was titled "Bisichet" (Trouble).[36] Coe recalled that the composition lived up to its title:

> It took months to learn. And the poor *bagana* (large ten-stringed lyre) player, he had the most difficulty going bum-bum-bum-bum [imitating bass oom-pah sound]. He was the sweetest guy.[37]

Although Coe learned that there were four modes based on pentatonic scales in Ethiopian secular music, he never mastered them and usually composed his pieces in a Western key. Coe also shortened songs so that Western audiences would be attracted to orchestra performances and could sit through them. He spent a great deal of time teaching the group to cohere:

> They took this up pretty quickly I think, and they learned to be an ensemble! I mean, that's what I think is the important part! Normally they would be solo players in a *tej bet* bar, and I guess they had songs, but they also created songs sort of like troubadours and created the news of the day or something to honor somebody. So to put them together was different.[38]

Other compositions by Coe included the "Oda Oak Oracle I–V" with a text by the young playwright Tsegaye Gabre-Medhin (quoted in the dedication to this book), who later became poet laureate of Ethiopia. Coe recalled that the piece received a scathing review in the *Ethiopian Herald*, which suggested that Ethiopian instruments were not intended to play foreign music.[39] The impact of Coe likely inspired musicians to innovate in their own ways; one orchestra member invented a collapsible *masenqo* with a hinged neck that could be folded to fit into a suitcase.

Coe was aware that the orchestra needed income and solicited engagements for the group; one of the first was a performance at a wedding. In

many ways, Coe's tenure reshaped the group both in the ethos of its performances and in its emerging public face:

> We got these jobs playing for Ethiopian social things and then we started
> doing performances for tourists, basically at the university and sometimes
> at the art center. And, of course, we gave concerts and I think it was a mix-
> ture, probably of both Ethiopian and Western. I think what happened, Ethi-
> opians began to see that this was a respectable group and that their mu-
> sic was worth hearing. . . . By the time I left [in mid-1966], it was a viable
> group. And the [Creative Arts Centre] director, Tesfaye Gessesse, had the
> wisdom and courage to hire this young man, Tesfaye Lemma.[40]

Tesfaye Lemma, continued

With Coe's departure imminent, the new Creative Arts Centre director, Tesfaye Gessesse, was searching for his successor and recalled being
amused by Tesfaye Lemma's youth, inability to play a traditional instrument, and lack of any professional experience:

> But I sensed that he had a deeply poetic nature, and I was impressed by
> his confidence that he could do something creative with the Orchestra. So,
> I decided to give him a chance.[41]

Tesfaye Lemma joined the Haile Selassie I University Creative Arts
Centre in 1966 and began work with the orchestra, which had been reduced to thirteen musicians during Coe's tenure. (See plate 8.3.) Tesfaye
was thrilled to receive the job, which rescued him from a time of financial
crisis and provided an exciting professional opportunity:

> Tesfaye Gessesse . . . hired me on fifty *birr* per month. And that money
> was enough to buy food and to rent a small house at that time. The life was
> very easy, and I enjoyed it. I enjoyed the orchestra. After I worked for eight
> months, they promoted me as supervisor of the orchestra.[42]

Thus, in 1966 Tesfaye Lemma inherited an orchestra that after three
years was accustomed to performing together. Coe had emphasized the
traditional nature of the orchestra, but Tesfaye's "goal was to change the
prevailing image of Orchestra Ethiopia as a relic of the past by making
the group popular on the stages of Addis Ababa's big theaters and in the
electronic media."[43] With a view of the group that was closer to the more

PLATE 8.3 Tesfaye Lemma on the campus of Haile Selassie I University, c. 1968. Courtesy of Charles Sutton.

innovative and experimental goals of founder El-Dabh,[44] Tesfaye's leadership solidified the growing reputation of the ensemble and musicians already members of the orchestra soon became his professional colleagues and lifelong friends.

Melaku Gelaw

One founding member of Orchestra Ethiopia was Melaku Gelaw, a traditional *krar* and *washint* virtuoso who was also an accomplished maker of musical instruments. Born in 1944 to a family of mixed Agau and Amhara descent, Melaku recalled that the way he learned to play the flute "was when I was guarding cattle" in the fields of the rural Lasta area of northern Wollo province where he grew up. Melaku left home as a young teenager in part because of his father's vociferous disapproval of his musical activities; he reports that although he had musical inclinations from an early age, if his father caught him with a *washint*, he would beat him and break the flute in half.[45] Melaku left home to finish school in a nearby provincial town and made a strong local reputation working as a secretary.

Eventually Melaku moved to Addis Ababa, where he learned to play the *krar* from an accomplished musician and auditioned for Hager Fikir Orchestra. That experience remains an uncomfortable memory, recounted in chapter 1: Melaku was rejected by the group for racial reasons.[46] Melaku subsequently heard about Orchestra Ethiopia being formed but had not signed up for an audition before the deadline. He asked the assistant to Tesfaye Gessesse to give him a chance to audition even though the positions had been filled. Someone who knew about his talent suggested to Halim El-Dabh that he audition Melaku: Melaku performed on *washint*, was greeted with applause, and was accepted into the orchestra. He was an active performer in Orchestra Ethiopia until 1968, when he left for economic reasons to teach at the National Music School and, subsequently, as a member of the faculty at the Yared School of Music for twenty-eight years.[47]

Melaku and Tesfaye Lemma established a close professional and personal relationship that they were able to sustain later as refugees in the United States. In 1995 Melaku's wife came to the United States to care for her pregnant sister, who died after giving birth, leaving Melaku's wife to care for the baby as well as her sister's older children. She applied for and received asylum; Melaku joined her along with their own eight children within a year.

Until his death in February 2018, Melaku performed at occasional concerts in the United States and had a band called Keneto. However, he did not play in restaurants or nightclubs like many musicians because he considered it to be undignified. Melaku enjoyed performing at universities and cultural centers and released a CD in Washington, DC.[48] Until health issues arose, he worked at a plywood manufacturing factory and continued to make and repair high-quality Ethiopian musical instruments at his home in Virginia. Melaku was proud of making "modern *krars*" that could be amplified. He also would have liked to contribute more to his new homeland and once said wistfully:

> If I had come here [to the United States] in my youth, I would have liked to do national service here. It could have been as a soldier or any way. I would have liked to have served the American people in some way if I could have done that as a young man.[49]

Melaku, in a word, would have aspired to be a sentinel musician.

Getamesay Abebe

Another veteran of Tesfaye Lemma's Orchestra Ethiopia was Getamesay Abebe. Born in 1943, he began his career as the apprentice to an older *azmari* in what is today the Arsi zone of the Oromia region several hours south of Addis Ababa. He recalled working in *tädj bet* (*tej bet*, drinking house) during his teenage years in the company of his *azmari* mentor and made two to three Ethiopian dollars a day, commenting drolly that "money had value then."[50] Eventually, Getamesay joined two of his siblings who lived in Addis Ababa. While working at the local cinema and playing *masenqo* in clubs during his first year in the capital, Getamesay heard about Orchestra Ethiopia, auditioned for Halim El-Dabh and was hired. Getamesay performed *masenqo* with Orchestra Ethiopia until 1968, when he left the ensemble to become head *masenqo* player for the Hager Fikir Orchestra, where he remained until he retired because of a health crisis in 2004. Getamesay toured with Hager Fikir's ensemble internationally and with the *Hizb le Hizb* (*People to People*, discussed in chapter 5) tour that saw defections when it came to the United States in 1987–88.[51] Three of Getamesay's ten children eventually immigrated to the United States, where he occasionally visited, but he retained his primary home in Addis Ababa.[52] Getamesay, who died in April 2016, is said to have always lived up to his name, which means "noble-seeming," always elegant and well dressed.

In 2007 Getamesay and Melaku, under the direction of Tesfaye, came together to record a CD titled *Reunion* with an American named Charles Sutton, whose colorful story enters this narrative later on.[53] (See plate 8.4.)

Tesfaye Lemma, continued

When Tesfaye assumed leadership of Orchestra Ethiopia in the fall of 1966, he had to struggle to attract an audience for the orchestra because he found Ethiopians more interested in Western instruments and global popular musical styles. At one New Year's Day show with other ensembles, including the Army, Police, and Imperial Bodyguard Bands, he recalled that these groups played for hours, but that the young audience hooted Orchestra Ethiopia from the stage before it had finished its third number.

Tesfaye tried composing new pieces for the orchestra, such as "Simish Man New" (lit., What is your name?), a lighthearted composition with the unconventional accompaniment of *embilta*, an ensemble of three end-blown flutes that played interlocking parts. Tesfaye's innovations were vividly remembered by Charles Sutton, an American who first heard Orchestra Ethiopia perform at the university after his arrival in Addis Ababa for Peace Corps service in September 1966:

> This is the kind of thing that Tesfaye did, and I don't want to give the impression at all that he was conservative, because he wasn't. He wouldn't

ቻርልስ ሳተን

ከመላኩ ገላው እና ጌታመሳይ አበበ ጋር
CHARLES SUTTON
with MELAKU GELAW & GETAMESAY ABBEBE

ዞር ገጠም
REUNION

PLATE 8.4 The CD *Reunion* (from left to right: Melaku Gelaw, Charles Sutton, Getamesay Abebe), c. 2007. Courtesy of Charles Sutton.

have asked me to play with the orchestra if he were conservative. If he were one of these educated people preserving tradition, I'm sure that the idea that a guy like me—a white American who would play with the orchestra—would never have been considered. But he was young and was open to try anything. . . . At that time, the instruments had been greatly eclipsed by Western influence, and he hoped that this might provide a renewed interest among Ethiopians in their own instruments. . . . [Orchestra Ethiopia] combined elements of the Western tradition of composition with traditional elements, and Tesfaye was the one who really achieved this kind of synthesis between these two things. The "Golden Age" of Tesfaye's talent was Orchestra Ethiopia.[54]

Charles went to the Creative Arts Centre to inquire about taking lessons on a traditional instrument, where he met Tesfaye Lemma. Soon, Charles began taking *masenqo* lessons with Getamesay Abebe, and Tesfaye would sometimes stop by during his lesson under the palm tree outside the center to listen to Charles's progress. After his lesson, Charles would go inside to watch the orchestra rehearsals from the back of the hall. By March 1967 Sutton, a talented guitar player and pianist, had become proficient on *masenqo*, and Tesfaye had made a calculated decision to invite Sutton to join the orchestra:

> It was a new experience for Ethiopians when they saw a *ferenj* (a foreigner) appreciating and performing their music. This brought good attention to the Orchestra. Especially in those days. Many people were not conscious about their culture. They didn't see their music and instruments as valuable. The younger people were more interested in rock music and in learning the guitar and keyboard. When I invited Charles to perform with the Orchestra, it was unusual and they woke up and said, "This is good music. An American is playing our music!" They came to have more respect for their music as a result.[55]

Sutton's presence with Orchestra Ethiopia attracted a great deal of publicity and proved to be a vital connection that helped sustain the ensemble into the future. It was also the start of deep friendships and continued collaborations among Tesfaye, Sutton, Getamesay, and Melaku.

Charles Sutton

I first heard stories about a Peace Corps volunteer named Charles Sutton when I arrived in Ethiopia in mid-1973: many remembered the *ferenj* musician who spoke fluent Amharic and was a virtuoso on the *masenqo*. However, I met Sutton only in the early 1990s, when I moved to New Haven, near where he lived in a small Connecticut town on the shore and both taught and performed as a freelance jazz musician.

Born in 1942 in New York City, Sutton grew up in Columbus, Ohio, and attended Harvard University.[56] After receiving his degree in English, Sutton joined the Peace Corps and arrived in Ethiopia in late September 1966, for service as an English teacher. Shortly after his arrival at the Haile Selassie I University campus, Sutton saw a poster advertising an Orchestra Ethiopia concert. Attending the concert encouraged him to learn to play an Ethiopian instrument; at first Sutton intended to study the six-stringed lyre, the *krar*, which he thought might be easier for him because of his experience as a guitarist. But the general manager, Tesfaye Gessesse, introduced Sutton to Getamesay, whose virtuosity and gracious demeanor encouraged Sutton to study the *masenqo*. Sutton began weekly lessons in the fall of 1966, and in March of the following year, Tesfaye Lemma invited Sutton to join the orchestra.[57]

Sutton became deeply involved and committed to expanding the orchestra's audience, realizing it was a means by which he could familiarize other Peace Corps volunteers with Ethiopian culture. Sutton arranged a welcome party for new Peace Corps arrivals at a local restaurant, where the volunteers ate their first Ethiopian food and met their Amharic teachers. After that dinner, the orchestra performed:

> Tesfaye and I worked together on the preparation of these special cross-cultural programs, which gave the newcomers an enchanting and unforgettable introduction to the country that would be their home for the next two years. We staged similar performances for the diplomatic community and for visiting dignitaries at the American Embassy.[58]

By the fall of 1967, the Peace Corps had reassigned Sutton, by then fluent in Amharic, to a position coordinating the local Amharic language program for the volunteers. Required to travel to various locales and to coach local teachers in their methods, on one trip north, in November–December 1967, Sutton gave speeches and solo *masenqo* concerts to audiences of secondary-school students:

> So, every place I would stop, there would be a secondary school, and I would go and say, "I could give this little show to entertain the kids." . . . And then I would play and sing and everything and then I would give a little talk and they went crazy over it. I still run into people . . . like taxi drivers who remember. They say, "oh you gave a speech when you were in Aksum." Or "you were in such and such a place when I was like in the eighth grade and I still remember it."[59]

Sutton also traveled with Tesfaye and the full orchestra to perform in provincial towns:

> We always went south. . . . We'd go to these places and the people really enjoyed it because they didn't have any entertainment there. Whenever they gave a performance I would play. Tesfaye wrote special pieces for me.[60]

Sutton's involvement with the orchestra proved to be far more crucial than a transitory publicity device. In April 1968, pleading budget constraints, the university terminated all the orchestra musicians' salaries and evicted them from the Creative Arts Centre.[61] Sutton then turned to the Peace Corps, which came to the ensemble's rescue, providing transport to performances and an office with a telephone at the Peace Corps headquarters in order to ensure that they would continue to receive invitations and could book appearances. Within a few days, Charles printed leaflets announcing that the orchestra was available for parties, receptions, and weddings and could be contacted at its new headquarters at the Peace Corps Office.[62] Sutton corresponded with embassies and arranged orchestra engagements for weddings and embassy events.[63] He next convinced the Peace Corps to renew his service for a third year and to allow him to be the orchestra's full-time administrator and business manager.[64]

At the end of his second year in Ethiopia, Sutton went on a scheduled monthlong home leave in the United States. Concerned about the orchestra's precarious financial position and also convinced that the ensemble could generate positive publicity for the Peace Corps, Sutton brought home with him photographs, recordings, and letters in support of the ensemble from various dignitaries.[65] He made a series of presentations to potential supporters, introducing the orchestra and its musicians, arguing that "we have to keep them together and preserve this ancient Ethiopian music."[66] Sutton also performed benefit concerts on behalf of the orchestra, donning Ethiopian traditional dress and playing his *masenqo* before US civic and charitable groups. The proceeds of $1,500 he collected through these efforts covered six months of salary for director Tesfaye and the fourteen people in the orchestra, sustaining its activities for six months.

Sutton also approached the Peace Corps to sponsor an Orchestra Ethiopia tour to the United States, which was approved and booked for twenty performances in the spring of 1969 in the eastern and midwestern United States. Upon his return to Ethiopia, Sutton approached businesses and civic groups in Addis Ababa who agreed to support the costs and in fact covered most of the orchestra's expenses for the tour, with Ethiopian Airlines providing free round-trip transportation from Addis Ababa to New York. Other Ethiopian businesses provided new costumes and appropriate clothing for the fifteen troupe members. Because of concerns that an ensemble named Orchestra Ethiopia would suggest that the group had official status, the group was billed as the Blue Nile Group for the tour.

On March 2, 1969, the Blue Nile Group appeared on the Ed Sullivan Show (CBS), which garnered an audience said to number forty million. The performance was just under three minutes and was introduced by Ed Sullivan as follows:

Now here, ladies and gentlemen, is the Blue Nile Orchestra from Ethiopia, which dates back 2000 years to Solomon and Sheba. Peace Corps volunteer Charles Sutton will introduce and narrate the selections. Let's give our Ethiopian visitors a very warm and very fine hand.[67]

The Blue Nile Group performed a medley of four brief selections chosen by Sullivan show staff from the orchestra's repertory during a daylong rehearsal to link the segments together for the live broadcast. The performance began with a solo by Sutton playing *masenqo* accompanied by the orchestra. Next came a solo by a dancer wearing a lion skin over his traditional white garb, "the dance of the lion hunter," followed by three performers on *embilta*, presented as "an ancient wind instrument of Ethiopia." The *embilta* players performed an elaborate choreography that was part of their usual performance practice. In closing, the entire orchestra accompanied "two young lovers expressing their affection for each other in a vigorous shoulder dance called *eskista*." The presentation highlighted the novelty of Sutton's participation and his role as cultural translator; it further exoticized the "primitivism" of numbers such as the lion dance from "an ancient land." The entire segment was staged to entertain a Western television audience with elaborate choreography and quick transitions.

The group's tour and Ed Sullivan Show telecast received a great deal of publicity both in the United States and in Ethiopia. There had been some concern about the tour prior to their departure, but it was resolved when, under the auspices of the Ministry of Education, the orchestra previewed the entire American concert program for dignitaries and prominent people in the arts at the Addis Ababa YMCA. All in attendance liked the show and thought the orchestra well prepared to make the trip. However, after the orchestra departed Ethiopia, the music director of Radio Ethiopia, who had not attended the pretour preview, strongly criticized the tour in the *Ethiopian Herald*, calling the orchestra's musicians "incompetent to perform in the US and the dupes of a foreign exploiter."[68] But members of the Ethiopian public, as well as a Ministry of Education spokesperson, countered with strong public support for the tour, and the *Ethiopian Herald* published a laudatory review of the Blue Nile Group's March 17, 1969, appearance at New York City's Town Hall performance space, which also had been noted in the *New York Times*.[69] The group arrived home as heroes. (See plate 8.5.) On their return to Addis Ababa on April 1, they quickly attracted a full calendar of bookings and contracts for regular employment at local hotels.[70] A recording made before the tour was published

PLATE 8.5 Photograph celebrating Orchestra Ethiopia's audience with
Emperor Haile Selassie I at the Jubilee Palace on September 25, 1969.
Courtesy of Charles Sutton.

as an LP titled *Orchestra Ethiopia,* later incorporated into the *éthiopiques*
23 (2007) reissue.[71]

Innovations Along with Signs of Struggle

Despite the favorable publicity, Haile Selassie I University declined to resume support for the ensemble, and no Ethiopian organization came forward to sponsor the group. Sutton departed Ethiopia in 1971 at the end of a
final Peace Corps contract extension, and another Peace Corps volunteer,
Marc Weishaus, took over as the orchestra administrator. Tesfaye also left
to study in the United States, dividing his time between working with the
Alvin Ailey American Dance Theater and auditing classes in composition
and ethnomusicology at Indiana University.[72] On his return in 1972, Tesfaye and his colleagues resumed activity with the ensemble and returned
to their former quarters at the Creative Arts Centre on the Haile Selassie I
campus. Tesfaye increased the number of musicians to sixteen and directed
orchestra performances at a wide variety of Addis Ababa hotels, including
Ghion, Hilton, Wabe Shebelle, and Ras.[73] Over the years, Tesfaye actively
collected Ethiopian musical instruments, carefully recording information
about each and writing a small book about them.[74]

Only the beginning of the revolution in 1974 and the imposition of curfews brought most public performances of the orchestra to a halt. Tourism shut down in response to the violence, and much of the diplomatic community, which had often hired the group to perform at official events, was recalled. However, the revolutionary government, in part influenced by socialist policies elsewhere, realized "that music plays a very important role in socialist culture for propaganda. We have to take care of these people."[75] The musicians of Orchestra Ethiopia were asked to perform on behalf of the revolution and were concerned that they might be imprisoned or killed if they said something wrong or oppositional.

The orchestra managed to survive through the first two years of the revolution by participating in the performance of revolutionary (socialist) songs at events and on television, pressed into service by the revolutionary government, which urgently needed new television shows to replace US dramas such as "Hawaii Five-O," abruptly taken off the air as symbols of capitalist decadence. Among the new programs were performances by musical ensembles such as Orchestra Ethiopia dramatizing the successes of the nascent revolution.

One such early effort was a musical drama centered on the character of "Mother Ethiopia," shown ill in bed, reduced by feudal graft and malfeasance to a weakened shadow of her former self. A young military officer dressed in a khaki uniform enters her room and orders her from her sickbed, accompanied by chanted invocations of a priest in the background. By the end of the drama, Mother Ethiopia miraculously recovers and joins the rousing chorus performed by the musicians of Orchestra Ethiopia.[76]

But the ensemble could not survive in the violent political and depressed economic climate of 1975 and formally disbanded later that year. However, it left an indelible mark on the lives and relationships of those who participated in the group over the years as well as a strong collective memory among many Ethiopians who had heard the ensemble in public presentations and on television. But for Tesfaye in particular, the ensemble represented an unfulfilled dream. During his years of leadership, the ensemble became, if not an official representative of Ethiopian traditional culture in a cosmopolitan setting, at least a musical organization known universally to Ethiopians at home and in the growing diaspora. Sutton observed in an interview that

I think it [Orchestra Ethiopia] combines elements of the Western tradition of composition with traditional elements, and Tesfaye was the one who really achieved this kind of synthesis between these two things. I think the contribution of John Coe and of Halim [El-Dabh], the founder, to get all these guys to play together and keep in good tempo and play a tune and all that kind of thing, that was a big challenge and that took a lot of hard work before Tesfaye came on the scene. So, in a sense, a stage was set. They had the training and preparation that he could really do something new and different with and that is what he did.[77]

Revolution and Orchestra Ethiopia's Path to Diaspora

With Orchestra Ethiopia disbanded, Tesfaye soon became general manager of the Ras Theatre, where he continued his innovative work during the revolution with cultural musicians whom he recruited from many regions of the country.[78] With no place to house his large collection of musical instruments acquired during the Orchestra Ethiopia years, he donated half of the instruments to the Yared School of Music and half to the City Hall Theatre.[79] Tesfaye observed that the constraints of revolutionary censorship were balanced to an extent by greater support for music and musicians under the new socialist state, where music was considered to have a special role in national propaganda:

> During Haile Selassie, they used to sing about various subjects but now all of our work was limited to just performing for the revolution. . . . The big leaders of the military, including Mengistu [Haile Mariam], used to give direction to art. But all their work concentrated on socialist propaganda.[80]

Tesfaye continued to compose songs but was cautious because he had made comments on the political situation well before the revolution with his song "Shimagile Negn" (I'm an old man), a veiled commentary on the advanced age of Emperor Haile Selassie I.[81] Although Tesfaye has said that he did not intend the song to be interpreted politically, it was rejected by censors. In 1975 Tesfaye again referred to political events in his composition "Almazin Ayiche" (Looking at Almaz), sung by Tilahun Gessesse. In this love song, Tesfaye masked political commentary in lyrics about the "three Almaz," using the popular name for girls or for a beloved (*almaz* translates as diamond), to refer to the three members of the military junta who were then vying for control: Atnafu Abate, Aman Andom, and Mengistu Haile Mariam. Shortly thereafter, the first two were assassinated and Mengistu took sole control. Although colleagues of Tesfaye feared for his life, he did not suffer consequences. The text of the song read

> While looking at the two *Almaz,*
> Here came the third one to my surprise,

As she made me forget the first two *Almaz*,
My decision was ruined through your choice.[82]

In 1987, when Tesfaye served as director of the traditional ensemble in the *People to People* tour of Europe and the United States, Mengistu Haile Mariam was deeply involved in preparing the ensemble at Congress Hall rehearsals for its performances abroad. Tesfaye recalls that Mengistu "didn't do any of his regular work. He was watching the program for three days, giving corrections."[83]

During the *People to People* tour to Washington, DC, as discussed in chapter 5, Tesfaye experienced a diabetic crisis and was rushed to a hospital in Maryland. Left in care of the Ethiopian Embassy when the troupe departed, Tesfaye recovered and escaped to receive asylum in the United States.[84]

During his early years in the United States, Tesfaye worked multiple jobs: as a parking lot attendant, security guard, and usher at the Kennedy Center, all the while seeking to gather financial resources so that he could return to musical activities. However, just months after seeking asylum in 1987, Tesfaye produced the first of what were to become annual Ethiopian New Year shows (titled "Inqutatash Bamerika," "New Year in America") at the Capitol Hilton Hotel. Sutton recalls that "Tesfaye put up handbills on 18th Street that he had written with magic marker in Amharic: 'Do you have a talent that you would like to bring before the public? Can you dance, sing, do comedy? Or play a musical instrument?' followed by his phone number. And that's how he got started and organized the first show. . . . These shows were tremendously popular . . . and would take in as much as $25,000 from one show. There was a magazine, *Elelta*, that you would get as part of a ticket."[85]

In 1994 Tesfaye founded the Center for Ethiopian Art and Culture (CEAC), a nonprofit cultural and educational organization dedicated to the presentation of the diverse cultures of peoples from Ethiopia. According to CEAC bylaws, it was founded (1) to support the promotion of Ethiopian art and culture in the United States; (2) to sponsor events by Ethiopian artists engaged in the areas of literature, dance, art, and theater; (3) to increase community awareness of the customs and traditions of Ethiopians who now reside in the United States; and (4) to assist in such other functions associated with the foregoing as the director of Center for Ethiopian Art and Culture shall from time to time deem fit and proper.[86] By September 1998 CEAC aspired to a broader agenda that included opening a new musical instrument museum (the Tesfa ["Hope"] Ethiopian Museum), establishing the first Ethiopian music and dance school in diaspora, which presented the Ethiopian coffee ceremony.[87] Here Tesfaye's continued role as a sentinel musician in the American diaspora is clear.

Under the auspices of CEAC, Tesfaye had also founded the new Nile Ethiopian Ensemble in 1994, embracing the name the orchestra had used during its 1969 tour to the United States. He recruited eight Ethiopian immigrant musicians and dancers for the ensemble.[88] Most were refugees from northern regions of Ethiopia, Amhara and other highland ethnic groups, but performed musical selections drawn from a wide variety of ethnic communities across the country.

Music and Musicians of the Nile Ethiopian Ensemble

The Nile Ethiopian Ensemble followed closely Orchestra Ethiopia's model from the past, with fast-paced numbers featuring dancers who wore costumes evoking traditional dress of various Ethiopian communities; between numbers, while the dancers changed clothes, singers performed to the accompaniment of *krar*, *masenqo*, and percussion. During its first year, the ensemble performed at thirty community centers and international events, twenty-five of which took place in the Washington, DC, metropolitan area.[89] On November 11, 1994, the Nile Ethiopian Ensemble, at my invitation, performed their standard program at Harvard University,[90] and their first anniversary celebration at the Capital Hilton Hotel on August 12, 1995, featured a special performance by Charles Sutton on the *masenqo*. For the next four years, the ensemble struggled to stay afloat financially, often booking out-of-town performances that had to be canceled for lack of funding.[91]

Purposefully innovative, the ensemble's instruments were modified for large audiences. Instrument sound boxes were made out of wood instead of skin to accommodate the use of an amplifier and the original gut strings were replaced with guitar strings. The ensemble continued to play Ethiopian traditional music and compositions by Tesfaye but also collaborated with other African musicians, participating in events such as Dance Africa in Chicago with African musicians from Ghana.[92]

The Nile Ethiopian Ensemble advertised itself as "a new generation of Ethiopian traditional musicians" and included several recent immigrants to the United States, all from a younger cohort whom Tesfaye had known in Ethiopia. A dancer and two musicians hired for the ensemble are still today among the most outstanding performers in traditional Ethiopian styles. We have already met the dancer in chapter 5, Ashenafi Mitiku, an expert in *bahelawi* music and dance, who also plays several of the cultural drums (small *kebero* and *atamo*).

After his arrival in Washington, DC, in 1993, Ashenafi first danced at Meskerem Restaurant on 18th Street in Adams Morgan and then joined the Nile Ethiopian Ensemble at its founding as their lead dancer. He performed at the Kennedy Center, Lincoln Center, World Music Institute in New York City, and in Chicago, and participated at the Nile Ethiopian Ensemble concert at Harvard University in 1994. "We performed [at] every place except the White House," Ashenafi recalled with a laugh.[93] The limited financial resources of the Nile Ethiopian Ensemble did not come close to fully supporting the musicians, and so Ashenafi took other jobs to sustain himself financially: in an Italian restaurant in Takoma Park, Maryland, and in an organic food co-op; eventually, he made a transition into real estate.[94]

In chapter 4, we encountered Setegn Atanaw, a veteran of the Blue Nile *Kinet* and later the lead *masenqo* player with the National Theatre Orchestra. Setegn left Ethiopia for Toronto in 1993 with the help of a sponsor. After performing at a Toronto restaurant for six months, Setegn received asylum in the United States, where he became a founding member of the Nile Ethiopian Ensemble in 1994.

Born in Ethiopia in 1976, Setegn grew up in a family of *azmari* in a small town south of Gondar.[95] Setegn attended a local church school and worked as a shepherd on his father's land. He learned to play *masenqo* from his father, transmits a great deal of traditional *azmari* lore, and commands a wide repertory of traditional *azmari* songs.[96]

Yet, despite his traditional training, Setegn is very much the modern *azmari*, versatile and conversant with different styles of music. He is proud of his reputation as a specialist in cultural music:

> I play *bahelawi* music, now I'm number one. I play everything. I play sometimes in English [laughter]. "Come on, baby. I wanna see you, baby. I need you, baby. Baby, come on, listen to me. Come on darling. Whoa. Whoa. Whoa!"[97]

A third prominent young musician who joined the Nile Ethiopian Ensemble not long before it disbanded in 1999 was Minale Dagnew Bezu. A veteran of the Gojjam Cultural Group Gish Abbay from 1983 to 1992, Minale defected during a cultural tour to the United States in 1993. Born in 1970 in Bahir Dar, Minale was initially a singer but shifted to *krar* when his voice changed at age fourteen. After his defection, he spent months performing in various American cities and eventually met his Ethiopian wife, who had come to the United States on a diversity visa. Although he did not work with Tesfaye for a long time, and economic pressures forced him to take a position as a valet in an area hotel, Minale was quite sympathetic to Tesfaye's efforts with the orchestra:

> My thinking is closer to Mr. Tesfaye because he's more dedicated for people to keep their heritage and culture. He wants to keep that culture for the next generation. . . .
>
> One of my aims is, even though I'm an American, is to try to keep my heritage by playing these cultural instruments. And if I can pass it on to my kids, I don't care if they choose to play the keyboard later on but I want them to know that I used to play one of the Ethiopian instruments called the *krar*. I want them not to forget that.[98]

Offspring of the Nile Ethiopian Ensemble

Throughout its American period, the Nile Ethiopian Ensemble was dogged by severe financial constraints and the lack of regular performance opportunities, as Tesfaye noted:

> I didn't get enough engagements, and the institutions, like the universities and schools, they don't pay reasonable money to keep my band together. . . . America is not convenient for foreign musicians.[99]

Tesfaye's diabetes worsened in the late 1990s, the blow that doomed the Nile Ethiopian Ensemble. Minale recalled that "Tesfaye was the one who kept the group going but then he got some health issues. . . . Tesfaye was dedicated to this."[100]

After the Nile Ethiopian Ensemble disbanded in 1999, Minale, Setegn, and Ashenafi began performing together at local restaurants in Washington, DC, eventually joining for performances at Dukem Ethiopian Restaurant on U Street.[101] In 2005 Minale collaborated with Dukem Ethiopian Restaurant owner Tefera Zewdie to choreograph biweekly folkloric music shows.[102] Dukem was praised by the musicians for paying good salaries, giving bonuses, and making the performers feel a big part of the organization.[103] Setegn performed on *masenqo* regularly at Dukem as well as at other DC metropolitan area establishments.

Dukem institutionalized two types of Ethiopian musical shows: the cultural show performed during the early evening and the jazz and popular music show started late and extended into early morning hours on the weekends. The audiences were quite different for the two shows. At cultural shows one found multicultural audiences incorporating the widest

PLATE 8.6 Musical ensemble at Dukem Ethiopian Restaurant, Washington, DC, including (left to right) Setegn Atanaw, Tsehay Amare, Solomon Bedany, and Minale Dagnew Bezu, c. 2007. Collection of author.

array of nationalities, including many Americans, Indians, South Americans, and West Africans, but few Ethiopians. In contrast, the late-evening shows, patronized mainly by Ethiopians, featured jazz and popular music, as well as neotraditional Ethiopian repertories accompanied by a synthesizer. (See plate 8.6.)

The Dukem Group was constrained by the small performance space available in a busy restaurant and as a result, always used a smaller number of musicians than the Nile Ethiopian Ensemble: Setegn and Minale were joined by a drummer playing on an electronic pad, along with one singer, while Ashenafi and two female dancers performed on the floor immediately in front of them. (See plate 3.6.) The musicians, who wore Ethiopian national dress, remained on stage playing throughout the show. Traditional songs performed by the solo singer in highland dress alternated with lively dance numbers. The cultural show was mounted twice a week beginning in 2005, early on Wednesday and Sunday evenings. It became very popular, but after the financial downturn in 2008, performances were cut back to a single Sunday evening performance and eventually discontinued entirely some years later.

Tsehay Amare

The singer for the Dukem Group was Tsehay Amare, born in 1974 in Wollo, Ethiopia. Tsehay is the niece of Alemayehu Eshete, who became famous across Ethiopia in the 1960s as "the Ethiopian Elvis." From age thirteen, Tsehay sang Ethiopian traditional music with the well-known Wallo-Lalibela *Kinet*. Her departure for Kenya in 1994 took place after the revolution ended, when restrictions on emigration had eased somewhat. After performing for two years in Nairobi, Tsehay moved on to sing at Canadian restaurants, and in 2004 she married an Ethiopian living in Washington, DC.[104]

After arriving in the United States, Tsehay worked as an aide in a nursing home in Virginia, but by the time of our first interview in 2007, she was employed full-time as a singer. She performed both traditional and modern styles, singing cultural music at Dukem in Washington, DC, and performed Ethiopian popular songs late in the evenings at a restaurant in nearby Falls Church, Virginia. Tsehay traveled to perform at weddings in many Ethiopian diaspora communities, including Atlanta, Seattle, Dallas, Columbus, Las Vegas, and more. Tsehay's circuitous migratory path to the United States, occurring as it did after the revolution ended, was not marked by the extreme hardships faced by musicians who escaped earlier. But she struggled to make a living, returning only once before 2007 to visit Ethiopia.[105]

Tsehay views her performances as having different purposes in Ethiopia and in the diaspora. In Ethiopia she seeks to promote peace and unity through her songs:

> I want to try to send a message to all the people. These days, the country has a lot of problems, political, even religious things. I wish I could send a message for the people: They have to be together in everything. If they do that, we can be together.[106]

In diaspora Tsehay sees her goal as helping Ethiopian immigrants to overcome the trauma of separation and to sustain traditional Ethiopian culture:

> Some of them are using the music to relax and forget any stress. They have a lot of things on their mind, and they come to listen to music and to forget everything. I'm glad I'm here for the people. They come to me and they say, "When we come here, we forget about our problems. Thank you so much." I'm glad I'm able to help them in this way. . . . You know, I want to

continue with the cultural songs because the people who are here like to listen to the traditional ones. That's why I am trying to keep that alive.[107]

Tsehay hopes to attract a wider audience for her music but is uncertain of how to achieve that goal:

I want to sing in English, but I want to sing about my culture. If I sing in English about my country, everybody can understand what I say. But you know the problem: I still don't speak English well enough.[108]

The Dukem Group

On many occasions at Dukem, members of the audience inquired about hiring the group to perform at parties or weddings. The contacts resulted in engagements and led Minale and his colleagues to consider giving the group a name, Dukem Group, printing a business card, and running the ensemble like a business.[109]

The Dukem Group performed at weddings in Ethiopian diaspora communities and at other venues for general audiences. One such occasion was an appearance under the name "the Upper Nile Ethiopian Ensemble" at the American Folk Festival in Bangor, Maine.[110] For this performance, an ensemble of six—Minale Dagnew Bezu, Setegn Atanaw, Tsehay Amare, Solomon Bedany, Ashenafi Mitiku, and another dancer, presented a forty-five-minute program. The compressed set represented much of geographic and ethnic Ethiopia, performing music and dance traditions from Gondar and Gojjam of the northern Amhara region, Gambela in the west, and Oromo from the largest region, Oromia, which stretches across much of central Ethiopia and extends south to the Kenyan border, and Gurage and Nilo-Saharan peoples of the Southern Nations, Nationalities, and Peoples' Region in the southwest. The musicians were festively dressed throughout with an emphasis on the then politically powerful Tigray region: Tsehay wore a white dress of rough white fabric known as *Mekele* cloth from its association with and manufacture in Mekele, Tigray, with embroidered crosses on the bodice; Solomon Bedany, who played the drums, had on a *Mekele* cloth top and pants; Minale wore traditional white national dress with a banner across his shirt with the red, green, and yellow colors of the Ethiopian flag; and Setegn wore an all-white outfit with a headband decorated in red, green, and yellow. Instead of his usual electric drum, Solomon played a set of small Ethiopian secular drums arranged on a stand, each drum, including the frame, covered with a leopard skin cloth that he had purchased from a friend. The musicians performed without pause, the dancers running offstage to change in an adjacent small tent. The two dancers wore the same "ethnic" outfits they used at Dukem, and the audience responded particularly enthusiastically to the energetic Oromo, Nilo-Saharan, and Gurage dances. The musicians and vocalist also contributed elaborate musical numbers during the costume changes, featuring *masenqo* and *krar* solos by Setegn and Minale and songs by Tsehay that showed off her virtuosity.[111]

Orchestral Genealogies and Signs of Connection

The line of descent from Orchestra Ethiopia to the Nile Ethiopian Ensemble to the Dukem / Upper Nile Ethiopian Ensemble is affirmed on one level by nominal connections: the name of each ensemble builds on a name used by a prior group. Tesfaye Lemma's musical legacy throughout is clear, sustained by his more than four hundred musical compositions and arrangements that reverberate in musical folklore shows performed in Dukem Ethiopian Restaurant. There, several veterans of the Nile Ethiopian Ensemble have performed familiar medleys of Ethiopian cultural music for both Ethiopians and tourists, with dancers in ethnic dress bringing ethnic communities' material cultures and bodily motions to life.

But deeper inquiry reveals many other important insights, not the least of which are the lifelong links among participating musicians sustained across boundaries of time and space. Orchestra Ethiopia, and the streams of musical and cultural performance that it has transmitted, also reflect what would otherwise be an unacknowledged encounter of Ethiopian expressive culture and music with the outside world. Somewhat ironically, a musical genre intended to convey ethnic particularism in service of Ethiopian nationalism proves to be, on deeper investigation, a modern, creative hybrid. If the life and work of Tesfaye, who lived between cultures long before he entered the American diaspora, is one center of a process drawing on a multiplicity of sources at home and abroad, so too was Orchestra Ethiopia. Here we have graphic examples of the process of "creative incorporation," a historical Ethiopian response to foreign influence that is both creative and transformative.[112]

That Tesfaye's efforts failed to establish audiences for an Ethiopian folklore orchestra in the United States also offers important insights into the changing world of Ethiopian diaspora music and culture. Tesfaye, who commanded enormous knowledge and inventiveness within the cultural music domain, lost his institutional anchor in Ethiopia and faced truly insurmountable barriers as he sought to establish an Ethiopian folklore orchestra in the United States. The United States did not provide even a modest audience for his brand of traditional African music, and the Nile Ethiopian Ensemble was unable to survive economically on the basis of approximately eighty public performances in their calendar between 1994 and 1998.[113] The orchestra's medley of Ethiopian ethnic music and dances, originally conceived in the 1960s and 1970s to celebrate diverse Ethiopian subcultures within an imperial framework of national unity, lost much of its appeal in the diaspora community, itself fiercely divided by Eritrean independence in 1991 and policies encouraging ethnic separatism at home. The Nile Ethiopian Ensemble's performances were received ambivalently at best amid the rapidly changing narratives of Ethiopian history, politics, and identity.[114]

But other structural changes also doomed Tesfaye's Nile Ethiopian Ensemble. Most concerts mounted for immigrant Ethiopian audiences in emerging Ethiopian communities throughout North America were aimed at a younger demographic, featuring a popular singer accompanied by a band that supported the audience's social dancing. At the same time, a new channel for traditional performance that did emerge in the late 1980s, as some Ethiopian Americans began to prosper, was not suited for a large ensemble: occasions such as weddings increased the demand for cultural musicians, but they mainly drew on solo instrumentalists or very small groups. The world of the Ethiopian cultural musician in the American diaspora came to resemble, albeit in distinctive late twentieth- and early-twenty-first-century settings, the career of the Ethiopian *azmari*, who traveled to perform at the behest of wealthy patrons, providing traditional music, song, and dance at life-cycle events. The Nile Ethiopian Ensemble did perform for some diaspora community events but was a large ensemble that incurred high travel costs and required substantial fees. Because the ensemble was mainly invited to perform at free and public Ethiopian community events without ticket sales, the ensemble proved not to be viable economically.

Although music has long been a site of political commentary and resistance at home in Ethiopia, none of the Nile Ethiopian Ensemble's musicians was prominently associated with political commentary through music. Tesfaye had made his strongest political statement by seeking asylum in the United States; his most political music consisted of compositions he created for the government in the early days of the revolution, before he became disillusioned with the revolution's course.[115]

Although he did not invent Orchestra Ethiopia from whole cloth, Tesfaye institutionalized the role of the orchestra in perpetuating Ethiopian traditional music and culture both at home and in diaspora. This template has ironically proven to be particularly generative in Ethiopia, continued through the revolutionary period, and proliferated in the postrevolutionary period until the present. In diaspora, Tesfaye's success was episodic and muted, marked in the end by great despair. Moments of triumph were few and far between, such as when Tesfaye received the Ethiopian Millennium Award from the *Ethiopian Yellow Pages* on the occasion of its Fourteenth Anniversary at Washington, DC, in 2007, an event that celebrated his contribution with a performance by the Dukem Group at that award ceremony.[116]

The early presence of Orchestra Ethiopia at Addis Ababa hotels, however, has continued and proliferated. At the Crown Hotel on old Debre Zeit road in the capital, there is a special large hall for cultural music performances constructed in the style of three large, connected rural houses with thatched roofs, a stage running along one side. A dozen musicians perform regular shows there, including instrumentalists playing two *krar*, one *masenqo*, and a traditional drum set. All these instruments have been modernized, with steel strings and amplification; a technician sits nearby, adjusting an amplifier. The instrumentalists accompany a male and female singer along with six dancers (three men and three women), who frequently leave the stage to dance around the perimeter of the tables at which their audience is seated. All are in national dress and the dancers move offstage to change to various regional and ethnic dress between musical numbers. Following Orchestra Ethiopia models, the repertory includes Amhara, Oromo, Gurage, and Harari musics and dances. With no narrator or other explanations for the audience, the instruments and singers maintain a continuous, lively stream of musical sound.[117]

Cultural music has also been extended into other lively new restaurant and entertainment venues in Addis Ababa's thriving world of tourism. In 2003 Yod Abyssinia Restaurant was established, called Yod (lit., witness or speak out) in the Gurage language of its owner, Tizazu Kore. Yod Abyssinia features live performance of songs and dances from a cross section of Ethiopian ethnic communities, attracting a large audience composed of both tourists and local people. An ensemble consisting of a quartet of traditional instrumentalists sits on the stage, and singers and dancers perform on different levels of the multitiered room where the dining tables are located. Individuals celebrating birthdays and anniversaries are called forward to the stage for recognition. Probably because of the large number of tourists in the audience and visitors from diaspora, the offspring of whom do not necessarily speak Ethiopian languages, Yod Abyssinia provides Amharic and English audio descriptions of the songs and dances, explaining their significance and ethnic provenance.[118] Other Addis Ababa restaurants, such as Hebir Ethiopia Cultural Restaurant on Bole Road, offer regular folklore performances of small traditional ensembles with singers.[119]

Orchestra Ethiopia is much more than a footnote in Ethiopian music history, and it is surely more significant than I could have anticipated when I first visited the ensemble at the Haile Selassie I University Creative Arts Centre in 1974. Beyond the many social and economic insights traced above, this extended case study provides powerful methodological lessons.

Close ethnographic work over time enables one to map complicated personal, political, economic, and musical factors that together provide a multitemporal narrative. Beyond offering a nuanced overview of the manner in which traditional music in general and individual musicians in particular have had a continued role in Ethiopian diasporic life, the study illustrates graphically how musicians associated with traditional repertories encountered very different economic and artistic opportunities in different locales over the last forty years. Multitemporal studies pay their biggest dividends as connections proliferate and lead the researcher in unexpected directions. An awareness of the potential for multitemporal research is particularly important at the start of projects when one has no idea whatsoever what might emerge. Although it may not be immediately obvious at any given moment during the research process, ethnography is continually in dialogue with history, and the data gathered in the present are always part of a longer historical continuum. When ethnography meets history, it provides multileveled perspectives that may be otherwise hidden.

One of the privileges of pursuing musical ethnography over time is that one's work may provide insights into and shed light on unexpected corners of the human experience. It enables one to appreciate the efforts of sentinel musicians such as Tesfaye Lemma, the interventions of outsiders such as Charles Sutton that would otherwise be invisible, and the depth of human relationships that grow out of musical collaboration. Ethnography and history prove not to be bound by casual encounters, but rather to be deeply joined to each other, their relationship unfolding over time in a complex and meaningful process.

✳ 9 ✳

Creativities

MUSICAL INVENTION AND
DIASPORIC CHALLENGES

Fät't'ärä
GENERAL MEANING: To create
MUSICAL MEANING: To compose, to improvise

Creativity shapes the agency of Ethiopians and the outcomes of both individual and collective actions in various domains of Ethiopian society.[1]
The Amharic words *fät'ari* (creator) and *fät'ära* (creativity) stem from the
same root *fät' t'ärä* (to create).[2] The phrase *yäfät'ära ch'ɔlota*, (lit., creative
artists) extends the notion of *fät'ara* to artistic creativity.[3] Beyond the deep
connection of the Ethiopian term *fät'ari* to the creator embedded in the
Ethiopian Christian worldview, *fät't'ärä* can, at times, like its English translation, move beyond creation or invention to imply fabrication or lying.[4]

As we have seen in the case of Orchestra Ethiopia, creative musical initiatives can emerge despite the daunting pressures of diaspora life, even
while such ventures may in the end be impossible to sustain. The diasporic
challenge of being caught between cultures can inhibit creativity for some,
while it can provide exposure to new cultural materials that others in the
arts may successfully explore. (See plate 9.1.) Domains such as religious
musical practices, which may at first appear to be resistant to change, on
closer scrutiny may be found to embrace innovations.

As we have seen in the discussion of "creative incorporation" in chapter 8, Ethiopian musicians experience and speak about creativity in terms
that take foreign influences into account. One can look to those involved
in musical creativity in order to witness the impact of new social and cultural settings on their creative efforts. An Ethiopian dancer who frequently
performs abroad notes that he values outside influences on his increasingly
transnational dance style and suggests that "One hand cannot clap. . . . You
need the other. . . . It is good to freely exchange."[5]

Mulatu Astatke, whose Ethio-jazz we explored in chapter 7, has de-

PLATE 9.1 Mount Dashen, the highest peak in Ethiopia, here creatively reimagined as an Ethiopian Mount Rushmore, carved with the faces of four powerful Ethiopian emperors (left to right): Yohannes IV (1872–89), Menelik II (1889–1913), Tewodros II (1855–68), and Haile Selassie I (1930–74). Courtesy of YohannesAramde.com.

veloped his own personal theory of creativity, on which he elaborated in an interview.[6] A creative person, according to Mulatu, is one who "starts something"; as the primary example of Ethiopian musical creativity, Mulatu named Saint Yared, the founder of Ethiopian Church music, whom he considers to be "the originator." Mulatu uses the Amharic word *fät'ari* to refer to someone "who creates something" and extends it to include a composer such as himself, who uses "new material with a new concept." He further notes that "there are two ways [in which one] can create," distinguishing between the "first creativity" of musicians from isolated locales, who invent their own traditions without outside influences, and a second form of creativity, such as his own (more similar to Levine's notion of creative incorporation), which permits a musician to absorb musical experiences from a wide variety of sources at home and worldwide and then to combine them in new ways. Mulatu views his own creativity as "definitely combining and giving a value to the first *fät'ära*." As an example, Mulatu cites the distinctive harmonies influenced by studies of Western music theory that he conceived based on the traditional Ethiopian modes (*qenyet*), which are used to accompany traditional Ethiopian melodies. Similarly, Mulatu has taken familiar Ethiopian rhythms, both from well-known Ethiopian regional musics and from dance, and transformed them within jazz.[7]

Just as musicians consider external influences vital to their creative processes, they link aspects of agency to creativity. In developmental psychology, creativity is in fact viewed as a component of individual agency, and "the creative individual is one who *regularly* solves problems or fashions products in a *domain,* and whose work is considered both novel and acceptable by knowledgeable members of a field."[8] In contrast, anthropologists have focused more on collective social notions for understanding creativity as "human activities that transform existing cultural practices in a manner that a community or certain of its members find of value."[9] The tripartite theory of agency set forth by Emirbayer and Mische, discussed in this volume's preface, implicitly includes what is termed the "creative reconstructive dimension of agency" as part of "the *projective* dimension of human agency."[10]

Diaspora life brings with it a range of new experiences that have catalyzed Ethiopian creativity in a variety of domains. But it is also the case that any opportunities for practicing musical creativity require stability and that the economic strains of diaspora life too often render creative music making out of reach despite accommodations of many sorts. Just as it takes two hands to clap, it takes economic stability to provide time and resources for musical creativity. In this chapter we will first consider the economic and social challenges to diasporic music making that demand their own full measure of creativity by the immigrant generation. Next, we will explore the manner in which individual musicians respond to such challenges, exploring creative initiatives in musical and cultural domains associated with traditional, popular, and sacred musics in the Ethiopian diaspora.

Economic Challenges to Diasporic Creativity

Throughout ethnographic interviews about music making with Ethiopian immigrants in diaspora, one encounters constant testimony about the economic challenges of pursuing a musical career. Even brief discussions of diasporic life inevitably turn to the difficulties of financial viability. It is clear that a great deal of effort in diaspora must be devoted to the most basic aspects of survival, as musicians struggle to gain a financial foothold to cover basic living expenses. Many older immigrant musicians despair over the impact of economic pressures on younger musicians' artistic aspirations and values:

It's very sad that most of the musicians are not in their own proper profession. Everybody is running for money instead of working for their own profession. . . . We could have been organizing and done something instead of everybody doing whatever he or she wanted to do. We have to differentiate between money and the art. If the art is developed, the money will come later on. If you perform good things, the person who sees that says "ah!" Without doing something you cannot have the appreciation.... I work for my own country not for the *genzeb* [money].[11]

We can take as an early example of the impact of financial constraints on performance opportunities the case of the Walias Band, which fled Ethiopia for the United States in 1981. The Walias Band performed regularly at Amha Eshete's Ibex Club in Washington, DC, during their initial period in the United States and soon after made what was likely the first musical tour by an Ethiopian ensemble across the country to perform for newly established Ethiopian immigrant communities. However, the band quickly encountered severe economic problems. The price of concert tickets were prohibitive for most Ethiopian immigrants, making it impossible to charge their audiences fees high enough to cover travel expenses:

Say I have to go somewhere, [for example,] Atlanta. Before that I was in Dallas, you know? I go Friday, Saturday I perform there, Sunday I will be at home. When we came with the Walias [in 1981], we went on Monday driving, not taking a plane. By the time we got to Atlanta, with hotel, food, everything, there was a lot of expense. And then, maybe the show is successful; the next week we have to stay in the hotel, we have to drive, we have to pay drivers. It was crazy. That's why it didn't work. Too much overhead.[12]

But even the critical mass of Ethiopians and Eritreans in the Washington, DC, metropolitan area has not provided support for the large number of immigrant musicians there who struggle to maintain their musical careers. Most popular traditional musicians who arrive in the United States are shocked to find out how difficult the economic challenges can be:

Over in Ethiopia, if you're a musician, you could do that full time. But here, in order to survive, you have to compromise. You cannot just play music, you have to have another kind of work, too. So, there might be a few fortunate musicians who can make a living out of music, but very few.[13]

Few cases detailing economic pressures on musicians have garnered more public attention than a story that began to circulate informally in the DC area around 2010. Word spread about an unnamed Ethiopian musician who for years had been seen playing a keyboard in his taxi while waiting for clients at Dulles Airport. Eventually, inquiries revealed that the musician was Hailu Mergia, a former member of the Walias Band, who had left a burgeoning Ethiopian musical career as a composer and arranger to settle in Washington, DC. In 2018 Hailu described to a reporter the activity that had attracted attention at Dulles Airport:

> "After I drop my customer, I grab my keyboard from the trunk and sit in the car and practice," Hailu said. "When I compose, I record it with my phone. I do it with my voice, whistling, whatever; and then I put it on the keyboard and record it in my car. I send it to the other musicians in my trio: 'Learn this line.'" [Hailu] pauses and smiles: "I always think: if you have a good bassline you can create anything."[14]

After a hiatus of several decades, Hailu was rediscovered and was able to start his musical career anew in Washington, DC.[15] The story is unusual only in its positive outcome.[16] Most Ethiopian taxi drivers interviewed in the one study carried out to date in the Washington, DC, metropolitan area are from middle-class backgrounds and had expected to hold white-collar jobs in diaspora; when they could not find work in their preferred professions, they used the Ethiopian immigrant network to locate opportunities in transportation industries.[17] Many musicians drive taxis in order to meet basic subsistence needs and find it to be an occupation that can accommodate musical performance schedules, although not without some constraints:

> Right now, I'm struggling and it's hard. . . . When I first came here, I had a taxi cab license, no job right now, so I have to drive a cab. . . . If you take taxi cab driving, for instance, if you don't work Friday nights and Saturday nights, you're not going to make much money. And if you are tired, you're not going to sing very well. You know that. For your voice to really come out the way it should, you have to have rested long enough, your body has to be relaxed.[18]

Many musicians routinely work two or more jobs to cover their living costs while sustaining dreams of creative initiatives they wish to undertake. "When I sing, I work at a nursing home and in different hospitals. I work in parking lots these days."[19] One accomplished church musician mused that

> the practicalities of living life here and keeping the tradition going are very tough. If I had time, I would like to contact other Ethiopians, but I don't have time. You know, I have dreams, a lot of dreams of *aqqwaqwam* [litur-

gical music and dance] because this is my profession. And so, I don't teach it because I can't, I don't have time, that's why.[20]

Even musicians who do locate some performance opportunities dis-cuss the continual financial strain within a community where only a few can afford fees to engage an entire band to perform. We have already seen in chapter 8 the negative impact of this reality on the Nile Ethiopian En-semble in its years of activity in the North American diaspora. In contrast to Ethiopia, where June through August is the rainy season, when travel is difficult, the summer months in the West are the high season for landing gigs for weddings and concerts in the diaspora.[21] Some immigrants who have prospered after decades in diaspora can pay the fees of ensembles fronted by well-known musicians who travel to perform at weddings, but "one-man bands" with a keyboardist who also sings are the most afford-able for the majority; traditional ensembles with *masenqo*, *krar*, and per-cussion, as well as dancers and a singer, are much too expensive to hire. "They cannot afford to take all those musicians," explained one singer.[22]

Musical Networks in the North American Diaspora

Bookings are made primarily through informal social networks. People contact musicians directly or contract with a vocalist, who then arranges for a keyboard player to accompany him or her. Indeed, pairs of musicians, such as a singer and an instrumentalist, tend to collaborate and travel to-gether.[23] Musicians who perform in weddings do not generally work on the concert circuit because, unless one is a major star, wedding perfor-mances reduce one's status and therefore one's financial prospects for other concert engagements.[24]

In part because of the dispersed nature of Ethiopian communities in urban locales across the United States and Canada, multiple informal net-works must be nurtured to sustain diasporic musical life. One excellent traditional *masenqo* player and singer who operates as a one-man band and is especially popular to hire for weddings confirmed that

> it's by word of mouth. People know me, they know I'm a good player [*masenqo*] and, when my name comes up, there'll always be somebody who has my phone number and people will be able to reach me.[25]

Those who emigrated from Ethiopia during or after their formative years inevitably draw on a variety of longtime personal ties. As we have seen in the cases of Yehunie Belay and Bezawork Asfaw, they and many others performed in ensembles during the revolutionary years and share that experience as well as the repertories they performed. For an older cohort of musicians, including Selam Seyoum Woldemariam, Moges Habte, and Ali Birra, the many excellent bands, including Walias, Ibex, Roha, Ethio Stars, and others that emerged in Addis Ababa and Asmara during the decades before the revolution, anchor lifelong musical collaborations and personal ties. The Yared School of Music in Addis Ababa spawned a good number of musicians, including Betelehem Melaku, Behailu Kassahun, and Beniam Bedru Hussein; Bezawork Asfaw did not attend the Yared School but did sing with one of their string quartets.[26] Informal networks are supplemented by individuals who represent musicians as promoters, but these individuals more often devote time to bringing musicians from Ethiopia who can command higher fees than those living in diaspora.

Although with a few exceptions such as Melaku Gelaw and Betelehem Melaku's father-daughter relationship, music making does not tend to be a hereditary profession. However, interviews revealed some unexpected familial connections: Tsehay Amare is the niece of the well-known Ethiopian pop singer Alemayehu Eshete, and keyboardist Behailu Kassahun is the brother of the star Ethiopian singer Abinet Agonafir. These ties have been refreshed as travel opportunities between homeland and diaspora reopened since the end of the revolution.

Among those of Orthodox Christian faith, years spent singing in church choirs established just before the revolution (to be discussed later in this chapter) link the musical experience and support networks of those who came of age during that time, including Hana Shenkute, Bezawork Asfaw, Getatchew Gebregiorgis, and Getahun Atlaw Garede. Many singers, as we have seen, share repertory, such as the large number of songs with lyrics composed by poet Alemtsehay Wedajo.[27]

New musical-social networks have also been established in the United States. If Mulatu Astatke was the first African student enrolled at the Berklee College of Music (at the time called Schillinger House) in the late 1950s, others have followed in his footsteps.[28] Moges Habte completed a correspondence course with Berklee while still in Ethiopia. In chapter 10 we will discuss the experiences of Abegasu Kibrework Shiota and Henock Temesgen, both in the Berklee alumni part of that international network.

To meet clerical and musical needs in the diaspora, the Ethiopian Orthodox Church initiated networks of traveling speakers and musicians. In addition to linking homeland and diaspora churches, this activity encouraged local musicians to reach out to a wider public and to perform at events such as festivals.

Newly established Ethiopian restaurants and non-Ethiopian eateries with Ethiopian clientele (such as Mr. Henry's in DC)[29] have long been sites of live performance. Other performance venues, such as Amha Eshete's Ibex Club in Washington, DC, were important nodes in performance networks.[30]

Musicians who are both skilled and fortunate perform part-time in restaurants and clubs if they live in major diaspora communities, especially the DC metropolitan area and West Coast diaspora centers, that can support regular, live musical performances. However, there is new competition for such opportunities as restaurants increasingly bring popular singers from "back home" on contract to perform for weeks at a time at the venue in order to attract more people.[31] A few musicians have established their own recording studios in their homes, producing and distributing albums for themselves and others mainly outside major American diasporic centers.[32]

Even given strong networks, personal challenges and financial pressures can derail the most promising career. Singer and multi-instrumentalist Betelehem Melaku has had to step back from performing as a one-woman band in order to work full-time as a health aide to help support her family:

> I cannot say that I am a musician because I have to work a lot, day by day, every day. . . . When you come to this country, you have to work, you have to pay your bills, you have to do a lot of tough things. . . . When I was back home, I was a little kid and I didn't have responsibility. I was just focusing on my school. After I came here, I had to help my family. I have to help myself because I have responsibilities and then I still keep doing my music, but you know I'm not satisfied. . . . I still do my music even if I don't make money on it. I love my music.[33]

Betelehem's father, the late, revered performer and instrument-maker Melaku Gelaw (d. 2018), had impressive performing networks but was very selective about where he performed. He, therefore, held a regular job in a nearby factory.[34]

Beyond the enormous ingenuity it takes to survive economically in a new homeland, most immigrants must also make enough money to remit funds to their families at home in Ethiopia. In the words of one musician,

> I have to help the family. Not only me, almost all of the people help their families because their income is not that much. Everything's expensive now.[35]

Another musician supports his siblings and extended family since the death of both his parents, sending home money for educational purposes.[36] Others also attest that most musicians send money home to their families.[37]

Musicians thus have to cultivate networks to line up performances. As noted in chapter 6, some of the more successful musicians have their own websites and a few also advertise their availability in community publications.[38] Others have business cards that they give to those who come to hear them perform and distribute them through Ethiopian shops and restaurants to advertise their availability for performances.[39] Some musicians advertise in the *Ethiopian Yellow Pages*, one of the most striking examples of combined economic and cultural creativity within the Ethiopian American community, a publication whose vice president is musician Yehunie Belay.

Commercial Networks and Creativity in Traditional Music: Yehunie Belay

First published in 1993 in Washington, DC, the *Ethiopian Yellow Pages* was founded by Yeshimebet "Tutu" Belay, an immigrant who came from Ethiopia to the United States with her family during the revolution.[40] Today president of the *Ethiopian Yellow Pages*, Tutu has built a major company that began as a community service and communications network rather than as a commercial venture.[41] The *Ethiopian Yellow Pages* advertises resources for immigrant services to the community, including lawyers offering counsel relevant to immigration and asylum; translation services for important documents; medical services; a monthly newsletter and website; and an annual exposition.[42] Tutu runs the business with her husband Yehunie Belay, who serves as vice president and is one of the most prominent traditional Ethiopian musicians active in the diaspora.

Born in 1968 in what was then Gojjam province, Yehunie began singing in his local revolutionary music ensemble when he was nine years old. He found his way into performance early on when he led groups of children around town singing traditional songs on holidays such as Christmas and New Year. Yehunie remembers being encouraged to perform by his teacher who, when he sang the Ethiopian national anthem at school, told him, "Oh, you are going to have a good voice. You'll be a good singer."[43]

Yehunie learned repertory from farmers and other workers in his area and then sang and danced on stage dressed in traditional garb. He performed in the well-known Gojjam *kinet* in Bahir Dar, then a provincial capital in the northwest, and was well aware of the network of revolutionary musical ensembles in neighboring regions: "Everywhere had its traditional *kinet*," he emphasized. In 1981 Yehunie released his first cassette in Ethiopia, *Yagere Lij* (Country boy). He recalls that during the "Derg time," the *kinet* performed traditional music, and so traditional things are what he saw and heard and are what he does. Although no one in his family was a musician, Yehunie became an accomplished performer, dramatizing his songs with costumes and choreography, knowing that "when you see the drama, it's good. You see a lot of culture."[44]

Yehunie was keenly aware that the Derg controlled everything during his apprenticeship with the *kinet*. "You had to serve them, and I was hoping to go straight to be[ing] an artist and a singer." When he asked for a two-week vacation to record his first album in the capital but stayed away for six weeks longer than the release time he had been granted, soldiers arrested him and jailed him in Addis Ababa. After a week, they returned Yehunie to Bahir Dar, where he was again imprisoned, but he was eventually allowed to return to the ensemble and to complete his cassette and make a television advertisement to publicize it. Yehunie's recording reached Ethiopian radio playlists, and he took advantage of the general instability just before the downfall of the Derg to move to the Ethiopian capital. In 1991 Yehunie received a contract for a concert tour in the United States. While in Los Angeles, Yehunie met Tutu, who was helping her brothers promote Yehunie's concerts. After four months in Los Angeles, Yehunie moved to Washington, DC, to perform at the Ambassel Restaurant, where he worked for a year, eventually releasing his first American CD (*Alo Lulo*) in 1994: "I wanted to show our beautiful culture to people."[45]

Yehunie juggles his work as vice president of the *Ethiopian Yellow Pages* with an active performing career as one of the best-known performers of Ethiopian traditional music. Although copies of the *Ethiopian Yellow Pages* are distributed both free in hard copy and online,[46] income from advertising fees, from other publications of their Feker Publishing Company, and Yehunie's active concert career have made Yehunie and Tutu among the most successful members of the Ethiopian diaspora community. When travel to Ethiopia opened up again in the 1990s, Yehunie and his family began to return regularly to their homeland for family visits, to carry out charitable work, and to give Yehunie time to pursue his creative work by learning new songs and producing new recordings. Here one can see the manner in which the worlds of economic initiative, sentinel activity, and musical creativity reinforce each other and converge.[47]

As Yehunie has noted, "my talent is in traditional music, explaining my culture."[48] As a specialist in *bahelawi* music, Yehunie performs only songs in Amharic and on his recordings focuses on repertory from the central highlands where he was born. However, on stage, Yehunie will often include traditional songs of communities from other regions, includ-

ing Oromo and Tigrayan songs; in this way, his traditional stage performances resemble the panoply of ethnic music and dance styles innovated
by Ethiopian traditional ensembles that emerged in the 1950s and 1960s.
Yehunie primarily performs publicly backed by a group of traditional instruments, especially *krar*, *masenqo*, and drums, but occasionally he will
employ a keyboardist playing a synthesizer.

Yehunie does compose, but only traditional songs, sometimes with
new melodies and lyrics in a traditional style. His songs often incorporate sounds that evoke the rural Ethiopian landscape, such as the chirping
of birds; a shepherd's flute plays on the title track for his CD *Alo Lulo*.
Yehunie often films "classic" music videos while in Ethiopia and releases
DVDs for each of his traditional CDs, a process that can require his presence abroad for a couple of months. A lively presence on stage, Yehunie
jokes that "whether they listen or not, I'm a good dancer."[49] His audience
is made up of Ethiopians living in diaspora and an enthusiastic public
in Ethiopia as well. Although he would like to attract a broader listening public, he is uncomfortable setting English lyrics to traditional tunes.

Very supportive of other traditional musicians, Yehunie gives a number
of them free space in the *Ethiopian Yellow Pages*:

> I'm trying to help my friends or artists and . . . I just put (in the *Yellow Pages*)
> more than ten artists with their names, pictures, and [phone] number. At
> least I can help them by this. If somebody needs them, they'll call them
> and contact them. And most of them do not pay money to advertise.[50]

Yehunie's commitment to traditional culture extends to his own home,
where he has made certain that his children have learned to speak and
read Amharic using the latest educational software. As vice president of
the *Ethiopian Yellow Pages*, he oversees management and graphics while
traveling internationally to perform at weddings and to appear at festivals
and concerts through various promoters across Europe, England, Australia, Sweden, and Israel. He and Tutu are active politically in Ethiopian
affairs at home and abroad and are generous philanthropists for worthy
causes. On the occasion of meeting Hillary Clinton during her campaign
for a US Senate seat, Yehunie presented her one of his CDs and then responded to her thank-you letter with the admonition: "Don't forget my
country."[51] (See plate 9.2.)

If Yehunie devotes time, creativity, and resources to his musical career,
to his business, and to active community building in both Ethiopia and the
United States, his story is a relatively unusual diaspora tale of economic
success, especially for an immigrant who came to the United States as an

PLATE 9.2 Yehunie Belay presenting his latest CD, *Kuku Melekote* (Cuckoo dove) to senatorial candidate Hillary Rodham Clinton in 2000. Courtesy of Yehunie Belay.

adult. He has continued also to innovate within his established traditional musical style.

Although musical creativity can be manifested in any musical style, from cultural to modern, and some of the most creative musicians are those of an older generation who have retained their primary residences in Ethiopia, especially Ethio-jazz innovator Mulatu Astatke, one does find an active contingent creating American and global popular styles among Ethiopians who arrived as young children in the United States. Here we can look at the career and music of Meklit Hadero to understand factors that shape musical creativity across repertories and generations.

Mobile Creativities: The Music of Meklit Hadero

Meklit Hadero was born in the Ethiopian capital, Addis Ababa, to a father from the Kambata ethnic community in south-central Ethiopia, in the region known since 1994 as the Southern Nations, Nationalities, and Peoples' Regional State;[52] her mother was from the Amhara ethnic group dominant in Ethiopian political life until the beginning of the revolution. Meklit spent much of her first year in the care of family members in Ethiopia after her parents departed for medical fellowships in East Germany shortly after her birth in 1980. She was reunited with her parents in Europe in 1981 and, a year later, the entire family received asylum in the United States. The trauma of this migration process has been described by Meklit's older sister, Meron, who has written about what she later learned about this experience from her parents:

> I don't remember that my mother prayed and fretted and did everything she could to get my baby sister out of Ethiopia, where she had to stay behind. I don't remember yet another complicated plan taking shape; that to get the right paperwork, we had to pretend that my aunt was her mother, someone else her father. When their plane from Addis Ababa to Paris refueled in Frankfurt and they walked off to join us there, I don't remember my mother's heart breaking when my sister didn't remember us anymore; we were unrecognizable to her after just several months apart.[53]

Meklit's family lived in a number of US locales such as Iowa, New York, and Florida, a peripatetic existence throughout which Meklit was exposed to Ethiopian music primarily through her parents' collection of cassettes. But Meklit was also early on "a student of the greats like Joni Mitchell and Bob Dylan" and had a "special affection" for Leonard Cohen's music, which she encountered through hearing Nina Simone's version of his song "Suzanne."[54] Meklit identifies herself as an Ethiopian American who lives "on both sides of the hyphen," an apt description of her musical identity a well.[55]

A graduate from Yale University in 2002 with a degree in political science, Meklit exemplifies a generation of Ethiopian musicians whose experience since their earliest years has been shaped by both their Ethiopian heritages and their American upbringings. She has resided since 2004 in the San Francisco Bay Area, composing her first song in 2005 and launching her musical career with the release of her first album in 2007. With six albums now in circulation, Meklit's 2017 release *When the People Move, the Music Moves Too* climbed to number four on the iTunes World Music Charts and number one on the North American College and Community Radio World Music Charts.[56] (See plate 9.3.) However, Meklit is aware that her career is untraditional, characterized by a great deal of genre crossing in her music and frequent artistic changes of course. Meklit believes that she has encountered barriers because some consider her jazz as "too world-music" and her world music as "too jazzy and pop." "One has to choose: jazz, rock, or folk!" Meklit protests. "What is this?" they say, "she does not fit a category."[57]

PLATE 9.3 *Meklit: When the People Move, the Music Moves Too* combines
influences of this singer-songwriter's several "sonic homes."
Courtesy of Meklit Hadero and Six Degrees Records. Photograph by John Nilsen.

A singer-songwriter known for her thoughtful lyrics,[58] one can track
Meklit's embrace of a number of styles through her CDs. Her first commercial release, *On a Day Like This,* moves through the course of a day,
narrating various moods and experiences in its ten songs.[59] But the tight
temporal focus of this CD belies its stylistic diversity as Meklit moves
from folk to jazz to blues, accompanying many songs with her acoustic
guitar and an ever-changing, unconventional band with electric guitar,
drum kit, bass, cello, viola, piano, a variety of woodwinds and brass, and
a Middle Eastern *ney.* Meklit credits her inspiration to multiple sources,
and her musical styles shift rapidly both within and among the songs.
She incorporates jazzy, New Orleans–like instrumental choruses (track 2,
"Float and Fall"), blues ballads (track 4, "You and the Rain"), and innovative covers of classics such as "Feeling Good" from the 1964 musical *The*

Roar of the Greasepaint—the Smell of the Crowd.[60] Meklit's treatment of "Feeling Good" is unconventional and borders on the cross-cultural, as it begins with a solo *ney* introduction followed by a long, unaccompanied vocal passage before settling in for the rest of the song.

Even on this first album, Ethiopian homeland influences are clearly apparent: included is the well-known Ethiopian song, "Abbay Mado" (Beyond the Nile).[61] Performed by Meklit in Amharic, "Abbay Mado," shaped by jazz, is the only song not in English on the album. Subsequent tracks in *On a Day Like This* have an Afro-Latin and Caribbean twist with occasional blue notes, use of the clave, and a big-band sound. Throughout, Meklit reshapes her vocals in the best blues style, inflecting different timbres and bending pitches. In sum, Meklit's first album moves across multiple repertories of various cultural origins, incorporating influences of African American, Latin, and Ethiopian origin.

One finds a similar heterogeneity of repertory and styles in Meklit's 2014 CD *Meklit: We Are Alive,*[62] which one listener summed up with the observation that Meklit is "constantly bringing together the tattered corners of a disparate and fragmented world."[63] The title song, "We Are Alive," incorporates elements of samba and a variety of sonic effects, "including a Casio that sounds like an electric kalimba."[64] Most songs on this CD are composed by Meklit, with the exception of a traditional Ethiopian tune "Kemekem" (I like your Afro), for which her video was named a Top 15 African Music Video of the Year by Okayafrica.[65] Along with a soul-influenced cover of Sting's "Bring on the Night," Meklit's rendition of "A Train" references and riffs on Duke Ellington's classic "Take the A Train."

Other tracks provide a glimpse of Meklit's growing engagement with Afrofuturism, the African American philosophy and aesthetic usually attributed to the creativity of jazz musician Sun Ra (1914–93). An "intersection of imagination, technology, the future, and liberation," the phenomenon preceded the introduction of the term *Afrofuturism,* which was coined by cultural critic Mark Dery in 1994.[66] Afrofuturism is a philosophical and artistic exploration that seeks "to unearth the missing history of people of African descent and their roles in science, technology, and science fiction."[67] Meklit's songs, such as "Stuck on the Moon" from *Meklit: We Are Alive,* embrace this aesthetic and signal the growing affinity of many younger Ethiopian American musicians with African American culture and tradition.

Meklit's most elaborate Afro-futurist musical collaboration to date has been with the Ethiopian diaspora ensemble CopperWire and is heard on the album *Earthbound,* an outcome of her work with hip-hop musician Gabriel Teodros and emcee and hip-hop pioneer Burntface (Elias Full-

more).[68] The three toured Ethiopia together during May 2011 for performances of Gabriel's "Colored People's Time Machine."[69] In 2012 they released the recording *Earthbound*, tracing the path of a "crew of rogues" in
a missing spacecraft (named *CopperWire*) stolen from an unknown location at an unknown time, with destinations of Addis Ababa and beyond
the solar system and Milky Way Galaxy. Gabriel has remarked that

> the music I think is different than anything we've ever touched on our
> own . . . and the universe we created is being expressed not only in music,
> but also film, literature, apps etc. The story of our first album, *Earthbound*,
> takes place in the year 2089. My character is half-human and half-alien (he's
> bilactical, if you will) and coming to Earth for the first time in his life.[70]

Afrofuturism is also clearly wedded to diasporic consciousness in
Meklit's 2017 CD *When the People Move, the Music Moves Too*,[71] especially
the arresting track "Supernova," also released as a music video.[72] Meklit
notes that "when someone asks you where you are from, you name a country and it means something. . . . But beyond place, there are older stories,
of hydrogen, helium, and the stars."[73]

Meklit links the development of her musical style to mobility and the
various places that have shaped her experience:

> I was born in Ethiopia, grew up in Brooklyn, and have lived for the past
> 14 years in the San Francisco Bay Area. These places are my sonic home-
> lands and I make music that touches all of them. I am inspired by the
> unique melodies, rhythms and scales of Ethiopia. I am moved by the im-
> provisation of jazz . . . the way it lets you make the music new every single
> time you play it, and the connection it gives me to the heart and history of
> the United States. I am a singer-songwriter at the core, deeply influenced
> by that American folk ethos that anyone can sing their truth if they can
> strum a chord or two.[74]

Meklit's experience as an Ethiopian-born musician raised in the United
States in the 1980s and 1990s included ample contact with Ethiopia through
recordings and emerging virtual sources and reflects a process of homeland
musical attraction common to many Ethiopian American musicians of her
generation. Visits to Ethiopia also followed after the end of the revolution
when travel restrictions relaxed. Although Meklit had visited Ethiopia in
2001, she first performed there in 2011.[75] Long familiar with the music of
Mulatu Astatke from his recordings and concert tours, Meklit had by 2011
begun performing Ethio-jazz herself. But her experience in Ethiopia made
clear to her the importance of her own creativity:[76]

In mid-2011, my band and I performed shows across Ethiopia. One evening I saw Dr. Mulatu Astatke, the Godfather of Ethio-jazz, in our Addis Ababa audience. We were over the moon at his presence. A legend was among us! Post-performance, he took me aside and asked an unexpected question: Why were we playing the music in exactly the same way it had been played forty years ago? . . . In that moment, standing next to the emptied-out theater, he both took me to task and tasked me. He told me I had to find something to contribute to this music.[77]

Although reinterpretation of music requires creativity, it is also the case that "Ethio-jazz comes from a hybrid soul."[78] One finds clear examples of hybridity in Meklit's own creative process: for instance, Meklit had long wanted to compose a *tizita* and finally took the opportunity to create such a song for a concert she gave at the Yerba Buena Center for the Arts in San Francisco in 2016. To commemorate the recent death of the music producer of the Beatles, George Martin, the so-called "fifth Beatle," Meklit accompanied her "Tizita" on a solo *krar*, sitting barefoot on a stool alone on the stage. She introduced her "Tizita" as follows:

"Tizita" is a song of longing and nostalgia; I wanted to write "Tizita" in English. Three months ago, when George Martin died, I was ready to write it. This is about him in memory of "Yesterday." This is a "Tizita," bitter is the sweetness that we all have somewhere. "Yesterday" is a "Tizita." My "Tizita" is a country I left when I was young. All those memories became this song, my heart's "Tizita."[79]

As in Mulatu's "traveling music" that emerged while he was living abroad, Meklit emphasizes that "I make music based in a life of migration."[80] "There is no such thing as a culture in a freezer," Meklit emphasizes, "but as we travel, we shift. But our memory stays intact."[81]

Beyond her active engagement as a performer across the world on the stage and in recordings, Meklit's musical identity is constructed of what she describes as two main parts: her creative work such as performing and composing and her intense commitment to cultural activism. Meklit articulates a philosophy that has guided her career as creator and activist:

I make the music I wish had existed when I was growing up. I want to create opportunities for other artists. I want to connect with other artists and thinkers. I want to lead with the idea, not the product.[82]

Meklit lives by this creed, and evidence is found in her extraordinary social activism. She is a founder and member since 2009 of the Arba Minch Collective, a network of multidisciplinary artists from the Ethiopian diaspora living in North America who provide each other ongoing support. As cofounder and composer-singer for the Nile Project Collective with Egyptian ethnomusicologist Mina Girgis from 2011 to 2015, Meklit brought together musicians from eleven Nile countries to create music collaboratively through a participatory leadership approach, modeling cross-cultural collaboration on both cultural and environmental levels.[83] In 2014 Meklit was the lead artist in HAFH—Home [Away From] Home—a project to bring together Ethiopian and Eritrean Artists in the Bay Area for a program and festival through the Yerba Buena Center for the Arts.[84] She thinks it vital that musicians engage with their communities, guard their traditions, and feels that "this I can do." This sentinel musician regularly mounts residencies with workshops to empower students on issues related to race and politics, and her TED talk "The Unexpected Beauty of Everyday Sounds" has attracted more than a million viewers.[85] None of these activities are accidental: Meklit emphasizes that "I'm on a fifty-year plan; don't look for the ten-year plan."[86]

Recreating Sacred Song: Merigeta Tsehai Birhanu

Creativity abounds in a full range of diasporic musical domains, even the seemingly most conservative. Innovations in the domain of Ethiopian Orthodox Church music have both transformed Ethiopian Christian ritual practices in diaspora and set into motion intense social changes.

We can enter into this domain through a discussion of the creativity of Tsehai Birhanu (b. 1938), a lifelong musical leader within the Ethiopian Church, trained from his early childhood to be a *merigeta*, the leader of musicians. A product of both traditional rural monasteries and modern universities in Ethiopia and the former Soviet Union, *merigeta* Tsehai held major positions in the Ethiopian Church during the early years of the revolution, including as administrator of the Arsi Diocese in Ethiopia's south and, from 1979 to 1982, as director of the Youth Department at the Patriarchal Head Office in Addis Ababa. But he also was the creative force behind the most dramatic musical innovation in modern Ethiopian Orthodox liturgical music and practice: in 1968, while still a student in Addis Ababa well before the revolution's start, *merigeta* Tsehai began composing hymns in the vernacular (Amharic) language. His hymns circulated at home in Ethiopia and, subsequently, worldwide. Known as *yä'ahud təmahərt bet mäzmur* (*ya'ihud temehert bet mezmur*, Sunday school songs), these

PLATE 9.4 Abebaye Lema leads the choir from Boston's Saint Michael's Ethiopian Orthodox Church in performing Amharic hymns. Collection of author.

hymns have been performed primarily by choirs of women and young people in Ethiopian Orthodox churches across the late twentieth- and twenty-first-century diaspora.[87] (See plate 9.4.) *Merigeta* Tsehai recalled that

> I composed this hymn book, while I was studying at the Holy Trinity College in Addis Ababa. I was assigned by the bishop to teach Bible and songs at every church in Addis Ababa. At that time, I was creating new hymns. One day it came into my mind that I had to print these songs that I am now teaching. I had to make a book according to the Saint Yared tradition. So I wrote the hymns down from September to September, according to the Ethiopian calendar. I sent my book to the bishop and he put his sign of approval on it to be sent to the Department of Evangelization. They said, "if it is published, it will be helpful for the younger generation of the church." . . . And it was published in 1968 EC [c. 1976]. Soon everybody, even the bishops, the archbishops, the scholars, they had that book.[88]

In 1982 *merigeta* Tsehai arrived for postgraduate studies at Princeton University and subsequently applied for and received asylum in the United States.[89] After completing a course of study at Princeton Theological Seminary, he performed clerical duties for the United States Catholic Conference Migration and Refugee Services in New York. From 2003 until his retirement in 2017, he served as priest, head musician, and administrator of St. Michael EOT Church in Mattapan (Boston), Massachusetts. During the years after he received asylum, *merigeta* Tsehai traveled widely to speak to Ethiopian Orthodox congregations across the United States and worked to found an Ethiopian monastery in Houston, Texas. From the 2000s forward, he made trips to Ethiopia to garner support for a church near his birthplace in the former Wollo Province of the country. *Merigeta* Tsehai's blend of superb musical training and continued transmission of a rare vocal style within Ethiopian Christian practice associated particularly with the Qoma Fasiledes monastery, at which he had been trained, render him a unique sentinel figure in perpetuating Ethiopian chant internationally. But, at the same time, *merigeta* Tsehai sensed early on the overwhelming cultural changes facing his church both at home and abroad over the last half century. The repertory of hymns he initiated have been crucial catalysts for changes in Ethiopian Christian diaspora life. It is striking that *merigeta* Tsehai credits Saint Yared for inspiring his innovations:

> If you are interested in what you are studying, your heart will be there every time, and you will be encouraged by the song. I studied deeply the song of, the hymn of Saint Yared and it created in me a composer.[90]

Merigeta Tsehai's Amharic hymns are set in a metered, strophic form with a refrain. The texts and melodies are both newly composed and based on scriptures and traditional chant, intended to be sung by a choir of women and children.

"A Voice Cried Out in the Wilderness" is one of the many hymns composed by *merigeta* Tsehai. Intended for the Ethiopian New Year that takes place in mid- to late September each year, the song's text implores the Virgin Mary to give a new year's blessing.

> A voice cried out in the wilderness,
> Saying prepare the way of God.
> If John told us his witness, let our heart be straight for our God.
> O Virgin Mary, bless for us our New Year.
>
> Every mountain and hill shall be made low; every valley shall be lifted up.
> Unless the mountain is not straight, there is no way to pass.

Let us prepare the way for our God; it will be for our benefit in the
world to come.
O Virgin Mary, bless for us our New Year.

Let us avoid every jealousy from our hearts and inherit righteousness
and compassion.
We have received the Holy Communion to inherit your kingdom.
O Virgin Mary, bless for us our New Year.

He who has two cloths, let him give one to anyone who has none.
Please sanctify us; not to perish with our sin.
O Virgin Mary, bless for us our New Year.

The new hymns were introduced to young people at church Sunday schools and as a result became known as "Sunday school songs" (*ya'ihud temehert bet mezmur*). During the revolution, when groups of more than three people were forbidden to convene, the Sunday schools provided one of the few opportunities for young people to gather without risk of arrest. The songs provided a central activity of these gatherings, quickly spreading across urban Ethiopian Orthodox churches.[91]

By the end of the revolution in the early 1990s, the Sunday school songs and members of the youth choirs that sang them had reached the diaspora, where they again provided an attractive entry for young people reluctant to participate in church rituals:

So, the problem is that everybody in the young generation comes here [to church] with a different idea. Some come for identity, some come for scholarship, whatever. And they don't want to learn Ge'ez and you can't force them. They don't want Ge'ez, only Amharic. Yeah, this is a problem. For them, Ge'ez is like Greek.[92]

Merigeta Tsehai's Sunday school songs in Amharic also brought new participants, women and girls, into church liturgical performance, which from its earliest days had been restricted to males.[93] As *Merigeta* Tsehai explained,

traditionally in Ethiopian Orthodox Church tradition, women do not sing. Even when attending the Mass they stand formally. They don't respond traditionally, especially in countryside. But since Emperor Haile Selassie was crowned, little by little they started to respond during the Mass. But traditionally they just stand firm and they listen. They don't understand the Ge'ez language. When the Mass is finished, they go home and that's it. But just now, very recently, since 1960 or something like that, they have started to follow the Gospel. But before it was not so. They just went to church, they listened to the Mass, and they went home after the Mass was dismissed.[94]

The youth choirs were dominated by women and young girls, sometimes joined by young male deacons. Women also learned to play the large church drum, *kebero*, to accompany the Sunday school songs, and some began to learn important sections of the Ge'ez liturgy as well. Although these changes were sparked in part by his own initiative, *merigeta* Tsehai remained ambivalent about the transformations underway:

> Traditionally it is not allowed for women to sing, and for them to participate with encouragement, never, ever! But now it is coming. For example, in the Catholic church women are reading the holy book but in Ethiopian Church, no! If the congregation sees this, they run away from the Church. No, we can't. Even here the women are participating with the men. Even in Ethiopia, not in the countryside now, but in the cities they do. Now we are losing our tradition. Time will tell in the future.[95]

Although *merigeta* Tsehai has spent the last several decades in the United States, his musical impact has continued to be felt in Ethiopia as well. A young deacon who assisted *merigeta* Tsehai at St. Michael EOT Church in Mattapan remarked after a visit to Ethiopia in 2010,

> these songs have been popular thanks to *merigeta* Tsehai, who started these Sunday school *mezmur* that are in Amharic. Now if you go through the streets of Addis Ababa, in the stores, in taxis, in whatever type of transportation you take, you hear these *mezmur*, Sunday school *mezmur* written in Amharic that are becoming very popular. Today more than twenty artists are publishing five, six CDs of this type, and *merigeta* Tsehai was the first to start it. So now it's more popular, you can hear it in the car, wherever you may be.[96]

Although he began his career as a musical innovator, the later years of *merigeta* Tsehai in diaspora have been devoted to shepherding his own small Boston congregation and helping to guard and guide Ethiopian Christianity across North America. He has been honored for his work by several civic organizations. (See plate 9.5.) His activities in diaspora

PLATE 9.5 *Merigeta* Tsehai Birhanu is honored with a Resolution and
Certificate of Special Congressional Recognition for his "years of dedicated
leadership and commitment to the Ethiopian Community in Greater Boston"
by the Chelsea City Council on December 4, 2006. Collection of author.

were focused on maintaining the traditional Ethiopian Christian liturgy
to the extent possible, a signal challenge given the shortage of clergy and
economic pressures of diaspora life. As one of the most accomplished
scholar-musicians of the Ethiopian Church worldwide, *merigeta* Tsehai
traveled widely:

> I go around the United States. When they celebrate holidays, for example,
> in Houston, Dallas, and Washington, they invite me, and I go there, and
> I give my service.[97]

Merigeta Tsehai's journey has been one he could not have imagined as
an orphan growing up in rural Ethiopia within traditional church schools.
His work, both at home in Ethiopia and abroad, is grounded spiritually
and emotionally in the traditional liturgy in which he was trained while
incorporating new materials and adjusting to new gender relations.

Diaspora realities have created many changes in Ethiopian Orthodox
Christianity in both its ritual practice and community life. The shortage

of trained clergy has sparked creativity in ritual pedagogy, as we have seen in the case of *liqa mezemran* Moges Seyoum in chapter 3. Women active in the Ethiopian Orthodox Church remain primarily involved in the Sunday school choirs, although many have begun to play important roles in church leadership.[98]

Efforts have been made to train young men in something approaching a traditional setting. Debre Haile Kidus Gabriel EOT Church in Decatur, Georgia, innovated a process of informally training young people in the Yared tradition. The head clergyman was training a handful of young boys who were to become deacons, but for a number of years, he took them under his wing and sought to emulate a traditional learning process during weekends when they were not in secular schools.[99] This was a novel attempt to close the gap in ritual knowledge and practice for second-generation Ethiopian Americans. The small group would carry out weekend night studies modeled on traditional Ethiopian monastery training and travel to other communities with their mentoring priest. Their learning process was subsequently emulated at other churches in the Atlanta metropolitan area, in Toronto, and in Los Angeles, as a grassroots educational initiative.[100]

Creativity Coming Full Circle

Some initiatives blend musical and economic creativity, bringing together musicians from across the spectrum of styles and using the collaborations to establish new economic traditions in the community. Most notable are the fundraisers now held regularly by Ethiopian churches, events that began in the early 2000s as churches sought to cover costs of new buildings and to accommodate their rapidly growing congregations. Events ranged from ticketed dinners with traditional Ethiopian cuisine that featured entertainment including comedians and liturgical singers to elaborate concerts with traditional and popular singers, which generated DVDs sold later to raise additional funds.[101] One musical memorial to Saint Yared mounted in 2006 by Debre Haile Kedus Gabriel EOT Church in Washington, DC, featured a dozen well-known popular singers who donated their talents to the concert, along with a number of prominent traditional instrumentalists and the church choirs singing Sunday school songs.[102]

In the past, musicians who performed in clubs and restaurants would not have been welcome to participate in a church event: "If you play at a nightclub, you can't come to church. But now the priest says, 'We appreciate God with music.'"[103]

As we have seen in this chapter, multiple new domains of creativity are emerging among musicians in the diaspora. Most notably, more Ethiopian singers have since the 2000s come for tours of various lengths across the United States and Canada, visiting clubs and mounting concerts, as well as church benefits, in major Ethiopian centers. During this time as well, diaspora Ethiopian musicians have begun to travel back to Ethiopia to perform concerts, with some returning by the first decade of the 2000s for extended visits or to reestablish residency in Ethiopia. The return of musicians to Ethiopia and the new horizons that have emerged as a result of the increasing transnational mobility of music and musicians are our subjects in chapter 10.

10

Horizons

REDISCOVERING HERITAGE AND
RETURNING TO HOMELAND

Admas

GENERAL MEANING: Horizon

MUSICAL MEANING: Name of an Ethiopian American band

The challenges of diaspora are shaped by the reality that its members can never know what the future will bring. If unexpected events in one's homeland force one to suddenly emigrate, how can one anticipate what future events might transpire and what their impact might be? What hopes exist for experiences that lie just beyond the horizon?[1] In this chapter we will explore new horizons at home in Ethiopia for musicians of the Ethiopian American diaspora. The multiple pressures shadowing return from diaspora to Ethiopia by prominent musicians can be viewed through a close look at the music, trajectories, and lives of members of the influential Admas Band, who made different decisions when confronted with the choice of remaining in diaspora or returning to Ethiopia. We will also track briefly the echoes of Ethiopian music in transnational circulation beyond the boundaries of the Ethiopian diaspora community.

While memories of the revolution that forced them to leave Ethiopia may have receded, most of the first generation of Ethiopian immigrants long for the homeland they left behind. Immigrants reside where their American children, now adults, have established their own lives and futures. Yet despite the passage of time, the trauma of displacement still exerts its hold and decades in diaspora have generated new sensibilities. Diaspora has over the course of decades reshaped a transnational "emotional community" that transcends the shifting allegiances of existing diaspora realities shaped by processes of descent, dissent, and affinity.[2] At the same time, many first-generation immigrants forced to leave their homeland during the revolution have refused to recognize the legitimacy of subsequent homeland governments and have a relationship to their homeland that can be termed "antagonistic."[3]

Conditions in the Ethiopian homeland have intermittently aroused hope for return while at the same time generating diasporic uncertainty and, at moments, active diasporic political action. At the end of the revolution in 1991, the Tigrayan forces that overthrew dictator Mengistu Haile Mariam assumed political control and imposed a system of ethnic federalism. Meles Zenawi, who formally became prime minister in 1995, remained in that office until his death at the age of fifty-seven in 2012. By 2015 homeland political leadership was again sufficiently unstable that there were public demonstrations led primarily by the majority Oromo population concerned that an urban development plan for the Ethiopian capital, Addis Ababa, would infringe on historical Oromo lands. After several years of mounting uncertainty and intermittent violence, the prime minister since 2012, Hailemariam Desalegn, resigned in February 2018 during a state of emergency and was replaced by forty-one-year-old Abiy Ahmed on April 2, 2018.[4] Prime Minister Abiy, who had extensive experience in multiple government posts and service as lieutenant colonel in the Ethiopian National Defense Force, was of Oromo descent and the son of a Muslim father and a Christian mother. His broad professional experience, multilingualism, and background bridging deep-seated ethnic and religious boundaries were further enhanced by advanced degrees in leadership and business and a doctorate in peace and security studies.[5] Upon taking office, Abiy moved decisively to reverse a number of unpopular measures: he ended an internet blackout, freed political prisoners, engaged with exiled Oromo opposition leaders, and appointed a new government with 50 percent female ministers and the first female president.[6] On July 9, 2018, at Abiy's initiative, Ethiopia and Eritrea signed a peace agreement, concluding the long-standing state of war that was still unresolved from the violent 1998–2000 border conflict and opening the borders to trade and travel.[7] Prime Minister Abiy also visited diaspora communities abroad, especially in the United States, and encouraged diaspora Ethiopians to return home. Abiy's implementation of dramatic changes in Ethiopia has been of a magnitude that diaspora Ethiopians compared to "the end of the Berlin Wall."[8] In order to permit members of the diaspora to participate more actively in the country's financial sector, Ethiopia passed legislation to liberalize the economy.[9] But resistance to Abiy's leadership also emerged among both Amhara and Oromo factions, which led to an unsuccessful coup attempt in late spring 2019 and, by the end of 2020, armed conflict with former leaders from the northernmost Tigray region.

Although the first generation of arrivals to the Ethiopian diaspora observed the new Ethiopian government of 2018 from afar with reactions ranging from excitement to concern, in contrast, many of the 1.5 generation who arrived in diaspora as children or teenagers had long ago embraced opportunities to visit Ethiopia.[10] Members of each generation are constantly redefining their emotional relationships to the homeland as well as their ties in diaspora. But among the many 1.5-generation Ethiopians who began to visit their homeland in the late 1990s, musicians have played special roles.

Like the community that produced and performed it, Ethiopian music has over these same years experienced a global spread. We have earlier traced the international dispersion of Ethiopian music a little more than a decade after the revolution began, catalyzed by the release of the 1986 LP *Ere Mela Mela*, and reaching yet more new audiences through the circulation of the *éthiopiques* CD series beginning in the later 1990s. During these decades as well, the number of international bands performing Ethiopian styles and repertories increased dramatically. By the early 2000s, with the revolution's end a decade earlier and the shock of Eritrean independence abating for many, a greater number of "diasporas," as members of the Ethiopian diaspora are called in Ethiopia, began to make regular trips to visit family and to renew homeland ties. By 2000 Ethiopian musicians from abroad also began to travel to perform in Ethiopia as communities at home greeted them with enthusiasm.

Diaspora communities emerge for different reasons and have different life spans. Processes of migration, arrival, and settlement in diaspora have long been shadowed by transnational connections and the question of return. There also exists the paradox that return is an outcome that transforms 1.5- and second-generation returnees into first-generation immigrants to their homelands.[11]

> If they [migrants] believe they are "returning" to a "homeland" to which they have an emotional and historical connection, then it is the ontology rather than the statistical measurement of return which is the overriding criterion.[12]

Many studies of return include second and subsequent generations, but this discussion will restrict itself to the first and 1.5 generations. Among Ethiopians, second-generation return is a topic very much in flux, in part because the transformation of second-generation Ethiopians in the American diaspora has been distinctively shaped by African American perspectives and cultural life.[13] One finds short-term return visits more common among younger diaspora Ethiopians than among their elders, but even that practice is complicated by the shifts of internal and national borders in the regions from which their families came.[14]

Weighing Return

Just as departures from Ethiopia rapidly increased as the revolution accelerated in 1975, returns to Ethiopia began to mount slowly during the decade after the revolution ended in 1991. Many diaspora members had long spoken hopefully of return, if only as a distant dream to occur decades in the future at the time of their retirement.[15] Others made visits to Ethiopia to take stock of the possibilities of return while considering what they had gained from diasporic experience:

> When you're out, you have a chance to expose yourself to a different culture, and then when you get back, you'll have a chance to see it differently and then appreciate it a lot. I [went back to visit] two years ago, gaining a fascinating understanding of my own culture, religion, and social issues. A great amount of culture is not shared with others that Ethiopia can contribute. An example would be a harmony of coexistence of Islam and Christianity.[16]

Along with a few adventuresome diaspora businesspeople who sensed an untapped opportunity,[17] a few musicians began to head back home in the 1990s, one of whom was Seleshe Damessae. A graduate of the Yared School of Music who had studied *krar* as a boy with his father, Seleshe lived in the northeastern United States for more than twenty years and performed widely in concerts across the United States and Europe. He also participated in Tesfaye Lemma's Nile Ethiopian Ensemble during its first year of activity in Washington, DC.[18] Seleshe returned to Ethiopia in the late 1990s and in 2000 founded the Gashe Abera Molla Association, which confronts social and environmental problems in Addis Ababa.[19] The organization is named after a character in one of Seleshe's songs—"Gashe Abera"—an old man who takes care of his local community. Seleshe is widely known in Ethiopia as Gashe Abera and has founded a lively movement to clean and beautify Ethiopian urban areas.[20] The Gashe Abera Molla initiative is today recognized across the country and has resulted in a reduction of trash in public spaces and increased the use of repurposed materials, such as old tires for rubbish bins and for public art.[21]

There is some skepticism among musicians who have remained in Ethiopia about the returnees. Melaku Belay, a traditional dancer who has both invigorated traditional dance performance at home and performed widely abroad, muses,

> those who ran away do not know themselves. Those who stay, do. It is important for the world to keep your uniqueness. To remain in your homeland gives value to your soul. To come and go is fine.[22]

Yet Melaku understands the forces that compelled musicians to leave and the changing circumstances that are now inviting their return. Wanting to sustain traditional music in a new way, he welcomes returnees:

> They come and can give an answer for young people who would run away. It was a fashion to run away. Now some are missing something, had enough of being away. It is important not to think of money; it is important to think of who we are and what we can give to others. I feel like I destroy my home when I go abroad.[23]

Musicians who have been living for years in diaspora comment on the growing practice of periodic return visits to Ethiopia.[24] Others comment as well on the increasing rate of permanent returns: "Now some of them, they start to return, you know, to move."[25] One of the older generation of Oromo musicians, Mohaammad Ibraahim Xawil, born in Harar in 1952, departed Ethiopia in 1990 for Jakarta, Indonesia. Moving on that same year to Seattle, then to Washington, DC, Mohaammad has returned to Ethiopia frequently for CD releases and to visit family, once staying six months:

> Nothing is like being back home all the time. Home is home. . . . I'm thinking to go back, but I have a family here. Kids here, I cannot just live forever there.[26]

Many musicians who have chosen not to return are in touch with family and also with professional circles in the homeland. Moges Seyoum notes that in the diaspora Ethiopian Orthodox Church,

> we get a lot of materials from Ethiopia—instruments and ritual items, everything we have now. The diaspora does not send much there, but they do hear what's going on.[27]

Musicians return to Ethiopia primarily for professional reasons, although some are concerned that with return may come professional isolation:

> We have a big chance in Ethiopia. . . . Here [in the United States] there is not very much chance, so that's why we work hard at different jobs. But if you go back to Ethiopia, probably you can focus on our profession. But I don't want to be stuck in the same small community. I want to be able to have an international community. I want to have a big band, a professional band, and go all over the world. That's what I want. That's my dream before I die.[28]

To understand the lure of return and the simultaneous ambivalence it arouses, it is worthwhile to recount the experience of a renowned diaspora ensemble that disbanded in the face of a decision between diaspora and return.

Admas's Dilemma: Abegasu Kibrework Shiota, Henock Temesgen, and Zakki Jawad

The year 2000 marked the release of a solo CD, *Indigo Sun*, by three prominent Ethiopian musicians long resident in the American diaspora; two were among the founders of the band Admas in 1984.[29] Admas occupied a distinctive musical niche in diaspora and was in great demand, performing and recording their own compositions as well as arranging and producing music for Ethiopian singers and instrumentalists working in the United States.[30]

Abegasu Kibrework Shiota was the anchor of Admas, a brilliant keyboardist and arranger born in Japan to an Ethiopian father and a Japanese mother. He returned to Ethiopia with his family when he was one year old. As a child, he acquired a Western classical music background and studied piano but became interested in popular music when he met Henock Temesgen during high school. Guitarist Henock, born to an Oromo family from the west of the country, was raised in the evangelical Mekane Yesus Church in Addis Ababa but attended a Catholic Boys School where he sang in choirs. He became interested in popular music when his brother, who attended the nearby British school, one day brought home an acoustic guitar obtained from his teacher. Abegasu and Henock lived in the same Addis Ababa neighborhood and formed a band that appeared for occasional shows at a local church. The two spent hours listening to the Beatles, the Bee Gees, and other Western groups; the close relationship of Emperor Haile Selassie I with the United States at the time meant easy access to Western popular music:

> We grew up listening to American songs all along, so that is what we liked to play back then, and we never learned traditional music when we were coming up. That was our focus and anytime we would compose or arrange any type of music we would automatically incorporate chords and you know we'd funk it up and make it hip. And that's how we started this incorporating the Western influence.[31]

Abegasu and Henock were also influenced by Mulatu Astatke's Ethiojazz and his success in fusing Latin influences with Ethiopian music; they were keenly aware that Mulatu had spent time at the Berklee College of Music in Boston, an experience to which they both aspired—and which eventually they emulated. They wanted to take music to the next step and "come up with a different sound." But the start of the revolution suddenly cut off all access to Western pop, and in 1980 Henock was sent to the United States to live with relatives. He switched from playing guitar to bass and began to perform professionally. Still at home in Addis Ababa, Abegasu worked as a professional keyboardist with two well-known Addis Ababa bands, the Dahlak Band and the Ethio Stars, finally arriving in the United States in 1984. He studied at the Berklee College of Music in the first half of the 1990s, where Henock also enrolled.[32]

Both Abegasu and Henock established their musical careers in the United States, making a first trip back to Ethiopia with singer Aster Aweke on a concert tour in the late 1980s.[33] Henock made a number of other visits to Ethiopia from 1988 onward and both performed as well in Europe, where they were often booked together with Salif Keita, King Sunny Ade, and other prominent African artists.

During the 1980s and 1990s, many Ethiopians migrated to the Washington, DC, area. Henock recalled that

> when I came here to Washington, DC, there were maybe two restaurants—there are now maybe forty or fifty. So through the years, Ethiopians increased a lot. A lot of my friends were here, a lot of my family was here, eventually all my brothers and sisters came here, everybody came here. The same with Abegasu, whose father was here. My mom was coming here, visiting us, my father was visiting us. . . . Playing with Aster in DC along with Abegasu every weekend for three years or so in an Ethiopian restaurant, you were always seeing an Ethiopian coming. There was not a big disconnect feeling, because one was always surrounded by and playing for the

community. Overall, I didn't feel like I lacked a lot or that I was isolated from the culture or the country.[34]

The third member of Admas joined the band only in 1997: the singer Zakki Jawad (known today professionally by the name Zedicus).[35] A friend of Abegasu from their teenage years in Addis Ababa, Zakki recalled that "the music is what introduced us."[36]

Born in Ethiopia in 1964, Zakki describes himself as a "performing songwriter" and can be heard singing lead vocals and playing guitar on Admas's 2000 album. With an Eritrean-Italian (Catholic) mother and a Harari (Muslim) father, Zakki's multicultural, multilingual, and multireligious upbringing equaled that of his two bandmates. His mother, Rosetta Josef, was an accomplished *krar* player and singer who worked as a nurse.[37] His father's career as a regional manager for North Africa and the Middle East for Ethiopian Airlines took the Jawad family abroad for years to Kenya and Lebanon; they returned to Ethiopia around 1970, where Zakki attended the British School (then the Sandford English School) in Addis Ababa. As noted in chapter 5, in 1977, during the Red Terror and at the start of the *zemecha* campaign that forced students to work in the countryside, the entire family moved to Egypt, where Zakki's father was managing Ethiopian Airlines.[38]

In 1983 Zakki left Egypt for college in Pune, India, a town about three hours from Mumbai. In 1985 he received a student visa and came to the United States to the University of the District of Columbia (UDC), where he received a bachelor's degree in ecological anthropology in 1990, hoping to return to Africa to help maintain the national parks. His interests had been shaped by a scouting program he participated in at the Sandford School:

> The best memories I have as a child were when we'd take trips, go camping out in the bush, in the wilderness, go to Langano, go to Arba Minch, go down south, you know, toward the Konso area. Camping . . . and it was just wonderful. For me, that was paradise on earth.[39]

The three musicians joined forces for the CD *Indigo Sun* in 2000, along with eight other artists performing on drums, saxophone, *djembe*, bongo, and various brass instruments.[40] The band was intensely international, including a percussionist (Dr. Djobi) from the Ivory Coast and an African American saxophone player (Melvin Smith) who also attended Berklee College of Music. Despite their longtime residency in diaspora, the three members of Admas were deeply concerned about tensions between Ethiopia and Eritrea that culminated in Eritrean independence at the end of the revolution and that exploded in another Ethiopian-Eritrean war in the late 1990s:

> The three of us are the founders of the group—me, Abegasu, and Zakki—we are all Ethiopians, well Zakki is half Ethiopian and half Eritrean, but we all consider ourselves the same. In the song "A Prize of Peace," we were trying to talk about what was going on between them [Ethiopia and Eritrea]. . . .[41] We are trying to say that we are all brothers and we should be together, there should be no fighting.[42]

Indigo Sun was overtly political in its message, dedicated "to those fighting in the Ethiopian/Eritrean war, many related by blood who lose their sanity before their lives."[43] The chorus of "A Prize of Peace" reads:

The prize / Peace is the prize
The places I've been / And oh! The hell I've seen
Lost to the wind—my senses fly / With my hands reaching for the sky
They'll have my blood / Back to the earth my bones return/ My bones
    return.[44]

The tracks of *Indigo Sun* blended pop, funk, and jazz with lively and unconventional voicings, as well as long improvisational passages. In "A Prize of Peace," the band incorporated a beat adapted from the Guyla region of Eritrea. *Indigo Sun* was also one of the first Ethiopian-produced diaspora albums to employ primarily English lyrics.[45]

Admas had its own studio in Washington, DC, which Abegasu oversaw and worked in as an arranger. (See plate 10.1.) The group first worked with another partner on the AIT Records label but later established their own label, C-Side Entertainment, which released *Indigo Sun* and other CDs.

Throughout their professional lives, Henock, Abegasu, and Zakki had been faced with decisions about where to live and perform, and by the early 2000s, difficult choices began to reemerge. The decisions taken demonstrate the complexity of diaspora life in general and the pervasive economic, social, and musical pressures confronting musicians.

By 1996 Henock and Abegasu both completed their degrees at the Berklee College of Music and wanted to work in New York City, which was closer to the large group of Ethiopian musicians and expatriate community in Washington, DC. They subsequently spent eight years in New York City, sharing an apartment with a bass player in Hell's Kitchen. But in 2003 the longtime roommates split up: Abegasu moved to Washington,

PLATE 10.1 Musicians gather in Washington, DC. Left to right: Mikyas Abebayehu, Abegasu Shiota, Zakki Jawad, Tsegaye B. Selassie, Abdi (Tesfaye) Nuressa, Kay Shelemay, Thomas "Tommy T" Gobena. Collection of author.

DC, to be near their studio; the bass player decamped to Orlando, Florida, and played for three years at Disney World before settling in Atlanta; Henock remained in New York City, resettling in Harlem. Henock loved his apartment on 121st Street, in a building where Dizzy Gillespie had once lived, and continued an active career that included gigs with the many Berklee alumni living in the New York metropolitan area.

Admas had broken new ground stylistically with an eclectic combination of styles. But their song "Won" from *Indigo Sun* forecast the choices the band would have to make between diaspora and homeland. The bilingual text reads:

> When we're one / We've won
> Overcome the subjugators / Overcome the mind oppressors
> Elevate the vindicators / Overcome the heathens
> Grows the leaf of union / On the trees of love
> Blows the breeze of one song / Sung by those beyond self
> When we're one / We've won
> *Waita yellelebet* (where there are no cries of agony)
> *Hazen yellelebet* (where there is no sorrow)
> *Hager ale alu* (they say there is a land)

Mehede new ahun (that is where I'll go)
Giqay chigir yesheshebet (where pain and suffering has no place)
Kifat yellelebet (and evil does not exist)
Ettager ale alu (they say there is a land)
Enihid b'andinet (together let us go).[46]

In 2003 Abegasu moved from Washington, DC, to Addis Ababa to set up a studio with the support of a generous patron. He was surprised at the number of concert venues in Addis Ababa and began performing several times a week at the Sheraton Hotel and elsewhere. At first, he did not tour much "because there was so much going on here," but he soon began to travel frequently with Ethiopian singers to Europe and the United States. He found that he had so much arranging work "that he could barely keep up with it." In the end, Abegasu concluded that he had been in a "learning mode" while in the United States, but that "what I am good at is Ethiopian music and it was good to come back. There are a lot of untapped things here."[47]

Henock remained in New York City. Before 9/11, he had performed a great deal in Europe and for the Ethiopian communities across the United States, but his contracts slowed down dramatically, as did music jobs in the United States, after the 2001 terrorist attacks. For a time Henock drove for a limousine service to cover his expenses, taking his guitar along with him and practicing while waiting for calls. Then, in 2006, Henock was offered a gig at the Sheraton Hotel in Addis Ababa.[48] (See plate 10.2.) This was not an easy decision, and many were surprised when Henock decided to leave New York City, because he used to tell his friends that "when I am eighty, you'll find me in Times Square walking with a cane." However, he had a positive musical experience at the Addis Ababa Sheraton, where he both performed and lived for six months.[49]

Henock and Abegasu began collaborating again in Addis Ababa, both traveling extensively to perform at festivals and concerts in Europe. Abegasu continued to arrange and produce recordings for Ethiopian musicians. In addition to performing, Henock presented workshops at the Yared School of Music and discovered that he loved to teach, noting that "it's the teaching and playing that feels worthwhile."[50] Initially concerned that the caliber of musicians in Addis Ababa would not equal that of New York City, Henock's perspective on his return to Ethiopia began to change: "Right now, I wouldn't live anywhere else," he said of Addis Ababa. "We are traveling a lot and I am more active here than I was there. When you move back, you get more authenticity."[51] Concerned about the lack of jazz instruction in Addis Ababa, in 2008 Henock started a school first known as

PLATE 10.2 Henock Temesgen performing at the Sheraton Hotel,
Addis Ababa, January 14, 2020. Collection of author.

the African Jazz School of Music (later renamed Jazzamba School of Music) with fellow musicians Abiy Woldemariam and Yonas Gorfe.[52] Soon Abegasu joined in the school initiative, along with Girum Mezmur, a superb Ethiopian guitarist and accordionist, who lives permanently with his Ethiopian American wife and family in Addis Ababa.

The sentinel activity of Girum Mezmur, who was born in Addis Ababa in 1974 and is a guitarist, producer, and teacher, provides insight into his impact on Henock and Abegasu's decisions to return to Ethiopia. At seventeen and a half Girum joined the Axumite band playing regularly at the Addis Ababa Hilton Hotel: "The Axumite band was a school for guitar for me," recalled Girum. He performed at the Hilton six nights a week from 1992 to 1998 and during the day attended the Yared School of Music. Also self-taught on the piano accordion when an instrument was left at his house by an uncle who departed for the United States to do graduate studies, Girum studied classical piano at the Yared School.

He soon became interested in the music of the 50s and 60s, especially of the Imperial Bodyguard Orchestra. "I had to take a choice," he said. "Many people left Ethiopia and came back rarely, but nowadays, people come for vacation after one year or two." Speaking about his Ethiopian-born wife, who lived for twelve years in the United States and has a US passport, Girum remarked, "Yes, she's a 'diaspora.' But staying here was a conscious choice for me." Girum ran nightly jazz jam sessions with the house band at a club known as the Coffee House from 1998 to 2008 and started a band that played there. Although by 2008 the club was open only one night a week because of financial pressures, Girum recalls that "Magic happened some nights when people came to jam. So much happened at the jam."[53]

The Coffee House closed in 2008, and Girum founded a new band named Afro Sound with Shewandagn Hailu and Tewodros Kassahun (Teddy Afro), from which the star took his stage name. In 2008 Girum partnered with Henock and others to start the Jazzamba School of Music. In 2011 they opened the Jazzamba Lounge, which hosted concerts three nights a week at the Itegue Taitu (Empress Taitu) Hotel compound in downtown Addis Ababa. Proceeds from this lounge supported the school, until much of the hotel was destroyed in a fire in 2015; the club then moved to another locale, Mama's Kitchen. After a period of great financial stress, the school closed in 2019.

Girum has remained permanently anchored in Addis Ababa, although he often travels internationally to perform. In May 2008, two months before the Coffee House closed, Girum founded the Addis Acoustic Project, an ensemble featuring accordion and traditional drums, along with a mandolin that Girum admired after hearing a venerable Ethiopian mandolin player, Ayele Mamo, on television. Henock performs on the double bass with the ensemble, which uses mandolin-like guitar techniques and includes a variety of musical elements from the Sudan and Latin music as a world-music-inflected jazz band that incorporates 1950s influences. Girum produces shows with Abegasu, arranging traditional Ethiopian songs for jazz settings. Both Henock and Abegasu credit Girum's presence with encouraging their return to Addis Ababa and acknowledge him as the anchor of the jazz scene in Ethiopia. Girum has composed jingle music for local commercials, as well as music for commercial films, and has performed with foreign musicians such as Angélique Kidjo from Benin. "Being adjustable is a matter of survival," says Girum.[54]

Zakki's life, however, was deeply rooted in Washington, DC, both personally and professionally, and he could not leave:

> Abegasu went for work, Henock was going for work, and they found the conditions very agreeable and I think they were just sort of seduced into staying at some point. They remained and I really fully support them in that decision. I wish I could do the same and I have been trying to, actually. . . . I don't have the tools necessary to make as reliable a living as Abegasu or Henock, because as you can see, I don't sing songs in Amharic, although with my Amharic, I do incorporate that into my music. But I don't pretend to be a traditional singer. I'm not. . . . Musically I see myself as a performing songwriter. Because I think my forte, rather than as an instrumentalist, is really as a composer. . . . So I can't make a living in Ethiopia doing that, and the kind of music I make, I'm not certain I'll be able to work regularly.[55]

Since 1996, Zakki has also held a professional position in the airline industry:

> It [airport work] is very accommodating as far as my music, my life as a musician goes. . . . The flexibility really has been key. I'm able to trade away days. Because sometimes I'm gone to Europe for ten days or so if I am touring with an Ethiopian act. If I don't have vacation time, I work for people and then they work for me.[56]

After Abegasu and Henock returned to Ethiopia, Admas did not immediately dissolve but rather was put on hold. The group recorded a second album with the star producer Bill Laswell just before Abegasu and Henock's departure, tentatively titled "Measured in Years," but it was never released. Zakki's career also began to move in other directions, including collaborations with Ethiopian musicians in diaspora such as Aster Aweke, Gigi Shibabaw, Tsegaye B. Selassie, and Neway Debebe. He worked with a wide variety of other musicians abroad, especially reggae bands, including the Jamaican band the Itals; Maxi Priest, a British-born reggae singer of Jamaican descent; and Ska musician Dave Wakeling of the English Beat.

In 2005 Zakki released his first album, *Zedicus*, its jewel box carrying an illustration of the thirteenth-century Indian minaret, Qtub Minar Tower.[57] The name Zedicus is based on a fictional character from a short story Zakki wrote while in high school. He adopted this professional name after Abegasu and Henock moved back to Ethiopia and he was on his own musically. "I write in my songs a lot about what I experience. A song like 'Rebel Soul,' for example, is about forging your own path."[58]

Zakki's songs often stake out political positions. Zakki explains that "I just feel it's my duty, given this forum that I'm allowed, to say something if someone will listen."[59] His 2005 song "Standing in the Middle," for instance, offers a critique of US government policy:

> They tell you what to believe
> In God we trust
> Information diseased
> Don't know what's going on overseas.[60]

Zakki describes his musical style in *Zedicus* as "world music on a bed of reggae." Deeply influenced by reggae as well as by both North and South Indian music from his years in India, Zakki's compositions often use the electric guitar to evoke the sound of the *sitar*, a North Indian plucked lute. He has also transposed Ethiopian modes to replicate Indian *raga*:

> Even in my Western music, you know, I borrow from the Ethiopian scales, and in particular the second album I'm working on, I think there was an influence on me when I went to India. I really love the way that a musician is allowed a position of reverence in their society. You can actually be raised as a musician, you can be groomed, you can be trained. In Ethiopia we do not. [By] most accounts you would be looked down on because it's more a matter of economics. My mother was very encouraging, because I remember that my earliest memories of my interest in music were in Lebanon. When I was four years old, and we lived in an apartment building, I would run down the stairs and say, "Papa, did you buy me a guitar?" I don't know why it was a guitar, but I was always fascinated with that instrument. And my dad never really took me seriously, and my mother was the first one who bought me a guitar. She had made a trip to Europe while we were living in Egypt of all places, so this is years later. So I had a late start. I really didn't get into it seriously until my mid-teens. I was sixteen when I got my first guitar.[61]

It is not surprising that Zakki embraced a wide range of musical influences:

> I listened to the standards, you know, like Earth, Wind & Fire, George Benson, Fleetwood Mac. I have a broad range of interests. I listened to Arabic music while we were there, although I wasn't really that into it. I think I was more into funk and soul—James Brown I loved. Michael Jackson, the early stuff, "Off the Wall" and "Thriller." And a lot of folk music, people like Joni Mitchell, Crosby, Stills, and Nash, Fleetwood Mac, the Bee Gees. I was really into them. Also Abba. I do like classical very much and I listen to it. I love Bach, Paganini, and Vivaldi. My father had a great influence on me because of his taste in music. Barry White is like a soundtrack of my youth in Addis. And the Temptations. My dad introduced me to Motown.[62]

Zakki and his band Abyssinia Roots have performed regularly at club venues in Washington, DC, and toured internationally. Prominent Ethiopian musicians in the band include Tsegaye B. Selassie as well as musicians from India, Italy, and Trinidad.

Zakki's song texts, usually set in English, link often to Africa. A notable example, and one that touches on themes relevant to Zakki's life as an Ethiopian in diaspora, can be heard in the song "Long Road":

> I've got a ticket, I wanna go to Sidamo
> I've got a ticket, I wanna be in Arussi
> I've got a ticket, show me the way to Dessie
> I've got a ticket to Dire Dawa and to Massawa
>
> Way past midnight, and I'm still walking
> It took so long for directions to your town
> At a local inn I sought help from an old man,
> He said, "Son, I can't show you the way,
> But the drink's on me."
>
> Would you mind telling me how do I get to Africa?
> 'Cause I keep on wandering
> Lose another day, on the wrong road
> I'm looking for a miracle or a ride
> 'Cause I know fourteen thousand miles is no joke
>
> And I know I can make it
> I'm halfway there already

I can clear it—over the ridge and
Anything the road brings.

Somebody said, "Take the long road"
And another said, "Head for the beach"
Never ceasing to reach for you, Africa.
In my thoughts I've never left you
I fear no strife, my gourd is full of His wisdom
Alone I've lumbered through furies in magical dreams
Where tears fell lost into the sea.

I'm on my way, I'm heading home
No Babylon can stop me now.

Got a ticket, I wanna go to Sidamo
Got a ticket, I wanna be in Arussi
I've got a ticket, show me the way to Dessie
I've got a ticket to Dire Dawa and to Massawa.[63]

In "Long Road," Zakki conveys a sense of extended mobility and expresses a deep diasporic longing for his homeland, inflected by the Rastafarian sentiment that Babylon cannot stop him now. Other songs on the album exhibit a reggae style and embed scattered Rastafarian references, such as "Rebel Soul," in which he implores Nyabinghi to "come and play your drums for me."[64] "Rebel Soul" also makes clear Zakki's continuing commitment to human rights, with his music as his weapon in that struggle:

Mother I'm growing my locks
I want to become a musician
I'll stand up for human rights—be a warrior
Guitar in my hand a spear.[65]

Rediscovering Heritage

The 1.5 generation of musicians arrived in the United States either as infants or young children, some years older than the second generation born to Ethiopian parents living in diaspora. We have already viewed the creativity of Meklit, part of the 1.5 generation, discussed in chapter 9; here we will explore the manner in which two other musicians from the 1.5 generation have chosen to return to a heritage they experienced as a child and absorbed from their parents. Although they increasingly affirm their growing connections to their homeland, they have at the same time attracted collaborators and listening publics outside the confines of the Ethiopian diaspora community.

WAYNA WONDWOSSEN

On June 25, 2008, Wayna Wondwossen opened her show at Busboys and Poets on 14th Street NW in Washington, DC.[66] The big restaurant had a special room with a stage at one end and small tables to accommodate drinks, food, and dessert for the audience at the performance. The wall behind the stage had large graphics of three well-known faces, each with a descriptive word underneath: "Watching" (Dalai Lama); "Waiting" (Gandhi); and "Dreaming" (Martin Luther King Jr.). Photographs hanging on the other sides of the rectangular room were primarily those of famous African American performers.[67]

"Is anyone else here an immigrant?" Wayna asked her audience as a preamble to her song "Slums of Paradise" that describes a young Ethiopian woman who aspires to a college education being forced into prostitution on the streets of Addis Ababa during the Ethiopian revolution. The song's chorus mourns revolutionary changes to Ethiopia in the face of its proud past:

Oh Lord how it used to be so beautiful / The origin of life we have now
    come to know
A picture of God's imagination / The cradle of our modern civilization
Rooted in the richest ancient history / With monarchies and military
    victories
Colorful with custom and tradition / A proud and independent African
    nation
That's what they say it's like / In the slums of paradise.[68]

Wayna was born in Addis Ababa and arrived in the United States with her mother as a three-year-old in 1977. After graduating from the University of Maryland with a degree in English and speech, she worked for several years as a speech writer at the Clinton White House until she left to pursue her musical career full time.[69]

Primarily known as singer-songwriter of R&B and soul, in 2004 Wayna released her first CD, *Moments of Clarity*, under the guidance of Ethiopian diaspora producers Abegasu and Tommy T. Although her first album does not draw on Ethiopian musical sources, she alludes to her heritage in the song "Slums of Paradise," quoted above, dramatizing the dissolution of Ethiopia during the revolution. "If it [my life] were a book, it would be a novella, because it's two stories where they're connected and the people don't necessarily know each other, but they are connected." She remembers her arrival as a child in the United States and being "bombarded with so much change" that she clung to her cousins who had arrived earlier to the suburban Maryland neighborhood where they lived and were already speaking only English: "And they say that in a matter of months I just completely morphed into this American. I regret that, so I'm working on getting my Amharic back."[70]

Despite her own early Americanization and membership in the African Methodist Episcopal Church,[71] her CD, *Moments of Clarity*, signals her ties to Ethiopia with visual markers: an Ethiopian cross decorates the face of the CD, and Wayna's name is signed in Amharic at the end of the liner notes' acknowledgments.

Having already visited Ethiopia twice for briefer periods, she traveled to Addis Ababa for three months between December 2006 and March 2007 to first perform there at a club called Harlem Jazz on Addis Ababa's lively Bole Road:

> It was quite an experience, just seeing how Ethiopians responded to Western music and then also being immersed in Ethiopian music all the time. So I think I observed my people as an adult really for the first time. And just came to a lot of internal realizations and a deeper kind of love for where I am from.[72]

Wayna's second album, *Higher Ground*, is modern R&B and soul; its fourth track is Minnie Riperton's classic song "Lovin' You."[73] Wayna's creative cover of that song, exploiting her extraordinary upper vocal range, garnered her a Grammy nomination in 2009. But only her third album, *The Expats* in 2013, makes explicit the convergence of her expatriate status and global musical interests through "her first sort of foray into Ethiopian music."[74] (See plate 10.3.) The second track, "Time Will Come," embeds clips from a speech of Emperor Haile Selassie I, with an introduction and instrumental interludes by Setegn Atanaw on the *masenqo*. If Wayna's earlier albums were directed at a global African American audience, *The Expats* and her subsequent work reach out to Ethiopians and to Ethiopian diaspora audiences.

Wayna has followed a dual path since 2015, enhancing her knowledge of Ethiopian music, language, and culture while touring as a backup singer

PLATE 10.3 Cover of Wayna Wondwossen's 2013 CD, *The Expats.*
Courtesy of Wayna Wondwossen.

with Stevie Wonder. The first time she sang in Amharic on stage was in fact with Stevie Wonder at his 2015 *Songs in the Key of Life* Tour, where Wayna performed several phrases of "Tizita."[75] Wayna is also expanding her own musical skills to include Ethiopian instruments:

> You know what? I actually bought a *krar* when I was in Ethiopia, an electric *krar*, and I really do want to learn to play. . . . I also have another kind of exciting project that I'm working on for later, which is I want to do a book and a CD that are sort of like an oral history project about Ethiopian women where we would interview every type of Ethiopian woman, from the upper class living in Bole, to the maid that works for her. And just to hear what their stories are, just to have a record of it. And then I would like to write a song about the people whose stories are the most compelling to me and do a kind of acoustic album. . . . So the thing that gets me really excited, telling the stories that aren't told, you know, the real story, like not

PLATE 10.4 Munit Mesfin in performance. Courtesy of Munit
Mesfin and photographer Luigi Ceccon.

what people show, but what's underneath. It would have a lot of traditional
instrumentation and then maybe some guitar and acoustic bass, too.[76]

MUNIT MESFIN

Just as Wayna has gravitated to Ethiopia for both musical inspiration and
performance opportunities, other 1.5-generation musicians have explored
their Ethiopian roots professionally. Return remains a viable option for
those who had earlier spent time in the country, such as Munit Mesfin,
born in Addis Ababa in 1981. At age ten, Munit accompanied her mother,
a public health specialist, to posts with UNICEF in India and Namibia.
Subsequently, Munit attended boarding school at Northfield Mount Her-
man in Massachusetts, eventually graduating from Smith College in 2003
and becoming a US citizen several years after that.[77]

In 2010 Munit moved with her Haitian American husband and first
child to Ethiopia. Her life had already involved "commuting a lot of back
and forth between Ethiopia and the United States" since 2007, when she
began performing with German guitarist Jörg Pfeil, who taught at the German Embassy School Addis Ababa. Known as "Munit and Jörg," the
"Ethio-Acoustic Soul Duo" released two albums, in 2008 and in 2013, respectively.[78] (See plate 10.4.)

But in addition to performing in Ethiopia and abroad, Munit devoted her time to aiding young women facing social issues, to building a sustainable arts economy in Ethiopia, and to promoting pan-Africanism. She served as creative music director for the radio drama "Yegna" (Ours), which sought to empower girls ages eleven to nineteen and worked to keep them in school by encouraging behavioral change and a shift in society's perceptions of girls' capacities and contributions through music and the arts. She was also a radio host for Afro FM 105.3 and an owner of Care Events and Communications, which put together several festivals, concerts, and conferences, celebrating Ethiopia's history through the arts on a broad range of social issues such as environmental protection and gender equity. Through these socially engaged efforts, Munit believed that she could help young women, their families, and the nation at large.[79]

In 2017 Munit relocated with her family to the United States but continued to tour occasionally with Jörg in Germany and South Africa, to work with Yegna, and also to perform with musicians in Addis Ababa, including her brother Jorga Mesfin and his band Asli Ethio Jazz. Reaffirming Ethiopia's importance in her life, one of her songs in her second album was "Hagere," which encourages all to go back home and be part of the solution to help Ethiopia and all Ethiopians to thrive. Munit continues to visit Ethiopia regularly to perform and to complete work on her first solo CD,[80] some of which she plans will be recorded with Ethiopian and non-Ethiopian musicians in the DC metropolitan area.

Munit is better positioned than most diaspora Ethiopians to move regularly between the diaspora and the homeland, a consequence of her decade in Ethiopia as a child and her bicultural and bilingual background. However, Munit acknowledges that living outside Ethiopia for most of her life has shaped her performance skills: "My throat is not tuned as an Ethiopian. . . . I didn't grow up there enough." But Munit's experience singing with many other musicians, including Wayna, with whom she performed in what she describes as her "first paying gig," has enabled Munit to present "Ethiopian things in Amharic, all original music, and some things in English as well since my global life requires it." In short, she feels that she has "brought back [to Ethiopia] music people liked to hear."[81]

Global Echoes

While 1.5-generation musicians such as Wayna and Munit have moved into creative dialogues between the United States and their natal homeland with the Ethiopian musical traditions that their parents left behind, a good number of non-Ethiopian musicians have discovered Ethiopian music since the 1990s largely through virtual sources. Much of this musical circulation has been conveyed by the *éthiopiques* CD series across the globe. American musicians were among the most receptive to these recordings early on, demonstrating the power of virtual connections to convey music over time and space, all the while shaping real-world musicking.

American jazz musician Russ Gershon, the founder and leader of the ten-piece jazz band Either/Orchestra, first encountered Ethiopian music when a friend gave him the recording *Ere Mela Mela*, a few years after its LP release. Gershon loved the music's sound as well as the voice of "Ere Mela Mela," singer Mahmoud Ahmed, "although it didn't change my life."[82] However, it took a second recording of the Ethiopian big-band sound from 1994, *Ethiopian Groove*, to again pique Gershon's interest and move him to musical action.[83] Gershon decided to include three compositions from *Ere Mela Mela*, which he arranged and titled "An Ethiopian Suite," on his ensemble's 2000 CD release *More Beautiful Than Death*.[84] At that point, the virtual world intervened again and Francis Falceto, producer of the *éthiopiques* series, encountered the 2000 Either/Orchestra recording:

> Thank you, Internet—for it is via the Web that the connection with the Either/Orchestra was made. It was in 2000, after a systematic search for information on Ethiopian music that I ended up at [the Accurate Records website] and then at the site of Either/Orchestra and of the label run by Russ Gershon. . . . The rest was a matter of a neat little story of luck, and of the necessary encounters. . . . To make a long story short, in 2005 the Either/Orchestra celebrated twenty years of existence, marked by an admirable output of recordings, recognised by a nomination at the Grammy Awards (for Best Arrangement of an Instrumental Composition). . . . This "Live in Addis" was recorded on 21 January 2004, during the third Ethiopian Music Festival.[85]

Gershon acknowledges the impact of Ethiopian music recordings on his work,[86] noting that Falceto

> offered a wealth of unreleased and never reissued recordings and his expertise about the personalities and history of Ethiopian pop and jazz. His contacts led to an invitation to the third Ethiopian Music Festival in Addis Ababa in January of 2004. No American big band had been in Ethiopia since Duke Ellington's in 1973 . . . and almost certainly no American artist had traveled to Addis Ababa to play Ethiopian songs for an Ethiopian audience.[87]

The Either/Orchestra became an emissary for Ethiopian music in the United States and elsewhere, for it incorporated arrangements of Ethiopian classics such as Girma Beyene's "Musiqawi Silt" into their live performances.[88] The ensemble also collaborated with Ethiopian diaspora musicians such as Hana Shenkute (singer and dancer), Minale Dagnew Bezu (*krar*), and Setegn Atanaw (*masenqo*) at major performances, including on one notable occasion in the Celebrity Series of Boston at the Berklee Performance Center.[89] In this and other instances, an entire performance was constituted from Ethiopian repertory, including arrangements from Mulatu Astatke's "Broken Flowers" film score.[90] Thus, the virtual domain served as the guide for live musicking, with Gershon using recordings as models from which he transcribed his own arrangements, always "adding some things not on the record."[91]

With the collaboration of three superb Ethiopian musicians at the 2006 Celebrity Series concert, whom Gershon termed "the workingest Ethiopian group in the US,"[92] Gershon incorporated repertory based on traditional modes and from several different ethnic communities. At a rehearsal for their upcoming public concert, the Either/Orchestra drummers Vincente Lebron and Pablo Bencid worked especially closely with Hana Shenkute, who demonstrated expertly how to perform the ethnic rhythms and the process by which the drummers could make the transitions between them.[93] The *chik chika* rhythm, with its fast two-against-three beat patterns, provided clear challenges to the ensemble drummers, one of whom commented that it was "kinda hard, man." Seeking clarification, Gershon asked Hana, "Where do you feel the one?" She responded by stamping the "one" with her foot and snapping the counter rhythm with her fingers.[94] The Latino drummers and Ethiopian musicians worked compatibly, a good-humored atmosphere established from the beginning of the rehearsal when trumpet player Tom Halter walked in carrying two *masenqo* that he had purchased the prior year during the orchestra's visit to Addis Ababa; the instruments were swaddled in Whole Foods and Trader Joe's shopping bags, eliciting laughter all around. As a result, the band decided to interpolate an amusing segment into the second half of the concert, with Setegn giving a mock *masenqo* lesson to several Either/Orchestra instrumentalists on stage, each then playing simple scales and melodies on a *masenqo*.[95]

The Celebrity Series concert thus fused aspects of the Ethiopian recordings with creative additions, such as the added electric *krar* and *masenqo*, all included on the detailed lead sheets that Gershon had prepared. To add variety to the program, and to take advantage of the skills of all three Ethiopian musicians with traditional Ethiopian music and dance, a "cultural segment" was added with Either/Orchestra percussion accompaniment. During the twenty-minute cultural segment, the percussionists improvised while Hana changed into garments appropriate to the ethnic music being performed—first Tigray, next Oromo, and finally, Gurage music and dance.[96]

The Either/Orchestra has continued to perform Ethiopian music for more than two decades, always moving into new territory. One major six-year project entailed reviving the music of Nerses Nalbandian and was performed at a memorial concert in Watertown, Massachusetts, on February 19, 2017. Nerses was the nephew of Kevork Nalbandian, the leader of the Armenian orphan band brought to Ethiopia from Jerusalem by the emperor in 1924. Nerses, who was born in Syria in 1915 and arrived in Ethiopia in 1938, influenced the development of Ethiopian music for decades to come.[97]

The Either/Orchestra is only one of many ensembles internationally to have encountered Ethiopian music and to have incorporated it in their live performances and recordings. If most Ethiopian musicians have sought to attract broader listening publics outside Ethiopia and its diaspora community, they could not have anticipated the rapidly growing affinity community that would be consuming and performing their music well into the twenty-first century. Although traditional musicians had long participated in cultural shows for tourists to Ethiopia and in Ethiopian restaurants in the United States, beyond the horizon the phenomenon referred to as "Ethio-groove" emerged among musicians worldwide.[98]

New Horizons

Éthiopiques had a central role in circulating Ethiopian music worldwide, and as a result it was perhaps inevitable that Falceto and Buda Musique would also take the lead in charting the echoes of Ethiopian music abroad on their new ÉthioSonic label's *Noise and Chill Out: Ethiopian Groove Worldwide*.[99] Among the twenty-eight tracks by ensembles performing Ethiopian music across the globe on this double CD, which include recordings from France, Australia, Japan, and numerous other locales, one or more Ethiopian musicians are heard on seventeen tracks, often an Ethiopian singer who performs in Amharic and another Ethiopian language.

The irony of this global Ethiopian music trend, suggests Ethiopian American musician Danny Mekonnen, is that Ethiopian music is now performed globally, but primarily by non-Ethiopians, who have effectively appropriated the Ethiopian sound; meanwhile, Ethiopian musicians are "exiled in a time lost, if not yet forgotten: frozen in the mobile physical-ity of vinyl records, digitized in the binary code of plastic CDs, immortalized in the ether of cyberspace."[100] The new global performance trend merits attention both because of its ubiquity and the issues it raises about what is either the embrace or appropriation of Ethiopian music by non-Ethiopians. Although many individuals and ensembles from outside Ethiopia are performing Ethiopian styles, it is not clear from the tracks on *Noise and Chill Out* that Ethiopians have been "exiled from their own repertories." Indeed, Danny Mekonnen, a 1.5-generation Ethiopian American saxophonist, founded and leads the multiethnic, Boston-area ensemble Debo Band, heard on that same ÉthioSonic album, featuring a first-generation Ethiopian immigrant singer, Bruck Tesfaye.

Collaborations between Ethiopian, Ethiopian diaspora, and non-Ethiopian musicians have become increasingly common. We have discussed in chapter 7 the more than decade-long collaboration of Dutch band The Ex with Ethiopian saxophonist Getatchew Mekuria (d. 2016) beginning in the early 2000s.[101] According to the notes that accompany their 2012 CD, released as a benefit for Getatchew, The Ex and the Ethiopian saxophonist performed almost one hundred concerts together in fifteen countries. In his own notes in that CD booklet, Getatchew wrote glowingly both of his collaboration with The Ex and the close professional and personal relationships they had forged:

> I just play Ethiopian music. With The Ex it is mix of styles and people. Music is a language. It's just what we created together. It is not just me, but the whole band. . . . The Ex band cares about my wife Ayaletch and also the family. Now we are like relatives.[102]

When The Ex went on tour for their fortieth anniversary in 2019, they once again collaborated with special guests from Ethiopia, this time the dance ensemble Fendika, led by Melaku Belay and Ethiopian circus performers.[103]

The growing impact of musicians from Ethiopia on the world music scene may have encouraged some from the diaspora to return home. Yet it is not surprising, as we have seen, that most of the returnees are those who lived and—in many cases—began their careers in Ethiopia before departing for diaspora during and after the revolution. Younger musicians have clearly begun to visit Ethiopia, as charted in chapters 8 and 9, but most do not remain for long periods, nor do they return to live there.[104] The ethnic background of some musicians has proven to be an impediment to returning—for instance, for much of the postrevolutionary period, Oromo musicians have been reluctant to return to Ethiopia out of concern about the political risks.[105] It is unclear whether push factors from the United States, such as the restrictive immigration policies implemented between 2016 and 2020, resulted in more musicians deciding to return to the Horn of Africa.

Whatever the pathways of individual musicians of the Ethiopian diaspora, considerable uncertainty remains about long-term diaspora musical prospects. The late Tesfaye Lemma, longtime director of Orchestra Ethiopia and one of the premier traditional musicians of the second half of the twentieth century both in Ethiopia and in the United States, speculated on the many challenges confronting diaspora Ethiopian musicians today:

> The Ethiopians were lucky, you know. In the hard time of the military government, a great number of Ethiopians, almost a million, descended to America, all over the United States. And this number, they consumed the music through weddings, birthdays, for Easter, New Year. They traveled from place to place and for the musicians, it didn't matter if they got business from Americans because they made more money from their community.
>
> But now because of the competition, most of them have gotten out of the music business and they tried to survive by working in any place. Most of them have no education or background except their music. . . . Some of them, they have stayed in this country over twenty years. They are middle-aged and their future is unknown.
>
> Really, I try to see a good future, but even if they, say, go to school in this country, they separate from their community because the Ethiopian community has no experience of jazz music or rock music. But the new generation might change. Most of the musicians are trying to be heard by Americans but they couldn't find the way. They can't do it. They try to imitate Americans, . . . African American singers and many others. They tried; they couldn't make it. Nobody listens to them and now they are far from Ethiopian listeners. I know some youngsters who go to America and music school but when they try something similar to Americans, they don't like it. Ah, now they have lost their way.
>
> Now this is really the problem with the new generation of musicians, and we can't continue like this. The Ethiopian singers, they are doing the same thing. And they get a mass audience, but the audience expects something better, something new, and the musicians couldn't respond for this kind of request. Now most of them don't have jobs.
>
> In the future I'm afraid for the new generation, [that] immigration

might stop anytime. The immigrants from Ethiopia are the source of income but now when . . . the new generation is born, they listen to African American music. They don't listen to Ethiopian music.[106]

Henock Temesgen recalled these pressures from his own years in the United States before his return to Ethiopia, grappling with challenges of finding an audience:

> One of the problems we had initially here was trying to fuse other influences with Ethiopian music because of the people that are here. It's very funny. When you go to Ethiopia, the people over there want to hear other stuff from other countries because they always hear the stuff over there. The people here, even people who've been here thirty, forty years, they are very nostalgic, they want to hear only the stuff from way back. So the moment we tried to change our arrangements initially and to bring other influences, these people really objected and the CDs didn't sell. People wanted more tradition. Nowadays it is changing; there are a lot of young singers coming and mixing different stuff, even people, kids who were born here and raised here, Ethiopians, are rapping in Amharic and in English. And the people over there are singing stuff based on reggae beats or different influences. So the States is changing a bit, but there is still the older generation that wants to hear stuff that is traditional or in that vein.[107]

Change is ever present in the life of Ethiopian diaspora musicians, each new development reshaping the horizon stretching before them. Change is also the single most powerful phenomenon shadowing the efforts of the ethnographer seeking to document and interpret the lives of diaspora musicians and their communities over the course of decades. Their stories can never be fully told, nor can any narrative reflect the most recent events. Even as one commits words and images to a page, circumstances have already begun to shift. For these reasons, it is vital to consider the broader lessons that have emerged from this study. In the afterword, we will return to the subject of the sentinel musician, exploring new perspectives and raising additional questions.

Afterword

SENTINEL MUSICIANS IN
GLOBAL PERSPECTIVE

The stories of sentinel musicians do not conclude with the end of the Ethiopian revolution, with the maturation of its diaspora, or with returns to the homeland. A strong tradition of musical leadership continues, exemplified most recently by the tragic death of the singer Hachalu Hundessa, a sentinel musician for Oromo people worldwide. Hachalu's murder was widely reported by the global media just as I was completing this book in the summer of 2020. Described as "more than just a singer and entertainer" and "a symbol for the Oromo people who spoke up about the political and economic marginalization that they had suffered under consecutive Ethiopian regimes," Hachalu had been receiving death threats and was shot by an assailant in Addis Ababa on June 29, 2020, an event that sparked violent protests across Ethiopia and its diaspora.[1] Only thirty-four years old (b. 1986) at the time of his death, Hachalu was sent to prison for five years at the age of seventeen for his political activities. His first album, *Sanyii Mootii* (Race of the king), followed his release from prison and made him an iconic figure. Hachalu recalled that "I did not know how to write lyrics and melodies until I was put behind bars. It is there that I learned."[2]

In the previous pages, we have taken a close look at the lives and experiences of many musicians from Ethiopia of different ages, ethnic backgrounds, regions, religions, and repertories. They share aspects of their Ethiopian pasts and the experience of the revolution, forced migration, and diaspora life in the United States. Yet narratives of their lives provide evidence of a broader pattern that transcends individual experiences.[3] Despite substantial struggles to sustain musical careers while confronting challenges of exile and resettlement, a striking number of these musicians have exhibited a powerful commitment to social and political action through their musical activity and beyond. A great number have acted as what I have termed sentinel musicians, individuals who have exercised initiative to guard the musical traditions and communities they represent and to guide others along challenging musical pathways.

Musical sentinels have been an important historical phenomenon in Ethiopia, as explained in the preface and discussed at many points throughout this book. They emerged from a feudal, hierarchical society ruled by a hereditary (male) aristocracy that survived until the later twentieth century. Centuries of political domination established a culture of control, with established authority concealing strong streams of resistance expressed through cultural channels that escaped official scrutiny. Here the flexibility of wax and gold both enabled double-layered linguistic expression and opened up a space in which subordinate forms of power emerged and prospered, albeit below a cover of conformity and consensus. Ethiopian minstrels, the *azmari*, lived at the center of these hidden channels of power, helping to shape and disseminate the flow of information and condemn aspects of life well beyond their control. Church musicians, too, the *debtera*, partook of ambiguity, working outside the church as merchants during their years of study and engaging in processes of healing long controversial within the religious hierarchy.[4] In Ethiopia, therefore, many musicians had long exercised personal agency at the very heart of the worlds that controlled them, finding ways both to criticize authority and, at other moments, to reinforce the existing hierarchy.

Quotidian issues also demanded the attention of musicians. Many have aided others less fortunate than themselves and, beyond their efforts in strictly musical domains, have addressed important social and political causes and founded institutions that continue to serve their communities. All this has been carried out by musicians living under difficult or even traumatic personal circumstances. Many offer testimonies about contributions of fellow musicians, alerting the scholar to the importance of their roles. For instance, singer Wayna Wondwossen recalled the help she received early in her career from keyboardist and producer Abegasu Kibrework Shiota:

> The first producer that I ever worked with in music in general was Abegasu Shiota. He was wonderful, I mean, just in terms of really just being a guide and sort of helping me navigate my way through everything.[5]

Other musicians, such as composer and ensemble director Tesfaye Lemma, moved aggressively in diaspora to help both individual musicians and the community at large. While struggling to recover from the trauma of his own defection and resettlement, Tesfaye established new institutions in Washington, DC, including the Nile Ethiopian Ensemble, the

CEAC, and the TESFA Museum for Musical Instruments. Only ill health ended Tesfaye's ambitious work.[6]

Some individuals discussed in these pages have transformed diaspora musical life by organizing it anew. Amha Eshete and Alemtsehay Wedajo used their knowledge of music and the arts to record performances for posterity, to establish major ethnic places and institutions, to fashion remarkable song texts, to mount large-scale public performances, and to build organizations for the advancement of music, poetry, dance, and drama.

We have seen already that the worlds of economic striving, sentinel activity, and musical creativity often converge. We can take as an example the case of Yehunie Belay, the remarkable traditional musician who, with the partnership of his wife Tutu, has given generously of himself and his resources to help connect his communities at home and abroad. Others, such as singer Telela Kebede, have displayed great courage over the decades, sustaining risky political stances at home along with efforts abroad to guide a younger generation in diaspora reeling from the challenges of forced migration.

Individual musicians have sometimes responded in more subtle ways to the needs of their community. Tsehay Amare has sought to meet the contrasting needs of her audiences in various places. She performs to help maintain traditional repertories in Ethiopia while seeking to offer comfort to those for whom she sings these songs in diaspora. The dynamic Ali Birra has forged new political pathways and enhanced community consciousness through his performances and recordings among Oromo people at home and abroad. The talented Mulatu Astatke, while maintaining his home in Addis Ababa, has spent years in the diaspora and performed regularly there, at the same time establishing new pedagogical initiatives and efforts to bring attention to indigenous traditions at home. Selam Seyoum Woldemariam resumed his musical career as a virtuoso guitarist a decade after his forced migration to the United States in 2000 and has been active both in supporting older colleagues and in sharing his experiences with young, upcoming musicians to help them break into the mainstream global sound.[7] Selam recalls that

> the first thing I did upon my arrival in the DMV area was to visit a very good friend, Tesfaye Lemma, at the nursing home. We used to meet every Friday and I used to take him out for lunch and a brisk stroll in the park. . . . Also, since my arrival in the US in April 2000, me and a good friend started to get together for lunch once a week. That started to grow in numbers and soon we were able to include musicians around the DMV area. We would reach 40 or 50 at times. . . . After a while, that same group

started to help musicians in need financially. Later on, as we became tech savvy, me and some fellow musicians formed another group—"DMV Musicians"—on Viber and started to communicate whatever info online, and by using Zelle money transfer, we became able to fundraise in minutes.... (We just sent some financial assistance to fellow musicians in Addis Ababa, who are facing hardship due to the pandemic.) Moreover, we are able to exchange information fast.[8]

Meklit Hadero has embraced as a central tenet of her career the use of her music and personal talents to support both Ethiopian and other immigrant communities from the Horn of Africa. A substantial cohort of both senior and younger musicians have also aggressively led the way into new musical domains, including Wayna Wondwossen, Getatchew Mekuria, Selam Seyoum Woldemariam, and The Weeknd, each projecting different aspects of Ethiopian sounds and worldviews into popular domains of which they have been a part.

It seems clear that the sensory acuity of all these individuals across their respective musical and artistic domains has sharpened their ability to perceive community needs and to conceive actions that would address those concerns. One wonders whether Ethiopian musicians arrived at this commitment to sentinel actions and social engagement at least in part from being part of a society so often in need. Likely the activity of musicians from the outside world who helped overcome the economic impact of drought and famine across the Horn of Africa in the mid-1980s through initiatives such as the Live Aid concert provided powerful models that enhanced initiatives already underway among musicians from the region.

Sentinel musicians of the Ethiopian diaspora have continued to change the worlds into which they were born by raising the level of respect among Ethiopians in general for musical professions. The great majority of the Ethiopian musicians today active in diaspora recounted family resistance to their desire to become musicians, but the situation has begun to shift. One of the most articulate appraisals of emerging new attitudes toward musicianship came from singer Aster Aweke, who, after decades of residency in the United States, has returned to live much of the time in Addis Ababa. Aster suggested that family resistance to her musical career was

because there was no future in it, and there was no role model then. And it's not because they wanted to show the force or power they have, it's just because they worried for you. They felt it was never decent, that you can't make a living. You only make money or a decent living by becoming a doc-tor, a nurse, or, you know, something higher. It was a culture that has now changed. Thanks to us.[9]

Sentinel Expectations: A Global and Transhistorical Perspective

In the early twenty-first century there is shared expectation in the global musical community that individual musicians will contribute to their communities and support each other; this attitude is widespread across many sectors of the performing arts, where the most successful are bound by conscience to support the many who are struggling. One professional manager for major performers internationally reports that he always discusses these responsibilities with the musicians with whom he works, linking the creative spirit to personal agency:

> Some things you do for music, some for career, and some for charity. You need to find the right balance between the three. There are so many artists who do great things for charity. Most have their own foundations to support their charity. . . . I think that musicians' engagement is widespread. I think that creative people have causes that are important to them and that they want to help wherever they can. They can't do everything but are trying to channel their efforts to one or to efforts that are important and meaningful to them, ranging from causes such as the homeless, education, and music in schools.[10]

Given a moment of reflection, most of us can probably cite a number of prominent musicians who, past or present, have, under political pressures and during times of extreme social stress, used their music to guard their traditions, to guide others, and to transform the world around them.

We can identify many who have become sentinels within their homelands as well as for other communities. Fela Kuti (1938–97), the Nigerian musician and political activist, innovated Afro-beat music and was a voice of resistance against authoritarian regimes and social inequality in his native land and elsewhere in Africa during the 1970s and 1980s. Perhaps best remembered for his 1989 antiapartheid album "Beasts of No Nation," Fela Kuti was frequently arrested and subjected to beatings by Nigerian governments that he accused of corruption. Surely a controversial figure, one who both fought for rights and was at moments unconventional and even transgressive in his own life, Fela Kuti was keenly aware of the power wedded to his responsibility as a musician. He once commented, "Music wants to dictate a better life, against a bad life."[11]

Many other musicians have exercised a strong moral impact through their performances and through their political actions. Here we can cite Umm Kulthum (d. 1975), characterized by her biographer Virginia Danielson as "the voice of Egypt" and known across the Middle East for her broadcasts beginning in the 1930s on early Egyptian radio, her concerts, and many sound recordings.[12] Umm Kulthum became an important symbol of her country and the Middle East at large because of her musical capacity to convey the sensory quality of *tarab* (enchantment), which moved listeners emotionally and reinforced their attachments to the Arab nation. But Umm Kulthum was also socially engaged as head of the Musicians' Union and of the Listening Committee for Egyptian radio. An outspoken voice in Egyptian political events, Umm Kulthum took an active role in philanthropy and benefit concerts to refill the Egyptian treasury after Egypt's defeat in the 1967 war.[13]

In recent years, a number of prominent musicians have established their moral authority and exercised agency as leaders of social and economic efforts to support human rights and other meritorious international causes. Bono (Paul David Hewson, b. 1960) comes to mind, the Irish musician who first made his musical reputation with the band U2 and who has over the years offered social leadership through both charitable donations and initiatives ranging from his activity with UNICEF, the Special Olympics, Oxfam, and collaborative recording projects in support of famine relief. Unlike Fela Kuti and Umm Kulthum, whose impact was largely restricted to their homelands or adjacent regions, Bono has been a global leader in generating help for the dispossessed.[14]

Although it may appear that musicians in the popular domain are the most prominent sentinel musicians internationally, there are many powerful examples of sentinel musicians from the global classical realm. The conductor-composer Leonard Bernstein was an extraordinary guide for many, with actions on behalf of civil rights and gender diversity; and, as founder of the Pacific Music Festival in Sapporo, Japan, he sought to deepen international understanding through intercultural musical exchange.[15] The renowned cellist Yo-Yo Ma has undertaken ambitious projects in education and cross-cultural communication through his long-standing Silkroad Project, founded in 1998, and is a proponent of global musical collaboration through the multicultural Silkroad Ensemble.[16]

There are many more musicians who are little known to a public outside their own cultural arenas but who deserve recognition for sentinel activity. Since becoming aware of the agency exercised by so many Ethiopian musicians in various domains associated with protecting and guiding traditions both old and new, I have been impressed more and more by how many musicians from local traditions across the globe also act in sentinel capacities. As in the Ethiopian case studies, especially common cross-culturally are musicians who work as guards.

A number of colleagues, aware of my interest in musical sentinels, have over the years shared information on parallels in a variety of other times and places. One remarked that

> when you spoke of sentinel musicians, it brought back memories of my childhood: I was part of a Vārakari group in Tamil Nadu, where the main *harikathā* exponent always had one or two watchmen-like musicians donning a uniform and singing along. I was performing with Sri Tukārām Ganapathi Mahārāj in Tamil Nadu, but he was borrowing from the Maharashtrian Sri Bapa Satarkar Mahārāj, whose performances were much more grandiose. I remember hundreds of people flanking his sides during his performances, us all dressed in white, with the only dresses of color belonging to the (one or) two watchmen-like guards, who would sing and dance just as we would, but were clothed in specific uniforms. They would walk on and off stage with the Mahārāj, and never left their side until the air of the performance was over.[17]

Other striking examples of musicians as sentinels can be traced across historical time and geographical space. Each case merits investigation for understanding the impact of musicians on their own societies. In the more distant past, numerous musicians served as guards or watchmen in locales stretching from England across Europe. Among them were the waits, guards who played instruments while standing watch in thirteenth- and fourteenth-century England; there were many types of waits and their responsibilities changed over the years in various locales.[18] Some, such as household watchmen called *vigilis*, played a type of shawm known as the wayte pipe. Royal *vigilis* were minstrels who had a variety of tasks that included piping the watch each night and guarding against danger.[19] By the early fifteenth century, the wait was a civic minstrel permanently employed by a town and, by later that century, many towns employed waits that included fine musicians who performed on ceremonial occasions. During the seventeenth and eighteenth centuries, the waits in some towns adopted particular melodies as their signature tunes, a practice also recalled from Ethiopia. Most waits were disbanded by the time of the Napoleonic wars and few existed after the Municipal Reform Act of 1835.[20]

The political engagement of the sentinel musician appears to be ubiquitous—the combination of acute sensory skills wedded to mobility allowed musicians to perceive widely and then advocate for and against courses of action. It is not surprising that many musicians have been engaged in political action and many examples can be found cross-culturally, such as the tragic death of Thomas Ashe during the Irish Rebellion of 1916 against British rule:

> In the years leading up to 1916, the leaders of the planned revolution were mostly poets, writers, musicians, and academics. . . . Thomas Ashe was a leader of the uprising who was a musician, teacher and activist. From Kerry (in southwest Ireland), he worked as a primary school teacher in Lusk, County Dublin. While at Lusk he founded a pipe band (bagpipes and drums) and was involved in a branch of the GAA (Gaelic Athletics Association). Both the Black Raven pipe band and Round Towers GAA club are still in existence today.[21]

Another instance is the phenomenon and impact of the *shomer* (guard) in the Yishuv, pre-Israel Palestine.[22] *Shomer* in Jewish religious law is a legal guardian entrusted with custody and care of another's property (Exodus 22:6–14). There is also a practice of guarding the body of the deceased prior to burial, a period during which reading psalms aloud is believed to offer comfort to the spirit of the departed. The notion of guard was institutionalized in *Hashomer*, the Jewish defense organization in Palestine, active from 1909 to 1920, in addition to other groups that guarded Jewish settlements and fought for independence. A genre of songs associated with those guards and soldiers, *Shirei Eretz Yisrael* (Songs of the Land of Israel), were composed and sung as part of the full spectrum of social activities in the Yishuv during the first half of the twentieth century.[23] These musicians and their songs were commemorated by Marc Lavry (1903–67), in his opera *Dan Hashomer* (Dan the Guard) Op. 158, first performed in 1945 by the Palestine Folk Opera.

Sentinel musicians are clearly found in many traditions and play important roles in their own societies. Indeed, the question may be posed: what musical traditions do *not* nurture musicians who assume responsibility within and beyond musical domains? It may as well be the case that not all sentinel musicians are necessarily positive guards and guides. We have only to recall the Sirens from Greek mythology, who lured sailors to their deaths through their songs, providing a name for auditory warning signals.

We can close with a final example extolling the Ethiopian *azmari* tradition in terms that emphasize these musicians' roles as guards and guides. In 2011 Brooklyn-born guitarist Tomás Doncker joined forces with several well-known Ethiopian diaspora musicians to produce a lively new recording.[24] Originally the score of a play that was never staged, the songs heard on the album, *Power of the Trinity*, express nostalgia for the times of Haile Selassie I, referring in tracks such as "Conscience of the World" and "Jah-Rusalem" to the late emperor's deep influence on the African diaspora. The album, described as a "soulful blend of R&B, spoken word and global urban sounds," incorporates performances by Ethiopian-born musicians long resident in the United States, including guitarist Selam Seyoum Woldemariam and vocalists Gigi and Tsegaye B. Selassie.[25]

Directly related to the theme of sentinel is the track "Azmari Man," composed by Doncker and Alan Grubner. The song's text invokes the historical role of the *azmari*, with a colorful musical setting enlivened by harmonica riffs and driving ostinatos. A recurrent refrain in Amharic weaves throughout the song referencing the historical association of the *azmari* with wax and gold (*sämənna wärq*), the system of double meanings long a hallmark of the *azmari*'s textual prowess and political savvy. If Doncker's evocation of the Ethiopian *azmari* is noteworthy for its extraordinary poetics and rich musical setting, the song also represents a rare public acknowledgment of the figure of the *azmari* in North American popular music, while touching on our central themes of mobility and sensory impact.

> *Azmari* man, *azmari* man, sing your sweet song disguised as truth.
> *Azmari* man, *azmari* man, guarding culture, protecting roots.
> Wandering minstrel, play your tune,
> Speak of liberation, coming soon,
> The evil downpresser don't know what you say
> Come like you would, anyway . . .
> Freedom of speech is what you preach
> When they come and lock you down
> Freedom of mind is what we find
> As you rise above the silence with your sacred sound . . .
> *Sämənna wärq.*[26]

Acknowledgments

A book such as this one, which has been in development for much of my career, accrues extraordinary debts. After the years of research that have fed into this manuscript, I am indebted to more individuals and institutions than I can even recall, let alone acknowledge sufficiently here.

My first debt is surely to the many musicians of the Ethiopian diaspora who shared details of their lives and music with me and permitted me to include their testimony in these pages. This book is dedicated to them. I am especially grateful to those who participated as interviewees for the project I carried out while serving as Chair in Modern Culture at the John W. Kluge Center at the Library of Congress. Their oral histories, sound recordings, and other materials are now safeguarded in the Ethiopian music collection I assembled in 2007–8 while in residence at the library. Most are also listed in this book, by date and place of interviews, under interviews and communications, and informal snapshots of many participants are included in plates 1.3 and 1.4 of chapter 1.

Many individuals went well beyond the boundaries of interviews to provide materials, guidance, and friendship. *Liqa mezemran* Moges Seyoum generously shared his deep musical, liturgical, and institutional knowledge of Ethiopian Orthodox Christianity and extended a full measure of personal hospitality. Behailu Kassahun volunteered a handwritten list of Washington, DC, metropolitan area musicians along with contact information that served as the basis for many of my interviews. Tesfaye Lemma, who died after a long illness in 2013, was a friend and colleague from 1974, when he welcomed me to rehearsals of Orchestra Ethiopia in Addis Ababa and arranged for me to study the *krar*, the Ethiopian lyre; I have treasured the hours we shared over the years in Addis Ababa and Washington, DC. Selam Seyoum Woldemariam is an extraordinary musician as well as a scholar of Ethiopian popular music history; I acknowledge his contributions both to Ethiopian music performance and to its study. Telela Kebede, a queen of Ethiopian music, shared both her memories and her memorabilia and organized an unforgettable evening at a Silver Spring Ethiopian restaurant with the cream of Ethiopian diaspora musical talent. Alemtsehay Wedajo shared her poetry and song lyrics, as well as many hours of discussion and fellowship in Washington, DC; her commitment to perpetuating the arts in the Ethiopian diaspora is a model for all. Betelehem Melaku, whom I first interviewed in Washington, DC, moved to Cambridge shortly thereafter and has enhanced my understanding of Ethiopian instrumental and vocal styles. Abdi Nuressa shared his own experiences and connected me with Oromo musicians in Washington, DC, and Atlanta. Hana Shenkute, Minale Dagnew Bezu, Tsehay Amare, Bezawork Asfaw, and Setegn Atanaw offered support from the beginning of the project in many contexts.

Other musicians not part of the Library of Congress archival project have been sources of information and inspiration. Mulatu Astatke spent a year in Cambridge as colleague and neighbor at Harvard's Radcliffe Institute, where he patiently sat for endless interviews with myself and the third member of our Radcliffe "Ethiopian cluster," historian Steven Kaplan. I thank Mulatu for sharing so much of himself and his music, as well as so many wonderful times over the years in Cambridge, Washington, DC, and Addis Ababa. I came to know *merigeta* Tsehai Birhanu well during his nearly fifteen years of leadership at St. Michael EOT Church in Mattapan, Massachusetts, and have drawn on his extraordinary knowledge of Ethiopian Orthodox musical performance and history as well as his feedback on my work. Ali Birra, master of Oromo music, along with his wife Lily Marcos-Birra, have been generous guides for this novice in Oromo studies and also provided me with contacts in many places. Abegasu Shiota, "Tommy T" Gobena, and Henock Temesgen visited the Harvard campus in 2003 and introduced me to the music of their innovative band, Admas; it is fitting that the last chapter of the book draws on their musicality and transnational pathways. I especially appreciate the time Abegasu and Henock devoted to a process of dialogical editing during my visit to Addis Ababa in January 2020. Girum Mezmur also contributed greatly to my understanding of musicians who chose to remain in Addis Ababa, and I am grateful for his insights and remarkable musical contributions. Collaborative projects carried out with the Harvard Office for the Arts provided opportunities to bring Aster Aweke to the Harvard campus in 2009, and Meklit Hadero in 2019, when both singers talked with me at length about their careers; I thank Aster for her hospitality as well in Addis Ababa. Meklit Hadero brought a new world of diasporic music to my attention and inspired me with both her musicality and her activism. Amha Eshete has graciously shared details of his own forced migration to the United States during my many visits to Addis Ababa, along with explaining his pivotal role in paving the way for other Ethiopian musicians in the United States. *Liqa* Berhanu Mekonnen, who died in 2007, was my teacher of Ethiopian chant in Addis Ababa in 1975 and provided the foundation on which much of my work in Ethiopian music was subsequently constructed. His expertise shared about so many aspects of Ethiopian ritual music and practice enriched my approach to music in ways that I could not have anticipated. Bishop Makarios, who now resides in New Jersey, provided advice and intellectual support from the time of my arrival in Addis Ababa in 1973 and, by the late 1970s, in the United States. Many others, whom I am unable to credit individually here, are included in references throughout the book.

A number of individuals not formally part of this project but deeply knowledgeable about Ethiopia, its diaspora, and its music offered a full measure of help and support. Tefera and Getatchew Zewdie, the owners of Dukem Ethiopian Restaurant in Washington, DC, were gracious hosts during my countless visits to their restaurant over the years and fielded my queries about musical life in the DC restaurant scene. Dr. Telahun Gebrehiwot helped restore my Amharic skills after the twenty-five-year gap in my visits to Ethiopia during and after the revolution and aided with translation of numerous song texts. I met Abebaye Lema at St. Michael EOT Church in Mattapan, Massachusetts, during my first visit there, and I frequently drew on her knowledge of the women's choirs and Sunday school songs. Dr. Meqdes Mesfin has provided endless clarifications and insights into diaspora life and the impact of homeland politics and has accompanied me to numerous diaspora concerts and events; I thank her also for her friendship. Russ Gershon, the founder and leader of the Either/ Orchestra in Somerville, Massachusetts, has provided many insights into the Ethiopian jazz world and its twenty-first-century life abroad, as has Danny Mekonnen, himself a member of the diaspora as well as my former Harvard student, who is the founder of Boston's Debo Band. Charles Sutton has offered endless clarifications, materials, and moral support for this project. Francis Falceto, the editor of the *éthiopiques* series, has graciously shared information available nowhere else.

I am deeply grateful to the institutions and fellowship agencies that have generously supported this complex, multinational project. They include a Radcliffe Institute Fellowship, 2007–8; National Endowment for the Humanities Fellowship, 2007–8; John Simon Guggenheim Memorial Foundation Fellowship, 2007–8; Chair in Modern Culture at the John W. Kluge Center of the Library of Congress, 2007–8; Rockefeller Foundation Bellagio Center Residency, 2012; and yearlong residency as the Marta Sutton

Weeks Fellow at the Stanford Humanities Center, 2015–16. Harvard University has provided sabbaticals and research support, most recently in 2019 with grants from the FAS Dean's Competitive Fund for Promising Scholarship and a Weatherhead Center for International Affairs Medium Grant for Faculty Research Projects. The Anne and Jim Rothenberg Fund for Humanities Research at Harvard University helped support this book's publication process, as did support from the Department of Music.

Each of the residential fellowships I held gave me access to new intellectual and human resources. The Kluge Center at the Library of Congress, then under the directorship of Dr. Carolyn Brown, provided support for my oral history project; I thank Mary Lou Reker, JoAnne Kitching, Robert Saladini, and Alicia Robertson. The American Folklife Center at the Library of Congress, its Archive of Folk Culture, and the Veterans History Project extended their facilities and resources; I greatly appreciated the assistance and collegiality of former director Peggy Bulger, Robert Patrick, Michael Taft, and Jonathan Gold. The Folger Shakespeare Library provided accommodations that facilitated my work at the library during the summers of 2007 and 2008. All the musicians who came to the Kluge Center for interviews and shared their wonder at seeing the Great Hall are credited in interviews and communications, but I am particularly grateful for the hospitality of *liqa mezemran* Moges Seyoum, Dr. Aklilu Haile, Bililign Mandefro, and Ms. Sergout Werku at the Debre Selam Kidist Mariam EOT Church in Washington, DC. The late art historian Marilyn Heldman provided a home away from home in Silver Spring, Maryland, during my numerous visits to the area from the early 2000s and shared experiences in the field in an American urban context that neither of us could have imagined when we first traveled together in rural Ethiopia during the fall of 1973. Dr. Itsushi Kawase provided visual documentation of diaspora musical events and has been exceedingly generous in sharing his audiovisual materials, translation skills, and companionship at late-night Ethiopian musical events in Washington, DC. Fentahun Tiruneh, Reference Specialist at the African and Middle Eastern Division, Library of Congress, provided invaluable support, suggestions, and friendship over the years.

A Radcliffe Fellowship year provided an opportunity to collaborate with longtime colleague in Ethiopian studies, historian Steven Kaplan, and with composer-performer Mulatu Astatke. In addition to the extensive interviews we carried out with Mulatu, Steven and I pursued ethnographic research together with Ethiopians in the Boston metropolitan area and visited churches and other Ethiopian institutions in the Northeast. We together hosted an interdisciplinary conference on the Ethiopian diaspora, from which we coedited a collection of articles in a special double issue, "Creating the Ethiopian Diaspora," in *Diaspora* (2006 [published 2011], reissued by Tsehai Press in 2015). I here remember with gratitude and affection the extraordinary presence of the late Judith Vichniac, then director of the Radcliffe Fellowship Program, as well as the stimulation of the other fifty fellows from across the disciplines.

At the Stanford Humanities Center, then director Caroline Winterer and her colleagues, including Robert Barrick, Andrea Davies, Kelda Jamison, Najwa Salame, Susan Sebbard, Patricia Terrazas, Andres Le Roux, and Sarah Ogilvie, offered a full measure of support and advice. I thank the other fellows from 2015–16, especially Katharina Piechocki, Jenna Gibbs, Gabriella Safran, the late Bernard (Barney) Bate, Niloofar Haeri, and Nancy Kollmann for stimulating and useful feedback. Karen Fung, curator of the African Collection at the Stanford University Libraries, provided expert assistance in locating materials in the Stanford collection. Shelley Fisher Fishkin, Rachael Hill, Charles Kronengold, Jesse Rodin, Anna Schultz, Issayas Tesfamariam, and Carol Vernallis provided a warm welcome to the Stanford community and offered sage advice on issues encountered in my work.

An invitation from Fumiko Ohinata at UNESCO to offer an intensive weeklong seminar in 2007 on the study of Ethiopian music and culture for professors from Ethiopian institutions countrywide provided unexpected insights into the study of Ethiopian music and musical life at home and abroad. Simeneh Betreyohannes Gebremariam offered wonderful support as my teaching fellow for that seminar and has continued to be a remarkable resource for many aspects of this study as he has pursued his own graduate studies on music of the Ethiopian revolution at the University of Michigan.

In each diaspora community, individuals extended themselves to aid my project and to introduce me to aspects of Ethiopian life in their locale. In Atlanta during late July 2009, I attended an Oromo Studies Conference and the annual Oromo games, where I was fortunate to experience the expertise and warm hospitality of Professor Mohammed Hassen and Aziza Hassen, who also located a knowledgeable taxi driver, Khalid Mohammed, who provided an informative daylong tour of Ethiopian communities in the Atlanta metropolitan area. This experience inspired my modus operandi during subsequent visits to many other diaspora locales, where I was able to hire a taxi driver from the community who was a longtime resident and deeply familiar with the community's history and growth. Dr. Hamza Abdurezak enabled me to meet and interview Ali Birra in Atlanta, and Jamal Sule shared information about musical life in that area.

During June 2010 and thanks to contacts made through Ali Birra, a longtime resident of Toronto, Canada, I visited the large Ethiopian, Eritrean, and Somali communities in Toronto. With the guidance of Abdul Hamid Mohammed, a former secretary of the Oromo community, I visited the main sites in that sprawling metropolitan area. While visiting community shops, I spotted flyers advertising a concert at a local club by Ethiopian American singer Mesfin Zeberga Tereda, whom I had interviewed in the Library of Congress project, and which I was able to attend.

During November 2010 in Los Angeles, California, I was introduced to the community and to Little Ethiopia by Berhanu Asfaw and Zena Asfaw Meqdes; Abba Tsige welcomed me to the St. Mary's EOT Church in Los Angeles.

In Minneapolis, Minnesota, during March 2011, Elizabeth Namarra and her sister Martha devoted considerable time to sharing their experience in diaspora and hosted me for a visit to their Oromo Evangelical Church. Jawar Muhammad and Arfasse Gammadaa offered hospitality during my visit and contacted Adamu Dinka Betal, who introduced me to the physical, institutional, and ethnic distribution of the local Oromo and Somali communities and to local musicians and shop owners.

During numerous visits to Houston, Texas (my childhood home), between 2007 and 2015, I visited Ethiopian shops, restaurants, and churches. In September 2013 I made a trip to Dallas, where, thanks to Danny and Mac Mekonnen, Wube Mekonnen graciously provided a tour of the institutional and commercial centers of the rapidly growing Ethiopian community in that metropolitan area.

I thank a Somali contact (who wishes to remain anonymous) for an excellent overview of various communities from the Horn of Africa in the Berkeley and Oakland, California, area during the fall of 2015.

I thank Dr. Nicola Scaldaferri for a stimulating visit to the Eritrean community in Milan, Italy, during April 2012.

While carrying out my ongoing research in Cambridge, Massachusetts, New York City, and the Washington, DC, metropolitan area and through the writing process, I have benefited from the continual advice and expertise of colleagues Solomon Addis Getahun, Getatchew Haile, Hamza Abdurezak, Mekonnen Firew Ayano, and Meley Mulugetta. Steven Kaplan has been an extraordinary colleague and collaborator in Ethiopian studies for decades, and I here once again acknowledge with deepest gratitude his generosity with materials, advice, and references throughout this often-shared research and writing process.

Colleagues across academia have provided a wealth of sources, materials, and welcome advice during the writing of this book; they are, of course, not responsible for the manner in which I have incorporated their suggestions. I thank Philip Bohlman, Benjamin Brinner, Brigid Cohen, Jean and John Comaroff, Virginia Danielson, Ganavya Iyer Doraiswamy, Margot Fassler, Rosalind I. J. Hackett, Ellen Harris, Jocelyne Guilbault, Getatchew Haile, the late Marilyn Heldman, David Kaminsky, Scott Kominers, Helen Lawlor, Panayotis (Paddy) League, Katherine Lee, Christie McDonald, Peter McMurray, Sarah Morelli, Daniel Neuman, Aniruddh Patel, Katharina Piechocki, Julie Rohwein, Gabriella Safran, Uri Schreter, Anna Schultz, Anthony Seeger, Judith Tick, and Audrey Wozniak.

An early, abbreviated version of chapter 3 was presented as a keynote for the Royal Musical Association Music and Philosophy Study Group during July 2015 at King's College, London, as well as at colloquia at University of California–Los Angeles and Stanford University. Papers on the sentinel concept and materials were presented in talks at the University of California–Berkeley (2015); New York University (2017); the University of Illinois (2019); UNICAMP Universidade Estadual de Campinas, Brazil (2019), and ICTM Cork, Ireland (2020). I am grateful for comments I received at these events. The section of chapter 7 discussing Mulatu Astatke's mobility is found in expanded form in my article "'Traveling Music': Mulatu Astatke and the Genesis of Ethiopian Jazz" in *Jazz Worlds/World Jazz* (2016).

Many research assistants contributed greatly to this project at all stages over the years. At Harvard, I thank Bridget Haile, Eric Lin, Ken Gichinga, Samantha Heinle (and the SHARP fellow program), Saskia Maxwell Keller, Marika Thompson, and Eloise Hodges for help with preparing interview transcripts, preparing the manuscript for this book, and other research tasks. Blayne Haggart aided with preparing transcripts at the Kluge Center at the Library of Congress. At Stanford, Miguel Isaias Samano located relevant articles in the *Ethiopian Herald* and Bitiya Elias Samuel helped translate song texts.

The last stages of manuscript completion and editing were especially challenging because of complications I experienced following hand surgery in fall 2019 as well as the COVID-19 pandemic that began some months thereafter. I could not have completed this manuscript without the devoted and creative help of Audrey Wozniak, Eloise Hodges, and Dr. Minji Kim. A number of colleagues helped me acquire or generously shared photographs that appear in these pages, including Ali Birra, Lily Marcos-Birra, Amha Eshete, Selam Seyoum Woldemariam, Francis Falceto, Yehunie Belay, Bezawork Asfaw, Meklit Hadero, Itsushi Kawase, Russ Gershon, Teffera (Teff) Girma, Teshome Mitiku, Munit Mesfin, Wayna

Wondwossen, Charles Sutton, Michael Gervers, Boris Adjemian, and the late Marilyn Heldman. I am deeply grateful to Michel Temteme Dagie for sharing his beautiful photograph of Ali Birra that appears on the cover. This image is taken from Michel's ongoing book project (*Faces of Ethiopian Music*), a photographic documentation through portraits of significant figures from Ethiopian music. I thank Scott Walker of the Harvard Map Collection for his indispensable collaboration in producing updated maps. Other institutions and individuals who graciously provided visual materials are acknowledged throughout the book.

For their comments and invaluable suggestions on the final draft of the manuscript, I thank Ellen Harris, Francis Falceto, Steven Kaplan, Mark Slobin, Selam Seyoum Woldemariam, Haden Smiley, Charles Sutton, and Timkehet Teffera. Two anonymous readers for the University of Chicago Press, whose identity I only learned as this book went to press, Beverley Diamond and Frank Gunderson, made suggestions that greatly improved the manuscript. For dialogical editing sessions and feedback, I thank Meklit Hadero, Zakki Jawad, Abegasu Shiota, Henock Temesgen, Kirubel Assefa, Munit Mesfin, and Mekbul Jemal Tahir. Of course, any mistakes or infelicities that remain are my own.

The constant support of my colleagues and the staff of the Harvard Department of Music contributed in countless ways to this long-term project. I owe special thanks for their intellectual and moral support to Carol Oja, Ingrid Monson, Kate van Orden, Judith Tick, and Braxton Shelley. I give a loud shout-out to the wonderful Harvard Music Department staff, led by Nancy Shafman and, including over the years this project was in process, Eva Kim, Karen Rynne, Brid Coogan, Kaye Denny, Charles Stillman, Lesley Bannatyne, and Kalan Chang, who all pitched in whenever necessary with timely support. The staff of the Eda Kuhn Loeb Music Library at many moments also provided needed resources and advice; I am grateful to Virginia Danielson, Sarah Adams, Liza Vick, Kerry Masteller, Elizabeth Berndt-Morris, Peter Laurence, and Robert Dennis.

I am deeply grateful to University of Chicago Press executive editor Elizabeth Branch Dyson for sage advice offered over the years that greatly improved this manuscript. Mollie McFee, University of Chicago Press editorial associate, has been an excellent and creative guide throughout the publication process. I thank Carol McGillivray and Geof Garvey for their management of the copyediting process, and Marilyn Bliss for her wonderful index. I acknowledge with gratitude the creative assistance of Dr. Minji Kim throughout the editing and production process.

Jack Shelemay has supported this seemingly endless project mightily and has provided innumerable insights and clarifications from his own deep knowledge of Ethiopian languages and culture; he has also shared many moments in Ethiopia and its diaspora along the way. That his own path has been shaped by the same forces that gave rise to the Ethiopian diaspora is one of life's great ironies. I cannot thank him enough for decades of love and support.

Appendix

AN OVERVIEW OF ETHIOPIAN DIASPORA COMMUNITIES ACROSS THE UNITED STATES

Beyond the large Ethiopian and Eritrean populations in Washington, DC, discussed in chapter 6, immigrants from the Horn of Africa have settled in many other locations across the United States.[1] Most are home to musicians, many of whom are engaged in community cultural and institutional life.

The Northeast
BOSTON, MASSACHUSETTS

Ethiopians live across the Boston metropolitan area, although many are found in both Cambridge and Boston's South End, with the total Ethiopian population of Greater Boston estimated at nine to twelve thousand.[2] In 1986 the Ethiopian Community Mutual Assistance Association (ECMAA) was established by Ethiopian refugees in Cambridge to serve their community. According to the ECMAA, the Boston Ethiopian population is 60 percent male, and 80 percent have limited English proficiency. The high cost of living in the Boston area results in severe housing pressures. The Ethiopian Community Association of Greater Boston, founded in 2011 and located in the Boston township of Roxbury, aids Ethiopian immigrants to become self-sufficient and to preserve and promote Ethiopian culture and traditions in the area.[3] An Eritrean Community Center is located in Roxbury, while Ethiopian and Eritrean restaurants are found across the metropolitan area in Cambridge, Somerville, Boston, and Malden. Ethiopian and Eritrean Orthodox churches as well as Ethiopian evangelical churches are scattered across the Boston metropolitan area. Most meet in the facilities of other organizations or churches, although St. Michael EOT Church in Boston's Mattapan section bought a small frame building in foreclosure that serves their congregation; it had previously been a synagogue and then an Armenian church. A congregant who had arrived in the area in

PLATE A.1 Betelehem "Betty" Melaku performs at a Harvard University concert in 2018. Collection of author.

1975 and who was well established put up her house as collateral in order to guarantee the church's mortgage.[4] The Ethiopian Evangelical Church in Boston (Roxbury) was founded in 2015, and the demographics of the evangelical churches tend to be younger. St. Mary's Ethiopian Orthodox Church has a predominantly Tigrayan membership that meets in the St. Stephen's Episcopal Church building in Boston's South End.[5]

Boston has long attracted Ethiopian musicians: Mulatu Astatke arrived in 1958 to study at what was then called the Schillinger House of Music, and the versatile Betelehem Melaku more than half a century later resides in Cambridge, where she performs traditional songs on *masenqo* and *krar* and entertains at weddings as a one-woman band, accompanying herself on the synthesizer.[6] (See plate A.1.)

From the early 2000s until his retirement in 2017, *merigeta* Tsehai Birhanu, a highly trained church musician discussed at length in chapter 9, led St. Michael EOT Church in Mattapan and was a sentinel musician both in Ethiopia before the revolution, and afterward in the diaspora. Boston is on the concert circuit for most touring Ethiopian musicians and is also the home to two major musical ensembles that perform Ethiopian music professionally—Danny Mekonnen's Debo Band, centered in Jamaica Plain, and Russ Gershon's Either/Orchestra, headquartered in Somerville.

NEW YORK, NEW YORK

New York is perhaps the most atypical Ethiopian diaspora locale. Estimated as home to around ten thousand Ethiopians across the metropolitan area, with most living in the Bronx and areas of New Jersey, the New York community is not as socially cohesive nor as heavily institutionalized as are other diaspora communities. The difference can be attributed to the fact that many Ethiopians tend to live in New York for shorter durations, often while working for international organizations; the economic pressures of New York City life also lead many to depart for other places. The main ethnic institutions are a handful of Ethiopian Orthodox churches.[7] After thirty years in residence at the Riverside Church in Manhattan, the EOT Church of Our Savior in 2014 bought a church building in the northwest Bronx that used to house a Lutheran congregation.[8] The Ethiopian community in New York City is most clearly represented by a number of Ethiopian restaurants in various neighborhoods of Manhattan and across the other boroughs and New Jersey townships.

The West Coast
LOS ANGELES, CALIFORNIA

The Ethiopian community in Los Angeles is one of the oldest in the North American diaspora, dating to the 1950s when a small cohort of students arrived to enroll in local colleges. Over time, it became quite diverse in its composition with fewer ethnic tensions between Ethiopian, Eritrean, and Oromo members than found in other diaspora communities. The Ethiopian community grew rapidly after the start of the revolution and remains "very spread out, no one lives in the one area."[9] With an estimated Ethiopian population of at least sixty thousand, Los Angeles has to date been the only US city to successfully establish a separate commercial neighbor-hood officially registered as "Little Ethiopia."[10]

In 1979 the first Ethiopian restaurant, Walia, opened in Los Angeles. By 1981 several more eateries were founded and over the years moved to the neighborhood located on Fairfax Avenue between Olympic and Pico Boulevards that would become known as Little Ethiopia.[11] The area's nu-merous restaurants, hair salons, and shops declare their national origin through the display of festive banners and the red, yellow, and green col-ors of the Ethiopian flag displayed in shop windows and interiors. There are occasional live performances by local Ethiopian musicians at a few restaurants, but performance permits can be difficult to obtain, and one restaurant owner reported that for this reason he has mainly used CDs rather than live musicians.[12] Since 2001, Little Ethiopia has sponsored an annual parade on Fairfax Avenue each September to celebrate the Ethio-pian New Year.[13]

In 1988 Saint Mary's EOT Church of Los Angeles was established and around 2005, began mounting annual *Timket* (Ethiopian Epiphany) cel-ebrations. By 2011 these events were the largest Ethiopian religious gath-erings in the United States, held in a parking lot adjacent to the Forum in the Inglewood area, usually on a Sunday afternoon in late January. "When the bishops dip their crosses into a plastic pool of water and sprinkle it on the bowed heads of believers . . . it blesses you the whole year," one par-ticipant explained.[14] This elaborate church procession attracts members of the Ethiopian diaspora from many communities in the western United States and beyond:

> Timket in LA is a big occasion. People come from all over the United States, Europe, and even Ethiopia. It is a very big cultural occasion. San Jose comes to LA that day, Las Vegas comes, Oakland comes. They all come to LA for Timket.[15]

SAN FRANCISCO BAY AREA, CALIFORNIA

Christian Amhara from the northern Ethiopian city, Gondar, first came to the Bay Area in the 1960s to study at area universities. Only decades later were they joined by Eritrean, Oromo, and Somali immigrants. Approxi-mately twenty thousand people from the Horn of Africa are today spread across a large geographical area stretching from the East and West Bay to the city of San Jose in Silicon Valley.[16] The early arrivals fleeing the revo-lution founded three Ethiopian Orthodox churches on Telegraph Avenue in Oakland, as well as evangelical churches. The later 1980s and homeland conflicts of 1992–1993 saw the entry of Oromo immigrants to the Bay Area and, in the early 1990s and again in the early 2000s, two waves of Somali refugees.[17] Today one finds members of different Ethiopian ethnic groups residing in the Temescal area of Oakland and patronizing a well-established commercial area on and adjacent to Telegraph Avenue, run by Ethiopian shop owners of diverse ethnic backgrounds. At local coffee shops on Telegraph Avenue, one can encounter Ethiopians, Eritreans, Oromo, and Somalis socializing together. In some instances, shared religious affiliations also encourage interactions that transcend different ethnic backgrounds: for instance, Ethiopians, Oromo, and Somali Muslims worship together at a large mosque at Telegraph and 31st Street, their religious needs outweighing ethnic rivalries.

It is clear that these relationships have emerged slowly in Oakland. "It takes time to build a community," one Somali interlocutor emphasized:

> At first there were no directions, no one to guide you. You worry about everything, how to get to work, how to live. But by the late 1990s and early 2000s, the community jelled. Now we are Americans. Let's pull together.[18]

The San Francisco Bay Area diaspora again provides a useful example of regional cooperation and innovation. For many years, the Oakland community successfully hosted a New Year (*Enkutatash*) celebration for their entire region until an annual $25,000 grant from a private San Francisco foundation ended in 2015. As a result, the greater San Francisco Bay Area *Enkutatash* celebration was canceled, and multiple artists and musicians rushed to fill the void. Ethiopian families in San Jose organized a musical celebration at nearby Lake Cunningham Regional Park; a San Francisco Ethiopian dance teacher organized dance and craft activities for local families with children; and the owner of an Oakland bar organized a night of music and dance featuring a visiting Ethiopian singer accompanied by the local Selamta Band. "There was nothing else going on so we figured we had to do something for our community," explained Oakland organizer Mekdem Sebhatu. The Selamta Band's lead bassist, Teddy Shawl, emphasized that the celebration was intended as a nondenominational unity event cutting across political and religious lines.[19] Here one finds a number of musicians acting as sentinels, taking decisive steps to unite their communities through musical initiatives.

Among the Ethiopian American musicians active in the San Francisco Bay Area is Meklit Hadero, who is discussed in chapter 9.

SEATTLE, WASHINGTON

Seattle is home to numerous immigrants from the Horn of Africa, with the Ethiopian Community in Seattle Agency incorporated in 1987 initiated by immigrants who sought to help their community.[20] The organization supports the social, cultural, and civic life of the Puget Sound Area and assists Ethiopians and Ethiopian Americans in preserving and sharing their cultural heritage.

A 2011 study estimated Seattle to be home to twenty-five to thirty thousand Ethiopians; eight to ten thousand Eritreans; and thirty to thirty-five thousand Somalis.[21] Religious institutions include Ethiopian and Eritrean Orthodox churches, Oromo evangelical churches, and mosques.[22] Many Seattle businesses today are still owned by Ethiopian immigrants who originally arrived in Seattle from northwestern Ethiopia. Their St. Gabriel EOT Church, constructed in 1999, is one of the largest Ethiopian Orthodox churches in the United States.

The Seattle community provides an example of diaspora interethnic tensions. Said to have begun with ten people who arrived from Ethiopia in 1971, the first wave of Eritrean refugees settled in Seattle in 1981, followed by successive waves of Ethiopians and Oromos, additional Eritreans, and Somalis.[23] The community did not cohere as a whole:

> We Somali, Ethiopian, and Eritrean exiles are like guests in somebody else's house. We each live in separate rooms and have little to do with one another. Out of respect for the host family, we are polite and try to keep our antagonisms out of sight.[24]

Investigations by US authorities of several Seattle residents of Somali descent after the 9/11 attacks for possible ties with terrorist group Al-Shabaab heightened suspicions locally that Somali immigrants harbored potential terrorists and reinforced the Somali community's tendency to look inward.[25] Fighting in the Horn of Africa between Somalia and Ethiopia sparked additional diasporic tensions, most markedly after Ethiopia's attack on Mogadishu in 2006. The complex social organization of the Seattle Somali community provides additional pressure toward fragmentation, with eighteen registered Somali social service centers, each run by a different Somali clan.[26] Thus in Seattle, the Somali immigrant community does not cooperate under a common leadership, let alone with other ethnic communities from the Horn of Africa.

Seattle's creative music scene has been home for Gabriel Teodros, a hip-hop artist who collaborates on occasion with his cousin Meklit Hadero;

both are discussed in chapter 9. His most recent album is *What We Leave Behind* in 2020.[27]

The Midwest

MINNEAPOLIS–ST. PAUL, MINNESOTA

Minneapolis–St. Paul is home to a large community from the Horn of Africa, with the first two immigrants said to have been Oromo men who arrived in 1972 and who both married Americans.[28] Oromo identity is a proud and independent one in Minnesota, articulated often and publicly.

Although Minneapolis–St. Paul today functions as the center of the international Oromo diaspora, with some forty thousand Oromo residing there, the Twin Cities also have the largest settlement of Somalis (eighty thousand) in the United States. The African Development Center (ADC) of Minnesota, established in Minneapolis in 2003, helps any and all of the hundred thirty thousand African immigrants and refugees in the Twin Cities to overcome economic, linguistic, cultural, and religious barriers.[29] The Oromo Community Center in St. Paul, founded as an informal mutual assistance association in 1985, later became the nonprofit organization Oromo Community of Minnesota to assist the growing numbers of Oromo immigrants in the Twin Cities.[30] Today, the headquarters for more than thirty-seven Oromo communities in diaspora, the organization purchased its own community center in St. Paul in 2008.[31]

The Somalis, the most numerous among the refugee communities from the Horn of Africa in the Minneapolis–St. Paul area, maintain the clearest social boundaries. When I visited Minneapolis–St. Paul in 2011, an unmarked mall on East 24th Street in South Minneapolis housed a religious bookshop, carpet shops, clothing stores, and California Studio, a well-stocked store with musical recordings. Despite the separation of Somalis from other ethnic communities in the area, California Studio marketed music for all the constituencies in Minnesota from the Horn of Africa, offering "Ethio-Oromo-Eritrean Music."[32]

Minneapolis Oromo are divided among Muslims, Christians, and those who practice Oromo traditional religion, *Waaqeffannaa*. Muslim Oromo attend any convenient local mosque, such as the Tawfiq Islamic Center in South Minneapolis, although many in the community aspire to build an Oromo mosque. Despite ethnic and religious separation, sociocommerscapes exist where members of all communities from the Horn of Africa in the Twin Cities do in fact interact across ethnic divisions. Despite the Somali majority, Oromo are so prominent and active in the Twin Cities that it has become known as the "Oromia Capital of America."[33]

There are several Oromo evangelical churches in Minneapolis– St. Paul, part of a network linking Oromo evangelical churches in Washington, DC, and other American locales.[34] A relationship between Oromo in the Wollega region of Ethiopia and Lutheran missions dates to the late nineteenth century, resulting in the conversion of many Oromo to Christianity. In 1952 the Ethiopian Evangelical Church Mekane Yesus (EECMY), also known as the Mekane Yesus Church, was founded in Addis Ababa as an umbrella for Lutheran Ethiopians. With the Twin Cities having long been a primary place of settlement for Scandinavians affiliated with Lutheran denominations, Minnesota attracted many Christian Oromo who were persecuted during the Ethiopian revolution for their affiliation with Mekane Yesus and who left the country seeking refuge in the United States.[35] The experience of Elizabeth Namarra, an Oromo evangelical music composer from Minneapolis, is recounted in chapter 5.

A number of other Oromo musicians live in Minneapolis, including singer Dawite Mekonnen. Born in Wollega in western Oromia, Dawite has released nine albums and performs mainly at private parties and weddings. Facing political problems at home in 1999, he escaped to Kenya and received asylum in the United States in 2001. First placed by Catholic sponsors in New Hampshire, he decided to join friends in Minnesota. Dawite juggles his music making with additional jobs to support his family but manages to produce a new album every two to three years. "At home music was a full-time job. Here, music is part time."[36] Dawite expresses hope to return to Wollega in the future.

CHICAGO, ILLINOIS

Musician Zeleke Gessesse was an early arrival to Chicago: "We came to Chicago as political refugees from Ethiopia," he said, recalling the arduous journey he endured to join relatives in Chicago in 1978.[37] Having formed a reggae band named Dallol while a teenager in Ethiopia, Zeleke quickly founded a new band of the same name in diaspora.[38] In 1986 he bought a music club named Wild Hare on North Clark Street in Chicago's Wrigleyville that "over the course of time . . . garnered not just a regional but a national and international reputation as one of the premier venues for reggae and Caribbean music."[39] The Wild Hare attracted major artists such as Rita Marley, Jimmy Cliff, and Toots and the Maytals until its closing in 2011, when Zeleke returned to Ethiopia. Zeleke was a sentinel musician, one of the few Ethiopian musicians in diaspora who fashioned a career performing international genres outside traditional Ethiopian styles.

Chicago appears to have provided an environment in which immigrants could depart from long-standing traditions both musical and culinary. An early Eritrean restaurant in Chicago, Mama Desta's Red Sea Restaurant, which closed in 2009, innovated musically by featuring a Senegalese *kora* player named Morikeba Kouyate, who performed there in the evenings.[40] Chicago-area Ethiopian restaurants also included new diaspora dishes on their menus, with the Ras Dashen restaurant offering a dessert of traditional Ethiopian flatbread (*injera*), topped with blueberries and ice cream.[41] Chicago's Ethiopian community is heterolocal in terms of residential areas as well as diverse in religious affiliations, supporting three Ethiopian Orthodox churches, a Mennonite Ethiopian church (Berhane Wongel), and several Oromo evangelical churches.

COLUMBUS, OHIO

Columbus has a rapidly growing Ethiopian community dating from the 1980s, estimated at twenty to twenty-five thousand. The Columbus community is heterolocal, spread across the east, northeast, and west of the city. The early population came from Sudanese refugee camps, followed by secondary migrations of individuals who sought to join family members already in Columbus. A primarily Christian community, the activity of Lutheran missions in northern Ethiopia attracted both rural Oromo and Tigrayans to Columbus.

The Southeast
ATLANTA, GEORGIA

If Minnesota is the informal center of the Oromo diaspora, Atlanta has a small but active Oromo population numbering around five thousand out of fifteen to twenty thousand immigrants from the Horn of Africa in the metropolitan area.[42] The Atlanta population from the Horn of Africa is also heterolocal, with Ethiopian and Oromo areas largely separate, part of the diverse population of DeKalb County, which extends northeast of Atlanta across towns such as Clarkston and Tucker. Ethiopian commercial places, including markets, restaurants, and even an *injera* bakery are found alongside shops serving a large Latino population living nearby.

Atlanta's Ethiopian communities do not always signal their identity through store names or ethnic decor; indeed, one cannot be certain of the ethnicity of a shop owner from the Horn of Africa unless one is told. With the exception of Somali shops that are scattered throughout Clarkston, Ethiopian, Oromo, and Eritrean institutions are difficult to identify without the assistance of a knowledgeable community member.

One does find Oromo concentrations in some apartment complexes, such as the Spring Chase Apartments in Stone Mountain, where many Oromo live; other apartment complexes house a blend of Somalis, Ethiopians, and Oromo along Indian Creek Drive. But the Oromo community is almost invisible unless you know where to look. At the same time, members of the Atlanta community from the Horn of Africa are assertive politically and a mixed group of Oromo professionals from the area emphasized that they wanted to be described in these pages as the "Oromo diaspora," not as part of the "Ethiopian diaspora."[43]

Although there are both Oromo Muslims and Oromo Christians living in the Atlanta metropolitan area, there are also efforts to practice indigenous Oromo religion, *Waaqeffannaa* (belief in one God), as part of a global initiative coordinated through a central office in Bergen, Norway. This group meets occasionally, coming together when a knowledgeable visitor is in town from Oromo communities in Ethiopia or Kenya. There are also three mosques in Clarkston alone, located mainly in houses that do not amplify the call to prayer nor widely advertise their presence.[44]

As in most diaspora communities I visited, I found active musicians in the Atlanta area. Jamal Sule is an Oromo musician who arrived in the United States in 1997 at age seventeen. A native of eastern Oromia, from the region around the ancient walled city of Harar, Jamal emphasizes differences among Oromo traditions and suggests that

> where you were born gives you a distinctive accent—and the music is different. Compare me and Abdi [Nuressa]—the same culture, but a different accent. Although the language is one, the music is different.[45]

The Southwest
DALLAS–FORT WORTH, TEXAS

The Mutual Assistance Association for the Ethiopian Community (MAAEC), serving the approximately thirty thousand Ethiopians in the Dallas–Fort Worth area, was founded in 1983, launching the first efforts to provide empowering programs and services for Ethiopians.[46] The organization has sponsored an annual Ethiopian Day every September since 2001. A central goal of MAAEC, for which it actively raises funds, is to build a community center to serve Ethiopians in Dallas and Fort Worth. Birhan "Mac" Mekonnen, a businessman who has served as executive director of the association, heads the fundraising initiative to establish a center "designed to bring Ethiopians together and keep the tradition and culture, to teach our children, making sure they know their roots."[47]

The Dallas Ethiopian community is characterized as "a good economic community and a big one. . . . The community is growing rapidly, and it is all over the city."[48] Many Ethiopians and Eritreans live in the north Dallas metropolitan area municipalities of Garland, Richardson, and Plano. However, their main commercial area, informally termed "Little Ethiopia-Eritrea," is located south of these residential areas.

Members of the Dallas Ethiopian and Eritrean communities encounter each other at commercial clusters with Ethiopian restaurants, an Ethiopian-run computer store, and a bakery. As in other Ethiopian diaspora locales, the food mart carries music and film videos. Ibex Ethiopian Bar and Cuisine is patronized by many Ethiopians, especially when it shifts to a nightclub format with a DJ on Saturday nights.[49] Desta Ethiopian Restaurant, in north Dallas south of Interstate 635, continues to attract a particularly devoted following after the widely publicized 2012 murders of its founders, Yared Lemma and Yenni Desta.[50] The restaurant features a singer on Saturday nights.

There are a handful of Ethiopian Orthodox churches in and around Dallas, the EOT Debre Meheret St. Michael Cathedral founded in 1991 in Garland being the largest.[51] There are also Ethiopian evangelical churches throughout the metropolitan area, such as the Ethiopian Evangelical Baptist Church that in June 2018 moved into a new site in Garland.[52] There is not a dedicated Ethiopian or Oromo mosque, but the Islamic Association of North Texas accommodates many Muslim members of the Ethiopian community for worship.

HOUSTON, TEXAS

Ethiopians arrived in Houston during the early years of the revolution, with an Ethiopian Community Organization founded in 1980 to represent and promote the Ethiopian community.[53] The number of Ethiopians and Eritreans in Houston is listed as 2,463 and 704, respectively, in data from the US Census Bureau 2010–14 American Community Survey Estimates.[54] However, these figures do not reflect numbers living across the entire metropolitan area, known as Greater Houston, which is one of the fastest-growing metropolitan areas in the country.

There are several Ethiopian Orthodox churches in Houston, with Debre Selam Medhane Alem EOT Church on Canemont Street featuring live streaming of their weekend services.[55] This active and rapidly growing Ethiopian Orthodox community purchased acreage in 1993 and conducted its services in a tent until August 6, 1995, when they laid the cornerstone for the current assembly hall; subsequently, they expanded the compound to seven acres to accommodate a new Sunday school building, a residential building for members of the clergy, and social spaces for its members and their children. This vibrant community has plans to build a much bigger edifice to accommodate its growing congregation.

A great concern of many Ethiopian Orthodox Christians in diaspora is the future of their esoteric liturgical tradition. There are no existing educational institutions for training Ethiopian Christian musicians and priests in the diaspora, and the harsh impact of the revolution on the homeland church has reduced the flow abroad of clergy trained in the traditional liturgy. The Houston community has initiated a drive to build a monastery where they can train new clergy and musicians and bury officials such as the patriarch of the American Synod, who died in the United States. Many churches affiliated with the American Synod are hosting benefits to support this construction.[56] The Washington, DC, Ethiopian theatrical company, Tayitu, founded and directed by poet and song lyricist Alemtsehay Wedajo, presented a benefit performance for this purpose.[57]

Houston has a number of Ethiopian restaurants, including Lucy Ethiopian Restaurant and Lounge on Southwest Freeway, which has a dance floor and bandstand in order to accommodate musicians from Ethiopia who stop in Houston on tours to sizable Ethiopian American communities. The facilities also permit the restaurant to host civic events such as those for the World Refugee Day. Despite its name, referring to the earliest hominid found in Ethiopia, Lucy has a modern décor with contemporary paintings.

Glossary

Term (popular spelling in parentheses). Definition

abugida. a writing system with consonant and vowel written as a unit
Abyssinia. traditional name for Ethiopia
ac'c'ir (*achir*). short vocal style
Achabir vocal style. vocal style associated with an Ethiopian highland monastery
Adare. people of Harar, eastern Ethiopia
adbar. protective spirit
ADC. African Development Center of Minnesota
Addis Acoustic Project. Addis Ababa, founded by Girum Mezmur in 2008
Adey/Soukous Club. Moges Habte's club in Washington, DC
Admas. Horizon; name of Ethiopian American band
AESAONE. All Ethiopian Sports Association One
Afaan Oromo. Cushitic language spoken by Oromo people, also called *Oromiffa*
Afran Qallo. 1960s Oromo band joined by Ali Birra in 1963
Agau (*Agaw*). indigenous highland people of Ethiopia
amba. a steep, flat-topped mountain in the Northern Ethiopian highlands
Amhara. people of northern and central highlands of Ethiopia
Amharic. one of the official languages of Ethiopia
ammakayənnät. agency
aqqwaqwam. Ethiopian Christian liturgical dance
Arba ləjoch (*Arba lijoch*). "40 Children," 1920s band of Armenian orphans
Arba Minch Collective. network of multidisciplinary artists from Ethiopian diaspora living in North America
atamo. small, laced drum
Axumite Band. Addis Ababa band in the 1990s
azmari. itinerant secular musician
azmari bet. "*azmari* house," small clubs for musical performance by *azmari*
azmatch. refrain of a song
Badme. town on Ethiopian-Eritrean border at center of 1998–2018 border dispute
bägäna (*bagana*). large lyre with ten strings
bahəl zämänawi (*bahel zemenawi*). modern cultural music

bahǝlawi (bahelawi). cultural or traditional music

balä zar. zar practitioner

bǝherawi sǝmmet. nationalistic feeling, patriotism

Berhane Wongel. Mennonite Ethiopian Church in Chicago, Illinois

bǝrr (birr). Ethiopian currency

Beta Israel. Ethiopian Jewish community that migrated to Israel

Bethlehem vocal style. dominant church vocal style, from Bethlehem monastery

Biftu Ganama. 1960s Oromo band

CEAC. Center for Ethiopian Arts and Culture, founded by Tesfaye Lemma in Washington, DC

chǝqchäqa (chik chika). two-against-three rhythm; argument or dispute

Coffee House. Addis Ababa performance venue that closed in 1998

COPWE. Commission for Organizing the Party of the Working People of Ethiopia

Däbo (Debo). collective effort; large musical ensemble; name of Boston area band

däbtära (debtera). Ethiopian church musician

Dahlak Band. Addis Ababa band, late 1970s

Dallol. a geothermal area in Ethiopia's Afar region; Zeleke Gessesse's band

Därg (Derg). committee or council; ruling committee during the Ethiopian revolution

däwäl (dawal). stone chimes struck to call rural congregants to prayer

Dehai Eritrea Online. news website, www.dehai.org

dǝms'. sound, voice

dǝms' magwaya. amplifier

dǝmsawi. vocalist

derdera. to play a harp

dida dǝms'. animal cry

duduk. Armenian double-reed aerophone

ECMAA. Ethiopian Community Mutual Assistance Association, Cambridge, Massachusetts

ECO. Ethiopian Community Organization, Houston, Texas

ǝddǝr (edir). neighborhood self-help organizations without religious ties

EDU. Ethiopian Democratic Union, underground organization during the revolution

ǝgǝr. leg

Either/Orchestra. jazz band, based in Somerville, Massachusetts, that performs Ethiopian music, founded by Russ Gershon in 1985

ǝnjära (injera). flat Ethiopian fermented bread made of *teff*

ǝmbilta (embilta). a set of three end-blown bamboo flutes

ǝngwǝrgwǝrro. song genre expressing melancholy or sorrow

Enkutatash. Ethiopian new year

EOT Church. Ethiopian Orthodox Tewahedo Church

EPRDF. Ethiopian People's Revolutionary Democratic Front, ruling party along with TPLF

EPRP. Ethiopian People's Revolutionary Party, underground organization during the revolution

Eritrea. country on northeastern Red Sea coast, formerly part of Ethiopia

ERSFNA. Eritrean Sports Federation in North America

ESAC. Ethiopian Social Assistance Committee, New York City

ESFNA. Ethiopian Sports Federation in North America

əskəsta (eskista). shoulder dance

ət'an. incense

Ethio-groove. Ethiopian music performed by non-Ethiopian bands worldwide

Ethio-jazz. Ethiopian jazz style innovated by Mulatu Astatke

Ethio Stars. Addis Ababa band, 1980s

etma asher. Sudanese Arabic expression for a husband after working hours

färänj (ferenj). foreigner

fät'ära. creativity

fät'ari. creator

fät't'ärä. to create, compose, improvise

Fendika. dancer Melaku Belay's traditional ensemble

Finfinnee. Oromo name for Addis Ababa

gänzäb (genzeb). money

Gash Abera Molla Association. organization that solves social and environmental
   problems in Addis Ababa, founded by Seleshe Damessae

Gə'əz (Ge'ez). liturgical language of Ethiopian Orthodox Church

gəbrä gäbb. morals or moral person

Gojjam. former province in northwestern Ethiopia

Gojjami. from Gojjam

Gondar. a city in northern Ethiopia

Gondari. from Gondar

Gurage. people of southwest Ethiopia

Guraginya. group of dialects spoken by Gurage people

gurri. trance dance associated with *zar* cult rituals; guttural sound accompanying
   dance

gwäshämärawi. percussion band

Habäsha or *Abäsha (Habesha* or *Abesha).* term derived from Abyssinia, referring
   primarily to highland Ethiopians and Eritreans

Hachalu Hundessa. revered Oromo singer murdered in 2020

HAFH. Home [Away From] Home, project to unite Ethiopian and Eritrean artists
   in the San Francisco Bay area

Haile Selassie I. emperor of Ethiopia, 1930–74

Harar. walled city in eastern Ethiopia

Harari. from Harar

həwas (hiwas). senses, bodily organs

   — *abalä zär.* [male] genitals, sex sense

   — *af.* mouth, sense of taste

   — *afəncha (afencha).* nose, sense of smell

   — *ayn.* eye, sense of sight

   — *ədj (ej).* hand, sense of touch

   — *əgər (eger).* leg or foot, sense of ambulation

   — *jor.* ear, sense of hearing

Həzb lä Həzb (Hizb le Hizb). People to People tour, 1987–88

hod. belly

hod babba. fear

hod chäräqa. magnanimous emotion

hod gäbba. forgetfulness

Horn of Africa. African peninsula extending east into Arabian sea, including Ethiopia, Eritrea, Somalia, and Djibouti

Ibex Band. Ethiopian band that succeeded Soul Ekos Band, led by Mahmoud Ahmed

Ibex Club. Amha Eshete's club in Washington, DC

Imperial Bodyguard Orchestra. the orchestra associated with Haile Selassie's Bodyguard

Issa-Somalian. clan from northern Somalia

Jan Meda Square. former Addis Ababa racing track that became a public space for celebration of events

Jazzamba School. Jazz school founded by Henock Temesgen, Abegasu Shiota, and Girum Mezmur

käbäro (kebero). large, oval Ethiopian kettle drum

Kəbrä Nägäst. Glory of the Kings, Ethiopian national epic

kaffetenya. higher-level urban administrative units that subsumed multiple *kebele* (See *Qäbäle*)

Kagnew Battalion. Ethiopian battalion that served in Korea during the Korean War

Kambata. ethnic group from southwest Ethiopia

khat. a stimulant leaf chewed in the Horn of Africa

kinät (kinet). revolutionary musical troupes

krar. six-stringed Ethiopian lyre

Kullo. people of Kaffa region

Lalibela. town in north-central Ethiopia with famous rock churches

leb. heart

leb ber. silver heart

leb defen. imbecile

leb mut. lacking wisdom

leb wäläd. inventive

lidet. Ethiopian Christmas celebration

liqä mäkwas. notables dressed like monarch

liqä mezemran (liqa mezemran). title, leader of the musicians

MAAEC. Mutual Assistance Association for Ethiopian Community, Inc., Dallas–Fort Worth area

Macha-Tulama Self-Help Association. Oromo self-help association in Ethiopia, 1960s

mahbär (mahber). Ethiopian Christian social welfare organizations

Mahlet. Ethiopian Christian ritual performed with instruments and dance

mäläkät (malakat). long, single-note trumpet used for royal proclamations

mänfäsawi mäzmuroch (menfesawi mezmuroch). indigenous spiritual songs

märägd. dancing during chanting of hymn with drum and sistrum

märigeta (merigeta). leader of musicians

mäsänqo (masenqo). one-string bowed lute

mäsob (mesob). traditional Ethiopian table or basket used for dining and to store *injera* (Ethiopian flatbread)

Mäsqäl (Masqal, Meskel). Ethiopian Christian Festival of the True Cross

mässariya. tool, instrument, implement, or arms

Masqala. traditional Oromo observance blended with *Masqal*

mäzmur (mezmur). song or portion of liturgy

Mekane Yesus Church. Lutheran Ethiopian Church

mələkkət (melekket). Ethiopian Christian notational signs based on Ge'ez syllabary

Mənilək II (Menelik II). emperor of Ethiopia, 1889–1913

muezzin. chanter of Muslim call to prayer

Mulu Wongel. Full Gospel Believers' Church, indigenous Pentecostal church

musiqa. music

nägarit (negarit). flat kettledrum

Nägarit Gazeta (Negarit Gazeta). Ethiopian government publication for federal laws

nät'älla. small shawl that covers the head and shoulders

ney. Middle Eastern end-blown flute

nikat. to awaken or be on one's guard, mass indoctrination sessions during the revolution

Nile Ethiopian Ensemble. Tesfaye Lemma's ensemble in Washington, DC, from 1994 to 1999

Nile Project Collective. collaborative group of musicians from eleven Nile countries

OCM. Oromo Community of Minnesota–St. Paul

OLF. Oromo Liberation Front

Orchestra Ethiopia. Ethiopian folk orchestra founded in 1963

Orominya. language of Oromo people, also known as Oromiffa or Afaan Oromo

Oromo. largest ethnolinguistic group, central and southern highlands

OSFNA. Oromo Sports Federation in North America

PMAC. Provisional Military Administrative Council; revolutionary ruling committee known as the Derg

qäbäle (kebele). neighborhood administrative unit

qal təməhərt. oral singing school

qangyeta. leader of the right side of the choir

qay. red

qəne (qene). improvised sacred poetry

qəñət (qenyet). secular tunings or modes

Qoma vocal style. vocal style from Qoma Fasiledes monastery

qum zema. plainchant

räjjim (rejjim). long vocal style

Re'ese Adbarat. church with cathedral status

Red Terror. bloody revolutionary period of urban killings during 1977–78

Roha Band. influential successor to Ibex Band in 1979

Saint Yared. revered founder of Ethiopian church music said to have lived in the sixth century

sämənna wärq. wax and gold

sämma. to hear, listen, or perceive

s'änatsəl (tsenatzel). sistrum

səddättäñña. refugee, displaced person, exile

s'əfat. slapping-style drum strokes in Ethiopian Christian tradition

sələt. melody, mode, line, pathway

səmmet. feeling, emotion, sense, sentiment

səmmet qäsäqäsä. to excite the emotions

səmmetawi. sentimental

Sənkəssar. Book of the Saints of the Ethiopian Orthodox Church

shämagəle. elder

shəbshäba. fast section of *Mahlet* with clapping

shəllälä (shillela). battle song

Somali Region. largest and easternmost region of Ethiopia

Soul Ekos Band. Ethiopian band, 1969–75

tabot. a flat, consecrated altar tablet

tädj bet (tej bet). drinking house

Tafari Mekonnen School. Addis Ababa school founded by Regent Tafari Mekonnen in 1925

taqqwara. very dark

Täwahədo (Tewahedo). unified

täym. brown

Taytu (Taitu) Betul. wife of Emperor Menelik II

teff. Eragrostis tef, indigenous Ethiopian grain

T'əmqät (Timket). baptism, Ethiopian Epiphany celebrating Christ's baptism

Tərənbuli. Ethiopian mercenaries in Libya

Tərəyətə Təbbəbat. special revolutionary-era concerts

Tesfa Ethiopian Museum. musical instrument museum briefly founded by Tesfaye Lemma in Washington, DC

təzətə (tizita). secular mode and song evoking remembrance and nostalgia

The Ex. Dutch band that collaborates with Ethiopian musicians

Tigray. northernmost Ethiopian region

Tigrinya. Semitic language spoken in Tigray

tizita, bati, anchihoye, ambasel. four secular Ethiopian modes or *qəñət*

TPLF. Tigray People's Liberation Front, ruling party that overthrew Derg in 1991

ululation. high trilling sound performed by women

UNHCR. United Nations High Commissioner for Refugees

Urjii Bakkalchaa. "Morning Star," 1960s Oromo band

Waaqeffannaa. Oromo indigenous religion

Walia (Walias) Band. Ethiopian jazz and funk band 1970s–90s

wanna. main, principal

Wäräda. administrative district of Addis Ababa

washənt (washint). bamboo flute

wäzäwwäzä. to dance, shake, agitate, or move to and fro

wazema. prelude, beginning, initial part

Wolayta. ethnic group in southwest Ethiopia

Wollega. former province in western Ethiopia, zone of new Oromia Region

Wollo. former province in northeastern Ethiopia

yä'ezra kwankwa (ya'ezra kwankwa). Ezra's language, *azmari argot*

ya'ihud temehert bet mezmur. Sunday school songs

yädəms' awətarec, yädəms' həwas. vocal cords

yäfät'ara chəlota. creative artists

yäfidel qərs' (yefidel qers'). conventional signs

— *änbər.* end of a musical phrase

— *ch'ərät.* drag or pull sound upward

— *därät.* chest, sing loudly in throat

— *dəfat.* mask voice when chant dips

— *dərs.* soften voice and let it die away
— *hədät.* voice flows without stopping
— *qənät.* straighten out voice at the end
— *qurt.* press voice downward
— *rəkrək.* a vocal slide or tremolo
— *yəzat.* stop abruptly

Yähagär Fəqər Mahbär (*Hager Fikir*). Association for the Love of Country; Ethiopian Patriotic Association

Yäkärmo Sew (*Yekermo Sew*). Mulatu Astatke composition featured in *Broken Flowers*, play by Tsegaye Gabre-Medhin

Yäkəbr Zäb (*Kebur Zebenya*). Imperial Bodyguard troops and orchestra, honor guard

yämusiqa mässariya. musical instrument

Yänəgus Təbbäqa. Imperial Bodyguard troops and orchestra, king's guard

Yared School. school of music in Addis Ababa

yäsərqosh bär. "stealth gate," entry for employees into the palace

Yerba Buena Center for the Arts. multicultural arts center in San Francisco

zämäch'a (*zemecha*). Development through Cooperation Campaign that sent young people to the countryside to educate peasantry

zämänawi (*zemenawi*). modern or popular music

zar. spirit possession rituals in Horn of Africa

zär. race

Zedicus. Zakki Jawad's professional name

zema. Ethiopian Christian chant

zema memher. chant teacher

zəmmamä. rhythmic motions of prayer staff

zəgubəñ. "close after me," revolutionary entertainment establishments

Notes

Editorial Policies

1. Wolf Leslau, *Concise Amharic Dictionary* (Wiesbaden, Ger.: Harrassowitz, 1976), xiii–xiv.

2. Thomas Leiper Kane, *Amharic-English Dictionary*, 2 vols. (Wiesbaden, Ger.: Harrassowitz, 1990).

Preface

1. The suggestion that local ethnography can speak to broader issues elsewhere is succinctly addressed by Jean and John Comaroff, "Ethnography on an Awkward Scale: Postcolonial Anthropology and the Violence of Abstraction," *Ethnography* 4, no. 2 (2003): 147–79, https://doi.org/10.1177/14661381030042001, who set forth a four-part methodological operation for *"mapping extensions of the phenomenal landscape"* [italics in the source]; they propose that such work "demands an ethnography that, once orientated to particular sites and grounded issues, is pursued on multiple dimensions and scales" (169). The light that this study sheds on musicians' roles cross-culturally is explored in the afterword.

2. Thomas P. Ofcansky, "Imperial Bodyguard," in *Encyclopaedia Aethiopica*, ed. Siegbert Uhlig (Wiesbaden, Ger.: Harrassowitz, 2007), 3:127–28. Henceforth, references to *Encyclopaedia Aethiopica* will be abbreviated to *EAe* in the notes.

3. Ofcansky, "Imperial Bodyguard," *EAe*, 3:127–28.

4. Ofcansky, "Imperial Bodyguard," *EAe*, 3:127–28.

5. Manuel DeLanda, *Assemblage Theory* (Edinburgh: Edinburgh University Press, 2016), 10–11.

6. *Jelis* (often called *griots* outside Africa) "are musicians, singers, public speakers, oral historians, praisers, go-betweens, advisers, chroniclers, and shapers of the past and the present" (Eric Charry, *Mande Music: Traditional and Modern Music of the Maninka and Mandinka of Western Africa* [Chicago: University of Chicago Press, 2000], 91).

7. Simon D. Messing, "The Highland-Plateau Amhara of Ethiopia" (PhD diss., University of Pennsylvania, 1957), 487. Messing does not offer any further details about the "secret musical note like a code," but it could well have drawn on the short melodic segments from the Ethiopian Orthodox Christian chant repertory that are the basis of the notational system *mələkkət* (*melekket*, signs) associated with the text and

melody of a specific liturgical chant. *Melekket* has an additional meaning of an identifying mark or a means of identification (Kane, *Dictionary*, 158).

8. For a discussion of African instruments that perform as speech surrogates, see Joseph S. Kaminski, "Surrogate Speech of the Asante Ivory Trumpeters of Ghana," *Yearbook for Traditional Music* 40 (2008): 117–35, https://www.proquest.com/docview /235107827/B6F298C9C99C4778PQ/1; and Adwoa Arhine, "Speech Surrogates of Africa: A Study of the Fante *Mmensuon*," *Legon Journal of the Humanities* 20 (2009): 105–22, https://www.ajol.info/index.php/ljh/article/view/121552. These articles discuss closely related traditions of Ghanaian Asante and Fante people in which ivory trumpets serve as speech surrogates. Kaminski details a case study of Asante ivory trumpets and Arhine discusses the Fante *mmensuon*, an ensemble in which the lead horn, *sese*, is used in the Fante court "as a talking instrument for recounting histories, singing appellations, uttering proverbs, and conveying messages, announcements and signals depending on the context" (Arhine, "Speech Surrogates," 116). Both articles discuss in passing other Ghanaian instruments such as the Asante *atumpan* drum that are speech surrogates as well as comparative examples from elsewhere on the African continent. An example that serves as a speech surrogate from outside Africa is the textless songs that convey specific semantic meaning among an indigenous people of northern Veracruz, Mexico, in Charles L. Boilés, "Tepehua Thought-Song: A Case of Semantic Signaling," *Ethnomusicology* 11, no. 3 (1967): 267–92, https://doi.org/10 .2307/850266.

9. Kane, *Dictionary*, 1016. For discussion of the *negarit*'s symbolic association with royal power from early dates, see Anaïs Wion, Anne Damon-Guillot, and Stéphanie Weisser, "Sound and Power in the Christian Realm of Ethiopia (Seventeenth–Eighteenth Centuries)," *Aethiopica* 19 (2016): 62–67, https://doi.org/10.15460 /aethiopica.19.1.904.

10. The *Nägarit Gazeta* first appeared in March 1942 as a monthly publication with the provision that no new law would be valid until published in the document, today an online platform (Theodor Vestal, "Nägarit Gazeṭa," *EAe*, 3:1106).

11. "Wax and gold" (*sämənna wärq*) uses the lost wax process of goldsmithing as a metaphor for hidden meanings; a clay mold is created around a wax form, which melts as it is replaced with molten gold (Donald N. Levine, *Wax and Gold: Tradition and Innovation in Ethiopian Culture* [Chicago: University of Chicago Press, 1965], 5).

12. Jenny Hammond, *Sweeter than Honey: Ethiopian Women and Revolution; Testimonies of Tigrayan Women* (Trenton, NJ: Red Sea, 1990), 141. The guitarist quoted here is identified only by her first name, Atsede; she learned to play the guitar as part of a revolutionary cultural troupe to be discussed in chapter 4.

13. Minale Dagnew Bezu, interview by author, January 7, 2008, Washington, DC.

14. The *Oxford English Dictionary* (OED) acknowledges this uncertain etymology, noting that the French words *sentinelle* and Italian *sentinella* are gendered feminine ("Sentinel, *n.*," *OED Online*, accessed January 21, 2020). However, other dictionaries, including the *Merriam-Webster*, suggest that Old Italian *sentinella* comes from *sentire*, "to perceive" in Latin, accessed January 21, 2020, https://www.merriam-webster.com /dictionary/sentinel.

15. Ewa A. Miendlarzewska and Wiebke J. Trost, "How Musical Training Affects Cognitive Development: Rhythm, Reward and Other Modulating Variables," *Frontiers in Neuroscience* 7 (2014): 1–18, https://doi.org/10.3389/fnins.2013.00279; and

Aniruddh D. Patel, "Why Would Musical Training Benefit the Neural Encoding of Speech? The OPERA Hypothesis," *Frontiers in Psychology* 2 (2011): 1–14, https://doi .org/10.3389/fpsyg.2011.00142.

16. Kane, *Dictionary*, 18; Wolf Leslau, *English-Amharic Context Dictionary* (Wiesbaden, Ger.: Harrassowitz, 1973), 1139. I thank Dr. Getatchew Haile for confirming the relationship between these two words. Both *həwas* and *səmmet* connote sensation.

17. Kane, *Dictionary*, 18, 462, and 472.

18. Thomas Campbell, *The Complete Poetical Works of Thomas Campbell: With a Memoir of His Life*, Lovell's Library, vol. 10, no. 526 (Boston: Phillips, Sampson, 1855), 161. The first reference to the sentinel stars was by Richard Lovelace in "To Lucasta" in *Lucasta: Postume Poems* (1659): "Like to the Sent'nel Stars, I watch all Night" (*OED*, s.v. "sentinel").

19. By the twentieth century, the term *sentinel* was also used to name devices that revealed hidden dimensions, such as those that signaled the depth of water through which a boat was sailing (*OED*, s.v. "sentinel"). Other permutations range from the sentinel crab of the Indian Ocean, and even the fanciful sentinel robots in comics featured on the Marvel Universe Wiki intended to save humanity from mutants. In computing, a sentinel character is used to mark the beginning or end of a block of data.

20. Jacques Attali, *Noise: The Political Economy of Music*, trans. Brian Massumi (Minneapolis: University of Minnesota Press, 1977), xi. I thank Jocelyne Guilbault for reminding me of this reference.

21. Attali, *Noise*, 11–12.

22. Fekade Azeze, "Mengistulore: Oral Literatures Depicting the Man, His Regime, Officials and Proclamations," in *Ethiopia: The Challenge of Democracy from Below*, ed. Bahru Zewde and Siegfried Pausewang (Addis Ababa: Forum for Social Studies, 2002), 149. I thank Mekonnen Firew Ayano for alerting me to this source.

23. Introductions in liner notes by W. A. D'Amat to Ali Birra, *Hin Yaadin: Bareeda Umma*, Awashsonic Music, c. 2009, compact disc, 5. Other musicians have rejected the role of prophet yet accept their responsibilities as inspirations and guides, none more emphatically than Bob Dylan in lyrics to one of his early songs, "Long Time Gone": "If I can't help somebody / With a word or song / If I can't show somebody / They are travelin' wrong / But I know I ain't no prophet / An' I ain't no prophet's son / I'm just a long time a-comin' / An' I'll be a long time gone" (Bob Dylan, *The Lyrics: 1961–2012* [New York: Simon and Schuster, 2016], 28–29).

24. For a discussion of individual agency and its potential for meaningful interventions, see Kay Kaufman Shelemay, "Ethnography as a Way of Life," *Ethnomusicology* 64, no. 1 (2020): 15–17.

25. Kane, *Dictionary*, 1260, defines the term as expressing "through the good offices of, by means of, through the mediation of."

26. Leslau, *Context Dictionary*, 30.

27. Mustafa Emirbayer and Ann Mische, "What Is Agency?," *American Journal of Sociology* 103, no. 4 (1998): 964, https://doi.org/10.1086/231294. They also suggest a reconceptualization of human agency "as a temporally embedded process of social engagement, informed by the past (in its habitual aspect), but also oriented toward the future (as a capacity to imagine alternative possibilities) and toward the present (as a capacity to contextualize past habits and future project within the contingencies of the moment). The agentic dimension of social action can only be captured in

its full complexity . . . if it is analytically situated within the flow of time. . . . We also argue that the structural contexts of action are themselves temporal as well as relational fields—multiple, overlapping *ways of ordering time*" (963).

28. Laura M. Ahearn, "Language and Agency," *Annual Review of Anthropology* 30 (2001): 112, https://doi.org/10.1146/annurev.anthro.30.1.109. John L. and Jean Comaroff, in *Of Revelation and Revolution*, vol. 2, *The Dialectics of Modernity on a South African Frontier* (Chicago: University of Chicago Press, 2009), 48, have usefully suggested that agency "refers to meaningful activity: activity to which intention may be ascribed before or after the event; which has consequences, intended or otherwise; which may be articulate or inarticulate, poetic or prosaic, verbal or visual or sensual. As this implies, it has many modalities."

29. Nicholas Cook, "Music as Performance," in *The Cultural Study of Music: A Critical Introduction*, 2nd ed., ed. Martin Clayton, Trevor Herbert, and Richard Middleton (New York: Routledge, 2012), 206.

30. In Amharic, *gəbrä gäbb* means "morals or a moral person" and *gəbrä gäbbənät* means "morals or morality" (Kane, *Dictionary*, 1976).

31. Dinaw Mengestu, *The Beautiful Things That Heaven Bears* (New York: Riverhead, 2007), 98.

32. Benjamin Piekut, "Actor-Networks in Music History: Clarifications and Critiques," *Twentieth-Century Music* 11, no. 2 (2014): 191–215, https://doi.org/10.1017/S147857221400005X.

Chapter One

1. I will use the expression "forced migration" to refer to the crises that impelled large numbers to migrate and will term the people who departed under these conditions "forced migrants" or "refugees." Although it is customary to differentiate between forced and voluntary migrants, the distinction is a difficult one to make in a region continually torn by political conflict, warfare, and natural disasters; thus, I will use the term *migrant* as well to refer to people involved in forced migrations. Although pull factors, such as growing family networks abroad and the lure of economic advantages, became more compelling in the years after the Ethiopian revolution ended in 1991 with fewer impediments to migration placed by the Ethiopian state, push factors remained very active instigators of individual decisions to migrate. A recent study of Somali migration also seeks to blur the refugee-migrant binary, finding that "for the majority of people on the move, these categories frequently overlap" (Cawo M. Abdi, *Elusive Jannah: The Somali Diaspora and a Borderless Muslim Identity* [Minneapolis: University of Minnesota Press, 2015], 9).

2. Even fewer scholars have charted the refugee experience and its musical outcomes. Among them is Adelaida Reyes, who, after noting that refugees "barely cast a shadow" in musical scholarship, provided a pioneering look at the pathways of Vietnamese refugees after their forced departures from Vietnam, through way stations in the Philippines and elsewhere, and on to new settlements in California, Paris, and beyond (Adelaida Reyes, *Songs of the Caged, Songs of the Free: Music and the Vietnamese Refugee Experience* [Philadelphia: Temple University Press, 1999], 1). More recent studies include Nadia Kiwan and Ulrike Hanna Meinhof, *Cultural Globalization and Music: African Artists in Transnational Networks* (New York: Palgrave Macmillan,

2011), which compares the transnational routes of musicians departing from Madagascar and North Africa.

3. Peter Gatrell, *The Making of the Modern Refugee* (Oxford: Oxford University Press, 2013), 10, https://doi.org/10.1093/acprof:oso/9780199674169.001.0001.

4. Stephen Greenblatt, *Cultural Mobility: A Manifesto* (Cambridge: Cambridge University Press, 2010), 250. James Clifford's approach to mobility through the lens of travel and traveling cultures has deeply influenced my approach in these pages, while at the same time providing evidence of disciplinary divides that have tended to understate the impact of mobility and migration on individual musical lives (James Clifford, *Routes: Travel and Translation in the Late Twentieth Century* [Cambridge, MA: Harvard University Press, 1997]).

5. Michel Agier, *On the Margins of the World: The Refugee Experience Today*, trans. David Fernbach (Cambridge, UK: Polity, 2008), 3–4, divides the experience of refugees into three stages: the stage of destruction, when events overrun daily life; that of confinement, the months and years of waiting in transit; and the moment of action, the still uncertain search for a new life.

6. The *duduk* is a double-reed aerophone played with the technique of circular breathing.

7. Cited in Asafa Jalata, *Oromia and Ethiopia: State Formation and Ethnonational Conflict, 1868–2004* (Trenton, NJ: Red Sea, 2005), 186, translated from the original Oromo text: *Durbbuman keenyalee kan kara yatuleen, Wannuma walisan kan jarrati walleen.* Asafa here cites an undated interview with the musician Ali Birra, who credited the verse to Oromo poet Abubakar Musa on his objections to the subordination of Oromo culture, the result of ethnic tensions that will be an important factor throughout this book. The Oromo are the largest Ethiopian ethnic community, making up well over a third of the population (Jan Hultin, "Oromo," *EAe*, 4:59). The Amhara, although a somewhat smaller population than the Oromo, dominated Ethiopia politically from the thirteenth century until the inception of the 1974 revolution (Donald N. Levine, "Amhara," *EAe*, 1:230). The Adare (Harari) are a small urban population that originally lived in the southeastern walled city of Harar (Camilla Gibb, "Harari Ethnography," *EAe*, 2:1026).

8. Martha Namarra, interview by author, March 13, 2011, Minneapolis, MN.

9. Jan Abbink, "Slow Awakening? The Ethiopian Diaspora in the Netherlands, 1977–2007," *Diaspora* 15, nos. 2–3 (2006 [pub. 2011]), 366, https://doi.org/10.1353/dsp.2011.0073.

10. Kay Kaufman Shelemay and Steven Kaplan, "Introduction," *Diaspora* 15, nos. 2–3 (2006 [pub. 2011]): 195–99, https://doi.org/10.1353/dsp.2011.0068. The documentary film *400 Miles to Freedom* by Avishai Yeganyahu Mekonen and Shari Rothfarb Mekonen (Los Angeles: Seventh Art, 2012), provides a chronicle of Avishai Mekonen's trauma as part of the Beta Israel forced migration to refugee camps in the Sudan and subsequently to Israel. See https://400milestofreedom.com/index.html for more information on the film. Full video is available on Kanopy, https://www.kanopy.com/product/400-miles-freedom.

11. Ahmed Ismail Yusuf, *Somalis in Minnesota* (St. Paul: Minnesota Historical Society Press, 2012), 20.

12. Greg Gow, *The Oromo in Exile: From the Horn of Africa to the Suburbs of Australia* (Carlton, Australia: Melbourne University Press, 2002), 10.

13. Migration Policy Institute, *The Ethiopian Diaspora in the United States*. Prepared for the Rockefeller Foundation–Aspen Institute Diaspora Program (Washington, DC: Migration Policy Institute, 2014).

14. In Bahru Zewde, "Embattled Identity in Northeast Africa: A Comparative Essay," in *Society, State, and History: Selected Essays*, ed. Bahru Zewde (Addis Ababa: Addis Ababa University Press, 2008), 363 and 366, Bahru discusses northeast Africa as a region with states that share an "embattled identity" shaped by colonial ambitions of the late nineteenth century, in which all "trans-frontier peoples [are] lost in this cartographic exercise." Bahru includes in this region Ethiopia, Eritrea, Djibouti, Somalia, and the Sudan. The years between 1896 and 1907 saw the expansion of the Ethiopian state under the Emperor Menelik II, which was conventionally regarded as a "Holy Crusade" to "restore" Ethiopia's historic grandeur and size. See also Harold G. Marcus, *A History of Ethiopia*, updated ed. (Berkeley: University of California Press, 2002), 104–5. Increasingly, later twentieth- and twenty-first-century scholars have viewed this era as one of Ethiopian colonial oppression. See, for example, Asafa, *Oromia and Ethiopia*, 84–85.

15. Solomon Addis Getahun, *The History of Ethiopian Immigrants and Refugees in America, 1900–2000: Patterns of Migration, Survival, and Adjustment* (New York: LFB Scholarly, 2007) provides a pioneering study of the Ethiopian American diaspora, while Gow, *Oromo in Exile*, does the same for the Oromo diaspora in Australia.

16. Jon Abbink, "Ethnic-Based Federalism and Ethnicity in Ethiopia: Reassessing the Experiment after 20 Years," *Journal of Eastern African Studies* 5, no. 4 (2011): 600, https://doi.org/10.1080/17531055.2011.642516.

17. As quoted in Abbink, "Ethnic-Based Federalism," 600.

18. Only the largest nationalities give their names to one of the regions, with an exception being the Southern Nations. Thus one finds, in alphabetical order, Afar Region; Amhara Region; Benishangul-Gumuz Region; Gambela Region; Harari Region; Oromia Region; Somali Region; Southern Nations, Nationalities, and Peoples' Region; and Tigray Region. During 2020, Sidama seceded from the Southern Nations, Nationalities, and Peoples' Region and was added as the tenth region. There are, in addition, two chartered cities, Addis Ababa (the capital) and Dire Dawa. There are nine ethnic communities in independent Eritrea.

19. Jon Abbink, "Ethnicity," *EAe*, 2:445.

20. Abbink, "Ethnic-Based Federalism," 601.

21. John Markakis, "Nationalities and the State in Ethiopia," *Third World Quarterly* 10, no. 4 (1989): 123–25.

22. References to physiognomy in Ethiopia were in the past characterized by different terms than in the West. "The skin color of most Amhara is regarded by them as brown (*täym*). . . . It is a mild insult to call a very dark person *taqqwara* (lit., 'dark'). European skin color is regarded as 'red' (*qay*), a common African attitude. The concept of 'white' coloring connotes paleness, . . . undernourishment, sickness, insipid weakness" (Messing, "Highland-Plateau Amhara," 566).

23. Melaku Gelaw, interview by author and Charles Sutton, August 14, 2007, Washington, DC.

24. Wolbert G. C. Smidt and Eloi Ficquet, "Ḥabäša," *EAe*, 5:339.

25. Minale Dagnew Bezu, interview by author, August 8, 2007, Washington, DC.

26. Zakki Jawad, interview by author, June 27, 2008, Washington, DC. Abyssinia

is a synonym used for Ethiopia until the middle of the twentieth century; it tends to designate the predominantly Christian and Semitic highland of Ethiopia and Eritrea (Rainer Voigt, "Abyssinia," *EAe*, 1:59).

27. Selam Seyoum Woldemariam, interview by author, September 7, 2007, Washington, DC.

28. Tekle Tewolde, interview by author, June 17, 2008, Washington, DC.

29. Abdi (Tesfaye) Nuressa, interview by author, July 16, 2008, Washington, DC. There are estimated to be more than thirty million Oromo in Ethiopia, divided into a number of communities located in the East, West, North, and South of Ethiopia (Jan Hultin, "Oromo Ethnography," *EAe*, 4:59–61).

30. A publication instrumental in recasting scholarly approaches to Ethiopia was Donald N. Levine, *Greater Ethiopia: The Evolution of a Multiethnic Society* (Chicago: University of Chicago Press, 1974). Subsequently, Donald L. Donham and Wendy James, eds., *The Southern Marches of Imperial Ethiopia: Essays in History and Social Anthropology*, 2nd ed. (Oxford, UK: James Currey, 2002), shifted focus from the northern highlands to southern regions and reevaluated the colonial impact of Ethiopian government actions on a range of southern peoples. Since the end of the Ethiopian revolution in 1991, a number of Ethiopian and foreign scholars have undertaken fieldwork in Ethiopia's south, accelerating the realignment of Ethiopian studies. Although Ethiopia has long nurtured indigenous scholars largely from Ethiopia's north, the last three decades have seen the flowering of intellectual leadership by an active cohort of scholars of Oromo descent, led by Mohammed Hassen, *The Oromo of Ethiopia: A History, 1570–1860* (Cambridge: Cambridge University Press, 1990); Asafa Jalata, ed., *Oromo Nationalism and the Ethiopian Discourse: The Search for Freedom and Democracy* (Lawrenceville, NJ: Red Sea, 1998); Mekuria Bulcha, *Contours of the Emergent and Ancient Oromo Nation: Dilemmas in the Ethiopian Politics of State and Nation-Building*. CASAS Book Series No. 84 (Cape Town, S. Africa: Centre for Advanced Studies of African Society, 2011); and others. Publications such as Ali Jimale Ahmed and Taddesse Adera, *The Road Less Traveled: Reflections on the Literatures of the Horn of Africa* (Trenton, NJ: Red Sea, 2008), suggest that studies crossing national borders in the Horn of Africa should be pursued in the future.

31. Teddy Afro, *Tikur Sew*, Adika Communication and Events and Belema Entertainment IFPI LZ10, 2012, compact disc. See also the music video "Tikur Sew," directed by Tamirat Mekonen and produced by Sabisa Films Production et al., 2012, on YouTube, 9:56, posted by Leyumct, June 10, 2012, https://www.youtube.com/watch?v=IuyfK7NLosY. For a discussion of the song as well as its complete Amharic text with English translation, see Rachael Hill, "Teddy Afro's 'Tikur Sew'—Ethnic Politics and Historical Narrative," *Africa Collective*, June 8, 2014.

32. Legesse Tigabu Mengie, "Ethnic Federalism and Conflict in Ethiopia: What Lessons Can Other Jurisdictions Draw?," *African Journal of International and Comparative Law* 23, no. 3 (2015): 464, https://doi.org/10.3366/ajicl.2015.0131.

33. Shelemay, field notes, Dukem Ethiopian Restaurant, July 2, 2008, Washington, DC. The annual Ethiopian soccer tournament sponsored by the Ethiopian Sports Federation in North America (ESFNA) began in 1983; see https://esfna.org/.

34. Getahun Atlaw Garede, interview by author, June 5, 2008, Washington, DC. In response to my comment, "Goodness, that's a complicated identity these days," Getahun responded with a smile, "I would say it's a blessing!"

35. Human Rights Watch, "Ethiopia: Events of 2018," *World Report 2019* (New York: Human Rights Watch, 2019), https://www.hrw.org/world-report/2019/country -chapters/ethiopia.

36. I have not included the Ethiopian Jews in this book other than in passing references in large part because very few have migrated to the United States. The story of their immigration to Israel is detailed in numerous sources and differs from that of other Ethiopians in that they are approached "less as Ethiopians abroad than as new, exotic Jews" (Shelemay and Kaplan, "Introduction," 206n3; Steven Kaplan, "*Tama Galut Etiopiya*: The Ethiopian Exile Is Over," *Diaspora* 14, nos. 2–3 (2005): 381–96, https://doi.org/10.1353/dsp.0.0018). The situation of Ethiopian Jewish refugees is very different from that of other Ethiopians of the revolutionary period, in that they began to have contact with the international Jewish community in the late nineteenth century.

37. See Kay Kaufman Shelemay, *A Song of Longing: An Ethiopian Journey* (Urbana: University of Illinois Press, 1991), for details of my marriage and subsequent residency in revolutionary Ethiopia.

38. Although I did make a short field trip to Toronto, Canada, and several prominent Canadian musicians such as Ali Birra and Abel Makkonen Tesfaye (The Weeknd) are discussed in this book, I was unable to carry out additional fieldwork in Canada. For this reason, I don't address the Ethiopian Canadian community. Archival resources were of limited help. One of the only archival collections existing when I began research in the early 1970s was that of Halim El-Dabh at the Library of Congress, dating from his residency in Ethiopia during the 1960s. At that time, El-Dabh founded Orchestra Ethiopia, a folklore orchestra that had an active performance career under Ethiopian imperial sponsorship. Until the beginning of the revolution, the orchestra maintained its activities under the direction of Tesfaye Lemma, who in summer 2007, deposited his collection of recordings at the Library of Congress. The genealogy of Orchestra Ethiopia in Ethiopia and in the US diaspora is reconstructed in chapter 8.

39. Thirty-two musicians from the Library of Congress project are pictured in plates 1.3 and 1.4. However, testimony is also found throughout this book from many other musicians interviewed either before or after my research at the Library of Congress or in different locales.

40. I have also cast the net wide enough to include individuals not of Ethiopian descent who were closely engaged with Ethiopian diaspora musical networks, institutions, or commercial music endeavors.

41. Getahun interview.

42. Notable among individuals interviewed from outside the Ethiopian community was Julius C. Jefferson Jr., who had performed as a jazz drummer with Ethiopian musicians at the Ibex Club and other Washington music venues while beginning his distinguished career at the Library of Congress (Julius C. Jefferson Jr., interview by author, August 7, 2007, Washington, DC). In 2020 Jefferson was acting chief of Research and Reference Services at the library, as well as president of the American Library Association.

43. This number includes only musicians in the cultural and modern categories and does not include either professional or amateur church musicians, who constituted an additional large number given the presence of more than a dozen DC-area Ethiopian Orthodox churches. I am indebted to Behailu Kassahun, who, during an interview early on in my research process in Washington, DC, gave me a handwritten

list of names and contact information for more than fifty immigrant musicians from the Horn of Africa in the area. Behailu also followed up by contacting many individuals to let them know about the project and that I would be in touch, contacts crucial to getting the project off to a fast and successful start. Behailu estimated that there were about one hundred fifty musicians from the region in the DC metropolitan area (Behailu Kassahun, interview by author, August 3, 2007, Washington, DC). Tesfaye Lemma independently estimated that there were around one hundred forty (Tesfaye Lemma, interview by author and Charles Sutton, August 15, 2007, Washington, DC).

44. It is possible that some musicians who did not respond to my requests for an interview or who said they were unable to participate in the study were undocumented. If a musician avoided scheduling an interview and a second query did not result in an appointment, I did not pursue their participation further.

45. For discussion of historical methods in ethnomusicology, see Bruno Nettl, "Historical Aspects of Ethnomusicology," *American Anthropologist* 60, no. 3 (1958): 518–32, https://doi.org/10.1525/aa.1958.60.3.02a00100; Alan P. Merriam, "Use of Music in Reconstructing Culture History," in *Reconstructing African Culture History*, ed. Creighton Gabel and Norman R. Bennett (Boston: Boston University Press, 1967), 85–114; Klaus P. Wachsmann, *Essays on Music and History in Africa* (Evanston, IL: Northwestern University Press, 1971); and Kay Kaufman Shelemay, "'Historical Ethnomusicology': Reconstructing Falasha Liturgical History," *Ethnomusicology* 24, no. 2 (1980): 233–58, https://doi.org/10.2307/851114.

46. Recent examples are Jonathan McCollum and David G. Herbert, eds., *Theory and Method in Historical Ethnomusicology* (Lanham, MD: Lexington, 2014); and Ann E. Lucas, *Music of a Thousand Years: A New History of Persian Musical Traditions* (Oakland: University of California Press, 2019).

47. Richard F. Mollica, *Healing Invisible Wounds: Paths to Hope and Recovery in a Violent World* (Nashville, TN: Vanderbilt University Press, 2008), 21, https://muse .jhu.edu/book/21116.

48. Bezawork Asfaw, *Lemenor*, Tizita Productions, 2002, compact disc. "Lemenor" can also be heard on YouTube, 10:17, posted by Ashenafi B., February 25, 2017, https:// www.youtube.com/watch?v=r8CwYvAsP4ki.

49. Text and melody by Moges Teka. English translation by Dr. Tilahun Gebrehiwot and author.

50. Fernand Braudel, *The Mediterranean and the Mediterranean World in the Age of Philip II*, trans. Siân Reynolds (New York: Harper and Row, 1972). See also Richard E. Lee, ed., *The Longue Durée and World Systems Analysis* (Albany: State University of New York Press, 2012), 244.

51. Notions of multitemporality have been extended to studies of the African postcolony, which criticizes social theory for failing "to account for *time as lived*, not synchronically or diachronically, but in its multiplicity and simultaneities, its presence and absences, beyond the lazy categories of permanence and change beloved of so many historians" (Achille Mbembe, *On the Postcolony* [Berkeley: University of California Press, 2001], 8).

52. Lee, ed., *Longue Durée*, 2–3, quoting Braudel, *Mediterranean*, 1:20–21.

53. See, for example, articles in Stephen Blum, Philip V. Bohlman, and Daniel M. Neuman, eds., *Ethnomusicology and Modern Music History* (Urbana: University of Illinois Press, 1991). Also, Ana María Ochoa Gautier, *Aurality: Listening and Knowledge in Nineteenth-Century Columbia* (Durham, NC: Duke University Press, 2014), draws

on archival and other written sources to reconstruct listening practices in nineteenth-century Columbia.

54. For historical reconstruction extending back to the fourteenth and fifteenth centuries based on a combination of oral traditions from musical domains, music transmitted through the twentieth century, written historical sources, and comparison to other extant Ethiopian liturgies, see Kay Kaufman Shelemay, *Music, Ritual, and Falasha History* (East Lansing: Michigan State University Press, 1989), and Kay Kaufman Shelemay and Peter Jeffery, eds., *Ethiopian Christian Liturgical Chant: An Anthology*, 3 vols. with CD (Madison, WI: A-R, 1993, 1994, 1997).

55. My reconstruction of Beta Israel history to the fourteenth and fifteen centuries was an exception in that it drew not just on oral testimonies about liturgical music and texts, but on indigenous Ethiopian historical sources as well as scholarly work of greater time depth. See Shelemay, *Music, Ritual, and Falasha History*.

56. David Armitage and Jo Guldi, "Le retour de la longue durée: une perspective anglo-américaine," *Annales: Histoire, Sciences Sociales* 70, no. 2 (2015): 289–318, https://doi.org/10.1353/ahs.2015.0033. One unusual example of *longue durée* reconstruction from recent musicological scholarship that has sought to pursue nonlinear but temporally deep history is Gary Tomlinson, *A Million Years of Music: The Emergence of Human Modernity* (Brooklyn, NY: Zone, 2015). Tomlinson's study is not based on conventional musical data but constructs a history of musical life from creative and nuanced readings of a full range of sources from across disciplines, ranging from archaeology to cognitive science. Tomlinson provides a reinterpretation of primary and secondary literature from scientific fields, theorizing an overview of music history that incorporates historical processes shot through with cultural initiatives, resulting in "spiraling feedback loops and loops-upon-loops, and burgeoning complexity from simple structures and actions" (19).

57. Lee, *Longue Durée*, 3.

58. To be sure, the focus on a single musician may render multitemporal work impossible if the individual stops performing, dies, or otherwise becomes unavailable. I thank Elizabeth Branch Dyson for suggesting that I warn any young scholars to whom this idea appeals that they would do well not to put all their eggs in one musician's basket!

59. Anthropologists have discussed differences in the duration of fieldwork. George M. Foster discussed the "repeated or continuous study" with periodic or return trips in George M. Foster, Thayer Scudder, Elizabeth Colson, and Robert V. Kemper, eds., *Long-Term Field Research in Social Anthropology* (New York: Academic, 1979), 9–10. Anthropologists of education have advocated long research engagements lasting from a few years to decades; they have documented on videotape "return interviews," to ascertain how long-term work with research associates can yield something more than what can be achieved in single interviews or multiple interviews within a short period of time. See also Joseph Tobin and Akiko Hayashi, "Return Interviews and Long Engagements with Ethnographic Informants," *Anthropology and Education Quarterly* 48, no. 3 (2017): 319, https://doi.org/10.1111/aeq.12202.

60. Mbembe, *On the Postcolony*, 15–16.

61. Sigurđur Gylfi Magnússon, "*The Singularization of History*: Social History and Microhistory within the Postmodern State of Knowledge," *Journal of Social History* 36, no. 3 (2003): 709–10, https://doi.org/10.1353/jsh.2003.0054.

62. One of the most widely circulated examples of the longitudinal study is the

"Up!" documentary film series that every seven years beginning in 1964 has tracked the impact of the British class system on the life experience of a small age cohort, most recently when the group turned sixty-three in 2019 ("63 Up," directed by Michael Apted, 2019). See Ty Burr, "'63 Up': A Film Series That Shows Life, Unforgettably, in Seven-Year Slices," *Boston Globe*, December 10, 2019, https://www.bostonglobe.com/2019/12/11/arts/63-up-film-series-that-shows-life-unforgettably-seven-year-slices/. Tobin and Hayashi, in "Return Interviews," have videotaped and published interviews from a series of return interviews, which differ from longitudinal studies in that they do not necessarily return to questions previously asked.

63. Issayas Tesfamariam, personal communication with author, May 24, 2016, Stanford, CA.

64. Anthony Seeger, "Long-Term Field Research in Ethnomusicology in the 21st-Century," *Em Pauta* 19, nos. 32–33 (2008): 10, https://seer.ufrgs.br/EmPauta/article/download/10742/6366.

65. Most of the music discussed here is accessible through postings on YouTube, on individual musicians' websites, or through the *éthiopiques* series of compact discs.

66. Koenraad Verboven, Myriam Carlier, and Jan Dumolyn, "A Short Manual to the Art of Prosopography," in *Prosopography Approaches and Applications: A Handbook*, ed. K. S. B. Keats-Rohan (Oxford, UK: Linacre College, Unit for Prosopographical Research, 2007), 39. I thank Ellen Harris for helping me identify a field that theorizes collective biography.

67. Karlijn Deene, "French Composers after the Franco-Prussian War (1870–1): A Prosopographical Study," in *Prosopography Approaches and Applications*, 568.

68. K. S. B. Keats-Rohan, "Biography, Identity and Names: Understanding the Pursuit of the Individual in Prosopography," in *Prosopography Approaches and Applications*, 141.

69. Randal Johnson, introduction to *The Field of Cultural Production: Essays on Art and Literature*, by Pierre Bourdieu (New York: Columbia University Press, 1993), 6.

70. Bruno Latour, *Reassembling the Social: An Introduction to Actor-Network-Theory* (Oxford: Oxford University Press, 2005).

71. The remaining number included foreign musicians who collaborated with Ethiopian musicians.

72. Struggles for political power in the Ethiopian past were often commemorated by singers, sometimes prematurely. James Bruce, a British traveler in Ethiopia during the 1770s, recounted a story about minstrels in the northeastern capital Gondar who had been supported by the local prince (Michael) and often sang his praises (*Bruce's Travels and Adventures in Abyssinia*, ed. J. Morison Clingan [Edinburgh: Adam and Charles Black, 1860]). However, when the patriarch excommunicated the prince, the singers joined in the ceremony and ridiculed Michael in virulent terms, "calling him crooked, lame, old and impotent" (256). Not long afterward, the prince overthrew the patriarch and returned victorious to Gondar, and the musicians welcomed him back. The prince, who had heard of their treachery, had his soldiers kill the musicians on the spot. But even in death musicians exercised their power: Bruce goes on to explain that several months later, the prince's horse threw him to the ground twice on the very spot where the musicians had been murdered, concluding that "everybody interpreted the accidents as an omen that Michael's power and fortune were gone from him for ever" (259).

Chapter Two

1. Correction to the song title given on *éthiopiques 1*, track 12, as "Yezemed yebaed" from Selam Seyoum Woldemariam, personal communication with author, June 16, 2020.

2. Shelemay, field notes, July 15, 2010, Either/Orchestra concert at the Lily Pad, Cambridge, MA.

3. I thank Francis Falceto for clarifying inclusive dates for Amha Records, as well as the date he obtained these materials for *éthiopiques*.

4. Francis Falceto, liner notes to *éthiopiques 1: Golden Years of Modern Ethiopian Music, 1969–1975*, Buda Musique 829512, 1997, compact disc. I thank Gilles Fruchaux of Buda Musique for clarifying the date of publication.

5. See https://rateyourmusic.com/artist/emilia.

6. According to my informal interview with Teshome Mitiku (Shelemay, field notes, August 22, 2007, Washington, DC), Teshome departed Sweden in the early 2000s for Washington, DC. However, according to information provided in correspondence between Falceto and Teshome, his date of immigration to the United States was in the early 1990s (Francis Falceto, personal communications with author, August 31, 2020 and October 3, 2020).

7. Gilles Deleuze and Félix Guattari, *A Thousand Plateaus: Capitalism and Schizophrenia*, trans. Brian Massumi (Minneapolis: University of Minnesota Press, 1987), 311. My reference to musical pathways relates primarily to the mobility of music and musicians and does not draw on that concept as used by Ruth Finnegan "as one possible metaphor for illuminating certain features of local music and its implications for urban life" (Ruth Finnegan, *The Hidden Musicians: Music-Making in an English Town* [Middletown, CT: Wesleyan University Press, 2007], 305).

8. Kane, *Dictionary*, 454.

9. Alain Gascon, "Horn of Africa," *EAe*, 3:67–68.

10. Edward Gibbon, *The Decline and Fall of the Roman Empire* (Chicago: Encyclopædia Britannica, 1952), 2:159–60.

11. Edward Ullendorff, *The Ethiopians: An Introduction to Country and People*, 3rd ed. (London: Oxford University Press, 1973), 75–77. Evidence from archaeology, linguistics, written epigraphic and literary sources, and oral traditions indicate that migrations from the east, north, and south "into, within, and to a minor extent, also from Ethiopia, Eritrea, and nearby regions" were common before 1400 (Alessandro Bausi, "Migrations before 1400," *EAe*, 5:427).

12. Thomas Faist, "The Mobility Turn: A New Paradigm for the Social Sciences?," *Ethnic and Racial Studies* 36, no. 11 (2013): 1638, https://doi.org/10.1080/01419870 .2013.812229.

13. Some might mark this revelatory moment decades earlier, in 1936, when Haile Selassie I, the first African ruler to speak before the League of Nations, denounced the brutal Italian invasion of his country. See, for example, Asfa-Wossen Asserate, *King of Kings: The Triumph and Tragedy of Emperor Haile Selassie I of Ethiopia*, trans. Peter Lewis (London: Haus, 2015), xi.

14. Lucy is the most famous of the *Australopithecus afarensis* genus fossils dating from three to four million years ago discovered in the Afar region of Ethiopia's northern Rift Valley (Berhane Asfaw "Australopithecus afarensis," *EAe*, 1:396).

15. "Do They Know It's Christmas" was a song released by the not-for-profit "Band

Aid" founded by Bob Geldof in 1984 (Bangshowbiz.com, "Bob Geldof: Band Aid Isn't a Good Song," *Washington Post*, May 22, 2015, https://www.washingtonpost.com /entertainment/bob-geldof-band-aid-isnt-a-good-song/2015/05/22/bf5b589e -0066-11e5-8c77-bf274685e1df_story.html). "We Are the World" was recorded by the group U.S.A. for Africa (United Support of Artists for Africa) in 1985 (Gavin Edwards, "'We Are the World': A Minute-by-Minute Breakdown," *Rolling Stone*, March 6, 2015, https://www.rollingstone.com/music/music-features/we-are-the-world-a -minute-by-minute-breakdown-54619/).

16. In 1991 the northern, formerly British, region of the country declared its independence as Somaliland and in 1998 the former Italian area known as Puntland at the tip of the Horn of Africa also declared its autonomy (Markus V. Höhne, "Somalia, Political History of," *EAe*, 4:707–10).

17. Frederick C. Gamst, "Djibouti," *EAe*, 2:179–83.

18. United Nations High Commissioner for Refugees, *Convention and Protocol Relating to the States of Refugees* (Geneva: UNHCR, 2010), 3, contains the text of the 1951 Convention Relating to the Status of Refugees, with an introductory note by the Office of the United Nations High Commissioner for Refugees.

19. Ban Ki-Moon, "With 16 Million Refugees Worldwide, Secretary General Calls for Redoubled Efforts to Address Causes," *United Nations Meetings Coverage and Press Releases*, June 17, 2008, https://www.un.org/press/en/2008/sgsm11643.doc.htm.

20. Christine P. Gambino, Edward N. Trevelyan, and John Thomas Fitzwater, "The Foreign-Born Population from Africa: 2008–2012," United States Census Bureau Report ACSBR/12–16, October 1, 2014, https://www.census.gov/library/publications /2014/acs/acsbr12-16.html. No doubt this figure significantly understates the actual number of immigrants from the Horn of Africa.

21. Getatchew Haile, "Amharic Poetry of the Ethiopian Diaspora in America: A Sampler," *Diaspora* 15, nos. 2–3 (2006 [pub. 2011]): 337, https://doi.org/10.1353 /dsp.2011.0069.

22. The term *gəzat*, from *agazä*, "to exile," was also used historically in Ethiopia, as was the noun *zäwari*, which means "wanderer" (Kane, *Dictionary*, 216, 1442). See also Solomon Addis Getahun, "*Sədät*, Migration, and Refugeeism as Portrayed in Ethiopian Song Lyrics," *Diaspora* 15, nos. 2–3 (2006 [pub. 2011]): 341–59, https://doi.org /10.1353/dsp.2011.0071.

23. Haile Gabriel Dagne, "Amba Gasän," *EAe*, 1:220–21.

24. Kane, *Dictionary*, 576–77.

25. Allan Louis Young, "Medical Beliefs and Practices of Begemder Amhara" (PhD diss., University of Pennsylvania, 1970), 231–32.

26. Somali culture in the region, which is particularly well known for migratory practices, has songs that justify mobility undertaken for purposes of earning a livelihood: "Traveling suits a man fine, if death is delayed departing him. He can't shelter in the warmth of a comforting wall, if there is no gain to be garnered." Text in Somali: *Ragga socodku waw door / Hadduu moodku daayee. / Derbi lama fadhiistiyo / Halkii kuu dartee / Kol haddaan wax daaqiyo* (Yusuf, *Somalis in Minnesota*, 4–5).

27. Telela Kebede, a star singer of the National Theatre who today lives in Silver Spring, Maryland, was born in 1938 in Kenya to Ethiopian parents who met there while in exile during the Italian occupation (Telela Kebede, interview by author, July 10, 2010, Washington, DC).

28. Solomon, "*Sədät*, Migration, and Refugeeism," 347.

29. Peter H. Koehn, *Refugees from Revolution: U.S. Policy and Third-World Migration* (Boulder, CO: Westview, 1991), 273.

30. Solomon, "Sədät, Migration, and Refugeeism," 343.

31. Solomon, "Sədät, Migration, and Refugeeism," 349.

32. John Urry, *Mobilities* (Cambridge, UK: Polity, 2007), 47.

33. See, for example, Sumanth Gopinath and Jason Stanyek, eds., *The Oxford Handbook of Mobile Music Studies*, 2 vols. (Oxford: Oxford University Press, 2014).

34. Russell King and Anastasia Christou, "Of Counter-diaspora and Reverse Transnationalism: Return Mobilities to and from the Ancestral Homeland," *Mobilities* 6, no. 4 (2011): 451–66, https://doi.org/10.1080/17450101.2011.603941.

35. Mimi Sheller and John Urry, "The New Mobilities Paradigm," *Environment and Planning A: Economy and Space* 38, no. 2 (2006): 211, https://doi.org/10.1068/a37268, citing Beverley Skeggs, *Class, Self, Culture* (London: Routledge, 2004), 49, and David Morley, *Home Territories: Media, Mobility, and Identity* (London: Routledge, 2000).

36. Paolo Marrassini, "Kəbrä Nägäst," *EAe*, 3:364–68.

37. However, there are surely moments in which the imaginary operates in the present as well. For instance, one can consider the ways in which individuals unable to depart the homeland during the revolution imagined diaspora life, as well as the equally rich nostalgia for an imagined life left behind among those abroad.

38. Recent archaeological work at Lalibela has established that the site was constructed in multiple phases, probably reflecting a long occupation sequence spanning at least eleven centuries (from the tenth to the twenty-first centuries). Claire Bosc-Tiessé et al., "The Lalibela Rock Hewn Site and Its Landscape (Ethiopia): An Archaeological Analysis," *Journal of African Archaeology* 12, no. 2 (2014): 141–64.

39. Niall Finneran, "Lalibela," *EAe*, 3:482.

40. Kirsten Stoffregen-Pedersen, "Jerusalem," *EAe*, 3:273–77.

41. Shelemay, *Music, Ritual, and Falasha History*, 24.

42. The Ethiopian Orthodox Church adheres to a christological doctrine that dates to the Council of Chalcedon in 451 CE and is shared by a number of Eastern Orthodox Churches, including the Syrian and the Armenian. The doctrine (*Tewahedo*) believes in the single nature of Christ, at once both divine and human.

43. Stoffregen-Pedersen, "Jerusalem," *EAe*, 3:274; Andrew Martinez, "Florence, Council of," *EAe*, 2:554.

44. Ulrich Braukämper, "Population History III: Migrations from the 15th to the 19th Century," *EAe*, 4:173.

45. Braukämper, "Population History," *EAe*, 4:173.

46. Marilyn E. Heldman, *The Marian Icons of the Painter Frē Ṣeyon* (Wiesbaden, Ger.: Harrassowitz, 1994), 140–41.

47. Heldman, *Marian Icons*, 142.

48. Frank Harrison, *Time, Place and Music: An Anthology of Ethnomusicological Observation c. 1550 to c. 1800* (Amsterdam: Frits Knuf, 1973), 50–51; Leonardo Cohen, *The Missionary Strategies of the Jesuits in Ethiopia (1555–1632)* (Wiesbaden, Ger.: Harrassowitz, 2009). See the beginning of chapter 3 for discussion of observations by Jesuits in Ethiopia.

49. C. Griffith Mann, "The Role of the Painted Icon in Ethiopian Culture," in *Ethiopian Art: The Walters Art Museum*, ed. Deborah E. Horowitz (Baltimore, MD: The Walters Art Museum, 2001), 126–27.

50. Donald Crummey, "The Politics of Modernization: Protestant and Catholic Missionaries in Modern Ethiopia," in *The Missionary Factor in Ethiopia*, ed. Samuel Rubenson, Getatchew Haile, and Aasulv Lande (Frankfurt: Peter Lang, 1998), 88-89.

51. See H. Marcus, *History of Ethiopia*, for details of the Italian presence in Ethiopia.

52. Solomon, "*Sədät*, Migration, and Refugeeism," 343-44.

53. H. Marcus, *History of Ethiopia*, 159.

54. Solomon, "*Sədät*, Migration, and Refugeeism," 345-47.

55. Giulia Bonacci, "Rastafari/Rastafarianism," *EAe*, 4:339-40.

56. Giulia Bonacci, "Šašämäne," *EAe*, 4:550-51.

57. Ewald Wagner, "Bilāl b. Rahāb al-Habašī," *EAe*, 1:583.

58. Jonathon Miran, "Red Sea Slave Trade in the Nineteenth Century," *EAe*, 4: 674-76.

59. Franz-Christoph Muth, "Aḥmad b. Ibrāhīm al-Ġāzī," *EAe*, 1:155-58.

60. Richard Pankhurst, "Slavery: Slave Trade from the Ancient Times to 19th Century," *EAe*, 4:674.

61. Shelemay, "Music," *EAe*, 3:1082-86.

62. Randi Rønning Balsvik, *Haile Selassie's Students: The Intellectual and Social Background to Revolution, 1952-1977* (East Lansing: African Studies Center, Michigan State University, 1985), 21.

63. Steven Kaplan, "Ethiopian Immigrants in the United States and Israel: A Preliminary Comparison." *International Journal of Ethiopian Studies* 5, no. 1 (2010): 75.

64. Sylvia Pankhurst, *Ethiopia: A Cultural History* (Essex, UK: Lalibela House, 1959), 534.

65. Earlier, in 1898, Emperor Menelik and Queen Victoria had exchanged phonograph messages. For information about this early technologically assisted exchange, see Abraham Demoz, "Emperor Menelik's Phonograph Message to Queen Victoria," *Bulletin of the School of Oriental and African Studies, University of London* 32, no. 2 (1969): 251-56. I thank Peter McMurray for bringing Demoz's documentation of this exchange to my attention.

66. Francis Falceto, *Abyssinie Swing: A Pictorial History of Modern Ethiopian Music* (Addis Ababa: Shama, 2001), 18, citing Casimir Mondon-Vidailhet, "La musique éthiopienne," in *Encyclopédie de la musique et dictionnaire du Conservatoire*, ed. Albert Lavignac and Lionel de la Laurencie (Paris: Librairie Delagrave, 1922), 3179-96.

67. Ani Aslanian, "In the Company of Emperors: The Story of Ethiopian Armenians," *Armenite*, October 6, 2014, https://thearmenite.com/2014/10/company -emperors-story-ethiopian-armenians/; Falceto, *Abyssinie Swing*, 29-32.

68. Aslanian, "In the Company of Emperors."

69. Donald Crummey, "Ethiopia, Europe and Modernity: A Preliminary Sketch," *Aethiopica* 3 (2000): 16, https://doi.org/10.15460/aethiopica.3.1.569.

70. Crummey, "Ethiopia," 16.

71. Aslanian, "In the Company of Emperors."

72. David Clay Large, *Between Two Fires: Europe's Path in the 1930s*, rev. ed. (New York: W. W. Norton, 1990), 148.

73. A contribution by Ethiopians in the virtual domain was to develop codes for digitizing languages known as *abugida*, such as Ge'ez, the Ethiopian Christian liturgical language, and many of the Brahmic scripts of India and Southeast Asia, in which each letter represents a consonant joined to a specific vowel (Nancy J. Hafkin, "'Whatsupoch' on the Net: The Role of Information and Communication Technology in

the Shaping of Transnational Ethiopian Identity," *Diaspora* 15, nos. 2–3 (2006 [pub. 2011]): 242n1). The name *abugida*, which is derived from the first four characters of the Ge'ez syllabary, is as a result used to refer to any language with a syllabary of this sort.

74. Hafkin, "'Whatsupoch' on the Net," 239–41.

75. Hafkin, "'Whatsupoch' on the Net," 233.

76. Crummey, "Ethiopia," 19.

Chapter Three

1. Harrison, *Time, Place and Music*, 50–51.

2. Changes since the revolution include the entry of women into liturgical performance in diaspora churches, where they can be seen standing with prayer staffs, singing along with the chant, and playing the liturgical drum, *käbäro* (*kebero*). These innovations will be discussed in chapter 9.

3. William A. Graham, *Beyond the Written Word: Oral Aspects of Scripture in the History of Religion* (Cambridge: Cambridge University Press, 1987), 164.

4. Eric Palazzo, "Art, Liturgy, and the Five Senses in the Early Middle Ages," *Viator* 41, no. 1 (2010): 25–56, https://doi.org/10.1484/J.VIATOR.1.100566.

5. For instance, although art historians have acknowledged the role of multiple senses and moved to develop broader theories drawing on the materiality of paintings and manuscripts, they have remained within the realm of the sacred when positing "how the sacred borrows 'some substantiality' from images and works of art in general 'in order to make its own substantiality present'" (Palazzo, "Art, Liturgy," 33). However, S. Brent Plate, in *Walter Benjamin, Religion, and Aesthetics* (New York: Routledge, 2005), 2–3, seeks "to rescue aesthetics as an originary point for the study of religion," exploring "the religiocultural constructions of perception . . . [of the] world on a material basis."

6. Steven Kaplan has anticipated this argument in part in his article "The Christianisation of Time in Fifteenth-Century Ethiopia," in *Religious Conversion: History, Experience and Meaning*, ed. Ira Katznelson and Miri Rubin (Farnham, UK: Ashgate: 2014), 81–98.

7. Kane, *Dictionary*, 18.

8. See Kay Kaufman Shelemay, "The Musician and Transmission of Religious Tradition: The Multiple Roles of the Ethiopian *Däbtära*," *Journal of Religion in Africa* 22, no. 3 (1992): 242–60, https://doi.org/10.1163/157006692X00167, for details of the *debtera*'s training and career. The musicians are responsible for performing the most elaborate musical content of the liturgy. The Mass, in contrast, is celebrated by the priests with a minimum of musical content.

9. See Shelemay and Jeffery, *Ethiopian Christian Liturgical Chant*, vols. 2 and 3, for details of Saint Yared's contributions and the findings that the Ethiopian Christian notational system dates to the period after the Islamic invasion in the mid-sixteenth century.

10. Berhanu Mekonnen, interview by author, June 2, 1975, Addis Ababa.

11. Gérard Colin, ed., *Le synaxaire éthiopien, mois de Genbot*, Patrologia Orientalis no. 211 (Turnhout, Belgium: Brepols, 1997), 242–45.

12. Abraham Habte Selassie, *Saint Yared and Ethiopian Ecclesiastical Music* (Washington, DC: Debre Selam Kidist Mariam Church, 1999), 5.

13. Hailu Habtu, "A Synopsis of Merigeta Lisana Worq's Book," in *T'ǝtawi Sǝra'ǝ'atä*

Mahlet Zä'abunä Yared Liq [The ancient hymn corpus of Chief Abuna Yared] (Addis Ababa: Makalé Maison des Études Éthiopiennes and Institut Tigréen des Langues, 1997), xvii.

14. Although Yared is traditionally said to have lived in the sixth century, we are able to date the first entry about this saint in the Synaxary only to around the year 1582. Moreover, the oldest extant visual images of Saint Yared are even later, dating to the rule of Queen Mentewab from 1730 to 1755. The institutionalization of the Yared myth evidently began in the late sixteenth century, after the Islamic invasion of 1529–43, around the same time as the inception of the musical notation system. For discussion of this historical reappraisal, see Marilyn E. Heldman and Kay Kaufman Shelemay, "Concerning Saint Yared," in *Studies in Ethiopian Languages, Literature, and History*, ed. Adam Carter McCollum (Wiesbaden, Ger.: Harrassowitz, 2017), 65–93.

15. Hailu, "Synopsis," xxii.

16. Abraham, *Saint Yared*, 17.

17. Messing, "Highland-Plateau Amhara," 573. One 1528 Ethiopian manuscript, *Mäzmurä Krestos* (Psalter of Christ), refers to the five senses in imitation of the Book of Psalms; it remains unpublished at the British Library, Or 534, http://www.bl.uk /manuscripts/FullDisplay.aspx?ref=Or_534. I thank Dr. Getatchew Haile for mentioning this source to me.

18. One allegorical device for representing the five senses in the European Middle Ages was the depiction of actual sensory organs, including an eye for sight, an ear for hearing, and others. Only in seventeenth-century Europe was a whole series of five senses depicted in this way. See Carl Nordenfalk, "The Five Senses in Late Medieval and Renaissance Art," *Journal of the Warburg and Courtauld Institutes* 48 (1985): 1–22. According to an expert in Ethiopian iconography, manuscript illumination, and painting, no such illustrations exist in Ethiopian artistic practice (Marilyn E. Heldman, personal communication with author, June 30, 2015).

19. Prepared by Kidanä Wäld Kəfle (c. 1862–1944), this entry was published as part of the entry for *hiwas* (senses): *Mäshafä Säwasəw Wägəs Wämäzgäbä Qalat Haddis* [A book of grammar and verb, and a new dictionary] (Addis Ababa, 1948 EC), 438, col. 25. See also Kane, *Dictionary*, 18, which lists seven senses, including *'əgər* (leg), which he translates as "motion," and *häfrätä səga* (genitalia). Kane adds that "others count only those above the neck, i.e. eyes, ears, nostrils and mouth."

20. The "seat of strength" is considered to be the knee (Messing, "Highland-Plateau Amhara," 571).

21. Kane, *Dictionary*, 18, s.v. *həwas*.

22. Kane, *Dictionary*, 36. In Kidanä Wäld Kəfle's *Mäshafä Säwasəw*, *abalä zär* (male genitals) is used to represent the sex sense.

23. Kane, *Dictionary*, 18, s.v. *həwas*.

24. The seating of women on the left likely relates to traditions that the left hand is reserved for unclean functions.

25. The (still limited) entry of women into Ethiopian Christian liturgical and musical performance in the years after the revolution marks changes that will be addressed in chapter 9.

26. Ethiopians are supposed to eat one meal a day during Lent without meat, egg, or milk products. Lent lasts fifty-six days in the Ethiopian tradition. On Easter Day, the fast is broken, the full liturgical performance resumes, and the full array of multiple senses are once again stimulated.

27. Hailu, "Synopsis," xxv.

28. See also Tom Boylston, *The Stranger at the Feast: Prohibition and Mediation in an Ethiopian Orthodox Christian Community* (Berkeley: University of California Press, 2018), especially chapter 2, "Fasting, Bodies, and the Calendar" (37–55), which discusses what Boylston terms "the ritual regime," "the system that connects bodies and patterns of work, exchange, and consumption to a much larger schematic vison of the world . . . through their connection to foundational religious events" (37).

29. For further details on *Mahlet,* see Ezra Gebremedhin, "Mahlet" *EAe* 3:659–660. Ethiopian chants are known as *mäzmur* (*mezmur,* portions), of which there are more than two dozen classified according to musical and liturgical criteria. For more details, see Shelemay and Jeffery, *Ethiopian Christian Liturgical Chant,* 1:6–7.

30. See Anne Damon, "Aqwaqwam ou la danse des cieux" [Aqwaqwam or the celestial dance], *Cahiers d'Études Africaines* 46, no. 182 (2006): 282, https://www.jstor .org/stable/4393575.

31. Sections of the Mass are conducted by priests and deacons within the Holy of Holies, an inner chamber today fitted with amplified sound so that the congregation can hear, but not see, what is happening.

32. Abraham, *Saint Yared,* 6.

33. The Mass does have Gospel portions read aloud, but its sensory load is subtler and more restrained, performed without instrumental accompaniment or dance, contrasting with the *Mahlet.*

34. Steven Kaplan has suggested that Emperor Zär'a Ya'əqob mobilized many forms of visual imagery, including icons of the Virgin Mary, in the service of the church ("Seeing Is Believing: The Power of Visual Culture in the Religious World of Aṣe Zär'a Ya'əqob of Ethiopia (1434–1468)," *Journal of Religion in Africa* 32, no. 4 [2002]: 413).

35. According to Messing, "Highland-Plateau Amhara," 553, water associated with baptism in the church, as well as common water in the church courtyard, is usually dispensed for healing. The use of holy water is considered to be a rebaptism, washing away any misdeeds or sins (380).

36. Shelemay and Jeffery, *Ethiopian Christian Liturgical Chant,* 2:4.

37. Messing, "Highland-Plateau Amhara," 368.

38. Alessandro Triulzi and Tamene Bitima, "On Some Masqala and Daboo Songs of the Macca Oromo," in "African Languages and Cultures," supplement, *Voice and Power* 3 (1996): 243–56, https://www.jstor.org/stable/586665.

39. Edward Ullendorff, *Ethiopia and the Bible: The Schweich Lectures of the British Academy 1967,* 3rd ed. (London: Published for the British Academy by the Oxford University Press, 1968), 103.

40. In *Deep Listeners: Music, Emotion, and Trancing* (Bloomington: Indiana University Press, 2004), Judith Becker has proposed a "habitus of listening" to capture "the interrelatedness of the perception of musical emotion and learned interactions with our surroundings. Our perceptions operate within a set of habits gradually established throughout our lives and developed through our continual interaction with the world beyond our bodies, the evolving situation of being-in-the-world" (71).

41. Johnson, introduction to *The Field of Cultural Production,* 5.

42. Kaplan, "Christianisation of Time," 82.

43. Messing, "Highland-Plateau Amhara," 572. In contrast, the full bodies of archangels and saints are lauded in the liturgy as entirely sacred. The allusion to the *tabot,* which is wrapped in cloth and kept within an inner chamber of the church accessible

only to the clergy, suggests that the human body, like sacred objects, may be heard, smelled, and even touched, but rarely seen.

44. Messing, "Highland-Plateau Amhara," 553. Women also give offerings of incense to pay homage to the Virgin Mary and to ensure their reciprocal relationship with her (Cressida Marcus, "The Production of Patriotic Spirituality: Ethiopian Orthodox Women's Experience of War and Social Crisis," *Northeast African Studies*, 8, no. 3 [2001]: 179–208, https://doi.org/10.1353/nas.2006.0008).

45. Interview with a church musician by author.

46. Messing, "Highland-Plateau Amhara," 579.

47. Imbakom Kalewold, *Traditional Ethiopian Church Education*, trans. Menghestu Lemma (New York: Teachers College Press, 1970), 2.

48. Kane, *Dictionary*, 168–69. *Märi* is joined to the word *geta*, meaning lord or master, also a term of respectful address for a man (Kane, *Dictionary*, 1991–92).

49. Moges Seyoum, interview by author, August 2, 2007, Washington, DC.

50. Moges S. interview, August 2, 2007.

51. Moges Seyoum, *Yeametu Wereboch* [Annual *wereb*], 2006, 6 compact discs.

52. Moges Seyoum, *Yaqeddus Yared Yazema Dersat Atäqalay Gäs'ata* [An essay on the chant of Saint Yared] (Washington, DC: Bäliqä Mäzämaran Mogas Sayum, 1992 EC).

53. Moges Seyoum, *Talaqu Itiyopayawi Liq Qaddus Yaredanna Yäzemawa Tarik Känämalakkatu* [Saint Yared: The great Ethiopian scholar and the history of the hymns and their notation] (Washington, DC, 2017).

54. Moges S. interview, August 2, 2007.

55. C. Marcus, "Production of Patriotic Spirituality," 180.

56. Moges S. interview, August 2, 2007.

57. Getahun interview.

58. Wayna Wondwossen, interview by author, May 8, 2008, Washington, DC.

59. Henock Temesgen, interview by author, March 7, 2003, Cambridge, MA. Although Aster Aweke in fact was raised primarily in the Ethiopian capital, her years in church choirs clearly shaped her vocal style. This topic is explored further in chapter 7. Similarly, one finds that many Egyptians credit renowned singer Umm Kulthum's vocal style and declamation of text to her background as the daughter of a Koran reader (Virginia Danielson, *The Voice of Egypt: Umm Kulthum, Arabic Song, and Egyptian Society in the Twentieth Century* [Chicago: University of Chicago Press, 1997]).

60. Bezawork Asfaw, interview by author, June 24, 2008, Washington, DC.

61. Kane, *Dictionary*, 1615. Most *azmari* are men, while the few female *azmari* singers, are usually accompanied by male instrumentalists. One of the few female *azmari* to attain fame was the six-stringed lyre (*krar*) player Asnaketch Werku (c. 1934–2011), also an actress and dancer. Asnaketch Werku, *éthiopiques 16: The Lady with the Krar*, Buda Musique 822652, 2003, compact disc, includes her music, while there exists a biography in Amharic of her life (Getachew Debalke, *Asnaketch Werku* [Addis Ababa: Alliance Ethio-Française and Shama, n.d.]).

62. Francisco Alvarez, *The Prester John of the Indies: A True Relation of the Lands of the Prester John, Being the Narrative of the Portuguese Embassy to Ethiopia in 1520*, ed. C. F. Beckingham and G. W. B. Huntingford (Cambridge, UK: Hakluyt Society, 1961), 1:443.

63. Alvarez, *Prester John*, 517.

64. James Bruce, *Travels to Discover the Source of the Nile*, ed. J. Morison Clingan

(Edinburgh: Adam and Charles Black, 1860), 36. The earliest mention of wandering singers whose profession is "to beg, to collect money" has been credited to Bahrey's "History of the Galla" in *Some Records of Ethiopia 1593–1646: Being Extracts from the History of High Ethiopia or Abassia, by Manoel de Almeida, together with Bahrey's History of the Galla*, ed. C. F. Beckingham and G. B. W. Huntingford (London: Hakluyt Society, 2010), 126. (Bahrey's "History" uses a name for Oromo people considered to be pejorative.) However, Francis Falceto has recently located an earlier mention of *azmari* in a mid-fifteenth-century juridical and administrative text (Falceto, personal communication, August 31, 2020). See also Manfred Kropp, "*Antiquae restitutio legis*: Zur Alimentation des Hofklerus und einer Zeugenliste als imago imperii und *notitia dignitatum* in einer Urkunde des Kaisers Zär'ä Ya'qob im *condaghe* der Hs. BM Or. 481, fol. 154," *Scrinium* 1, no. 1 (2005): 120, 125, and 135, https://doi.org/10.1163/18177565 -90000131. I thank Francis Falceto for advising me of this new source.

65. Bruce, *Travels to Discover*, 1860.

66. For details of Tessema Eshete's stay in Berlin, see the notes by Francis Falceto and Wolfgang Bender that accompany thirty-two remastered songs on Tessema Eshete, *éthiopiques 27: Centennial of the First Ethiopian Music Recordings*, Buda Musique 860192, 2011, compact disc. Tessema was sent to Berlin to learn to drive a car that Germany presented to Emperor Menelik II in 1908. While in Berlin, Tessema recorded songs for Beka Records, believed to be the first recordings of an Ethiopian singer released commercially (Falceto and Bender, "The Life and Work of Tessema Eshete, First Ethiopian Singer to Record Commercially," liner notes to *éthiopiques 27*, 17–18).

67. See C. Marcus, "Production of Patriotic Spirituality," 203, for a detailed case study of the communicative relationship of *Gondari* women with the Virgin Mary through Marian song performances.

68. Tessema Eshete was the son of Ato Eshete Gobe, an *azmari* at the Ethiopian court in the southwestern city of Harar, who was unusual in being schooled in reading and writing Amharic. When his father died, Tessema was transferred to the orphanage in the palace of Emperor Menelik II in Addis Ababa. His selection for the trip to Germany on behalf of the emperor emerged from this youthful contact with Menelik's court. It is likely that the exposure to early sound recording in Berlin enhanced Tessema's rising social and professional status on his return to Ethiopia, where he married a noblewoman and eventually became the first Ethiopian Minister of Posts, Telegraphs, and Telephones. See Falceto and Bender, "Life and Work of Tessema Eshete," 17–19; see also Francis Falceto and Haylu Habtu, additional notes in PDF on *éthiopiques 27* CD, 2–55.

69. Falceto and Haylu, additional notes in PDF on *éthiopiques 27* CD, 16.

70. Falceto and Haylu, additional notes in PDF on *éthiopiques 27* CD, 8.

71. The title of the song, "Medina," is a cognate with Arabic meaning "capital city." There is no mention of a city in the song text and, because the idiom *yämädina sält* refers to musical accompaniment to poetry, the title may be an example of the type of double meaning exploited throughout the lyrics (Kane, *Dictionary*, 331–32).

72. Falceto and Haylu, additional notes in PDF on *éthiopiques 27* CD, 4.

73. Graziani, who was notorious for his brutality, became governor general of Italian Somaliland in 1935 and subsequently commanded the force that invaded Ethiopia and reached Addis Ababa in 1936. When the war ended in May 1936, Graziani was made viceroy of Ethiopia (Shawki El Gamal, "Graziani, Rudolfo," *EAe* 2:877–78). On February 19, 1937, a failed assassination attempt against Graziani resulted in the kill-

ing of thousands of Ethiopians in retribution; some four thousand houses in Addis Ababa were burned down, some with their occupants locked inside (Ian Campbell, *The Plot to Kill Graziani: The Attempted Assassination of Mussolini's Viceroy* [Addis Ababa: Addis Ababa University Press, 2010], 246).

74. Falceto, *Abyssinie Swing*, 46, citing the Ethiopian Press and Information Office, *La civilisation de l'Italie fasciste en Éthiopie* (Addis Ababa: Berhanena Selam, 1938). See, for example, praise poems transcribed from the Amharic oral tradition glorifying Bälay Zälläqä, who played a prominent role in the resistance movement against the Italians between 1935 and 1941, in Getie Gelaye, "Amharic Praise Poems of Däǧǧazmač Bälay Zälläqä and the Patriots of Goǧǧam during the Italian Occupation of Ethiopia, 1936–1941," in *Proceedings of the 15th International Conference of Ethiopian Studies, Hamburg 2003*, ed. Siegbert Uhlig (Wiesbaden, Ger.: Harrassowitz, 2006), 587–97.

75. Setegn Atanaw, interview by author and Itsushi Kawase, September 4, 2007, Washington, DC.

76. The *zar* cult is usually led by women as both healers and patients and is practiced by members of all religious groups (Simon D. Messing, "Group Therapy and Social Status in the Zar Cult of Ethiopia," *American Anthropologist* 60, no. 6 [1958]: 1120–26, https://www.jstor.org/stable/665379). See also the film by Itsushi Kawase, *When Spirits Ride Their Horses*, self-produced, 2012, 28 min., www.itsushikawase.com. The film presents excerpts from a *zar* cult ceremony in Gondar, Ethiopia, in the home of a female medium who exorcises a powerful spirit. The ceremony, held on the night before the Ethiopian Christian New Year, is accompanied by a *masenqo* player who sings and plays the song "Oh Lord, give us plenty of peace and joy." There is dancing by the medium and other participants, accompanied by the *masenqo*, drums, clapping, and ululation.

77. Timkehet Teffera, "The *Masinqo*: Its Meaning, Role and Its Multi-Functionality in Song and Dance," in *Studia Instrumentorum Musicae Popularis IV*, ed. Gisa Jähniche (Münster, Ger.: MV-Wissenschaft, 2016), 295–316. Timkehet discusses the songs and dance performed by the *azmari* in the *zar* cult ritual filmed by anthropologist Itsushi Kawase in Gondar (299–300). See also Itsushi Kawase, "The Azmari Performance during Zar Ceremonies in Northern Gondar, Ethiopia—Challenges and Prospects for the Documentation," *Cultures sonores d'Afrique* 5 (2012): 65–80.

78. Kaplan, "Zar," *EAe*, 4:185–87; Timkehet, "*Masinqo*," 299–300.

79. Setegn interview. The Apocalypse of Ezra (also known as 4 Ezra) is a book of visions composed by a Jewish author around 100 CE and ascribed to the biblical figure of Ezra the Scribe (Steven Kaplan, "Ezra, Apocalypse of," *EAe*, 2:482). Ezra is also said to have initiated the argot spoken by *azmari* known as *yä'ezra kwankwa* (Ezra's language). Setegn interview; see also Wolf Leslau, *Ethiopian Argots* (The Hague: Mouton, 1964).

80. Itsushi Kawase, personal communication with author, September 4, 2007, Washington, DC.

81. Getatchew Gebregiorgis, interview by author, July 2, 2008, Washington, DC.

82. Like many other Ethiopian musicians born in the years before and during the Ethiopian revolution, Ashenafi started his career as a dancer and drummer with a performance ensemble associated with an urban *kebele*, a local watch organization that exerted often repressive control over its population and their vital resources.

83. Ashenafi Mitiku, interview by author, August 28, 2007, Washington, DC.

84. Timkehet, "*Masinqo*," 304.

85. Constance Classen, "McLuhan in the Rainforest: The Sensory Worlds of Oral

Cultures," in *The Empire of the Senses: The Sensual Culture Reader*, ed. David Howes (London: Bloomsbury, 2005), 161.

86. Shelemay, field notes, May 26, 1997, Boston, MA.

87. Getahun interview.

Chapter Four

1. An important contribution to this subject is John Morgan O'Connell and Salwa El-Shawan Castelo-Branco, eds., *Music and Conflict* (Urbana: University of Illinois Press, 2010), which "explores the significance of music for understanding conflict" (vii). The essays in Jonathan Ritter and J. Martin Daughtry, eds., *Music in the Post-9/11 World* (New York: Routledge, 2007), chart "musical commentary on 9/11 . . . in other unexpected places in the world" (vii). To observe the response of musicians and their music to ongoing situations of violence requires the presence of the ethnographer, which is often impossible to achieve except in rare circumstances, as in Oliver Y. Shao's fifteen-month residency between 2011 and 2015 as a volunteer and researcher in the large Kakuma refugee camp of northwestern Kenya, not far from the Sudanese, Ugandan, and Ethiopian borders (Oliver Y. Shao, "A Cosmopolitan Social Justice Approach to Education," *Africa Today* 63, no. 2 [2016]: 107–11, https://www.jstor.org/stable/10.2979/africatoday.63.2.14).

2. Ironically, the fiction of a revolution devoid of music was probably inadvertently set into motion by the individual responsible for bringing Ethiopian music to a global listening public, *éthiopiques* CD series editor Francis Falceto. In the notes to the first volume of his extended CD series, *Golden Years of Modern Ethiopian Music, 1969–1975*, Falceto wrote that lively musical life in Ethiopia was "brutally extinguished in 1974 by the fall of the Emperor and the arrival of a particularly brutal military junta. The golden era's days were numbered, and the country would soon wake up to a new regime of repression" (Falceto, liner notes to *éthiopiques 1*, 18).

3. See David McDonald's discussion of his encounter in Israel-Palestine with "two disparate cultural narratives: one of occupation and the other of exile" (*My Voice Is My Weapon: Music, Nationalism, and the Poetics of Palestinian Resistance* [Durham, NC: Duke University Press, 2013], 8).

4. Falceto and Haylu, additional notes in PDF on *éthiopiques 27* CD, 16.

5. Kane, *Dictionary*, 297. See also Simeneh Betreyohannes Gebremariam, "The Azmari Tradition in Addis Ababa: Change and Continuity," *Northeast African Studies* 18, nos. 1–2 (2018): 36, https://www.muse.jhu.edu/article/732604.

6. A description of a coronation procession for Emperor Susenyos, who ruled from 1607 to 1632, was left by a Portuguese Jesuit, Pedro Páez, then in Ethiopia (Isabel Boavida, Hervé Pennec, and Manuel João Ramos, eds., *Pedro Páez's History of Ethiopia, 1622*, trans. Christopher J. Tribe [Farnham, UK: Ashgate, 2011], 1:159), providing details of the musical expression of power:

On Sunday morning, the emperor came out richly dressed in brocade and crimson satin, with a gold chain round his neck, from which hung a very fine cross; he was riding a powerful horse that was very well decked out. . . . He was preceded by all his captains, each with his troop drawn up in order with men on foot in the vanguard and then those on horseback, all dressed for celebration with many banners and playing their drums, trumpet, shawms and flutes, which they have in their own fashion.

7. Such a painting is reproduced in the catalog from an exhibition I curated in 1985 at the Jewish Museum in New York City (Kay Kaufman Shelemay, ed., *The Jews of Ethiopia: A People in Transition* [Tel Aviv: Beth Hatefutsoth, 1986; New York: Jewish Museum, 1986], 15).

8. Pankhurst, *Ethiopia*, 588. See chapter 2 in the present volume for additional discussion of the anthem composed by an Armenian immigrant to Ethiopia, Kevork Nalbandian, who arrived from Jerusalem with the *Arba Lijoch* in 1924.

9. Pankhurst, *Ethiopia*, 588. It may not be coincidental that several of the main figures responsible for the assassination attempt on Italian viceroy Graziani during the Italian occupation of Ethiopia had been students at the Tafari Mekonnen School in the late 1920s and early 1930s, where they were imbued with a patriotic spirit (I. Campbell, *Plot to Kill*, 12–18). One was Moges Asgedom, who was born in Eritrea, and whose only published photograph appears to be in a band uniform (I. Campbell, *Plot to Kill*, 15). A friend recalled that "the spirit of resistance was with Moges from an early period" (I. Campbell, *Plot to Kill*, 15–16). Abriha Deboch, another student at Tafari Mekonnen School, also wears the same band uniform in a photograph (I. Campbell, *Plot to Kill*, 19). However, these identical uniforms do not match available photographs of school or municipality ensembles.

10. There were multiple instances in which *azmari* leveled criticism against Ethiopian social and political life from the eighteenth until the early twentieth centuries, culminating in their resistance to the Italian occupation that began in 1935 (Simeneh, "*Azmari* Tradition," 38–39). For a discussion of *azmari* as targets of Italian occupiers, see also 47–48.

11. Bahru Zewde, "Hagär Fəqər Tiyatər," *EAe*, 2:966.

12. Asfa-Wossen, *King of Kings*, 204.

13. Bahru Zewde, *A History of Modern Ethiopia, 1855–1991*, 2nd ed., Eastern African Studies (Oxford, UK: James Currey, 2001), 684–85.

14. Pankhurst, *Ethiopia*, 424.

15. Pankhurst, *Ethiopia*, 424.

16. *Azmari* come from multiple ethnic communities and regions, many of Amhara descent, but a significant number as well from Oromo, Tigray, and Eritrean communities (Simeneh, "*Azmari* Tradition," 35–36; Cynthia Tse Kimberlin, "*Masinqo* and the Nature of *Qəñət*" [PhD diss., University of California-Los Angeles, 1976], 15). See also Cynthia Tse Kimberlin, "Mäsinqo," *EAe*, 3:835. *Azmari* sing in their respective ethnic languages, which serve to differentiate their ethnic community of descent, as do the different sound-box shapes, sizes, and decorations of their instrument's spike head. The Tigray *azmari* are said to favor the largest sound box; Amhara, ones of medium size; and Oromo, the smallest (Kimberlin, "Mäsinqo," 835). Most *azmari* are Christians, and one Ethiopian scholar who interviewed them during the mid-1960s in the highlands has written that most *azmari* he spoke with attended church schools for four or five years in their youth (Ashenafi Kebede, "Azmari, Poet-Musician of Ethiopia," *Musical Quarterly* 61, no. 1 [1975]: 53, https://doi.org/10.1093/mq/LXI.1.47). In "*Masinqo* and the Nature of *Qəñət*," 21–22, Kimberlin discusses one *azmari* of Muslim faith.

17. For instance, a song of praise, "Səma," recorded in 1908 for Emperor Menelik

II (1844–1913), who had assumed the Ethiopian throne in 1889, celebrated the king's status as an innovator with strong interests in new technologies:

> Now, the train gallops, and the telephone speaks
> A prophet, my heart suspects, is Menelik
> When had these things happened before?
> The son of the king of Shewa
> The King of the Habeshas, you Menelik are a prophet
> You leave the past behind, and know what is ahead.

Trans. Haylu Habtu in Falceto and Haylu, in additional notes in PDF on *éthiopiques* 27 CD, 64.

18. Marcel Griaule, *Burners of Men: Modern Ethiopia*, trans. Edwin Gile Rich (London: J. B. Lippincott, 1935), 126.

19. It was customary for Ethiopians to be given a horse's name alongside their baptismal name. Many Ethiopian heroes are lauded in song by their horse's names.

20. Asfa-Wossen, *King of Kings*, 204. See also Richard Pankhurst, "The Early History of Ethiopian Horse-Names," *Paideuma* 35, no. 1 (1989): 197–206.

21. Asfa-Wossen, *King of Kings*, 199.

22. The Haile Selassie I Theatre Orchestra, for example, influenced countless musicians both through its live performances and, until the present, through recordings. Ethiopian American Debo Band leader Danny Mekonnen recalled its influence on his own ensemble, founded in the early 2000s in Boston: "The Haile Selassie Theater Orchestra was a big influence on me as I was thinking of putting a project together. It was the predominant orchestra while [Emperor] Haile Selassie was in power and was basically a stage band under the direction of an Armenian composer who was living in Ethiopia named Nerses Nalbandian. . . . It was a modern, full ensemble. They wore tuxedos and had a string section, but they were also playing folk music. That sort of piqued my interest" (Alex Spoto, "Debo Band's Danny Mekonnen on His Music's Ethiopian Roots: The Boston Band Digs Deep into Ethiopian Musical History," *Spin*, July 12, 2012, https://www.spin.com/2012/07/debo-bands-danny-mekonnen -his-musics-ethiopian-roots/).

23. Falceto, liner notes to *éthiopiques 17: Tlahoun Gèssèssè*, Buda Musique 822662, 2004, compact disc, 25.

24. "Alchalkum" (I can't take it anymore): "How long should I bear your ill? / How long are you going to make me suffer? / I can't take it anymore, I've had enough. / I can't take it anymore, I've had enough." The double meaning of "Alchalkum" was so closely associated with resistance against the government that its performance was once again banned under the 1975 revolutionary regime of the Derg. This song can be heard on YouTube, 5:15, posted by Tilahun Gessesse-Topic, April 7, 2020, https:// www.youtube.com/watch?v=pqiHA_6Xu6E.

25. Addis Ababa was known as Finfinnee among the Oromo, who from the seventeenth century onward lived nearby and transmitted oral traditions about the medical properties of the thermal springs in the area (Kevin O'Mahoney and Wolbert Smidt, "Finfinnee," *EAe*, 2:544). Emperor Menelik II established his residence on a mountain overlooking Finfinnee in 1879, but it was his queen, Taytu (Taitu), who in 1887 named the area below near the hot springs amid flowering mimosa trees "Addis

Ababa" (lit., new flower), which became the name of the new capital (O'Mahoney and Smidt, "Finfinnee," 545).

26. Asafa Jalata, "The Emergence of Oromo Nationalism and Ethiopian Reaction," in *Oromo Nationalism and the Ethiopian Discourse: The Search for Freedom and Democracy*, ed. Asafa Jalata (Lawrenceville, NJ: Red Sea, 1998), 5–7. Gow (*Oromo in Exile*, 62–63), who interviewed many Oromo musicians in the Australian diaspora, dates the band Urjii Bakkalchaa earlier, to 1960, and says that it was founded by the poet Abubakar Musa and only later nicknamed "Afran Qalloo," "*qaloo* being the name of the father of four Oromo sub-groups: *oborraa, babilee, dagaa and alaa.*" See also Gow, *Oromo in Exile*, 64–70, for details about other Oromo musicians and the bands they subsequently established. In "Macha-Tulama Association 1963–1967 and the Development of Oromo Nationalism," in *Oromo Nationalism and the Ethiopian Discourse: The Search for Freedom and Democracy*, ed. Asafa Jalata (Lawrenceville, NJ: Red Sea, 1998), 187, Mohammed Hassen notes that there were no Western-educated leaders to head the Oromo nationalist movement until the 1970s, which may account for the prominent role of musicians and musical performance in the early Oromo nationalist movement. Oromo Liberation Front (OLF) cultural and musical troupes, through traditional and modern music, poems, and speeches, explained the nature of Ethiopian colonialism and the necessity for liberation (Asafa, "Emergence of Oromo Nationalism," 16).

27. Oromo are indigenous Cushitic peoples who were early inhabitants of the Horn of Africa; by the fourteenth century, many had migrated from the south to the central and northern highland plateau (Mohammed Hassen, *The Oromo of Ethiopia: A History, 1570–1860*, African Studies Series 66 [Cambridge: Cambridge University Press, 1990], xi–xiii). A number of regional and tribal groups compose the broader Oromo community, a community united by the Afaan Oromo language. In terms of religious affiliations, although most Oromo today are Muslims, many are Ethiopian Orthodox, an increasing number are affiliated with evangelical and Protestant Christian denominations, and a smaller but growing group maintains the indigenous Oromo religion, *Waqafaana* (Elizabeth and Martha Namarra, interviews by author, March 13, 2011, Minneapolis, MN).

28. Asafa, "Emergence of Oromo Nationalism," 6–7.

29. Lily Marcos-Birra, "A Short Untold History of Ali Birra: A Legendary Oromo Singer," in *Ali Birra: A Fifty Year Journey for the Love of Music and His People*, ed. Mohammed Hassen and Lily Marcos-Birra (Dallas, TX: CreateSpace, 2013), 7.

30. Marcos-Birra, "Short Untold History," 17–18. The spelling of Oromo names is complex due to vowel gemination and is not at all consistent. Spellings vary among sources, so whenever possible I have adopted the spelling selected by the individual in question. The use of Latin script for writing Afaan Oromo dates to 1974, when a newly founded Oromo cultural committee petitioned the military junta to use the Latin script they had recently adopted for several official publications, including a dictionary and newspaper. Between 1942 and 1974, Afaan Oromo was officially banned by the Ethiopian government for virtually all purposes, from oral uses to the production of literature (P. T. W. Baxter, "Ethiopia's Unacknowledged Problem: The Oromo," *African Affairs* 77, no. 308 [1978]: 288). The new Latin script, called *Qubee*, was intended to restore the Oromo language after a long period of restrictions under the monarchy. However, the military government insisted on use of the Amharic syllabary, leading to ongoing conflicts between the government and the Oromo, and directly galvaniz-

ing the founding of the Oromo Liberation Front in 1974. The cultural committee was initially successful in starting a number of musical groups across Oromo communities, which held the first public performances of Oromo music and dance, but such events resulted in imprisonment, torture, and murder of many of the participants. *Qubee* was officially adopted as the official Oromo script only in 1991 after the fall of the Derg (Asafa, *Oromia and Ethiopia*, 188).

31. The Oromo text and English translation are provided in Mohammed Hassen, "Ali Mohammed Birra Is a Gift to the Oromo People and to the World of Music," in *Ali Birra: A Fifty Year Journey*, 59–60. The English translation is credited to Taha Ali Abdi, noting that "it is almost impossible to capture the most accurate translation of the [Oromo] lyrics in English."

32. Urjii Bakkalchaa evidently sparked other Oromo bands, and Ali also founded Hiryyaa Jaalalaa (A Friend of Love) in 1964 (Gow, *Oromo in Exile*, 630).

33. Marcos-Birra, "Short Untold History," 24.

34. Mohammed, "Ali Mohammed Birra Is a Gift," 63–64.

35. Thomas Osmond, "A Few Remarks about the Song 'Awash,'" in liner notes to Ali Birra, *éthiopiques 28: Great Oromo Music*, Buda Musique 860233, 2013, compact disc, 30–32.

36. Ali Birra, interview by author, August 2, 2009, Atlanta, GA.

37. Nagaso Gidada, "Oromo Historical Poems and Songs: Conquest and Exploitation in Western Wallaga, 1886–1927," *Paideuma* 29 (1983): 327–40, https://www.jstor.org/stable/41409898; Alessandro Triulzi, "Social Protest and Rebellion in Some *Gäbbar* Songs from Qellam, Wällägä," in *Modern Ethiopia/L'Éthiopie moderne: From the Accession of Menelik II to the Present*, ed. Joseph Tubiana (Rotterdam, Neth.: Balkema, 1980), 177–96.

38. Ali Birra's first trip back to Ethiopia took place more than a decade after the revolution ended; by then, his home was in Toronto, Canada (Ali interview). In recent years, Ali and his wife Lily have divided their time between Bishoftu, Oromia Region and Toronto (Ali Birra and Lily Marcos-Birra, personal communication with author, June 16, 2020).

39. Selam Seyoum Woldemariam, interview by author, August 26, 2007, Washington, DC.

40. Martha Z. Tegegn, "Part Two: Exclusive Interview with Ethiopian Legend Teshome Mitiku," *Tadias*, August 12, 2010, http://www.tadias.com/08/12/2010/part-two-exclusive-interview-with-ethiopian-legend-teshome-mitiku/.

41. Shiferaw Bekele and Sophia Dege-Müller, "Revolution of 1974," *EAe*, 4: 384–85.

42. Beleke and Dege-Müller, "Revolution of 1974," 385.

43. Kane, *Dictionary*, 1758.

44. H. Marcus, *History of Ethiopia*, 192; Kane, *Dictionary*, 1617.

45. Dirk Bustorf, "Zämäča," *EAe*, 5:122.

46. Simeneh Betreyohannes, "Music and Politics in Twentieth Century Ethiopia: Empire, Modernization and Revolution" (MA thesis, Addis Ababa University, 2008), 102. The *zemecha* choir resembles musical initiatives mounted in the 1930s by authoritarian governments of that period, for example, in Brazil, which introduced collective singing known as orpheonic song to promote the political interests of the regime (Flávio Oliveira, "Orpheonic Chant and the Construction of Childhood in Brazilian Elementary Education," in *Brazilian Popular Music and Citizenship*, ed. Idelber Avelar

and Christopher Dunn [Durham, NC: Duke University Press, 2011], 57–58). I thank Haden Smiley for pointing out this similarity.

47. In 1987 Ethiopia was renamed the "People's Democratic Republic of Ethiopia with Derg strongman Mengistu Haile Mariam as its president" (Beleke and Dege-Müller, "Revolution of 1974," 384–85).

48. One of the most brutal periods of the revolution took place in the mid-1980s, when the Derg imposed resettlement and villagization processes. As many as six hundred thousand people were moved from areas in the northeast that had been the site of a famine in 1984–85 to "underpopulated" regions in the south and west of the country, and many from the south, a region where there was widespread disease of the economically important ensete plant (*Ensete ventricosum*), were moved to the west. Villagization involved moving scattered homesteads into designated villages in areas adjacent to their homes (Wendy James et al., eds., *Remapping Ethiopia: Socialism and After* [Oxford, UK: James Currey, 2002], 19).

49. Clergy were also humiliated by being forced to clean the streets in urban areas (personal observation, 1975, Addis Ababa). In 1976 the Ethiopian patriarch Abuna Thewophilos was arrested for consecrating bishops without the approval of the Derg and was subsequently executed. *Merigeta* Tsehai Birhanu composed a *qene* (improvised liturgical poetry in Ge'ez) at that time in memory of the Abuna's death, an instance of political content embedded in a liturgical portion (Tsehai Birhanu, personal communication with author, August 30, 2006, Cambridge, MA).

50. See discussion later in this chapter on adjustments that urban hotels made to accommodate performances that lasted throughout curfew hours.

51. When her family returned to newly liberated Ethiopia in 1941, Telela's father received rewards of land and a political position from the emperor in Sidamo Province, about 160 miles south of Addis Ababa.

52. Telela Kebede, interview by author with Mimi Wondimiye (daughter), August 22, 2007, Washington, DC.

53. The founding of the Haile Selassie I National Theatre is usually dated to the construction of a building that served "as a focus for the Emperor's Silver Jubilee celebrations in 1955" (Jane Plastow, "Theatre: Theatre in Ethiopia," *EAe*, 4:940). However, the testimony of Telela, as well as that of Mulatu Astatke (interview by author and Steven Kaplan, September 12, 2007, Cambridge, MA), and Getatchew Mekuria ("Oral History: Getatchew Mekuria," liner notes to *Getatchew Mekuria, The Ex and Guests, Moa Anbessa*, Terp Records AS-11, 2006, compact disc), indicates an active history for the National Theatre stretching back into the late 1940s.

54. Ethiopian cultural music used only indigenous instruments, such as the one-stringed bowed lute (*masenqo*) and the six-stringed lyre (*krar*), which accompanied a solo singer in a heterophonic texture. In contrast, the modern music groups use Western musical instruments and draw on traditional Ethiopian tunings harmonized in a Western manner.

55. The performance of traditional tunes accompanied by Western instruments became known as *bahel zemenawi* (modern cultural music).

56. Telela is associated with a number of songs she popularized. In the late 1950s, Telela performed a version of "Shäggaw Təranbuli" (The handsome Ethiopian from Tripoli), mentioned in chapter 2, which told of Ethiopians and Eritreans who had been recruited to serve with Italian colonial forces between 1911 and the 1930s in Libya. Transmitted by traditional Ethiopian minstrels to the modern singers at the

National Theatre, the song describes the return of a soldier from Tripoli wearing Western trousers and drinking an expensive brand of mead (Solomon, "*Sedät*, Migration, and Refugeeism," 344–45).

57. Until the postrevolutionary period and the independence of Eritrea, Ethiopia had been divided into fourteen provinces. A new policy of ethnic federalism was adopted in 1994 (John M. Cohen, "'Ethnic Federalism' in Ethiopia," *Northeast African Studies* 2, no. 2 [1995]: 157–88).

58. Kane, *Dictionary*, 963.

59. This translation was prepared by the author in collaboration with Bitiya Elias Samuel.

60. Simeneh Betreyohannes writes that Getachew Debalke told him during an interview that he was moved by his observations of the worsening famine while traveling in the north and wanted to criticize the government for neglecting the crisis (Simeneh, "Music and Politics," 112, citing an interview with Getachew Debalke, December 1, 2008).

61. Research has documented the widespread presence of private drinking houses with live music performed by women during the period of urbanization in Ethiopia and Eritrea in the 1940s and 1950s. Known as *suwa* houses in Asmara, Eritrea, these modest venues served beer and featured female singers and *krar* players (Christine Matzke, "Of Suwa Houses and Singing Contests: Early Urban Women Performers in Asmara, Eritrea," in *African Theatre: Women*, ed. Jane Plastow [Bloomington: Indiana University Press, 2002], 29–46).

62. Telela interview, August 22, 2007. Telela's modest private club (*azmari bet*) that she ran between 1974 and 1976 in Addis Ababa featured her singing to *masenqo* (bowed lute) accompaniment and serving guests food that she had prepared herself; one of the small tables substituted for the *kebero* (drum). Although *masenqo* player Elias Tebabal usually accompanied Telela's singing, another *azmari* recalls performing with Telela at her house as well (Woretaw Wubet, interview by author, August 1, 2007, Washington, DC).

63. Telela interview, July 10, 2010.

64. Mimi Wondimiye, interview by author, August 22, 2007, Washington, DC.

65. Telela interview, August 22, 2007.

66. Abubakar Ashakih and Judith Ashakih, *Gift of Incense: A Story of Love and Revolution in Ethiopia* (Trenton, NJ: Red Sea, 2005), 232. Midnight curfews were instituted erratically as early as December 1973. In March 1974 curfew expanded to 11 p.m.–6 a.m. and, by June, from dusk (6 p.m.) to dawn (Ashakih and Ashakih, *Gift of Incense*, 232–33). Although the Venus Nightclub operation was erratic under the curfews, Abubakar rescued a number of musicians who were in difficult positions during the revolution, including guitarist Selam Seyoum Woldemariam, who was stranded in Asmara during the fighting. "Abubakar Ashakih called me, invited me, he sent me a ticket. My first beautiful experience in music started in the Venus Nightclub" (Selam interview, September 7, 2007).

67. John W. Harbeson, *The Ethiopian Transformation: The Quest for the Post-imperial State*, Westview Special Studies on Africa (Boulder, CO: Westview, 1988), 142. Many students became part of the opposition to the Derg as a result of their negative experiences when new policies were imposed in the countryside.

68. Moges Habte, interview by author, August 27, 2007, Washington, DC. There is some question about the extent of the disruption of the government ensembles asso-

ciated with the emperor and patriotism at the beginning of the revolution. In "Music and Politics," 75, Simeneh writes that "despite what many scholars have thought and said, the previously prominent ensembles were not, in fact, disbanded, but were rather used intensively to serve the new national agenda. Many artists worked with the government voluntarily, especially during the first few years of the Revolution." Whatever the extent of musicians' collaboration with the revolutionary government during its early years in power, following the violence that began in late 1975, many were unwilling to participate and sought alternatives. A number of musicians living in the diaspora made repeated efforts to contribute money to a fund to support musicians impoverished by the revolution (Moges H. interview, August 27, 2007).

69. Tibebeselassie Tigabu, "Remembering the Giant Roha," blogpost, *Reporter*, July 4, 2015.

70. Tibebeselassie, "Remembering the Giant Roha." Dawit Yifru also notes that he arranged "Lomi Tera Tera" for Telela Kebede during the period of the creeping coup and was imprisoned for four months as a result. Selam Seyoum Woldemariam recalls that this distressing moment for musicians occurred during the 1970s but does not remember the Roha Band confronting problems at the Hilton during the 1980s (personal communication, June 16, 2020).

71. Selam Seyoum Woldemariam, interview by author, September 5, 2007, Washington, DC. Quotation amended June 16, 2020, by Selam Seyoum Woldemariam, personal communication.

72. Moges Habte (b. 1950, Addis Ababa) attended the Yared School of Music and completed a correspondence course as well with the Berklee College of Music in Boston. In addition to his performance activities, he opened a music shop named Ethio Sound in central Addis Ababa's Masqal Square, which he sold on his departure from Ethiopia. Moges came to the United States at the invitation of Amha Eshete to perform at Amha's Blue Nile Restaurant on 16th Street in Washington, DC. (Amha's sentinel role will be detailed further in chapter 5.) When the Walias Band arrived and began a US tour in 1981, Amha opened Ibex Club on Georgia Avenue. In 1982 Moges and two other musicians left the band after the tour and received asylum in the United States. When Moges departed Ethiopia for the 1981 tour, he sent his wife and daughter to Djibouti so that they could later join him in the US (Moges H. interview). See also the discussion of the early tour in chapter 5.

73. Aklilu Zewdi, interview by author, June 16, 2006, Addis Ababa.

74. Beniam Bedru Hussein, interview by author, June 26, 2008, Washington, DC.

75. Moges H. interview.

76. Moges H. interview.

77. Simeneh, "*Azmari* Tradition," 50–51. Kane, *Dictionary*, 1673, defines zəgubəñ as "whorehouse."

78. Selam interview, September 5, 2007.

79. Kane, *Dictionary*, 766.

80. Harbeson, *Ethiopian Transformation*, 137.

81. By July 1977 the Derg began to reassert control of urban terror from the *kebele* (Jacob Wiebel, "'Let the Red Terror Intensify': Political Violence, Governance and Society in Urban Ethiopia, 1976–78," *International Journal of African Historical Studies* 48, no. 1 [2015]: 24, https://www.jstor.org/stable/44715382).

82. Solomon, *History of Ethiopian Immigrants*, 51–52.

83. H. Marcus, *History of Ethiopia*, 196. I was an eyewitness to the Red Terror while visiting Addis Ababa during December 1977 and January of 1978. Every morning one would see bodies in the street with signs identifying them as enemies of the state. Violence was so rampant that most residents planning to go anywhere in the city would telephone someone at the destination (and those even living along the way) to find out what route would be safest to take. The local *kebele* in the neighborhood in which we lived (Wäräda [District] 1; Kane, *Dictionary*, 1515) was armed and present around the clock on the ground floor of our apartment building, scrutinizing everyone who came and left.

84. Kane, *Dictionary*, 1440.

85. Solomon Addis Getahun, "The Transformation of the *Azmari, Liqa Maquwas*, from the Despicable to the Admirable and Sought after Profession" (paper presented at the *First International Conference on Azmari in Ethiopia*, Stiftung Universität, Hildesheim, Ger., January 6–8, 2012).

86. Harbeson, *Ethiopian Transformation*, 180; O. Nikolayeva, "Cultural Reforms in Ethiopia," in *Ten Years of the Ethiopian Revolution*, ed. Nikolai Ivanovich Gavrilov, trans. Nadezhda Burova (Moscow: Progress, 1986), 157.

87. Simeneh, "Music and Politics," 75.

88. Nikolayeva, "Cultural Reforms in Ethiopia," 158.

89. Simeneh, "Music and Politics," 76.

90. Simeneh, "Music and Politics," 76.

91. Simeneh, "Music and Politics," 76.

92. Solomon, "Transformation of the *Azmari*." I thank Solomon for sharing a draft of this paper and giving me permission to quote from it.

93. Abegasu Kibrework Shiota and Henock interviews by author, both March 7, 2003, Cambridge, MA.

94. Ashenafi interview.

95. Bezawork interview.

96. Minale interview, August 8, 2007.

97. Yehunie Belay, interview by author, July 22, 2007, Washington, DC.

98. Setegn interview.

99. Tsehay Amare, interview by author, August 9, 2007, Washington, DC.

100. Simeneh, "Music and Politics," 77.

101. Leslau, *Context Dictionary*, 1402; Kane, *Dictionary*, 976. Another performing arts group in which music was an important component was known as the circus. It emerged in Ethiopia in 1991, at the very end of the revolution, through the initiatives of an American and a French Canadian working with agencies to ensure migration of the Ethiopian Jews (Beta Israel community) from Ethiopia to Israel. One was a juggler, who taught the children to juggle and perform shows for their families while they were in temporary housing in Addis Ababa. After the Ethiopian Jewish community migrated to Israel in May 1991, the circus initiative caught on with other children in the Ethiopian capital. Supported by the expatriate community, and recognized in 1993 by the new postrevolutionary government, the circus initiative eventually spread throughout the country (Leah Niederstadt, "Fighting HIV with Juggling Clubs: An Introduction to Ethiopia's Circuses," *African Arts* 42, no. 1 [2009]: 76–87, https://doi .org/10.1162/afar.2009.42.1.76), for a nuanced history and case study of the circuses and their eventual role in HIV/AIDS education in Ethiopia.

102. Woretaw interview.

103. Selam interview, September 5, 2007. A higher-level administrative unit termed *kaffetenya* oversaw the local *kebele*.

104. Bezawork's Amhara family intermarried with Oromo, Tigray, and Harari families. As a result, she speaks Amharic and understands Oromo and Tigrinya.

105. Bezawork interview.

106. Bezawork interview.

107. Kane, *Dictionary*, 1025.

108. Bezawork interview.

109. Solomon, *History of Ethiopian Immigrants*, 52.

110. Bezawork interview.

111. Bezawork interview.

112. See discussion of the *People to People* initiative in chapter 5.

113. Bezawork interview. In diaspora, much of Bezawork's energy was devoted to bringing her two young sons to join her and to supporting her family remaining in Ethiopia, which experienced many tragedies. Her sister died of cancer and left four children; her brother-in-law was killed by the Derg. Her father, mother, and brother died within a period of several months in 2003.

114. Simeneh, "Music and Politics," 68–69.

115. Simeneh, himself descended from an *azmari* family from the north, argues that the first *azmari bet* were established in the northern provincial capital of Gondar about twenty years earlier than those in Addis Ababa. At their peak in the later 1990s and early 2000s, as many as thirty *azmari bet* may have been in Addis Ababa (Simeneh, "Music and Politics," 72–73). I thank Francis Falceto for confirming that he documented the first *azmari bet* in Addis Ababa only in March 1993 (personal communication, August 31, 2020).

Chapter Five

1. Abonesh Adinew, "Harar Dire Dawa," track 9 of *Balageru*, Boku Productions and Bete Arodyon BA0001, 2000, compact disc. "Harar Dire Dawa" has lyrics by Sisay Asefe and Abraham Wolde, with melody by Sisay Asefe. Harar is a historic eastern city in the Harari region; Dire Dawa, slightly north of Harar, is one of two Ethiopian chartered cities (the other is Addis Ababa); Jijiga is the capital of the Somali region; Moyale is a town on the Ethiopian border with Kenya in Oromia; Illubabor is a former province and today the southwestern zone of the Oromia region; Gondar is a northwestern city in the Amhara region and the former capital of Begemder province. The final word in each line is taken from the verb *dänäbbärä*, to bolt, flee in fright, or run away (Kane, *Dictionary*, 1798).

2. Abonesh "Abiti" Adinew, interview by author, August 14, 2007, Washington, DC.

3. Alessandro Triulzi, "Battling with the Past—New Frameworks for Ethiopian Historiography," in *Remapping Ethiopia: Socialism and After*, ed. Wendy James et al. (Oxford, UK: James Currey, 2002), 280.

4. Reyes, *Songs of the Caged*, xv.

5. The mass forced migrations from Vietnam and Ethiopia in fact coincide in their inception during the mid-1970s; these migrations also are parallel in their decades-long durations to follow and their establishment of major diasporas in the United States.

6. Koehn, *Refugees from Revolution*, 104.

7. Solomon, *History of Ethiopian Immigrants*, 76.

8. Amha Eshete, interview by author, June 19, 2006, Addis Ababa.

9. There were three other music shops, owned by Armenians and Greeks (Arefaynie Fantahun, "Amha Eshete: Pioneer of Ethiopia's Music Industry," *Music in Africa*, June 20, 2016, https://www.musicinafrica.net/magazine/amha-eshete-pioneer-ethiopias -music-industry).

10. Arefaynie, "Amha Eshete."

11. In 1908, as described in chapter 3, *Azmari Tessema Eshete* was recorded in Germany; the surviving recordings have been edited and were reissued by Francis Falceto in collaboration with Wolfgang Bender in 2011 on *éthiopiques 27*.

12. *Tadias* staff, "Amha Eshete and Contribution of Amha Records to Modern Ethiopian Music," *Tadias*, May 25, 2012, http://www.tadias.com/05/25/2012/the -legacy-of-amha-eshete-amha-records-contribution-to-modern-ethiopian-music/.

13. Falceto, liner notes to *éthiopiques 10: Tezeta, Ethiopian Blues and Ballads*, Buda Musique 822222, 2002, compact disc, 20.

14. I thank Francis Falceto for clarifying these numbers (Falceto, personal communication, August 31, 2020).

15. Amha interview, June 19, 2006.

16. *Tadias* staff, "Amha Eshete."

17. *Tadias* staff, "Amha Eshete."

18. *Tadias* staff, "Amha Eshete."

19. In November 1986 French record producer Francis Falceto met Amha in Washington, DC, eventually licensed distribution rights to Amha's originals, and in 1997 launched publication of the now internationally circulated series *éthiopiques* through Buda Musique in Paris. Amha notes that without Francis Falceto, "this music would have been buried and stayed buried somewhere in the suburbs of Athens, Greece where all the [EMI] masters were stored until then" (*Tadias* staff, "Amha Eshete").

20. The situation of Somali Ethiopians became even more complex after the revolution ended in 1991 with the partition of Somalia. The fall of longtime Somali dictator Siad Barre in 1991 contributed to the state of chaos that forced a mass exodus from Somalia and adjacent regions of the Ethiopian Ogaden (Yusuf, *Somalis in Minnesota*, 12–14).

21. Many Ethiopians made their way south and settled for long periods in various regions of Africa, such as Uganda and South Africa. Ironically, postrevolutionary Ethiopia has also hosted hundreds of thousands of refugees from other regions of Africa in displaced-person camps and other sites across the country, such as outlying neighborhoods of Addis Ababa and other cities. Ethiopia is said to have hosted the largest number of refugees in Africa, more than seven hundred thousand, of whom more than one hundred thousand are Eritreans. Conflicts in Somalia, Eritrea, and South Sudan have driven many refugees from these regions across the borders into Ethiopia. Many other African refugees from across the continent stopped in Ethiopia on their way north through the Sudan and Libya in an effort to cross the Mediterranean to seek asylum in Europe (Mark Anderson, "Ethiopia Hosts Largest Number of Refugees in Africa," *Guardian*, August 20, 2014, https://www.theguardian.com/global -development/2014/aug/20/ethiopia-largest-number-refugees-africa; James Jeffrey, "Stuck in Limbo in Ethiopia, Africa's Biggest Refugee Camp," *Deutsche Welle*, November 13, 2015, https://www.dw.com/en/stuck-in-limbo-in-ethiopia-africas-biggest -refugee-camp/a-18848086; Stefania Prandi, "Eritrean Refugees in Ethiopia," *Al-*

Jazeera, March 10, 2016, https://www.aljazeera.com/indepth/inpictures/2016/03
/eritrean-refugees-ethiopia-160306065928790.html).

22. Steven Kaplan and Chaim Rosen, "Ethiopian Jews in Israel," *American Jewish
Year Book* 94 (1994): 100, https://www.jstor.org/stable/23605644. By mid-1984,
ten thousand Ethiopian Jews had crossed into the Sudan, and many were airlifted
to Israel in a secret initiative known as "Operation Moses" (Ahmed Karadawi, "The
Smuggling of the Ethiopian Falasha to Israel through Sudan," *African Affairs* 90, no.
358 [1991]: 23–49; Ruth K. Westheimer and Steven Kaplan, *Surviving Salvation: The
Ethiopian Jewish Family in Transition* [New York: New York University Press, 1992],
24–29). A subsequent airlift of more than fourteen thousand Ethiopian Jews from
Addis Ababa to Israel during the closing months of the Ethiopian revolution, known
as "Operation Solomon," brought to Israel almost all of the Beta Israel community
known to remain in Ethiopia at that time (Westheimer and Kaplan, *Surviving Salvation*, 32). Nearly forty-five thousand Beta Israel came to Israel between 1972 and 1993
(Kaplan and Rosen, "Ethiopian Jews in Israel," 69). At several points after Operation
Solomon, groups of Ethiopians known as Falas Mura, converts to Christianity of Beta
Israel descent, were brought to Israel (Gadi BenEzer, *The Ethiopian Jewish Exodus:
Narratives of the Migration Journey to Israel, 1977–1985*, Routledge Studies in Mem-
ory and Narrative 9 [London: Routledge, 2002]; and Kaplan and Rosen, "Ethiopian
Jews in Israel"). For a discussion of reasons that the Sudanese government opened its
borders to Ethiopian refugees, see Teshome G. Wagaw, "Caught the Web: The Horn
of Africa and the Migration of Ethiopian Jews," *Northeast African Studies* 13, nos. 2–3
(1991): 115–16, https://www.jstor.org/stable/43660093. At the end of 2013, Israel's
Central Bureau of Statistics estimated that 135,000 Ethiopian Jews lived in Israel, of
whom 85,900 were born in Ethiopia (Lidar Gravé-Lazi, "CBS Report: 135,000 Ethiopians Living in Israel at End of 2013," *Jerusalem Post*, November 19, 2014, https://
www.jpost.com/israel-news/cbs-report-135000-ethiopians-living-in-israel-at-end
-of-2013-382266).

23. Canada was also a popular choice and was frequently used as a way station for
those seeking asylum in the United States. A large Ethiopian and Eritrean community
was established in Toronto by the 1980s; an increasing number in the 2000s moved
west to Edmonton and Calgary, Alberta.

24. Solomon, *History of Ethiopian Immigrants*, 86–96.

25. Solomon, *History of Ethiopian Immigrants*, 96–97.

26. Solomon, *History of Ethiopian Immigrants*, 98.

27. Solomon, *History of Ethiopian Immigrants*, 64.

28. Koehn, *Refugees from Revolution*, 165.

29. I first learned of Elizabeth Namarra's musical career through a University of
Minnesota project initiated by ethnomusicologist Mirjana (Minja) Laušević, who died
in 2007. During her brief tenure at the University of Minnesota, Minja carried out a
team research project with her students on musical traditions of communities living in
the Twin Cities. She documented music of local Oromo musicians as part of this effort,
and I am grateful for having had access to this work. I thank Anna Schultz for direct-
ing me to the website (personal communication, January 18, 2013). Formerly housed
in http://www.cla.umn.edu/twocities/rprojs/eastafrica/ea-index.asp and https://
wiki.umn.edu/WorldInTwoCities/WebHome, these sites have been taken down.

30. Tormod Engelsviken, "Mission, Pentecostalism, and Ethiopian Identity: The

Beginnings of the Mulu Wongel Believers' Church," *Norsk Tidsskrift for Misjons-vitenskap* 68, no. 4 (2014): 208–9, https://mfopen.mf.no/mf-xmlui/handle/11250/2470839. The Full Gospel Believers' Church (FGBC) remained underground during the last two years of the Emperor Haile Selassie I's rule. After a brief period of recognition by the military government beginning in early 1975, the FGBC was again harassed and forced underground. A well-known FGBC singer, Tesfaye Gabbiso, was held in prison for seven years without trial and subjected to torture, a case that was widely reported by human-rights organizations (Jörg Haustein, *Writing Religious History: The Historiography of Ethiopian Pentecostalism* [Wiesbaden, Ger.: Harrassowitz, 2011], 198–99). See also Lila W. Balisky, *Songs of Ethiopia's Tesfaye Gabbiso: Singing with Understanding in Babylon, the Meantime, and Zion* (Eugene, OR: Pickwick, 2018), which documents Tesfaye Gabbiso's life and repertory in detail.

31. Elizabeth interview.

32. See Gow, *Oromo in Exile*, 9–10, for details about the history of the Oromo community in Australia.

33. Gow, *Oromo in Exile*, 126.

34. Teha Shabo, quoted in Gow, *Oromo in Exile*, 17.

35. Asfa-Wossen, *King of Kings*, 137–57, and Kirsten Stoffregen-Pedersen, *The History of the Ethiopian Community in the Holy Land from the Time of Emperor Tewodros II till 1974*, Studia Oecumenica Hierosolymitana, vol. 2, ed. Geries Sa'ed Khoury (Jerusalem: Ecumenical Institute for Theological Research, 1983).

36. Abbink, "Slow Awakening," 172.

37. Abbink, "Slow Awakening," 176.

38. The presence of Eritreans is particularly visible in Milan, where there is a sizable Eritrean commercial neighborhood. The community holds major events, such as a celebration of the Festival of the True Cross (*Masqal*) each September. Other locales in Italy have Eritrean and Ethiopian populations and, since the 1990s, have witnessed interest in activities such as bringing *azmari* from Ethiopia to perform (Shelemay, field notes, Milan, Italy, April 18, 2012). I thank Nicola Scaldaferri for facilitating my contact with the Eritrean community in Milan. For a portrait of the Eritrean diaspora in Italy, see the documentary film, *Asmarina: Voices and Images of a Postcolonial Heritage*, dir. Alan Maglio and Medhin Paulos (Milan, Italy, 2015), https://asmarinaproject.com/.

39. Tesfaye Lemma, who directed the traditional ensemble on that tour, recalls that Derg chairman Mengistu Haile Mariam came to three days of rehearsals before their departure for the tour and offered "corrections": "He used to think that all Americans would come to see the show, but I told him maybe some Peace Corps volunteers, maybe some teachers who have experience with Ethiopia might come, but it is very hard to get an audience. But they didn't believe me. They were very ignorant about America" (Tesfaye interview, August 15, 2007). Tesfaye's knowledge came from having spent two years in the United States between 1971 and 1973, studying at Indiana University and having a residency with the Alvin Ailey Dance Troupe in New York City. See chapter 8 for further discussion of Tesfaye's career and contribution.

40. The *Live Aid* concert was linked by satellite to one hundred ten nations and raised more than $125 million for famine relief. The event featured some seventy-five acts such as Elton John, Madonna, Sting, and Eric Clapton, along with a simultaneous concert at Philadelphia's John F. Kennedy Stadium. Controversy surrounded the mounting of *Live Aid*, in part because the money raised for the famine was paid to the brutal regime of Mengistu Haile Mariam and did not go to famine victims directly; in

addition, many were concerned about the Ethiopian government's brutality in conducting the war with Eritrea and the government's forced resettlement of Ethiopians in regions distant from their natal villages (*Spin* staff, "Live Aid: The Terrible Truth," *Spin*, July 13, 2015, https://www.spin.com/featured/live-aid-the-terrible-truth-ethiopia-bob-geldof-feature/, which republishes a *Spin* article by Robert Keating originally published in July 1986).

Ethiopian musicians resented their exclusion from the concert: "I really respect their trying to help Ethiopia. They came over, they gave money, and they did quite a lot. But they should also have had Ethiopian artists and musicians to be involved on this project, but they never did that. I had a BBC interview about this and I said, 'it's great. But it only promotes themselves.' And, you know, also, Ethiopia. But since they are doing musical promotion, we have beautiful culture and art. Why don't they help one guy out as an artist and add an Ethiopian musician to that concert? Or put one Ethiopian popular singer in the show?" (Mulatu Astatke, interview by author and Steven Kaplan, December 4, 2007, Cambridge, MA).

41. Tesfaye interview, August 15, 2007.

42. Mulatu arranged the show, its set, and costumes and had an agreement that the performance "would be based on Ethiopian music and nothing else" (Mulatu Astatke, interview by author and Steven Kaplan, October 30, 2007, Cambridge, MA). He selected the musicians in collaboration with a committee and also played conga drums with dance numbers. Tesfaye, an expert in traditional instruments and music, played a role in selecting the traditional musicians and composed some music for the show as well.

43. The complete show was filmed in Germany during the 1987–88 tour and can be viewed on YouTube in nine parts as the "*People to People* Tour." See discography.

44. Mulatu Astatke, interviews by author and Steven Kaplan, October 17 and 30, 2007.

45. Bezawork interview.

46. Mulatu interview, October 30, 2007.

47. Mulatu interview, October 30, 2007.

48. Mulatu interview, October 30, 2007.

49. Tesfaye interview, August 15, 2007.

50. Mulatu Astatke, interview by author and Steven Kaplan, September 9, 2007, Cambridge, MA.

51. Getatchew interview.

52. Getatchew interview.

53. Getatchew did not perform with a *kebele kinet* because he was in the jail of Kebele 27, in the Mercato (market) area.

54. Getatchew interview.

55. Badme is a town on the Eritrean-Ethiopian border that was the focal point of an armed territorial dispute that began in May 1998 and was not formally resolved until 2018. See further discussion later in this chapter.

56. Getatchew interview.

57. See Baxter, "Ethiopia's Unacknowledged Problem," 283–96, for an early scholarly analysis of the longtime divide; there is a copious literature on many incidents that have exacerbated Ethiopian government–Oromo relations over the years and related human-rights issues (Firew Kebede Tiba, "Oromo Struggle: Causes of the Conundrum and towards a Covenant," *O Pride*, July 30, 2012, https://www.opride

.com/2012/07/30/the-oromo-struggle-in-ethiopia-causes-of-the-conundrum-and -towards-a-covenant/).

58. Trevor Trueman, "Persecuted in Ethiopia: Hunted in Hargeisa," Oromia Support Group Report 47, Oromo Relief Association UK, February 2012, https://www .oromoreliefassociationuk.com/?p=128.

59. *Human Rights in Ethiopia: Through the Eyes of the Oromo Diaspora* (Minneapolis, MN: Advocates for Human Rights, 2009), 1.

60. Human Rights Watch, *World Report 2017* (New York: Human Rights Watch, 2017), 251–56, https://www.hrw.org/sites/default/files/world_report_download /wr2017-web.pdf.

61. Jeffrey Gettleman, "Meles Zenawi, Prime Minister of Ethiopia, Dies at 57," *New York Times*, August 21, 2012, https://www.nytimes.com/2012/08/22/world/africa /meles-zenawi-ethiopian-leader-dies-at-57.html.

62. Jason Burke, "'These Changes Are Unprecedented': How Abiy Is Upending Ethiopian Politics," *Guardian*, July 8, 2018, https://www.theguardian.com/world /2018/jul/08/abiy-ahmed-upending-ethiopian-politics. In 2019 Abiy Ahmed won the Nobel Peace Prize for his dramatic initiatives in the Horn of Africa, including making peace with Eritrea. But as this book goes to press in 2021, armed conflict between government forces and those of the Tigray region have led to protests against Abiy Ahmed's government at home and abroad.

63. Selam interview, September 5, 2007.

64. Selam founded the Selamino Music Centers at two locations in downtown Addis Ababa and was very successful in the music business.

65. Selam interview, September 5, 2007.

66. According to Amnesty International, by early 1999, the situation had "developed into a systematic, country-wide operation to arrest and deport anyone of full or part Eritrean descent" ("Ethiopia/Eritrea: Amnesty International Witnesses Cruelty of Mass Deportations," news release no. AFR 25/02/99, *Amnesty International*, January 29, 1999, https://www.amnesty.org/download/Documents/140000/afr 250021999en.pdf).

67. Selam interview, September 5, 2007.

68. Wayna Wondwossen, interview by author, May 30, 2008, Washington, DC; Meklit Hadero, interview by author, December 11, 2015, Stanford, CA; Danny Mekonnen, personal communication with author, spring 2006, Cambridge, MA; Tekle interview.

69. Abdi (Tesfaye) Nuressa, interview by author, June 18, 2008, Washington, DC; Melaku Gelaw, interview by author and Charles Sutton, August 14, 2007, Washington, DC; Betelehem "Betty" Melaku, interview by author, August 18, 2007, Washington, DC.

70. Teshome Mitiku, interview by author, August 22, 2007, Washington, DC.

71. Moges H. interview, August 27, 2007; Abegasu interview, March 7, 2003; Minale interview, August 8, 2007; Yehunie interview, July 22, 2007; Abonesh interview.

72. Seleshe Damessae, interview by author, 1978, New York, NY.

73. Henock interview, March 7, 2003; Tsehai Birhanu, interview by author, March 20, 2007, Cambridge, MA.

74. Tsegaye B. Selassie, interview by author, July 1, 2008, Washington, DC; Thomas "Tommy T" Gobena, interview by author, March 7, 2003, Cambridge, MA; Sayem Osman, interview by author, June 12, 2008, Washington, DC.

75. Beniam interview; Munit Mesfin, interview by author, May 21, 2014, Addis Ababa; Hermela Mulatu, interview by author, June 14, 2008, Washington, DC.

76. Abraham Habte Selassie, interview by author, June 12, 2008, Washington, DC; Getahun interview.

77. Ashenafi interview. See also LaDena Schnapper, ed., *Teenage Refugees from Ethiopia Speak Out (in Their Own Voices)* (New York: Rosen, 1997).

78. Mohaammad Ibraahim Xawil, interview by author, June 17, 2008, Washington, DC.

79. Zakki interview.

80. Abebaye Lema, interview by author, April 21, 2008, Cambridge, MA; Mesfin Zeberga Tereda, interview by author, August 18, 2007, Washington, DC. The diversity immigrant visa lottery mandated by the Immigration Act of 1990 (Pub. L. 101–649), which provided for fifty-five thousand "diversity immigrants" annually, was instituted in 1995.

81. Koehn, *Refugees from Revolution*, 150–51. Koehn compares the processes of migration during the Ethiopian and Iranian revolutions, the latter of which began in 1978, resulting in the overthrow of longtime Iranian ruler Mohammad Reza Shah Pahlavi, in early 1979.

82. Koehn, *Refugees from Revolution*, 162.

83. Koehn, *Refugees from Revolution*, 203n147.

84. Koehn, *Refugees from Revolution*, 183.

Chapter Six

1. The US Refugee Act established an Office of Refugee Resettlement in the Department of Health and Human Services and raised the number of refugees admitted from 17,400 to 50,000 annually. Official Ethiopian resettlement numbers, no doubt quite low, totaled 31,182 between 1980 and 1999; the two years with the highest numbers were in 1980–81 at 3,500 and 1991 at 4,085. Migration continued at a high level through 1993, after which it diminished slightly but continued until the present (Solomon, *History of Ethiopian Immigrants*, 103).

2. See William Safran, "Diasporas in Modern Societies: Myths of Homeland and Return," *Diaspora* 1, no. 1 (1991): 83–99, for a fundamental discussion of diaspora. My approach here draws in a general way on the five variables that Kim D. Butler ("Defining Diaspora, Refining a Discourse," *Diaspora* 10, no. 2 [2001]: 195) proposed for the purposes of diaspora analysis:

1. Reasons for, and conditions of, the dispersal
2. Relationship with the homeland
3. Relationship with host lands
4. Interrelationships within communities of the diaspora
5. Comparative studies of diasporas

3. For an overview of the Ethiopian diaspora and its study, see Kay Kaufman Shelemay and Steven Kaplan, "Introduction," *Diaspora* 15, nos. 2–3 (2006 [pub. 2011]): 191–213.

4. Mark Slobin, "Music in Diaspora: The View from Euro-America," *Diaspora* 3, no. 3 (1994): 243. See also Mette Louise Berg and Susan Eckstein, special issue, "Re-

imagining Diasporas and Generations," *Diaspora* 18, nos. 1–2 (2009, pub. 2015), and Daniel Fittante, "Connection without Engagement: Paradoxes of North American Armenian Return Migration," *Diaspora* 19, nos. 2–3 (2010, pub. 2017): 147–60.

5. Ethiopian lives both at home and abroad were dramatically affected by the Derg's actions, including the adoption of a Marxist-Leninist ideology; a move away from the West toward an alliance with the Soviet Union; and nationalizations of businesses and private enterprise in February 1975, of all rural land in March, and of urban property in July of that same year (H. Marcus, *History of Ethiopia*, 192–96).

6. Elias Negash, interview by author, January 30, 2016, Los Altos, CA. See also Ryan Phillips, "East Africans in Oakland: Sharing Ethiopian Music with the World," *Oakland North*, April 10, 2012, https://oaklandnorth.net/2012/04/10/east-africans -in-oakland-sharing-ethiopian-music-with-the-world/.

7. See Elias's website, https://www.eliasnegash.com/. Another Ethiopian musician who immigrated to Berkeley, California, as a teenager in the late 1980s recalls taking music classes with Elias Negash: "When I came to the States, he was the only one who played jazz" (Kirubel Assefa, personal communication with author, May 14, 2020).

8. Danny, personal communication with author.

9. Solomon, *History of Ethiopian Immigrants*, 114–15.

10. Solomon, *History of Ethiopian Immigrants*, 115.

11. Before that time, only Mama Desta had opened a venue in Washington, DC, that served Ethiopian bread, *injera*, and tea. The efforts by Mama Desta and Amha Eshete were surely among the very first Ethiopian restaurants established outside Ethiopia, presaging what was to become a very successful culinary trend. For a longer discussion of the Ethiopian art of cooking and cuisine, characterized as "the most visible projection of Ethiopia's diasporic community," see James McCann, "A Response: *Doro Fänta*: Creativity vs. Adaptation in the Ethiopian Diaspora," *Diaspora* 15, nos. 2–3 (2006 [pub. 2011]): 385, https://doi.org/10.1353/dsp.2011.0075. The first Ethiopian restaurant in the United States, and evidently the first outside Ethiopia worldwide, was opened in Long Beach, California, in 1966 by Beyene Guililat; it operated only for six months before it closed (Harry Kloman, *Mesob across America: Ethiopian Food in the U.S.A.* [New York: iUniverse, 2010], 147 and 150).

12. Tesfaye Lemma, interview by author, August 20, 2007, Washington, DC.

13. Amha Eshete, personal communication with author, June 1, 2015. In my earlier article, "Music in the Ethiopian American Diaspora: A Preliminary Overview," in *Proceedings of the 16th International Conference of Ethiopian Studies: July 2–6, 2007, Trondheim, Norway*, ed. Svein Ege et al. (Wiesbaden, Ger.: Harrassowitz, 2009), 1153–64, https://dash.harvard.edu/handle/1/4269154, I mistakenly gave the name of Amha's Ibex Club as Kilimanjaro. Kilimanjaro was another Washington, DC, club, founded by Victor and Shirley Kibunja in 1987, who thereafter established Kilimanjaro clubs in New York City and Nairobi, Kenya. I thank Alecia Kibunja of Washington, DC, for contacting me and for sending me the correct information about her parents' club, which offered music and a variety of African cuisines. I regret my earlier error.

14. When Amha left the United States to return to Ethiopia in 1993 (Falceto, personal communication, August 31, 2020), he sold the first floor of his club to saxophonist Moges Habte, who had long played at the club and who reopened it as the Adey Ethiopian Club and Restaurant. The club had a difficult financial time, and the new owners changed the name to Soukous African Club to attract other Africans. The club

was shut down by police and its liquor license revoked after the fatal shooting of a DC policeman on its doorstep in 1997 (Moges H. interview; Vincent Morriss, "City Moves to Shut Down Go-Go Club," *Washington Times*, February 7, 1997). Moges remembers gratefully the kindness of the building's owner, who did not hold him to the fourteen years remaining on his lease.

15. Amha's former wife remained in Washington, DC; his children live in New York City and Los Angeles (Amha interview, June 19, 2006).

16. Amha interview, June 19, 2006.

17. There was an earlier, brief American tour arranged for the Nile Ethiopian Ensemble, which performed on the Ed Sullivan Show in 1969. This subject will be discussed in chapter 8.

18. Wilbur Zelinsky and Barrett A. Lee, "Heterolocalism: An Alternative Model of the Sociospatial Behaviour of Immigrant Ethnic Communities," *International Journal of Population Geography* 4, no. 4 (1998): 281–98, https://doi.org/10.1002/(SICI) 1099-1220(199812)4:4<281::AID-IJPG108>3.0.CO;2-O. However, in some of the cities, apartment complexes attracted a significant number of Ethiopian immigrants, such as the Telegraph Avenue housing division known as Keller Plaza largely occupied by Ethiopians in Oakland, California, and the large concentration of Somalis living in a group of high-rises known as the Cedars, which stand along Cedar Avenue in Minneapolis, Minnesota (Shelemay, field notes, October 31, 2015, Oakland, CA; and March 12, 2011, Minneapolis, MN).

19. Associated Press, "Little Ethiopia Taking Root in D.C. Area," *Deseret News*, November 6, 2005, https://www.deseret.com/2005/11/6/19920410/little-ethiopia -taking-root-in-d-c-area.

20. Estimates for the Ethiopian population in the DC metropolitan area vary widely and depend on their dates, the separate records kept for Eritrean immigrants after the country's 1993 independence, and the difficulty of counting the many Ethiopians who moved to the city from their documented arrival elsewhere in the United States. In "Ethiopian Ethos and the Making of Ethnic Places in the Washington Metropolitan Area," *Journal of Cultural Geography* 20, no. 2 (2003): 21–42, https://doi.org/10.1080 /08873630309478274, Elizabeth Chacko provides figures gathered in 2001 that estimate forty-five to fifty thousand Ethiopians in Washington, DC. However, by the turn of the Ethiopian millennium in September 2007, most in the community offered informal estimates as high as two hundred fifty thousand, a figure also cited by the press in 2010 (Misty Showalter, "Inside Washington D.C.'s 'Little Ethiopia,'" *CNN World: Marketplace Africa*, October 22, 2010, http://edition.cnn.com/2010/WORLD/africa /10/22/little.ethiopia.washington/).

21. Associated Press, "Little Ethiopia Taking Root in D.C. Area." See also http:// www.ethiopiancommunitydc.org and https://www.ecdcus.org/. One can track the organization of the various diaspora communities from the founding dates of community organizations. For instance, see the Ethiopian Community in Seattle agency, incorporated in 1987 by immigrants who sought to help others, http://ecseattle.org.

22. Moges H. interview.

23. Associated Press, "Little Ethiopia Taking Root in D.C. Area."

24. Dan Reed, "DC's 'Little Ethiopia' Has Moved to Silver Spring and Alexandria," *Greater Greater Washington*, September 14, 2015, https://ggwash.org/view/39188/dcs -little-ethiopia-has-moved-to-silver-spring-and-alexandria.

25. In Ge'ez the word *Täwahǝdo*, popularly spelled *Tewahedo* (Kane, *Dictionary*,

994), means unified and is included in the formal title of the Ethiopian Orthodox Church. Some large diaspora churches today take the title *däbr* (*debre*), literally mount or mountain, a traditional designation in Ethiopia for a large monastic church built on land given by the emperor (Kaplan, "Däbr," *EAe*, 2:6–7). Ethiopian churches tend to be named after saints or the Virgin Mary.

26. Chacko, "Ethiopian Ethos," 29.

27. Chacko, "Ethiopian Ethos," 25.

28. Ray Oldenburg, *The Great Good Place: Cafés, Coffee Shops, Community Centers, Beauty Parlors, General Stores, Bars, Hangouts, and How They Get You through the Day* (New York: Paragon House, 1989), xvii; and Ray Oldenburg, *Celebrating the Third Place: Inspiring Stories about the "Great Good Places" at the Heart of Our Communities* (New York: Marlowe, 2001).

29. Chacko, "Ethiopian Ethos," 25.

30. Chacko, "Ethiopian Ethos," 28. Chacko builds on the notion of heterolocalism in Zelinsky and Lee, "Heterolocalism," and Joseph Wood's concept of place making in "Vietnamese American Place Making in Northern Virginia," *Geographical Review* 87, no. 1 (1997): 58–72, https://doi.org/10.1111/j.1931-0846.1997.tb00060.x. In "Ethiopian Ethos," 24, Chacko suggests that "ethnic place-making in metropolitan areas has been loosened from its traditional central city moorings," and it differs from one immigrant community to another.

31. While still living in Dallas, in 1987 Moges Seyoum made trips to officiate at DSK Mariam EOT Church in Washington, DC, at the time of its founding, finally relocating from Dallas to Washington, DC, in 1989 (Moges Seyoum, personal communication with author, August 8, 2020).

32. See Walle Engedayehu, "The Ethiopian Orthodox Tewahedo Church in the Diaspora: Expansion in the Midst of Division," *African Social Science Review* 6, no. 1 (2014): 115–33.

33. Shelemay, field notes, March 12, 2011, Minneapolis, MN.

34. The internet has in part, but not completely, replaced the longtime mode of advertising through posters and flyers displayed and distributed by local shops.

35. Chris Roberts, "Somali Music Is Here, but Hard to Find," *MPR News*, August 30, 2006, https://www.mprnews.org/story/2006/08/21/ethnicmusicsomalian.

36. McCann, "Response: *Doro Fänta*," 385. The expression of personhood through taste-based metaphors characterizes other traditions such as the Anatolian Greek diaspora in the United States as explicated in Panayotis League, "Grooving Heavy, Dancing Drunk: Gustemic Metaphor and Mimetic Polytemporality in Anatolian Greek Music," *Ethnomusicology* 63, no. 3 (2019): 393–417.

37. Sarah Reiss, "How Dallas Got So Many Ethiopian Restaurants," *D Magazine*, June 2011, https://www.dmagazine.com/publications/d-magazine/2011/june/how-dallas-got-so-many-ethiopian-restaurants/.

38. The concert featured Yehunie Belay and Mohaammad Xawil (Shelemay, field notes, July 3, 2008, Arlington, VA).

39. Shelemay, field notes, September 26, 2009, Cambridge, MA.

40. Elias interview.

41. Phillips, "East Africans in Oakland."

42. "ESFNA 2015 in the DC-Maryland-Virginia Area," *Ethiopian Sports Federation in North America*, February 3, 2015, https://www.esfna.net/news_article/show/474279-esfna-2015-in-the-dc-maryland-virginia-area.

43. Shelemay, field notes, June 29–July 5, 2008, Washington, DC.

44. Kirubel Assefa, personal communication with author. Kirubel, a well-known jazz musician who lives in southern California, oversaw planning of musical events for ESFNA between 2008 and 2015.

45. Eritrean Sports Federation in North America (ERSFNA), https://www.eritreansports.com/.

46. Oromo games in late July and early August 2009 in Atlanta were quite parallel to the ESFNA events (Shelemay, field notes, July 30–August 3, 2009, Atlanta, GA). The 2009 soccer tournament was held at James R. Hallford Stadium in Clarkston, Georgia, a football stadium often used for soccer that holds fifteen thousand. Many Oromo musicians arrived to perform during the week, including Abdi Nuressa, Ali Birra, Kemer Yusuf, Mohammed Sheba, Muktar Usman, Habtamu Lamu, Elemo Ali, and the Oz. Concerts were held at various sites in the adjacent area, including the Lions of Judah Event Center and the Atrium Nightclub (both on Memorial Drive in Stone Mountain, Georgia) and Studio 72 (Tucker, Georgia). Concerts began at midnight or later after the end of evening competitions and dinner.

47. Indeed, the OSFNA website http://www.osfna.org/news/ has a note on its home page that anyone trying to host concerts during OSFNA week should contact OSFNA to partner with them. For a payment of 10% percent of the profits, OFSNA will advertise the concert in the field, on their website, and on their Facebook page.

48. https://esfna.org/about/.

49. AESAONE, All Ethiopian Sports Association One, June 9, 2017, www.aesaone.org. This website is no longer available.

50. Hafkin, "'Whatsupoch' on the Net," 222.

51. Hafkin, "'Whatsupoch' on the Net," 223–24. In 1987 Hafkin facilitated the Economic Commission for Africa's African Information Society Initiative that established the first email connectivity in more than ten African countries (Internet Hall of Fame, "Timeline," http://www.internethalloffame.org/internet-history/timeline).

52. Hafkin, "'Whatsupoch' on the Net," 232–33.

53. *Afaan Oromo* does not use the Ethiopic syllabary but is written in the Latin alphabet.

54. I thank Samantha Heinle, who researched Ethiopian musicians online as my research assistant during summer 2014, for compiling this information under the auspices of the Harvard SHARP Program.

55. Yehunie Belay and Yeshimebet "Tutu" Belay, interviews by author, August 30, 2007, Washington, DC; Steven Kaplan, "Vital Information at Your Fingertips: The *Ethiopian Yellow Pages* as a Cultural Document," *Diaspora* 15, nos. 2–3 (2006 [pub. 2011]): 247–63, https://doi.org/10.1353/dsp.2011.0074. The book includes sections on accountants, advertising, airlines, bank, beauty, chiropractors, computer and communication technology, construction, education, groceries, health and doctors, lawyers, money transfer, music and entertainment, printing and publishing, real estate, restaurants and hotels, shops, and travel, shipping, and moving (https://ethiopianyellowpages.com/).

56. Hafkin, "'Whatsupoch' on the Net," 221–45. See also Victoria Bernal, "Eritrea On-Line: Diaspora, Cyberspace, and the Public Sphere," *American Ethnologist* 32, no. 4 (2005): 660–75, https://doi.org/10.1525/ae.2005.32.4.660; Bernal, "Eritrea Goes Global: Reflections on Nationalism in a Transnational Era," *Cultural Anthropology* 19, no. 1 (2004): 3–25, https://doi.org/10.1525/can.2004.19.1.3.

57. Bernal, "Eritrea On-Line," 660. Bernal notes that conflict is a central dynamic of discussions in Eritrean cyberspace, likely because the diaspora and Eritrea itself "were formed through violence" (662). The site www.dehai.org discussed by Bernal thus served as "an arena of nonviolent conflict in a violent world but also as a multiplier of outrage and as a vehicle for mobilizing action in situations of conflict" (662). Dehai was created and maintained by Eritreans in Washington, DC, who jokingly referred to the city as "the capital of Eritrea" (664). There were yearly Dehai retreats in the United States that brought users face to face, although there was no access to the internet within Eritrea until the year 2000. After the Eritrean-Ethiopian 1998–2000 border war, Dehai fragmented into multiple other sites. Dehai is a transliteration of the Tigrinya word that literally means "voice" but that is also used to mean "news." The site, officially in English, aimed to provide an independent public forum for discussion and debate about Eritrea separate from Ethiopians and not under an official organization such as the Eritrean People's Liberation Front (663–65).

58. *Tadias* staff, "Spotlight: Trace Muzika, a New Channel from Ethiopia and Diaspora," *Tadias*, July 31, 2020, http://www.tadias.com/07/31/2020/spotlight -trace-muzika-a-channel-dedicated-to-music-from-ethiopia-diaspora/. See also Habeshaview, https://www.habeshaview.com/hv/about/.

59. Protests after contested Ethiopian elections in 2005 led the government to crack down on print media and gave rise to blogging efforts online. The government next blocked many blogs and arrested bloggers, action that gained international attention and criticism (Hafkin, "'Whatsupoch' on the Net," 240–41). The appointment of new prime minister Abiy Ahmed in April 2018 resulted in a relaxation of government policy restricting journalists and bloggers, after the resolution of several notorious cases of governmental action in February 2018. Most prominent was the pardoning of a group of journalists known as Zone 9 bloggers, who spent one and a half years in prison accused of campaigns against the government. See "The Zone 9 Bloggers, Update," *Electronic Frontier Foundation*, September 20, 2015, https://www.eff.org/offline/zone-9 -bloggers. However, after the murder of Oromo musician Hachalu Hundessa at the end of June 2020, violent protests ensued and internet service across the country was shut down for weeks (Abdi Latif Dahir, "Hachalu Hundessa, Ethiopian Singer and Activist, Is Shot Dead," *New York Times*, June 30, 2020, https://www.nytimes.com /2020/06/30/world/africa/ethiopia-hachalu-hundessa-dead.html).

60. Endale Getahun, telephone interview by author, December 10, 2019. Endale broadcasts in Amharic and presents twelve shows in different languages by immigrant producers who speak their own languages ranging from Somali to Spanish. Previously he produced an Ethiopian television show and Ethiopian music program in Washington, DC.

61. Endale telephone interview. Endale also reports drawing on recordings from YouTube, characterizing himself as an "end user." "I tend to play what they like—the old, traditional musicians such as Aster [Aweke] and Tilahun [Gessesse]. . . . They request songs and even the younger ones like the old songs. The old music is most enjoyed by my audience."

62. Hafkin, "'Whatsupoch' on the Net," 224–25.

63. Selam Gebrekidan, "Ethiopia and Eritrea Declare an End to Their War," *New York Times*, July 9, 2018, https://www.nytimes.com/2018/07/09/world/africa /ethiopia-eritrea-war.html; Elias Meseret, "Ethiopia and Eritrea Restore Relations after Ending 20-Year Border War," *Christian Science Monitor*, July 9, 2018, https://www

.csmonitor.com/World/Africa/2018/0709/Ethiopia-and-Eritrea-restore-relations
-after-ending-20-year-border-war.

64. Aaron Maasho, "At Concert, Ethiopia, Eritrea Leaders Preach Peace, Love, Unity," *Reuters*, July 15, 2018, https://www.reuters.com/article/us-ethiopia-eritrea -idUSKBN1K50ZB. In addition to Ali Birra, musicians performing were Hachalu Hundessa, Ittiqaa Tafarii, Galaanaa Gaaromsaa, Kemer Yusuf, Tadele Gemechu, Getachew H. Mariam, and Tadele Roba.

65. Asafa, *Oromia and Ethiopia*, 210–17. The relationship between the Oromo, who are the largest ethnic group in Ethiopia but were long on the margins of power, and the Amhara, who long controlled the monarchy, had also been quite strained for decades. But during late spring of 2018, the installation of Abiy Ahmed as the first prime minister of partial Oromo descent brought about changes accomplished in part with the cooperation of Amhara factions long opposed to Tigrayan rule. This political rapprochement between Oromo and Amhara against the Tigrayan-dominated government in power since 1991 began to shift longtime antagonisms as well between Oromo and Amhara communities in diaspora. However, deep-seated political divides and historical discrimination against Oromo left a variety of disgruntled factions, including those from diaspora who returned to Ethiopia to participate in the 2018 transition.

66. Donna Stefanik, "Refugee Alliance Gets New Digs: Women's Agency Expects to Boost Service by 500 Clients a Year." *Skanner* 10, no. 111, Seattle edition, June 25, 2003, 1.

67. "Ethiopian Group Stages Protest in Downtown Dallas," *Dallas Morning News*, November 20, 2013, https://www.dallasnews.com/news/2013/11/21/ethiopian -group-stages-protest-in-downtown-dallas/. A number of Ethiopian Americans are entering the US political arena at local, state, and, increasingly, national levels. They include Joe Neguse, of Eritrean descent, who was elected by Colorado's Second District to the House of Representatives in 2018 (see https://neguse.house.gov/about), and Yohannes Abraham, who was selected to oversee Joe Biden's presidential transition team (Samuel Getachew, "Ethiopian-American to run Biden's Transition Team," *Reporter*, June 27, 2020, https://www.thereporterethiopia.com/article/ethiopian -american-run-bidens-transition-team). In 2018 the Ethiopian American magazine *Tadias* headlined the election of Ethiopian American Alex Assefa as a state legislator in the Nevada State Assembly; of Eritrean American Joe Neguse to Congress; and of Ilhan Omar of Minnesota as the first Somali American to be elected to the US Congress (Tadias staff, "Alex Assefa, Joe Neguse and Ilhan Omar: Ethiopian, Eritrean and Somali Make History," *Tadias*, November 8, 2018, http://www.tadias.com/11/08 /2018/alex-assefa-joe-neguse-lhan-omar-ethiopian-eritrean-somali-make-history -us-election/).

68. The emergence of corporations such as Uber and Lyft have adversely affected the burgeoning Ethiopian taxi industry, reducing clientele as well as the value of taxi medallions (Roger Lowenstein, "Uber, Lyft and the Hard Economics of Taxi Cab Medallions," *Washington Post*, May 24, 2019, https://www.washingtonpost.com/business /economy/uber-lyft-and-the-hard-economics-of-taxi-cab-medallions/2019/05/24 /cf1b56f4-7cda-11e9-a5b3-34f3edf1351e_story.html).

69. Moges Seyoum and Kahele Wondaferaw, interview by author and Steven Kaplan, January 27, 2007, Washington, DC.

70. Seble W. Argaw, interview by Steven Kaplan and author, October 5, 2007, Cambridge, MA. Also see the discussion of domestic violence among Ethiopian immigrant couples in Israel and North America, especially notes 49–52, in Steven Kaplan, "Ethi-

opian Immigrants in the United States and Israel: A Preliminary Comparison," *International Journal of Ethiopian Studies* 5, no. 1 (Spring–Summer 2010): 79–80.

71. Seble interview. *Adbar* is defined in the organization's website as an Ethiopian word for a female goddess (https://www.ethiopianwomen.org/who-we-are-1), but the word is more usually glossed as "protective spirit" (Kane, *Dictionary*, 1307). Other Ethiopian women's organizations have been established in the United States, including the Ethiopian Women's Organization for All Women, founded in Dallas, Texas, in 2004, https://www.ethiowomen.org/.

72. Charles Schaefer, "*Maḥbär*," *EAe*, 3:650; Dirk Bustorf and Charles Schaefer, "Əddər," *EAe*, 2:225–27. For example, in August 2008, the Dallas Ethiopian community established the Ethiopian Community EDIR. This traditional organization, http://www.edirdfw.org/page/about-us/, assists participants in covering funeral expenses.

73. When flying on Ethiopian Airlines to Addis Ababa for a visit in December 2017, I witnessed an elderly, grief-stricken Ethiopian woman returning to her homeland to bury a relative who had died in diaspora. She accidentally left the cash given to her by her *mahber* in one of the plane's bathrooms, from which it had disappeared by the time she realized the loss and returned to retrieve it, a devastating upset for the woman and her accompanying family. I do not know if the money was ever returned.

74. Kaplan, "Ethiopian Yellow Pages," 257–58.

75. Martha Z. Tegegn, "Part Three Exclusive: Teshome Mitiku Plans to Return to Ethiopia," *Tadias*, August 19, 2010, http://www.tadias.com/08/19/2010/part-three-exclusive-teshome-mitiku-plans-to-return-to-ethiopia/.

76. Abonesh interview.

77. Terrence Lyons, "Transnational Politics in Ethiopia: Diasporas and the 2005 Elections," *Diaspora* 15, nos. 2–3 (2006 [pub. 2011]): 265–84, https://doi.org/10.1353/dsp.2011.0076.

78. The events were described in detail by Abonesh and her husband, Negash Shifrew, in a joint interview. Both gave permission for details of this experience to be shared in print.

79. The DVD is *Yäqəddus yared mätasäbiya bä'əwəq yäkinä-təbäb säwoch* [Reflections of Holy Yared, the Best-Known Artistic Person] (Washington, DC: Kedus Gabriel EOT Cathedral, n.d.).

80. The Hamlin Fistula Clinic in Ethiopia, https://hamlinfistula.org/, is renowned for its innovative and free treatment of fistula, a common and disabling complication during pregnancy and delivery among Ethiopian women.

81. Negash interview.

82. Posted on Ethio Entertainment Facebook page on September 8, 2012; the post is no longer available. Abonesh has since returned to live in Ethiopia.

Chapter Seven

1. Kane, *Dictionary*, 18.

2. Nina Sun Eidsheim, *Sensing Sound: Singing and Listening as Vibrational Practice* (Durham, NC: Duke University Press, 2015), 12. Other points raised by Eidsheim are quite congruent with directions I take in this chapter. She suggests transferring "the privilege of authorship to the listener" and that "to focus analytically on the listener allows us to read and interrogate the impact of a piece of music as it is experienced by a listener who is encultured in a given way" (5). Here I pay ample attention to inter-

pretation by listeners while seeking to understand as well the agency of those who conceive and perform sound. Although Eidsheim works with vocal repertories with which she has long been a practitioner, her concern for the contexts of music making and her articulated affinity for anthropologist Clifford Geertz's maxim of "thick description" lends her work on song as a "relational sphere" and about the "integral part that music plays in how we forge our relations to one another" a rich resource for ethnomusicologists (1, 3). Eidsheim's emphasis on the importance of raising acousmatic questions and the impossibility of giving a single answer about what one perceives when one hears is a welcome model for my effort here to address sound from multiple listening perspectives. In addition, her focus on vocality and timbre has led me to query the relationship between vocal and instrumental sounds. See also Nina Sun Eidsheim, *The Race of Sound: Listening, Timbre, and Vocality in African American Music* (Durham, NC: Duke University Press, 2019).

3. Kane, *Dictionary*, 1730. *Mässariya*, from the root *sära* (work), is used interchangeably for tool, instrument, implement, or arms (Kane, *Dictionary*, 210), implicitly recognizing the materiality of both instruments and the voice. A twentieth-century term for musical instrument is *yämusiqa mässariya* (Leslau, *Context Dictionary*, 821).

4. Hermela Mulatu, interview by author, July 3, 2008, Washington, DC. Mulatu has received recognition across the global Ethiopian diaspora, including the 2006 SEED (Society of Ethiopians Established in Diaspora) Award, an honorary doctorate from his alma mater Berklee College of Music (May 1, 2012), and the 2017 Ethiopian Canadian Bikila Award for Lifetime Achievement. In 2019 he was awarded the Ordre des Arts et des Lettres from the French Ministry of Culture.

5. Mulatu had long been known for his constant travel and was featured in a poster advertising Ethiopian Airlines in the early 1970s. The caption to the advertisement with Mulatu's portrait read "Ethiopian Airlines. Going to great lengths to please" and was used as the cover photo for the album *Mulatu of Ethiopia* (Worthy Records W-1020, 1972, LP). See Kay Kaufman Shelemay, "'Traveling Music': Mulatu Astatke and the Genesis of Ethiopian Jazz," in *Jazz Worlds/World Jazz*, ed. Philip V. Bohlman and Goffredo Plastino (Chicago: University of Chicago Press, 2016), 246. Mulatu's ability to continue to travel during the revolutionary years is credited by the musician to his international reputation: "That is why they gave me the passport." His work as a jazz musician with strictly instrumental music also served to screen him from political controversy: "Toot, toot, toot: it doesn't mean anything" (Mulatu Astatke, interview by author and Steven Kaplan, November 6, 2007, Cambridge, MA). Mulatu noted that he was allowed to travel and perform in the former Soviet Union and across Eastern Europe during the revolution because of the burgeoning Soviet-Ethiopian alliance during the era, especially when Soviet presence in Ethiopia increased in 1978 during the Ethiopian-Somali War. He recorded an LP with Polijazz in Europe in 1989 (Mulatu Astatke, interview by author and Steven Kaplan, October 2, 2007, Cambridge, MA).

6. Ben Sisario, "Film Puts a New Focus on the Master of 'Ethiojazz,'" *New York Times*, October 13, 2005, https://www.nytimes.com/2005/10/13/arts/music/film-puts-a-new-focus-on-the-master-of-ethiojazz.html.

7. As discussed in chapter 2, the earliest historical antecedent for Ethio-jazz dates from 1896, when in celebration of the Ethiopian victory over the Italian forces at the Battle of Adwa, Czar Nicholas II of Russia sent a full complement of brass band instruments to Ethiopian emperor Menelik II (Falceto, *Abyssinie Swing*, 18; Timkehet Teffera, "Canvassing Past Memories through *Təzəta*," *Journal of Ethiopian Studies* 46

[December 2013]: 31–66, www.jstor.org/stable/44326314). The 1924 arrival of the Armenian orphans and the establishment of Ras Tafari's Royal Marching Band (1924–29), followed by the founding of the Imperial Bodyguard Orchestra in 1929, had an impact on performance practice, for Ethiopian traditional music largely consisted of instrumentalists who performed alone or as accompaniment to a singer or dancer. By the 1940s, a popular brass ensemble had been established at the National Theatre (then the Haile Selassie I National Theatre) in Addis Ababa (Selam Seyoum Wolde-mariam, "The Origin and Development of Zemenawi Music in Ethiopia from 1896–1974" [bachelor's thesis, Addis Ababa University, 1988], 38–39). Other bands soon appeared on the Ethiopian musical scene, notably "The Imperial Bodyguard Band Jazz Symphony" (*Yakebur Zebegna Orchestra Yajazz Symphony*), also established in 1950 with a large brass section (47). The bodyguard jazz ensemble is said to have been the first popular band to have performed publicly at the Ras Hotel in 1950, playing versions of big-band repertory and some arrangements of Ethiopian songs (50–52).

8. Falceto, *Abyssinie Swing*, 53.

9. Mulatu interview, September 12, 2007.

10. Mulatu Astatke, interview by author and Steven Kaplan, September 25, 2007, Cambridge, MA.

11. Mulatu interview, September 12, 2007.

12. Mulatu's first album was *Afro-Latin Soul*, featuring Mulatu and his Ethiopian Quintet and singer Louis Rodriguez on Worthy Records W-1014, 1966, LP. He next released *Afro-Latin Soul*, vol. 2, Worthy Records W-1015, 1966, LP, and *Mulatu of Ethiopia*, Worthy Records W-1020, 1972, LP.

13. Mulatu interview, September 25, 2007.

14. The others are "Yegelle Tezeta," "Gubelye," and "Ethanopium," all of which are included, along with "Yekermo Sew" on the film's soundtrack album, *Music from Broken Flowers*, Decca 988 3781, 2005, compact disc. All except for "Ethanopium" are performed by Mulatu. "Yekermo Sew" is also available on *éthiopiques 4: Ethio Jazz and Musique Instrumentale 1969–1974*, Buda Musique 829642, 1998, compact disc. The original "Yekermo Sew" recording is dated by *éthiopiques* editor Francis Falceto to a 45 rpm recording issued in Addis Ababa at the end of 1969, although it was also released by producer Amha Eshete on *Ethiopian Modern Instrumental Hits*, Amha Records AELP 10, 1972, LP (Falceto, liner notes to *éthiopiques 4*, 18). A different rendition of "Yekermo Sew" was recorded at Omega Recording Studios in Rockville, Maryland, in 1992 and was released on Mulatu's *Assiyo Bellema*, Ethio-Grooves Records, 1994, cassette.

15. The play, *Yekermo Sew*, was composed near the end of Tsegaye Gabre-Medhin's tenure as vice director of arts at the Haile Selassie I National Theatre between 1959 and 1970. During this period, Tsegaye innovated by writing plays about the lives of ordinary people in contrast to dramas about major historical figures popular in prior decades. *Yekermo Sew* is "a sombre piece examining the degradation of city life among the poor and the aspiring petit bourgeoisie" (Jane Plastow, *African Theatre and Politics: The Evolution of Theatre in Ethiopia, Tanzania and Zimbabwe—a Comparative Study* [Amsterdam: Rodopi, 1996], 96). The plot focuses on two brothers who live in poverty in Addis Ababa, whose uncle tries to persuade them to leave dissolute city life for the countryside. By the end of the play, one of the brothers considers a return to the family farm and the traditional lifestyle of an earlier generation (Plastow, *African Theatre and Politics*, 95–96).

16. Kane, *Dictionary*, 1384.

17. Mulatu Astatke, interview by author, November 9, 2007, Cambridge, MA.

18. A rarely performed vocal version of "Yekermo Sew" exists, initially recorded by Seyfu Yohannes with the Soul Ekos Band in 1962–63 EC (c. 1970–71) on *éthiopiques 24, Golden Years of Modern Ethiopian Music, 1969–1975*, track 13 (Buda Musique 860176, 2008), as well as on YouTube, 4:01, posted by Mirkuzz, July 9, 2011, https://www.youtube.com/watch?v=-tnCCfCCQVQ. A 2015 recording, "Yekermo Sew: A Tribute to Seifu Yohannes and Tsegaye Gabre-Medhin" by duo Munit and Jörg, recorded and directed by Michael Tsegaye, is also available on YouTube, 3:53, posted by Munit– Jörg, January 2, 2015, https://www.youtube.com/watch?v=bN6HrFq8_wM.

The following song lyrics by Tsegaye Gabre-Medhin (as sung by Munit) provide insight into the retrospective (and introspective) nature of the play (text courtesy of Munit Mesfin; transcription and translation by author):

1. *Bäfəqər yazänä bämən yədäsätal*
   yədäsätal

   What could possibly cheer up a person who has been saddened by love?

   Mäls ənkwan bayəsät'əm yäkärmo sew
   yawqal yawqal

   Even if he won't give a reply, the man from the last year knows, he knows.

2. *Yämiyastäkəz fəkər səntun ədanəzəzo*
   ədanəzəzo

   The kind of love that makes one reminisce, reminisce.

   Yäkärmo sew fəkər mät'äyäq näw yəzo
   yəzo

   The love from last year's person, that's the one to get hold of and ask.

3. *Täqaqfo mäch'anäq gəlp' əyätäyayu*

   Rather than cuddling and worrying while seeing eye to eye

   Säwoch' sälä fäqər, əsti täwäyayu

   People, let's talk about love (do talk about love)

4. *Bäsämän fəkər käto midgämwo*

   That we get so exhausted from a delirious love,

   Yät'ənt näw yamənaw wäyəs yäkärmo
   säw

   Is it one from the future or is it from last year's person?

[repeat verses 1–4]
[repeat verses 1–2]

Also see the partial translation of the play at Tsegaye Gabre-Medhin and Nafkote Tamirat, "Drama, Translations: Yekermo Sew," *Rusted Radishes 6* (2018), http://www.rustedradishes.com/yekermo-sew/. That the composition "Yekermo Sew" was first released in Addis Ababa in 1969 places the work's genesis firmly in the late 1960s and Mulatu confirms that he composed "Yekermo Sew" in Ethiopia after his return from New York City, but he cannot be certain of the precise date. "You know, traveling and playing . . . sometimes you forget things" (Mulatu interview, November 9, 2007).

19. Mulatu interview, December 4, 2007. In "Canvassing Past Memories," 38, Tim-

kehet has noted that the two types of *tizita* tunings are known as *abəy* (foremost, main, major, leading) and *nə'us* (small or minor) but have been translated by traditional music teachers in the 1960 as major and minor. Mulatu at first told me that "Yekermo Sew" was set in *anchihoye* mode but a few minutes later corrected it to *tizita* minor (Mulatu Astatke, interview by author and Steven Kaplan, September 19, 2007, Cambridge, MA).

20. Mulatu interviews, November 9, 2007, and December 4, 2007. While the modes of the Ethiopian Orthodox Church tradition can be confirmed through analysis of the indigenous notational system back to the sixteenth century, as well as Ethiopian Christian oral traditions that propose an even earlier dating (see Shelemay and Jeffery, *Ethiopian Christian Liturgical Chant*; and Heldman and Shelemay, "Concerning Saint Yared"), the systematization of the secular modes (*qəñət* [*qenyet*]) appears to be a twentieth-century innovation. A recent study based on analysis of early recordings and measurement of modal pitch content in performance persuasively shows that the system of four pentatonic modes (*ambasel, anchihoye, bati,* and *tizita*) was likely formalized in the late 1950s or early 1960s as part of pedagogical processes necessary to train musicians in a range of urban musical institutions, including various westernized music ensembles with continual elaboration at the Yared School of Music, founded in 1966–67 (Stéphanie Weisser and Francis Falceto, "Investigating *Qəñət* in Amhara Secular Music: An Acoustic and Historical Study," *Annales d'Éthiopie* 28 [2013]: 314, https://doi.org/10.3406/ethio.2013.1539).

21. David H. Rosenthal, *Hard Bop: Jazz and Black Music, 1955–1965* (New York: Oxford University Press, 1992), 29 and 36.

22. Mulatu interview, September 12, 2007.

23. Rosenthal, *Hard Bop*, 48.

24. "I liked his voicings and I was just searching when I was in New York . . . and then suddenly this guy was playing at Birdland. I just started listening to him" (Mulatu interview, September 12, 2007).

25. Richard R. Smith, "Fender," *Grove Music Online*, October 16, 2013, https://doi .org/10.1093/gmo/9781561592630.article.A2249505.

26. Tony Bacon and Lynn Wheelwright, "Electric Guitar," *Grove Music Online*, January 31, 2014, https://doi.org/10.1093/gmo/9781561592630.article.A2256412.

27. Mulatu also continued to have unusual resources for hearing a wide range of foreign music at home in Ethiopia, especially after the revolution. Immediately after the revolution ended, c. 1991–95, Mulatu contracted to organize recordings that had been purchased by the emperor or that he had received as gifts over the years. This collection had miraculously survived the revolution in a room of the former palace with "different musics: jazz, classic, and operas, [as well as] interviews with Eisenhower, with Kennedy and a lot of stuff." Three or four people assisted Mulatu in categorizing the recordings according to genres such as jazz, light music, poetry, and so on. According to Mulatu, there were no recordings of church music nor foreign popular music. "I don't know if he (the emperor) listened to them or not," Mulatu related, "but I was just listening and observing and learning from it. There was some modern music, all music, and the first guy who made a recording of *masenqo* and singing." The latter likely included an original set of recordings of Tessema Eshete, later published as *éthiopiques* 27; see chapter 3 for discussion of this landmark set (Mulatu interview, September 19, 2007).

28. Mulatu Astatke, interview by author and Steven Kaplan, November 30, 2007, Cambridge, MA.

29. Mulatu interview, November 9, 2007.

30. Mulatu interview, November 30, 2007.

31. Alex Spoto, "Debo Band's Danny Mekonnen on His Music's Ethiopian Roots: The Boston Band Digs Deep into Ethiopian Musical History," *Spin*, July 12, 2012, https://www.spin.com/2012/07/debo-bands-danny-mekonnen-his-musics-ethiopian-roots/.

32. Dawit Gebre, interview by author, April 14, 2016, Stanford, CA.

33. See *éthiopiques 26: Mahmoud Ahmed and the Imperial Bodyguard Band (1972–74)*, Buda Musique 860191, 2010, compact disc; and "Tilahun Gessesse with the Ethiopian Imperial Bodyguard Band," YouTube, 11:51, posted by Dave HM, February 16, 2014, https://www.youtube.com/watch?v=Q4OrljuSVKM.

34. From 2003 until 2017, St. Michael EOT Church in Boston's Mattapan neighborhood was led by *merigeta* Tsehai Birhanu, an accomplished practitioner of the Qoma style (Shelemay, field notes, July 23, 2006, and November 12, 2011, Cambridge, MA; and Tsehai interview, March 20, 2007).

35. Shelemay and Jeffery, *Ethiopian Christian Liturgical Chant*, 2:4–6.

36. Betelehem "Betty" Melaku, interviews by author, August 12 and August 20, 2019, Cambridge, MA.

37. Nate Chinen, "Getatchew Mekurya, 81, Ethiopian Saxophonist with Global Reach Dies," *New York Times*, April 11, 2016, https://www.nytimes.com/2016/04/12/arts/music/getatchew-mekurya-ethiopian-jazz-saxophonist-dies-at-81.html.

38. Getatchew's saxophone recording of a *shillela* can be heard on *éthiopiques 14: Negus (King) of the Ethiopian Sax*, Buda Musique 822562, 2003, compact disc. "Shellela" provided the core sample for "I Came Prepared," track 4 with guest artist Damian Marley on Somali-Canadian rapper K'naan's (Keinan Abdi Warsame) album, *Troubadour*, A&M Octone Records B001247802, 2009, compact disc (Chinen, "Getatchew Mekurya"). I witnessed a live, solo performance of "Shillela" during a set performed by Getatchew at the Middle East Nightclub in Cambridge, Massachusetts, on December 12, 2006, that brought the house down with its expressive speech and song-like inflections (Shelemay, field notes, Middle East Nightclub, December 12, 2006, Cambridge, MA).

39. Getatchew Mekuria, liner notes to *Getatchew Mekuria, The Ex and Guests—Moa Anbessa*.

40. Chinen, "Getatchew Mekurya."

41. Mulatu's Ethio-jazz was originally recorded by Amha Eshete for Amha records but was rereleased and widely circulated as *éthiopiques 4*. Getatchew's early singles and compilation albums were produced by Philips in a series of 1972 recordings but were also later acquired for *éthiopiques 14* and rereleased in 2003. Getatchew made subsequent recordings with the Dutch ensemble The Ex in 2006: *Getatchew Mekuria, The Ex and Guests—Moa Anbessa*, and in 2012, *Getatchew Mekuria, The Ex and Friends—Y'Anbessaw Tezeta*, Terp Records AS-21/22, 2012, compact disc.

42. *Ere Mela Mela*, Kaifa Records LPKF 20, 1975, LP; reissued CRAM 047, 1986, LP. Crammed Discs released an eclectic mix of music "from the four corners of the planet," believing that "borders between genres are no longer indispensable," http://www.crammed.be/index.php?id=32. Although by the mid-1980s political restrictions and regulations of the later revolutionary period had severely constrained the performing careers of these Ethiopian musicians at home and on their foreign travel, *Ere Mela Mela* served as their messenger when it was released by Crammed Discs and

garnered international attention, including number five on the list of top albums for 1986 in the *New York Times* (Robert Palmer, "The Pop Life: Peter Case Heads a List of the Top Albums of 1986," *New York Times*, January 7, 1987, https://www.nytimes.com /1987/01/07/arts/the-pop-life-peter-case-heads-a-list-of-the-top-albums-of-1986 .html).

43. *éthiopiques 7: Erè Mèla Mèla*, Buda Musique 829802, 1999, compact disc. In 1975 the *Ere Mela Mela* LP caught the ear of Falceto, the producer of *éthiopiques* series, a decade later in 1984, catalyzing his long engagement with Ethiopian and Eritrean recordings. In addition to singer Mahmoud Ahmed, a veteran of the Imperial Body-guard Orchestra for most of the decade before the revolution, the brilliant group of Ibex Band musicians who participated in the original 1975 recording included Theodros Mitiku (brother of the singer Teshome Mitiku, who appeared in chapter 2) and Fekade Amde Maskal (both on tenor saxophone); guitarist Selam Seyoum Wolde-mariam; drummer Tesfaye "Hodo" Mekonnen; keyboardist Haile Maryam Gebre Ghiorgis; bassist, Giovanni Rico; and percussionist Girma Tchibsa (Falceto, liner notes to *éthiopiques 7: Erè Mèla Mèla*). Guitarist Selam Seyoum Woldemariam recalls the original recording and its subsequent life as "the first CD ever in Ethiopia" (Selam interview, September 5, 2007).

44. Jon Pareles, "In Every Note, Passion That Needs No Translation," *New York Times*, July 27, 2014, https://www.nytimes.com/2014/07/28/arts/music/mahmoud -ahmed-kicks-off-summer-concert-series.html. Mahmoud Ahmed did not acquire this vocal style in church, however; he was of Gurage ethnicity and was born into a Muslim family.

45. *éthiopiques 16: The Lady with the Krar* features the music of Asnaqetch Werqu, Buda Musique 82265-2, 2003, compact disc. The CD includes "Mèla Mèla" on track 4. Asnaqetch's rendition has a slightly different text, although the thematic content is similar to that of the version Mahmoud Ahmed performed.

46. Falceto, liner notes to *éthiopiques 7*, 10.

47. Robert Palmer, "Ethiopian Funk from Mahmoud Ahmed," *New York Times*, July 30, 1986, https://www.nytimes.com/1986/07/30/arts/the-pop-life-evolution -of-psychobilly-on-new-cramps-album.html. The article begins midway down.

48. Kane, *Dictionary*, 1246, lit., "muttering, a poem or song expressing melancholy or sorrow."

49. Kane, *Dictionary*, 1948.

50. As noted earlier, Weisser and Falceto's investigation of mode in Amhara secular music suggests that the four modes (*qenyet*) appear to be fairly recent (Weisser and Falceto, "Investigating Qəñət," 303). They cite Katell Morand ("Solitudes habitées. Le chant, le souvenir et le conflit chez les Amhara du Goggam (Éthiopie)" [PhD diss., Université de Paris Ouest Nanterre, 2012], 98), who found during fieldwork among *azmari* in Gojjam that *tizita* as a song title was largely unknown. Another comparison by Weisser of renditions of *tizita* melodies by various musicians shows substantial differences in the intervals used, as well as variance within the performance of an individual musician as determined by the context (Weisser and Falceto, "Investigating Qəñət," 306–7).

51. These concerts were named *Tərəyatə Təbbəbat*; the word *təbbəbat* indicates that the event was "skillful or learned" (Leslau, *Context Dictionary*, 230; Kane, *Dictionary*, 2149). On these programs, which were organized by Alemtsehay Wedajo, Bezawork

sang with Mahmoud Ahmed and Muluken Melesse, a famous singer born in 1954 who later gave up popular song for a ministry at an evangelical church (Bezawork interview).

52. Bezawork interview. One can only speculate that Bezawork's rendition of "Tizita" effectively "went viral" to the limited extent possible in revolutionary Ethiopia prior to the internet.

53. Timkehet, "Canvassing Past Memories," 43. *Under African Skies: Ethiopia,* a BBC Two documentary about Ethiopian music during the revolution, first screened in 1989, featured a segment exploring the background of the *tizita* sentiment in Ethiopian culture, the portrayal of the *tizita* affect in visual arts, and a performance of the ballad by Bezawork Asfaw. "Under African Skies: Ethiopia," YouTube, 57:58, posted by Adamant Critique, August 30, 2016, https://www.youtube.com/watch?v=5N09oe9eK6c.

54. Timkehet, "Canvassing Past Memories," 43–44.

55. Bezawork Asfaw, "Tizita," track 5 of *Yetizitawoch Tizita* (Tizita of Tizitas), Nahom Favorite, vol. 23, Nahom Records 8 84501 39120 7, 2010, compact disc. Transcribed and translated by Timkehet in "Canvassing Past Memories," 44.

56. Falceto, liner notes to *éthiopiques 10,* 24. I thank Timkehet for bringing this source to my attention.

57. There are also many instrumental versions of the song, including a 2008 recording by a female violin trio trained at Yared School of Music, a division of Addis Ababa University, track 12 on *Instrumental Music: Asatamia Akafafay,* Master Sound/Yared School of Music, 2008, compact disc. Getatchew recorded a solo saxophone version of "Tizita," track 8 of *Getatchew Mekuria, The Ex and Guests—Moa Anbessa.*

58. Alemtsehay Wedajo, interview by author, June 9, 2008, Washington, DC.

59. Excerpt from Michael Belayneh's "Tibeb New Tizita" (Wise Tizita), lyricist Getinet Eniyew. On track 10 of *Yetizitawoch Tizita,* Nahom Favorite, vol. 23. Text transcribed by Timkehet in "Canvassing Past Memories," 41.

60. Afework Tekle (1932–2012), one of the most revered Ethiopian painters of the twentieth century, commented on his own painting dedicated to "Tizita," titled "Remembrances," that "the painting is symbolic and allegorical as the song (Tizita) itself" (comment made by Afework in a segment of the documentary *Under African Skies: Ethiopia,* transcribed by Timkehet in "Canvassing Past Memories," 35).

61. Getinet Eniyew's poem "Läkas məsst norwal" (What a termite it is!) from his *Anthology of Poems: Iwuqetin Filega* [In search of wisdom] (Addis Ababa, 2001), 64–65. Timkehet quotes the complete Amharic text with English translation in "Canvassing Past Memories," 41–42.

62. Aster Aweke, *Aster,* Triple Earth Records Terra 107, 1989, LP; reissued Columbia Records CK 46848, 1990, compact disc, track 3. Translation by Aster Aweke in the liner notes.

63. See discussion of song performance and affective arousal in Kay Kaufman Shelemay, *Let Jasmine Rain Down: Song and Remembrance among Syrian Jews* (Chicago: University of Chicago Press, 1998), 215–16.

64. Although Stéphanie Weisser and Francis Falceto did not find evidence of widespread transmission of the song "Tizita" among musicians from early dates, they did find its melodic and modal characteristics in recordings dating to 1939 (Weisser and Falceto, "Investigating Qəñət," 304).

65. Kane, *Dictionary*, 462. Additional meanings include "to grant one's prayer" and "to act as a witness."

66. Kane, *Dictionary*, 464; Leslau, *Context Dictionary*, 382, 412, 1139. I thank Dr. Getatchew Haile for confirming the relationship between these terms.

67. Kane, *Dictionary*, 464.

68. Kane, *Dictionary*, 18.

69. Stéphanie Weisser, "Emotion and Music: The Ethiopian Lyre *Bagana*," *Musicae Scientiae* 16, no. 1 (2011): 3–18. Note Weisser's use of a descriptive system to characterize categories of response to music based on Alf Gabrielsson, "Emotions in Strong Experiences with Music," in *Music and Emotion: Theory and Research*, ed. Patrik N. Juslin and John A. Sloboda (Oxford: Oxford University Press, 2001), 431–49.

70. Weisser, "Emotion and Music," 5.

71. Weisser, "Emotion and Music," 4.

72. Weisser, "Emotion and Music," 6. Weisser uses the term *derdera* (*dərdər*, from *däräddärä*, "to play a harp or similar instrument"; Kane, *Dictionary*, 1752) for this instrumental introduction. *Azmatch* is another term for "introduction," which has as one of its meanings a refrain of a song (Kane, *Dictionary*, 1278).

73. Weisser, "Emotion and Music," 9.

74. Weisser, "Emotion and Music," 9–12.

75. Weisser, "Emotion and Music," 11.

76. Harrison, *Time, Place and Music*, 51.

77. Weisser, "Emotion and Music," 11.

78. Weisser, "Emotion and Music," 16.

79. Messing, "Highland-Plateau Amhara," 573.

80. Messing, "Highland-Plateau Amhara," 573.

81. Aster Aweke, interview by author, April 6, 2009, Cambridge, MA.

82. Anupa Mistry, "The Dark Knight Returns: A Conversation with The Weeknd," *Pitchfork*, August 31, 2015, https://pitchfork.com/features/interview/9711-the-dark-knight-returns-a-conversation-with-the-weeknd/. The Weeknd visited Ethiopia and performed there in 2018. He also donated funds to support the Ethiopic studies program at University of Toronto. See Lucianna Ciccocioppo, "With Support from The Weeknd, U of T's Ethiopic Program Soars Past $500,000 Endowment Goal," *U of T News* (University of Toronto), November 2, 2020, https://www.utoronto.ca/news/support-weeknd-u-t-s-ethiopic-program-soars-past-500000-endowment-goal.

83. Abbink, "Ethnicity," *EAe*, 2:444.

84. In chapter 3, we discussed how the sound and words of Oromo musician Ali Birra provided a musical counterpoint to Amhara hegemony and highland dominance that began well before the revolutionary period. If Oromo musicians have often refused to sing in Amharic, it is also the case that musicians of other ethnic identities refused to perform in Afaan Oromo. Asafa (*Oromia and Ethiopia*, 186) writes,

> in the early 1960s, at an Oromo wedding in Dire Dawa an Oromo asked an Adare musical group hired for entertainment to sing in Afaan Oromoo. A member of the group replied that their instruments did not know Afaan Oromoo, yet the entire group could speak it. Their refusal and irritating comment indicated how even the Adare despised the Oromo, their language, and culture. This event annoyed the Oromo guests and led them to form a committee that raised money and organized the Afran Qallo Musical Group.

85. György Martin, "Dance Types in Ethiopia," *Journal of the International Folk Music Council* 19 (1967): 23–27, https://www.jstor.org/stable/942181.

86. Probably a reference to the northern Somali Issa clan who also live in Ethiopia.

87. Kullo is an informal name for Dawro and Konta people who live in Ethiopia's Southern Nations, Nationalities, and Peoples' Region.

88. In the literature from the 1960s and 1970s and earlier dates, the Oromo are called by a name considered to be pejorative, Galla. I have replaced the term *Galla* with *Oromo* in the quote for that reason. The Martin project ("Dance Types in Ethiopia") was amplified by Tibor Vadasy, who spent two years in Ethiopia as a choreographer and folk-dance teacher at the Yared School of Music, publishing three articles: "Ethiopian Folk-Dance," *Journal of Ethiopian Studies* 8, no. 2 (1970): 119–46; "Ethiopian Folk-Dance II: Tegré and Guragé," *Journal of Ethiopian Studies* 9, no. 2 (1971): 191–217; and "Ethiopian Folk-Dance III: Wällo and Galla," *Journal of Ethiopian Studies* 11, no. 1 (1973): 213–31. These studies are problematic because of the strong evolutionary model that underpins the typology and description of the dances. For more recent studies, see Cynthia Tse Kimberlin, "Dances," *EAe*, 2:81–84; and a preliminary study from an engineering perspective that analyzed video clips to test classification of Ethiopian dances: Karpaga Selvi Subramanian and Andargie Mekonnen, "Content Based Classification of Ethiopian Traditional Dance Videos Using Optical Flow and Histogram of Oriented Gradient," *International Journal of Innovations in Engineering and Technology* 6, no. 3 (2016): 371–80, http://ijiet.com/wp-content/uploads/2016/02/57.pdf.

89. Ashenafi interview.

90. Hamza Aburedzek, interview by author, August 4, 2009, Cambridge, MA.

91. The Ethiopian calendar, based on a Roman Julian model, runs approximately seven and a half years behind the Gregorian calendar adopted in the West. Thus, the Ethiopian millennial year began in early September 2007 of the Gregorian calendar, both in Ethiopia and in its diaspora.

92. Shelemay, field notes, September 8, 2007, Washington, DC; see also Shelemay, "Music in the Ethiopian American Diaspora."

93. Each ethnic community also has associated dress conventions that are usually presented stereotypically in folkloric dance presentations. Highland women and men wear white cotton garments, and Amhara women wear long dresses with long sleeves, embroidered on the bodice or with colorful woven borders or both. Oromo women are often represented in performance wearing shorter cotton dresses with short sleeves and according to recent conventions on stage, occasionally with one shoulder bare; sometimes these dresses, often brown or a muted earth tone, are decorated with cowrie shells. Tigray women wear white cotton dresses with embroidery similar to, but usually shorter in length than, those of highland Amhara women, which are often tailored from the textured cloth traditionally woven in Mekele, Tigray. Gurage women, in contrast, are often represented for dance performances in knee-length skirts over long white pants, wearing turbans.

94. See "Oromia," YouTube, 3:35, posted by Dammee tube, November 3, 2019, https://www.youtube.com/watch?v=atarcw77jGk, for a recording of Ali Birra performing this anthem in Addis Ababa (Finfinnee). The song is set in a martial style of a Western anthem and is performed by Ali with chorus.

95. When I was speaking about "performing identity" with examples of comparative national anthems at Hamline University in Minnesota, where there are the largest Oromo and Somali populations in the United States, a student of dual Oromo and

Somali descent raised his hand during the question-and-answer period. Knowing that I was an Ethiopianist, he volunteered the information that Ali Birra's "Oromiyaa" was the unofficial Oromo national anthem and that it was sung at the beginning of the local Oromo radio show every Sunday (Fathi Hassan, interview by author, March 15, 2011, St. Paul, Minnesota).

96. Gow, *Oromo in Exile*, 57.

97. Text and translation from Gow, *Oromo in Exile*, 57. Text revised by Mekonnen Firew Ayano.

98. Betelehem interview, August 20, 2019.

99. Mekbul Jemal Tahir, telephone interview by author, August 20, 2020. See Melaku Belay's Fendika group performing an updated version of the Oromo lion dance in "Fendika: Best Oromo Dance," YouTube, 7:09, posted by Tenaadam, September 14, 2016, https://www.youtube.com/watch?v=I64XBcawthU.

100. Gideon Goldenberg, "Gurage," *EAe*, 2:924–28.

101. The plant is called false banana because it does not produce edible fruit, but it is processed as the main crop and staple food of the region (Alke Dohrmann and Manfred Metz, "Ənsät," *EAe*, 2:316). According to an accomplished Gurage dancer, the characteristic cutting motion can be done in different ways, but "when I see the motions, I always relate it to carving the banana tree roots" (Mekbul interview). See "Best of Ethiopian Gurage Cultural Dance," YouTube, 4:30, posted by *Ethio Youth Media TV*, October 23, 2013, https://www.youtube.com/watch?v=PIVhuYL FWgE.

102. Worku Nida, "Gurage Ethno-historical Survey," *EAe*, 2:929.

103. Mekbul interview.

104. Mekbul interview.

105. Henock interview, March 7, 2003.

106. Thomas "Tommy T" interview, March 7, 2003.

Chapter Eight

1. This chapter draws both on methods of multitemporal ethnography and on those of prosopography set forth in chapter 1. It is also influenced by theories of *agencement* (usually glossed as assemblage in translation), referring to "the action of matching or fitting together a set of components (*agencer*), as well as to the result of such an action: an ensemble of parts that mesh well together" (Manuel DeLanda, *Assemblage Theory* [Edinburgh: Edinburgh University Press, 2016], 1). I acknowledge the impact of the concept of *agencement* and the framework of assemblage theory largely derived from the philosophical writings of Deleuze and Guattari in *A Thousand Plateaus*, as well as DeLanda's subsequent commentary thereon in framing both my analysis and its presentation in this chapter. However, this theoretical framework carries with it an idiosyncratic terminology that can obscure its most important points and for this reason I prefer not to employ it here. Rather, I track parallels to assemblage theory in this note for readers who wish to pursue it further. For instance, consistent with DeLanda's expansion of Deleuze and Guattari's assemblage theory, individuals here are presented within their own historical parameters in seeking to understand the transformations they have effected (DeLanda, *Assemblage Theory*, 13). The ensemble presented is constituted of heterogeneous components (musicians) and emerges from the interaction among these parts (DeLanda, *Assemblage Theory*, 20–21). Spatial boundaries (degree

of territorialization and deterritorialization of the assemblage) become crucial in the movement of Orchestra Ethiopia both within various geographical and virtual settings in Ethiopia as well as across the diaspora. Aspects of musical style lend characteristics (degree of coding and decoding) that are associated with and help define the ensemble as a whole (DeLanda, *Assemblage Theory*, 22).

2. Tesfaye Lemma, the director, arranger, and composer for Orchestra Ethiopia, collaborated in designing the notation with two Orchestra Ethiopia musicians, Nigussu Retta and Abebe Wolde, who had studied at the Yared Music School in Addis Ababa, where traditional and Western music were combined in a joint curriculum (Kay K. Shelemay, "A New System of Musical Notation in Ethiopia," in *Ethiopian Studies: Dedicated to Wolf Leslau on the Occasion of His Seventy-Fifth Birthday, November 14th, 1981*, ed. Stanislav Segert and Andras T. E. Bodrogligeti [Wiesbaden, Ger.: Harrassowitz, 1983]), 571–82.

3. For an overview of Ethiopian modernism and the ways in which it emerged at early dates and was distinctive, see Crummey, "Ethiopia."

4. Levine, *Greater Ethiopia*, 64–8. See also Levine, "On Cultural Creativity," 215–20, for a revisiting of his own theory of creative incorporation, with its roots in the work of Enrico Cerulli, *Storia della letteratura etiopica* [A history of Ethiopian literature] (Milan: Nuova Accademia, 1956), 12–13.

5. Tesfaye Lemma's central role with the *People to People* tour and his defection during their appearances in the United States were detailed in chapter 5.

6. Benjamin Piekut, "Actor-Networks in Music History: Clarifications and Critiques," *Twentieth-Century Music* 11, no. 2 (2014): 213, https://doi.org/10.1017/S14 7857221400005X.

7. Shelemay, "New System of Musical Notation." See also Cynthia Tse Kimberlin, "Orchestra Ethiopia 1963–1975: Halim El-Dabh, Catalyst for Music Innovation and Preservation," in *Multiple Interpretations of Dynamics of Creativity and Knowledge in African Music Traditions: A Festschrift in Honor of Akin Euba on the Occasion of His 70th Birthday*, ed. Bode Omojola and George Dor (Point Richmond, CA: MRI, 2005), 187–210. A historical recording of performances by Orchestra Ethiopia has been released on compact disc, with detailed notes written by Charles Sutton, as *éthiopiques 23: Orchestra Ethiopia* (Francis Falceto, CD editor) Buda Musique 860152, 2007, compact disc. On August 15, 2007, Tesfaye Lemma deposited his collection of recordings to the Archive of Folk Culture at the Library of Congress (Shelemay, field notes, August 15, 2007, Washington, DC).

8. Tesfaye interview, August 15, 2007.

9. Charles Sutton, "Tezeta," additional notes in PDF on *éthiopiques 23* CD, 4.

10. Tesfaye interview, August 15, 2007.

11. Sutton, "Tezeta," additional notes in PDF on *éthiopiques 23* CD, 4.

12. Tesfaye interview, August 15, 2007.

13. Tesfaye interview, August 15, 2007.

14. Asfa-Wossen, *King of Kings*, 174–75.

15. Bahru Zewde, "Mäkwännən Habtäwäld," *EAe*, 3:684–85.

16. Tesfaye interview, August 20, 2007.

17. Bahru Zewde, "Hagär Fəqər Tiyatər," *EAe*, 2:966.

18. Tesfaye interview, August 20, 2007.

19. Tesfaye interview, August 20, 2007. The four Wollo songs are the names of what are today cited as the four tuning systems or modes in Ethiopian secular music. Schol-

ars have questioned the time depth of the terminology associated with the mode concept *qenyet* and the lack of evidence for the transmission of four modes demonstrated
among musicians from various regions of the highland plateau despite their prominent mention in scholarly literature from the 1970s (Weisser and Falceto, "Investigating *Qəñət*"; Ashenafi Kebede, "The Music of Ethiopia: Its Development and Cultural
Setting" [PhD diss., Wesleyan University, 1971]). Indeed, in their analysis of recordings made in Ethiopia by Italians during the 1939 occupation, Weisser and Falceto find
that only two of the ostensible four secular modes were named. They suggest that it
is possible that the "four *qəñət* theory" grew out of pedagogical innovations around
the middle of the twentieth century, the time of the founding of ensembles such as
the Hager Fikir, the Haile Selassie I Theatre Orchestra, and Orchestra Ethiopia, all of
which needed to teach traditional music to members of their new ensembles (Weisser
and Falceto, "Investigating *Qəñət*," 308–9, 313–14). Two individuals may have contributed to codifying the modal system for pedagogical purposes. One was the Armenian
musician Nerses Nalbandian (1915–77), who taught at the Yared School of Music in
Addis Ababa in 1954, introducing studies of both Ethiopian traditional and Western
musics (Samson Hovhannisyan, "Armenian Orphans and Ethiopian Music: Contribution and Development," *PanARMENIAN*, June 9, 2016, http://www.panarmenian
.net/eng/details/207201). I thank Francis Falceto for information on Nerses Nalbandian (Falceto, personal communication, August 31, 2020). The second less likely
and slightly later possibility is Ashenafi Kebede (1938–98), an Ethiopian trained at
the Eastman School of Music and subsequently at Wesleyan University, who served
as director of the Yared School of Music in Addis Ababa from 1963 to 1968 (Cynthia
Tse Kimberlin, "The Scholarship and Art of Ashenafi Kebede (1938–68)," *Ethnomusicology* 43, no. 2 [1999]: 322–34, https://doi.org/10.2307/852737). Tesfaye Lemma's
explanation of the four modes is consistent with the tradition in which he participated
in the mid-1960s. Charles Sutton, to be discussed later in this chapter, began studying *masenqo* in Addis Ababa with traditional *azmari* Getamesay Abebe; he recalls
that his teacher Getamesay taught him the four modes, each named for a song that
exemplified its content: *tizita*, *bati*, *ambasel*, and *anchihoye* (Charles Sutton, personal
communication with author, August 6, 2018). Clearly, explanations of the Ethiopian
secular modal system as divided into four named modes were well established and in
circulation by the mid-1960s.

20. This ensemble had a major impact on Mulatu Astatke in the 1950s (Mulatu interview, September 12, 2007). Telela Kebede performed with both traditional (*bahelawi*)
and popular (*zemenawi*) Haile Selassie I Theatre Ensembles from the time of their
founding (Telela interview, August 22, 2007).

21. Sutton, liner notes to *éthiopiques 23*, 29.

22. Sutton, "Tezeta," additional notes in PDF on *éthiopiques 23* CD, 4.

23. Philip Caplan (1917–69) was born in Charleston, West Virginia. He received his
master of fine arts in 1947 from Yale University and his PhD in 1960 from the University of Denver. Long active in community theater and a teacher at multiple universities both in the United States and abroad, he established the Creative Arts Centre and
served as its first director ("In Memoriam," *Southern Speech Journal* 35, no. 2 [1969]:
191–92, https://doi.org/10.1080/10417946909372048).

24. Elisabeth Biasio, "Gäbrä Krəstos Dästa," *EAe*, 2:617–18.

25. Tesfaye interview, August 15, 2007.

26. El-Dabh also composed the music long used for the sound and light show

performed at the Sphinx and the Great Pyramids of Giza, Egypt, http://www
.halimeldabh.com.

27. Halim El-Dabh, interview by author, March 5, 2007, Cambridge, MA. According
to Sutton ("Tezeta," additional notes in PDF on *éthiopiques* 23 CD, 2), El-Dabh arrived
in Ethiopia in December 1962, traveled the country for a period of time and was subsequently put in charge of the music program at the Creative Arts Center in early 1963.

28. El-Dabh interview, March 5, 2007.

29. Denise Seachrist, *The Musical World of Halim El-Dabh* (Kent, OH: Kent State
University Press, 2003), 85–86. Other sources have characterized El-Dabh as a more
contemporary composer, citing music he had composed for the Martha Graham Dance
troupe or melodies he borrowed from Leonard Bernstein's compositions (John Coe,
interview by author, June 8, 2007, Cambridge, MA).

30. Sutton, "Tezeta," additional notes in PDF on *éthiopiques* 23 CD, 2.

31. Late one evening in 1975 during the Ethiopian revolution, I received a telephone
call from an official at Radio Voice of the Gospel, telling me that he feared that their
archives would be destroyed by revolutionary forces. He asked me to come with any
blank tapes I had and make copies of any recordings I wished to save. I went to the
station the next day and for hours worked with a technician there, trying to identify
recordings of particular historical interest and value. The recordings had very sparse
documentation, all of which I copied out. This information became part of the electronic record after I deposited the tapes in the Archive of World Music at Loeb Music
Library, Harvard University. In late 2004 I received an email from Halim El-Dabh's
assistant, David Badagnani, who had recognized some of El-Dabh's compositions recorded for Radio Voice of the Gospel from my collection's finding guide. The ensemble was called "The El-Dabh Orchestra," not Orchestra Ethiopia (David Badagnani, personal communication with author, January 23, 2005). I arranged for copies
of these materials to be sent to El-Dabh, who did not have copies of the radio tapes.

32. Sutton, "Tezeta," additional notes in PDF on *éthiopiques* 23 CD, 2.

33. Sutton, "Tezeta," additional notes in PDF on *éthiopiques* 23 CD, 2–3.

34. Coe interview.

35. Coe interview.

36. *Bəsəchət*, which Coe glossed as "Trouble," is usually translated as vexation, irri-
tation, frustration, aggravation, or exasperation (Kane *Dictionary*, 900).

37. Coe interview.

38. Coe interview.

39. Coe interview. Coe's score for "Oda Oak Oracle I–V" does not include an Amharic text (only English translation), but it does indicate in the prefatory matter that
he quoted "themes" from a range of Ugandan tribal musics; no source is cited for these
melodies. Coe's compositions are written for traditional Ethiopian instruments such
as *kebero* (drum), *washint* (flute), *embilta* (a set of three end-blown flutes), *masenqo*,
krar, and *bagana*. One composition ("Meskel") includes parts for *taiko* (Japanese
drum) and *s'änatsəl* (*tsenatzel*, sistrum).

40. Coe interview.

41. Sutton, "Tezeta," additional notes in PDF on *éthiopiques* 23 CD, 4.

42. Tesfaye interview, August 15, 2007.

43. Sutton, "Tezeta," additional notes in PDF on *éthiopiques* 23 CD, 4.

44. Sutton, "Tezeta," additional notes in PDF on *éthiopiques* 23 CD, 5.

45. Melaku's father later reconciled with his son after attending one of his per-

formances at the Creative Arts Centre. When the orchestra played music from the northern city of Gondar, Melaku was astonished to see his father stand up and sway to the rhythm. He later told his son, "I don't consider this to be an *azmari* or common minstrelsy. This is something else and I give you my blessing" (Melaku G. interview, August 14, 2007).

46. Melaku G. interview, August 14, 2007.

47. See Betelehem Melaku, "In Memory of Melaku Gelaw," at https://bettymelaku music.wixsite.com/mysite/bio.

48. *Melaku Gelaw*, C-Side Entertainment, 2001, compact disc and cassette tape.

49. Melaku G. interview, August 14, 2007. Melaku's wife was a dancer with Orchestra Ethiopia in its early years, and his daughter Betelehem is a musician who trained at the Yared School on Ethiopian instruments and violin. Betelehem today lives in Cambridge, Massachusetts, and performs as a one-woman band for Ethiopian celebrations and weddings (Betelehem interview, August 18, 2007).

50. Getamesay Abebe, interview with author and Charles Sutton, July 18, 2008, Cambridge, MA.

51. See *People to People* Tour, Part 9 at 2:04–2:40 for a solo performance by Getamesay on the *masenqo*, www.youtube.com/watch?v=8pn-wd1xx4I.

52. Getamesay interview.

53. *Reunion* with Charles Sutton, Melaku Gelaw, and Getamesay Abebe, 2007, compact disc.

54. Charles Sutton, interview with author, August 16, 2007, Washington, DC. Tesfaye Lemma also brought in other new personnel for the orchestra. He retained only one singer previously with the ensemble, Almaz Getatchew from Wolleta, who was said to have been "vivacious and feisty." He added two new singers, Teshay Endale and Yeshe Mebrate, both of whom were young and "gave the orchestra some sex appeal." According to Sutton, there was a contrast between them and the very old men who played the *embilta* (Sutton, "Tezeta," additional notes in PDF on *éthiopiques* 23 CD, 5).

55. Tesfaye, quoted by Sutton, "Tezeta," additional notes in PDF on *éthiopiques* 23 CD, 6. Sutton first performed with Orchestra Ethiopia on March 24, 1967.

56. Sutton graduated from Harvard in 1966, although he entered in 1960 and is listed as class of 1964, having taken two years off to study classical guitar in Washington, DC, with Sophocles Papas and jazz guitar at the Berklee College of Music (Sutton interview, August 16, 2007).

57. See Charles Sutton, liner notes to *Reunion* [*Zoro Gät'äm*], self-produced, 2007, compact disc.

58. Sutton, "Tezeta," additional notes in PDF on *éthiopiques* 23 CD, 6.

59. Sutton interview, August 16, 2007.

60. Sutton interview, August 16, 2007.

61. Sutton, "Tezeta," additional notes in PDF on *éthiopiques* 23 CD, 7.

62. Sutton interview, August 16, 2007.

63. Tesfaye interview, August 15, 2007.

64. Sutton, "Tezeta," additional notes in PDF on *éthiopiques* 23 CD, 7.

65. Sutton interview, August 16, 2007. Updated by Charles Sutton, personal communication with author, May 1, 2020.

66. Tesfaye interview, August 15, 2007.

67. Transcribed by author and Sutton from a video clip, courtesy of Charles Sutton.

68. Sutton, "Tezeta," additional notes in PDF on *éthiopiques* 23 CD, 8.

69. Anna Kisselgoff, "Blue Nile Dancers a Peace Corps Find," *New York Times*, March 18, 1969, https://www.nytimes.com/1969/03/18/archives/blue-nile-dancers -a-peace-corps-find.html.

70. Sutton, "Tezeta," additional notes in PDF on *éthiopiques 23* CD, 9.

71. Charles Sutton recalls that "the recording had been made by VOA [Voice of America] folklorist and recordist Leo Sarkesian, who arranged for a thousand LPs to be pressed by Tempo Records in Hollywood. The LPs were shipped to Ethiopia, arriving several months after we came back from the tour. I went to the minister of finance to ask if he would allow the albums to come into the country tax-free, so that all sales proceeds could go to the orchestra. To my surprise, the minister replied that granting such a request would exceed his authority. It could be granted only by the emperor. It was thus that the entire orchestra got an audience with His Imperial Majesty on September 25, 1969, during which, speaking on the orchestra's behalf, I petitioned H.I.M. to allow the free entry of the records into Ethiopia. He consented, saying that he would take care of paying the tax himself. The records sold out almost immediately and now are collectors' items" (Sutton, personal communication, May 1, 2020).

72. Tesfaye recalled sitting in on classes offered by Indiana anthropologist Alan Merriam (Tesfaye interview, August 20, 2007).

73. Tesfaye interview, August 15, 2007.

74. Tesfaye Lemma, *Itəyop'iya muziqa mäsrayawəch mädjmäriya ətəm* [Ethiopian musical instruments] (Addis Ababa: Tesfaye Lemma, 1975). This booklet was evidently funded by ads sponsored by Addis Ababa institutions and businesses and sold for three Ethiopian *birr* at the time of publication. It includes photographs of musical instruments in Tesfaye's personal collection, drawn from central and northern Ethiopia (Shoa, Gondar, Gojjam, Wollo, Tigray), southern Ethiopia (Wollamo, Konso, Gidole), and southwestern Ethiopia (Wollega, Gambela). Short descriptions of each in Amharic and English accompany the photographs. A second booklet was evidently planned (according to the introductory note by Mekbib Kifle on p. 6) but never issued.

75. Tesfaye interview, August 15, 2007.

76. I watched this televised performance at my home in Addis Ababa and recorded it, eventually depositing the recording with my other Ethiopian materials in Harvard University's Archive of World Music. The recording had a surprising afterlife, as did the others I was able to rescue from the threatened Radio Voice of the Gospel archive. In 2006 Sutton drove from Connecticut to meet El-Dabh during the composer's visit to New York City. Although the two had spoken on the phone a few times in the early 2000s, they had never met before. During that visit, El-Dabh's assistant David Badagnani, who had accompanied El-Dabh on the trip, played recordings of the orchestra I earlier had sent to El-Dabh that I had salvaged from Radio Voice of the Gospel. He also played the recording I had made of the Orchestra Ethiopia's 1975 performance of "Mother Ethiopia" on revolutionary television, which I had also sent to El-Dabh; the latter recording caught Sutton's attention. With my permission, Sutton made a copy of my television show recording and shared it with Tesfaye Lemma. Tesfaye was, of course, the composer and director of the orchestra in 1975, but he had been unaware that any recording of this performance had survived. At Badagnani's request and with my gratitude, Tesfaye and Sutton prepared detailed notes on each track I had rescued from Radio Voice of the Gospel, as well as my own revolutionary day recording, in order to ensure that the Harvard Archive had these notes for future scholarly study. Although I had known Tesfaye since meeting him in Ethiopia in 1974 and had seen

him many times over his years in the United States, it never occurred to me to tell him about the spontaneous recording I had made of Orchestra Ethiopia in my Addis Ababa living room. For a fuller discussion of this series of revelations enabled by the survival of archival recordings, see Kay Kaufman Shelemay, "Learning from the Eda Kuhn Loeb Music Library," *Harvard Library Bulletin* 18, nos. 1–2 (2007): 37–41, http://nrs.harvard.edu/urn-3:HUL.InstRepos:34917354. I am grateful to Sutton, Badagnani, and Tesfaye for recognizing the importance of both sets of recordings and providing detailed documentation for future users.

77. Sutton interview, August 16, 2007.

78. Charles Sutton, personal communication with author, February 17, 2008.

79. The City Hall Theatre put their part of the collection in storage, where it was ruined, but the Yared School of Music instrument collection remains on display.

80. Tesfaye interview, August 15, 2007.

81. Simeneh, "Music and Politics," 119.

82. Simeneh, "Music and Politics," 115.

83. Tesfaye interview, August 15, 2007.

84. Three other musicians had defected from the troupe in Washington, DC: Elias Arega, *krar* player; Teka Gulima, drummer; and Getatchew Gebregiorgis, the lead dancer whose story was recounted in chapter 5.

85. Sutton, personal communication, May 1, 2020.

86. Center for Ethiopian Art and Culture By-laws (Washington, DC, 1994), 1–2, in author's collection. CEAC was incorporated a few years earlier in 1991. I thank Charles Sutton for this information (personal communication with author, March 4, 2021). CEAC had a board of directors headed by Tesfaye Lemma as executive director, along with academics specializing in Ethiopian studies, Cynthia Tse Kimberlin, the late University of Chicago sociologist Donald Levine, and myself. Other board members were LaDena Schnapper, the immigration sponsor and "American mother" of dancer Ashenafi Mitiku (chapter 5), and Charles Sutton. Two Ethiopian immigrants on the board were Dr. Tedla W. Giorgis, a psychologist who immigrated to the United States as a teenager and retired early from the position as director of multicultural services division of the Department of Mental Health in Washington, DC, to return to Ethiopia in 2010 as an adviser to the Ethiopian Federal Ministry of Health, and Sara Workeneh, a movement therapist and lecturer in dance movement therapy at the Center for Dance, Music and Theatre at Goucher College in Baltimore, Maryland.

87. Tesfaye Lemma, letter to *Elelta* 2 (1998): 1.

88. Here one can see a close relationship to assemblage theory in tracing relations of interiority (those connecting parents and offspring) to relations of exteriority, not defined by identity but by other, variable parameters (DeLanda, *Assemblage Theory*, 2).

89. Tesfaye Lemma, letter, 1.

90. Program notes for Nile Ethiopian Ensemble Performance, Harvard University, Cambridge MA, November 11, 1994; and Shelemay, field notes, November 11, 1994.

91. "The Nile Ethiopian Ensemble, 1998 Calendar of Events," *Elelta* 2 (1998): 11.

92. Ashenafi interview; Setegn interview. Seleshe Damessae, an accomplished *krar* player who came to the United States in the 1970s, spent a year as artist in residence with the Nile Ethiopian Ensemble during its inaugural year in 1994. He participated in a performance event held for CEAC's "First Anniversary Celebration" (Tesfaye Lemma, *Second Anniversary, September 1996* [Washington, DC: CEAC, 1996], 4).

93. Ashenafi interview.

94. Ashenafi has a network of other Ethiopian dancers in Washington, DC, California, and Denver and connects with other musicians and dancers performing with troupes in Addis Ababa. He has visited Ethiopia several times since coming to the United States (Ashenafi interview).

95. Setegn's first language was a special *azmari argot* known as *yä'ezra kwankwa* (lit., Ezra's language). His family is Amhara and also speaks standard Amharic (Setegn interview).

96. Setegn plays the four *qenyet* but also mentions performing twenty-five *qenyet* "of his own" (Setegn interview). He is said to perform eight types of the *ambasel* mode (Itsushi Kawase, personal communication with author, September 4, 2007, Washington, DC). Setegn presents himself as a composer and an arranger, as well as a singer.

97. Setegn interview.

98. Minale Dagnew Bezu, interview by author, August 13, 2008, Washington, DC. Minale is one of the few musicians who eventually succeeded in working full-time in music, in large part because use of the *krar* in both Ethiopian cultural and popular music is widespread: "Now I'm not doing another work. . . . I'm just a musician, but before when I was with the Nile Ethiopian Orchestra. . . . I used to valet-park at the Marriott Hotel. I was a busboy in Las Vegas at one point for four months."

99. Tesfaye interview, August 20, 2007.

100. Minale interview, August 13, 2008. Tesfaye spent his last years at Rock Creek Manor, a nursing home in Washington, DC. Many friends and fellow musicians visited him during these years, such as the poet Alemtsehay Wedajo, who used to take him out to lunch regularly. Tesfaye deposited his collection of Ethiopian recordings in the archive of the American Folklife Center at the Library of Congress. Charles Sutton served as Tesfaye's legal guardian during his years at Rock Creek Manor, driving down regularly from Connecticut to visit Tesfaye and to handle his affairs. Tesfaye died on February 1, 2013. In May 2013 his book, *Yä'itəyop'iya Muziqa Tarik* [The history of Ethiopian music], was published in Washington, DC; an Ethiopian edition was issued by Shama Books in Addis Ababa. According to an obituary posted by the Ethiopian Heritage Society in North America, Tesfaye Lemma's "artistic achievements and contributions are known throughout Ethiopia and within the Ethiopian Diaspora in the United States and beyond. Consequently, he earned the nick name 'The Father of Traditional Ethiopian Music'" (Ethiopian Heritage Society in North America, "Ethiopia Loss Tesfaye Lemma," press release, February 8, 2013, http://ehsna.org/ethiopia-loss-tesfaye-lemma-ehsna-pr/).

101. Ashenafi has had a regular job dancing at cultural music performances with the ensemble at Dukem Ethiopian Restaurant in Washington, DC, since 2001 (Ashenafi interview).

102. Minale interview, August 13, 2008.

103. Minale interview, August 13, 2008.

104. Tsehay interview, August 9, 2007.

105. Tsehay interview, August 9, 2007.

106. Tsehay interview, August 9, 2007.

107. Tsehay interview, August 9, 2007.

108. Tsehay interview, August 9, 2007.

109. This initiative was in part due to financial pressures, which reduced performances at area restaurants.

110. Shelemay, field notes, August 28–30, 2009, Bangor, ME.

111. Shelemay, field notes, August 28–30, 2009, Bangor, ME.

112. See Levine, *Wax and Gold*, 64–68, for an expansion of this term. See also Donald N. Levine, "On Cultural Creativity in the Ethiopian Diaspora," *Diaspora* 15, nos. 2–3 (2006 [pub. 2011]): 215–20, https://doi.org/10.1353/dsp.2011.0070.

113. Tesfaye Lemma, "CEAC Events," *Elelta* 2 (1998): 11, 13–14.

114. John Sorenson, *Imagining Ethiopia: Struggles for History and Identity in the Horn of Africa* (New Brunswick, NJ: Rutgers University Press, 1993), 38–76.

115. Shelemay, "Learning from the Eda Kuhn Loeb," 37–41.

116. "Who Is Tesfaye Lemma?," *Immigrant Connect Chicago*, http://immigrantconnect .medill.northwestern.edu/blog/2010/07/15/who-is-tesfaye-lemma/.

117. Shelemay, field notes, June 21, 2006, Addis Ababa.

118. Shelemay, field notes, May 24, 2014, Addis Ababa.

119. Abegasu Kibrework Shiota, interview by author, June 20, 2006, Addis Ababa; Shelemay, field notes, December 26, 2017, Addis Ababa.

Chapter Nine

1. Shelemay and Kaplan, "Introduction," 201–3.

2. Kane, *Dictionary*, 2341.

3. Leslau, *Context Dictionary*, 267.

4. A recent monograph compares the Western ideas about creativity to indigenous concepts among *Kangra* female singers in the Himalayas (Kirin Narayan, *Everyday Creativity: Singing Goddesses in the Himalayan Foothills* [Chicago: University of Chicago Press, 2016], 29–30).

5. Melaku Belay, interview by author, May 22, 2014, Addis Ababa.

6. Mulatu Astatke, interview by author and Steven Kaplan, October 23, 2007, Cambridge, MA.

7. Shelemay, "Traveling Music," 307–8.

8. Howard Gardner, *Frames of Mind: The Theory of Multiple Intelligences* (New York: Basic, 2004), xxxi.

9. Renato Rosaldo, Smadar Lavie, and Kirin Narayan, "Introduction: Creativity in Anthropology," in *Creativity/Anthropology*, ed. Smadar Lavie, Kirin Narayan, and Renato Rosaldo (Ithaca, NY: Cornell University Press, 1993), 5.

10. Emirbayer and Mische, "What Is Agency?," 984. The impact of projection is particularly marked in Amharic, where one tense, the imperfect, can convey the present or the future in the main affirmative clause: for example, the verb *yəsäbəral* can mean "he breaks, he is breaking, he will break" (Wolf Leslau, *Amharic Textbook* [Wiesbaden, Ger.: Harrassowitz, 1967], 108). As noted in this volume's preface, agency is *ammakayənnät* (Kane, *Dictionary*, 1260; Leslau, *Context Dictionary*, 30).

11. Telela interview, August 22, 2007.

12. Moges H. interview, August 27, 2007.

13. Woretaw interview.

14. Rebecca Bengal, "Hailu Mergia: The Ethiopian Jazz Legend Who Jams in His Taxi," *Guardian*, March 1, 2018, https://www.theguardian.com/music/2018/mar/01 /hailu-mergia-the-ethiopian-jazz-legend-who-jams-in-his-taxi. *Hailu Mergia and His Classical Instrument*, first released by Tango Recordings, was rereleased by Awesome Tapes from Africa, ATFA006, 2013, compact disc. Hailu Mergia and the Walias,

Tch Belew, Kaifa Records LPKF 45, 1977, LP, first released in Ethiopia, was also re-released in 2014 by Awesome Tapes from Africa, ATFA012, reviving Hailu's career.

15. Drew DiPrinzio, "Hailu Mergia on Music and Memory. The Organ and Accordion Master Reflects on Life before His Upcoming Concert in Washington, D.C.," *Seven Thirty DC*, June 6, 2019, https://medium.com/seventhirty-dc/hailu-mergia -on-music-and-memory-cd491109b35f.

16. Others involved in musical careers discussed doing business such as arranging tours while driving their taxis: "I can do a lot of business while I'm driving . . . I call here and I call there" (Tekle interview).

17. Elizabeth Chacko, "Ethiopian Taxicab Drivers: Forming an Occupational Niche in the US Capital," *African and Black Diaspora* 9, no. 2 (2016): 204, https://doi.org /10.1080/17528631.2015.1083177. The growth of Uber, Lyft, and other new transportation companies has dramatically altered the financial situation of many Ethiopian and other immigrant taxi drivers, especially those who paid for expensive medallions that lost virtually all their value since 2013 (Jack Newsham and Dan Adams, "Amid Fight with Uber, Lyft, Boston Taxi Ridership Plummets," *Boston Globe*, August 19, 2015, https://www.bostonglobe.com/business/2015/08/19/boston-taxi -ridership-down-percent-this-year/S9dZMELMye6puzTTYoDIrL/story.html; Scott Kirsner, "Uber-Lyft Fee to Help Taxi Has So Far Funded Only Consultants," *Boston Globe*, March 29, 2019, https://www.bostonglobe.com/business/2019/03/29 /uber-and-lyft-fee-that-supposed-help-taxi-drivers-has-only-funded-consultants /Tcby2tPg1OpaUazb3TrXtM/story.html).

18. Abraham interview.

19. Mohaammad interview, June 17, 2008.

20. Moges S. interview, August 2, 2007.

21. Behailu interview.

22. Abonesh interview.

23. Hana Shenkute, interview by author, August 30, 2007, Washington, DC. Some older traditional musicians will not perform in clubs or restaurants: "I don't consider it a dignified thing to go into restaurants and drinking houses and play a lot like people do. I don't want to do that. No way will I play in a drinking house or a restaurant. I like to play any place that has distinction and dignity. I choose according to the place and according to the status that it has" (Melaku G. interview, August 14, 2007). Others will not sing in restaurants because they consider it detrimental to their profile as a concert and recording artist or problematic because of ethnic background: "I do not perform in restaurants. I just do concerts and big weddings. . . . An artist should be somewhat reserved for some occasions. Therefore, I don't want to be seen every night. If you go to an Ethiopian restaurant, you can just go and see a musician by drinking beer basically. There is no entrance, there is no nothing . . . I'd rather people come to see me on certain occasions. A lot of restaurants around this area don't think they need Oromo music" (Abdi interview, July 16, 2008).

24. Tekle interview. Indeed, while individuals who hire a famous singer to perform at a wedding gain status from that event, the singer loses status as a result even if the gig brings a financial profit. However, instrumentalists who accompany a singer at a wedding maintain their status because "they are in the background." A small group of promoters mount concerts and sell drinks at those events, but they are generally perceived as lacking in power and do not represent top talent. In contrast, promot-

ers gain power by working with musicians who are starting out and by helping them build their reputations.

25. Woretaw interview. Similar sentiments were expressed by Tsehay (interview, August 9, 2007); Abdi (interview, July 16, 2008); and Wayna (interview, May 30, 2008).

26. Bezawork interview.

27. Alemtsehay Wedajo, interview by author, July 12, 2010, Washington, DC. Poets and lyricists are convened monthly by Alemtsehay, who in August 2000 founded the Tayitu Cultural and Educational Center in Washington, DC (Tayitu.org), which serves as the center of activity in Ethiopian poetry, music, and drama.

28. Mulatu Astatke received an honorary doctorate from the Berklee College of Music on May 12, 2012. Berklee Media Relations, "Eagles, Alison Krauss, Mulatu Astatke Receive Honorary Degrees at Commencement," Berklee press release, May 12, 2012, https://www.berklee.edu/news/4435/eagles-alison-krauss-mulatu-astatke-receive -hono.

29. Mr. Henry's has been located at 601 Pennsylvania Avenue SE, on Capitol Hill since 1966 and has launched the careers of singers such as Roberta Flack (Katherine Flynn, "Mr. Henry's in Washington, D.C.," *National Trust for Historic Preservation*, July 9, 2015, https://savingplaces.org/stories/historic-bars-mr-henrys-in -washington-d-c#.Xd7cApNKiX0).

30. Moges H. interview.

31. Beniam interview.

32. Jamal Sule, interview by author, July 30, 2009, Atlanta, GA.

33. Betelehem interview, August 18, 2007.

34. Melaku G. interview, August 14, 2007.

35. Mesfin interview.

36. Minale interview, August 8, 2007. An increasing number of diaspora Ethiopians also make investments in Ethiopia, especially in single-family housing and in the hospitality sector. See also Yannick Roland Nene Ngoma Tchibinda, "Diaspora Direct Investments: The Challenges of the African Diaspora," *Journal IKSAD* 4, no. 14 (2018): 709, https://dergipark.org.tr/en/pub/iksad/issue/51710/671372; and Elizabeth Chacko and Peter H. Gebre, "Leveraging the Diaspora for Development: Lessons from Ethiopia," *GeoJournal* 78, no. 3 (2013): 495–505, https://doi.org/10.1007 /s10708-012-9447-9.

37. Hana interview.

38. Mesfin interview.

39. Minale interview, August 8, 2007.

40. Yeshimebet interview. See also Kaplan, "Vital Information," 247–63.

41. Kaplan, "Vital Information," 249.

42. Emily Wax, "Ethiopian Yellow Pages: Life, by the Book," Style section *Washington Post*, June 8, 2011, https://www.washingtonpost.com/lifestyle/style/ethiopian -yellow-pages-life-by-the-book/2011/06/01/AGM64YMH_story.html.

43. Yehunie Belay, interview by author, August 22, 2007, Washington, DC.

44. Yehunie interview, August 22, 2007. Yehunie mentioned that there are not many hereditary musicians in the region (Amhara Region, formerly Gojjam province) from which he came and compared his emergence to the story of the sheep and the goat: "The goat bleats louder, so from a sheep family comes a goat!" In 2011 Yehunie was the subject of *Sew Bageru*, a short documentary video that recorded his return to his hometown Fenote Selam decades after his departure ("Yehunie Belay 'Sew Bageru': A

Short Documentary," YouTube, 15:32, posted by *Bawza TV*, March 28, 2012, https://www.youtube.com/watch?v=AQ0hpLU1vvw).

45. Yehunie interview, August 22, 2007; Yehunie Belay, *Alo Lulo*, [self-produced], 1994, compact disc. *Alo Lulo* is a "trilling sound of joy" (Kane, *Dictionary*, 1102).

46. Yehunie, interview by Steven Kaplan, October 26, 2007, Washington, DC.

47. For several years beginning in around 2009, Yehunie opened an Ethiopian restaurant named Little Ethiopia in Washington, DC, where he also performed traditional music. The restaurant closed in the mid-2010s.

48. Yehunie interview, August 22, 2007.

49. Yehunie interview, August 22, 2007.

50. Yehunie interview, July 22, 2007.

51. Yehunie, interview, July 22, 2007.

52. This is one of the nine regional states into which Ethiopia was divided in 1991 at the end of the revolution.

53. Meron Hadero, "To Walk in Their Shoes," in *The Displaced: Refugee Writers on Refugee Lives*, ed. Viet Thanh Nguyen (New York: Abrams, 2018), 84–85.

54. Siddharta Mitter, "For Meklit Hadero, Keeping It Real and Varied," *Boston Globe*, July 10, 2011, http://archive.boston.com/ae/music/articles/2011/07/10/meklit_hadero_forges_ahead_with_vision_and_innovation/.

55. Meklit interview.

56. See Meklit's website, https://www.meklitmusic.com/bio.

57. Meklit interview.

58. See Meklit's website for the lyrics to many of her songs, https://www.meklitmusic.com/lyrics.

59. Meklit Hadero, *On a Day Like This*, Porto Franco Records PFR015, 2010, compact disc.

60. Meklit interview. The song "Feeling Good," composed in 1964 by Anthony Newley and Leslie Bricusse and published by Musical Comedy Productions, entered Meklit's repertory through her engagement with the work of singer Nina Simone, who included a rendition of the song in her 1965 studio album *I Put a Spell on You*, Philips PHS 600-172, 1965, LP. See Patrick Corcoran, "Nina Simone's 'I Put A Spell On You' Turns 55," *Albumism*, May 31, 2020, https://www.albumism.com/features/nina-simone-i-put-a-spell-on-you-turns-55-anniversary-retrospective.

61. The song was popularized by renowned Ethiopian singer Mahmoud Ahmed on the album *Ere Mela Mela*, the long history of which was discussed in chapter 7. "Abbay Mado" is on the original vinyl recordings from 1975 and 1986, as well as on the 1999 *éthiopiques* 7 CD.

62. Meklit, *We Are Alive*, Six Degrees Record 657036 120426, 2014, compact disc.

63. Walter Mosley, "Seeking a Unified Field," liner notes to *We Are Alive*.

64. Product overview of *We Are Alive* by Meklit, *Barnes & Noble*. This webpage is no longer available.

65. *Okayafrica*, "Okayafrica's Top 15 Music Videos of 2015," *Okayafrica*, December 21, 2015, https://www.okayafrica.com/african-music-videos-2015-top-15/?rebelltitem=11#rebelltitem11. See also https://www.meklitmusic.com/press. Meklit's "Kemekem" music video is available on YouTube, 5:25, posted by Meklit, April 21, 2015, https://www.youtube.com/watch?v=qC8feW4gomo.

66. Ytasha L. Womack, *Afrofuturism: The World of Black Sci-Fi and Fantasy Culture* (Chicago: Chicago Review Press, 2013), 9 and 16, citing Mark Dery, "Black to

the Future: Interviews with Samuel R. Delany, Greg Tate, and Tricia Rose," in *Flame Wars: The Discourse of Cyberculture*, ed. Mark Dery (Durham, NC: Duke University Press, 1994), 180.

67. Womack, *Afrofuturism*, 17.

68. Gabriel Teodros (b. 1981) is an Ethiopian American rapper from Seattle and a cousin of Meklit Hadero. Burntface is an African and Black Power collective with two dozen musicians, singers, rappers, web designers, activists, teachers, and visual artists. Burntface was originally an Ethiopian rap group begun by Elias aka "The Profit" while he was in college in Atlanta; they released an underground classic recording *U Abesha?* (Are you Ethiopian?). The rap group grew into a collective that incorporated both Ethiopian and African American rappers with Burntface communities in Elias's base, Los Angeles, as well as Seattle, Houston, New York, New Orleans, San Diego, Tanzania, and Addis Ababa. For more details on Burntface and its "revolutionary marketing," see Elias, "The Burntface Movement: Futuristic African Rap Music," *Tadias Online*, 2003, http://www.tadias.com/v1n5/AE_2_2003-3.html, concerning his use of art as a tool for social awareness and the uplift of Africa as well as "for profit."

69. Gabriel Teodros, "Colored People's Time Machine," YouTube, 2:57, posted by Gabriel Teodros, April 17, 2013, https://www.youtube.com/watch?v=cuIxAkZXsKI. See also Gabriel Teodros, *Colored People's Time Machine*, Fresh Chopped Beats FCB-053; MADK Productions FCB-053, 2012, compact disc.

70. Leigh Bezezekoff, "Song of the Day: Gabriel Teodros—Mind Power," *KEXP*, February 24, 2012 (this article is no longer available online). As described in liner notes to *Earthbound*, Porto Franco Records PFR041, 2012, compact disc, by award-winning science fiction author Nnedi Okorafor, CopperWire members Teodros, Meklit, and Burntface are characters of Ethiopian descent who "journey to Earth in the year 2089 to learn what it means to be human. They include mad scientist Scholar Black (Burntface), alien-human hybrid Getazia (Gabriel Teodros), and interstellar telepath Ko Ai (Meklit Hadero). The album uses metaphors of intergalactic distances to talk about diasporic and cultural connection and disconnection. The album also uses sonified light curves (that is, the sound of stars, processed through Fourier analysis into frequencies that can be heard by humans)" prepared by supernova analyst Jon Jenkins of the SETI Institute and NASA Kepler Mission Labs ("Gabriel Teodros," *Wikipedia*, https://en.wikipedia.org/wiki/Gabriel_Teodros). See also https://copperwire.bandcamp.com/album/earthbound.

71. Meklit, *When the People Move, the Music Moves Too*, Six Degrees Records 657036 126923, 2017, compact disc.

72. Meklit, "Supernova," YouTube, 5:43, posted by Meklit H., July 9, 2018, https://www.youtube.com/watch?v=MvHnrEh63SE.

73. Shelemay, field notes, Meklit in Concert, "This Was Made Here: A Diasporic Odyssey," May 21, 2016, Yerba Buena Center for the Arts, San Francisco, CA. Meklit again sonified Jon Jenkins's SETI data as a model for the structure and construction of this piece of which the listener might otherwise be unaware (Shelemay, field notes, Meklit during Harvard University Residency, March 28, 2019, Cambridge, MA).

74. Meklit Music website, FAQ, https://www.meklitmusic.com/faq.

75. Shelemay, field notes, Meklit during Harvard University Residency, March 26, 2019, Cambridge, MA.

76. Meklit Music website, Story, https://www.meklitmusic.com/bio; Meklit interview.

77. Concert program book, "Meklit Hadero: This Was Made Here: A Diasporic Odyssey," *Yerba Buena Center for the Arts Forum*, San Francisco, CA, May 19–21, 2016, https://ybca.org/wp-content/uploads/2019/07/YBCA_Meklit_Playbill_Final_Web.pdf, 5; Meklit interview. Meklit describes her own moments of creativity as "moments of discipline and mystery," when she "catches" melodies while doing things, such as sitting in silence and listening to the sounds around her: "I keep banks of melodies on my phone," she says. "If I catch a melody, I'll sing it into my phone. Then you don't start with a blank page." Yet, at the same time, Meklit believes that her creative process truly starts with rhythm (Shelemay, field notes, Meklit during Harvard University Residency, March 27 and 28, 2019).

78. Shelemay, field notes, Meklit in Concert, May 21, 2016.

79. Shelemay, field notes, Meklit in Concert, May 21, 2016.

80. Shelemay, field notes, Meklit during Harvard University Residency, March 28, 2019.

81. Shelemay, field notes, Meklit in Concert, May 21, 2016.

82. Shelemay, field notes, Meklit during Harvard University Residency, March 28, 2019.

83. Julie Caine, "The Nile Project: Producing Harmony in Divided Region," *NPR Music*, September 14, 2014, https://www.npr.org/2014/09/14/347733976/the-nile-project-producing-harmony-in-a-divided-region.

84. See Meklit Music website, Culture Projects, "Home [Away From] Home" segment, accessed January 26, 2021, https://www.meklitmusic.com/artsculture.

85. Meklit, "The Unexpected Beauty of Everyday Sounds," TED Fellows Retreat, August 2015, https://www.ted.com/talks/meklit_hadero_the_unexpected_beauty_of_everyday_sounds?language=en.

86. Meklit interview. In September 2019 Meklit assumed the position of Chief of Program at Yerba Buena Center for the Arts, https://ybca.org/person/meklit-hadero/.

87. The first women's choirs, encouraged by Emperor Haile Selassie I, were established in the late 1960s at two religious institutions closely associated with the imperial family, Holy Trinity Cathedral and Beta Maryam Church in Addis Ababa.

88. Tsehai Birhanu, interviews by author, April 12, 2008, and September 17, 2008, Cambridge, MA; Tsehai Birhanu, *Mäzmur Səbhat* [Songs of praise] (Addis Ababa: Ethiopian Orthodox Church, c. 1968 EC). *Merigeta* Tsehai provided me with texts of a number of his hymns during more than a decade of our regular interaction in Cambridge, Massachusetts, until his retirement (celebrated in Cambridge on May 27, 2017) and subsequent departure to live in New Jersey near his children. *Merigeta* Tsehai's initiative occurred during the 1960s when "the spiritual song movement" arose across Ethiopian churches among university students and other young adults. These indigenous spiritual songs (*menfesawi mezmuroch*) were composed by young people and popular among them. It seems likely that the strong impetus for songs of a new genre across Ethiopian Catholic and evangelical churches sparked a response in the Ethiopian Orthodox Church itself (Balisky, *Songs of Ethiopia's Tesfaye Gabbiso*, 3).

89. *Merigeta* Tsehai served as an official of the Ethiopian Orthodox Church while it was under extreme pressure during the Ethiopian revolution. Composers of Christian hymns such as Tesfaye Gabbiso of the evangelical Kale Heywet Church spent years in prison from 1979 to 1987 (Balisky, *Songs of Ethiopia's Tesfaye Gabbiso*, 83).

90. Tsehai Birhanu, interview by author, October 26, 2010, Cambridge, MA.

91. One cleric who grew up in the church during the years of the revolution (b. 1972) and both taught in the Sunday school and trained a Sunday school youth choir, credited Emperor Haile Selassie I with having encouraged the establishment of Sunday schools at Meskaye Hizunan Medhane Alem Monastery High School, which he attended in order to attract youth to be engaged in the church. "He brought some ecclesiastical scholars to teach the youth a modern way of singing in the church . . . You know, these high-ranking communities sent their children into high school and then they are reluctant to attend religious ceremonies and to participate in churches. So he [Emperor Haile Selassie I] knew all the psychology, and then, in a very special way, he drew their attention into the church" (Getahun interview).

92. Tsehai interview, October 26, 2010.

93. Shelemay, "Musician and Transmission of Religious Tradition," 242–60.

94. Tsehai interview, November 26, 2010.

95. Tsehai interview, October 26, 2010.

96. Gabriel Alemayehu, interview by author, October 26, 2010, Cambridge, MA.

97. Tsehai interview, October 26, 2010.

98. Women with professions outside the church have made great contributions. Tenisay "Mary" Alemu Walker, a hairdresser in the Boston metropolitan area, put up her house as collateral for the building purchased by the St. Michael EOT Church in Mattapan, Boston, acknowledging that "there are a lot of women who have done a lot in the church" (Tenisay "Mary" Alemu Walker, interview by author, January 14, 2007, Cambridge, MA). Women already had performed as choir singers, *bagana* players, and on the *kebero*, but their roles increased during the 1980s in diaspora. When *merigeta* Tsehai arrived in Boston in 2003, he invited accountant Abebaye Lema to begin the St. Michael choir (Abebaye Lema, interview by author, August 8, 2006, Cambridge, MA). In Indianapolis, chemist Aster Bekele founded her own church (Aster Bekele, telephone interview by author, August 24, 2015). All three are women who practice other professions but who are active in creating institutional structures and empowering change.

99. Dawit interview.

100. Initially, there was significant backlash against this program, according to one of the participating youths.

101. Shelemay, field notes, May 30, 2008, Washington, DC; *Yäqəddus Yared Mättasäbiya Bä'əwuq Yäkinut'əbäb Säwoch* [Holy Yared's memorial with well-known artists], c. 2008, DVD. Fundraisers have been held as well by DHK Gabriel Church in Atlanta (Dawit interview).

102. Singers included Bezawork Asfaw, Yehunie Belay, and Abonesh Adinew, and instrumentalists included Minale Dagnew Bezu and Setegn Atanaw.

103. Minale interview, January 7, 2008. Some older singers, however, still do not approve of the fusion of popular and sacred repertories and refuse to participate in events like the DHK Gabriel benefit (Telela interview, August 22, 2007).

Chapter Ten

1. I use the word *horizon* here in its conventional English meaning while acknowledging the importance of the term to Edmund Husserl's phenomenology, in which *horizon* is extended to include "co-given aspects," including internal horizon and external horizon (Joel Smith, "Phenomenology," *Internet Encyclopedia of Philosophy*, https://www.iep.utm.edu/phenom/).

2. Michel Maffesoli, *The Time of the Tribes: The Decline of Individualism in Mass Society* (London: Sage, 1996), 18; Kay Kaufman Shelemay, "Musical Communities: Rethinking the Collective in Music," *Journal of the American Musicological Society* 64, no. 2 (2011): 349–90, https://doi.org/10.1525/jams.2011.64.2.349. Here the experience of decades in a new environment produces unfamiliar sensibilities, transforming local attachments into emotions.

3. Stéphane Dufoix, *Diasporas*, trans. William Rodarmor (Berkeley: University of California Press, 2008): 62–64. Dufoix proposes four "ideal types" of diaspora categorized by the collective experience with the homeland: centroperipheral mode (where the diaspora community is in a host country closely linked with the original homeland); enclaved mode (which operates locally and has networks of like associations, but not linked by formal nationality); atopic mode (which recognizes their common origin but links to several countries and not to a single homeland); and antagonistic mode (an exile polity, formed by groups who refuse to recognize the current regime in their country of origin). Ethiopian diaspora communities may be said to occupy a continuum, with those who left during the revolution clearly well within the antagonistic mode, and with degrees of antagonistic relationship with the homeland that vary with the date and circumstance of departure as well as ethnic origin. Other factors, such as the independence of Eritrea, has shifted diaspora-homeland relations, as has the establishment of ethnic federalism in the mid-1990s.

4. Reuters, "Africa's Youngest Leader Is Riding a Wave of Hope from the Young People Who Got Him There," *Free Zone Channel*, June 2, 2018.

5. UNESCO, "World Press Freedom Day 2019: H. E. Dr. Abiy Ahmed," UNESCO, https://en.unesco.org/world-press-freedom-day-2019/he-dr-abiy-ahmed.

6. Abdi Latif Dahir, "Ethiopia's New 50% Women Cabinet Isn't Just Bold—It's Smart," *Quartz Africa*, October 16, 2018, https://qz.com/africa/1426110/ethiopias -new-cabinet-is-50-women/; Laurel Wamsley, "Ethiopia Gets Its 1st Female President," *NPR*, October 25, 2018, https://www.npr.org/2018/10/25/660618139 /ethiopia-gets-its-first-female-president.

7. Daniel Otieno, "After Making Peace, Ethiopia and Eritrea Now Focus on Development," *Africa Renewal*, December 2018, https://www.un.org/africarenewal /magazine/december-2018-march-2019/after-making-peace-ethiopia-and-eritrea -now-focus-development. The Eritrean diaspora also saw the truce as opening up a possibility for them to return home. The Eritrean diaspora is global, including approximately one hundred seventy thousand Eritrean refugees living in Ethiopia, across the Middle East, and in Europe, as well as large numbers in the United States (Caron Creighton, "Eritrean Diaspora Watches Ethiopia Thaw with Hope, Mistrust," *AP News*, July 21, 2018, https://apnews.com/e03f26d58dea4fe2a442a9fe0a8925a4).

8. Ed Cropley, "As Ethiopia's 'Wall' Comes Down, Exiles Dream of Going Home," *Reuters World News*, July 20, 2018, https://www.reuters.com/article/us-ethiopia -diaspora-idUSKBN1KA1W5; Ezega staff reporter, "Eight Ethiopian Political Parties Sign to Join Prosperity Party," *Ezega News*, December 1, 2019, https://www.ezega .com/News/NewsDetails/7501/Eight-Ethiopian-Political-Parties-Sign-to-Join -Prosperity-Party. This agreement established the new Prosperity Party to succeed the former ruling party, EPRDF.

9. Haleluya Hadero, "Ethiopia's Financial Reforms Hold Promise for Its Diaspora Business Community," *Quartz Africa*, August 10, 2019, https://qz.com/africa /1684528/ethiopia-opens-financial-sector-investments-to-diaspora/.

10. Rebecca Haile, who left Ethiopia suddenly and under violent circumstances in 1976 at the age of ten for asylum in the United States, first returned in May 2001, twenty-five years later. She writes of her own ambivalent, dual diaspora identity, neither fully American nor fully Ethiopian, and dedicates her book to the second generation, "to my children and their cousins, who will decide for themselves how to define their relationship to Ethiopia" (Rebecca G. Haile, *Held at a Distance: My Rediscovery of Ethiopia* [Chicago: Academy Chicago, 2007]).

11. Russell King and Anastasia Christou, "Of Counter-diaspora and Reverse Transnationalism: Return Mobilities to and from the Ancestral Homeland," *Mobilities* 6, no. 4 (2011): 456, https://doi.org/10.1080/17450101.2011.603941. Studies of young Vietnamese who immigrated to the United States during the mid-1970s (contemporaneous with the immigration of the first Ethiopians displaced by the revolution), and who then later returned to Vietnam, confronted the paradox that the returnees were disappointed to find that they felt like foreigners at home (Deborah Reed-Danahay, "'Like a Foreigner in My Own Homeland': Writing the Dilemmas of Return in the Vietnamese American Diaspora," *Identities* 22, no. 5 [2015]: 603, https://doi.org/10.1080/1070289X.2014.975713).

12. King and Christou, "Of Counter-diaspora," 452.

13. American-born Ethiopians of the second generation and those brought to the United States as babies or in early childhood tend to have incorporated US notions of race into their lives. Sonya Damtew, who arrived in Portland, Oregon, from Ethiopia at the age of sixteen in 1978 recalls, "Before coming here, I understood class and gender. . . . Race I had to learn. I had to learn it the hard way. . . . African American is birth and tradition, but it's also who people say you are. . . . It's not enough to be African, because that's just who you are by yourself. If you are African American, then you are part of a community" (Nikole Hannah-Jones, "African Immigrants Help Shape Portland's Small Black Community," *Oregonian*, January 19, 2009, https://www.oregonlive.com/news/2009/01/african_immigrants_help_shape.html). Yet diasporic creativity can accommodate a dual African and African American identity in unexpected ways, as the case of Mulugeta Abate's Seattle restaurant Lovage (which closed in 2017) demonstrated: "I do an East African bowl, I call it an East African bowl and it's probably the closest thing. I take collard greens, and either beef or lamb, for most of the bowls here we do rice, quinoa, rice noodles. For that bowl, I'd do a little bit of *injera*. . . . I think the first exposure people have to a culture is either through music or through food." Transcribed from a video interview in Aida Solomon, "I Am Ethiopia: The Fusion Flavors of Chef Mulugeta Abate," *Seattle Globalist*, August 5, 2014, https://www.seattleglobalist.com/2014/08/05/ethiopia-chef-mulugeta-abate-lovage/28199.

14. King and Christou, "Of Counter-diaspora," 458–59.

15. Abraham interview.

16. Getahun interview.

17. Anders Kelto, "Ethiopia's Economy Benefits from Returning Diaspora," *Public Radio International: The World*, February 20, 2013, https://www.pri.org/stories/2013-02-20/ethiopias-economy-benefits-returning-diaspora.

18. Publication for CEAC Second Anniversary Celebration (Washington, DC, September 1996), 4; Seleshe Damessae, *Tesfaye: A Future Hope*, Music of the World CDT-107, 1994, compact disc reissue, first released in Canada in 1987.

19. Dagnachew Teklu, "Ethiopia: International Year of Volunteers Launched," *Daily*

Monitor, December 18, 2000, https://allafrica.com/stories/200012180129.html. See also Angel Romero, "Artist Profiles: Seleshe Damessae," *World Music Central*, August 21, 2016, https://worldmusiccentral.org/tag/gashe-abera-molla/.

20. Shelemay, field notes, May 21, 2014, Addis Ababa.

21. Nita Bhalla, "Cleaning Up the Streets of Addis," *BBC News*, May 8, 2001, http://news.bbc.co.uk/2/hi/africa/1319359.stm, which contains photographs of several important sites transformed by the Gashe Abera Molla project.

22. Melaku B. interview, May 22, 2014.

23. Melaku B. interview, May 22, 2014.

24. Minale interview, August 8, 2007; Sayem interview.

25. Moges H. interview.

26. Mohaammad interview.

27. Moges S., interview, August 2, 2007. Most of the choirs performing Sunday school songs at Ethiopian American churches wear robes ordered from and manufactured in Ethiopia.

28. Mohaammad interview.

29. Admas, *Indigo Sun*, C-Side Entertainment, 2000, compact disc.

30. Notable among their early productions was Aster Aweke's introductory international CD, *Aster*.

31. Abegasu, Henock, and Thomas "Tommy T" interviews, March 7, 2003. Western music also entered Ethiopia through the presence of US troops at Kagnew Station in Eritrea. Abegasu recalled that before the revolution "there were a lot of Americans living and working and teaching. We got a lot of music even in our radio stations, in the national radio program that was playing Top 40 music. That was interrupted and we didn't get anything for a long time. After that, when the military government took over, they didn't want anything coming from the West. I left a little later, so I was here anyway, now it's open again and there is open access to music from here [the West]."

32. Abegasu and Henock interviews, March 7, 2003.

33. The BBC Two documentary, *Under African Skies: Ethiopia*, begins with a short clip of Aster Aweke walking along a street in Washington, DC, and then singing in a concert; she is accompanied by a backup band including Abegasu and Henock (Abegasu and Henock interviews, March 7, 2003). See also chapter 7, n. 53, for the YouTube link.

34. Henock interview, March 7, 2003.

35. During a session of dialogical editing with Abegasu and Henock in Addis Ababa on January 14, 2020, the two mentioned that they had originally founded Admas with Tewodros Aklilu, a keyboardist who performed with the band from 1984 to 1987 (Abegasu Kibrework Shiota and Henock Temesgen, personal communications with author, January 14, 2020, Addis Ababa; Field notes, January 14, 2020, Addis Ababa). Tewodros has performed since 2009 with the Abugida Band that backs up Ethiopian songwriter and performer Teddy Afro. See Tewodros's LinkedIn page: https://www.linkedin.com/in/tewodros-aklilu-20a70261.

36. Zakki interview.

37. No recordings survive of Rosetta Josef's performances, although Zakki has strong memories of regular coffee ceremonies at their homes abroad in which expatriate wives would gather over coffee, incense would be burning, and his mother would play her *krar* and sing. "Just wonderful memories," recalled Zakki (Zakki interview).

38. Zakki interview. Because there were no English middle schools in Cairo after

their move to Egypt, Zakki and his elder brother were sent back to Ethiopia for school, but because of the dangerous situation, they were moved to stay with their uncle, a priest in a Catholic monastery near Debre Birhan in the Rift Valley.

39. Zakki interview.

40. Admas, *Indigo Sun*.

41. The 1998–2000 war over the Ethiopian-Eritrean border area.

42. Henock interview, March 7, 2003.

43. Dedication on Admas, *Indigo Sun* CD cover. The Ethiopian-Eritrean war from 1998 to 2000, fought at great cost of life and resources over desolate border lands, was not formally resolved until 2018. Several songs from *Indigo Sun* are available for listening on https://myspace.com/admasband/music/album/indigo-sun-3024277.

44. Liner notes to Admas, *Indigo Sun*.

45. Admas's debut album, *Sons of Ethiopia*, originally issued as one thousand vinyl copies in 1984 that quickly went out of print (African Heritage Records AR-1001, 1984, LP) was reissued by Frederiksberg Records FRB 007 in 2020. The original recording can be heard online at YouTube, 39:36, posted by Cream Over Misery, December 3, 2016, https://www.youtube.com/watch?v=RcX5tnFX5rE. For a review of *Admas: Sons of Ethiopia*, see Chris Richards, "In 1984, These D.C. Ethiopian Expats Made a Truly Rare Record. Now the World Can Hear It," *Washington Post*, Style, July 30, 2020, https://www.washingtonpost.com/lifestyle/style/in-1984-these-dc-ethiopian-expats-made-a-truly-rare-record-now-the-world-can-hear-it/2020/07/29/837911c0-d0e7-11ea-8d32-1ebf4e9d8e0d_story.html. I thank Hedy Bookin-Weiner for bringing Richards's article to my attention. An Admas album produced in the early 2000s by Bill Laswell was never released.

46. Liner notes to Admas, *Indigo Sun*.

47. Abegasu Kibrework Shiota, interview by author, May 24, 2014, Addis Ababa.

48. The Addis Ababa Sheraton Hotel was built and owned by Sheikh Mohammed Hussein Al-Amoudi, who had an Ethiopian mother and a Yemini father. Al-Amoudi, who was under detention in Saudi Arabia from November 2017 until late January 2019, supported the work of many musicians who returned from diaspora, hiring many to perform at the Sheraton Hotel (Yohannes Anberbir and Summer Said, "Saudi Arabia Releases Ethiopian Billionaire Al Amoudi," *Wall Street Journal*, January 27, 2019, https://www.wsj.com/articles/saudi-arabia-releases-ethiopian-billionaire-al-amoudi-11548614361).

49. Henock Temesgen, interview by author, May 25, 2014, Addis Ababa.

50. Henock interview, May 25, 2014.

51. Henock interview, May 25, 2014.

52. Founders webpage, Jazzamba School of Music, https://jazzambaschoolofmusic.org/jazzamba-founders. In 2015 Henock also established a biweekly group called Debo (Coming together) that has continued with weekly sessions at the Ghion Hotel (Danny Mekonnen, personal communication with author, April 23, 2015, Cambridge, MA; Henock, personal communication, January 14, 2020).

53. Girum Mezmur, interview by author, May 20, 2014, Addis Ababa.

54. Girum Mezmur, interviews by author, May 28, 2014, and January 17, 2020, Addis Ababa; Henock personal communication, January 14, 2020.

55. Zakki interview.

56. Zakki interview.

57. *Zedicus*, C-Side Entertainment 783707153704, 2005, compact disc.

58. Zakki interview. During the early years of Zakki's band, Tommy T Gobena, the brother of Henock Temesgen, performed as the bass player. Tommy T then moved on to join Gogol Bordello, a well-known ensemble that draws on Gypsy music, cabaret, and punk traditions. Tommy T has also published his own albums, including *The Prester John Sessions*, Easy Star Records ES-1021, 2009, compact disc, based on Ethiopian traditional music mixed with funk, jazz, dub, and reggae. Tommy T has made significant contributions as a sentinel musician, notably as UNICEF's national ambassador to Ethiopia: "Tommy's ambassadorship has come at a time when UNICEF Ethiopia is seeking to engage with a wide range of the diaspora groups to get their understanding and support for children's issues in Ethiopia. . . . They can relay information fast to their communities and have also a strong awareness raising capacity" ("UNICEF Appoints Thomas 'Tommy T' Gobena as Its National Ambassador to Ethiopia," *UNICEF Ethiopia*, October 14, 2015, https://unicefethiopia.wordpress .com/2015/10/14/unicef-ethiopia-appoints-thomas-tommy-t-gobena-as-its-new -ambassador/).

59. Zakki interview.

60. *Zedicus*, track 11, "Standing in the Middle."

61. Zakki interview.

62. Zakki interview.

63. *Zedicus*, track 3, "Long Road."

64. Nyabinghi is the name of both a Rastafarian ritual and the sacred music for drums played at that ritual (Giulia Bonacci, "Rastafari/Rastafarianism," *EAe*, 4:339).

65. *Zedicus*, track 5, "Rebel Soul."

66. See restaurant website at https://www.busboysandpoets.com.

67. Shelemay, field notes, June 25, 2008, Washington, DC.

68. Liner notes to Wayna Wondwossen, *Moments of Clarity*, book 1, Quiet Power Productions 825346715629, 2004, compact disc.

69. Wayna interview, May 30, 2008.

70. Wayna interview, May 30, 2008.

71. Wayna had been baptized in the Ethiopian Orthodox Church.

72. Wayna interview, May 30, 2008. During her 2006–7 visit to Addis Ababa, Wayna also performed several shows with Abegasu and his band at the Addis Ababa Hilton, the Sheraton, and at the Alliance Ethio-Française.

73. Wayna Wondwossen, *Higher Ground*, Quiet Power Productions 4621, 2008, compact disc.

74. Wayna interview, May 30, 2008; *The Expats*, Y2 Music, 2013, compact disc.

75. Wayna's performance of "Tizita" with Stevie Wonder, 2015 *Songs in the Key of Life Tour*, on YouTube, 4:00, posted by Ethiobeats, October 6, 2015, https://www .youtube.com/watch?v=Iz7HhVEKoDM.

76. Wayna interview, May 30, 2008.

77. Munit interview. I thank Munit for corrections offered to this biography in a communication with me on October 19, 2020.

78. *Jörg and Munit: Just the Two of Us, Live at the Coffee House*, [self-produced] 2008, compact disc; *Munit + Jörg 2*, [self-produced] 2013, digital. See also https:// munitandjorg.bandcamp.com/album/munit-jorg-2. In 2014 Jörg returned to Germany.

79. Jolly Papa, "Jolly Papa Interview: Munit Mesfin," *Jolly Papa*, April 10, 2019, https://www.mixcloud.com/JollyPapa/munit-mesfin-jolly-papa-interview/.

80. Munit sought to raise funds on Indiegogo in 2018 to underwrite *Munit: The Solo Album, Positive Vibes Project*, self-produced, 2018–19. See Jolly Papa, "Jolly Papa Interview: Munit Mesfin."

81. Jolly Papa, "Jolly Papa Interview: Munit Mesfin."

82. Gershon remembers receiving the LP in 1988 or 1989 from a friend. Russ Gershon, interview by author, August 16, 2010, Cambridge, MA.

83. *Ethiopian Groove: The Golden Seventies*, Blue Silver Records BSD 195, 1994, compact disc. I thank Francis Falceto for clarifying Russ Gershon's second source (Francis Falceto, Personal communication with author, September 13, 2020). "It blew my mind," said Gershon, who got it from a friend who had picked up the recording in France (Gershon interview, August 16, 2010).

84. Either/Orchestra, *More Beautiful than Death*, Accurate Records AC 3282, 2000, compact disc.

85. Francis Falceto, "This Is Ethiopian Music," liner notes to *éthiopiques 20: Either/ Orchestra. Live in Addis*, Buda Musique 860121, 2005, compact disc, 17–21.

86. Gershon interview, August 16, 2010.

87. Russ Gershon, "Ten Americans in Addis," liner notes to *éthiopiques 20*, 24. While in Addis Ababa, the Either/Orchestra met Mulatu Astatke, who sat in as a guest playing percussion and vibes at their concert; Mulatu is heard on *éthiopiques 20* on track 3 of CD 2 in the song "Keset Eswa Betcha." Mulatu performed in concert with the Either/Orchestra on September 29, 2007, at the Somerville Theatre in Somerville, Massachusetts (Gershon interview, August 16, 2010).

88. "Musiqawi Silt," composed by Girma Beyene and performed by the Walias Band, is on *éthiopiques 13: Ethiopian Groove, the Golden Seventies*, Buda Musique 822552, 2003, compact disc.

89. Shelemay, field notes, January 28, 2006, Boston, MA. All three musicians had performed for years at Dukem Ethiopian Restaurant in Washington, DC, Hana singing late-night popular music and jazz on weekends from 11 p.m. until 3 a.m., and Minale and Setegn joining a traditional singer, drummer, and dancers on Wednesday nights for a "cultural show." Here other musical networks overlap: Hana Shenkute, *Hana*, AIT Records AIT004, 1995, compact disc, was produced and arranged by Henock Temesgen.

90. Mulatu Astatke's score for Jim Jarmusch's film *Broken Flowers* is discussed in chapter 7. See also the beginning of chapter 2 for a description of a "secret" Either/ Orchestra concert at the Lily Pad in Cambridge, Massachusetts (Shelemay, field notes, July 15, 2010, Cambridge, MA).

91. Russ Gershon, interview by author, January 27, 2006, Cambridge, MA.

92. Gershon, interview, January 27, 2006.

93. Shelemay, field notes, January 27, 2006, Somerville, MA.

94. Shelemay, field notes, January 27, 2006, Somerville, MA. Hana, who arrived in the United States from Ethiopia in 1994, remarked that she had enjoyed performing with the Either/Orchestra, which was her first experience working with American musicians: "I liked it, it changed and challenged me" (Hana interview).

95. Shelemay, field notes, January 27, 2006, Somerville, MA, and January 28, 2006, Boston, MA.

96. Hana performed in the costumes regularly used by the cultural dancers in the

Dukem folklore show, which she evidently had borrowed for the Boston performances. She wore a traditional long white cotton dress with embroidery for the Tigray segment with a *nät'älla* (small cloth shawl) covering her hair. For the Oromo number, she changed to a brown dress decorated with cowrie shells with one shoulder bare. The final segment was from Gurage tradition, for which she wore pants under a short dress along with a turban on her head. Hana performed dance motions associated with each ethnic group as she sang their songs (Shelemay, field notes, January 28, 2006, Boston, MA).

97. Aram Arkun, "Intercontinental Mélange: From Ethiopia to Watertown via Jerusalem and Either/Orchestra," *Armenian Mirror-Spectator*, February 23, 2017, https://mirrorspectator.com/2017/02/23/intercontinental-melange-from-ethiopia-to-watertown-via-jerusalem-and-eitherorchestra/.

98. Danny A. Mekonnen, "Ethio-Groove on the World-Stage: Music, Mobility, Mediation," *Callaloo* 33, no. 1 (2010): 299–313, www.jstor.org/stable/40732822.

99. *Noise and Chill Out: Ethiopian Groove Worldwide*, ÉthioSonic 860215, 2012, compact disc. For an overview of the musicians from across the globe presented on *Noise and Chill Out*, see Francis Falceto's liner notes to the two-CD set, with twenty-eight tracks representing both released and unreleased cuts from ensembles such as the Imperial Tiger Orchestra of Switzerland performing Mulatu's Ethio-jazz and the Kronos Quartet presenting an arrangement based on a song performed by Getatchew Mekuria.

100. Danny, "Ethio-Groove on the World-Stage," 301.

101. See the discussion in chapter 7 about Getatchew Mekuria's performance with The Ex, including saxophone versions of the *shillela* and *tizita* (Shelemay, field notes, Middle East Nightclub, December 12, 2006, Cambridge, MA). Both the 2006 and 2012 CDs by The Ex gave Getatchew top billing on the cover.

102. Getatchew Mekuria, liner notes to *Getatchew Mekuria, The Ex and Guests, Moa Anbessa*, Terp Records AS11, 2006, compact disc, 5. In 2014, when Getatchew was no longer well enough to travel, The Ex organized a "Celebration of Getatchew Mekuria" concert series in Ethiopia and in 2017 published a photobook in a final tribute to him: The Ex, *Getatchew Mekuria (1935–2016), the Lion of Ethiopian Saxophone: A Lifelong Musical History in Photos, from the Municipality Band to The Ex* (Amsterdam: Terp Records and Ex Records, 2017).

103. The concert was titled "The Ex: 40 Years, the Ethiopia Connection, Special Guests Fendika and Circus Debre Berhan." In 1991 circus troupes in Ethiopia were introduced by two expatriates working with Ethiopian Jewish children in Addis Ababa shortly before they were airlifted to Israel, a practice that quickly spread and led to the establishment by 1993 of more than a dozen troupes nationwide. For a discussion of the postrevolutionary Ethiopian circus tradition, which primarily involves acrobatics, juggling, costumes, music, and dance but no animals nor high wire acts, see Niederstadt, "Fighting HIV with Juggling Clubs," 77.

104. Others who have returned include Hana Shenkute in 2010. Abonesh Adinew returned to Ethiopia after the traumatic closure of her Washington, DC, restaurant and opened a café in Addis Ababa (Henock and Abegasu, personal communications, January 14, 2020).

105. Even as late as 2016, Oromo musicians were charged with terrorism for "inciting song lyrics" and were imprisoned (Endalk, "Ethiopian Musicians Charged with Terrorism for 'Inciting' Song Lyrics," *Advox Global Voices*, July 14, 2017, https://advox.globalvoices.org/2017/07/14/ethiopian-musicians-charged-with-terrorism

-for-inciting-song-lyrics/). However, the call by Prime Minister Abiy Ahmed to diaspora Oromo to return home has had a positive impact on Oromo musicians.

106. Tesfaye interview, August 20, 2007.

107. Henock interview, March 7, 2003.

Afterword

1. *BBC News*, "Hachalu Hundessa: Deadly Protests Erupt after Ethiopian Singer Killed," June 30, 2020, https://www.bbc.com/news/world-africa-53233531; Bekele Atoma, "More than an Entertainer," *BBC News*, BBC Afaan Oromo, June 30, 2020, https://www.bbc.com/news/world-africa-53233531; and *BBC News*, "Hachalu Hundessa: 'Eighty-One Killed' in Protests over Ethiopian Singer's Death," July 1, 2020, https://www.bbc.com/news/world-africa-53243325.

2. Hachalu Hundessa, *Sanyii Mootii* (Race of the king), was released in Ethiopia in 2009. The music video can be viewed on YouTube, 5:50, posted by Eyoss, n.d., https://www.youtube.com/watch?v=GkHrvbHD9Vo. See also *BBC News*, "Hachalu Hundessa: Ethiopia Singer Buried amid Ethnic Unrest," July 2, 2020, https://www.bbc.com/news/world-africa-53262998.

3. The evidence from multiple biographies, following the methods of prosopography, allows us to establish shared patterns and concerns.

4. Shelemay, "Musician and Transmission of Religious Tradition," 242–60.

5. Wayna interview, May 30, 2008.

6. We have also witnessed the remarkable creativity and contributions of foreign musicians active in Ethiopia, most notably that of the American Peace Corps volunteer Charles Sutton, who, beyond performing as a virtuoso on the *masenqo* for audiences internationally, intervened to garner financial support to rescue Orchestra Ethiopia during several periods of crisis. Sutton also extended himself beyond all measure as a friend and personal guide for Ethiopian musicians who migrated to the United States, most prominently for Tesfaye.

7. Selam Seyoum Woldemariam, personal communication with author, June 16, 2020. Selam founded and participated in a number of bands over two decades in diaspora, performing regularly for eight years as Selamino at restaurants in the DC metropolitan area.

8. Selam, personal communication, June 16, 2020.

9. Aster A. interview.

10. Bruce Eskowitz (COO, Red Light Management), personal communication with author, November 19, 2019, Boston, MA.

11. Hank Bordowitz, *Noise of the World: Non-Western Musicians in Their Own Words* (Brooklyn, NY: Soft Skull, 2004), 167–72.

12. Danielson, *Voice of Egypt*.

13. Virginia Danielson, "Performance, Political Identity, and Memory: Umm Kulthum and Gamal Abd al-Nasir," in *Images of Enchantment: Visual and Performing Arts in the Middle East*, ed. Sherifa Zuhur (Cairo: American University in Cairo Press, 1998), 116.

14. Nathan Farrell, "Celebrity Politics: Bono, Product (RED) and the Legitimising of Philanthrocapitalism," *British Journal of Politics and International Relations* 14, no. 3 (August 2012): 392–406.

15. I thank my former advisee, Stephanie Lui, who introduced me to the Pacific

Music Festival as the subject of her Harvard senior thesis in 2005. The Pacific Music Festival has been held every summer since its inception until the period of the pandemic, hosting more than 3,600 musicians from seventy-seven countries and regions from the classical music world. See https://www.pmf.or.jp/en/.

16. See www.silkroad.org for an overview of the organization's efforts.

17. Ganavya Iyer Doraiswamy, personal communication with author, March 28, 2016, Los Angeles, CA.

18. I thank Margot Fassler and Daniel Neumann for suggesting that I investigate European watchmen and dawn song traditions, as well as for providing sources. See David Klausner, "Civic Musicians in Wales and the Marches, 1430–1642" in *Music and Medieval Manuscripts: Paleography and Performance; Essays Dedicated to Andrew Hughes*, ed. John Haines and Randall Rosenfeld (Aldershot, UK: Ashgate, 2004), 279–99.

19. Klausner, "Civic Musicians," 279–99. In seventeenth- and eighteenth-century Germany, town musicians were "part of a network of civic employees that helped guard the town from outside attack, keep peace within the walls, and warn inhabitants of fires and threats from outside. The network included bell ringers, night watchmen, gate guards, callers of hours, alarm sounders, civic drummers, and musical tower guards (*Türmer*). These varied employees communicated by making sounds of one kind or another with bells, trumpets, drums, clappers, and their voices" (Tanya Kevorkian, "Town Musicians in Baroque Society and Culture," *German History* 30, no. 3 [2012]: 355, https://doi.org/10.1093/gerhis/ghs048). There were also early watch traditions that involved dawn-songs (*albas*) from courtly France that included stock elements such as the watchman's warning song; similar but independent traditions are found in Germany and England. See Paul Battles, "Chaucer and the Traditions of Dawn-Song," *Chaucer Review* 31, no. 4 (1997): 318–19, https://www.jstor.org/stable/25095986.

20. Richard Rastall, "Wait [wayt, wayte]," *Grove Music Online*, 2001, https://www.doi.org/10.1093/gmo/9781561592630.article.29801.

21. Helen Lawlor, personal communication with author, October 23, 2017. See also Declan Kiberd and P. J. Mathews, *Handbook of the Irish Revival: An Anthology of Irish Cultural and Political Writings 1891–1922* (Dublin: Abbey Theatre Press, 2015), 380. Also see Bríona Nic Dhiarmada, *The 1916 Irish Rebellion* (Notre Dame, IN: Notre Dame Press, 2016). I thank Helen Lawlor for suggesting sources on this subject.

22. I thank Philip Bohlman, who suggested this parallel. See Ari Teperberg, "Dan Hashomer (Dan the Guard), Opera, Op.158 (1941–2)," *Marc Lavry Heritage Society*, http://www.marclavry.org/2011/06/01/dan-hashomer-dan-guard-opera-op-158/.

23. Oz Almog, *The Sabra: The Creation of the New Jew*, trans. Haim Watzman (Berkeley: University of California Press, 2000), 239. See also Jardena Gertler-Jaffe, "With Song and Hard Work: Shirei Eretz Yisrael and the Social Imaginary," *University of Toronto Journal of Jewish Thought* 6 (2017): 131–52, which details ways in which these songs, and their composers and performers, established new social networks and were instrumental in forming the Israeli national culture after the War for Independence (1947–49). A major source on music and culture in Israel also suggests that the songs of the land of Israel and their accompanying performance rituals based on communal singing became one of the great signifiers of its period and of emerging Israeli national culture (Motti Regev and Edwin Seroussi, *Popular Music and National Culture in Israel* [Berkeley: University of California Press, 2004], 17–18). Of relevance here is that many of the composers of these songs were immigrants to Palestine from eastern and central Europe (Regev and Seroussi, *Popular Music*, 142).

24. I thank Selam Seyoum Woldemariam for sending me a copy of this CD. I am also grateful to Selam and Tomás for clarifying textual content of the song "Azmari Man" and for permission to reproduce these materials here.

25. *Tadias* staff, "Brooklyn to Ethiopia: Doncker, Gigi, Selam, Laswell, and More," *Tadias*, September 28, 2011, updated October 9, 2011, http://www.tadias.com/09/28/2011/brooklyn-to-ethiopia-tomas-donckers-musical-journey-featuring-gigi-selam-laswell-more/.

26. Tomás Doncker, "Azmari Man," track 8 in *Power of the Trinity*, True Groove Records, 2011, compact disc. See also Tomás Doncker, "The Power of the Trinity," YouTube, 6:25, posted by Shine a Light Productions, July 17, 2011, https://www.youtube.com/watch?v=KAr4WWVDgA4.

Appendix

1. While I carried out short field trips to a dozen diaspora communities with populations from the Horn of Africa in the United States as well as Toronto, Canada, I did not visit the Ethiopian diaspora community in Las Vegas, Nevada, which has an Ethiopian and Eritrean population estimated at forty thousand (Max Darrow, "Board of County Commissioners Approves Measure to Designate Cultural Districts," *3 News Las Vegas*, September 18, 2019, https://news3lv.com/news/local/board-of-county-commissioners-approves-measure-to-designate-cultural-districts). I also was unable to visit one of the largest Ethiopian Orthodox churches outside Ethiopia in Aurora, Colorado, a Denver suburb: Dagmawit Gishen St. Mary Church, which was founded in 1993, completed construction of a new building on January 14, 2007. The church seats one thousand and houses a separate museum space to showcase Ethiopian relics, along with an education center that was inaugurated in 2015. A video of the church exterior and interior accompanied by music of Sunday school songs is found at "Life in America," YouTube, 43:50, posted by EBSTV Worldwide, September 28, 2015, https://www.youtube.com/watch?v=5yxZm9bxlJY.

2. Ethiopian Community Mutual Assistance Association (ECMAA), Cambridge, MA, http://www.krichevsky.com/maac-3/prof-Ethiopian.html.

3. Ethiopian Community Association of Greater Boston, https://www.facebook.com/Ethiopian-Community-Association-of-Greater-Boston-276072052416645/info/?tab=overview.

4. Tenisay Mary interview.

5. Shelemay, field notes, September 14, 1999, Boston, MA.

6. The daughter of the late *krar* and *washint* virtuoso and instrument maker Melaku Gelaw, Betelehem "Betty" Melaku participated with three other Boston-area immigrant musicians in a Harvard course titled "Social Engagement in Music" that I taught collaboratively with Carol Oja and Michael Uy during spring 2019. A graduate of the Yared School in Addis Ababa, Betelehem has taught her eldest son Samuel to play the *masenqo*. I first interviewed Betelehem on August 18, 2007, in Washington, DC, shortly before she moved with her family to Cambridge, Massachusetts.

7. An Ethiopian Social Assistance Committee (ESAC) that supports women's rights and culture with an archive was founded in 2012, https://esacnyc.com/.

8. Denis Slattery, "After Passing the Collection Plate for 30 Years, a Bronx Congregation Finally Raised Enough Money to Buy a Church of Its Own," *New York Daily*

News, May 22, 2014, https://www.nydailynews.com/new-york/bronx/30-years-bronx-ethiopian-congregation-finally-buys-church-article-1.1802754.

9. Berhanu Asfaw and Zena Asfaw, interview by author, November 10, 2010, Los Angeles, CA.

10. See "Little Ethiopia, Los Angeles," *Los Angeles Almanac*, http://www.laalmanac.com/LA/la702.php. Efforts are underway to officially name the Las Vegas Spring Valley neighborhood as "Little Ethiopia." See Kelcie Grega, "Little Ethiopia Seeks Recognition as Cultural District," *Las Vegas Sun*, December 17, 2019, https://lasvegassun.com/news/2019/dec/17/little-ethiopia-seeks-recognition-as-cultural-dist/.

11. See Kloman, *Mesob across America*, 152–54.

12. Berhanu Asfaw arrived in Los Angeles during the 1980s and opened his restaurant Messob in 1989. (Berhanu Asfaw, interview by author, November 10, 2010, Los Angeles, CA).

13. Shelemay, field notes, November 10, 2010, Los Angeles, CA. African and Caribbean members of the Los Angeles community participate in the parade as well. Berhanu Asfaw reports that his restaurant's clientele is quite diverse, with Ethiopians accounting for only around 10 percent of his customers, while many whites, Indians, and other African immigrants from other African countries patronize the restaurant (Berhanu A. interview).

14. Kate Linthicum, "Ethiopian Community Gathers to Celebrate Timket," *Los Angeles Times*, January 22, 2011, https://www.latimes.com/local/la-xpm-2011-jan-22-la-me-beliefs-ethiopian-epiphany-20110122-story.html.

15. Berhanu A. interview.

16. So many immigrants have come to the Bay Area from Gondar, Ethiopia, that Ethiopians jokingly refer to Silicon Valley as "Azezo," a town just south of Gondar.

17. Anonymous, interview by author, October 31, 2015, Oakland, CA.

18. Anonymous interview.

19. Waringa Kamau, "Oakland's Enkutatash Festival Is Cancelled, but Ethiopians Celebrate in Other Ways," *Oakland North*, September 11, 2015, https://oaklandnorth.net/2015/09/11/oaklands-enkutatash-festival-is-cancelled-but-ethiopians-celebrate-in-other-ways/.

20. http://ecseattle.org/about-us.

21. Sandra M. Chait, *Seeking Salaam: Ethiopians, Eritreans, and Somalis in the Pacific Northwest* (Seattle: University of Washington Press, 2011), 34. The number of Ethiopians evidently includes three thousand Oromo (Chait, *Seeking Salaam*, 198). A 2010 article says that estimates of the number of Somalis in Seattle vary widely, from several thousand to more than thirty thousand (Jennifer Ott, "Somali Community in Seattle," *HistoryLink.org*, November 19, 2010, https://www.historylink.org/File/9634).

22. Chait, *Seeking Salaam*, 152–53.

23. Chait, *Seeking Salaam*, 10.

24. Abdihakim Hassan, interview in Seattle, 2006, quoted in Chait, *Seeking Salaam*, 36. Elsewhere in the northwest, Portland, Oregon, about 173 miles from Seattle, has about three to four thousand Ethiopians and Somalis, and two to three thousand Eritreans (Chait, *Seeking Salaam*, 32). Small communities such as Portland absorbed refugees from the Horn of Africa in the 1980s and 1990s, enhancing Portland's African American community of around thirty-five thousand. In 2013 Africans made up around four thousand of this number.

25. Chait, *Seeking Salaam*, 67–69.

26. Chait, *Seeking Salaam*, 69.

27. Gabriel Teodros, *What We Leave Behind*, self-produced, 2020, digital, https://www.gabrielteodros.com/discography#what-we-leave-behind.

28. Bayissa K. Gerbi and Dawite Mekonnen, interviews by author, March 12, 2011, Minneapolis, MN.

29. African Development Center of Minnesota, https://www.adcminnesota.org/mission-and-history.

30. Oromo Community of Minnesota, https://www.oromomn.org/.

31. Toronto, Canada, is also a major Oromo Center.

32. Shelemay, field notes, March 12, 2011, Minneapolis, MN.

33. Solomon, *History of Ethiopian Immigrants*, 125.

34. Samuel Taye, interview by author, July 30, 2009, Atlanta, GA.

35. Solomon, *History of Ethiopian Immigrants*, 128–29.

36. Dawite interview.

37. Howard Reich, "Wild Hare: A Chicago Reggae Landmark Prepares to Close," *Chicago Tribune*, April 18, 2011, https://www.chicagotribune.com/news/ct-xpm-2011-04-18-ct-live-0419-jazz-wild-hare-20110418-story.html.

38. Dallol is a geothermal area in the northern Afar region of Ethiopia that is recognized as one of the hottest regions on earth. See B. Cavalazzi, R. Barbieri, F. Gómez, B. Capaccioni, K. Olsson-Francis, M. Pondrelli, A.P. Rossi, et al., "The Dallol Geothermal Area, Northern Afar (Ethiopia) — An Exceptional Planetary Field Analog on Earth," *Astrobiology* 19, no. 4 (2019): 553–78.

39. Reich, "Wild Hare."

40. Morikeba Kouyate, interview by author, November 10, 2011, Cambridge, MA. Morikeba is a seventh-generation *griot* from Senegal who arrived in Chicago in 1991. During 1993–94, he played *kora* from 7 to 10 p.m. at Mama Desta's Red Sea Restaurant.

41. McCann, "Response: *Doro Fänta*," 387.

42. Khalid Mohammed, interview by author, August 1, 2009, Atlanta, GA; Mohammed Hassen, interview by author, July 31, 2009, Atlanta, GA.

43. Oromo professionals, group discussion with author, July 30, 2009, Atlanta, GA.

44. Khalid interview.

45. Jamal interview.

46. "By-Laws of the Mutual Assistance Association for the Ethiopian Community Inc.," Dallas–Fort Worth, TX, November 13, 2011, https://d3ciwvs59ifrt8.cloudfront.net/e10cfb1b-5201-43b6-b7f2-9ab4fd1a411e/44e8c91e-c7b8-462f-9747-55fe5cb2b8cb.pdf. DFW International Community Alliance also estimated that there are approximately three thousand Eritreans in the Dallas–Fort Worth area, http://www.dfwinternational.org/community_profiles/Ethiopia. Its website is, however, no longer available.

47. Cristina Daglas, "Texas: Spotlight on Birhan Mekonnen," *Tadias*, August 31, 2014, http://www.tadias.com/08/31/2014/a-thriving-ethiopian-community-in-dallas-texas-d-magazine-profiles-birhan-mac-mekonnen/; originally published in *D Magazine*.

48. Wube Mekonnen, interview by author, September 22, 2013, Dallas, TX.

49. Scott Reitz, "At Ibex Ethiopian, the Dishes (and the Vibe) are Communal," *Dallas Observer*, August 4, 2011, https://www.dallasobserver.com/restaurants/at-ibex-ethiopian-the-dishes-and-the-vibe-are-communal-6422710.

50. Jennifer Emily, "Family of Slain Ethiopian Couple Keeps Dallas Restaurant Going," *Dallas Morning News*, December 30, 2013, https://www.dallasnews.com/news /2013/12/30/family-of-slain-ethiopian-couple-keeps-dallas-restaurant-going/.

51. This is the church that Moges Seyoum helped found under a different name soon after his arrival in Dallas in 1982.

52. Elvia Limon, "Ethiopian Evangelical Baptist Church Gets New Texas Site," *AP News*, May 30, 2018, https://apnews.com/38dd21e91bc645b6ae8d5d0d8399e88d. See also the church's website, https://www.eecdallas.org.

53. Ethiopian Community Organization in Houston, https://ecohouston.org.

54. Houston Population Information, https://www.houstontx.gov/ispeakhouston /HoustonPopulationDetailedEthnicity.pdf.

55. The church celebrated its twenty-fifth year in 2019 according to its website, http://houstonmedhanealem.org.

56. Dawit interview.

57. Alemtsehay interview, July 12, 2010. For information on Tayitu Cultural and Educational Center, see www.Tayitu.org.

Discography

ALBUM TITLE	ARTIST	LABEL/NUMBER	YEAR	FORMAT
Afro-Latin Soul	Mulatu Astatke and His Ethiopian Quintet	Worthy Records W-1014	1966	LP
Afro-Latin Soul, vol. 2	Mulatu Astatke	Worthy Records W-1015	1966	LP
Alo Lulo	Yehunie Belay	[self-produced]	1994	CD
Aster	Aster Aweke	Triple Earth Records Terra 107; Columbia Records CK 46848	1989; 1990	LP; CD
Assiyo Bellema	Mulatu Astatke	Ethio-Grooves Records	1994	Cassette
Balageru	Abonesh Adinew	Boku Productions and Bete Arodyon BA0001	2000	CD
Colored People's Time Machine	Gabriel Teodros	Fresh Chopped Beats FCB-053; MADK Productions FCB-053	2012	CD
Earthbound	CopperWire with Meklit Hadero, Gabriel Teodros, and Burntface	Porto Franco Records PFR041	2012	CD
Ere Mela Mela	Mahmoud Ahmed and the Ibex Bands	Kaifa Records LPKF 20	1975	LP
Ere Mela Mela	Mahmoud Ahmed	Crammed Discs CRAM 047	1986	LP reissue
Ethiopian Groove: The Golden Seventies	Various	Blue Silver Records BSD 195	1994	CD
Ethiopian Modern Instrumental Hits	Various	Amha Records AELP 10	1972	LP
éthiopiques 1: Golden Years of Modern Ethiopian Music 1969–1975	Various	Buda Musique 829512	1997	CD

ALBUM TITLE	ARTIST	LABEL/NUMBER	YEAR	FORMAT
éthiopiques 4: Ethio Jazz and Musique Instrumentale 1969–1974	Mulatu Astatke	Buda Musique 829642	1998	CD
éthiopiques 7: Erè Mèla Mèla	Mahmoud Ahmed	Buda Musique 829802	1999	CD
éthiopiques 10: Tezeta, Ethiopian Blues and Ballads	Various	Buda Musique 822222	2002	CD
éthiopiques 13: Ethiopian Groove, the Golden Seventies	Various	Buda Musique 822552	2002	CD
éthiopiques 14: Negus of the Ethiopian Sax	Getatchew Mekuria	Buda Musique 822562	2003	CD
éthiopiques 16: The Lady with the Krar	Asnaketch Werku	Buda Musique 822652	2003	CD
éthiopiques 17: Tlahoun Gèssèssè	Tilahun Gessesse	Buda Musique 822662	2004	CD
éthiopiques 20: Either/Orchestra Live in Addis	Either/Orchestra	Buda Musique 860121	2005	CD
éthiopiques 23: Orchestra Ethiopia	Orchestra Ethiopia	Buda Musique 860152	2007	CD
éthiopiques 24: Golden Years of Modern Ethiopian Music (1969–1975)	Various	Buda Musique 860176	2008	CD
éthiopiques 26: Mahmoud Ahmed and the Imperial Bodyguard Band (1972–74)	Mahmoud Ahmed and the Imperial Bodyguard Band	Buda Musique 860191	2010	CD
éthiopiques 27: Centennial of the First Ethiopian Music Recording	Tessema Eshete	Buda Musique 860192	2011	CD
éthiopiques 28: Great Oromo Music	Ali Birra	Buda Musique 860233	2013	CD
The Expats	Wayna Wondwossen	Y2 Music	2013	CD
Getatchew Mekuria, The Ex and Guests, Moa Anbessa	Getatchew Mekuria	Terp Records AS-11	2006	CD
Getatchew Mekuria, The Ex and Friends, Y'Anbessaw Tezeta	Getatchew Mekuria	Terp Records AS-21/22	2012	CD
Hailu Mergia and His Classical Instrument	Hailu Mergia	Tango Recordings; Awesome Tapes from Africa ATFA006	1985; 2013	Cassette reissue
Hana	Hana Shenkute	AIT Records AIT004	1995	CD

ALBUM TITLE	ARTIST	LABEL/NUMBER	YEAR	FORMAT
Higher Ground	Wayna Wondwossen	Quiet Power Productions 4621	2008	CD
Hin Yaadin: Bareeda Umma	Ali Birra	Awashsonic Music	c. 2009	CD
Indigo Sun	Admas	C-Side Entertainment	2000	CD
Instrumental Music	Asatamia Akafafay	Master Sound/Yared School of Music	2008	CD
I Put a Spell on You	Nina Simone	Philips PHS 600-172	1965	LP
Jörg and Munit: Just the Two of Us, Live at the Coffee House	Munit Mesfin and Jörg Pfeil	[self-produced]	2008	CD
Lemenor	Bezawork Asfaw	Tizita Productions	2002	CD
Melaku Gelaw	Melaku Gelaw	C-Side Entertainment	2001	CD and cassette tape
Moments of Clarity, Book 1	Wayna Wondwossen	Quiet Power Productions 825346715629	2004	CD
More Beautiful than Death	Either/Orchestra	Accurate Records AC 3282	2000	CD
Mulatu of Ethiopia	Mulatu Astatke	Worthy Records W-1020	1972	LP
Munit + Jörg 2	Munit Mesfin and Jörg Pfeil	[self-produced] https://munitandjorg .bandcamp.com/releases	2013	Digital
Music from Broken Flowers	Mulatu Astatke and others	Decca 988 3781	2005	CD
Nahom Favorite, vol. 4: Yetizitawoch Tizita	Various	Nahom Records 884501406611	2010	CD
Noise and Chill Out: Ethiopian Groove Worldwide	Various	ÉthioSonic 860215	2012	CD
On a Day like This	Meklit Hadero	Porto Franco Records PFR015	2010	CD
Power of the Trinity	Tomás Doncker	True Groove Records	2011	CD
The Prester John Sessions	Tommy T	Easy Star Records ES-1021	2009	CD
Reunion	Charles Sutton, Melaku Gelaw, and Getamesay Abebe	[self-produced]	2007	CD

ALBUM TITLE	ARTIST	LABEL/NUMBER	YEAR	FORMAT
Sons of Ethiopia	Admas	African Heritage Records AR-1001; reissued Frederiksberg Records FRB 007	1984; 2020	LP; LP
Tch Belew	Hailu Mergia and the Walias	Kaifa Records LPKF 45; rereleased by Awesome Tapes from Africa ATFA012	1977; 2014	LP; CD
Tesfaye: A Future Hope	Seleshe Damessae	Music of the World CDT-107	1994	CD reissue
Tikur Sew	Teddy Afro	Adika Communication and Events/Belema Entertainment IFPILZ10	2012	CD
Troubadour	K'naan	A&M Octone Records B001247802	2009	CD
We Are Alive	Meklit Hadero	Six Degrees Records 657036 120426	2014	CD
What We Leave Behind	Gabriel Teodros	[self-produced] https://gabrielteodros.bandcamp.com/album/what-we-leave-behind	2020	Digital
When the People Move, the Music Moves Too	Meklit Hadero	Six Degrees Records 657036 126923	2017	CD
Yeametu Wereboch (6-disc set)	Moges Seyoum	[self-produced]	2006	CD
Yetizitawoch Tizita, Nahom Favorite, vol. 23	Various	Nahom Records 8 84501 39120 7	2010	CD
Zedicus	Zedicus	C-Side Entertainment 783707153704	2005	CD

Music Videos and Live Recordings

TITLE	ARTIST	LINK
"Alchalkum"	Tilahun Gessesse	https://www.youtube.com/watch?v=pqiHA_6Xu6E
Best Oromo Dance (Lion)	Fendika	https://www.youtube.com/watch?v=I64XBcawthU
Best of Ethiopian Gurage Cultural Dance	Ethio Youth	https://www.youtube.com/watch?v=PIVhuYLFWgE
"Colored People's Time Machine"	Gabriel Teodros	https://www.youtube.com/watch?v=cu1xAkZXsKI
"Kemekem" (I like your Afro)	Meklit Hadero	https://www.youtube.com/watch?v=qC8feW4gomo
"Lemenor"	Bezawork Asfaw	https://www.youtube.com/watch?v=r8CwYvAsP4k
"Oromia"	Ali Birra	https://www.youtube.com/watch?v=atarcw77jGk
People to People Tour 1987/1988	National Theatre Troupe of Ethiopia	Part 1 https://www.youtube.com/watch?v=p3vWc7sqz8c
		Part 2 https://www.youtube.com/watch?v=XU97CpI3Aqc
		Part 3 https://www.youtube.com/watch?v=rzxQMnh2kRQ
		Part 4 https://www.youtube.com/watch?v=8atNSkE2v8M
		Part 5 https://www.youtube.com/watch?v=NXHECcg_O8k
		Part 6 https://www.youtube.com/watch?v=FMU4Xz_37jI
		Part 7 https://www.youtube.com/watch?v=DSODt9Pug0c
		Part 8 https://www.youtube.com/watch?v=OIkxZwX7NDo
		Part 9 https://www.youtube.com/watch?v=8pn-wd1xx4I
"Sanyii Mootii" (Race of the king)	Hachalu Hundessa	https://www.youtube.com/watch?v=GkHrvbHD9Vo
Sons of Ethiopia [Full Album]	Admas	https://www.youtube.com/watch?v=RcX5tnFX5rE
"Supernova"	Meklit Hadero	https://www.youtube.com/watch?v=MvHnrEh63SE
"The Power of the Trinity"	Tomás Doncker	https://www.youtube.com/watch?v=KAr4WWVDgA4
"Tikur Sew"	Teddy Afro	https://www.youtube.com/watch?v=IuyfK7NLosY
"Tilahun Gessesse with the Ethiopian Imperial Bodyguard Band"	Tilahun Gessesse	https://www.youtube.com/watch?v=Q4OrljuSVKM

TITLE	ARTIST	LINK
"Tizita"	Wayna and Stevie Wonder	https://www.youtube.com/watch?v=Iz7HhVEKoDM
"Yekermo Sew"	Munit and Jörg	https://www.youtube.com/watch?v=bN6HrFq8_wM
"Yekermo Sew"	Seyfu Yohannes	https://www.youtube.com/watch?v=-tnCCfCCQVQ

Interviews and Communications

(Ethiopian names are alphabetized by first name)

Abdi (Tesfaye) Nuressa. Interview by author, June 18, 2008. Washington, DC.
———. Interview by author, July 16, 2008. Washington, DC.
Abebaye Lema. Interview by author, August 8, 2006. Cambridge, MA.
———. Interview by author, April 21, 2008. Cambridge, MA.
Abegasu Kibrework Shiota. Interview by author, March 7, 2003. Cambridge, MA.
———. Interview by author, June 20, 2006. Addis Ababa.
———. Interview by author, May 24, 2014. Addis Ababa.
———. Personal communication with author, January 14, 2020. Addis Ababa.
Abonesh "Abiti" Adinew. Interview by author, August 14, 2007. Washington, DC.
Abraham Habte Selassie. Interview by author, June 12, 2008. Washington, DC.
Aklilu Zewdi. Interview by author, June 16, 2006. Addis Ababa.
Alemtsehay Wedajo. Interview by author, June 9, 2008. Washington, DC.
———. Interview by author, July 12, 2010. Washington, DC.
Ali Birra. Interview by author, August 2, 2009. Atlanta, GA.
Ali Birra and Lily Marcos-Birra. Personal communication with author, June 16, 2020.
Amha Eshete. Interview by author, June 19, 2006. Addis Ababa.
———. Personal communication with author, June 1, 2015.
Anonymous. Interview by author, October 31, 2015. Oakland, CA.
Ashenafi Mitiku. Interview by author, August 28, 2007. Washington, DC.
Aster Aweke. Interview by author, April 6, 2009. Cambridge, MA.
Aster Bekele. Telephone interview by author, August 24, 2015.
Badagnani, David. Personal communication with author, January 23, 2005.
Bayissa K. Gerbi. Interview by author, March 12, 2011. Minneapolis, MN.
Behailu Kassahun. Interview by author, August 3, 2007. Washington, DC.
Beniam Bedru Hussein. Interview by author, June 26, 2008. Washington, DC.
Berhanu Asfaw and Zena Asfaw. Interview by author, November 10, 2010. Los Angeles, CA.
Berhanu Mekonnen. Interview by author, June 2, 1975. Addis Ababa.
Betelehem "Betty" Melaku. Interview by author, August 18, 2007. Washington, DC
———. Interview by author, August 12, 2019. Cambridge, MA.

———. Interview by author, August 20, 2019. Cambridge, MA.

Bezawork Asfaw. Interview by author, June 24, 2008. Washington, DC.

Coe, John. Interview by author, June 8, 2007. Cambridge, MA.

Danny Mekonnen. Personal communication with author, Spring 2006. Cambridge, MA.

———. Personal communication with author, April 23, 2015. Cambridge, MA.

Dawit Gebre. Interview by author, April 14, 2016. Stanford, CA.

Dawite Mekonnen. Interview by author, March 12, 2011. Minneapolis, MN.

Doraiswamy, Ganavya Iyer. Personal communication with author, March 28, 2016. Los Angeles, CA.

Elias Negash. Interview by author, January 30, 2016. Los Altos, CA.

El-Dabh, Halim. Interview by author, March 5, 2007. Cambridge, MA.

Elizabeth Namarra. Interview by author, March 13, 2011. Minneapolis, MN.

Endale Getahun. Telephone interview by author, December 10, 2019.

Eskowitz, Bruce. Personal communication with author, November 19, 2019. Boston, MA.

Falceto, Francis. Personal communication with author, August 31, 2020.

———. Personal communication with author, September 13, 2020.

———. Personal communication with author, October 3, 2020.

Fathi Hassan. Interview by author, March 15, 2011. St. Paul, MN.

Gabriel Alemayehu. Interview by author, October 26, 2010. Cambridge, MA.

Gershon, Russ. Interview by author, January 27, 2006. Cambridge, MA.

———. Interview by author, August 16, 2010. Cambridge, MA.

Getahun Atlaw Garede. Interview by author, June 5, 2008. Washington, DC.

Getamesay Abebe. Interview by author and Charles Sutton, July 18, 2008. Cambridge, MA.

Getatchew Gebregiorgis. Interview by author, July 2, 2008. Washington, DC.

Girum Mezmur. Interview by author, May 20, 2014. Addis Ababa.

———. Interview by author, May 28, 2014. Addis Ababa.

———. Interview by author, January 17, 2020. Addis Ababa.

Hamza Aburedzek. Interview by author, August 4, 2009. Cambridge, MA.

Hana Shenkute. Interview by author, August 30, 2007, Washington, DC.

Henock Temesgen. Interview by author, March 7, 2003. Cambridge, MA.

———. Interview by author, May 25, 2014. Addis Ababa.

———. Personal communication with author, January 14, 2020. Addis Ababa.

Heldman, Marilyn E. Personal communication with author, June 30, 2015.

Hermela Mulatu. Interview by author, June 14, 2008. Washington, DC.

———. Interview by author, July 3, 2008. Washington, DC.

Issayas Tesfamariam. Personal communication with author, May 24, 2016. Stanford, CA.

Jamal Sule. Interview by author, July 30, 2009. Atlanta, GA.

Jefferson, Julius C., Jr. Interview by author, August 7, 2007. Washington, DC.

Kawase, Itsushi. Personal communication with author, September 4, 2007. Washington, DC.

Khalid Mohammed. Interview by author, August 1, 2009. Atlanta, GA.

Kirubel Assefa. Personal communication with author, May 14, 2020.

Lawlor, Helen. Personal communication with author, October 23, 2017.

Martha Ketsela. Interview by author, August 28, 2007. Washington, DC.

Martha Namarra. Interview by author, March 13, 2011. Minneapolis, MN.

Mekbul Jemal Tahir. Telephone interview by author, August 20, 2020.

Meklit Hadero. Interview by author, December 11, 2015. Stanford, CA.

Melaku Belay. Interview by author, May 22, 2014. Addis Ababa.

Melaku Gelaw. Interview by author and Charles Sutton, August 14, 2007. Washington, DC.

Mesfin Zeberga Tereda. Interview by author, August 18, 2007. Washington, DC.

Mimi Wondimiye. Interview by author, August 22, 2007. Washington, DC.

Minale Dagnew Bezu. Interview by author, August 8, 2007. Washington, DC.

———. Interview by author, January 7, 2008. Washington, DC.

———. Interview by author, August 13, 2008. Washington, DC.

Moges Habte. Interview by author, August 27, 2007. Washington, DC.

Moges Seyoum. Interview by author, August 2, 2007. Washington, DC.

———. Personal communication with author, August 8, 2020.

Moges Seyoum and Kahele Wondaferaw. Interview by author and Steven Kaplan, January 27, 2017. Washington, DC.

Mohaammad Ibraahim Xawil. Interview by author, June 17, 2008. Washington, DC.

Mohammed Hassen. Interview by author, July 31, 2009. Atlanta, GA.

Morikeba Kouyate. Interview by author, November 10, 2011. Cambridge, MA.

Mulatu Astatke. Interview by author, November 9, 2007. Cambridge, MA.

———. Interview by author and Steven Kaplan, September 9, 2007. Cambridge, MA.

———. Interview by author and Steven Kaplan, September 12, 2007. Cambridge, MA.

———. Interview by author and Steven Kaplan, September 19, 2007. Cambridge, MA.

———. Interview by author and Steven Kaplan, September 25, 2007. Cambridge, MA.

———. Interview by author and Steven Kaplan, October 2, 2007. Cambridge, MA.

———. Interview by author and Steven Kaplan, October 17, 2007. Cambridge, MA.

———. Interview by author and Steven Kaplan, October 23, 2007. Cambridge, MA.

———. Interview by author and Steven Kaplan, October 30, 2007. Cambridge, MA.

———. Interview by author and Steven Kaplan, November 6, 2007. Cambridge, MA.

———. Interview by author and Steven Kaplan, November 30, 2007. Cambridge, MA.

———. Interview by author and Steven Kaplan, December 4, 2007. Cambridge, MA.

Munit Mesfin. Interview by author, May 21, 2014. Addis Ababa.

———. Personal communication with author, October 19, 2020.

———. Personal communication with author, October 23, 2020.

Negash Shifrew. Interview by author, August 14, 2007. Washington, DC.

Oromo professionals. Group discussion with author, July 30, 2009. Atlanta, GA.

Samuel Taye. Interview by author, July 30, 2009. Atlanta, GA.

Sayem Osman. Interview by author, June 12, 2008. Washington, DC.

Schultz, Anna. Personal communication with author, January 18, 2013.

Seble W. Argaw. Interview by Steven Kaplan and author, October 5, 2007. Cambridge, MA.

Selam Seyoum Woldemariam. Interview by author, August 26, 2007, Washington, DC.

———. Interview by author, September 5, 2007. Washington, DC.

———. Interview by author, September 7, 2007. Washington, DC.

———. Personal communication with author, June 16, 2020.

Seleshe Damessae. Interview by author, 1978. New York, NY.

Setegn Atanaw. Interview by author and Itsushi Kawase, September 4, 2007. Washington, DC.

Sutton, Charles. Interview with author, August 16, 2007. Washington, DC.

———. Personal communication with author, February 17, 2008.

———. Personal communication with author, August 6, 2018.

———. Personal communication with author, May 1, 2020.

———. Personal communication with author, March 4, 2021.

Tekle Tewolde. Interview by author, June 17, 2008. Washington, DC.

Telela Kebede. Interview by author with Mimi Wondimiye (daughter), August 22, 2007. Washington, DC.

———. Interview by author, July 10, 2010. Washington, DC.

Tenisay "Mary" Alemu Walker. Interview by author, January 14, 2007. Cambridge, MA.

Tesfaye Lemma. Interview by author and Charles Sutton, August 15, 2007. Washington, DC.

———. Interview by author, August 20, 2007. Washington, DC.

Teshome Mitiku. Interview by author, August 22, 2007. Washington, DC.

Thomas "Tommy T" Gobena. Interview by author, March 7, 2003. Cambridge, MA.

Tsegaye B. Selassie. Interview by author, July 1, 2008. Washington, DC.

Tsehai Birhanu. Personal communication with author, August 30, 2006. Cambridge, MA.

———. Interview by author, March 20, 2007. Cambridge, MA.

———. Interview by author, April 12, 2008. Cambridge, MA.

———. Interview by author, September 17, 2008. Cambridge, MA.

———. Interview by author, October 26, 2010. Cambridge, MA.

———. Interview by author, November 26, 2010. Cambridge, MA.

Tsehay Amare. Interview by author, August 9, 2007. Washington, DC.

Wayna Wondwossen. Interview by author, May 8, 2008. Washington, DC.

———. Interview by author, May 30, 2008. Washington, DC.

Woretaw Wubet. Interview by author, August 1, 2007. Washington, DC.

Wube Mekonnen. Interview by author, September 22, 2013. Dallas, TX.

Yehunie Belay. Interview by author, July 22, 2007. Washington, DC.

———. Interview by author, August 22, 2007. Washington, DC.

———. Interview by author, August 30, 2007. Washington, DC.

———. Interview by Steven Kaplan, October 26, 2007. Washington, DC.

Yeshimebet "Tutu" Belay. Interview by author, August 30, 2007. Washington, DC.

Zakki Jawad. Interview by author, June 27, 2008. Washington, DC.

Field Notes

November 11, 1994. Nile Ethiopian Ensemble Performance at Harvard University, Cambridge, MA.

May 26, 1997. Boston, MA.

September 14, 1999. Boston, MA.

January 27, 2006. Somerville, MA.

January 28, 2006. Boston, MA.

June 21, 2006. Addis Ababa.

July 23, 2006. Cambridge, MA.

December 12, 2006. Middle East Nightclub, Cambridge, MA.

August 15, 2007. Washington, DC.

August 22, 2007. Washington, DC.

September 8, 2007. Washington, DC.

May 30, 2008. Washington, DC.

June 25, 2008. Washington, DC.

June 29–July 5, 2008. Washington, DC.

July 2, 2008. Dukem Ethiopian Restaurant, Washington, DC.

July 3, 2008. Arlington, VA.

July 30–August 3, 2009. Atlanta, GA.

August 28–30, 2009. Bangor, ME.

September 26, 2009. Cambridge, MA.

July 15, 2010. Either/Orchestra concert at The Lily Pad, Cambridge, MA.

November 10, 2010. Los Angeles, CA.

March 12, 2011. Minneapolis, MN.

November 12, 2011. Cambridge, MA.

April 18, 2012. Milan, Italy.

May 21, 2014. Addis Ababa.

May 24, 2014. Addis Ababa.

October 31, 2015. Oakland, CA.

May 21, 2016. Meklit in Concert, "This Was Made Here: A Diasporic Odyssey." Yerba Buena Center for the Arts, San Francisco, CA.

December 26, 2017. Addis Ababa.

March 26, 27, and 28, 2019. Meklit Hadero, during Harvard University Residency, Cambridge, MA.

January 14, 2020. Addis Ababa.

Bibliography

(Ethiopian names are alphabetized by first name)

Abbink, Jan. "Slow Awakening? The Ethiopian Diaspora in the Netherlands, 1977–2007." *Diaspora* 15, nos. 2–3 (2006 [published 2011]): 361–80. https://doi.org/10.1353/dsp.2011.0073.

Abbink, Jon. "Ethnic-Based Federalism and Ethnicity in Ethiopia: Reassessing the Experiment after 20 Years." *Journal of Eastern African Studies* 5, no. 4 (2011): 596–618. https://doi.org/10.1080/17531055.2011.642516.

———. "Ethnicity." In *Encyclopaedia Aethiopica*. Edited by Siegbert Uhlig, 2:444–46. Wiesbaden, Ger.: Harrassowitz, 2005.

Abdi, Cawo M. *Elusive Jannah: The Somali Diaspora and a Borderless Muslim Identity*. Minneapolis: University of Minnesota Press, 2015.

Abdi Latif Dahir. "Ethiopia's New 50% Women Cabinet Isn't Just Bold—It's Smart." *Quartz Africa*, October 16, 2018. https://qz.com/africa/1426110/ethiopias-new-cabinet-is-50-women/.

———. "Hachalu Hundessa, Ethiopian Singer and Activist, Is Shot Dead." *New York Times*, June 30, 2020. https://www.nytimes.com/2020/06/30/world/africa/ethiopia-hachalu-hundessa-dead.html.

Abraham Demoz. "Emperor Menelik's Phonograph Message to Queen Victoria." *Bulletin of the School of Oriental and African Studies, University of London* 32, no. 2 (1969): 251–56.

Abraham Habte Selassie. *Saint Yared and Ethiopian Ecclesiastical Music*. Washington, DC: Debre Selam Kidist Mariam Church, 1999.

Abubakar Ashakih and Judith Ashakih. *Gift of Incense: A Story of Love and Revolution in Ethiopia*. Trenton, NJ: Red Sea, 2005.

Admas. Liner notes. *Indigo Sun*. C-Side Entertainment, 2000. Compact disc.

Agier, Michel. *On the Margins of the World: The Refugee Experience Today*. Translated by David Fernbach. Cambridge, UK: Polity, 2008.

Ahearn, Laura M. "Language and Agency." *Annual Review of Anthropology* 30 (2001): 109–37. https://doi.org/10.1146/annurev.anthro.30.1.109.

Ahmed, Ali Jimale, and Taddesse Adera. *The Road Less Traveled: Reflections on the Literatures of the Horn of Africa*. Trenton, NJ: Red Sea, 2008.

Aida Solomon. "I Am Ethiopia: The Fusion Flavors of Chef Mulugeta Abate." *Se-*

attle Globalist, August 5, 2014. https://www.seattleglobalist.com/2014/08/05
/ethiopia-chef-mulugeta-abate-lovage/28199.

Almog, Oz. *The Sabra: The Creation of the New Jew.* Translated by Haim Watzman.
Berkeley: University of California Press, 2000.

Alvarez, Francisco. *The Prester John of the Indies: A True Relation of the Lands of the
Prester John, Being the Narrative of the Portuguese Embassy to Ethiopia in 1520.*
Edited by C. F. Beckingham and G. W. B. Huntingford. 2 vols. Cambridge, UK:
Hakluyt Society, 1961.

Amnesty International. "Ethiopia/Eritrea: Amnesty International Witnesses Cruelty of Mass Deportations." News release no. AFR 25/02/99, January 29, 1999.
https://www.amnesty.org/download/Documents/140000/afr250021999en
.pdf.

Anderson, Mark. "Ethiopia Hosts Largest Number of Refugees in Africa." *Guardian*, August 20, 2014. https://www.theguardian.com/global-development
/2014/aug/20/ethiopia-largest-number-refugees-africa.

Arefaynie Fantahun. "Amha Eshete: Pioneer of Ethiopia's Music Industry." *Music in
Africa*, June 20, 2016. https://www.musicinafrica.net/magazine/amha-eshete
-pioneer-ethiopias-music-industry.

Arhine, Adwoa. "Speech Surrogates of Africa: A Study of the Fante *Mmensuon*." *Legon Journal of the Humanities* 20 (2009): 105–22. https://www.ajol.info/index
.php/ljh/article/view/121552.

Arkun, Aram. "Intercontinental Mélange: From Ethiopia to Watertown via Jerusalem and Either/Orchestra." *Armenian Mirror-Spectator*, February 23, 2017.
https://mirrorspectator.com/2017/02/23/intercontinental-melange-from
-ethiopia-to-watertown-via-jerusalem-and-eitherorchestra/.

Armitage, David, and Jo Guldi. "Le retour de la longue durée: une perspective
anglo-américaine." *Annales: Histoire, Sciences Sociales* 70, no. 2 (2015): 289–318.
https://doi.org/10.1353/ahs.2015.0033.

Asafa Jalata. "The Emergence of Oromo Nationalism and Ethiopian Reaction." In
*Oromo Nationalism and the Ethiopian Discourse: The Search for Freedom and De-
mocracy.* Edited by Asafa Jalata, 1–26. Lawrenceville, NJ: Red Sea, 1998.

———. *Oromia and Ethiopia: State Formation and Ethnonational Conflict, 1868–
2004.* Trenton, NJ: Red Sea, 2005.

———, ed. *Oromo Nationalism and the Ethiopian Discourse: The Search for Freedom
and Democracy.* Lawrenceville, NJ: Red Sea, 1998.

Asfa-Wossen Asserate. *King of Kings: The Triumph and Tragedy of Emperor Haile Selassie I of Ethiopia.* Translated by Peter Lewis. London: Haus, 2015.

Ashenafi Kebede. "Azmari, Poet-Musician of Ethiopia." *Musical Quarterly* 61, no. 1
(1975): 47–57. https://doi.org/10.1093/mq/LXI.1.47.

———. "The Music of Ethiopia: Its Development and Cultural Setting." PhD diss.,
Wesleyan University, 1971.

Aslanian, Ani. "In the Company of Emperors: The Story of Ethiopian Armenians."
Armenite, October 6, 2014. https://thearmenite.com/2014/10/company
-emperors-story-ethiopian-armenians/.

Associated Press. "Little Ethiopia Taking Root in D.C. Area." *Deseret News*, November 6, 2005. https://www.deseret.com/2005/11/6/19920410/little-ethiopia
-taking-root-in-d-c-area.

Attali, Jacques. *Noise: The Political Economy of Music.* Translated by Brian Massumi. Minneapolis: University of Minnesota Press, 1977.

Avishai Yeganyahu Mekonen and Shari Rothfarb Mekonen. *400 Miles to Freedom.* Documentary film. Los Angeles: Seventh Art, 2012. 60 min. https://www .kanopy.com/product/400-miles-freedom.

Bacon, Tony, and Lynn Wheelwright. "Electric Guitar." *Grove Music Online,* January 31, 2014. https://doi.org/10.1093/gmo/9781561592630.article.A2256412.

Bahrey. "History of the Galla." In *Some Records of Ethiopia 1593–1646: Being Extracts from the History of High Ethiopia or Abassia, by Manoel de Almeida, together with Bahrey's History of the Galla.* Edited by C. F. Beckingham and G. B. W. Huntingford, 109–32. London: Hakluyt Society, 2010.

Bahru Zewde. "Embattled Identity in Northeast Africa: A Comparative Essay." In *Society, State, and History: Selected Essays.* Edited by Bahru Zewde, 363–74. Addis Ababa: Addis Ababa University Press, 2008.

———. "Hagär Fəqər Tiyatər." In *Encyclopaedia Aethiopica.* Edited by Siegbert Uhlig, 2:966. Wiesbaden, Ger.: Harrassowitz, 2005.

———. *A History of Modern Ethiopia, 1855–1991.* 2nd ed. Eastern African Studies. Oxford, UK: James Currey, 2001.

———. "Mäkwännən Habtäwäld." In *Encyclopaedia Aethiopica.* Edited by Siegbert Uhlig, 3:684–85. Wiesbaden, Ger.: Harrassowitz, 2007.

Balisky, Lila W. *Songs of Ethiopia's Tesfaye Gabbiso: Singing with Understanding in Babylon, the Meantime, and Zion.* Eugene, OR: Pickwick, 2018.

Balsvik, Randi Rønning. *Haile Selassie's Students: The Intellectual and Social Background to Revolution, 1952–1977.* East Lansing: African Studies Center, Michigan State University, 1985.

Bangshowbiz.com. "Bob Geldof: Band Aid Isn't a Good Song." *Washington Post,* May 22, 2015. https://www.washingtonpost.com/entertainment/bob -geldof-band-aid-isnt-a-good-song/2015/05/22/bf5b589e-0066-11e5-8c77 -bf274685e1df_story.html.

Ban Ki-Moon. "With 16 Million Refugees Worldwide, Secretary General Calls for Redoubled Efforts to Address Causes." *United Nations Meeting Coverage and Press Releases,* June 17, 2008. https://www.un.org/press/en/2008/sgsm11643 .doc.htm.

Barnes and Noble. Product overview of *We Are Alive* by Meklit. https://www .barnesandnoble.com/w/we-are-alive-meklit/27347266. No longer available.

Battles, Paul. "Chaucer and the Traditions of Dawn-Song." *Chaucer Review* 31, no. 4 (1997): 317–38. https://www.jstor.org/stable/25095986.

Bausi, Alessandro. "Migrations before 1400." In *Encyclopaedia Aethiopica.* Edited by Siegbert Uhlig, 5:427–29. Wiesbaden, Ger.: Harrassowitz, 2014.

Baxter, P. T. W. "Ethiopia's Unacknowledged Problem: The Oromo." *African Affairs* 77, no. 308 (1978): 283–96.

BBC News. "Hachalu Hundessa: Deadly Protests Erupt after Ethiopian Singer Killed." June 30, 2020. https://www.bbc.com/news/world-africa-53233531.

———. "Hachalu Hundessa: 'Eighty-One Killed' in Protests over Ethiopian Singer's Death." July 1, 2020. https://www.bbc.com/news/world-africa-53243325.

———. "Hachalu Hundessa: Ethiopia Singer Buried amid Ethnic Unrest." July 2, 2020. https://www.bbc.com/news/world-africa-53262998.

Becker, Judith. *Deep Listeners: Music, Emotion, and Trancing.* Bloomington: Indiana University Press, 2004.

Bekele Atoma. "More than an Entertainer." *BBC News*, June 30, 2020. https://www.bbc.com/news/world-africa-53233531.

BenEzer, Gadi. *The Ethiopian Jewish Exodus: Narratives of the Migration Journey to Israel, 1977–1985.* Routledge Studies in Memory and Narrative 9. London: Routledge, 2002.

Bengal, Rebecca. "Hailu Mergia: The Ethiopian Jazz Legend Who Jams in His Taxi." *Guardian*, March 1, 2018. https://www.theguardian.com/music/2018/mar/01/hailu-mergia-the-ethiopian-jazz-legend-who-jams-in-his-taxi.

Berg, Mette Louise, and Susan Eckstein, eds. "Re-imagining Diasporas and Generations." Special issue, *Diaspora* 18, nos. 1–2 (2009 [published 2015]).

Berhane Asfaw. "Australopithecus afarensis." In *Encyclopaedia Aethiopica.* Edited by Siegbert Uhlig, 1:396. Wiesbaden, Ger.: Harrassowitz, 2003.

Berklee Media Relations. "Eagles, Alison Krauss, Mulatu Astatke Receive Honorary Degrees at Commencement." Berklee press release, May 12, 2012. https://www.berklee.edu/news/4435/eagles-alison-krauss-mulatu-astatke-receive-hono.

Bernal, Victoria. "Eritrea Goes Global: Reflections on Nationalism in a Transnational Era." *Cultural Anthropology* 19, no. 1 (2004): 3–25. https://doi.org/10.1525/can.2004.19.1.3.

———. "Eritrea On-Line: Diaspora, Cyberspace, and the Public Sphere." *American Ethnologist* 32, no. 4 (2005): 660–75. https://doi.org/10.1525/ae.2005.32.4.660.

Betelehem Melaku. "In Memory of Melaku Gelaw." Betelehem Melaku website. https://bettymelakumusic.wixsite.com/mysite/bio.

Bezezekoff, Leigh. "Song of the Day: Gabriel Teodros—Mind Power." *KEXP*, February 24, 2012.

Bhalla, Nita. "Cleaning Up the Streets of Addis." *BBC News*, May 8, 2001. http://news.bbc.co.uk/2/hi/africa/1319359.stm.

Biasio, Elisabeth. "Gäbrä Krəstos Dästa." In *Encyclopaedia Aethiopica.* Edited by Siegbert Uhlig, 2:617–18. Wiesbaden, Ger.: Harrassowitz, 2003.

Blum, Stephen, Philip V. Bohlman, and Daniel M. Neuman, eds. *Ethnomusicology and Modern Music History.* Urbana: University of Illinois Press, 1991.

Boavida, Isabel, Hervé Pennec, and Manuel João Ramos, eds. *Pedro Páez's History of Ethiopia, 1622.* 2 vols. Translated by Christopher J. Tribe. Farnham, UK: Ashgate, 2011.

Boilés, Charles L. "Tepehua Thought-Song: A Case of Semantic Signaling." *Ethnomusicology* 11, no. 3 (1967): 267–92. https://doi.org/10.2307/850266.

Bonacci, Giulia. "Rastafari/Rastafarianism." In *Encyclopaedia Aethiopica.* Edited by Siegbert Uhlig, 4:330–40. Wiesbaden, Ger.: Harrassowitz, 2010.

———. "Šašämäne." In *Encyclopaedia Aethiopica.* Edited by Siegbert Uhlig, 4:550–51. Wiesbaden, Ger.: Harrassowitz, 2010.

Bordowitz, Hank. *Noise of the World: Non-Western Musicians in Their Own Words.* Brooklyn, NY: Soft Skull, 2004.

Bosc-Tiessé, Claire, Marie-Laure Derat, Laurent Bruxelles, François-Xavier Fauvelle, Yves Gleize, and Romain Mensan. "The Lalibela Rock Hewn Site and Its Landscape (Ethiopia): An Archaeological Analysis." *Journal of African Archaeology* 12, no. 2 (2014): 141–64.

Boylston, Tom. *The Stranger at the Feast: Prohibition and Mediation in an Ethiopian Orthodox Christian Community.* Berkeley: University of California Press, 2018.

Braudel, Fernand. *The Mediterranean and the Mediterranean World in the Age of Philip II.* Translated by Siân Reynolds. New York: Harper and Row, 1972.

Braukämper, Ulrich. "Population History III. Migrations from the 15th to the 19th Century." In *Encyclopaedia Aethiopica.* Edited by Siegbert Uhlig, 4:172–75. Wiesbaden, Ger.: Harrassowitz, 2010.

Bruce, James. *Travels and Adventures in Abyssinia.* Edited by J. Morison Clingan. Edinburgh: Adam and Charles Black, 1860.

———. *Travels to Discover the Source of the Nile.* Edited by J. Morison Clingan. Edinburgh: Adam and Charles Black, 1860.

Burke, Jason. "'These Changes Are Unprecedented': How Abiy Is Upending Ethiopian Politics." *Guardian,* July 8, 2018. https://www.theguardian.com/world /2018/jul/08/abiy-ahmed-upending-ethiopian-politics.

Burr, Ty. "'63 Up': A Film Series That Shows Life, Unforgettably, in Seven-Year Slices." *Boston Globe,* December 10, 2019. https://www.bostonglobe.com/2019 /12/11/arts/63-up-film-series-that-shows-life-unforgettably-seven-year -slices/.

Bustorf, Dirk. "Zämäča." In *Encyclopaedia Aethiopica.* Edited by Siegbert Uhlig, 5:121–22, Wiesbaden, Ger.: Harrassowitz, 2014.

———, and Charles Schaefer. "Əddər." In *Encyclopaedia Aethiopica.* Edited by Siegbert Uhlig, 2:225–27. Wiesbaden, Ger.: Harrassowitz, 2005.

Butler, Kim D. "Defining Diaspora, Refining a Discourse." *Diaspora* 10, no. 2 (2001): 189–219.

"By-Laws of the Mutual Assistance Association for the Ethiopian Community Inc." Dallas/Fort Worth, TX. November 13, 2011. https://d3ciwvs59ifrt8.cloudfront .net/e10cfb1b-5201-43b6-b7f2-9ab4fd1a411e/44e8c91e-c7b8-462f-9747 -55fe5cb2b8cb.pdf.

Caine, Julie. "The Nile Project: Producing Harmony in a Divided Region." *NPR Music News,* September 14, 2014. https://www.npr.org/2014/09/14/347733976 /the-nile-project-producing-harmony-in-a-divided-region.

Campbell, Ian. *The Plot to Kill Graziani: The Attempted Assassination of Mussolini's Viceroy.* Addis Ababa: Addis Ababa University Press, 2010.

Campbell, Thomas. *The Complete Poetical Works of Thomas Campbell: With a Memoir of His Life.* Lovell's Library. Vol. 10, no. 526. Boston: Phillips, Sampson, 1855.

Cavalazzi, B., R. Barbieri, F. Gómez, B. Capaccioni, K. Olsson-Francis, M. Pondrelli, A. P. Rossi, et al. "The Dallol Geothermal Area, Northern Afar (Ethiopia)—An Exceptional Planetary Field Analog on Earth." *Astrobiology* 19, no. 4 (2019): 553–78.

Center for Ethiopian Art and Culture By-Laws. Washington, DC, 1994.

Cerulli, Enrico. *Storia della letteratura etiopica.* Milan: Nuova Academia, 1956.

Chacko, Elizabeth. "Ethiopian Ethos and the Making of Ethnic Places in the Washington Metropolitan Area." *Journal of Cultural Geography* 20, no. 2 (2003): 21–42. https://doi.org/10.1080/08873630309478274.

———. "Ethiopian Taxicab Drivers: Forming an Occupational Niche in the US Capital." *African and Black Diaspora* 9, no. 2 (2016): 200–13. https://doi.org/10 .1080/17528631.2015.1083177.

———, and Peter H. Gebre. "Leveraging the Diaspora for Development: Lessons from Ethiopia." *GeoJournal* 78, no. 3 (2013): 495–505. https://doi.org/10.1007/s10708-012-9447-9.

Chait, Sandra M. *Seeking Salaam: Ethiopians, Eritreans, and Somalis in the Pacific Northwest.* Seattle: University of Washington Press, 2011.

Charry, Eric. *Mande Music: Traditional and Modern Music of the Maninka and Mandinka of Western Africa.* Chicago: University of Chicago Press, 2000.

Chinen, Nate. "Getatchew Mekurya, 81, Ethiopian Saxophonist with Global Reach Dies." *New York Times*, April 11, 2016. https://www.nytimes.com/2016/04/12/arts/music/getatchew-mekurya-ethiopian-jazz-saxophonist-dies-at-81.html.

Ciccocioppo, Lucianna. "With Support from The Weeknd, U of T's Ethiopic Program Soars Past $500,000 Endowment Goal." *U of T News* (University of Toronto), November 2, 2020. https://www.utoronto.ca/news/support-weeknd-u-t-s-ethiopic-program-soars-past-500000-endowment-goal.

Classen, Constance. "McLuhan in the Rainforest: The Sensory Worlds of Oral Cultures." In *The Empire of the Senses: The Sensual Culture Reader.* Edited by David Howes, 147–63. London: Bloomsbury, 2005.

Clifford, James. *Routes: Travel and Translation in the Late Twentieth Century.* Cambridge, MA: Harvard University Press, 1997.

Corcoran, Patrick. "Nina Simone's 'I Put A Spell On You' Turns 55." *Albumism*, May 31, 2020. https://www.albumism.com/features/nina-simone-i-put-a-spell-on-you-turns-55-anniversary-retrospective.

Cohen, John M. "'Ethnic Federalism' in Ethiopia." *Northeast African Studies* 2, no. 2 (1995): 157–88.

Cohen, Leonardo. *The Missionary Strategies of the Jesuits in Ethiopia (1555–1632).* Äthiopistische Forschungen. Vol. 70. Wiesbaden, Ger.: Harrassowitz, 2009.

Colin, Gérard ed. *Le Synaxaire Ethiopien, Mois de Genbot.* Patrologia Orientalis no. 211. Turnhout, Belgium: Brepols Publishers, 1997.

Comaroff, Jean and John. "Ethnography on an Awkward Scale: Postcolonial Anthropology and the Violence of Abstraction." *Ethnography* 4, no. 2 (2003): 147–79. https://doi.org/10.1177/14661381030042001.

Comaroff, John L. and Jean. *Of Revelation and Revolution.* Vol. 2, *The Dialectics of Modernity on a South African Frontier.* Chicago: University of Chicago Press, 2009.

Cook, Nicholas. "Music as Performance." In *The Cultural Study of Music: A Critical Introduction.* 2nd ed. Edited by Martin Clayton, Trevor Herbert, and Richard Middleton, chapter 16. New York: Routledge, 2012.

CopperWire. Liner notes. *Earthbound.* Porto Franco Records PFR041, 2012. Compact disc.

Creighton, Caron. "Eritrean Diaspora Watches Ethiopia Thaw with Hope, Mistrust." *AP NEWS*, July 21, 2018. https://apnews.com/e03f26d58dea4fe2a442a9fe0a8925a4.

Cropley, Ed. "As Ethiopia's 'Wall' Comes Down, Exiles Dream of Going Home." *Reuters World News*, July 20, 2018. https://www.reuters.com/article/us-ethiopia-diaspora-idUSKBN1KA1W5.

Crummey, Donald. "Ethiopia, Europe and Modernity: A Preliminary Sketch." *Aethiopica* 3 (2000): 7–23. https://doi.org/10.15460/aethiopica.3.1.569.

———. "The Politics of Modernization: Protestant and Catholic Missionaries in Modern Ethiopia." In *The Missionary Factor in Ethiopia*. Edited by Samuel Rubenson, Getatchew Haile, and Aasulv Lande, 85–89. Frankfurt: Peter Lang, 1998.

D'Amat, W. A. "Introduction." In liner notes. *Hin Yaadin: Bareeda Umma*. Awashsonic Music, c. 2009. Compact disc.

Daglas, Cristina. "Texas: Spotlight on Birhan Mekonnen." *Tadias*, August 31, 2014. http://www.tadias.com/08/31/2014/a-thriving-ethiopian-community-in -dallas-texas-d-magazine-profiles-birhan-mac-mekonnen/.

Dagnachew Teklu. "Ethiopia: International Year of Volunteers Launched." *Daily Monitor*, December 18, 2000. https://allafrica.com/stories/200012180129 .html.

Dallas Morning News. "Ethiopian Group Stages Protest in Downtown Dallas." November 21, 2013. https://www.dallasnews.com/news/2013/11/21/ethiopian -group-stages-protest-in-downtown-dallas/.

Damon, Anne. "Aqwaqwam ou la danse des cieux" [Aqwaqwam or the celestial dance]. *Cahiers d'Études Africaines* 46, no. 182 (2006): 261–90. https://www .jstor.org/stable/4393575.

Danielson, Virginia. "Performance, Political Identity, and Memory: Umm Kulthum and Gamal 'Abd al-Nasir." In *Images of Enchantment: Visual and Performing Arts in the Middle East*. Edited by Sherifa Zuhur, 109–22. Cairo: American University in Cairo Press, 1998.

———. *The Voice of Egypt: Umm Kulthum, Arabic Song, and Egyptian Society in the Twentieth Century*. Chicago: University of Chicago Press, 1997.

Danny A. Mekonnen. "Ethio-Groove on the World-Stage: Music, Mobility, Mediation." *Callaloo* 33, no. 1 (2010): 299–313. www.jstor.org/stable/40732822.

Darrow, Max. "Board of County Commissioners Approves Measure to Designate Cultural Districts." *3 News Las Vegas*, September 18, 2019. https://news3lv .com/news/local/board-of-county-commissioners-approves-measure-to -designate-cultural-districts.

Deene, Karlijn. "French Composers after the Franco-Prussian War (1870–1): A Prosopographical Study." In *Prosopography Approaches and Applications: A Handbook*. Edited by K. S. B. Keats-Rohan, 567–78. Oxford, UK: Linacre College, Unit for Prosopographical Research, 2007.

DeLanda, Manuel. *Assemblage Theory*. Edinburgh: Edinburgh University Press, 2016.

Deleuze, Gilles, and Felix Guattari. *A Thousand Plateaus: Capitalism and Schizophrenia*. Translated by Brian Massumi. Minneapolis: University of Minnesota Press, 1987.

Dery, Mark. "Black to the Future: Interviews with Samuel R. Delany, Greg Tate, and Tricia Rose." In *Flame Wars: The Discourse of Cyberculture*. Edited by Mark Dery, 179–222. Durham, NC: Duke University Press, 1994.

Dinaw Mengestu. *The Beautiful Things That Heaven Bears*. New York: Riverhead, 2007.

DiPrinzio, Drew. "Hailu Mergia on Music and Memory. The Organ and Accordion Master Reflects on Life before His Upcoming Concert in Washington, D.C." *Seven Thirty DC*, June 6, 2019. https://medium.com/seventhirty-dc/hailu -mergia-on-music-and-memory-cd491109b35f.

Dohrmann, Alke, and Manfred Metz. "Ǝnsät." In *Encyclopaedia Aethiopica*. Edited by Siegbert Uhlig, 2:316–18. Wiesbaden, Ger.: Harrassowitz, 2005.

Donham, Donald L., and Wendy James, eds. *The Southern Marches of Imperial Ethiopia: Essays in History and Social Anthropology*. 2nd ed. African Studies Series 51. Oxford, UK: James Currey, 2002.

Dufoix, Stéphane. *Diasporas*. Translated by William Rodarmor. Berkeley: University of California Press, 2008.

Dylan, Bob. *The Lyrics: 1961–2012*. New York: Simon and Schuster, 2016.

EBSTV Worldwide. "Life in America, Dagmawit Gishen (Saint Mary) Ethiopian Church in Denver Colorado." YouTube, September 28, 2015. https://www.youtube.com/watch?v=5yxZm9bxlJY.

Edwards, Gavin. "'We Are the World': A Minute-by-Minute Breakdown." *Rolling Stone*, March 6, 2015. https://www.rollingstone.com/music/music-features/we-are-the-world-a-minute-by-minute-breakdown-54619/.

Eidsheim, Nina Sun. *The Race of Sound: Listening, Timbre, and Vocality in African American Music*. Durham, NC: Duke University Press, 2019.

———. *Sensing Sound: Singing and Listening as Vibrational Practice*. Durham, NC: Duke University Press, 2015.

Elias. "The Burntface Movement: Futuristic African Rap Music." *Tadias Online*, 2003. http://www.tadias.com/v1n5/AE_2_2003-3.html.

Elias Meseret. "Ethiopia and Eritrea Restore Relations after Ending 20-Year Border War." *Christian Science Monitor*, July 9, 2018. https://www.csmonitor.com/World/Africa/2018/0709/Ethiopia-and-Eritrea-restore-relations-after-ending-20-year-border-war.

Emily, Jennifer. "Family of Slain Ethiopian Couple Keeps Dallas Restaurant Going." *Dallas Morning News*, December 30, 2013. https://www.dallasnews.com/news/2013/12/30/family-of-slain-ethiopian-couple-keeps-dallas-restaurant-going/.

Emirbayer, Mustafa, and Ann Mische. "What Is Agency?" *American Journal of Sociology* 103, no. 4 (1998): 962–1023. https://doi.org/10.1086/231294.

Endalk. "Ethiopian Musicians Charged with Terrorism for 'Inciting' Song Lyrics." *Advox Global Voices Advocacy*, July 14, 2017. https://advox.globalvoices.org/2017/07/14/ethiopian-musicians-charged-with-terrorism-for-inciting-song-lyrics/.

Engelsviken, Tormod. "Mission, Pentecostalism, and Ethiopian Identity: The Beginnings of the Mulu Wongel Believers' Church." *Norsk Tidsskrift for Misjonsvitenskap* 68, no. 4 (2014): 195–215. https://journals.mf.no/ntm/article/view/4319/3636.

Ethiopian Heritage Society in North America (EHSNA). "Ethiopia Loss Tesfaye Lemma." Press release, February 8, 2013. http://ehsna.org/ethiopia-loss-tesfaye-lemma-ehsna-pr/.

Ethiopian Press and Information Office. *La civilisation de l'Italie fasciste en Éthiopie*. Addis Ababa: Berhanena Selam, 1938.

Ethiopian Sports Federation in North America. "ESFNA 2015 in the DC-Maryland-Virginia Area." February 3, 2015.

Ezega staff reporter. "Eight Ethiopian Political Parties Sign to Join Prosperity Party." *Ezega News*, December 1, 2019. https://www.ezega.com/News/NewsDetails/7501/Eight-Ethiopian-Political-Parties-Sign-to-Join-Prosperity-Party.

Ezra Gebremedhin. "Mahlet." In *Encyclopaedia Aethiopica.* Edited by Siegbert Uhlig, 3:659–60. Wiesbaden, Ger.: Harrassowitz, 2007.

Faist, Thomas. "The Mobility Turn: A New Paradigm for the Social Sciences?" *Ethnic and Racial Studies* 36, no. 11 (2013): 1637–46. https://doi.org/10.1080 /01419870.2013.812229.

Falceto, Francis. *Abyssinie Swing: A Pictorial History of Modern Ethiopian Music.* Addis Ababa: Shama, 2001.

———. Liner notes. *éthiopiques 1: Golden Years of Modern Ethiopian Music, 1969– 1975.* Buda Musique 829512, 1997. Compact disc.

———. Liner notes. *éthiopiques 4: Ethio Jazz and Musique Instrumentale 1969–1974.* Buda Musique 829642, 1998. Compact disc.

———. Liner notes. *éthiopiques 7: Erè Mèla Mèla.* Buda Musique 829802, 1999. Compact disc.

———. Liner notes. *éthiopiques 10: Tezeta, Ethiopian Blues and Ballads.* Buda Musique 822222, 2002. Compact disc.

———. Liner notes. *éthiopiques 17: Tlahoun Gèssèssè.* Buda Musique 822662, 2004. Compact disc.

———. Liner notes. *Noise and Chill Out: Ethiopian Groove Worldwide.* ÉthioSonic 860215, 2012. Compact disc.

———. "This Is Ethiopian Music." In liner notes. *éthiopiques 20: Either/Orchestra. Live in Addis,* 17–21. Buda Musique, 860121, 2005. Compact disc.

———, and Wolfgang Bender. "The Life and Work of Tessema Eshete, First Ethiopian Singer to Record Commercially." In liner notes. *éthiopiques 27: Centennial of the First Ethiopian Music Recording,* 1–29. Buda Records 860192, 2011. Compact disc.

———, and Haylu Habtu. Additional notes in pdf. *éthiopiques 27: Centennial of the First Ethiopian Music Recording.* Buda Musique 860192, 2011. Compact disc.

Farrell, Nathan. "Celebrity Politics: Bono, Product (RED) and the Legitimising of Philanthrocapitalism." *British Journal of Politics and International Relations* 14, no. 3 (August 2012): 392–406.

Fekade Azeze. "Mengistulore: Oral Literatures Depicting the Man, His Regime, Officials and Proclamations." In *Ethiopia: The Challenge of Democracy from Below.* Edited by Bahru Zewde and Siegfried Pausewang, 149–66. Uppsala, Swed.: Nordiska Afrikainstitutet; Addis Ababa: Forum for Social Studies, 2002.

Finnegan, Ruth. *The Hidden Musicians: Music-Making in an English Town.* Middletown, CT: Wesleyan University Press, 2013.

Finneran, Niall. "Lalibela." In *Encyclopaedia Aethiopica.* Edited by Siegbert Uhlig, 3:482–84. Wiesbaden, Ger.: Harrassowitz, 2007.

Firew Kebede Tiba. "Oromo Struggle: Causes of the Conundrum and Towards a Covenant." *O Pride,* July 30, 2012. https://www.opride.com/2012/07/30/the-oromo -struggle-in-ethiopia-causes-of-the-conundrum-and-towards-a-covenant/.

Fittante, Daniel. "Connection without Engagement: Paradoxes of North American Armenian Return Migration." *Diaspora* 19, no. 2–3 (2010 [published 2017]): 147–69.

Flynn, Katherine. "Mr. Henry's in Washington, D.C." *National Trust for Historic Preservation,* July 9, 2015. https://savingplaces.org/stories/historic-bars-mr -henrys-in-washington-d-c#.XmJH-CFKjIU.

Foster, George M., Thayer Scudder, Elizabeth Colson, and Robert V. Kemper, eds. *Long-Term Field Research in Social Anthropology.* New York: Academic, 1979.

"Gabriel Teodros." *Wikipedia.* https://en.wikipedia.org/wiki/Gabriel_Teodros.

Gabrielsson, Alf. "Emotions in Strong Experiences with Music." In *Music and Emotion: Theory and Research.* Edited by Patrik N. Juslin and John A. Sloboda, 431–49. Oxford: Oxford University Press, 2001.

Gambino, Christine P., Edward N. Trevelyan, and John Thomas Fitzwater. "The Foreign-Born Population from Africa: 2008–2012." United States Census Bureau Report ACSBR /12–16, October 1, 2014. https://www.census.gov/library/publications/2014/acs/acsbr12-16.html.

Gamst, Frederick C. "Djibouti." In *Encyclopaedia Aethiopica.* Edited by Siegbert Uhlig, 2:179–83. Wiesbaden, Ger.: Harrassowitz, 2005.

Gardner, Howard. *Frames of Mind: The Theory of Multiple Intelligences.* New York: Basic, 2004.

Gascon, Alain. "Horn of Africa." In *Encyclopaedia Aethiopica.* Edited by Siegbert Uhlig, 3:67–69. Wiesbaden, Ger.: Harrassowitz, 2007.

Gatrell, Peter. *The Making of the Modern Refugee.* Oxford: Oxford University Press, 2013. https://doi.org/10.1093/acprof:oso/9780199674169.001.0001.

Gershon, Russ. "Ten Americans in Addis." In liner notes. *éthiopiques 20: Either/Orchestra. Live in Addis,* 22–29. Buda Musique 860121, 2005. Compact disc.

Gertler-Jaffe, Jardena. "With Song and Hard Work: Shirei Eretz Yisrael and the Social Imaginary." *University of Toronto Journal of Jewish Thought* 6 (2017): 131–52.

Getachew Debalke. *Asnaketch Werku.* Addis Ababa: Alliance Ethio-Française and Shama, n.d.

Getatchew Haile. "Amharic Poetry of the Ethiopian Diaspora in America: A Sampler." *Diaspora* 15, nos. 2–3 (2006 [published 2011]): 213–337. https://doi.org/10.1353/dsp.2011.0069.

Getatchew Mekuria and Terrie Ex. Liner notes. *Getatchew Mekuria, The Ex and Guests, Moa Anbessa.* Terp Records AS-11, 2006. Compact disc.

Getie Gelaye. "Amharic Praise Poems of Däǧǧazmač Bälay Zälläqä and the Patriots of Goǧǧam during the Italian Occupation of Ethiopia, 1936–1941." In *Proceedings of the 15th International Conference of Ethiopian Studies, Hamburg 2003.* Edited by Siegbert Uhlig, 587–97. Wiesbaden, Ger.: Harrassowitz, 2006.

Getinet Eniyew. *Anthology of Poems: Iwuqetin Filega* [In search of wisdom]. Addis Ababa, 2001.

Gettleman, Jeffrey. "Meles Zenawi, Prime Minister of Ethiopia, Dies at 57." *New York Times,* August 21, 2012. https://www.nytimes.com/2012/08/22/world/africa/meles-zenawi-ethiopian-leader-dies-at-57.html.

Gibb, Camilla. "Harari Ethnography." In *Encyclopaedia Aethiopica.* Edited by Siegbert Uhlig, 2:1026–28. Wiesbaden, Ger.: Harrassowitz, 2005.

Gibbon, Edward. *The Decline and Fall of the Roman Empire.* Vol. 2. Chicago: Encyclopædia Britannica Books, 1952.

Goldenberg, Gideon. "Gurage." In *Encyclopaedia Aethiopica.* Edited by Siegbert Uhlig, 2:924–28. Wiesbaden, Ger.: Harrassowitz, 2005.

Gopinath, Sumanth, and Jason Stanyek, eds. *The Oxford Handbook of Mobile Music Studies.* 2 vols. Oxford: Oxford University Press, 2014.

Gow, Greg. *The Oromo in Exile: From the Horn of Africa to the Suburbs of Australia.* Carlton, Australia: Melbourne University Publishing, 2002.

Graham, William A. *Beyond the Written Word: Oral Aspects of Scripture in the History of Religion*. Cambridge: Cambridge University Press, 1987.

Gravé-Lazi, Lidar. "CBS Report: 135,000 Ethiopians Living in Israel at End of 2013." *Jerusalem Post*, November 19, 2014. https://www.jpost.com/israel-news/cbs-report-135000-ethiopians-living-in-israel-at-end-of-2013-382266.

Greenblatt, Stephen. *Cultural Mobility: A Manifesto*. Cambridge: Cambridge University Press, 2010.

Grega, Kelcie. "Little Ethiopia Seeks Recognition as Cultural District." *Las Vegas Sun*, December 17, 2019. https://lasvegassun.com/news/2019/dec/17/little-ethiopia-seeks-recognition-as-cultural-dist/.

Griaule, Marcel. *Burners of Men: Modern Ethiopia*. Translated by Edwin Gile Rich. London: J. B. Lippincott, 1935.

Hafkin, Nancy J. "'Whatsupoch' on the Net: The Role of Information and Communication Technology in the Shaping of Transnational Ethiopian Identity." *Diaspora* 15, nos. 2–3 (2006 [published 2011]): 221–45. https://doi.org/10.1353/dsp.2011.0072.

Haile Gabriel Dagne. "Amba Gasän." In *Encyclopaedia Aethiopica*. Edited by Siegbert Uhlig, 1:220–21. Wiesbaden, Ger.: Harrassowitz, 2003.

Haile, Rebecca G. *Held at a Distance: My Rediscovery of Ethiopia*. Chicago: Academy Chicago, 2007.

Hailu Habtu. "A Synopsis of Merigeta Lisana Worq's Book." In *T'ǝtawi Sǝra'ǝ'atä Mahlet Zä'abunä Yared Liq* [The ancient hymn corpus of Chief Abuna Yared], xiii–xxxiii. Addis Ababa: Makalé Maison des Études Éthiopiennes and Institut Tigréen des Langues, 1997.

Haleluya Hadero. "Ethiopia's Financial Reforms Hold Promise for Its Diaspora Business Community." *Quartz Africa*, August 10, 2019. https://qz.com/africa/1684528/ethiopia-opens-financial-sector-investments-to-diaspora/.

Hammond, Jenny. *Sweeter than Honey: Ethiopian Women and Revolution; Testimonies of Tigrayan Women*. Trenton, NJ: Red Sea, 1990.

Hannah-Jones, Nikole. "African Immigrants Help Shape Portland's Small Black Community." *Oregonian*, January 19, 2009. Updated March 27, 2019, by Benjamin Brink. https://www.oregonlive.com/news/2009/01/african_immigrants_help_shape.html.

Harbeson, John W. *The Ethiopian Transformation: The Quest for the Post-imperial State*. Westview Special Studies on Africa. Boulder, CO: Westview, 1988.

Harrison, Frank. *Time, Place and Music: An Anthology of Ethnomusicological Observation c.1550 to c.1800*. Amsterdam: Frits Knuf, 1973.

Haustein, Jörg. *Writing Religious History: The Historiography of Ethiopian Pentecostalism*. Wiesbaden, Ger.: Harrassowitz, 2011.

Heldman, Marilyn E. *The Marian Icons of the Painter Frē ṣeyon*. Wiesbaden, Ger.: Harrassowitz, 1994.

———, and Kay Kaufman Shelemay. "Concerning Saint Yared." In *Studies in Ethiopian Languages, Literature, and History*. Edited by Adam Carter McCollum, 65–93. Wiesbaden, Ger.: Harrassowitz, 2017.

Hill, Rachael. "Teddy Afro's 'Tikur Sew'—Ethnic Politics and Historical Narrative." *Africa Collective*, June 8, 2014.

Höhne, Markus V. "Somalia, Political History of." In *Encyclopaedia Aethiopica*. Edited by Siegbert Uhlig, 4:707–10. Wiesbaden, Ger.: Harrassowitz, 2010.

Houston Population Information. https://www.houstontx.gov/ispeakhouston
/HoustonPopulationDetailedEthnicity.pdf.

Hovhannisyan, Samson. "Armenian Orphans and Ethiopian Music: Contribution
and Development." *PanARMENIAN*, June 9, 2016. http://www.panarmenian
.net/eng/details/207201/.

Hultin, Jan. "Oromo." In *Encyclopaedia Aethiopica*. Edited by Siegbert Uhlig, 4:59.
Wiesbaden, Ger.: Harrassowitz, 2010.

———. "Oromo Ethnography." In *Encyclopaedia Aethiopica*. Edited by Siegbert
Uhlig, 4:59–61. Wiesbaden, Ger.: Harrassowitz, 2010.

Human Rights in Ethiopia: Through the Eyes of the Oromo Diaspora. Minneapolis,
MN: Advocates for Human Rights, December 2009.

Human Rights Watch. "Ethiopia: Events of 2018." *World Report 2019*. New York:
Human Rights Watch, 2019. https://www.hrw.org/world-report/2019/country
-chapters/ethiopia.

———. *World Report 2017*. New York: Human Rights Watch, 2017. https://www
.hrw.org/sites/default/files/world_report_download/wr2017-web.pdf.

Imbakom Kalewold. *Traditional Ethiopian Church Education*. Translated by
Menghestu Lemma. New York: Teacher's College Press, 1970.

"In Memoriam." *Southern Speech Journal* 35, no. 2 (1969): 191–92. https://doi.org
/10.1080/10417946909372048.

James, Wendy, Donald L. Donham, Eisei Kurimoto, and Alessandro Triulzi, eds. *Remapping Ethiopia: Socialism and After*. Oxford, UK: James Currey, 2002.

Jeffrey, James. "Stuck in Limbo in Ethiopia, Africa's Biggest Refugee Camp."
Deutsche Welle, November 13, 2015. https://www.dw.com/en/stuck-in-limbo-in
-ethiopia-africas-biggest-refugee-camp/a-18848086.

Johnson, Randal. Introduction to *The Field of Cultural Production: Essays on Art and
Literature*, by Pierre Bourdieu, 1–25. New York: Cambridge University Press,
1993.

Jolly Papa. "Jolly Papa Interview: Munit Mesfin." *Jolly Papa*, April 10, 2019. https://
www.mixcloud.com/JollyPapa/munit-mesfin-jolly-papa-interview/.

Kamau, Waringa. "Oakland's Enkutatash Festival Is Cancelled, but Ethiopians Celebrate in Other Ways." *Oakland North*, September 11, 2015. https://oaklandnorth
.net/2015/09/11/oaklands-enkutatash-festival-is-cancelled-but-ethiopians
-celebrate-in-other-ways/.

Kaminski, Joseph S. "Surrogate Speech of the Asante Ivory Trumpeters of Ghana."
Yearbook for Traditional Music 40 (2008): 117–35. https://www.jstor.org/stable
/20465070.

Kane, Thomas Leiper. *Amharic-English Dictionary*. 2 vols. Wiesbaden, Ger.: Harrassowitz, 1990.

Kaplan, Steven. "The Christianisation of Time in Fifteenth-Century Ethiopia." In
Religious Conversion: History, Experience and Meaning. Edited by Ira Katznelson
and Miri Rubin, 81–98. Farnham, UK: Ashgate, 2014.

———. "Däbr." In *Encyclopaedia Aethiopica*. Edited by Siegbert Uhlig, 2:6–7. Wiesbaden, Ger.: Harrassowitz, 2005.

———. "Ethiopian Immigrants in the United States and Israel: A Preliminary Comparison." *International Journal of Ethiopian Studies* 5, no. 1 (Spring-Summer
2010): 71–92.

———. "Ezra, Apocalypse of." In *Encyclopaedia Aethiopica*. Edited by Siegbert Uhlig, 2:482. Wiesbaden, Ger.: Harrassowitz, 2005.

———. "Seeing Is Believing: The Power of Visual Culture in the Religious World of Aşe Zär'a Ya'eqob of Ethiopia (1434–1468)." *Journal of Religion in Africa* 32, no. 4 (2002): 403–21.

———. "*Tama Galut Etiopiya*: The Ethiopian Exile Is Over." *Diaspora* 14, nos. 2–3 (2005): 381–96. https://doi.org/10.1353/dsp.0.0018.

———. "Vital Information at Your Fingertips: The *Ethiopian Yellow Pages* as a Cultural Document." *Diaspora* 15, nos. 2–3 (2006 [published 2011]): 247–63. https://doi.org/10.1353/dsp.2011.0074.

———. "Zar." In *Encyclopaedia Aethiopica*. Edited by Siegbert Uhlig, 4:185–87. Wiesbaden, Ger.: Harrassowitz, 2010.

———, and Chaim Rosen. "Ethiopian Jews in Israel." *American Jewish Year Book* 94 (1994): 59–109. https://www.jstor.org/stable/23605644.

Karadawi, Ahmed. "The Smuggling of the Ethiopian Falasha to Israel through Sudan." *African Affairs* 90, no. 358 (1991): 23–49.

Kawase, Itsushi. "The Azmari Performance during Zar Ceremonies in Northern Gondar, Ethiopia—Challenges and Prospects for the Documentation." In *Cultures sonores d'Afrique V*. Edited by Junzo Kawada, 65–80. Tokyo: University of Foreign Studies, 2012.

———, dir. *When Spirits Ride Their Horses*. 2012. 26 min. www.itsushikawase.com /horses.html.

Keats-Rohan, K. S. B. "Biography, Identity and Names: Understanding the Pursuit of the Individual in Prosopography." In *Prosopography Approaches and Applications: A Handbook*. Edited by K. S. B. Keats-Rohan, 139–82. Oxford, UK: Linacre College, Unit for Prosopographical Research, 2007.

Kelto, Anders. "Ethiopia's Economy Benefits from Returning Diaspora." *Public Radio International: The World*, February 20, 2013. Hosted by Aaron Schachter. https://www.pri.org/stories/2013-02-20/ethiopias-economy-benefits -returning-diaspora.

Kevorkian, Tanya. "Town Musicians in Baroque Society and Culture." *German History* 30, no. 3 (2012): 350–71. https://doi.org/10.1093/gerhis/ghs048.

Kiberd, Declan, and P. J. Mathews. *Handbook of the Irish Revival: An Anthology of Irish Cultural and Political Writings 1891–1922*. Dublin: Abbey Theatre Press, 2015.

Kidanä Wäld Kəfle. *Mäshafä Säwasəw Wägəs Wämäzgäbä Qalat Haddis* [A book of grammar and verb, and a new dictionary]. Addis Ababa, 1948 EC.

Kimberlin, Cynthia Tse. "Dances." In *Encyclopaedia Aethiopica*. Edited by Siegbert Uhlig, 2:81–84. Wiesbaden, Ger.: Harrassowitz, 2005.

———. "Mäsinqo." In *Encyclopaedia Aethiopica*. Edited by Siegbert Uhlig, 3:834–36. Wiesbaden, Ger.: Harrassowitz, 2007.

———. "*Masinqo* and the Nature of *Qeñet*." PhD diss., University of California–Los Angeles, 1976.

———. "Orchestra Ethiopia 1963–1975: Halim El-Dabh, Catalyst for Music Innovation and Preservation." In *Multiple Interpretations of Dynamics of Creativity and Knowledge in African Music Traditions: A Festschrift in Honor of Akin Euba on the Occasion of His 70th Birthday*. Edited by Bode Omojola and George Dor, 187–210. Point Richmond, CA: MRI, 2005.

———. "The Scholarship and Art of Ashenafi Kebede (1938–1968)." *Ethnomusicology* 43, no. 2 (1999): 322–34. https://doi.org/10.2307/852737.

King, Russell, and Anastasia Christou. "Of Counter-diaspora and Reverse Transnationalism: Return Mobilities to and from the Ancestral Homeland." *Mobilities* 6, no. 4 (2011): 451–66. https://doi.org/10.1080/17450101.2011.603941.

Kirsner, Scott. "Uber-Lyft Fee to Help Taxi Has So Far Funded Only Consultants." *Boston Globe*, March 29, 2019. https://www.bostonglobe.com/business/2019 /03/29/uber-and-lyft-fee-that-supposed-help-taxi-drivers-has-only-funded -consultants/Tcby2tPg1OpaUazb3TrXtM/story.html.

Kisselgoff, Anna. "Blue Nile Dancers a Peace Corps Find." *New York Times*, March 18, 1969.

Kiwan, Nadia, and Ulrike Hanna Meinhof. *Cultural Globalization and Music: African Artists in Transnational Networks*. New York: Palgrave Macmillan, 2011.

Klausner, David. "Civic Musicians in Wales and the Marches, 1430–1642." In *Music and Medieval Manuscripts: Paleography and Performance: Essays Dedicated to Andrew Hughes*. Edited by John Haines and Randall Rosenfeld, 279–99. Aldershot, UK: Ashgate, 2004.

Kloman, Harry. *Mesob across America: Ethiopian Food in the U.S.A.* New York: iUniverse, 2010.

Koehn, Peter H. *Refugees from Revolution: U.S. Policy and Third-World Migration*. Boulder, CO: Westview, 1991.

Kropp, Manfred. "'*Antiquae restitutio legis*': Zur Alimentation des Hofklerus und einer Zeugenliste als *imago imperii* und *notitia dignitatum* in einer Urkunde des Kaisers Zär'ä Ya'qob im *condaghe* der Hs. BM Or. 481, fol. 154." *Scrinium* 1, no. 1 (2005): 115–47. https://doi.org/10.1163/18177565-90000131.

Large, David Clay. *Between Two Fires: Europe's Path in the 1930s*. Rev. ed. New York: W. W. Norton, 1990.

Latour, Bruno. *Reassembling the Social: An Introduction to Actor-Network-Theory*. Oxford: Oxford University Press, 2005.

League, Panayotis. "Grooving Heavy, Dancing Drunk: Gustemic Metaphor and Mimetic Polytemporality in Anatolian Greek Music." *Ethnomusicology* 63, no. 3 (2019): 393–417.

Lee, Richard E., ed. *The Longue Durée and World-Systems Analysis*. Albany: State University of New York Press, 2012.

Legesse Tigabu Mengie. "Ethnic Federalism and Conflict in Ethiopia: What Lessons Can Other Jurisdictions Draw?" *African Journal of International and Comparative Law* 23, no. 3 (2015): 462–75. https://doi.org/10.3366/ajicl.2015 .0131.

Leslau, Wolf. *Amharic Textbook*. Wiesbaden, Ger.: Harrassowitz, 1967.

———. *Concise Amharic Dictionary*. Wiesbaden, Ger.: Harrassowitz 1976.

———. *English-Amharic Context Dictionary*. Wiesbaden, Ger.: Harrassowitz, 1973.

———. *Ethiopian Argots*. The Hague, Neth.: Mouton, 1964.

Levine, Donald N. "Amhara." In *Encyclopaedia Aethiopica*. Edited by Siegbert Uhlig, 1:230–32. Wiesbaden, Ger.: Harrassowitz, 2003.

———. *Greater Ethiopia: The Evolution of a Multiethnic Society*. Chicago: University of Chicago Press, 1974.

———. "On Cultural Creativity in the Ethiopian Diaspora." *Diaspora* 15, nos. 2–3 (2006 [published 2011]): 215–20. https://doi.org/10.1353/dsp.2011.0070.

————. *Wax and Gold: Tradition and Innovation in Ethiopian Culture*. Chicago: University of Chicago Press, 1965.

Limon, Elvia. "Ethiopian Evangelical Baptist Church Gets New Texas Site." *AP News*, May 30, 2018. https://apnews.com/38dd21e91bc645b6ae8d5d0d8399 e88d.

Linthicum, Kate. "Ethiopian Community Gathers to Celebrate Timket." *Los Angeles Times*, January 22, 2011. https://www.latimes.com/local/la-xpm-2011-jan-22 -la-me-beliefs-ethiopian-epiphany-20110122-story.html.

Los Angeles Almanac. "Little Ethiopia, Los Angeles." http://www.laalmanac.com /LA/la702.php.

Lowenstein, Roger. "Uber, Lyft and the Hard Economics of Taxi Cab Medallions." *Washington Post*, May 24, 2019. https://www.washingtonpost.com/business /economy/uber-lyft-and-the-hard-economics-of-taxi-cab-medallions/2019 /05/24/cf1b56f4-7cda-11e9-a5b3-34f3edf1351e_story.html.

Lucas, Ann E. *Music of a Thousand Years: A New History of Persian Musical Traditions*. Oakland, CA: University of California Press, 2019.

Lyons, Terrence. "Transnational Politics in Ethiopia: Diasporas and the 2005 Elections." *Diaspora* 15, nos. 2–3 (2006 [published 2011]): 265–84. https://doi.org /10.1353/dsp.2011.0076.

Maasho, Aaron. "At Concert, Ethiopia, Eritrea Leaders Preach Peace, Love, Unity." *Reuters*, July 15, 2018. https://www.reuters.com/article/us-ethiopia-eritrea -idUSKBN1K50ZB.

Maffesoli, Michel. *The Time of the Tribes: The Decline of Individualism in Mass Society*. London: Sage, 1996.

Maglio, Alan, and Medhin Paolos, dir. *Asmarina: Voices and Images of a Postcolonial Heritage*. Documentary film. Milan, Italy, 2015. https://asmarinaproject.com.

Magnússon, Sigurður Gylfi. "*The Singularization of History*: Social History and Microhistory within the Postmodern State of Knowledge." *Journal of Social History* 36, no. 3 (2003): 701–35. https://doi.org/10.1353/jsh.2003.0054.

Mann, C. Griffith. "The Role of the Painted Icon in Ethiopian Culture." In *Ethiopian Art: The Walters Art Museum*. Edited by Deborah E. Horowitz, 121–37. Lingfield, UK: Third Millennium, 2001.

Marcos-Birra, Lily. "A Short Untold History of Ali Birra: A Legendary Oromo Singer." In *Ali Birra: A Fifty Year Journey for the Love of Music and His People*. Edited by Mohammed Hassen and Lily Marcos-Birra, 7–51. Dallas, TX: CreateSpace, 2013.

Marcus, Cressida. "The Production of Patriotic Spirituality: Ethiopian Orthodox Women's Experience of War and Social Crisis." *Northeast African Studies* 8, no. 3 (2001): 179–208. https://doi.org/10.1353/nas.2006.0008.

Marcus, Harold G. *A History of Ethiopia*. Updated ed. Berkeley: University of California Press, 2002.

Markakis, John. "Nationalities and the State in Ethiopia." *Third World Quarterly* 11, no. 4 (1989): 118–30.

Marrassini, Paolo. "Kəbrä Nägäst." In *Encyclopaedia Aethiopica*. Edited by Siegbert Uhlig, 3:364–68. Wiesbaden, Ger.: Harrassowitz, 2007.

Martha Z. Tegegn. "Part Two: Exclusive Interview with Ethiopian Legend Teshome Mitiku." *Tadias*, August 12, 2010. http://www.tadias.com/08/12/2010/part -two-exclusive-interview-with-ethiopian-legend-teshome-mitiku/.

———. "Part Three Exclusive: Teshome Mitiku Plans to Return to Ethiopia." *Tadias*, August 19, 2010. http://www.tadias.com/08/19/2010/part-three -exclusive-teshome-mitiku-plans-to-return-to-ethiopia/.

Martin, György. "Dance Types in Ethiopia." *Journal of the International Folk Music Council* 19 (1967): 23–27. https://www.jstor.org/stable/942181.

Martinez, Andrew. "Florence, Council of." In *Encyclopaedia Aethiopica*. Edited by Siegbert Uhlig, 2:554–55. Wiesbaden, Ger.: Harrassowitz, 2005.

Matzke, Christine. "Of *Suwa* Houses and Singing Contests: Early Urban Women Performers in Asmara, Eritrea." In *African Theatre: Women*. Edited by Jane Plastow, 29–46. Bloomington: Indiana University Press, 2002.

Mbembe, Achille. *On the Postcolony*. Berkeley: University of California Press, 2001.

McCann, James. "A Response: *Doro Fänta*: Creativity vs. Adaptation in the Ethiopian Diaspora." *Diaspora* 15, no. 2 (2006 [published 2011]): 381–88. https://doi .org/10.1353/dsp.2011.0075.

McCollum, Jonathan, and David G. Herbert, eds. *Theory and Method in Historical Ethnomusicology*. Lanham, MD: Lexington, 2014.

McDonald, David A. *My Voice Is My Weapon: Music, Nationalism, and the Poetics of Palestinian Resistance*. Durham, NC: Duke University Press, 2013.

Meklit Hadero. "The Unexpected Beauty of Everyday Sounds." TED Fellows Retreat, August 2015. https://www.ted.com/talks/meklit_hadero_the _unexpected_beauty_of_everyday_sounds.

"Meklit Hadero: This Was Made Here: A Diasporic Odyssey." Yerba Buena Center for the Arts Forum, San Francisco, CA, May 19–21, 2016. https://ybca.org/wp -content/uploads/2019/07/YBCA_Meklit_Playbill_Final_Web.pdf.

Mekuria Bulcha. *Contours of the Emergent and Ancient Oromo Nation: Dilemmas in the Ethiopian Politics of State and Nation-Building*. CASAS Book Series No. 84. Cape Town, S. Africa: Centre for Advanced Studies of African Society, 2011.

Meron Hadero. "To Walk in Their Shoes." In *The Displaced: Refugee Writers on Refugee Lives*. Edited by Viet Thanh Nguyen, n.p. New York: Abrams, 2018.

Merriam, Alan P. "Use of Music in Reconstructing Culture History." In *Reconstructing African Culture History*. Edited by Creighton Gabel and Norman R. Bennett, 85–114. African Research Studies 8. Boston: Boston University Press, 1967.

Messing, Simon D. "Group Therapy and Social Status in the Zar Cult of Ethiopia." *American Anthropologist* 60, no. 6 (1958): 1120–26. https://www.jstor.org/stable /665379.

———. "The Highland-Plateau Amhara of Ethiopia." PhD diss., University of Pennsylvania, 1957.

Miendlarzewska, Ewa A., and Wiebke J. Trost. "How Musical Training Affects Cognitive Development: Rhythm, Reward and Other Modulating Variables." *Frontiers in Neuroscience* 7 (2014): 1–18. https://doi.org/10.3389/fnins.2013.0 0279.

Migration Policy Institute. *The Ethiopian Diaspora in the United States*. Prepared for the Rockefeller Foundation–Aspen Institute Diaspora Program (RAD). Washington, DC: Migration Policy Institute, 2014.

Miran, Jonathan. "Red Sea Slave Trade in the Nineteenth Century." In *Encyclopaedia Aethiopica*. Edited by Siegbert Uhlig, 4:674–76. Wiesbaden, Ger.: Harrassowitz, 2010.

Mistry, Anupa. "The Dark Knight Returns: A Conversation with The Weeknd."

Pitchfork, August 31, 2015. https://pitchfork.com/features/interview/9711-the
-dark-knight-returns-a-conversation-with-the-weeknd/.

Mitter, Siddharta. "For Meklit Hadero, Keeping It Real and Varied." *Boston Globe*, July 10, 2011. http://archive.boston.com/ae/music/articles/2011/07/10/meklit
_hadero_forges_ahead_with_vision_and_innovation/.

Moges Seyoum. *Talaqu Itiyopəyawi Liq Qəddus Yaredənna Yäzemawə Tarik Känämələkkətu* [Saint Yared: The great Ethiopian scholar and the history of the hymns and their notation]. Washington, DC, 2017.

———. *Yaqeddus Yared Yazema Dersat Atäqalay Gäs'əta* [An essay on the chant of Saint Yared]. Washington, DC: Bäliqä Mäzämәran Mogәs Sәyum, 1992.

Mohammed Hassen. "Ali Mohammed Birra Is a Gift to the Oromo People and to the World of Music." In *Ali Birra: A Fifty Year Journey for the Love of Music and His People*. Edited by Mohammed Hassen and Lily Marcos-Birra, 52–95. Dallas, TX: CreateSpace, 2013.

———. "Macha-Tulama Association 1963–1967 and the Development of Oromo Nationalism." In *Oromo Nationalism and the Ethiopian Discourse: The Search for Freedom and Democracy*. Edited by Asafa Jalata, 183–222. Lawrenceville, NJ: Red Sea, 1998.

———. *The Oromo of Ethiopia: A History, 1570–1860*. African Studies Series 66. Cambridge: Cambridge University Press, 1990.

Mollica, Richard F. *Healing Invisible Wounds: Paths to Hope and Recovery in a Violent World*. Nashville, TN: Vanderbilt University Press, 2008.

Mondon-Vidailhet, Casimir. "La musique éthiopienne." In *Encyclopédie de la musique et dictionnaire du Conservatoire*. Edited by Albert Lavignac and Lionel de la Laurencie, 3179–96. Paris: Librairie Delagrave, 1922.

Morand, Katell. "Solitudes habitées: le chant, le souvenir et le conflit chez les Amhara du Goggam (Éthiopie)." PhD diss., Université de Paris Ouest Nanterre, 2012.

Morley, David. *Home Territories: Media, Mobility, and Identity*. London: Routledge, 2000.

Morriss, Vincent. "City Moves to Shut Down Go-Go Club." *Washington Times*, February 7, 1997.

Mosley, Walter. "Seeking a Unified Field." In liner notes. Meklit Hadero, *We Are Alive*, n.p. Six Degrees Records 657036 120426, 2014. Compact disc.

Muth, Franz-Christoph. "Aḥmad b. Ibrāhīm al-Ġāzī." In *Encyclopaedia Aethiopica*. Edited by Siegbert Uhlig, 1:155–58. Wiesbaden, Ger.: Harrassowitz, 2003.

Nagaso Gidada. "Oromo Historical Poems and Songs: Conquest and Exploitation in Western Wallaga, 1886–1927." *Paideuma* 29 (1983): 327–40. https://www.jstor
.org/stable/41409898.

Narayan, Kirin. *Everyday Creativity: Singing Goddesses in the Himalayan Foothills*. Chicago: University of Chicago Press, 2016.

Nettl, Bruno. "Historical Aspects of Ethnomusicology." *American Anthropologist* 60, no. 3 (1958): 518–32. https://doi.org/10.1525/aa.1958.60.3.02a00100.

Newsham, Jack, and Dan Adams. "Amid Fight with Uber, Lyft, Boston Taxi Ridership Plummets." *Boston Globe*, August 19, 2015. https://www.bostonglobe
.com/business/2015/08/19/boston-taxi-ridership-down-percent-this-year
/S9dZMELMye6puzTTYoDIrL/story.html.

Ngoma Tchibinda, Yannick Roland Nene. "Diaspora Direct Investments: The Challenges of the African Diaspora." *Journal of Institute of Economic Development and Social Researches* 4, no. 14 (2018): 706–13. https://dergipark.org.tr/en/pub/iksad/issue/51710/671372.

Niederstadt, Leah. "Fighting HIV with Juggling Clubs: An Introduction to Ethiopia's Circuses." *African Arts* 42, no. 1 (2009): 76–87. https://doi.org/10.1162/afar.2009.42.1.76.

Nic Dhiarmada, Bríona. *The 1916 Irish Rebellion*. Notre Dame, IN: Notre Dame Press, 2016.

Nikolayeva, O. "Cultural Reforms in Ethiopia." In *Ten Years of the Ethiopian Revolution*. Edited by Nikolai Ivanovich Gavrilov. Translated by Nadezhda Burova, 149–60. Moscow: Progress, 1986.

"The Nile Ethiopian Ensemble, 1998 Calendar of Events." *Elelta* 2 (1998): 11.

Nordenfalk, Carl. "The Five Senses in Late Medieval and Renaissance Art." *Journal of the Warburg and Courtauld Institutes* 48 (1985): 1–22.

Ochoa Gautier, Ana María. *Aurality: Listening and Knowledge in Nineteenth-Century Colombia*. Durham, NC: Duke University Press, 2014.

O'Connell, John Morgan, and Salwa El-Shawan Castelo-Branco, eds. *Music and Conflict*. Urbana: University of Illinois Press, 2010.

Ofcansky, Thomas P. "Imperial Bodyguard." In *Encyclopaedia Aethiopica*. Edited by Siegbert Uhlig, 3:127–28. Wiesbaden, Ger.: Harrassowitz, 2007.

Okayafrica. "Okayafrica's Top 15 Music Videos of 2015." *Okayafrica*, December 21, 2015. https://www.okayafrica.com/african-music-videos-2015-top-15/?rebelltitem=11#rebelltitem11.

Oldenburg, Ray. *Celebrating the Third Place: Inspiring Stories about the "Great Good Places" at the Heart of Our Communities*. New York: Marlowe, 2001.

———. *The Great Good Place: Cafés, Coffee Shops, Community Centers, Beauty Parlors, General Stores, Bars, Hangouts, and How They Get You through the Day*. New York: Paragon House, 1989.

Oliveira, Flávio. "Orpheonic Chant and the Construction of Childhood in Brazilian Elementary Education." In *Brazilian Popular Music and Citizenship*. Edited by Idelber Avelar and Christopher Dunn, 44–63. Durham, NC: Duke University Press, 2011.

O'Mahoney, Kevin, and Wolbert Smidt. "Finfinnee." In *Encyclopaedia Aethiopica*. Edited by Siegbert Uhlig, 2:544–46. Wiesbaden, Ger.: Harrassowitz, 2005.

Osmond, Thomas. "A Few Remarks about the Song 'Awash.'" In liner notes. Ali Birra, *éthiopiques 28: Great Oromo Music*, 30–32. Buda Musique 860233, 2013. Compact disc.

Otieno, Daniel. "After Making Peace, Ethiopia and Eritrea Now Focus on Development." *Africa Renewal*, December 2018. https://www.un.org/africarenewal/magazine/december-2018-march-2019/after-making-peace-ethiopia-and-eritrea-now-focus-development.

Ott, Jennifer. "Somali Community in Seattle." *HistoryLink.org*, November 19, 2010. https://www.historylink.org/File/9634.

Palazzo, Eric. "Art, Liturgy, and the Five Senses in the Early Middle Ages." *Viator* 41, no. 1 (2010): 25–56. https://doi.org/10.1484/J.VIATOR.1.100566.

Palmer, Robert. "Ethiopian Funk from Mahmoud Ahmed." *New York Times*, July 30, 1986. https://www.nytimes.com/1986/07/30/arts/the-pop-life-evolution-of-psychobilly-on-new-cramps-album.html.

———. "The Pop Life: Peter Case Heads a List of the Top Albums of 1986." *New York Times*, January 7, 1987. https://www.nytimes.com/1987/01/07/arts/the-pop-life-peter-case-heads-a-list-of-the-top-albums-of-1986.html.

Pankhurst, Richard. "The Early History of Ethiopian Horse-Names." *Paideuma* 35, Afrika-Studien 1 (1989): 197–206.

———. "Slavery: Slave Trade from Ancient Times to the 19th Century." In *Encyclopaedia Aethiopica*. Edited by Siegbert Uhlig, 4:673–74. Wiesbaden, Ger.: Harrassowitz, 2010.

Pankhurst, Sylvia. *Ethiopia: A Cultural History*. Essex, UK: Lalibela House, 1959.

Pareles, Jon. "In Every Note, Passion That Needs No Translation." *New York Times*, July 27, 2014. https://www.nytimes.com/2014/07/28/arts/music/mahmoud-ahmed-kicks-off-summer-concert-series.html.

Patel, Aniruddh D. "Why Would Musical Training Benefit the Neural Encoding of Speech? The OPERA Hypothesis." *Frontiers in Psychology* 2 (2011): 1–14. https://doi.org/10.3389/fpsyg.2011.00142.

Phillips, Ryan. "East Africans in Oakland: Sharing Ethiopian Music with the World." *Oakland North*, April 10, 2012. https://oaklandnorth.net/2012/04/10/east-africans-in-oakland-sharing-ethiopian-music-with-the-world/.

Piekut, Benjamin. "Actor-Networks in Music History: Clarifications and Critiques." *Twentieth-Century Music* 11, no. 2 (2014): 191–215. https://doi.org/10.1017/S147857221400005X.

Plastow, Jane. *African Theatre and Politics: The Evolution of Theatre in Ethiopia, Tanzania and Zimbabwe—a Comparative Study*. Amsterdam: Rodopi, 1996.

———. "Theatre: Theatre in Ethiopia." In *Encyclopaedia Aethiopica*. Edited by Siegbert Uhlig, 4:940–42. Wiesbaden, Ger.: Harrassowitz, 2010.

Plate, S. Brent. *Walter Benjamin, Religion, and Aesthetics*. New York: Routledge, 2005.

Prandi, Stefania. "Eritrean Refugees in Ethiopia." *Al-Jazeera*, March 10, 2016. https://www.aljazeera.com/indepth/inpictures/2016/03/eritrean-refugees-ethiopia-160306065928790.html.

Rastall, Richard. "Wait [wayt, wayte]." *Grove Music Online*, 2001. https://www.doi.org/10.1093/gmo/9781561592630.article.29801.

Reed, Dan. "DC's 'Little Ethiopia' Has Moved to Silver Spring and Alexandria." *Greater Greater Washington*, September 14, 2015. https://ggwash.org/view/39188/dcs-little-ethiopia-has-moved-to-silver-spring-and-alexandria.

Reed-Danahay, Deborah. "'Like a Foreigner in My Own Homeland': Writing the Dilemmas of Return in the Vietnamese American Diaspora." *Identities* 22, no. 5 (2015): 603–18. https://doi.org/10.1080/1070289X.2014.975713.

Regev, Motti, and Edwin Seroussi. *Popular Music and National Culture in Israel*. Berkeley: University of California Press, 2004.

Reich, Howard. "Wild Hare: A Chicago Reggae Landmark Prepares to Close." *Chicago Tribune*, April 18, 2011. https://www.chicagotribune.com/news/ct-xpm-2011-04-18-ct-live-0419-jazz-wild-hare-20110418-story.html.

Reiss, Sarah. "How Dallas Got So Many Ethiopian Restaurants." *D Magazine*, June 2011. https://www.dmagazine.com/publications/d-magazine/2011/june/how-dallas-got-so-many-ethiopian-restaurants/.

Reitz, Scott. "At Ibex Ethiopian, the Dishes (and the Vibe) Are Communal." *Dallas Observer*, August 4, 2011. https://www.dallasobserver.com/restaurants/at-ibex-ethiopian-the-dishes-and-the-vibe-are-communal-6422710.

Reuters. "Africa's Youngest Leader Is Riding a Wave of Hope from the Young People Who Got Him There." *Free Zone Channel*, June 2, 2018.

Reyes, Adelaida. *Songs of the Caged, Songs of the Free: Music and the Vietnamese Refugee Experience*. Philadelphia: Temple University Press, 1999.

Richards, Chris. "In 1984, These D.C. Ethiopian Expats Made a Truly Rare Record. Now the World Can Hear It." Review of *Admas: Sons of Ethiopia*. *Washington Post*, Style, July 30, 2020. https://www.washingtonpost.com/lifestyle/style/in -1984-these-dc-ethiopian-expats-made-a-truly-rare-record-now-the-world -can-hear-it/2020/07/29/837911c0-d0e7-11ea-8d32-1ebf4e9d8e0d_story .html.

Ritter, Jonathan, and J. Martin Daughtry, eds. *Music in the Post-9/11 World*. New York: Routledge, 2007.

Roberts, Chris. "Somali Music Is Here, but Hard to Find." *MPR News*, August 30, 2006. https://www.mprnews.org/story/2006/08/21/ethnicmusicsomalian.

Romero, Angel. "Artist Profiles: Seleshe Damessae." *World Music Central*, August 21, 2016. https://worldmusiccentral.org/tag/gashe-abera-molla/.

Rosaldo, Renato, Smadar Lavie, and Kirin Narayan. "Introduction: Creativity in Anthropology." In *Creativity/Anthropology*. Edited by Smadar Lavie, Kirin Narayan, and Renato Rosaldo, 1–8. Ithaca, NY: Cornell University Press, 1993.

Rosenthal, David H. *Hard Bop: Jazz and Black Music, 1955–1965*. New York: Oxford University Press, 1992.

Safran, William. "Diasporas in Modern Societies: Myths of Homeland and Return." *Diaspora* 1, no. 1 (1991): 83–99.

Samuel Getatchew. "Ethiopian-American to Run Biden's Transition Team." *Reporter*, June 2, 2020. https://www.thereporterethiopia.com/article/ethiopian -american-run-bidens-transition-team.

Schaefer, Charles. "*Maḥbär*." In *Encyclopaedia Aethiopica*. Edited by Siegbert Uhlig, 3:649–50. Wiesbaden, Ger.: Harrassowitz, 2007.

Schnapper, LaDena, ed. *Teenage Refugees from Ethiopia Speak Out (in Their Own Voices)*. New York: Rosen, 1997.

Seachrist, Denise. *The Musical World of Halim El-Dabh*. Kent, OH: Kent State University Press, 2003.

Seeger, Anthony. "Long-Term Field Research in Ethnomusicology in the 21st-Century." *Em Pauta* 19, nos. 32–33 (2008): 3–20. https://seer.ufrgs.br/EmPauta /article/view/10742/6366.

Selam Gebrekidan. "Ethiopia and Eritrea Declare an End to Their War." *New York Times*, July 9, 2018. https://www.nytimes.com/2018/07/09/world/africa /ethiopia-eritrea-war.html.

Selam Seyoum Woldemariam. "The Origin and Development of Zemenawi Music in Ethiopia from 1896–1974." BA thesis, Addis Ababa University, 1988.

Shao, Oliver Y. "A Cosmopolitan Social Justice Approach to Education." *Africa Today* 63, no. 2 (2016): 107–11. https://www.jstor.org/stable/10.2979/africatoday .63.2.14.

Shawki El Gamal. "Graziani, Rudolfo." In *Encyclopaedia Aethiopica*. Edited by Siegbert Uhlig, 2:877–78. Wiesbaden, Ger.: Harrassowitz, 2005.

Shelemay, Kay Kaufman. "Ethiopian Musical Invention in Diaspora: A Tale of

Three Musicians." *Diaspora* 15, nos. 2–3 (2006 [published 2011]): 303–20. https://doi.org/10.1353/dsp.2011.0067.

———. "Ethnography as a Way of Life." *Ethnomusicology* 64, no. 1 (2020): 1–18.

———. "'Historical Ethnomusicology': Reconstructing Falasha Liturgical History." *Ethnomusicology* 24, no. 2 (1980): 233–58. https://doi.org/10.2307/851114.

———, ed. *The Jews of Ethiopia: A People in Transition.* Tel Aviv: Beth Hatefutsoth; New York: The Jewish Museum, 1986.

———. "Learning from the Eda Kuhn Loeb Music Library." *Harvard Library Bulletin* 18, nos. 1–2 (2007): 37–41. http://nrs.harvard.edu/urn-3:HUL.InstRepos: 34917354.

———. *Let Jasmine Rain Down: Song and Remembrance among Syrian Jews.* Chicago: University of Chicago Press, 1998.

———. "Music." In *Encyclopaedia Aethiopica.* Edited by Siegbert Uhlig, 3:1082–86. Wiesbaden, Ger.: Harrassowitz, 2007.

———. *Music, Ritual, and Falasha History.* East Lansing: Michigan State University Press, 1989.

———. "Musical Communities: Rethinking the Collective in Music." *Journal of the American Musicological Society* 64, no. 2 (2011): 349–90. https://doi.org/10.1525 /jams.2011.64.2.349.

———. "The Musician and Transmission of Religious Tradition: The Multiple Roles of the Ethiopian *Däbtära.*" *Journal of Religion in Africa* 22, no. 3 (1992): 242–60. https://doi.org/10.1163/157006692X00167.

———. "Music in the Ethiopian American Diaspora: A Preliminary Overview." In *Proceedings of the 16th International Conference of Ethiopian Studies: July 2–6, 2007, Trondheim, Norway.* Edited by Svein Ege, Harald Aspen, Birhanu Teferra, and Shiferaw Bekele, 1153–64. Wiesbaden, Ger.: Harrassowitz, 2009. https:// dash.harvard.edu/handle/1/4269154.

———. "A New System of Musical Notation in Ethiopia." In *Ethiopian Studies: Dedicated to Wolf Leslau on the Occasion of His Seventy-Fifth Birthday, November 14th, 1981.* Edited by Stanislav Segert and Andras T. E. Bodrogligeti, 571–82. Wiesbaden, Ger.: Harrassowitz, 1983.

———. *A Song of Longing: An Ethiopian Journey.* Urbana: University of Illinois Press, 1991.

———. "'Traveling Music': Mulatu Astatke and the Genesis of Ethiopian Jazz." In *Jazz Worlds/World Jazz.* Edited by Philip V. Bohlman and Goffredo Plastino, 239–57. Chicago: University of Chicago Press, 2016. https://dash.harvard.edu /handle/1/34361554.

———, and Peter Jeffery, eds. *Ethiopian Christian Liturgical Chant: An Anthology.* 3 vols. with CD. Madison, WI: A-R, 1993, 1994, 1997.

———, and Steven Kaplan. "Introduction." *Diaspora* 15, nos. 2–3 (2006 [published 2011]): 191–213. https://doi.org/10.1353/dsp.2011.0068.

———, and Steven Kaplan, eds. *Special Issue: Creating the Ethiopian Diaspora: Perspectives from Across the Disciplines. Diaspora* 15, nos. 2–3 (2006 [published 2011]).

Sheller, Mimi, and John Urry. "The New Mobilities Paradigm." *Environment and Planning A: Economy and Space* 38, no. 2 (2006): 207–26. https://doi.org/10 .1068/a37268.

Shiferaw Bekele and Sophia Dege-Müller. "Revolution of 1974." In *Encyclopaedia Aethiopica*. Edited by Siegbert Uhlig, 4:384–85. Wiesbaden, Ger.: Harrassowitz, 2010.

Showalter, Misty. "Inside Washington D.C.'s 'Little Ethiopia.'" *CNN World: Marketplace Africa*, October 22, 2010. http://edition.cnn.com/2010/WORLD/africa /10/22/little.ethiopia.washington/.

Simeneh Betreyohannes Gebremariam. "The *Azmari* Tradition in Addis Ababa: Change and Continuity." *Northeast African Studies* 18, no. 1–2 (2018): 31–57. https://www.muse.jhu.edu/article/732604.

———. "Music and Politics in Twentieth Century Ethiopia: Empire, Modernization and Revolution." MA thesis, Addis Ababa University, 2008.

Sisario, Ben. "Film Puts a New Focus on the Master of Ethiojazz." *New York Times*, October 13, 2005. https://www.nytimes.com/2005/10/13/arts/music/film -puts-a-new-focus-on-the-master-of-ethiojazz.html.

Skeggs, Beverley. *Class, Self, Culture*. London: Routledge, 2004.

Slattery, Denis. "After Passing the Collection Plate for 30 Years, a Bronx Congregation Finally Raised Enough Money to Buy a Church of Its Own." *New York Daily News*, May 22, 2014. https://www.nydailynews.com/new-york/bronx/30 -years-bronx-ethiopian-congregation-finally-buys-church-article-1.1802754.

Slobin, Mark. "Music in Diaspora: The View from Euro-America." *Diaspora* 3, no. 3 (1994): 243–51.

Smidt, Wolbert G. C., and Eloi Ficquet. "Ḥabäša." In *Encyclopaedia Aethiopica*. Edited by Siegbert Uhlig, 5:339–40. Wiesbaden, Ger.: Harrassowitz, 2014.

Smith, Joel. "Phenomenology." *Internet Encyclopedia of Philosophy*. https://www .iep.utm.edu/phenom/.

Smith, Richard R. "Fender." *Grove Music Online*, October 16, 2013. https://doi.org /10.1093/gmo/9781561592630.article.A2249505.

Solomon Addis Getahun. *The History of Ethiopian Immigrants and Refugees in America, 1900–2000: Patterns of Migration, Survival, and Adjustment*. New York: LFB Scholarly, 2007.

———. "*Sedät*, Migration, and Refugeeism as Portrayed in Ethiopian Song Lyrics." *Diaspora* 15, nos. 2–3 (2006 [published 2011]): 341–59. https://doi.org/10.1353 /dsp.2011.0071.

———. "The Transformation of the *Azmari, Liqa Maquwas*, from the Despicable to the Admirable and Sought after Profession." Paper presented at the First International Conference on Azmari in Ethiopia, Stiftung Universität, Hildesheim, Ger., January 6–8, 2012.

Sorenson, John. *Imagining Ethiopia: Struggles for History and Identity in the Horn of Africa*. New Brunswick, NJ: Rutgers University Press, 1993.

Spin staff. "Live Aid: The Terrible Truth." *Spin*, July 13, 2015. https://www.spin.com /featured/live-aid-the-terrible-truth-ethiopia-bob-geldof-feature/.

Spoto, Alex. "Debo Band's Danny Mekonnen on His Music's Ethiopian Roots: The Boston Band Digs Deep into Ethiopian Musical History." *Spin*, July 12, 2012. https://www.spin.com/2012/07/debo-bands-danny-mekonnen-his-musics -ethiopian-roots/.

Stefanik, Donna. "Refugee Alliance Gets New Digs: Women's Agency Expects to Boost Service by 500 Clients a Year." *Skanner* 10, no. 111, Seattle edition, June 25, 2003.

Stoffregen-Pedersen, Kirsten. *The History of the Ethiopian Community in the Holy Land from the Time of Emperor Tewodros II till 1974.* Studia Oecumenica Hierosolymitana. Vol. 2. Edited by Geries Sa'ed Khoury. Jerusalem: Ecumenical Institute for Theological Research, 1983.

———. "Jerusalem." In *Encyclopaedia Aethiopica.* Edited by Siegbert Uhlig, 3:273–77. Wiesbaden, Ger.: Harrassowitz, 2007.

Subramanian, Karpaga Selvi, and Andargie Mekonnen. "Content Based Classification of Ethiopian Traditional Dance Videos Using Optical Flow and Histogram of Oriented Gradient." *International Journal of Innovations in Engineering and Technology* 6, no. 3 (2016): 371–80. http://ijiet.com/wp-content/uploads/2016/02/57.pdf.

Sutton, Charles. Liner notes. *éthiopiques 23: Orchestra Ethiopia.* Buda Musique 860152, 2007. Compact disc.

———. "Tezeta." Additional notes in pdf. *éthiopiques 23: Orchestra Ethiopia*, 1–12. Buda Musique 860152, 2007. Compact disc.

———. Liner notes. *Reunion* [*Zoro Gät'äm*], [not on label], 2007. Compact disc.

Tadias staff. "Alex Assefa, Joe Neguse and Ilhan Omar: Ethiopian, Eritrean and Somali Make History." *Tadias*, November 8, 2018. http://www.tadias.com/11/08/2018/alex-assefa-joe-neguse-lhan-omar-ethiopian-eritrean-somali-make-history-us-election/.

———. "Amha Eshete and Contribution of Amha Records to Modern Ethiopian Music." *Tadias*, May 25, 2012. http://www.tadias.com/05/25/2012/the-legacy-of-amha-eshete-amha-records-contribution-to-modern-ethiopian-music/.

———. "Brooklyn to Ethiopia: Doncker, Gigi, Selam, Laswell, and More." *Tadias*, September 28, 2011. Updated October 9, 2011. http://www.tadias.com/09/28/2011/brooklyn-to-ethiopia-tomas-donckers-musical-journey-featuring-gigi-selam-laswell-more/.

———. "Spotlight: Trace Muzika, a New Channel for Music from Ethiopia and Diaspora." *Tadias*, July 31, 2020. http://www.tadias.com/07/31/2020/spotlight-trace-muzika-a-channel-dedicated-to-music-from-ethiopia-diaspora/.

Teperberg, Ari. "Dan Hashomer (Dan the Guard), Opera." *Marc Lavry Heritage Society.* https://marclavry.org/composition/dan-hashomer-dan-guard-opera-op-158.

Tesfaye Lemma. "CEAC Events." *Elelta* 2 (1998): 11–14.

———. *Itəyop'iya Muziqa Mäsrayawəch Mädjmäriya Ətəm* [Ethiopian musical instruments]. Addis Ababa, 1975.

———. Letter. *Elelta* 2 (1998): 1.

———. *Second Anniversary, September 1996.* Washington, DC: CEAC, 1996.

———. *Yä'itəyop'iya Muziqa Tarik* [The history of Ethiopian music]. Edited by Alemayehu Gebrehiwot. Washington, DC: Nafqot Ethiopia, 2013.

Teshome G. Wagaw. "Caught in the Web: The Horn of Africa and the Migration of Ethiopian Jews." *Northeast African Studies* 13, nos. 2–3 (1991): 109–26. https://www.jstor.org/stable/43660093.

The Ex. *Getatchew Mekuria (1935–2016), the Lion of Ethiopian Saxophone: A Lifelong Musical History in Photos, from the Municipality Band to The Ex.* Amsterdam: Terp Records and Ex Records, 2017.

Tibebeselassie Tigabu. "Remembering the Giant Roha." Blogpost. *Reporter*, July 4, 2015.

Timkehet Teffera. "Canvassing Past Memories through *Təzəta.*" *Journal of Ethiopian Studies* 46 (December 2013): 31–66. www.jstor.org/stable/44326314.

———. "The Masinqo: Its Meaning, Role and Its Multi-Functionality in Song and Dance." In *Studia Instrumentorum Musicae Popularis IV.* Edited by Gisa Jähnichen, 295–316. Münster, Ger.: MV-Wissenschaft, 2016.

Tobin, Joseph, and Akiko Hayashi. "Return Interviews and Long Engagements with Ethnographic Informants." *Anthropology and Education Quarterly* 48, no. 3 (2017): 318–27. https://doi.org/10.1111/aeq.12202.

Tomlinson, Gary. *A Million Years of Music: The Emergence of Human Modernity.* Brooklyn, NY: Zone, 2015.

Triulzi, Alessandro. "Battling with the Past—New Frameworks for Ethiopian Historiography." In *Remapping Ethiopia: Socialism and After.* Edited by Wendy James, Donald L. Donham, Eisei Kurimoto, and Alessandro Triulzi, 276–88. Oxford, UK: James Currey, 2002.

———. "Social Protest and Rebellion in Some *Gäbbar* Songs from Qellam, Wällägä." In *Modern Ethiopia/L'Éthiopie moderne: From the Accession of Menelik II to the Present.* Edited by Joseph Tubiana, 177–96. Rotterdam, Neth.: Balkema, 1980. [Proceedings of the 5th International Conference of Ethiopian Studies, Nice, Fr., December 19–22, 1977.]

———, and Tamene Bitima. "On Some Masqala and Daboo Songs of the Macca Oromo." *African Languages and Cultures.* Supplement, no. 3 (1996): 243–56. https://www.jstor.org/stable/586665.

Trueman, Trevor. "Persecuted in Ethiopia: Hunted in Hargeisa." Oromia Support Group Report 47. *Advocacy for Oromia,* February 2012. https://advocacy4oromia.org/witnesses/persecuted-in-ethiopia-hunted-in-hargeisa/.

Tsegaye Gabre-Medhin. *Oda Oak Oracle: A Legend of Black Peoples, Told of Gods and God, of Hope and Love, and of Fears and Sacrifices.* London: Oxford University Press, 1965.

———, and Nafkote Tamirat. "Drama, Translations: Yekermo Sew." *Rusted Radishes* 6 (2018). http://www.rustedradishes.com/yekermo-sew/.

Tsehai Birhanu. *Mäzmur Səbhat* [Songs of praise]. Addis Ababa: Ethiopian Orthodox Church, c. 1968.

Ullendorff, Edward. *Ethiopia and the Bible: The Schweich Lectures of the British Academy 1967.* London: Published for the British Academy by the Oxford University Press, 1968.

———. *The Ethiopians: An Introduction to Country and People.* 3rd ed. London: Oxford University Press, 1973.

Under African Skies: Ethiopia. BBC Two documentary, YouTube video, 57:58. Posted by Adamant Critique, August 30, 2016. https://www.youtube.com/watch?v=5N09oe9eK6c.

UNESCO. "World Press Freedom Day 2019: H. E. Dr. Abiy Ahmed." UNESCO. https://en.unesco.org/commemorations/worldpressfreedomday/media resources.

"UNICEF Appoints Thomas 'Tommy T' Gobena as Its National Ambassador to Ethiopia." *UNICEF Ethiopia,* October 14, 2015. https://unicefethiopia.wordpress.com/2015/10/14/unicef-ethiopia-appoints-thomas-tommy-t-gobena-as-its-new-ambassador/.

Urry, John. *Mobilities.* Cambridge, UK: Polity, 2007.

Vadasy, Tibor. "Ethiopian Folk-Dance." *Journal of Ethiopian Studies* 8, no. 2 (1970): 119–46.

———. "Ethiopian Folk-Dance II: Tegré and Guragé." *Journal of Ethiopian Studies* 9, no. 2 (1971): 191–217.

———. "Ethiopian Folk-Dance III: Wällo and Galla." *Journal of Ethiopian Studies* 11, no. 1 (1973): 213–31.

Verboven, Koenraad, Myriam Carlier, and Jan Dumolyn. "A Short Manual to the Art of Prosopography." In *Prosopography Approaches and Applications: A Handbook*. Edited by K. S. B. Keats-Rohan, 35–69. Oxford, UK: Linacre College, Unit for Prosopographical Research, 2007.

Vestal, Theodor. "Nägarit Gazeṭa." In *Encyclopaedia Aethiopica*. Edited by Siegbert Uhlig, 3:1106–7. Wiesbaden, Ger.: Harrassowitz, 2007.

Voigt, Rainer. "Abyssinia." In *Encyclopaedia Aethiopica*. Edited by Siegbert Uhlig, 1:59–65. Wiesbaden, Ger.: Harrassowitz, 2003.

Wachsmann, Klaus P. *Essays on Music and History in Africa*. Evanston, IL: Northwestern University Press, 1971.

Wagner, Ewald. "Bilāl b. Rahāb al-Habašī." In *Encyclopaedia Aethiopica*. Edited by Siegbert Uhlig, 1:583. Wiesbaden, Ger.: Harrassowitz, 2003.

Walle Engedayehu. "The Ethiopian Orthodox Tewahedo Church in the Diaspora: Expansion in the Midst of Division." *African Social Science Review* 6, no. 1 (2014): 115–33.

Wamsley, Laurel. "Ethiopia Gets Its 1st Female President." *NPR*, October 25, 2018. https://www.npr.org/2018/10/25/660618139/ethiopia-gets-its-first-female-president.

Wax, Emily. "Ethiopian Yellow Pages: Life, by the Book." *Washington Post*, June 8, 2011. https://www.washingtonpost.com/lifestyle/style/ethiopian-yellow-pages-life-by-the-book/2011/06/01/AGM64YMH_story.html.

Wayna Wondwossen. Liner notes. *Moments of Clarity*, book 1. Bowie, MD: Quiet Power Productions 825346715629, 2004. Compact disc.

Weisser, Stéphanie. "Emotion and Music: The Ethiopian Lyre *Bagana*." *Musicae Scientiae* 16, no. 1 (2011): 3–18. https://doi.org/10.1177/1029864911416493.

———, and Francis Falceto. "Investigating Qəñat in Amhara Secular Music: An Acoustic and Historical Study." *Annales d'Éthiopie* 28 (2013): 299–322. https://doi.org/10.3406/ethio.2013.1539.

Westheimer, Ruth K., and Steven Kaplan. *Surviving Salvation: The Ethiopian Jewish Family in Transition*. New York: New York University Press, 1992.

"Who Is Tesfaye Lemma?" *Immigrant Connect Chicago*, July 10, 2010. http://immigrantconnect.medill.northwestern.edu/blog/2010/07/15/who-is-tesfaye-lemma/.

Wiebel, Jacob. "'Let the Red Terror Intensify': Political Violence, Governance, and Society in Urban Ethiopia, 1976–78." *International Journal of African Historical Studies* 48, no. 1 (2015): 13–29. https://www.jstor.org/stable/44715382.

Wion, Anaïs, Anne Damon-Guillot, and Stéphanie Weisser. "Sound and Power in the Christian Realm of Ethiopia (Seventeenth–Eighteenth Centuries)." *Aethiopica* 19 (2016): 61–89. https://doi.org/10.15460/aethiopica.19.1.904.

Womack, Ytasha L. *Afrofuturism: The World of Black Sci-Fi and Fantasy Culture*. Chicago: Chicago Review Press, 2013.

Wood, Joseph. "Vietnamese American Place Making in Northern Virginia." *Geographical Review* 87, no. 1 (1997): 58–72.

Worku Nida. "Gurage Ethno-historical Survey." In *Encyclopaedia Aethiopica*. Edited by Siegbert Uhlig, 2:929–33. Wiesbaden, Ger.: Harrassowitz, 2005.

Yäqəddus yared mätasäbiya bä'əwəq yäkinä-təbäb säwoch [Reflections of Holy Yared, the best-known artistic person]. Washington, DC: Kedus Gabriel EOT Cathedral, n.d.

Yehunie Belay. "'Sew Bageru': A Short Documentary." YouTube, 15:32. Posted by *Bawza TV*, May 28, 2012. https://www.youtube.com/watch?v=AQ0hpLU 1vvw.

Yohannes Anberbir and Summer Said. "Saudi Arabia Releases Ethiopian Billionaire Al Amoudi." *Wall Street Journal*, January 27, 2019. https://www.wsj.com/articles /saudi-arabia-releases-ethiopian-billionaire-al-amoudi-11548614361.

Young, Allan Louis. "Medical Beliefs and Practices of Begemder Amhara." PhD diss., University of Pennsylvania, 1970. Ann Arbor, MI: University Microfilms, 1970 [1972 copy]. Microfilm.

Yusuf, Ahmed Ismail. *Somalis in Minnesota*. People of Minnesota series. St. Paul: Minnesota Historical Society Press, 2012.

Zelinsky, Wilbur, and Barrett A. Lee. "Heterolocalism: An Alternative Model of the Sociospatial Behaviour of Immigrant Ethnic Communities." *International Journal of Population Geography* 4, no. 4 (1998): 281–98. https://doi.org/10.1002 /(SICI)1099-1220(199812)4:4<281::AID-IJPG108>3.0.CO;2-O.

"The Zone 9 Bloggers, Update." Offline cases, *Electronic Frontier Foundation*, September 20, 2015. https://www.eff.org/offline/zone-9-bloggers.

Index

Note: Ethiopian names are alphabetized by first name. Page numbers in italics refer to plates and figures. A *t* after a page number indicates a table.

"Abbay Mado" (Meklit Hadero), 218

Abbink, Jan, 107–8

Abdi (Tesfaye) Nuressa, *16*, *238*, 286; on ethnicity, 11; migration path, 116, 117*t*; performance during Oromo soccer tournament, 337n46

Abebaye Lema, 222, 364n98; migration path, 117*t*, 119

Abebe Wolde, 351n2

Abegasu Kibrework Shiota, 210, 234–43, *238*; in BBC documentary, 367n33; career in US, 234–39; mentorship of Wayna Wondwossen, 246, 258; migration path, 117*t*, 118; performances at Ibex Club, 123; performances in *kinet*, 95; on prerevolutionary musical life in Ethiopia, 367n31; return to Ethiopia, 239–43

Abel Makkonen Tesfaye. *See* Weeknd

Abinet Agonafir, 210

Abiti Restaurant (Washington, DC), 145

Abiy Ahmed, 13, 114, 140, 230, 332n62, 338n59, 339n65, 371–72n105

Abiy Woldemariam, 240

Abonesh "Abiti" Adinew, *16*, 99, 364n102; migration path, 117*t*, 118; political difficulties in diaspora, 144–46; return to Ethiopia, 371n104

Abraham, Yohannes, 339n67

Abraham Habte Selassie, *16*; migration path, 117*t*, 118

Abraham Wolde, 327n1

Abriha Deboch, 319n9

Abubakar Ashakih, 324n66

Abubakar Musa, 83, 301n7, 321n26

Abugida Band, 367n35

Abyssinia as term, 302–3n26

Abyssinia Roots (band), 244

ac'c'ir vocal style, 158

Achabir vocal style, 158

Adare (Harari) people of Ethiopia, 301n7

Adbar Women's Alliance (AWA), 142, 340n71

Addis Ababa Restaurant (Silver Spring), *126*

Addis Acoustic Project, 241–42

Ade, King Sunny, 235

Adey Ethiopian Club and Restaurant (Washington, DC), 334n14

admas, 229–32

Admas Band, 229, 234–39, 242, 367n35

Adwa, Battle of, 12, 40, 144, 341n7

Afaan Oromo language, 60, 84, 168, 321n27, 348n84

Afework Tekle, 347n60

Afran Qallo (band), 82, 321n26, 348n84

African Americans: jazz musicians, 154–55; rap groups, 362n68; second-

African Americans (*continued*)
generation Ethiopian Americans influenced by, 218, 231–32, 236, 247, 255–56, 366n13; spirituals, 4; Washington, DC, community, 125, 246
African Development Center (ADC) of Minnesota, 283
African immigrants to the United States, 33–34. *See also* Ethiopian immigrants to the United States
Afrofuturism, 218, 362n70
Afro-Latin Soul (Mulatu Astatke album), 342n12
Afro Sound (band), 241
Agau people of Ethiopia, 8, 182
agency: creativity likened to, 205–6, 261; Ethiopian concept of, xxvi; forced migration and, xxii; meanings of, 300n28; nonmusical activities, xxvii; power of musical, xxi, 26; projective dimension of, 206, 358n10; reconceptualization of, 299–300n27; of sentinel musicians, xxv, 27, 77, 257–58; theory of, 206; types of, xxvi
Agier, Michel, 301n5
Aḥmad b. Ibrāhīm al-Ġāzi, 43
AIT Records, 237
Al-Amoudi, Sheikh Mohammed Hussein, 368n48
"Alchalkum" (Tilahun Gessesse), 82, 320n24
Alemayehu Eshete, 101, 102, 198, 210
Alemtsehay Wedajo, *16*, 34, 346n51, 357n100; migration path, 117t; as sentinel musician, 18, 259; song texts by, 18, 163, 210; Tayitu founded by, 288
Alexandria, Virginia, 127, 143
Ali Birra, *84*, 210, 301n7; Derg's appropriation of popularity, 84–85; emigration of, 85; importance to Oromo people, xxvi, 82–85, 167, 348n84, 350n95; performance during Oromo soccer tournament, 337n46; as sentinel musician, 168, 259; vocal style, 157
All Ethiopian Sports Association One (AESAONE), 137
Almaz Getatchew, 354n54

"Almazin Ayiche" (Tesfaye Lemma), 192–93
Almaz Restaurant (Washington, DC), 126
Alo Lulo (Yehunie Belay CD), 213
Al-Shabaab terrorist group, 282
Alvarez, Father Francisco, 67
Aman Andom, 192
ambasel pentatonic mode, 152, 344n20, 352n19
Ambassel Restaurant (Washington, DC), 213
American Folklife Center Archives, Library of Congress, 15, 18–19
Amha Eshete, 101–4, *102*; entrepreneurial activity in Ethiopia, 30, 101–3, 123, 342n14, 345n41; entrepreneurial activity in the United States, 103–4, 123–24, 163, 207, 211, 334n11; migration path, 116, 117t; return to Ethiopia, 123, 334n14; as sentinel musician, 18, 103–4, 116, 211, 259, 325n72
Amhara people of Ethiopia, 8; in author's study, 27; dances of, 168; dress conventions, 349n93; as early immigrants to San Francisco area, 280; forced migration of, 7, 100–101; highland hegemony of, 59–61, 157; prerevolutionary dominance of, 7, 301n7; relations with Oromo, 339n65, 348n84; vocal style, 157
Amha Records, 30, 103, 342n14, 345n41
Amharic language, 10, 60, 80, 358n10
ammakayənnät, xxvi. *See also* agency
anchihoye pentatonic mode, 152, 344n20
Apocalypse of Ezra, 317n79
aqqwaqwam, 65, 208–9
Arba Minch Collective, 221
Arhine, Adwoa, 298n8
Ark of the Covenant, 37
Armenian community in Ethiopia, 86
Armenian genocide, 44
Armenian orphan brass band *Arba Lijoch*, 44–47, 78–79, 342n7
Asafa Jalata, 301n7
Asante people of Ghana, 298n8
Ashe, Thomas, 264
Ashenafi Kebede, 352n19, 357n101

Ashenafi Mitiku, *16*, 72, 356n86; in
Dukem Group, 196–97, 199–200; on
Ethiopian religion's influence on
dance styles, 71; migration path, 117*t*,
118–19; network of dancers, 357n94;
in Nile Ethiopian Ensemble, 194–95;
performances in *kinet*, 95, 317n82
Asli Ethio Jazz (band), 250
Asnaqetch Werqu (Asnaketch Werku),
160, 315n61, 346n45
Assefa, Alex, 339n67
assemblage theory, xxii, 350–51n1
Assiyo Bellema (Mulatu Astatke cas-
sette), 342n14
Aster (Aster Aweke album), 163, 367n30
Aster Aweke, 338n61; in BBC docu-
mentary, 367n33; collaborations with
Zakki Jawad, 242; on family's resis-
tance to her musical career, 260–61;
influence of, 166; performances at
Ibex Club, 123; performances with
Abegasu Kibrework Shiota and
Henock Temesgen, 235; "Tizita" per-
formed by, 163–64; vocal style, 67,
315n59
Aster Bekele, 364n98
Atlanta, Ethiopian and Eritrean immi-
grants in, 15, 130, 140, 285–86
Atnafu Abate, 192
Ato Eshete Gobe, 316n68
"A Train" (Meklit Hadero's performance
of), 218
Atrium Nightclub (Atlanta), 337n46
Atsede, 298n12
Attali, Jacques, xxv–xxvi
atumpan (Asante drum), 298n8
Aurora, Colorado, Ethiopian immi-
grants in, 374n1
Australia, Oromo refugee community
in, 106–7
Avishai Mekonen, 301n10
Axumite Band, 241
Ayele Mamo, 241
azmari, *68*; ambiguous social sta-
tus of, 68, 78; apprentice system of,
183–84; career of, 201; definition of,
xxii; early mentions of, 316n64; eth-
nic backgrounds of, 319n16; female,

88–90, 315n61, 324n62; historical descriptions of, 67–68; as information
conduit, xxii, 80, 258, 264–65; Italy's
execution of during Ethiopian occupation, 69; Patriotic Association's
professional company, 79; performance at *zəgubəñ*, 92; political and
social commentary by, 27, 67–68, 78,
79–80, 192–93, 258, 307n72, 319n10;
post-revolution resurgence, 98; praise
songs of, 80, 319–20n17; repertory
of, 68–69, 195; sensory world of, 67–
70; Telela Kebede as, 88–90; *yä'ezra
kwankwa* argot, 317n79, 357n95
azmari bet, 98, 324n62, 327n115
"Azmari Man" (Tomás Doncker and
Alan Grubner), 265

"Back to Africa" movement, 42
Badagnani, David, 353n31, 355n76
bägäna (*bagana*), 67, 70, 164–65, 180
bahəlawi (*bahelawi*) music: diaspora
performers, 18; Dukem Group performances, 196–97, 199–200; Ethiopian government emphasis on, 11,
94–95; failure to find an audience in
diaspora, 200–201; Orchestra Ethiopia's performance of, 171–203; revival
of performances in Ethiopia, 201–
3; Telela Kebede's performances of,
88; Yehunie Belay's performances of,
213–14
bahəl zämänawi (*bahel zemenawi*)
music, 18, 95, 323n55
Bahrey, 316n64
Bahru Zewde, 302n14
Bälay Zälläqä, 317n74
Bapa Satarkar Mahārāj, Sri, 263
Barre, Siad, 328n20
bati pentatonic mode, 152, 344n20,
352n19
"Beasts of No Nation" (Fela Kuti), 261
Beatles, 32
Becker, Judith, 314n40
Behailu Kassahun, *16*, 210, 304–5n43;
migration path, 117*t*
bəherawi səmmet, 164
Bencid, Pablo, 252

Beniam Bedru Hussein, *16*, 210; migration path, 117*t*, 118
Berhane Wongel Mennonite Ethiopian Church (Chicago), 285
Berhanu Asfaw, 375nn12–13
Berklee College of Music (formerly Schillinger House), 150, 153, 155, 210, 235, 237
Bernal, Victoria, 338n57
Bernstein, Leonard, 262, 353n29
Beshah Tekle-Maryam, 175
Beta Israel (Ethiopian Jews), 5, 14, 38, 104, 301n10, 304n36, 306n55, 326n101, 329n22
Betelehem (Betty) Melaku, *16*, 210, *278*, 278–79, 354n49, 374n6; financial challenges, 211; migration path, 116, 117*t*
Bethlehem (*ac'c'ir*) vocal style, 158
Bezawork Asfaw, *16*, 209–10, 346n51, 364n102; economic hardships in diaspora, 327n113; exclusion from *People to People* tour, 109; on life during Red Terror years, 96–98; migration path, 116, 117*t*; performance of "Lemenor," 20, 21; performance of "Tizita," 161–63; performances at Ibex Club, 123; performances in *kinet*, 95
Bezunesh Bekele, 82, 109
Biftu Ganama (band), 82
Bilāl b. Rahāb al-Habašī, 43
biographies, collective, 24–28
Birhan "Mac" Mekonnen, 141, 286
"Birraa dhaa Barihe" (Ali Birra), 83
"Bisichet (Trouble)" (John Coe), 180
Blue Nile Group (Orchestra Ethiopia billed as), 188–89
Blue Nile *Kinet*, 95, 195
Blue Nile Restaurant (San Francisco), 122
Blue Nile Restaurant (Washington, DC), 123, 325n72
Bono, 262
Boston/Cambridge area, Ethiopian immigrants in, 15, 18, 133, 142, 277–79
Bourdieu, Pierre, 26, 60–61
Boylston, Tom, 314n28

Brancaleon, Nicolò, 39; "Saint George and Scenes of His Martyrdom," *40*
brass instruments in Ethiopian court, 44–47, 341–42n7
Braudel, Fernand, 20–21
Brazil, orpheonic song in, 322n46
Bricusse, Leslie, 361n60
"Bring on the Night" (Meklit Hadero's performance of), 218
Broken Flowers (film and soundtrack), 151–52, 252, 342n14, 370n90
Bruce, James, 67, 307n72
Bruck Tesfaye, 254
Buda Musique, 253, 328n19
Burntface (Elias Fullmore), 218–19, 362n68, 362n70
Busboys and Poets (Washington, DC), 246
Butler, Kim D., 333n2

California Studio music shop (Minneapolis), 130, 283
Cambridge, Massachusetts. *See* Boston/Cambridge area, Ethiopian immigrants in
Campbell, Thomas, "The Soldier's Dream," xxv
Caplan, Philip, 176, 178, 180, 352n23
Care Events and Communications, 250
Caribbean music and musicians, 152. *See also specific performers*
Catholic Charities USA, 122–23
Catholic Relief Services, 136
Celebrity Series of Boston concert, 252–53
Center for Ethiopian Art and Culture (CEAC), 193–94, 259, 356n86
Chacko, Elizabeth, 127, 128, 335n20, 336n30
chəqchäqa (*chik chika*) rhythm, 77, 154, 161, 169–70, 252
Chicago, Ethiopian immigrants in, 284–85
chik chika rhythm. See *chəqchäqa* (*chik chika*) rhythm
circuses, Ethiopian, 254, 326n101, 371n103

City Hall Theatre (Addis Ababa), 71, 118, 167, 192, 356n79

Cliff, Jimmy, 284

Clifford, James, 301n4

Clinton, Hillary Rodham, 214, 215

Coe, John, 178–81, 179, 191–92, 353n39

Coffee House (Addis Ababa), 241

Cohen, Leonard, 216

"Colored People's Time Machine" (Gabriel Teodros), 219

Columbus, Ohio, Ethiopian immigrants in, 285

Comaroff, Jean, 297n1, 300n28

Comaroff, John, 297n1, 300n28

Commission for Organizing the Party of the Working People of Ethiopia (COPWE), 93

conflict and music, studies of, 77

"Conscience of the World" (Tomás Doncker), 265

CopperWire, 218–19, 362n70

Coptic Church of Egypt, 39

coup attempt (1960), xxii, 79

Crammed Discs, 160, 345–46nn42–43

Creative Arts Centre. See Haile Selassie I University Creative Arts Centre

creative incorporation, 172, 200, 204, 205

Crown Hotel (Addis Ababa), 202

C-Side Entertainment, 237

cultural fields concept, 26

däbtära (debtera). See Ethiopian Orthodox church musicians

Dagmawit Gishen St. Mary Church (Aurora, Colorado), 374n1

Dahlak Band, 235

Dallas–Fort Worth, Ethiopian immigrants in, 15, 132, 286–87, 336n31, 376n46

Dallol (band), 284

Dance Africa, 194

Dan Hashomer (Marc Lavry), 264

Danielson, Virginia, 262

Danny Mekonnen, 253–54, 279, 320n22; migration path, 116, 117t, 122

David, King of Israel, 78

Davis, Miles, 154

däwäl (dawal), 156, 156

"Dawal" (Mulatu Astatke), 155–56

Dawite Mekonnen, 284

Dawit Yifru, 91, 325n70

debo, 121

Debo Band, 116, 254, 279, 368n52

Debre Haile Kedus Gabriel EOT Church (Washington, DC), 227

Debre Haile Kidus Gabriel EOT Church (Decatur, Georgia), 227

Debre Selam Medhane Alem EOT Church (Houston), 287–88

Debre Selam St. Michael EOT Church (Boston), 129

debtera. See Ethiopian Orthodox church musicians

Dehai Eritrea Online, 139, 338n57

DeLanda, Manuel, 350–51n1

Deleuze, Gilles, 350–51n1

dəms', 149–50, 156

Derg: clergy abuse by, 323n49; co-optation of Ali Birra's popularity, 84–85; establishment of power, 86–87; exit visas under, 101, 103; forced resettlement under, 323n48; government-imposed curfews, 87, 90, 91–92, 191, 324n62; Marxist-Leninist ideology of, 334n5; musical life under, 90–98, 114–15, 155, 192–93, 201, 212–13, 224, 324–25n68; neighborhood administrative units, 92–93; overthrow of, 113; People to People concert tour sponsored by, 108–10; Red Terror years, 87, 91, 93, 97, 104, 111, 119, 121, 236, 323n49, 326n83; repression of music and musicians, 87–96; revolutionary songs, 93–94, 95–96; rural land reform and peasant associations, 86–87, 90, 104, 236, 323n48. See also Ethiopian revolution

Dery, Mark, 218

Desta Ethiopian Restaurant (Dallas), 287

diaspora communities: creative challenges and invention in, 204–28; ethnic identity issues in, 8–11, 12–13, 27,

diaspora communities (*continued*)
166–68, 349–50n95; importance of
ethnic places, 124, 128–40, 335n21,
336n30; migration's impact on musical expression, 4; mobility modalities, 36–48; phenomenon of, 121,
333n2; places and politics in, 121–46,
282; refugees' trauma stories, 20; returnees, 366n11; studying through
biography, 24–28; types of, 365n3.
See also Ethiopian immigrants to the
United States; *specific peoples*
Djibouti, 33; Ethiopian refugees in, 105,
107; map of, 6
Doncker, Tomás, 264–65
Donham, Donald L., 303n30
"Do They Know It's Christmas?" (Bob
Geldof), 32, 308–9n15
double meanings. *See* "wax and gold"
linguistic practice
Dr. Djobi, 236
DSK Mariam EOT Church (Washington, DC), 62, 63–65, 71, 127, 129,
336n31
duduk (Armenian wind instrument),
4, 301n6
Dufoix, Stéphane, 365n3
Dukem Ethiopian Restaurant (Washing-
ton, DC), 72, 125, 132, *133*, 135, *137*, 196–
98, *197*, 357n101, 370n89, 370–71n96
Dukem Group, 196–200, 202
Dylan, Bob, 216, 299n23

Earthbound (Meklit Hadero CD), 218–
19
əddər (*edir*), 142
Ed Sullivan Show, The, 188–89, 335n17
Eidsheim, Nina Sun, 340–41n2
Either/Orchestra, 29, *30*, 251–53, 279,
370n87
El-Dabh, Halim, 176–78, *177*, 180, 183,
184, 191–92, 304n38, 352–53nn26–27,
355n76
Elemo Ali, 337n46
Eleta (magazine), 193
Elias Arega, 356n84
Elias Negash, 122, 133–34
Elias Tebabal, 324n62

Elias "The Profit," 362n68
Elizabeth Namarra, 105–6, *106*, 284,
329n29; migration path, 116, 117*t*
Ellington, Duke, 125, *126*, 251
El-Shawan Castelo-Branco, Salwa, 318n1
əmbilta (*embilta*), 43, 184, 189
Emilia, 31
Emirbayer, Mustafa, 206, 299–300n27
Endale Getahun, 139, 338nn60–61
Endru, Wilson, 91
English Beat, 243
əngwərgwərro, 161
EOT Church of Our Savior (Bronx,
New York), 279
EOT Debre Meheret St. Michael Cathe-
dral (Dallas), 287
Ephrem, H. E. Blata, 79
Ephrem Tamiru, 123
"Ere Mela Mela" (Mahmoud Ahmed),
160, 251, 346n45
Ere Mela Mela (Mahmoud Ahmed
album), 160–63, 231, 251,
345–46nn42–43, 361n61
Eritrea: ethnic communities in, 302n18;
independence of, 7, 12, 33, 139, 140,
201, 230, 237, 365n3; Italian colo-
nial presence in, 32–33, 40–41, 108;
map of, 6; Massawa Red Sea port,
39; truce with Ethiopia, 365n3; US
troops in, 367n31
Eritrean civil war, 368n43; end of, 6–7;
refugees from, 104, 105, 114–16, 119
Eritrean Community Center (Roxbury,
Massachusetts), 277
Eritrean diaspora in Italy, 108, 330n38
Eritrean immigrants to the United
States and Canada: in author's study,
27; in Boston, 277; in Dallas–Fort
Worth area, 376n46; diaspora's possibility of return, 365n3; intangible
ethnic places, 137–39; in Los Angeles,
279, 280; in New York, 14–15; in San
Francisco, 280, 281; in Seattle, 282,
375n24; situational ethnicity of, 10–
11; soccer federation, 135–37; tensions
with Ethiopians, 140, 282; in Toronto,
329n23; in Washington, DC, 15, 116,
277, 335n20, 338n57

Eritrean Sports Federation in North America (ERSFNA), 135, 137

əskista (eskista), 168, 189

Ethio-jazz and jazz musicians, 103, 123; Elias Negash, 122; Girum Mezmur, 241–42; historical antecedent, 341n7; Jazzamba School of Music founded by Henock Temesgen, 239–40; Meklit Hadero, 216–21; Mulatu Astatke, 150–56, 204–5, 215, 219–20, 235, 345n41, 371n99; sonic quality, 158–61; Teshome Mitiku, 29–30. See also popular music in Ethiopia; specific performers and ensembles

Ethiopia: Addis Ababa's history, 320–21n25; border changes to, 33; calendar, 61, 349n91; current conflict in, 332n62; ethnic communities' characteristic rhythms and meters, 168–70; ethnic communities in, 7, 8–11, 166–68, 339n65, 348n84; ethnic dress conventions, 197, 199, 253, 349n93, 370–71n96; ethnic federalism in, 7–9, 9, 27, 140, 201, 302n18; exile and refugeeism in history and imagination, 33–35; famine relief concerts for, 108, 260, 330–31n40; folklore ensembles, 167–68; Italian occupation of, 32–33, 34–35, 40–41, 69, 79, 308n13, 316–17n73; Jesuits in, 39; linguistic communities in, 8, 10; map of, 6; media censorship in, 338n59; musicians' ambivalent position in, 27; musicians' political heritage, 78–82; Muslim invasion of, 39, 43; naming customs in, 320n19; origin myth of, 37; post-revolution history of, 230; Protestant missionaries in, 39–40; protests and governmental change, 2017–2018, 13; refugees hosted by, 328n21; Rift Valley archaeological discoveries, 32, 308n14; scholarly approaches to, 303n30; skin color perceptions in, 302n22; tourism in, 202–3; war with Eritrea, 6–7, 368n43; waves of migration from, 119, 121–22, 229–32; West Indian immigrants to, 42. See also Derg; Ethiopian revolution; specific peoples

Ethiopian Community Association of Greater Boston, 277

Ethiopian Community Center, 125

Ethiopian Community Development Council, 125

Ethiopian Community in Seattle Agency, 282

Ethiopian Community Mutual Assistance Association (ECMAA), 277

Ethiopian dances: in cultural ensemble performances, 173, 176, 189, 194–95, 197–98, 200, 201, 202–3; ethnicity and, 167, 168–70; kinet performances, 94, 95, 97, 118, 212; in liturgical performance, 55–56, 57–59, 61, 63, 73; in People to People tour, 108–11; as sensory practice, 70–72; in zar cult, 70

Ethiopian Democratic Union, 104

Ethiopian Evangelical Church (Roxbury, Massachusetts), 278

Ethiopian Evangelical Church Mekane Yesus (EECMY), 284

Ethiopian evangelical congregations, 73, 105–6, 284, 330n30

Ethiopian Folk Dance and Music Ensemble, 110

Ethiopian Groove (CD), 251

Ethiopian Herald, 189

Ethiopian immigrants to the United States: 1.5 generation, 231–32, 245–50, 254; adjustment difficulties, 110, 112; in American political life, 339n67; asylum pathways, 99–120; author's study of, 14–19, 24–28; burial concerns, 142–43; career as musician viewed by, 260–61; challenges confronting diaspora Ethiopian musicians today, 255–56; communities of, 15, 33, 122, 277–88; comparative perspective, 143–44; defections, 108–12, 116, 118, 145; economic and occupational patterns, 141; economic challenges to diasporic creativity, 206–9, 211–12; enumeration of, 7, 33; ethnic arenas, 132–37; ethnic institutions, 129–30; ethnic place-making, 128–40; ethnic places, 143; ethnic sociocommerscapes, 130–32, 135, 143;

Ethiopian immigrants to the United
States (*continued*)
first-generation, 229–30, 231–32; gender issues, 141–43; generational differences in musical creativity, 215;
growth of diaspora, 15; identity issues
for, 8–11, 166–68; influence of African American perspective on, 231–
32; intangible ethnic places, 137–40,
212–15; investments in Ethiopia made
by, 360n36; lack of support for traditional Ethiopian music, 200–201;
Little Ethiopias as third spaces, 143,
280; longing for homeland, 229–30;
multiethnic, 13, 27; musical networks,
209–12, 259–60; occasions for music,
201; periodic return visits to Ethiopia
by, 233, 247; politics of, 136–37, 140–
41, 144–46, 201, 229–30, 236–37, 243,
282; reasons for, 119–20; refugee clusters, 122–23; religious participation
of, 73, 221–22, 224–27; remittances
sent by, 138, 211–12; restaurant and
nightclub gigs, 183, 196–98, 209, 235,
359n23, 372n7; returnees to Ethiopia,
15, 228, 229–56; second-generation,
218, 231–32, 236, 247, 255–56, 366n13.
See also *specific cities and regions*; *specific names and ethnic groups*
Ethiopian music, popular. *See* popular music in Ethiopia; *zämänawi*
(*zemenawi*) music
Ethiopian music, traditional. See
bahǝlawi (*bahelawi*) music
Ethiopian Orthodox Church and
churches: Christianization of calendar, 61; clergy sent to West Indies,
42; cultural dominance of, 7; diaspora challenges, 226–27; diaspora-
homeland communication, 233; doctrine of, 310n42; emperor as head of,
61, 78, 87; fundraisers held in, 227;
historical contacts with Christian
world abroad, 39; loss of prestige under Derg rule, 87, 100; in the United
States, 129; in Washington, DC, 62,
63–65, 129. *See also specific churches*
Ethiopian Orthodox Church liturgical

performance: absence of spoken text
in, 58; amplification in, 58; centrality
of music in, 129; changes in diaspora,
73; dance in, 55–56, 57–59, 61, 63, 73;
Epiphany, 59; fasting and, 56–57;
gender separation and women's participation, 56, 58; instruments used
in, 50, 57–58; Lenten season, 56–57,
313n26; *Mahlet*, 57t, 57–59; *Mäsqäl*
(*Masqal*), 60, 62, 133, *134*; multisensory aspect of, 49–51, 55–62, 155–56;
Portuguese Jesuit description of, 49;
processions and movement, 55–56,
62; ritual hierarchy of senses, 57–59;
secular influence of, 59–61; sound
world of, 150, 155–59; *Timket*, 280;
transmission of, 65–66; vernacular hymns for, 221–25, 363n88; vocal
styles, 156–58, 166
Ethiopian Orthodox church musicians:
healing powers of, 27, 53, 54, 62–63,
69, 70, 258; Italy's execution of during
Ethiopian occupation, 69; migration
paths of, 118; outside the church, 62–
67, 111, 210, 258; training and demands
of, 18, 63, 64–65, 73, 222–23, 227, 288;
Tsehai Birhanu as, 221–27
Ethiopian Patriotic Association (Hager
Fikir), 79, 81, 96, 101–3; musical ensemble, 175–76, 182, 184, 352n19
Ethiopian People's Revolutionary
Democratic Front (EPRDF), 140
Ethiopian People's Revolutionary Party,
93, 104
Ethiopian restaurants, community importance of, 14–15, 123–24, 125, 130–
32, 196–98, 211. *See also specific restaurants and communities*
Ethiopian revolution: airlift of Ethiopian Jews during, 329n22; author's
experience during, 14; "creeping
coup," 14, 86, 101; early days of, 86;
end of, 113, 230; famine preceding, 32,
86, 108, 324n60; political engagement
of musicians during, 27–28, 77–78,
88–89, 192–93; refugees from, 5–6, 7,
33, 35, 100–104, 119; voluntary migration during, 43–44. *See also* Derg

Ethiopian Social Assistance Committee (ESAC), 374n7

Ethiopian-Somali war, 5–6, 104, 119, 141

Ethiopian Sports Federation in North America (ESFNA), 134–36; venues, 136t

Ethiopian state cultural ensembles, 11, 81, 88, 93–96, 108–10, 167–68, 170, 175–76

"Ethiopian Suite, An" (Russ Gershon), 251

Ethiopian vocal and instrumental timbral characteristics, 156–59, 166

Ethiopian Women's Organization for All Women, 340n71

Ethiopian Yellow Pages, 139, 202, 212–15, 337n55

éthiopiques CD series, 30, 103, 124, 160, 190, 231, 251, 253, 328n19, 342n14, 345n41

ÉthioSonic label, 253

Ethio Sound music shop (Addis Ababa), 325n72

Ethio Stars, 210, 235

etma asher, 105

Europe, Ethiopian communities in, 107–8

Ex, 254, 345n41, 371nn101–2

Expats, The (Wayna Wondwossen CD), 247, 248

Ezra, Saint, 70

Faist, Thomas, 32

Falas Mura, 329n22

Falceto, Francis, 30, 251, 253, 316n64, 318n2, 328n19, 342n14, 346n43, 346n50, 347n64, 352n19, 370n83, 371n99

"Fano Tesemara ende Ho Chi Minh ende Che Guevara" (Teshome Mitiku), 30

Fante people of Ghana, 298n8

fät't'ärä, 204–6

"Feeling Good": Meklit Hadero's performance of, 217–18; Nina Simone's performance of, 361n60

Fekade Amde Maskal, 346n43

Feker Publishing Company, 213

Fendika dance ensemble, 254

Finnegan, Ruth, 308n7

Flack, Roberta, 360n29

forced migration: agency and, xxii; causes of, 33–34, 36, 87, 100–101; defections, 108–12, 116, 118, 145; impact of, 99–100; Indian Ocean slave trade, 42–43; lack of choice about resettlement destination, 107; meaning of, 300n1; for religious reasons, 105–6; role of music in, 3; routes leaving Ethiopia, 99, 104–5; of Vietnamese, 100; war and, 7, 14, 33; waves from Ethiopia, 119, 121–22, 140. See also specific people

Foster, George M., 306n59

fukera-shilella, 95

Full Gospel Believers' Church (FGBC), 330n30

Gabriel Teodros, 218–19, 282–83, 362n68, 362n70

Galaanaa Gaaromsaa, 339n64

Garvey, Marcus, 42

Gashe Abera Molla Association, 232

gəbrä gäbb, 300n30

Gebra Masqal, Emperor of Ethiopia, 53, 54

Gebre Kristos Desta, 176

Gedewon, 52

Geertz, Clifford, 341n2

Ge'ez liturgical language, 50, 66, 73, 80, 225, 311n73

Geldof, Bob, 108, 308–9n15

German Cultural Institute (Addis Ababa), 178

Gershon, Russ, 29, 30, 251–53, 279

Getachew Debalke, 88–89, 94, 324n60

Getachew H. Mariam, 339n64

Getahun Atlaw Garede, 16, 210; migration path, 117t, 118

Getamesay Abebe, 183–84, 185, 185–87, 352n19

Getatchew Gebregiorgis, 16, 113, 210, 356n84; defection of, 111–12; Ethiopian liturgical music's influence on, 71; migration path, 116, 117t

Getatchew Mekuria: The Ex and, 254, 371nn101–2; Kronos Quartet's performance of music by, 371n99; on National Theatre, 323n53; as sentinel musician, 260; sonic quality on saxophone, 159–61
Getinet Eniyew, 347n61
gǝzat, 309n22
Ghion Hotel (Addis Ababa), 190, 368n52
Gibbon, Edward, 31–32
Gigi Shibabaw, 242, 265
Gillespie, Dizzy, 238
Girgis, Mina, 221
Girma Beyene, 252
Girma Tchibsa, 346n43
Girum Mezmur, 240–42
Gish Abbay *Kinet*, 94, 95, 195–96, 212
Gogol Bordello, 369n58
Gow, Greg, 302n15, 321n26
Graham, William, 50–51
Graziani, Rodolfo, 69, 316–17n73, 319n9
Great Britain, Ethiopian community in, 107
Greenblatt, Stephen, 4
Griaule, Marcel, 80
Grubner, Alan, 265
Guattari, Félix, 350–51n1
Gurage people of Ethiopia, 144–46, 202, 346n44; characteristic dance movements, 169, 199, 200, 253, 350n101, 370–71n96; dress conventions, 349n93, 370–71n96
Guraginya language, 144, 169
gurri, 70, 72
gwäshämärawi, 98

Habesha as term, 8–10
habitus concept, 60–61, 314n40
Habtamu Lamu, 337n46
Hachalu Hundessa, 257, 338n59, 339n64, 372n2
HAFH (Home [Away From] Home) festival, 221
Hafkin, Nancy J., 337n51
"Hagere" (Munit Mesfin), 250
Hager Fikir. *See* Ethiopian Patriotic Association

Haile, Rebecca, 366n10
Hailemariam Desalegn, 114, 230
Haile Maryam Gebre Ghiorgis, 346n43
Haile Selassie I, Emperor of Ethiopia, 205; Amharization under, 157; Armenian orphan band hired by, 44–47, 45; authority of, 355n71; coronation of, 42; cosmopolitan interests of, 44–45, 47, 78–79, 175–76, 235, 320n22; early life, 41–42; educational expansion under, 44; encouragement of the establishment of Sunday schools, 364n91; exile abroad, 34–35, 308n13; Imperial Bodyguard and Orchestra, xxi–xxii, 78–79; influence on world music, 265; modernization under, 81; music's importance to, 78–79; Orchestra Ethiopia and, 176; overthrow of, 7, 32, 33, 35, 86, 101; record collection of, 344n27; regime's increasing insularity, 81–82, 83–84; repression of evangelical congregations, 330n30; songs in praise of, 80
Haile Selassie I National Theatre (Addis Ababa), 81, 88, 152, 167; founding of, 323n53; orchestra of, 320n22, 342n7, 352n19. *See also* National Theatre
Haile Selassie I University Creative Arts Centre (Addis Ababa), 173, 176, 180, 185–86, 190
Hailu Mergia, 92, 123, 208
Halter, Tom, 252
Hana (Hana Shenkute CD), 370n89
Hana Shenkute, 16, 210, 252–53, 370n89, 370n94, 370–71n96; migration path, 117t; return to Ethiopia, 371n104
Harambee Music Shop (Addis Ababa), 101
"Harar Dire Dawa," 327n1; Abonesh Adinew's performance of, 99, 145
Harlem Jazz (Addis Ababa), 247
Harnett National Studios, 153
Harvard University, 194, 195
Harvard University Archive of World Music, 355n76
Hebir Ethiopia Cultural Restaurant (Addis Ababa), 203
Henock Temesgen, 210, 234–43, 240; in BBC documentary, 367n33; ca-

reer in the United States, 234–39; on challenges confronting diaspora Ethiopian musicians, 256; Debo established by, 368n52; Hana Shenkute and, 370n89; migration path, 117t, 118; performances at Ibex Club, 123; performances in *kinet*, 95; return to Ethiopia, 239–43

Hermela Mulatu, *16*, 150; migration path, 117t, 118

hǝwas (*hiwas*), xxiv, 49, 51, 164–65, 299n16. *See also* sensory thought and practice, Ethiopian

Higher Ground (Wayna Wondwossen CD), 247

Hilton Hotel (Addis Ababa), 91–92, 114–15, 190, 241, 325n70

Hiryyaa Jaalalaa (band), 322n32

hiwas. See *hǝwas* (*hiwas*)

holy water, healing power of, 61, 314n35

Horn of Africa: British and French colonial interests in, 32–33; changes in nomenclature, 5–7; competing ethnic and national identities from, 13, 27, 141, 302n14; droughts and famines in, 32, 260; forced migration from, 3; immigrants to San Francisco area, 280–81; map of, *6*; as metaphor for isolation, 31–32; military mercenaries from, 41; musicians' ambivalent position in, 27; refugee outflow after 1974, 33, 119–20, 121; refugees to the United States from, 104–5; as regional designation, 7, 31–33; as research concern, 11–13; scholarly approaches to, 303n30; *zar* cult in, 70. *See also specific countries and peoples*

hotels, Addis Ababa: bands in, 85, 91–92, 114–15; cultural ensembles at, 202; Orchestra Ethiopia's performances in, 190. *See also specific hotels and bands*

Houston, Ethiopian immigrants in, 15, 130, 287–88

Husserl, Edmund, 364n1

Ibex Band, 91, 114, 210, 346n43

Ibex Club (Washington, DC), 123, 124, 163, 207, 211, 304n42, 325n72, 334n13

Ibex Ethiopian Bar and Cuisine (Dallas), 287

imagined mobility, 36, 37–38

Imperial Bodyguard, founding of, xxi–xxii

Imperial Bodyguard Orchestra, 45–47, 78–79, 81, *81*, 84, 97, 144–45; disbanding of, 91; founding of, xxii, 342n7; implication in 1960 coup attempt, 82; influence of, 241; jazz ensemble, xxii, 85, 152, 342n7; marching band, 174; members implicated in 1960 coup attempt, xxii; singers with, 157–58

Imperial Tiger Orchestra, 371n99

incense: in Ethiopian liturgical services, 50, 59, 61, 156, 315n44; secular uses of, 61; in *zar* cult, 70

Indian music, 243, 263

Indian Ocean slave trade, 42–43

Indigo Sun (Admas Band CD), 234, 236–37, 238–39

information and communication, music as conduit for, xxii–xxiii, xxiv, 80, 258

internet: restrictions in Ethiopia, 139, 338n59; as virtual ethnic space, 137–39, 338n57; virtual mobility and, 47–48

Islamic Association of North Texas, 287

Israel, songs of guards in pre-Israel Palestine, 264, 373n23

Itals, 242

Italy: Eritrean diaspora in, 108, 330n38; historical relations with Ethiopia, 39; occupation of Ethiopia and Eritrea, 32–33, 34–35, 40–41, 69, 79, 308n13, 316–17n73

Itegue Taitu Hotel (Addis Ababa), 241

Itsushi Kawase, 317n77

Ittiqaa Tafarii, 339n64

"Jah-Rusalem" (Tomás Doncker), 265

Jamal Sule, 286

James, Wendy, 303n30

"Japanwan Wodǝdjǝ" (Tilahun Gessesse), 41

Jarmusch, Jim, 151–52, 370n90

Jazzamba School of Music (Addis Ababa), 239–40, 241

Jefferson, Julius C., Jr., 16, 304n42
jeli (Mali musicians), xxii, 297n6
Jenkins, Jon, 362n73
Jerusalem: Armenian orphan band
 brought to Ethiopia from, 44–45;
 Ethiopian clerics' visit to, 39; Ethi-
 opian community in, 107, 118; in
 Ethiopian imagination, 37–38
Jesuits, 39, 49
Jews, Ethiopian. See Beta Israel (Ethio-
 pian Jews)
Johanson, Donald, 32
Jorga Mesfin, 250

käbäro (kebero), 155, 225, 312n2
Kagnew Battalion, 41
Kale Heywet Church, 363n89
Kambata people of Ethiopia, 215
Kaminski, Joseph S., 298n8
Kane, Thomas Leiper, 56, 313n19
Kaplan, Steven, 18, 314n34
Karamara Hotel (Addis Ababa), 118–19
Kassa Woldemariam, 178
kebele. See qäbäle (kebele)
Kebele 19 Kinet, 95
kebero. See käbäro (kebero)
Kəbrä Nägäst, 37
Kedus Gabriel EOT Church (Washing-
 ton, DC), 145
Keita, Salif, 235
"Kemekem" (Meklit Hadero's perfor-
 mance of), 218
Kemer Yusuf, 337n46, 339n64
Keneto (band), 183
Kenya: Ethiopian refugees in, 104, 105–
 7; map of, 6
Ketema Mekonnen, 123
Kibunja, Victor and Shirley, 334n13
Kidanä Wäld Kəfle, 313n19
Kidjo, Angélique, 242
Kilimanjaro Club (Washington, DC),
 334n13
Kimberlin, Cynthia Tse, 356n86
kinät (kinet) musical troupes, 93–96, 94,
 98, 212–13
Kirubel Assefa, 337n44
Kisêdjê people of Brazil, 23–24
K'naan, 345n38

Koehn, Peter H., 119
Korean War, Ethiopian battalion in, 41
Kouyate, Morikeba, 285, 376n40
krar: amplification of, 88, 183; author's
 lessons on, 173; azmari performances
 on, 67; Meklit Hadero as performer,
 220; Melaku Astatke as performer
 and maker of, 182–83, 211; Minale
 Dagnew Bezu as performer, 195–96,
 200; popularity of, 357n98; use in
 Ethiopian cultural music, 323n54;
 Wayna Wondwossen as performer,
 248–49; as weapon of resistance, xxiv
Kronos Quartet, 371n99
Kuku Melekote (Yehunie Belay CD), 215
Kuti, Fela, 153, 261

Lalibela, rock-hewn churches of, 37–38,
 38, 310n38
Lalibela Cultural Troupe, 95
Las Vegas, Ethiopian immigrants in,
 374n1
Laswell, Bill, 242, 368n45
Latour, Bruno, 26
Laušević, Mirjana (Minja), 329n29
Lavry, Marc, 264
Lebron, Vincente, 252
"Lemenor" (Bezawork Asfaw), 20
Lemenor (Bezawork Asfaw CD), 21
leprosy, 34
Levine, Donald N., 172, 205, 303n30,
 356n86
Library of Congress, John W. Kluge
 Center, 15, 18
Libya, 41
Lidet celebration, 50
Lily Pad (Cambridge, Massachusetts),
 29, 31
Lions of Judah Event Center (Atlanta),
 337n46
liqä mäkwas, 78
liqä mezemran, 63, 65. See also Moges
 Seyoum
Live Aid concert, 108, 260, 330–31n40
"Lomi Tera Tera": Getachew Debalke as
 lyricist, 94; Telela Kebede's perfor-
 mance, 88–89, 325n70
"Long Road" (Zakki Jawad), 244–45

"Long Time Gone" (Bob Dylan), 299n23

longue durée studies, 4, 77, 306n56, 306n58, 306–7n62; author's research process, 14–19; biographical data in, 24–28; Braudel's notion of, 20–21; difficulties of, 21–22, 23; insights from, 203; shape of, 24

Los Angeles, Ethiopian and Eritrean immigrants in, 15, 143, 144, 279–80; Little Ethiopia district, 280

Lovage Restaurant (Seattle), 366n13

Lovelace, Richard, 299n18

"Lovin' You" (Wayna Wondwossen), 247

Lucy Ethiopian Restaurant and Lounge (Houston), 288

"Lucy in the Sky with Diamonds" (the Beatles), 32

Lutheran Ethiopians, 284, 285

Ma, Yo-Yo, 262

"Maal Ja'an" (Ali Birra), 84

Macha-Tulama Self-Help Association, 82–83

mahbär (mahber), 142

Mahlet, 57t, 57–59

Mahmoud Ahmed, 346n43, 346n51; in *People to People* tour, 109; performance of "Ere Mela Mela," 160, 251, 361n61; vocal style, 157–58, 160–61, 251

Makeda, Queen of Ethiopia, 37

Makonnen Habte-Wold, 79, 175

Mama Desta's Red Sea Restaurant (Chicago), 285, 334n11, 376n40

Mama's Kitchen (Addis Ababa), 241

märägd, 57t, 57

märigeta (merigeta), 63, 65, 73. *See also* Ethiopian Orthodox church musicians; Tsehai Birhanu

Maritu Legesse, 109

Marley, Damian, 345n38

Marley, Rita, 284

Martha Graham Dance Company, 353n29

Martha Ketsela, *16*, 108; migration path, 117t

Martha Namarra, 106, *106*

Martin, George, 220

Martin, György, 167

Maru Grocery (Houston), 130

mäsänqo (masenqo): amplification of, 88; *azmari* performances on, 67–70, *68*, 319n16; collapsible, 180; Getamesay Abebe as performer, 184; Setegn Atanaw as performer, 195, 200, 247; Sutton as performer, 185–87, 194; Telela Kebede as performer, 324n62; use in Ethiopian cultural music, 323n54; use in *zar* cult, 70; Wollo performers, 175–76

Masekela, Hugh, 153

Mäsqäl (Masqal), 60, 62, 133, *134*

mäzmur (mezmur), 314n29. *See also yä'əhud təməhərt bet mäzmur*

Mäzmurä Krestos, 313n17

McDonald, David, 318n3

Mecca, pilgrimage to, 39

Mekdem Sebhatu, 281

Meklit Hadero, 281, 282–83, 362n70; creative path of, 245; on creativity, 363n77; migration path, 116, 117t, 215–16; musical style of, 215–21; as sentinel musician, 260

Meklit: We Are Alive (Meklit Hadero CD), 218

Mekuria Bulcha, 100

Melaku Belay, 233, 254

Melaku Gelaw, *16*, 182–83, 184, *185*, 210, 354n49; father's reconciliation with, 353–54n45; financial challenges, 211; migration path, 116, 117t

mələkkət (melekket). *See* notation, Ethiopian musical

Meles Zenawi, 114, 230

Mendes, Sergio, 154

Menelik, 37

Menelik II, Emperor of Ethiopia, xxvi, 205, 316n66, 316n68; *azmari* songs praising, 68, 319–20n17; brass instruments received from Czar Nicholas II of Russia, 341n7; modernization of educational system under, 44; Queen Victoria and, 311n65; residence of, 320–21n25; Teddy Afro's song praising, 12; unification of Ethiopia, 60, 302n14

Menelik II Lyceum (Addis Ababa), 44

menfesawi mezmuroch, 363n88

Mengistu Haile Mariam, 86, 87, 93, 94, 94, 110, 119, 192–93, 230, 330n39, 330–31n40

merigeta. See Ethiopian Orthodox church musicians; *märigeta (merigeta)*

Meron Hadero, 216

Mesfin Zeberga Tereda, 17; migration path, 117t, 119

Meskerem Restaurant (Washington, DC), 195

Messing, Simon D., 297–98n7

Messob Restaurant (Los Angeles), 375nn12–13

mezmur. See *mäzmur (mezmur)*

Michael Belayneh, 163

Michael Tsegaye, 343n18

microhistorical studies, 22–23, 24

migration: conflict-driven, 5–7; *longue durée* studies of, 4, 14–19, 20–21, 77; overview of patterns, 116–20; processes of mapping and naming, 5–13; pull and push factors in, 300n1; studies of musicians', 3–4; as transformative experience, 4–5. *See also* forced migration; virtual migration; voluntary migration

Migration Policy Institute, 7, 236–37

Mikyas Abebayehu, 238

military mercenaries, 41

Mimi Wondimiye, 89, 90

Minale Dagnew Bezu, 9–10, 17, 197, 252, 357n98, 364n102; in Dukem Group, 196–97, 199–200; migration path, 117t, 118; in Nile Ethiopian Ensemble, 195–96; performances in *kinet*, 95

Minneapolis–St. Paul, Minnesota: Oromo immigrants in, 15, 106, 130, 140, 143, 283–84; Somali immigrants in, 5–6, 15, 130, 143, 283–84, 335n18

Mische, Ann, 206, 299–300n27

Mitchell, Joni, 216, 244

mmensuon (Fante ensemble), 298n8

mobilities: Ethiopian sound and, 149–70; modalities of, 35–48; pathways of, 29–31; politics and, 46–47; relation-ship between spatial and social, 32. *See also* forced migration; migration

modal jazz, 153–54

modes in Ethiopian music: creative incorporation of, 205; in Ethio-jazz, 152–54, 344n19; Indian *raga* and, 243; nostalgia and, 20; sacred–secular links, 66–67; Setegn Atanaw on, 357n96; systematization of, 344n20, 346n50, 351–52n19; Yared as reputed organizer of, 52, 66. See also *qəñet (qenyet); specific modes*

Moges Asgedom, 319n9

Moges Habte, 17, 210; on Addis Ababa hotel bands, 91–92; club owned by, 334–35n14; migration path, 108, 116, 117t, 118, 325n72; performances at Ibex Club, 123

Moges Seyoum, 17, 63–66, 64, 129, 227, 233, 336n31; Dallas church cofounded by, 65, 377n51; migration path, 65, 116, 117t; as sentinel musician, 73

Mohaammad Ibraahim Xawil, 17, 233, 336n38; migration path, 117t, 119

Mohammed Hassen, 321n26

Mohammed Sheba, 337n46

Moments of Clarity (Wayna Wond-wossen CD), 246–47

Morand, Katell, 346n50

More Beautiful Than Death (Either/Orchestra), 251

Mr. Henry's Restaurant (Washington, DC), 211, 360n29

Muktar Usman, 337n46

Mulatu Astatke, 151, 161, 278, 352n20; access to foreign music in Ethiopia, 344n27; constant travel of, 341n5; cultural mobility of, 150; Either/Orchestra and, 252, 370n87; Ethio-jazz style of, 150–56, 160, 215; influence of, 166, 219–20, 235; interviews with, 18; on National Theatre, 323n53; *People to People* tour and, 108–10, 331n42; on personal price of defecting, 110; personal theory of creativity, 204–5; preference for instrumental works, 155; as sentinel musician, 151, 259 multitemporal ethnographic studies, 19–24, 305n51

Mulugeta Abate, 366n13

Muluken Melesse, 346–47n51

Munit and Jörg, 249, 343n18

Munit Mesfin, 249, 249–50, 343n18; migration path, 117t, 118

Murray, Bill, 151

musical signatures and codes, xxii, 165, 297n7

"Musiqawi Silt" (Girma Beyene), 252

Muslims: Ethiopian, 43, 59–60, 86, 129–30, 143, 281, 286; Indian Ocean slave trade of, 43; passage through Ethiopia and Eritrea, 39

Mutual Assistance Association for the Ethiopian Community (MAAEC), 286

"My Mother Is Ethiopia" (Woretaw Wubet), 95–96

nägarit (negarit): in court processions, xxiii, 43, 78; use as speech surrogate, xxiii

Nägarit Gazeta (Negarit Gazeta), xxiii

Nalbandian, Kevork, 45–46, 253, 319n8

Nalbandian, Nerses, 86, 253, 320n22, 352n19

national anthem of Ethiopia, 79

National Folk Festival (Richmond, Virginia, 2007), 66

National Theatre (Addis Ababa), 89, 95, 97–98, 111, 161–62

negarit. See nägarit (negarit)

Neguse, Joe, 339n67

Netherlands, Ethiopian community in, 107

Neway Debebe, 109, 242

Newley, Anthony, 361n60

New York, Ethiopian and Eritrean immigrants in, 14–15, 144, 237, 279

ney, 217–18

Nicholas II, Czar of Russia, 44, 341n7

Nigussie Te'amwork, 162

Nigussu Retta, 351n2

nikat, 96–97

Nile Ethiopian Ensemble, 194–96, 201, 209, 232, 258, 335n17; offspring of, 196–200

Nile Project Collective, 221

Noise and Chill Out: Ethiopian Groove Worldwide (CD), 253, 371n99

nomenclature, changes in geographical, 5–7

non-Ethiopian musical collaborators, 29–30, 250–53

nostalgia: of Ethiopian soldiers who served in Korea, 41; of refugees, 99–100; tizita mode and, 20, 153–54, 161–64, 347n53

notation, Ethiopian musical, 297–98n7; Moges Seyoum's book on, 65; oral tradition's importance to, 58; Orchestra Ethiopia's hybrid system, 171, 173, 351n2, 352n19; system of, 158, 159t; Yared's reputed invention of, 52, 58

Nyabinghi, 245, 369n64

Oakland, Ethiopian immigrants in, 19, 130, 134, 280–81, 335n18. See also San Francisco Bay area, Ethiopian immigrants in

O'Connell, John Morgan, 318n1

"Oda Oak Oracle I–V" (John Coe), 180, 353n39

Okorafor, Nnedi, 362n70

Oldenburg, Ray, 128

Omar, Ilhan, 339n67

On a Day Like This (Meklit Hadero CD), 217–18

oral tradition and transmission: about bagana, 165; of Ethiopian history, xxvi, 308n11; of Ethiopian ritual musics, 21, 51; Ethiopian senses according to, 55t, 166; as important communication channel in Ethiopia, xxiv; of life experiences, 24–25; longue durée studies and, 21–22; Mahlet's dependence on, 58; of saints' lives and proverbs, 60

Orchestra Ethiopia, 81, 108, 171–203, 190, 204; "afterlife" of, 173, 200–203; American tour as Blue Nile Group, 188–89; changes over time, 171–72;

Orchestra Ethiopia (*continued*)
Coe's compositions for, 180; Coe's
leadership of, 178–81, 191–92; as cultural model, 202; disbanding in 1975,
173, 191; early 1970s activity, 190–91;
early repertoire, 177; El-Dabh's leadership of, 176–78, 183, 184, 191–92,
304n38; establishment of, 176–78;
Ethiopian revolution and, 172–73,
191, 355n76; Getamesay Abebe in,
183–84; impact of, 173, 203; medleys
performed by, 170; Melaku Gelaw in,
182–83; "Mother Ethiopia" television performance, 191, 355n76; multiple lives of, *174*; Nile Ethiopian
Ensemble and, 194–96; notational
system developed by, 171, 173, 351n2,
352n19; Sutton in, 186–88; Sutton's
appraisal of, 191–92; Sutton's fundraising for, 188, 372n6; Tesfaye Lemma's compositions for, 184, 187; Tesfaye Lemma's leadership of, 181–82,
184–86, 190–91, 304n38, 354n54
Orchestra Ethiopia (LP), 189–90
"Oromiyaa" (Ali Birra), 168, 350n95
Oromo Community Center (St. Paul),
283
Oromo Community of Minnesota, 283
Oromo immigrants to the United States
and Canada: in Atlanta, 130, 140, 285–
86; in author's study, 27; in Los Angeles, 279; in Minneapolis, 15, 106, 130,
140, 143, 283–84; Muslims, 130; numbers of, 143, 144; in Oakland, 130; refugee paths, 105–7; reluctance to return to Ethiopia, 233, 255, 371–72n105;
in San Francisco, 280, 281; in Seattle,
282, 375n21; soccer federation, 135–36,
137; tensions with other Ethiopians,
282; in Toronto, 15, 130, 376n31
Oromo Liberation Front (OLF), 113,
140, 321n26, 322n30
Oromo people of Ethiopia, 8, 301n7,
321n27; Ali Birra's importance to,
xxvi, 167, 168, 259, 350n95; Amharization of, 60; cultural variety of, 11;
dances of, 167, 168, 199–200; dress
conventions, 349n93, 370–71n96;

forced migration, 105–7, 113–14, 140,
283–84; growth of political power,
140; Hachalu Hundessa as sentinel
musician, 257; Hachalu Hundessa's
importance to, 257; linguistic and
ethnic identity, 10; *Masqala* ceremony, 60; Menelik II viewed by, 12;
name spellings, 321–22n30; pejorative name for, 349n88; population
of, 303n29; relations with Amhara,
339n65, 348n84; self-determination
aspirations of, 12, 82–85, 100, 230,
321n26; vocal style, 157
Oromo Sports Federation in North
America (OSFNA), 135, 337n46
Oz, 337n46

Pacific Music Festival, 372–73n15
Páez, Pedro, 318–19n6
Pankhurst, Sylvia, 79–80
Papas, Sophocles, 354n56
Peace Corps volunteers in Ethiopia,
179–80, 184–89, 372n6
Pentecostal Church Mulu Wongel, 105
People to People international concert
tour, 98, 108–12, 150, 184, 193, 330n39,
331nn42–43; defections during, 109–
12, 116
Pfeil, Jörg, 249
Philips Records, 345n41
physical travel, 36, 39–42
Police Band, 91
Polijazz, 341n5
popular music in Ethiopia, 80–81, 150,
234–35; Amha Eshete's entrepreneur-
ial activity, 101–3; development of
jazz instruction, 240–41; hotel bands,
85, 91–92, 114–15, 190, 240–41
Portland, Oregon, Ethiopian immi-
grants in, 375n24
Power of the Trinity (Tomás Doncker
CD), 265
Prester John myth, 39
Prester John Sessions, The (Tommy T
album), 369n58
Prestige Records, 154
Priest, Maxi, 242–43
Princeton Theological Seminary, 222–23

"Prize of Peace, A" (Admas Band), 237
prophets, musicians as, xxvi
proprioception, 150
prosopography, 25–28
proverbs, Ethiopian, 60, 61
Puntland, 309n16

qäbäle (*kebele*), 92–97, 161, 317n82,
    325n81, 326n83
qəne (*qene*), 52, 65, 323n49
qəñet (*qenyet*), 66, 205, 344n20, 346n50,
    352n19, 357n96
Qoma Fasiledes monastery, 223
Qoma vocal style, 158
qum zema, 57t, 57

race and racial awareness, 8
Radio Ethiopia, 189
radio stations, diaspora, 139, 338nn60–61
Radio Voice of the Gospel (Ethiopia),
    177, 178, 353n31, 355–56n76
raga, 243
räjjim (*rejjim*) vocal style, 158
rap, Ethiopian, 362n68
Ras Band, 85
Ras Dashen Restaurant (Chicago), 285
Ras Hotel (Addis Ababa), 91, 114, 190
Rastafarian religion, 42
Ras Tafari Makonnen. *See* Haile Selassie
    I, Emperor of Ethiopia
Ras Tafari's Royal Marching Band
    (S. M. Negus Tafari's Royal Marching
    Band), 45, 45, 342n7
Ras Theatre (Addis Ababa), 145, 167,
    192
"Rebel Soul" (Zakki Jawad), 243, 245
Red Terror. *See* Derg
refugees: exile within Ethiopia, 34–35;
    music studies on, 300n2; UN defini-
    tion of, 33. *See also* forced migration;
    specific peoples and locations
reggae, 42, 242–43, 245, 256, 284, 369n58
rejjim. See räjjim (*rejjim*) vocal style
religious ritual as sensory experience,
    50–51. *See also* Ethiopian Orthodox
    Church liturgical performance
repatriation to Ethiopia, 228, 229–32; 1.5
    diaspora generation, 231–32, 245–50;

desire for, 229; factors in weighing,
    232–34, 238–39, 254–55; first diaspora
    generation, 231–32; paradox of be-
    coming an immigrant to one's home-
    land, 231–32; political difficulties,
    229–30, 339n65; reasons for musi-
    cians', 233, 234, 239–42, 249–50; skep-
    ticism among those who remained in
    Ethiopia, 233
Retroz (band), 122
return mobility, 37, 228, 229–56
Reunion (CD), 184, 185
Reyes, Adelaida, 100, 300n2
rhythms, Ethiopian characteristic, 77,
    154, 161, 168–70
Rico, Giovanni, 346n43
Riperton, Minnie, 247
Riverside Church (New York), 14, 129,
    279
Rodriguez, Louis, 342n12
Roha Band, 91, 114–15, 210, 325n70
Rosetta Josef, 236, 367n37

St. Gabriel EOT Church (Seattle), 129,
    282
St. Mary's EOT Church (Boston), 278
St. Mary's EOT Church (Los Angeles),
    129, 280
St. Michael's EOT Church (Boston),
    222, 223, 225, 277, 279, 345n34, 364n98
sämənnawärq. See "wax and gold" lin-
    guistic practice
sämma, xxiv, 164
San Diego, Somali immigrants in, 5–6
San Francisco Bay area, Ethiopian im-
    migrants in, 19, 143, 144, 221, 280–81
San Jose, Ethiopian immigrants in, 19
Sanyii Mootii (Hachalu Hundessa al-
    bum), 257, 372n2
Sarkesian, Leo, 355n71
Saudi Arabia, Ethiopian migrants in, 141
Sayem Osman, 17; migration path, 117t,
    118
Schillinger House. *See* Berklee College
    of Music
Schnapper, LaDena, 118–19, 356n86
Seattle, Ethiopian immigrants in, 15,
    140, 282–83, 366n13, 375n21

security guards, xxiv. *See also* Imperial Bodyguard, founding of

səddättäñña, 34

Seeger, Anthony, 23–24

s'əfat, 57*t*, 57–58

Selamino Music Centers (Addis Ababa), 332n64

Selam Seyoum Woldemariam, *17, 115,* 210; Abubakar Ashakih and, 324n66; collaboration with Tomás Doncker, 265; on "creeping coup," 325n70; on ethnic identity, 11; on importance of *Ere Mela Mela,* 346n43; life during Derg years, 114–16; migration path, 108, 116, 117*t*; as sentinel musician, 259–60, 372n7

Selamta Band, 281

Seleshe Damessae, 232, 356n92; migration path, 117*t*, 118

səlt, 29, 31

səmmet, xxiv, 164, 299n16

Sənkəssar, 52

sensory thought and practice, Ethiopian, xxiv, 49–73; in *azmari* performance, 67–70; *bagana* and, 164–65; bodily organs linked to senses, 51, 164–66, 313n18; as conceptual model, 73, 149; cross-cultural differences, 71; in Ethiopian secular dance, 72; hearing, 57–58; leg and foot motion as sense, 55–56, 59, 70–72, 149; as lived experience, 60; music's ability to alleviate pain, 53–54, 165; in religious ritual, 49–51, 57–61, 72–73, 155–56; ritual hierarchy of senses, 57–59; sentinel musicians' role shaped through, 63–66, 73; seven senses, 55*t*, 55–57; sex organs as sense, 55, 56, 59; sight, 58–59; smell, 58–59; tales and depictions of Saint Yared, 51–54; taste, 56–57; touch, 59; tracking across boundaries, 60–61; transmission of, 59–61; upper vs. lower body, 61; Western notions compared with, 54–55; in *zar* cult event, 70, 72

sentinel, etymology and meanings of, xxiv–xxv

sentinel musicians: agency and flexibility of, xxii, xxv, 3, 4, 27, 77; author's use of, xxv; concept of, xxi–xxvii; economic difficulties, 112, 206–9; ethnic identity and, 167; German town musicians, 373n19; global and transhistorical perspective, 261–65; as information conduit, xxii; interviews with, 18; in medieval and Renaissance Europe, 263, 373n19; as pivotal figures, xxiii, xxv, 104, 123–24, 151, 193–94, 198–99, 225–26, 241, 258–59; political engagement of, 30–31, 78–82, 84–85, 89–90, 145–46, 214–15, 243, 257–58, 259, 263–64; respect for, 260–61; role in times of conflict, xxiii–xxiv, 77–78; sensory powers' importance to, 51, 63, 73; social activism and engagement of, xxvii, 221, 250, 257, 260; visiting foreign musicians as, 46, 372n6

sentinel stars, xxv, 299n18

sese (Fante horn), 298n8

Setegn Atanaw, *17, 197,* 364n102; career in Ethiopia, 95; collaborations with Either/Orchestra, 252; collaboration with Wayna Wondwossen, 247; in Dukem Group, 196–97, 199–200; on Ethiopian modes, 357n96; languages spoken by, 357n95; migration path, 117*t*, 195

Sew Bageru (documentary), 360n44

Seyfu Yohannes, 101, 343n18

"Shäggaw Tərənbuli," 41; Telela Kebede's performance of, 323–24n56

Shambel Belayneh, 109, 123

Shao, Oliver Y., 318n1

Shaw, George Bernard, *Androcles and the Lion,* 180

shəbshäba, 57*t*, 58

Shelemay, Kay, 238

shəllälä (*shillela*), 159, 345n38, 371n101

shepherds, xxiv, xxvi

Sheraton Hotel (Addis Ababa), 239, 240, 368n48

Shewandagn Hailu, 241

shillela. See *shəllälä* (*shillela*)

"Shimagile Negn" (Tesfaye Lemma), 192

Shirei Eretz Yisrael, 264, 373n23
shomer, 264
Shriver, Sargent, 179
Silkroad Ensemble, 262
Silver, Horace, 154–55
Silver Spring, Maryland, 125, 143
Simeneh Betreyohannes, 324n60,
   325n68, 327n115
"Simish Man New" (Tesfaye Lemma),
   184
Simone, Nina, 216
Sirens (Greek mythical beings), 264
Sisay Asefe, 327n1
sistrum, 53, 54, 57–58
sitar, 243
"Slums of Paradise" (Wayna Wond-
   wossen), 246, 247
Smith, Melvin, 236
soccer tournaments, Ethiopian, 133–35,
   135, 337n46
social media, 138
Solomon, King, 37
Solomon Addis Getahun, 302n15
Solomon Bedany, 197, 199–200
Somalia: border war with Ethiopia, 5–6,
   104, 119, 141; Ethiopian refugees in, 5,
   105; Italian colonial presence in, 32–
   33; map of, 6; partition of, 328n20
Somali immigrants to the United States,
   281, 282; in Minneapolis, 5–6, 15,
   130, 143, 283–84, 335n18; in Portland,
   375n24; in Seattle, 375n21; tensions
   with Ethiopians, 141, 282
Somaliland, 309n16, 316–17n73; map of, 6
Somali language, 80
Somali people of Ethiopia, 8; forced migration, 104, 283–84, 328n20; migration practices of, 309n26
"Song for My Father" (Horace Silver),
   154–55
Sons of Ethiopia (Admas album), 368n45
Sonya Damtew, 366n13
Soukous African Club (Washington,
   DC), 334–35n14
Soul Ekos Band, 29, 30–31, 101, 343n18
sound recordings: as virtual ethnic
   space, 137, 139. See also *specific labels,
   titles, and performers*

speech surrogates, instruments as, xxii–
   xxiii, 298n8
"Standing in the Middle" (Zakki
   Jawad), 243
Sting, 218
Sudan, refugee camps in, 104–5, 329n22
Sun Ra, 218
"Supernova" (Meklit Hadero), 219
Susenyos, Emperor of Ethiopia, 318–
   19n6
Sutton, Charles, *185*, 190, 193, 355n71,
   356n86; in Ethiopia, 184–89; fund-
   raising for Orchestra Ethiopia, 188,
   372n6; on instruction in Ethiopian
   modal system, 352n19; musical legacy,
   203; on Orchestra Ethiopia's impor-
   tance, 191–92; performance with Nile
   Ethiopian Ensemble, 194; as Tesfaye
   Lemma's legal guardian, 357n100
suwa houses, 324n61
"Suzanne" (Cohen), 216

tabot, 61, *62*, 69, 314–15n43
Tadele Gemechu, 339n64
Tadele Roba, 339n64
Tadias, 339n67
tädj bet (*tej bet*), 178, 180, 183–84
Tafari Mekonnen School (Addis
   Ababa), 79, 173, 319n9
Taha Ali Abdi, 322n31
Takoma Park, Maryland, 127
"talking" drums, xxiii. See also *nägarit*
   (*negarit*)
Tawfiq Islamic Center (South Minne-
   apolis), 283
taxi drivers, Ethiopian immigrant, 141,
   207–9, 339n68, 359nn16–17
Tayitu Cultural and Educational Center
   (Washington, DC), 288, 360n27
Teddy Afro (Tewodros Kassahun), 140,
   241, 367n35; protests against, 12
Teddy Mitiku, 116
Teddy Shawl, 281
Tedla W. Giorgis, 356n86
Tefera Zewdie, 125, 196
tej bet. See *tädj bet* (*tej bet*)
Teka Gulima, 356n84
Tekle Tesfa-Ezghi, 103

Tekle Tewolde, 17; migration path, 116, 117t

Telela Kebede, 17, 88–90, 90, 309n27; azmari bet of, 324n62; migration path, 116, 117t; on National Theatre, 323n53; performances with National Theatre ensembles, 352n20; as sentinel musician, 259; "Shäggaw Tərənbuli" performed by, 323–24n56

television stations, diaspora, 139

Tempo Records, 355n71

tərənbuli, 41

Tesfa Ethiopian Museum (Washington, DC), 193, 259

Tesfaye Gabbiso, 330n30, 363n89

Tesfaye Gessesse, 181, 186

Tesfaye "Hodo" Mekonnen, 346n43

Tesfaye Lemma, 182; CEAC and, 356n86; on challenges confronting diaspora Ethiopian musicians, 255–56; compositions of, 184, 187, 192–93, 201; defection of, 110, 193; estimate of Ethiopian musicians in Washington, DC, area, 305n43; instruments collected by, 190, 192, 355n74, 356n79; life in the United States, 193–94, 202; migration path, 116, 117t, 193; musical legacy, 200–202, 203, 258–59; musical studies, 173–75, 176, 190; Nile Ethiopian Ensemble founded by, 194–96, 232, 258; Orchestra Ethiopia and, 172, 181–82, 184–86, 201–2, 304n38, 351n2, 354n54, 355–56n76; People to People tour and, 108, 330n39, 331n42; as Ras Theatre director, 192; as sentinel musician, 201–2, 259; Sutton's help to, 357n100, 372n6

Teshay Endale, 354n54

Teshome Mitiku, 30; on Ethiopian community in Washington, DC, 143; migration path, 30–31, 85, 116, 117t, 308n6; performances with Either/Orchestra, 29; Soul Ekos Band and, 29, 30, 101

Tessema Eshete, 68–69, 316n66, 316n68, 344n27

Tewodros II, Emperor of Ethiopia, 205

Tewodros Aklilu, 367n35

Tewodros Kassahun. See Teddy Afro (Tewodros Kassahun)

təzəta (tizita) pentatonic mode, 20, 153–54, 161–64, 346n50, 347n53; tunings, 344n19

Theodros Mitiku, 346n43

Thewophilos, Abuna, 323n49

Tigrayan immigrants to the United States, 278, 285

Tigrayan people of Ethiopia, xxiii, 8, 230; characteristic meter used by, 168; dress conventions, 199, 349n93, 370–71n96; ethnic tensions with Oromo and Amhara, 339n65

Tigray People's Liberation Front (TPLF), xxiii, 140

Tigrinya language, 8, 80

"Tikur Sew" (Teddy Afro), 12

Tilahun Gessesse, 41, 192, 338n61; in Imperial Bodyguard Orchestra, 82, 157–58, 174; in People to People tour, 109; vocal style, 166

"Time Will Come" (Wayna Wondwossen), 247

Timkehet Teffera, 317n77, 347n61

Timket celebrations, 280

Tizazu Kore, 202

"Tizita": Aster Aweke's performance, 163–64; Bezawork Asfaw's performance, 161–63; early transmission history of, 347n64; instrumental versions, 347n57, 371n101; Meklit Hadero's performance, 220; Michael Belayneh's performance, 163; Wayna Wondwossen's performance, 248–49

tizita mode. See təzəta (tizita) pentatonic mode

Tomlinson, Gary, 306n56

"Tommy T" Gobena, 238, 246, 369n58; migration path, 117t, 118

Toots and the Maytals, 284

Toronto, Ethiopian immigrants in, 15, 130, 195, 304n38, 322n38, 329n23, 374n1, 376n31

Town Hall (New York), 189

Trace Muzika music channel, 139

Tsegaye B. Selassie, 17, 238, 242, 265; migration path, 117t, 118

Tsegaye Gabre-Medhin, 153, 154, 155, 180, 342n15
Tsehai Birhanu, *merigeta* (Father), 221–27, 226, 279, 323n49, 345n34, 363nn88–89, 364n98; migration path, 117*t*, 118; religious training of, 222–23; vernacular hymns of, 221–25
Tsehay Amare, 17, 95, 197, 210; in Dukem Group, 198–200; as sentinel musician, 259
Tukārām Ganapathi Mahārāj, Sri, 263

Ullendorff, Edward, 32
Umm Kulthum, 262, 315n59
Under African Skies: Ethiopia (documentary), 347n53, 367n33
"Unexpected Beauty of Everyday Sounds, The" (Meklit Hadero TED talk), 221
United Nations Refugee Convention, 1951, 33
Up! documentary film series, 306–7n62
Ure, Midge, 108
Urjii Bakkalchaa (band), 82, 83, 321n26, 322n32
Urry, John, 36
US Office of Refugee Resettlement, 122
US Refugee Act of 1980, 121, 333n1

Vadasy, Tibor, 349n88
Venus Nightclub (Addis Ababa), 90, 324n62
vibrato style, Ethiopian, 159–60
Victoria, Queen of England, 311n65
Vietnamese people: forced migration, 100; returnees, 366n11
vigilis, 263
Village Gate nightclub (New York), 153
virtual migration, 37
virtual mobility, 47–48
"Voice Cried Out in the Wilderness, A" (Tsehai Birhanu), 223–24
voluntary migration, 43–47; diversity visas, 119, 195, 333n80; Ethiopian students, 35, 43–44, 47, 65, 119, 121–22, 150, 235, 236; factors in, 36–37, 85, 89, 96, 98, 100; foreign musicians, 44–47

Waaqeffannaa religion, 283, 286, 321n27
Wabe Shebelle Hotel (Addis Ababa), 190
waits, 263
Wakeling, Dave, 243
Walias Band, 91–92, 114, 124, 207, 208, 210, 325n72
Walker, Tenisay "Mary" Alemu, 364n98
Wallo–Lalibela *Kinet*, 198
wanna, xxi
Washington, DC, Ethiopian and Eritrean immigrants in, 15, 16–17, 31, 125–40; Amha Eshete's central role, 104, 123–24; churches and mosques, 129–30; community growth, 235–36; cross-racial contacts, 144; defections from *People to People* concert tour, 109–12, 116; economic challenges, 206–9, 211–12; Ethiopian Millennium concert, 167–68; ethnic institutions, 125, 129–30, 193–201; ethnic sociocommerscapes, 125, 130–32; interviews with, 15; Little Ethiopia district, 143; migration pathways of, 100; migration waves, 125; number of active musicians, 18–19, 305n43; population of, 335n20; settlement areas, 125, 127, 127; Tesfaye Lemma's cultural work, 258–59
washint, 182–83
"wax and gold" linguistic practice: ambiguity of, 258; *azmari* use of, 27, 67–68, 79–80, 265; meaning of, xxiii; as metaphor, 137, 298n11; in popular songs, 88–89, 192–93
Wayna Wondwossen, 17, 246–49, 248; Abegasu Kibrework Shiota's mentorship of, 258; migration path, 116, 117*t*; as sentinel musician, 260
wäzäwwäzä, 99
wazema, 3
"We Are Alive" (Meklit Hadero), 218
"We Are the World" (Bob Geldof), 32, 309n15
weddings, musical entertainment at, 188, 198, 199, 201, 209, 214, 279, 284, 354n49, 359nn23–24
Weeknd, 157, 166, 260

Weishaus, Marc, 190
Weisser, Stéphanie, 164–65, 346n50, 347n64, 348n72, 352n19
West African music and musicians, 152. *See also specific performers*
West Indies, Rastafarians in, 42
When the People Move, the Music Moves Too (Meklit Hadero CD), 216, 217, 219
White, Barry, 244
Wild Hare Club (Chicago), 284
women as musicians: as *azmari*, 88–90, 315n61; in diaspora, 364n98; participation in Ethiopian Orthodox liturgical performance, 56, 58, 59, 157, 224–25, 227, 312n2, 363n87; in private drinking houses, 324n61; in royal encampments, 67
women as refugees, problems of, 105, 141–43, 340n71
"Won" (Admas Band), 238–39
Wonder, Stevie, 248
Woretaw Wubet, 17, 95–96; migration path, 117t
Workeneh, Sara, 356n86
world music, Ethiopian music and, 122, 216, 243, 253–55, 260
Wright, Jeffrey, 151

yä'əhud təməhərt bet mäzmur (*ya'ihud temehert bet mezmur*), 221–25
yä'ezra kwankwa language, 317n79, 357n95
yäfidel qərs' (*yefidel qers'*), 158, 159t
"Yäkärmo Säw (Yekermo Sew)" (Mulatu Astatke), 152–56, 342n14, 342n15, 343n18
Yäkəbr Zäb (honor guard), xxi. *See also* Imperial Bodyguard, founding of
Yänəgus Təbbäqa (king's guard), xxi. *See also* Imperial Bodyguard, founding of
Yared, Saint, 157, 205, 223, 313n14; accounts of life, 52–53, 58; contribution and impact of, 51–54, 63, 65, 66, 73; Ethiopian dance and, 71; miniature portrayal of, 53, 54
Yared Lemma, 287
Yared School of Music (Addis Ababa), 183, 192, 210, 239, 241, 351n2, 356n79

Yätäbabbärut music group, 95–96
Yehunie Belay, 17, 209–10, 215, 336n38, 364n102; *Ethiopian Yellow Pages* and, 139, 212–15; on lack of hereditary Amhara musicians, 360n44; migration path, 117t, 118; performances in *kinet*, 95; performances of *bahelawi* music, 213–14; as sentinel musician, 259
"Yekermo Sew: A Tribute to Seifu Yohannes and Tsegaye Gabre-Medhin," 343n18
Yenni Desta, 287
Yeshe Mebrate, 354n54
Yeshimebet "Tutu" Belay, 259; *Ethiopian Yellow Pages* and, 139, 212–15
"Yezemed yebada" (Teshome Mitiku), 29
Yod Abyssinia Restaurant (Addis Ababa), 202
Yohannes IV, Emperor of Ethiopia, 205
Yonas Gorfe, 240
YouTube, 138

Zakki Jawad (Zedicus), 17, 238, 367–68nn37–38; migration path, 117t, 119, 236–37; post-Admas Band career, 242–45
zämäch'a (*zemecha*), 86, 90, 104, 236; choirs, 86–87, 322n46
zämänawi (*zemenawi*) music, 81, 98; diaspora performers, 18; global spread of, 231; instruments used in, 323n54; neotraditional (*bahel zemenawi*), 95, 323n55; public performances of, 167–68; Telela Kebede's performance of, 88
Zär'a Ya'əqob, Emperor of Ethiopia, 61, 314n34
zar cult, 70, 72, 317nn76–77
zäwari, 309n22
Zedicus. *See* Zakki Jawad
Zedicus (Zakki Jawad CD), 243
zəgubəñ, 92
Zeleke Gessesse, 284
Zelwecker, Franz, 81
zemecha. See *zämäch'a* (*zemecha*)
zemenawi. See *zämänawi* (*zemenawi*) music
zəmmamä, 57t, 57
Zone 9 bloggers, 338n59